CW01664099

Graham A. Reid

LONDON, 30th April, 2008.

Beacon Fire and Shooting Star

The Literary Culture of the Liang (502–557)

Harvard-Yenching Institute
Monograph Series 63

Beacon Fire and Shooting Star

The Literary Culture of the Liang (502–557)

Xiaofei Tian

Published by the Harvard University Asia Center
for the Harvard-Yenching Institute
Distributed by Harvard University Press
Cambridge (Massachusetts) and London 2007

Printed in the United States of America

The Harvard-Yenching Institute, founded in 1928 and headquartered at Harvard University, is a foundation dedicated to the advancement of higher education in the humanities and social sciences in East and Southeast Asia. The Institute supports advanced research at Harvard by faculty members of certain Asian universities and doctoral studies at Harvard and other universities by junior faculty at the same universities. It also supports East Asian studies at Harvard through contributions to the Harvard-Yenching Library and publication of the *Harvard Journal of Asiatic Studies* and books on premodern East Asian history and literature.

Tian, Xiaofei.

Beacon fire and shooting star : the literary culture of the Liang (502-557) / Xiaofei Tian.

p. cm. -- (Harvard-Yenching Institute monograph series ; 63)

Includes bibliographical references and index.

ISBN 978-0-674-02602-5 (alk. paper)

1. Chinese literature--Northern and Southern dynasties, 386-589--History and criticism. 2. China--Civilization--221 B.C.-960 A.D. I. Title. II. Title: Literary culture of the Liang (502-557).

PL2289.T74 2007

895.1'09--dc22

2007029588

Index by the author

Printed on acid-free paper

Last number below indicates year of this printing

16 15 14 13 12 11 10 09 08 07

謹以此書獻給我的知己

宇文所安

Acknowledgments

Writing this book was an extraordinary pleasure, made doubly so by the assistance I received along the way. The book grew out of my dissertation. Since then, it has undergone many transformations. It would not have assumed its present form without the interdisciplinary academic community of which I am privileged to be a member, as I have benefited immensely from interacting with my colleagues at Harvard. I want to thank Peter Bol, Sun Joo Kim, and Michael Szonyi for their insights on Chapter 7. I feel most indebted to Wilt Idema, who read the entire manuscript and gave valuable suggestions. I am deeply grateful to Philip Kuhn and Michael Puett for their unfailing support.

I am fortunate to also have colleagues in the field who have provided me with intellectual stimulation and warm friendship over the years. As parts of the book have been presented at various conferences and workshops, I am thankful to the organizers of these events and to my discussants, audiences, and readers, particularly Robert Ashmore, Alan Berkowitz, Robert Campany, Alan Chan, Kang-i Sun Chang, Jack Chen, Cynthia Chennault, Nicola Di Cosmo, Grace Fong, Lu Yang, Scott Pearce, Graham Sanders, Wendy Swartz, Lillian Tseng, Paula Varsano, Wang Ping, Ellen Widmer, Yang Su-jen, Robin Yates, and J. R. Ziemer. Special thanks are due to David Knechtges for going through the manuscript with scrupulous care and offering extremely helpful feedback.

Material for chapter five first appeared in an article, "Illusion and Illumination: A New Poetics of Seeing in Liang Dynasty Court Literature," in *Harvard Journal of Asiatic Studies* 65.1 (2005), and I thank the editors for permission to use it. The anonymous readers' illuminating comments and Joanna Handlin Smith's thorough editing helped sharpen the argument.

Finally, my thanks go to my family for their loving support. This book is dedicated to my husband, Stephen Owen, with love and gratitude.

X.F.T.

Contents

Note on Sources

For poetry and prose citations, I use primarily Lu Qinli's 逯欽立 *The Poetry of the Pre-Qin, Han, Wei, Jin, and Southern and Northern Dynasties* (*Xian Qin Han Wei Jin nanbeichao shi* 先秦漢魏晉南北朝詩) and Yan Kejun's 嚴可均 *Complete Prose of Antiquity, the Three Dynasties, Qin, Han, the Three Kingdoms, and the Six Dynasties* (*Quan shanggu sandai Qin Han sanguo liuchao wen* 全上古三代秦漢三國六朝文). These anthologies are divided into different volumes by dynasties, such as *Complete Liang Poetry* (*Quan Liang shi* 全梁詩) and *Complete Liang Prose* (*Quan Liang wen* 全梁文). In identifying the source of a text from Lu Qinli or Yan Kejun's anthologies, I shall not refer to the complete title but cite only the relevant volume title, followed by *juan* and page numbers (e.g., *Quan Liang shi* 1.12). In the notes, the abbreviation *T* is used for *Taishō shinshū Daizōkyō* 大正新修大藏經.

Beacon Fire and Shooting Star

The Literary Culture of the Liang (502–557)

Introduction

In autumn 2004, a splendid exhibition of Chinese artifacts entitled "China: Dawn of a Golden Age, 200–750 AD" opened at the Metropolitan Museum at New York. This exhibition brought together more than three hundred works of art from forty-six Chinese museums and cultural institutions; reportedly it had taken seven years to prepare. Strolling down the gallery hall, I paused for a long time in front of a standing stele with twin seated Buddhas made in 545, the eleventh year of the Datong era of Emperor Wu of the Liang (Liang Wudi 梁武帝, r. 502–49). As I was admiring the work, a middle-aged Chinese man also stopped in front of the stele. After examining the little plaque identifying the piece, he mused aloud to what appeared to be his family: "Liang dynasty—what dynasty was that? I have never heard of it before."

The Liang dynasty 梁, lasting from 502 to 557, was one of the most brilliant and creative periods in Chinese history, yet also one of the most underestimated and misunderstood. This was, moreover, the period when the cultural images of the "North" and "South," still with immense resonance after more than a millennium, finally took shape in the Chinese cultural imagination. This book examines the cultural context of literary production in the Liang dynasty as well as many of the literary works themselves. In doing so, it addresses a set of interrelated cultural and literary historical issues, re-evaluates and challenges established claims about this period, and explores the reasons for its subsequent neglect and denigration. In the end, what this book uncovers about the Liang dynasty not only deepens our understanding of medieval China but also leads to a number of fascinating questions about Chinese cultural politics and the ideological inclinations of contemporary literary studies, both in- and outside China.

If the Liang is not well known to the average Chinese, who usually possesses a good basic knowledge of imperial Chinese history by way of school education and through literary works disseminated in print or orally (as in the old but still flourishing entertainment form of storytelling), films, and TV programs, it is primarily because this dynasty is subsumed under the more general period designations for early medieval China. After the collapse of the Han empire in the late second century, China was divided among three kingdoms: Wei in the north, Shu Han in the southwest, and Wu in the south. In 265, the Wei ruler was overthrown by a powerful minister, Sima Yan 司馬炎, who subsequently founded the Jin dynasty and unified China. The unity was, however, soon to be interrupted: in 317, the royal house of the Jin dynasty reestablished itself to the south of the Yangzi River after the invasion of non-Chinese peoples of the north, with the city of Jiankang 建康 (modern Nanjing) as the new capital. Subsequently, southern China witnessed a succession of five dynasties: Eastern Jin 東晉 (317–420), Song 宋 (420–79), Qi 齊 (479–502), Liang, and Chen 陳 (557–89). These five dynasties, along with the earlier southern kingdom of Wu, which had also taken Jiankang as its capital, are generally referred to as the Six Dynasties (*liuchao* 六朝). During the same period, northern China went through a series of non-Chinese regimes, until Yang Jian 楊堅 (541–604), a tough-minded general, consolidated the North toward the end of the sixth century and founded the Sui 隋. In 589 Yang Jian conquered the last of the Southern Dynasties and once again brought China under the rule of a single dynasty.

This long period of division was subsequently known as the Northern and Southern Dynasties (*nanbeichao* 南北朝), or, according to the customary periodization in modern literary and historical studies, was collectively referred to as the "Wei, Jin, and Northern and Southern Dynasties" (*Wei Jin nanbeichao* 魏晉南北朝). Wedged between Han and Tang, the two energetic and enduring empires, this period has traditionally been considered a social and political "dark age," a stage of preparation for the brilliant accomplishments of the Tang literary masters, and consequently a phase of transition, an almost four-century-long hyphen between great empires. In the words of a modern scholar, "From the literary historical perspective, the literature of this period indeed does not seem to be magnificent and wide-ranging when compared with the grand literature of Han and Tang, and it is naturally less prominent."[1] Concessions to the cultural splendors of this period tend to focus on a few canonized authors and works or on achievements in the visual arts, such as calligraphy, painting, and sculpture. The collective term "Wei, Jin, and Northern and Southern Dynasties" can, however, hardly do justice to the important social and cultural changes that took place in these centuries; and the conventional account of literary history that revolves around a small, fixed cluster of great writers and great works cannot but obscure the complexities of the larger picture, as well as limit our understanding of those writers and works themselves. This book intends to break down the generalizations by focusing on one segment of the long hand-scroll, to give an in-depth exploration of the cultural and literary world of the Liang.

The inevitable question is: Why the Liang? Except for the last few turbulent years, the Liang prospered under the peaceful rule of Emperor Wu, who was on the throne for forty-seven years. His was one of the longest reigns in all imperial Chinese history, and it was nothing short of a miracle in the Northern and Southern Dynasties, a period characterized by quick changes of rulers and violent palace coups. The Liang, however, remained a stable regime for nearly half a century; the capital, Jiankang, was the world's most populous city in its day, a flourishing cultural and commercial center. Emperor Wu's enthusiastic patronage of literature, the arts, and learning was a major factor in making the Liang court "the most catholic and sophisticated intellectual milieu of pre-Tang China."[2] Literary activities, such as writing, editing, anthologizing, and cataloguing, were carried out on an unprecedented scale. In more ways than one, the Liang marked the zenith of the Southern Dynasties, and it proves to be one of the rare cases in which dynastic periodization happily coincides with an intellectually and culturally coherent period. Even though the Chen dynasty managed to rule the South for another thirty years or so, the fall of the Liang was truly the end of

1. Wu Yun, *Wei Jin nanbeichao*, p. 1.
2. Dudbridge, *Lost Books*, p. 69.

an era. The Liang poetic style remained a dominant influence until the early eighth century, but the old balance of power, maintained for over two hundred years between North and South, had been tipped; socially and culturally the Chen was a mere afterglow of the Liang, lacking in magnitude, boldness, and imagination.

It is necessary to state from the outset what this book is not. It is not a conventional literary history of the Liang. A conventional literary history attempts to give a balanced treatment of all genres of literature, usually including writings not considered "literature" at the time, such as the *zhiguai* 志怪 (accounts of the strange) narrative. Instead, a significant portion of this book is devoted to the contextualization of literature. Such a contextualization is more important to our understanding of the Liang literary culture than a detailed study of each literary genre flourishing in this period. By "literary culture," I refer not only to the literary writings themselves but also to the physical process of literary production such as text copying and transmitting, to cultural activities such as book collecting, anthologizing, cataloging, and various forms of literary scholarship, and to the intricate interaction of religion (particularly Buddhism) and literature. This book also aims to explore the impact of social and political structures on the literary world, a world that is not separate from the other spheres of society but remains an intimate part of society. To use the terms of traditional disciplines, I would describe this book as a social and cultural history of the Liang literature. As such, this book hopes to be at once narrower in range than a conventional literary history and larger in its vision of the cultural and literary world of the Liang. In the end, only by situating literary texts into the milieu in which they were born can we better understand them; when we do so, literary texts, insofar as they articulate a way of seeing the world, also illuminate the social, historical, and cultural "contexts" that frame them.

When it comes to treating the literary texts themselves, this book puts more stress on poetry than on other genres, although prose pieces, especially *fu*, also get substantial exposure. The reason for focusing on poetry is simple: poetry, especially poetry in the five-syllable line, was indisputably the major genre of this period; this contrasts sharply with the Han dynasty, when the *fu* form was the dominant literary genre. But poetry was the center of attention of Liang writers in both theory and practice. In addition to the early sixth-century *Gradations of Poets* (*Shi pin* 詩品), an important work of literary criticism in Chinese literary history, much discussion of literature from the Liang revolves around poetry. As Zhong Rong 鍾嶸 (d. 518) declared in the preface to *Gradations of Poets*, "Poetry in the five-syllable line occupies the most important position in literature, being particularly flavorful among the various modes of literary expression" 五言居文辭之要，是眾作之有滋味者也.[3] Changes in poetry in this period also had a larger, more far-reaching impact on the later development of Chinese literature than did contemporary *fu* and other prose forms. Indeed, as is widely recognized by scholars, in the fifth and sixth centuries even the *fu* experienced an increasing "poeticization" (*shihua* 詩化).[4]

One of the most important poetic developments during this period was the conscious attention to prosody on the part of poets. And yet, prosody is not closely related to the intellectual and cultural issues of the time and belongs properly to a more specialized study of the poetry of the period. Since there are already many detailed studies of this topic in various languages, this book does not treat this issue as a central concern. Instead, it endeavors to pinpoint what lies beneath the "new transformation" (*xinbian* 新變) the poets of this period were so intent upon achieving and did in fact achieve.

Liang literature was a continuation and development of the efforts of previous generations. The Liang writers' most immediate predecessors were the poets of the Yongming era 永明 (483–93) of the Qi dynasty, of whom Shen Yue 沈約 (441–513) and even Emperor Wu of the Liang himself (then simply Xiao Yan 蕭衍) were among the foremost. Shen Yue lived into the Liang, widely respected as the grand old master of letters and exerting formidable influence in the recognition and promotion of younger talents. He passed away in 513, the same year that saw

3. Zhong Rong, *Shi pin jizhu*, p. 36.

4. See, e.g., Ma Jigao, *Lidai*, pp. 73–74; Wang Lin, *Liuchao*, pp. 25–28; and Li Lixin 李立信, "Lun liuchao fu zhi shihua" 論六朝賦之詩化, in *Disanjie*, pp. 95–110. The poeticization is manifested for the most part in formal terms, namely, the brevity of a later *fu* in sharp contrast with the immensity of a Han *fu*, and the liberal use of lines of five and seven syllables, which leads to the result that at times a *fu* reads more like a poem in lines of miscellaneous lengths (*zayan shi* 雜言詩).

the birth of Yu Xin 庾信 (513–81), who was to become the most important poet of the late sixth century.

Despite the fortuitousness of the "overlap," Shen Yue's death did not constitute a milestone that marked the end of an epoch in literary history. Lacking a powerful, dominant voice, the literary landscape in the first half of the Liang was rather diffuse and varied. Whereas He Xun 何遜 (d. ca. 518), with his lucid and exquisite poems, was clearly writing in the tradition of the Yongming generation, there were also avid followers of the early fifth-century poets Xie Lingyun 謝靈運 (385–433) and Bao Zhao 鮑照 (d. 466), each known for a distinctly individual style. The contemporary literary scene was succinctly summarized by Xiao Zixian 蕭子顯 (483–537), a descendent of the Qi royal family, in his famous commentary on "The Biographies of Men of Letters" in *The History of the Southern Qi* (*Nan Qi shu* 南齊書). Following an analysis of the contemporary world of letters, Xiao Zixian articulated his own literary values, but his description of what poetry should be was not as important as his display of a highly self-conscious critical sensibility and a strong sense of a need for change, innovation, and originality. In this, Xiao Zixian was characteristic of his age.

Modern scholars tend to divide Liang writers into three camps: the conservatives, the radicals, and those holding a middle course. Such clear-cut distinctions are, however, an anachronistic misunderstanding of the age—perhaps a result of observing the intertwined literary and political partisanship commonly seen in late imperial China. A closer examination of the Liang shows that many writers moved freely between these putative "camps," that there was a consensus regarding the literary canon, and that certain beliefs about literature were held in common. In other words, there existed various preferences and tastes in the Liang, but no opposing "schools." What have been construed as conflicting viewpoints and styles were more precisely a function of personal predilections, individual talents, and generational changes. The true transformation in literature occurred in the 530s, when Emperor Wu's third son, Xiao Gang 蕭綱 (503–51), then a grown man, moved back to the capital from his provincial post and brought his literary coterie. In 531, as a consequence of his elder brother's untimely death, Xiao Gang was made the crown prince. The poetry written by Xiao Gang and his courtiers quickly became the new fashion in the capital and was subsequently dubbed the "Palace Style" (*gongti* 宮體), a reference to the Spring Palace, the residence of the heir apparent. Not only did this style define the literary scene of the second half of the Liang dynasty, it also was a crucial turning point in the history of Chinese poetry.

The most persistent criticism directed at Palace Style poetry and of the Liang dynasty in general is decadence (*tuifei* 頹廢). Nothing is further from the truth. "Decadence" indicates a sense of decay: a sumptuousness moving to excess, over-ripeness, a physical decomposition as a sign of spiritual abandon and moral dissolution. However, the self-conscious quest for newness, the energetic endeavors at innovation, and the immense cultural confidence demonstrated by the Liang court, both in relation to its literary precursors and to its neighbor state in the North, demonstrate the inaccuracy of the term "decadence" as a characterization of Liang literary culture. Nor does such criticism capture the quality of the political life of the period. Emperor Wu was a diligent monarch who desired to make the most of the existing social structure and implemented reforms that energized the Southern Dynasties political system. He was also well known for his support of cultural projects and his promotion of rites and music, an important aspect of the ideal Confucian sage-emperor. The quick dissolution of the Liang empire was as baffling and painful to contemporaries as it was problematic for historians of later times, who faced the task of constructing a narrative out of accidents, drawing a moral lesson, and justifying the dynastic downfall by pinpointing the ruler's fatal mistakes. In the conventional *grand récit*, two things are singled out to bear the blame for the collapse of the Liang: Palace Style poetry, and Emperor Wu's devotion to Buddhism. In both cases, imperial attention is considered to have been distracted from its proper object (i.e., governance), misplaced, and squandered. It is high time for us to break out from such age-old paradigms and examine the Liang cultural world in a new light.

The book is divided into eight chapters. Chapter 1, "The Rule of Emperor Wu," aims to provide general background for the literary and cultural activities of the Liang dynasty. This backdrop is essential for understanding the rise of what I call a cultural elite in this period, the subject of Chapter 3. Chapter 1 narrates the long, colorful life of Emperor Wu and delineates the social background of the Liang. Particular emphasis is placed on the political configuration of Liang society: how the hierarchical distinction between gentry and commoners, northern immigrants and local southerners, created a series of economic and political problems, and how Emperor Wu worked under the constraints of the entrenched structure of the Southern Dynasties and sought to make the inherited system function better to the advantage of the state. One long-standing misperception of the Qi and Liang royal families is that they came from a humble background; this chapter argues for a more precise distinction between commoners (*hanren* 寒人) and members of the minor gentry (*hanshi* 寒士) and calls for the contextualization of these loosely used terms to facilitate a more accurate understanding of the complex array of cultural and political forces clashing and negotiating with one another in sixth-century southern China. In the end, political values came to be closely intertwined with cultural values, as a new set of criteria for evaluating people, which emerged in Emperor Wu's reforms of bureaucratic recruitment and in his general promotion of scholarly and literary undertakings, encouraged cultural accomplishments and opened up a road for traditionally marginalized members of the lower gentry and native southerners. Another point of focus in this chapter is Emperor Wu's religious agenda. Throughout his reign, employing both theoretical and institutional means, Emperor Wu had attempted to establish a Buddhist polity, with himself as the *dharmarāja* (dharma king), or "emperor bodhisattva," in whom spiritual authority and secular authority converged and were concentrated. The composition and cataloguing of Buddhist works, the imposition of vegetarianism on the Buddhist clergy, and the spectacular public displays of religious fervor such as masses, assemblies, and lectures on sūtras all contributed to the construction of this new role for the sovereign. Emperor Wu's religious thought and practice were to have a lasting influence on the subsequent development of Chinese Buddhism.

The next two chapters, "Mapping the Cultural World," I and II, attempt to draw a larger picture of the social and cultural transitions in the first half of the sixth century. Chapter 2 concentrates on the materiality of the textual world in this period by discussing textual production and transmission, book collecting and cataloguing, encyclopedia compilation and anthology making; the following chapter shifts the focus to the social context of literary discourse and attempts to map the diversified literary landscape. Liang writers were intensely aware of the changes occurring in literary history and had a strong interest in defining their own position against those of previous generations. This period witnessed an unprecedented flourishing of editing, collating, anthologizing, and cataloguing activities, through which the Liang writers "fixed" (in several senses of the word) received manuscripts, organized knowledge, and constructed a literary historical narrative. One important characteristic of the period was the rise of a cultural elite, which was constituted mainly by members of the lower gentry and native southerners. These traditionally marginalized social groups now obtained distinction and prestige through cultural accomplishments and transported the family politics of the old Southern Dynasties aristocracy into a new realm by making "cultural accomplishments" (*wen* 文) their family business and by establishing close ties with one another through intermarriage.

Chapter 3 also aims to dispel a long-established misconception of this period as being characterized by several rival literary schools, the most prominent of which are taken to have been represented by the princely brothers Xiao Tong 蕭統 (501–31) and Xiao Gang, respectively. This chapter shows that such a rivalry is largely an ideological construction, created out of a need for a dramatized, but also much simplified, literary historical narrative.

Chapter 4, "The Pleasure of the Superfluous," turns attention to Liang Palace Style poetry and discusses its reception and interpretation in relation to a fundamental issue in Chinese literary discourse, namely, the "use" of literature or the lack thereof. In order to discover what Palace Style poetry *is*, we must first clarify what it is *not*. This chapter questions the standard definition of Palace Style poetry as a poetry about palace ladies, boudoir objects, and romantic passion and challenges the conventional belief that *The New Songs of the Jade Terrace* (*Yutai xinyong* 玉臺新詠), a poetry anthology compiled by the court poet Xu Ling 徐陵 (507–83), is the representative anthology of Palace Style poetry. This chapter also examines the ideological interests that have contributed to and are in turn well served by these perceptions of Palace Style poetry. One of the issues discussed is the enigmatic case of the originator of the Palace Style, Xu Chi 徐摛 (474–551), and his "appraisal" of a boil. Like a boil itself, Xu Chi's "appraisal" is a superfluous thing, floating outside the system of what is traditionally regarded as "literature" and symbolizing, to a certain extent, the fate of Palace Style poetry itself. Serving no practical function in the management of the state, resisting political allegory and canonization, many Palace Style poems are furthermore about useless, superfluous objects such as dust, a broken bridge, and reflections in water; as such, they pose a serious threat to a totalizing cultural system that demands any surplus be appropriated and contained.

Chapter 5, "Illusion and Illumination: A New Poetics of Seeing," proposes a new interpretation of the "Palace Style" by situating the Liang court literature in the context of the Buddhist doctrines embraced by the Liang royal house and aristocrats. This literature, profoundly influenced by Buddhist teachings about meditative concentration and visualization, is about the representation of a new way of perceiving the phenomenal world and about the presentation of highly particular moments. Central to the discussion of the new poetics of seeing is the Buddhist concept of *nian* 念, a "thought-instant," that is, a momentary thought *and* the fleeting moment such a thought takes. Liang Palace Style poetry is ultimately about those instants when the poet's prolonged, concentrated gaze illuminates the phenomenal world as what it truly is, namely, the world as transient, relative, constantly changing, and illusory. The chapter focuses on a group of literary texts about candles and candle-lit scenes, not only because candles and lamps were favorite subjects for the Liang court but also because the fleeting images of light and shadow, observed by the court poets with fascination and intensity, best illustrate the new poetics of seeing embodied in this body of literature.

Chapter 6, "'Suppression of the Light': Xiao Gang, Prince and Poet," continues the discussion of the changed perception of the phenomenal world in the Liang, but it centers on the life and work of one major Palace Style writer, Prince Xiao Gang. Gifted with a bold imagination, an extraordinary power of observation, and a sensitivity to the poetic word, Xiao Gang has nevertheless been one of the most misunderstood and underestimated poets in Chinese literary history. Despite the persistent criticism of his works, Xiao Gang exerted a palpable influence on the contemporary literary scene as well as on later generations; the popularity of his writings is evidenced by the survival of a relatively large quantity of his poems through preservation in encyclopedias and anthologies.

Chapter 7, "The Cultural Construction of the North and South," looks at the construction of the cultural images of the North and South in the late Six Dynasties. In the Chinese cultural imagination, the North and South have long been associated with a set of fixed characteristics or gender stereotypes: the North is tough, austere, and masculine; the South soft, sensuous, and feminine. And yet, instead of reflecting reality, these images are no more than cultural constructs first formed during the early medieval period. This chapter discusses a series of forms of literary representation closely related to the fashioning of the gendered images of the North and South: namely, the birth of a poetic subgenre, "frontier poetry" (*biansai shi* 邊塞詩), in the South; the embodiment of the Southland (Jiangnan 江南) in the image of lotus picking in a group of poems authored by both southern and northern poets; and, last but not the least, the performance and preservation of the so-called northern and southern folk songs in the southern court. These forms of literary representation, on one hand, followed their own generic conventions quite independent of "external reality"; on the other hand, they were also embedded in a web of contemporary forms of cultural representation determined by larger historical forces. This chapter argues that the construction of the cultural images of the "North" and "South" in the literature of this period, situated within a larger historical and cultural context, is a consequence of the active construction of regional identities in discursive forms. The process had started as early as in the third and fourth centuries but did not reach its culmination in the late Northern and Southern Dynasties; rather, it became firmly established only in the Sui and Tang, the dynasties that unified China and brought the North and South together.

Chapter 8, "Parting Ways," deals with southern poets' responses to the trauma, diaspora, and destruction of the old social and cultural order caused by the Hou Jing Rebellion, which broke out in 548 and eventually led to the fall of the Liang. Many sorthern poets were forced to live in the North as captives or detainees: some of them, such as Xu

Ling and Shen Jiong 沈炯 (502–60), eventually returned to the South; others, for example, Yan Zhitui 顏之推 (ca. 531–91) and Yu Xin, never went home again. Such emigration contributed to the fusion of the northern and southern cultures and made a true comparison of North and South possible; it also enabled these poets, survivors of traumatic historical and social changes, to obtain a distance across time and space to reflect on, and make sense of, what had happened to their state, their families, and themselves.

This chapter centers on "survivors' accounts" by Shen Jiong, Yan Zhitui, and Yu Xin, because each is representative of his times in terms of personal experiences and literary style. Shen Jiong's poems and *fu* written upon homecoming to the South present a vivid picture of the trauma suffered by his homeland and himself. Even more fascinating are the two permanently displaced writers, Yan Zhitui and Yu Xin. Yan Zhitui to a large extent represents the average sorthern courtier: well educated, sophisticated, proud of his elite clan lineage, and keen to pass on the family's cultural heritage to his descendents. To Yan Zhitui, the fall of the Liang was more than just the collapse of one dynasty; it equaled the devastation of civilization itself. Yet, his sense of responsibility to family and clan ultimately transcended that to the state. Consequently, Yan Zhitui was intent on the survival of his family on many levels: physical, moral, and cultural, and he sought to deal with his grief over the fall of the South in a rational, pragmatic way. In many ways, Yan Zhitui's writings provide the perfect foil for those of Yu Xin. If Yan Zhitui was prosaic in his sentiments and in his choice of literary medium, Yu Xin was the quintessential poet. He, too, served a series of official posts in the North, although, unlike Yan Zhitui, he seemed never to have accepted the fate of the South with the same kind of resignation. Taken together, Shen Jiong's, Yan Zhitui's, and Yu Xin's writings speak eloquently to us of personal human tragedies against a vast canvas of war, destruction, and displacement. Although their experiences were certainly not new in Chinese history, the extent and psychological complexity of their surviving writings were unprecedented.

Although the Liang dynasty officially ended in 557 with the abdication of Emperor Jing 敬帝 (r. 555–57), it enjoyed a political afterlife as the Latter Liang for another thirty years, and its cultural legacy lived on much longer. The Epilogue, "The Aftermath and the Romanticization of the Liang," looks at how the Liang was romanticized during the Tang and how the most enduring image of the Liang—melancholy, sensuous, and decadent—was in fact fashioned by the late Tang poets and reflects the cultural ambience of the late Tang rather than of the Liang dynasty itself. The Liang was an energetic era, characterized not by decadence but by a robust spirit, fascinated with beginnings and innovations.

The title of this book, *Beacon Fire and Shooting Star*, is taken from Yu Xin's poetry. In the last year of his life, Yu Xin, an exile in the North, composed a quatrain upon the Sui army's advance into the South. He imagined looking toward the riverbank and the Shooting Star Fortress, a stronghold to the west of Jiankang, only to see raging beacon fires, a signal of an invading army, flaming along the Yangzi River. In another poem by Yu Xin lamenting the fall of Jiangling 江陵 (in modern Hubei), the capital of the Liang in its last years, to the Western Wei army, the beacon fire and shooting star are embedded in a parallel couplet:

流星夕照境	The shooting star at dusk shines over the land,
烽火夜燒原	throughout the night beacon fires burn on the plains.[5]

A shooting star was traditionally an omen of war; under certain circumstances, it indicated the demise of the army commander. It is an image of blazing light, brilliant, terrifying, transitory, leaving behind a more intense darkness than existed before its passage. Parallel to the beacon fires, the flaming heavenly body both complements and contrasts with the light emanating from the earth, which spreads gradually throughout the land, signifying more destruction and wreckage.

Yu Xin's vision of the South is thus a darkening land lit up in a moment of terrible beauty. In contrast to what is illumined by the broad light of day, the landscape visible in the light of the shooting star and beacon fires can only be a fraction of the whole—a fitting allegory for a book that intends to reconstruct the ever-elusive history of a bygone age. In more ways than one, this book is about light, shadow, and the illuminating power of the poetic word long after the end of an

5. Yu Xin, no. 12 of "In Imitation of 'Singing of My Feelings'" ("Ni Yonghuai" 擬詠懷), in *Quan bei Zhou shi* 3.2368.

era. Surrounded by its "context" of war and destruction, Yu Xin's couplet reminds us of a much smaller light, the light from candles and lamps: they represent fragile human efforts to dispel the darkness not for the purpose of warning like beacon fires but for the peaceful pleasures of daily life: eating, drinking, reading, writing, playing chess—a miniature battle, but also only a game. Beacon fire and shooting star contextualize the flickering candlelight, which forms the center of this book's attention, for in the end, as well exemplified by Yu Xin's parallel couplet, war and destruction are transient, but the poetic word lives on, set ablaze in the midst of the ruins of the poet's homeland.

❧

Long after the Liang fell, its cultural achievements remain an important legacy, and yet, this legacy is both troubled and troubling, intertwined with problems of contemporary cultural politics and illustrating some perennial issues of Chinese society. The splendor of the southern empire lies hidden in bits and pieces of its once vast textual production and is refracted through the multiple lenses of interpretations of later ages seeking to make sense of that corpus through their own ideological assumptions. The reconstruction of the past is largely an act of reassembling the fragments that have survived the ravages of time. What is pieced back together can never be the perfect original, but the pleasure lies in the knowledge of the limitations and the freedom of inference and imagination.

CHAPTER ONE
The Rule of Emperor Wu

Toward the end of summer 2003, in the Temple of Pure Mercy (Jingci si 淨慈寺) by the West Lake in the city of Hangzhou, I came across a group of elderly women kneeling on mats and praying to the Buddha. Some of them were murmuring in low voices with their eyes closed, but many of them were holding a small booklet and reading from it silently, their lips moving with earnestness. As one of them turned a page, I caught a glimpse of the cover of the booklet. It was *The Liang Emperor's Confession* (*Liang huang chan* 梁皇懺), a work attributed to Emperor Wu of the Liang.[1] According to popular belief, he wrote it to redeem the soul of his wife, Chi Hui 郗徽 (468–99).

It is difficult to know when or how the legend began. It was certainly in existence as early as the seventh century. The gossipy history of the Southern Dynasties, *The Southern History* (*Nan shi* 南史), compiled by

1. On the authenticity of the attribution, see Xu Liqiang, "*Liang huang chan* chutan." Xu concludes that the confession was originally intended for monks and nuns for having eaten meat or drunk alcohol and could have been part of Emperor Wu's advocacy of vegetarianism. Based on a section on Buddhist confession from the Southern Qi prince Xiao Ziliang's 蕭子良 (460–94) *Jingzhuzi* 淨住子, *Liang huang chan* was first mentioned in the Japanese Monk Enchin's 圓珍 (814–91) catalogue of Chinese Buddhist writings compiled in 858. The present text was edited by the Yuan monk Zhisong Boting 智松柏庭 in 1338. *Liang huang chan* remains one of the most popular confessions performed in confession rituals in Chinese Buddhist communities today.

the early Tang historian Li Yanshou 李延壽 and presented to the throne in 659, gives the following account:

The empress had an extremely jealous disposition. After she died, she was transformed into a dragon and entered the well in the imperial harem. Sometimes she appeared to the emperor in his dreams; sometimes she would manifest her form in bright, splendid light. Whenever the emperor was going to fall ill, the dragon would stir up the well water and make it splash. The emperor had a hall constructed over the well. Piles of clothes were left in the hall; there was a silver well-pulley and a golden urn, which was constantly filled with all kinds of delicacies as a sacrifice. Because of this, the emperor never established an empress during his reign.[2]

后酷妒忌，及終，化爲龍入于後宮井，通夢於帝．或見形，光彩照灼．帝體將不安，龍輒激水騰涌．於露井上爲殿，衣服委積，常置銀鹿盧金瓶灌百味以祀之．故帝卒不置后．

Wei Shu 韋述 (d. 757) in *An Account of the Two Capitals* (*Liangjing ji* 兩京記) recorded an anecdote about Empress Chi throwing herself into the well in a rage because the emperor did not immediately grant her the title of empress. She subsequently turned into a poisonous dragon. As the story goes, the emperor shed bitter tears, granted her the title "Heavenly Dragon Queen," and had a sacrificial hall built at the site of the well.[3] This anecdote was, however, clearly a fabrication: the empress had died several years before the emperor ascended the throne. The Buddhist dimension of these stories is nevertheless obvious: poisonous dragons are a Buddhist symbol of passions and desires; Buddhists also believe that suicides are not reincarnated as human beings.

The memory of Emperor Wu apparently remained vivid throughout the centuries primarily because of his Buddhist faith and his great contributions to Chinese Buddhism. Although orthodox Confucian scholars condemned the emperor's devotion to Buddhism and saw it as a fundamental cause of the collapse of the Liang, in the popular imagination he became a sympathetic figure. A late seventeenth-century novel,

2. *Nan shi* 11.339. The story was repeated in Xu Song's 許嵩 *Jiankang shilu* 建康實錄 (18.502), a compilation of historical materials about the Six Dynasties completed after 756.

3. *Taiping guangji* 418.3406. There is no hint even in the racy *Southern Histories* that the empress committed suicide.

entitled *The Romance of Emperor Wu of the Liang Coming from the West* (*Liang Wudi xilai yanyi* 梁武帝西來演義),[4] describes Emperor Wu as the incarnation of Arhat Calamus and Chi Hui as the incarnation of the Bright Monarch Narcissus, born into the human world to cultivate their Buddha natures and fulfill their destinies. Feng Menglong's 馮夢龍 (1574–1646) 1620 short-story collection includes a piece entitled "Emperor Wu of the Liang Returns to the Land of Extreme Bliss Through Ceaseless Cultivation" ("Liang Wudi leixiu gui jile" 梁武帝累修歸極樂).[5] Both fictional accounts cast the emperor's devotion to Buddhism in a positive light. These accounts are significant in that Emperor Wu is treated as a person apart from his function as ruler: kingship is merely a test, a role played by Emperor Wu for the sake of achieving Buddhahood, which requires one to experience the utmost of what "the world of red dust" has to offer. This sets him apart from other kings and emperors portrayed in late imperial Chinese historical fiction; the tension between the person and the sovereignty he assumes provides the driving force for these narratives.

Emperor Wu of the Liang was an extraordinary and complicated character, both as a man and as an emperor. He had a unique vision of kingship, and his religious faith was inseparable from his intellectual pursuits and his political aspirations. The length of his reign is noteworthy in an age characterized by rebellions, intrigues, short-lived rulers, and bloodshed. Traditional historians were often baffled by his nearly impeccable conduct as a monarch and his disastrous end. Buddhism, particularly mistrusted by Confucian-minded scholars, became a convenient scapegoat. Another conventional allegation was Emperor Wu's laxity in meting out penalties. His disposition to mercy was seen as a hindrance to the proper legal exigencies of the state. A careful investigation,

4. Reprinted from the 1673 Yongqing tang 永慶堂 edition in *Guben xiaoshuo jicheng* 古本小說集成, vols. 12–13. After the Yongqing tang edition, there were two more reprints: the 1819 Baoqing ge 抱青閣 edition and the 1851 Yuguo tang 裕國堂 edition. The novel is also known as *Liang Wudi yanyi* 梁武帝演義 or *Liang Wudi zhuan* 梁武帝傳. Emperor Wu also figures in other literary forms of late imperial China such as drama and *baojuan* 寶卷.

5. For a translation of the complete story into English by Shuhui Yang and Yunqin Yang, see Feng Menglong, *Stories Old and New*, pp. 643–67. The translation of the title used here is the Yangs'.

however, reveals that his devotion to Buddhism and his leniency were probably the least important causes of the fall of the dynasty.

This chapter offers a general background of the period by sketching several aspects of the reign of Emperor Wu: administrative, economic, military, and religious. I begin, however, with an account of the first half of Emperor Wu's life, before he took the throne. The Liang dynasty began with him, and with his death in 549, the empire fell apart. Almost every significant event of the Liang happened during Emperor Wu's long and colorful life.

LIFE BEFORE ENTHRONEMENT

Emperor Wu's name was Xiao Yan (464–549). His family was a northern immigrant family that settled in Wujin 武進 (in modern Jiangsu), which was subsequently renamed Southern Lanling 南蘭陵 after the Xiaos' place of origin, Lanling (in modern Shandong). The Xiaos of Lanling claimed to be descendents of Xiao He 蕭何 (d. 193), a famous Western Han prime minister, although such a claim is dubious at best.[6] Xiao Yan's more immediate ancestors had served in a series of low official posts. Xiao Yan's father, Xiao Shunzhi 蕭順之 (d. 492), was a distant cousin of Xiao Daocheng 蕭道成 (427–82), the founding emperor of the Qi. Since the stepmother of Liu Yu 劉裕 (356–422), the founding emperor of the Song dynasty, was also a Xiao of Lanling, the three southern dynasties—Song, Qi, and Liang—were related by blood or marriage.

Xiao Shunzhi was granted the title Marquis of Linxiang County after Xiao Daocheng became emperor in 479. In 490, the eighth year of the Yongming (Eternal Brilliance) era of Emperor Wu of the Qi (Xiao Ze 蕭賾, the son of Xiao Daocheng; r. 483–93), Xiao Shunzhi was sent to suppress the rebellion of the emperor's fourth son, Xiao Zixiang 蕭子響 (469–90). Before Xiao Shunzhi set out from the capital, Xiao Changmao 蕭長懋 (458–93), Crown Prince Wenhui 文惠太子, who had always disliked his aggressive younger brother, reportedly asked Xiao Shunzhi to execute the prince on the spot, a request Xiao Shunzhi honored. This,

6. For a detailed discussion of the origin of the surname Xiao, the Xiao clan of Lanling, and its immigration to the South, see Cao Daoheng, *Lanling Xiao shi*, pp. 1–9; and Cao Daoheng and Fu Gang, *Xiao Tong pingzhuan*, 3–9.

however, was clearly not what the emperor himself wanted. According to *The Southern History*, the emperor's grief and resentment at the slaying of his son unsettled Xiao Shunzhi so much that he died shortly afterward, "in shame and fear."[7]

Xiao Yan began his career serving under the minister Wang Jian 王儉 (452–89), a member of the great aristocratic Wang clan.[8] Wang Jian reportedly much admired Xiao Yan and predicted that "the young Master Xiao will become a palace attendant [i.e., one of the emperor's confidential advisors] before he reaches thirty years old. After that, his advancement will be immeasurable."[9]

The 480s was a good decade for the young Xiao Yan, as he became a frequent visitor to the salon of Xiao Ziliang, Prince of Jingling 竟陵. Xiao Ziliang was a genteel man, a lover of literature, and a devout Buddhist. His Western Villa, situated on Rooster Cage Hill to the northwest of the imperial palace, was a center for both cultural and religious activities.[10] He summoned scholars to compile *An Epitome of Books of the Four Categories* (*Sibu yaolue* 四部要略) in a thousand scrolls, invited famous monks to lecture on Buddhism, and asked his guests to compose poems at parties. Of the numerous men of letters gathered around Prince Jingling, the "Eight Companions of the Prince of Jingling" (*Jingling bayou* 竟陵八友) were the most illustrious. They were Xiao Yan, Shen Yue, Fan Yun 范雲

7. *Nan shi* 44.1109. *Nan Qi shu*, compiled by a descendent of the Qi royal family during the reign of Emperor Wu of the Liang, states that the prince was "granted death" (by the emperor) and thus cleared Xiao Shunzhi of any responsibility (*Nan Qi shu* 40.706). It is impossible to ascertain what really happened, but in this case *Nan shi* might be closer to the truth, since its author was writing in the seventh century and, unlike the author of the *Nan Qi shu*, did not have to worry about political consequences.

8. According to the *Liang shu* (1.2), Xiao Yan's first post was under the Southern Leader of Court Gentlemen (the Prince of Baling, Xiao Ze's thirteenth son) as an administrator in the Law Section. Since the Prince of Baling was appointed the Southern Leader of Court Gentleman in the spring of 489, Xiao Yan's appointment under the prince must have been very brief, for Wang Jian died shortly afterward. *Nan shi* does not record this appointment.

9. *Liang shu* 1.2; *Nan shi* 6.168.

10. There is a great deal of scholarly literature on the Prince of Jingling and his salon. On the scholars and their activities at the Western Villa, see Lin Jiali, *Shen Yue yanjiu*, pp. 400–431. See also Liu Yuejin, *Menfashizu*, pp. 27–70; Jansen, *Höfische Öffentlichkeit*; and Cao Daoheng, "Liang Wudi."

(451–503), Ren Fang 任昉 (460–508), Xie Tiao 謝朓 (464–99), Wang Rong 王融 (467–93), Lu Chui 陸倕 (470–526), and Xiao Chen 蕭琛 (d. 529).[11] Of the eight, Shen Yue, Xie Tiao, and Wang Rong were particularly interested in prosody and were largely responsible for the so-called Yongming style of poetry with their innovations in rules governing the use of tones and rhymes. These prosodic innovations were to have a profound impact on Liang poetry. Ren Fang was a great master of prose style. Shen Yue, Ren Fang, and Fan Yun also enjoyed a reputation for promoting younger literary talents. Their influence in the world of letters around the turn of the sixth century was immense. Of this memorable group, Xiao Yan distinguished himself for one rather unique trait: he was good at horse riding.[12] When he joked with Ren Fang that after he became one of the high lords of state, he would make Ren a Record Keeper, Ren Fang quipped back: "When I rise to the position of one of the high lords of state, I'll make *you* a member of the cavalry."[13]

If Emperor Wu of the Qi's reign had lasted longer or if Crown Prince Xiao Wenhui had succeeded to the throne, Xiao Yan might have been known to us only as one of the Eight Companions of a refined prince, but history took a surprising turn. The death of the rebellious prince Xiao Zixiang at the hand of Xiao Yan's father broke the circle of the Eight Companions. Xiao Zilong 蕭子隆 (474–94), a younger brother of the slain prince, was sent to take his place as the governor of Jingzhou 荆州. Xie Tiao was appointed his literary tutor, and Xiao Yan served as his consultant. They departed from the capital city to take their posts in the spring of 491. Many poems were composed at the farewell parties. Xiao Chen, the youngest of the Eight Companions, got so drunk at the banquet that he had to finish his poem properly the next day.[14]

11. According to his *Liang shu* biography, Xiao Chen's birth year was 478, but he would then have been too young to participate in the salon. On this dating problem, see Cao Daoheng and Liu Yuejin, *Nanbeichao*, p. 257.

12. Wang Rong was said to have vigorously practiced his riding skills in the last years of his life to prepare himself for a more active political and military life (*Nan Qi shu* 47.823).

13. *Liang shu* 14.252. After Xiao Yan's enthronement, Ren Fang was indeed appointed Record Keeper.

14. *Quan Liang shi* 15.1804. Other extant poems written for Xiao Yan are by Wang Rong, Wang Yan 王延, Ren Fang, and Zong Guai 宗夬 (456–504); see *Quan Qi shi* 2.1396, 2.1377–78; and *Quan Liang shi* 5.1599, 2.1554. Lu Qinli 逯欽立 mis-

Neither Xie Tiao nor Xiao Yan stayed long in Jingzhou. Xie Tiao was recalled by the emperor, because he had grown too close to the prince; Xiao Yan hurried back to the capital when he learned of his father's illness in 492.[15] By the time he arrived, it was already too late.

In the capital, events developed in unexpected ways. In the early spring of 493, the crown prince died at the age of thirty-five; half a year later, the emperor himself fell gravely ill. The eldest son of the crown prince, Xiao Zhaoye 蕭昭業 (473–94), was the rightful heir to the throne, but he was young and did not have a good reputation. Wang Rong, one of the Eight Companions, became involved in a conspiracy to put the Prince of Jingling on the throne. Wang Rong had always held a high opinion of Xiao Yan, allegedly saying of him: "One day the administration of the whole realm will surely fall to this person." Xiao Yan, by contrast, did not think much of Wang Rong: "An extraordinary cause must be carried out by an extraordinary person. Rong is not someone who can assist a young ruler. I can foresee his failure."[16] Both men, it turned out, were very perceptive.

At the emperor's deathbed in the Hall of Continuing Prosperity, all the courtiers and princes were waiting anxiously. The Prince of Jingling had been with the dying emperor for days, erecting bronze lotus flowers on the four corners of the emperor's bed and bringing in monks to chant sūtras outside the hall. Since the heir apparent was not present, all the courtiers were speculating in whispers whether the Prince of Jingling should be enthroned in his place. Wang Rong, wearing full armor underneath a crimson robe, had had an imperial edict forged ordering that the entourage of the heir apparent should not be admitted to the dying

---

takenly identified Wang Yan as Wang Yanzhi 王延之 (421–84), who had already died by this time. For Xiao Yan's poem in response to Ren Fang, Wang Rong, and Zong Guai, see *Quan Liang shi* 1.1528.

15. The date of Xiao Shunzhi's death is recorded in *The Master of the Golden Tower* (*Jinlouzi* 金樓子) by Xiao Yi 蕭繹 (508–55), Xiao Yan's seventh son, as the tenth year of the Yongming era (*Jinlouzi* 1.49).

16. *Liang shu* 1.2; *Nan shi* 6.169. Sima Guang's 司馬光 (1019–86) monumental historical work *Zizhi tongjian* 資治通鑑 recorded a slightly different version of the conversation between Xiao Yan and Fan Yun, which, however, confirms Xiao Yan's low esteem of Wang Rong's political talent: "Wang Yuanchang [Wang Rong's style name] does not have the ability to save the world" (*Zizhi tongjian* 138.4332).

emperor's presence. The Prince of Wuling, the fifth and eldest of the surviving brothers of the dying emperor, said out loud: "If we go by the oldest heir, then it should be me; but if we go by the proper heir, then it should be the eldest son of the crown prince!"[17] At this point the emperor recovered consciousness and summoned the heir apparent, who came in with all his armed guards. The attempted coup failed. Shortly after, the twenty-six-year-old Wang Rong was granted permission to commit suicide. His death marked the beginning of a series of intrigues, rebellions, and murders following the end of the era of Eternal Brilliance.

Xiao Luan 蕭鸞 (452–98; later Emperor Ming 明帝, r. 494–98), an ambitious nephew of the founding emperor, began to play a prominent political role. *The Southern History* claims that Xiao Yan intended to help Xiao Luan dispose of the descendents of Emperor Wu because Emperor Wu had provoked the death of his father.[18] It is, however, impossible for us to know what passed through Xiao Yan's mind, nor is it easy to discern, between the euphemistic *Liang shu* and the sensationalizing *Nan shi*, how deeply Xiao Yan was involved in Xiao Luan's designs on the throne. Xiao Luan asked Xiao Yan for advice when he was planning to summon Xiao Zilong, whom Xiao Yan had served briefly in Jingzhou, to the capital city. This was the only clear instance of Xiao Yan's assistance to Xiao Luan in his plan to purge the princes. Xiao Luan had a small circle of confidants, which apparently did not include Xiao Yan.

One thing is unmistakable: Xiao Yan played his cards well in the highly volatile and dangerous political situation following Emperor Wu's death. He came to be trusted by Xiao Luan, though Xiao Luan may also have wanted to gain the support of the private army of several thousand soldiers that Xiao Yan and his brothers had inherited from their father.[19] Xiao Yan was soon sent to the northwestern border to watch over Cui Huijing 崔慧景 (438–500), the governor of Yuzhou 豫州, who was seen as a potential rebel. Instead of taking immediate military action against Cui Huijing, Xiao Yan brought the situation under control by diplomacy. This was his first political triumph.

17. The Prince of Wuling's name was Xiao Ye 蕭曄 (467–94) (*Nan Qi shu* 35.626).

18. *Nan shi* 6.169; *Liang shu* 1.2.

19. See Xiao Yan's preface to his "Xiaosi fu" 孝思賦, in *Quan Liang wen* 1.2948.

Almost exactly a year after Xiao Zhaoye ascended the throne, Xiao Luan deposed him and proclaimed Xiao Zhaoye's younger brother Xiao Zhaowen 蕭昭文 (480–94) emperor; three months later, Xiao Luan himself ascended the throne. In early 495, the Northern Wei invaded Qi, and Xiao Yan distinguished himself in battle by his courage and resolve. Later that same year, Xiao Yan was appointed palace cadet under the crown prince and put in charge of Stone Fort, the main fortification for the defense of the capital. According to *The Southern History*, he was well aware of the emperor's suspicious nature and dismissed all his retainers. Perhaps as a result, the emperor often praised Xiao Yan's modest lifestyle to the other courtiers. From 495 to 497, Xiao Yan kept a low profile in the capital. During this time, he wrote a poem and sent it to his old friend Xie Tiao.[20] In the poem, beneath the modest claim that he had done nothing to deserve the award of his current post and that there was nothing for him to do since the world was at peace, one may easily detect a sense of wistfulness about his situation. Xiao Yan was obviously not satisfied with being a "caged bird" and was biding his time.

Xiao Yan did not have to wait long. In 497, he was dispatched to Xiangyang 襄陽 (in modern Hubei) on a military campaign under the command of Cui Huijing to counter a Northern Wei invasion of Yongzhou 雍州. Although the campaign was not successful, it proved advantageous for Xiao Yan. In the autumn, Xiao Luan, Emperor Ming of the Qi, made Xiao Yan the governor of Yongzhou; shortly thereafter the emperor passed away. Emperor Ming's successor was his adolescent son, the notorious Xiao Baojuan 蕭寶卷 (483–502), who was to be given the posthumous title Marquis of Darkness in the East (Donghun hou 東昏侯). Six ministers were entrusted with the responsibility of managing state affairs.

The histories portray Xiao Baojuan as a tyrant who never hesitated to kill his ministers. He was at the same time no more than an uncontrollable adolescent who took his father's dying words very much to heart: Emperor Ming had told him that he should "never put off doing things until it was too late"—a lesson he drew from the hesitation of the young ruler he himself had deposed only a few years earlier. Xiao Baojuan's ministers were both fighting among themselves and conspiring with other

20. *Quan Liang shi* 1.1528.

princes. Soon all six ministers were executed, for good or bad reasons. Several rebellions broke out and were suppressed. Meanwhile Xiao Yan spent his time getting ready for war: hiring soldiers, preparing weapons, cutting down trees and bamboo, and gathering rushes for making boats. Most important, he united around him the local great clans of Yongzhou, whose support and participation in his plot against the Qi proved crucial to Xiao Yan's eventual ascendance to power.[21] Xiao Yan also tried to persuade his elder bother Xiao Yi 蕭懿 to join him, but Xiao Yi refused. In the winter of 500, Xiao Yi was granted permission to commit suicide by the emperor. Another younger brother, Xiao Rong 蕭融, was also executed.

On the night Xiao Yan learned of Xiao Yi's death, he summoned his generals and decided to rise against the Qi. Xiao Yingzhou 蕭穎胄 (453–501), a distant relative of the Qi royal family serving the emperor's brother Xiao Baorong 蕭寶融 (488–502) at Jingzhou, responded. Together they made Xiao Baorong the new emperor, and Xiao Yan pressed his troops toward the capital. Although it encountered much resistance along the way, by the autumn of 501 Xiao Yan's army was outside Jiankang. In the ninth month, Xiao Yan's first son, Xiao Tong, was born to his concubine Ding Lingguang 丁令光 (485–525) back in the power base at Xiangyang; in the tenth month, Eastern Residence City, a fortress to the southeast of Jiankang, surrendered; shortly thereafter, Xiao Yingzhou died of illness in Jingzhou, making it easier for Xiao Yan to bring the political situation under his personal control.

The crowning victory took place on December 28, 501, when a mutiny took place in the imperial palace. The young emperor's head was cut off by his generals. Wrapped in yellow oilcloth, it was sent to Xiao Yan by none other than his old friends Fan Yun and Liu Hui 劉繪 (458–502), who had also been a frequent guest at the Prince of Jingling's residence in the 480s.

By this point, it was quite clear to everyone where the "mandate of heaven" had fallen. Shen Yue and Fan Yun, former members of the

21. For Xiao Yan's alliance with the great clans of Yongzhou, see Yasuda Jirō's study in *Chūgoku chūseishi kenkyū*, pp. 203–45; idem, "The Changing Aristocratic Society," pp. 42–48; Jansen, *Höfische Öffentlichkeit*, p. 201; and Zhang Yihe, *Diyu jituan*, pp. 80–85.

Eight Companions, were the key figures in urging Xiao Yan to take the throne.[22] Shen Yue also played a crucial role in the decision of Xiao Yan on how to deal with Xiao Baorong, the puppet emperor. Xiao Yan had wanted to send him to a fief in the far south, but Shen Yue quoted the warlord Cao Cao 曹操 (155–220): "Don't suffer true woes for the sake of a false reputation." Xiao Baorong was killed, along with his four surviving brothers.

Despite his execution of the descendents of Xiao Luan, Xiao Yan intended to change the culture of political violence. The Song emperors had been particularly ruthless about killing their own family members: almost every emperor of the Song had committed at least one act of fratricide; some of them killed their brothers, cousins, or uncles by the dozens. Born toward the end of the Song, Xiao Yan lived through the Qi and witnessed the mass murders committed by Xiao Luan and Xiao Baojuan. His resolve to differ from his predecessors began with his magnanimity toward Xiao Daocheng's grandsons. He delivered a long speech to them explaining why he had decided to spare their lives (against, as he claimed, the counsel of almost all his ministers) and on why they should serve the new dynasty happily.[23] The discourse seemed to be a combination of sincerity and diplomacy—the most notable trait in Emperor Wu's politicking. Indeed, all of Xiao Daocheng's grandsons were appointed to prominent positions. If Xiao Yan, in his role as emperor, has often been accused of too much leniency toward members of his own family, it was partly because of his increasingly strong Buddhist vision of kingship and partly because he had seen with his own eyes that the so-called precautionary executions had been completely ineffective, in fact disastrous. The modern historian Zhou Yiliang 周一良 gave as reasons for Xiao Yan's leniency that he did not face the same level of political threat from the royal house as had the previous dynasty and was of a much younger age (which made him more confident) when he was enthroned than had been the founding emperors of Song and Qi. Zhou Yiliang also observed that unlike the Song and Qi emperors, Emperor Wu never killed any of the generals who helped him found the dynasty. To put the statement differently, none of those gen-

22. *Liang shu* 13.234, 14.253.
23. Ibid., 35.507–9.

erals ever rose against him, perhaps in no small measure because these generals came from the regional great clans who had been prevented from participating in the central government under Song and Qi and now were only too happy about being given a chance under Emperor Wu's rule. Both the changed circumstances and Emperor Wu's skill at managing people were powerful factors that contributed to the peace of his rule.[24]

On April 25, 502, the thirty-eight-year-old Xiao Yan was enthroned. He changed the name of the dynasty from Qi to Liang and inaugurated the Heaven's Inspection (Tianjian 天監) era. After making the ritual sacrifice in the southern suburbs of Jiankang, he said to Fan Yun, who was riding beside his sedan: "On this day, I feel as if harnessing six horses with rotten ropes as reins." Fan Yun answered: "I only hope Your Majesty will grow more and more cautious every day."[25] Indeed, following a succession of fifteen emperors in eighty-two years, with the average rule of each monarch lasting a little over five years, no one, including Emperor Wu himself, could have imagined that he would be on the throne for nearly half a century.

IMAGINARY FAMILY TREES

Two months before Xiao Yan mounted the throne, he wrote a memorial to the emperor regarding the foundation of a bureaucratic state: the recruitment system (considering that the fourteen-year-old emperor was a mere pawn, the memorial was addressed more to the ministers). In the memorial, Xiao Yan lamented the corrupted state of family genealogies, which formed the basis for selection and appointment of officials:

> Moreover, genealogies are full of errors, with all kinds of forgery and counterfeiting. No one pays any attention to the distinction between gentry members and commoners. Therefore, those with a falsified family background enter the gentry class, and people embellishing their appearances are turned into elegant gentlemen.[26]

譜牒訛誤, 詐僞多緒, 人物雅俗, 莫肯留心. 是以冒襲良家, 即成冠族; 妄修邊幅, 便爲雅士.

---

24. Zhou Yiliang, *Lunji*, pp. 339–42.
25. *Liang shu* 7.231.
26. Ibid., 1.22.

Xiao Yan's concern here was the recruitment system, but his memorial touched on an issue that had much wider repercussions.

Medieval Chinese society was characterized by a rigidly defined social hierarchy. The basic distinction was between gentry (*shi* 士) and commoners (*shu* 庶), and the social status of a household was indicated on the household register, customarily called the "yellow register" (*huang ji* 黄籍).[27] There has been some debate about the exact definition of *shi*. For instance, David Johnson argues that *shi* denoted "a loose category of people whose status [was] earned rather than a coherent group with ascribed status" and posits that *shi* was not among the categories used on the registers. Although no household registers survive from the Southern Dynasties to confirm or refute such claims, the constant references to the distinction between *shi* and *shu* in Southern Dynasties sources show that the difference seemed much more transparent to people at the time than it is to us now.[28] The example of the Song

27. The conventional explanation for the term "yellow register" is that the registers were written on paper dyed yellow. The yellow dye was an insecticide, and so yellow paper lasted longer than plain white paper. Records of yellow paper being used for official documents can be traced to the third century. See *Sanguo zhi* 14.459; and *Jin shu* 36.1078. In 676 Emperor Gaozong of the Tang issued an edict commanding that all communiqués from the Department of State Affairs be written on yellow paper, since documents on white paper had suffered frequent damage from insects (*Jiu Tang shu* 5.101). For a good exposition of the terms "yellow registers" and "white registers," arguing that the designation yellow "may be an indication more than simply the color of the document," since "'yellow' was symbolic of the emperor," see Crowell, "Northern Émigrés," pp. 180–81. In this case, however, the quality of material on which a document is written coincides with the importance of the document and with the symbolic significance of the color of the material. Crowell further speculates that the material used for the registers may not have been paper at all. This suggestion deserves further investigation, since Shen Yue clearly stated that registers from 328 (the third year of the Xianhe era) till the Song were on strips of paper that were closely joined with detailed notes in red ink 朱筆隱注, 紙連悉縫 (*Quan Liang wen*, 27.3110). Finally, it is important to remember that the term "yellow registers" seemed to be used primarily in relation to the "white registers," which are discussed below. For the kind of household information recorded in the "yellow registers," see Crowell, p. 182; and Zheng Xin, *Wei Jin nanbeichao*, pp. 212–16.

28. For instance, the famous Song minister Wang Hong 王弘 (379–432) initiated a discussion at court about the proper punishments for *shi* as opposed to *shu* (*Song shu* 42.1318–21). Shen Yue's lament about the lack of distinction between *shi*

general Zong Yue 宗越 (408–65) is well known: he originally belonged to a "secondary [gentry] household" (*cimen* 次門), but after an administrator sorted out the echelons of the local clans of Xiangyang, he was demoted to "conscriptable household" (*yimen* 役門) rank; only by petitioning the emperor in 447 did he recover the "secondary household" status.[29] Another military figure, Wu Nian 武念, was described as being from a "three-five household" (*sanwu men* 三五門).[30] "Three-five," according to Hu Sanxing 胡三省 (1230–1302), referred to the rule that one of every three male adults or two of every five in a household should be conscripted.[31] In both cases, the distinction between *shi* and *shu* households did not appear to be related to mere officeholding, since Zong Yue had begun his official career as a commandery clerk, and Wu Nian had served as a commandery military officer.

Although within the *shi* class itself there were further fine distinctions such as "exalted household" (*gaomen* 高門) and "secondary household," the most important difference between *shi* and *shu* appears to be that the gentry enjoyed, if not an absolute, then at least a partial exemption from taxation and corvée duty and had privileged access to offices. Even peasants working for gentry families were exempt from state taxation and service. Taxation and corvée were onerous enough for farmers that many willingly attached themselves to local gentry landowners, basically as serfs. Some gentry families had hundreds of peasants working their land (variously referred to as *jiatong* 家僮, *tongke* 僮客, *tongpu* 僮僕, *tongshi* 僮使, or *tongshu* 僮豎).[32] Tao Kan 陶侃 (259–334), the great-grandfather of the famous Eastern Jin poet Tao Yuanming 陶淵明 (365?–427), had "several dozens of concubines and over a thousand servants"; even Tao Yuanming's uncle Tao Dan 陶淡, a

and *shu* in the Song and Qi due to the corruption of household registers further reveals that household registers were indeed used to identify a person's social status, which in turn determined a person's conscription status (*Quan Liang wen* 27.3110).

29. *Song shu* 83.2109.

30. Ibid., 83.2112.

31. *Zizhi tongjian* 125.3947.

32. For a detailed discussion, see Tang Changru, "Clients and Bound Retainers." See also Zheng Xin, *Wei Jin nanbeichao*, pp. 140–65.

recluse, owned over a hundred servants.[33] These servants, or farmhands, along with their families, were called *yinhu* 蔭户, "protected households."

The state struggled constantly with wealthy gentry families over control of land and people. In 457, Liu Zishang 劉子尚, a Song prince, wrote to the emperor:

> Despite the old ban on taking land for private ownership, popular custom never took it seriously. People held hills and owned lakes, preserving them for family interest. The laxity of the ban has become more and more serious in recent years. The rich and powerful may occupy a whole mountain; the poor and weak have no place to do woodcutting, nor can they fish in the privately owned lakes. This is indeed a profound impairment to governing and should be completely abolished. We should perfect the previous rules and enforce the old ban.[34]
>
> 山湖之禁, 雖有舊科, 民俗相因, 替而不奉. 熂山封水, 保爲家利. 自頃以來, 頹弛日甚. 富強者兼嶺而占, 貧弱者薪蘇無託. 至漁采之地, 亦又如兹. 斯實害治之深弊, 爲政所宜去絶, 損益舊條, 更申恒制.

The "old ban" referred to an imperial edict issued in 336: "Those who hold hills and lakes for private ownership will be punished as robbers. Anyone who occupies as much land as three square feet will be executed in the marketplace." Liu Zishang's contemporary Yang Xi 羊希 (d. 467), who was serving as central aide to the Imperial Secretary, argued that the 336 edict was too severe and could not possibly be implemented. Yang Xi also pointed out that if the government confiscated all private land, it would cause immense resentment and social disturbance. He suggested that government officials be granted an amount of land in accordance with their official ranks:

> Those who already own land should not take more; but if their land falls short of the stipulated amount they are allowed to occupy more to fulfill their allotment. . . . Anyone who violates the rules [by taking more land than their allotted amount beyond what they already have], even if it is only one square

33. *Jin shu* 66.1779, 64.2460. When the famous poet Xie Lingyun, a scion of the great aristocratic Xie clan, traveled for sightseeing, his followers numbered several hundreds. They cut down trees and opened up roads for him in the mountains and caused such an uproar that the local magistrate at first thought that mountain bandits were coming (*Song shu* 67.1775).

34. *Song shu* 54.1537.

foot, will be punished as a common thief, and his land will be confiscated. The edict of the second year of the Xiankang 咸康 era [336] should be abolished.[35]

若先已占山，不得更占；先占闕少，依限占足.... 有犯者，水土一尺以上，並計贓，依常盜律論. 停除咸康二年壬辰之科.

Six Dynasties historian Charles Holcombe has remarked: "In contrast to the late T'ang, the Northern and Southern Dynasties period seems to be characterized not so much by great private estates as by notable government efforts to prevent them."[36] And yet, the government's efforts to thwart gentry accumulation of land and dependent households attest to the seriousness of this problem for the central state during this period.

The problem was further complicated by discrimination against native southerners in the fourth century. After the Jin royal house was forced to flee non-Chinese invaders in the 310s and a vast number of northerners moved to the South, the northern immigrants (or "lodged people," *qiaomin* 僑民) "at the least, enjoyed lighter tax and corvée obligations, and in fact they may have been completely exempt."[37] The term "white registers" (*bai ji* 白籍), of which there is little record in dynastic histories, is believed to have originated in this period.[38] Scholars speculate that in order to differentiate the northern immigrants from the native southerners, the immigrants were recorded on white registers instead of the yellow registers and under their original home counties instead of under their places of settlement, which were referred to as "immigrant or lodged or settler commanderies or counties" (*qiao junxian* 僑郡縣).[39] Due to the scarcity of records, scholars disagree about the

35. *Song shu* 54.1537. The text, however, refers to the second year of the Xiankang era as the *renchen* 壬辰 year, which was 332, not 336. One of the two dates is clearly an error.

36. Holcombe, *In the Shadow*, p. 61.

37. Crowell, "Northern Émigrés," p. 184.

38. One mention of the term occurs in the decree issued by Emperor Cheng of the Jin in 341 (*Jin shu* 7.183; see Crowell, "Northern Émigrés," pp. 190–91). Another mention can be found in Fan Ning's 范甯 (339–401) memorial to the throne, discussed below.

39. "White registers" were supposedly written on white paper. Zhou Yiliang (*Zhaji*, p. 246) believes that the use of white paper, which was less durable than yellow paper, may have reflected the "temporary nature" of these registers. If this speculation is true, then it certainly reveals an optimistic attitude on the part of the Eastern Jin court (i.e., they would recover North China in the near future).

exact functioning of the white registers, but two things seem certain—the white registers were used to differentiate the northern immigrants from the native southerners, and the northern immigrants benefited from their special status.[40]

The privileges of the northern immigrants were, however, a drain on state income. As hopes of recovering the North grew dimmer, the central government adopted, among other procedures such as re-examination of household registers (*jianji* 檢籍) and registration of unregistered households (*kuohu* 括户), a measure known as "residence determination" (*tuduan* 土斷). Although not a new policy, for the Southern Dynasties governments residence determination was designed to bring the northern immigrants under the administrative units of their current residence and to prevent further dislocation of the population. As William Crowell summarizes, "Residence determination meant that a person who was a native of one area but who was actually residing in another was to be made a legal resident of the latter place."[41] Once made a legal resident, the person would be obliged to pay taxes and fulfill corvée duty. As Fan Ning suggested to Emperor Xiaowu 孝武帝 of the Jin (r. 373–96):

> In antiquity land was divided into different units to strengthen the hearts of the people; sage-kings made the rules, which did not differentiate between yellow and white registers. When the Chinese heartland was lost to invaders and fell into chaos, people immigrated to the south. Since they hoped to return to their home regions one day, the government allowed them to register under their places of origin. Since then, a long time has passed, and people have settled down in their new life. All the cypresses planted by the grave mounds [of the first-generation immigrants] have grown into big trees. Although this is not

40. See Crowell, "Northern Émigrés," pp. 182–83.

41. Ibid., p. 187. Yasuda Jirō ("The Changing Aristocratic Society," pp. 38–39) makes a most interesting case for two kinds of "residence determination" in the Southern Dynasties: "registration according to current territorial status" (*xiantu tuduan* 現土土斷) and "registration accompanied by conversion to territorial identity" (*shituhua tuduan* 實土化土斷). The former implies the complete abolition of the attribution of immigrant commandaries and counties (*qiao junxian*) and the integration of the immigrants into the local administrative units; the latter means converting the shadow governments of the immigrant commanderies and counties into administrative units with real territory. This would certainly explain the frequency of residence determination during the Southern Dynasties.

their homeland, in reality people have already settled in. Now is the time to correct their administrative units and to determine households according to where they are.[42]

古者分土割境，以益百姓之心；聖王作制，籍無黃白之別. 昔中原喪亂，流寓江左，庶有旋反之期，故許其挾注本郡. 自爾漸久，人安其業，丘壟墳柏，皆已成行，雖無本邦之名，而有安土之實. 今宜正其封疆，以土斷人戶.

Residence determination was carried out several times during the Eastern Jin, most effectively in 364 (known as the "*gengxu* regulations") and then again in 413 under the leadership of Liu Yu, the powerful general who was to become the founding emperor of the Song in 420. According to Liu Yu, the 364 "residence determination" had been so successful that it greatly improved the fiscal situation of the state.[43] Throughout the Song, Qi, and Liang dynasties, residence determination occurred periodically, such as at Yongzhou in 457, and at South Xuzhou 南徐州 in 502, as soon as Emperor Wu of the Liang was enthroned.[44] The last imperial edict on residence determination was issued in 560 by Emperor Wen of the Chen dynasty 陳文帝 (r. 560–66), but it was most likely aimed not at the old northern immigrants but at people who had been dislocated because of the Hou Jing Rebellion and the subsequent wars that broke out in the South.

The privileges enjoyed by the northern émigrés were not limited to exemptions from taxes and corvée: the southerners faced discrimination in official appointments, a prominent phenomenon in the fifth century. For instance, when the founding emperor of the Qi tried to appoint southerner Zhang Xu 張緒 chief administrator, he was opposed by Wang Jian on the grounds that "few southerners have been appointed to this post." Qiu Lingju 丘靈鞠, a talented fifth-century poet and a native of the Wu commandery 吳郡, allegedly told his friends:

"I should go back to the east and dig up the grave of Gu Rong [顧榮, d. 312]. The Southland stretches thousands of square miles and has produced all sorts of

42. *Jin shu* 75.1986.

43. *Song shu* 2.30. The "*gengxu* regulations" were decreed on the *gengxu* day of the third month in the second year of the Xingning era of Emperor Ai of the Jin (April 18, 364).

44. Crowell, "Northern Émigrés," p. 189–204; Wang Zhongluo, *Wei Jin nanbeichao shi*, pp. 326–28.

gentlemen with panache. Then that Gu Rong let all those carpetbaggers cross the Yangzi River and obstruct the path of people like us—his crime cannot be redeemed even by death!"

我應還東掘顧榮冢. 江南地方數千里, 士子風流, 皆出此中. 顧榮忽引諸傖渡, 妨我輩塗轍. 死有餘罪.

Gu Rong, also a native of Wu commandery and a scion of an elite southern family, was a key figure in the establishment of the Eastern Jin.[45] As discussed below, Emperor Wu of the Liang made considerable efforts to improve the political situation of the southerners.[46]

Residence determination was but one of the many methods the central government used to increase tax revenues and its control of the population. People found just as many ways to evade taxes. In 480, in a memorial to the emperor regarding the "yellow register problem," Yu Wanzhi 虞玩之 recounted some of the subterfuges for avoiding taxes: the poor ran away from their home regions, "in blatant disregard of residence determination"; there were households that lived close to one another and never registered, pretending they were one big family; some bald people pretended to be monks. One of the more serious offenses was for a household to change its registers and "insinuate themselves into the gentry class, so that in the past they served others but now they have servants of their own."[47] In response, the emperor established the Office of Correcting Registers (Jiaoji guan 校籍官); officials of the office were required to discover several fraudulent household registers

45. *Nan Qi shu* 33.601, 52.890. See Zhou Yiliang's fine analysis of this issue in his articles "Nanchao jingnei zhi gezhongren ji zhengfu duidai zhi zhengce" 南朝境內之各種人及政府對待之政策 and "*Nan Qi shu* 'Qiu Lingju zhuan' shishi jianlun nanchao wenwu guanwei ji qingzhuo" 南齊書丘靈鞠傳試釋兼論南朝文武官位及清濁, in idem, *Lunji*, pp. 58–72, 102–26.

46. The southerners were not the only victims of political discrimination: "later" northern immigrants were much scorned by the descendents of earlier settlers and were called *huangcang* 荒傖 or *canghuang* 傖荒 (something like "newly arrived carpetbaggers"). A passage from Shen Yue's *Song shu* (65.1720–21) states: "Northerners who crossed the Yangzi River later were treated by the government as *canghuang*. Even though they had great abilities, they were more often than not excluded from the 'pure paths' [prestigious offices]." Even an illustrious family background was of no help in such cases. Southern Dynasties society was thus enclosed in a complicated web of hierarchies determined by many factors.

47. *Nan Qi shu* 34.609.

every day. Many households claiming to belong to the gentry class were removed from the gentry registers (*queji* 却籍). The Tang Yuzhi 唐寓之 Rebellion in 486 was very much a result of general resentment at the government's intensified efforts to correct "forged" or "erroneous" registers.[48] The rebels were called the "white bandits" (*baizei* 白賊), presumably a reference to their immigrant "white register" status.[49] Social pressure forced Emperor Wu of the Qi to decree in 490 that all registers be restored to the status quo ante, of the Shengming era (477–78).[50] This was a capitulation on the part of the central government. The failure to remove falsifiers from the gentry registers did not, as the modern historian Tang Changru suggests, help commoners; it merely reinforced the conventional social hierarchy and weakened the state.[51]

The matter of household registration was a crucial issue in this period; both state interests and the interests of a social class—the gentry—were closely tied to it. Zhu Dawei's article on the dramatic decrease in taxpaying households and taxpayers in the South, in sharp contrast with their dramatic increase in the North, concludes that it was primarily a consequence of the failure of the Southern Dynasties to control the alarming number of "protected households" attached to the rich and powerful.[52] In analyzing the state's efforts to regain taxpayers, however, Zhu Dawei looked mainly at the policy of registering "hidden households" (*jiankuo yinhu* 檢括隱户 or *kuohu* 括户) without paying much attention to residence determination or, even more important, to what was seen as the increasingly urgent need for genealogical studies (*puxue* 譜學).

48. Under the influence of the Marxist theory about class conflict, many modern Chinese scholars have debated whether this rebellion should be classified as a "peasant rebellion" instead of a "gentry rebellion." Zhu Dawei (*Liuchao shilun*, pp. 437–56) argues forcefully against the "peasant rebellion" theory. *Nan shi* (77.1928) states clearly: "All those who had been removed from the gentry registers were sent to distant places to serve garrison duty, and people were very resentful. Some escaped to avoid the woes [of being sent away]. On account of this, a Fuyang man Tang Yuzhi gathered people and started an uprising. . . . All those who had been removed from the gentry registers in the three Wu regions went to join him; he got together a crowd of thirty thousand people."

49. *Nan Qi shu* 56.975.

50. Ibid., 34.610.

51. Tang Changru, *Wei Jin nanbeichao shi luncong*, p. 571.

52. Zhu Dawei, *Liuchao shilun*, pp. 302–36.

Expertise in genealogical studies began in the late fourth century with Jia Bi 賈弼, who pursued it out of a private passion.[53] His work on genealogies, in 712 scrolls, was only the beginning of many such compilations in the Southern Dynasties.[54] The quick development of genealogical studies, as scholars have pointed out, is a peculiar and noteworthy feature of historiography in the Southern Dynasties, and many historians have discussed their significance in the social and political life of the Six Dynasties elite.[55] Most scholars emphasize that the gentry class desired to maintain a closed system in order to hold on to its political and cultural privileges, but in fact economic factors (i.e., the right to seize land and own a private labor force without paying taxes) might have played much more prominent roles in the gentry's determination to protect their position. The government, for its part, viewed genealogical studies as a tool for controlling the population and increasing its revenues. What we see during this period is an ongoing struggle between the state and the great families; it was a problem that Emperor Wu of the Liang had to deal with as soon as he mounted the throne.

At the beginning of the Tianjian reign, Emperor Wu received a report that three large prefectures—South Xuzhou, Yingzhou 郢州, and Jiangzhou 江州—had not submitted "yellow registers" for nearly two years. Shen Yue sent a memorandum to the emperor, reminding him of the importance of accurate genealogies.[56] He suggested that the Jin dynasty registers be utilized in the process of obtaining accurate genealogies and pointed out the lamentable state into which those old registers had fallen:

53. Jia Bi's passion became a family specialty. His grandson Jia Yuan 賈淵 (441–502) was an expert in genealogy. Jia Yuan was almost executed in 494 because he had sold the genealogy of the great Wang clan of Langye to a "carpetbagger" Wang Taibao 王泰寶, who, of course, intended to insert his own name into it (*Nan Qi shu* 33.907).

54. *Nan shi* 59.1462.

55. See Zhou Yiliang, "Wei Jin nanbeichao shixue fazhan de tedian" 魏晉南北朝史學發展的特點, in *Wei Jin nanbeichao lunji*, pp. 395–400. For a nice summary of the modern study of genealogy studies, see Li Chuanyin, "Nanchao puxue yu zhengzhi."

56. Du You, *Tong dian* 通典 3.59–61. See also *Quan Liang wen* 27.3110.

All the old registers from the Jin are in the charge of the Census Section of the Chancellery. They are called "the Jin registers" and are stored in the Eastern and Western Storehouses. Since no one consults them any more, the keepers no longer take care of them. They are pawed by dogs and nibbled at by rats, become wet and moldy in the rain, and become unbound and scattered on the floor. The doors to the storehouses are not even locked. These registers are accurate and detailed and really should be protected and treasured, since one may consult them to check out official ranks from high to low.

晉代舊籍, 並在下省左人曹, 謂之晉籍, 有東西二庫. 既不係尋檢, 主者不復經懷, 狗牽鼠齧, 雨濕沾爛, 解散於地, 又無扃縢. 此籍精詳, 實宜保惜, 位高官卑, 皆可依按.

Shen Yue described how any moderately well-to-do commoner family would try to change its household register by bribery. According to Shen Yue, the practice, which enabled the "low-born" to join the gentry class and hence elude state taxation and conscription, cost about ten thousand cash, but the returns clearly outweighed the payment. The forged registers, which recorded what office an ancestor served in which year, were apparently full of ludicrous errors:

All those cheating methods are invented by ignorant commoners, who are unable to distinguish era names or recognize official ranks. Some of them put the Yixi era [405–18] before the Ningkang era [373–75]; some put the Long'an era [397–401] after the Yuanxing era [402–4]. Often there was no such office in the period designated or such a fief in such a year. The Yuanxing reign only lasted for three years, and yet they claimed a "fourth year of the Yuanxing reign." Or an imperial edict's date does not correspond to the calendar. There are tens of thousands of such errors, and yet the directors who examined the registers were not aware of them, let alone those incompetent clerks!

凡此姦巧, 並出愚下, 不辨年號, 不識官階. 或注義熙在寧康之前, 或以隆安在元興之後. 此時無此府, 此年無此國. 元興唯有三年, 而猥稱四年. 又詔書甲子, 不與長厤相應. 如此詭謬, 萬緒千端. 校籍諸郎, 亦所不覺. 不才令史, 更何可言.

Falsification, however, was only one problem for those attempting to fix the registers. The registers were, according to Shen Yue, written in such small characters that they caused eyestrain. Sometimes, Shen Yue hypothesized, if three brothers appeared on three separate registers, one might be removed from the gentry register while the status of the other two remain unchanged. Those who felt they had been wrongly removed appealed to the government in such overwhelming numbers that the government gave up and allowed all of them to be re-registered as gentry.

Shen Yue suggested that registers from before the Jingping 景平 era (423), especially the Jin registers, be used in collating registries. Since the examination of registers provided an opportunity for making forgeries and effecting changes, Shen Yue asked that no one be allowed to do collating and copying alone; whenever a director entered the storehouse to check a register, there should always be two clerks present; further, when the director left, he should sign out. Shen Yue also proposed that scholars familiar with genealogies and ranks be assigned to the Census Section in charge of collating and correcting genealogies, using the Jin registers as well as the Song registers predating the Jingping reign as references.

Shen Yue's memorandum drew the emperor's attention forcefully to genealogical studies. The learned scholar and writer Wang Sengru 王僧孺 (465–522), at the time serving as palace aide to the censor in chief, was asked to mend *The Genealogies of a Hundred Families* (*Baijia pu* 百家譜). "[The posts of] director and clerks were established, and the Genealogy Bureau [*Puju* 譜局] was thereupon founded."[57] If we may trust this record, it was during the Liang dynasty that genealogical studies were transformed from a function of private interests and needs into a state-sponsored activity.

Years later, when Xiao Tong was compiling the *Wen xuan* 文選, he included under the category of "Accusation" Shen Yue's 490 critique of Wang Yuan 王源, a member of the elite, for marrying his daughter to the son of a wealthy man, Man Zhangzhi 滿璋之, who, according to Shen Yue, had claimed falsely to be the descendent of the Wei Defender in Chief Man Chong 滿寵 (d. 242). Man Zhangzhi himself was an attendant gentleman (a relatively lowly secretarial post) in a

57. See also Ma Duanlin 馬端臨, *Wenxian tongkao* 12.126. A variant reading for the sentence is: "The Genealogy Bureau from then on became stricter." The fourth-century genealogy expert Jia Bi was granted "clerks and scribes" to help him copy his work, but no "Genealogy Bureau" was mentioned (*Nan Qi shu* 33.907). The eighth-century writer Liu Fang's 柳芳 "Treatise on Surnames and Genealogies" ("Xingxi lun" 姓系論) stated in vague terms: "The genealogy studies by the Jia family and Wang family appeared. Henceforth a Genealogy Bureau was established, staffed with a director and so forth" (*Xin Tang shu* 199.5677).

princely establishment, but his family background was suspect: "It is impossible to tell whether his clan belongs to the gentry class or the commoners."[58] Shen Yue suggested that Wang Yuan not be allowed to hold office again for the rest of his life. This critique has sometimes been read as evidence of a snobbish desire on the part of the Southern Dynasties elite to keep their privileged class closed to outsiders; and yet, in the context just described, Shen Yue's critique was probably much more pragmatic. Rather than a sentimental attachment to the existing social order or an attempt to maintain the purity of the northern émigré lineages as a symbol of their political legitimacy, Shen Yue's impeachment of the intermarriage of a high-level gentry household and a wealthy, tax-paying commoner's household was an effort to keep the two distinct and to defend the state's economic interests.[59]

In the Song, Emperor Xiaowu 孝武帝 (r. 454–64) had tried in vain to abolish the privileges of the gentry by forcing members of the gentry class who had intermarried with commoners to serve as soldiers. This policy met with stubborn resistance. Instead of serving in the army, many simply ran away. After the emperor ordered that those who absconded be executed if captured, those who fled turned into bandits.[60] Emperor Wu of the Liang did not want to repeat the failures of the previous dynasties in securing human and material resources. The lack of a large number of taxpaying households to boost revenues and build a powerful army hindered him from carrying out reforms in a forceful manner. Hence he could only resort to more temperate means, such as strengthening genealogy studies and correcting household registers in order to catch those who tried to pass for gentry members and elude taxation. The Liang, however, was trapped in a system that would have taken much more than genealogical studies to fix.

---

58. Xiao Tong, *Wen xuan* 40.1815.

59. Cheng Zhangcan stresses Shen Yue's "great family/aristocracy complex" (*shizu qingyijie* 世族情意結) and his efforts to resuscitate the declining moral sense of the gentry class; see his article in "*Wen xuan*" *xue*, pp. 338–50. Another modern scholar, Wu Jianhui ("Lun Shen Yue"), considers Shen Yue politically "reactionary" and "conservative." For an English translation and discussion of Shen Yue's impeachment, see Johnson, *The Medieval Chinese Oligarchy*, pp. 9–11; and Mather, "Intermarriage," pp. 221–26.

60. *Song shu* 82.2104; *Zizhi tongjian* 129.4058–59.

THE POLITICAL CULTURE OF THE LIANG

The memorial on recruitment Xiao Yan wrote just before he ascended the throne reveals his deep engagement in building a better political recruitment system. It has often been said that the Southern Dynasties witnessed the rise of men of humble lineage (*hanren*).[61] Another observation, frequently cited since it was first made by Yan Zhitui, is that Emperor Wu preferred to employ "the low-born" (*xiaoren* 小人, here used in the original sense of the term).[62] In striking contrast with these characterizations, *The Southern History* states: "The only men of humble family background who rose to high official positions in the Liang dynasty were [Chen] Qingzhi [484–539] and Yu Yao" 梁世寒門達者唯慶之與俞藥.[63] We might ask then what really happened in the Liang? The apparent contradiction between these claims needs to be examined.

There were in fact much finer social distinctions within both *shi* and *shu*, so much so that the term *han* (humble) means virtually nothing unless it is located in a specific context. For instance, the term *hanmen*, "a humble lineage," was usually applied to a commoner, but it was also used by Jiang Xue 江斅 (fl. early fifth century), who claimed that he had come from "a waning clan of humble lineage" (*hanmen cuizu* 寒門悴族). This same Jiang Xue, however, had been chosen to marry a Song princess. According to Shen Yue, "Those who marry princesses must be scions of noble families and need not all be talented."[64] Therefore, Jiang Xue's claim is one of modesty and cannot be taken literally.[65] Zhang Zuan 張纘 (499–549), a descendent of the Western Jin writer Zhang Hua 張華 (232–300), was a cousin at some remove from Emperor Wu and was the emperor's son-in-law; yet, the *Nan shi* describes him as being from *hanmen*.[66] In this case, we can understand the phrase only

61. See Tang Changru, "Nanchao hanren de xingqi" 南朝寒人的興起, in idem, *Wei Jin nanbeichao shi luncong*, pp. 543–77.

62. Yan Zhitui, *Yanshi jiaxun* 11.292.

63. *Nan shi* 61.1501.

64. *Song shu* 52.1505.

65. Ibid., 41.1290.

66. *Nan shi* 56.1386.

comparatively, in relation to the very top echelon of the gentry class, such as the Wang clan of Langye 琅琊王氏.

Similarly, we would not be able to grasp the *Southern History* statement cited above unless we distinguish "commoners" (*hanren*) from "members of the minor gentry" (*hanshi* or *houmen* 後門): the former term was applied to commoners as opposed to various phrases indicating gentry members;[67] the latter term was often used in relation to the top elite (*jiazu* 甲族 or *gaomen*). Chen Qingzhi, who rose to a prominent position through military accomplishments, had been Emperor Wu's page, and Yu Yao had also been a servant. Thus both were true commoners (*hanren*), not members of the minor gentry (*hanshi*). The phrase *hanshi*, on the other hand, might be used as a derogative term or in reference to low-ranking officials. *The Southern History* recorded two similar anecdotes in which the minister Chu Yuan 褚淵 (435–82) was satirized for his disloyalty to the Song royal house.[68] In both cases, Chu Yuan angrily retaliated by calling the critic an "impudent *hanshi*." The adversary in the first version of the anecdote, Liu Xiang 劉祥, may indeed have qualified as a *hanshi*, but in the second version the person being called a *hanshi* was none other than Xie Chaozong 謝超宗 (d. 483), a member of the Xie clan of Chenjun 陳郡謝氏, one of the top elite clans in the Southern Dynasties. In both cases the *hanshi* in question replied ironically: "I could not bring myself to be a murderer [like you]—how can I help being a *hanshi*?" Here the term *hanshi* was clearly used to refer to official rank. In other words, Liu Xiang/Xie Chaozong was saying: "You murdered the Song loyalists Yuan and Liu, so you were promoted; I could not bring myself to do such a thing, which is why I remain a low official." By shifting the implication of *hanshi* from "humble family background" to "low official rank," Liu Xiang/Xie Chaozong rebutted Chu Yuan's angry vilification. These two anecdotes

67. For instance, "At the time there was a *hanren* called Yao Yin at Shanyin, who also had noble inclinations and was valued by members of the gentry" 時山陰又有寒人姚吟，亦有高趣，爲衣冠所重 (*Song shu* 93.2295). Or: "[If anyone breaks the decree,] a member of the gentry shall be deprived of his office, and a *hanren* shall be whipped one hundred times" 人士免官，寒人鞭一百 (*Nan Qi shu* 56.978).

68. See *Nan shi* 15.430, 19.543. The first anecdote first appears in *Nan Qi shu* 36.639.

demonstrate the elasticity of the term *hanshi* and the necessity of contextualizing its meaning.

In contrast to Song and Qi emperors, who had frequently trusted true commoners with great power, Emperor Wu of the Liang tended to promote not *hanren* but *hanshi*.[69] One case in point is that both *Song shu* 宋書 and *Nan Qi shu* have a section called "Biographies of the Special Favorites" ("Enxing zhuan" 恩倖傳 or "Xingchen zhuan" 倖臣傳), which records a series of low-born people who became close to emperors and wielded great power, but *Liang shu* contains no such section. *Nan shi* added Zhou Shizhen 周石珍, Lu Yan 陸驗, and Xu Lin 徐麟, all three serving under Emperor Wu of the Liang, to its "Biographies of the Special Favorites," but none rose to a prominent position or was influential.[70] The four most powerful ministers during Emperor Wu's reign, Zhou She 周捨 (471–524), Xu Mian 徐勉 (466–535), He Jingrong 何敬容 (d. 549), and Zhu Yi 朱异 (483–549), were all members of the gentry. Of the four, He Jingrong came from the highest stratum of the Southern Dynasties elite: his family, the He clan of Lujiang 盧江何氏, produced famous ministers, scholars, and recluses for many generations. He Jingrong himself was married to the daughter of Emperor Wu of the Qi as "a scion of an illustrious clan" (*mingjiazi* 名家子).[71] Zhou She was the eighth-generation descendent of Zhou Yi 周顗 (269–322), the well-known "three-day-sober vice president of the Imperial Secretariat" of the Eastern Jin; his father, Zhou Yong 周顒 (d. 485), was a famous conversationalist and a Buddhist theorist, whose work on prosody contributed to the establishment of the "Yongming style."[72] Xu Mian was once called a *hanshi* by Emperor Wu of the Liang himself,[73] but Zhu Yi was the only one among the four ministers who not only was of a relatively humble origin but also was a native southerner. Yet even Zhu Yi's father had been a county magistrate, and his maternal grandfather, Gu Huan

69. As Zhou Yiliang (*Lunji*, p. 346) says, those chosen by Emperor Wu came from the middle to lower levels of the gentry class and should not be confused with *hanren* or *shuren* (commoners).

70. *Nan shi* 77.1935–37.

71. *Liang shu* 31.531.

72. *Nan Qi shu* 22.730–34.

73. *Nan shi* 60.1479.

顧歡, was a renowned scholar and writer.[74] In other words, Zhu Yi was a *hanshi*, not a *hanren*. Zhu Yi and Xu Mian might be regarded as "low born" (*xiaoren*) only in comparison with the top echelon of the Southern Dynasties elite, but they were nevertheless members of the gentry, not commoners.

Emperor Wu never intended to demolish the hierarchy that divided gentry from commoner; indeed, such an attempt would have been beyond his power. His chief aim was to make the inherited system work to the advantage of the state, and in that he succeeded to a remarkable degree. He was devoted to appointing people with suitable abilities to appropriate positions, which led him to ignore some of the conventional social prejudices against the lower gentry, native southerners, and later northern immigrants referred to contemptuously as "newly arrived carpetbaggers."[75] As Yasuda Jirō aptly put it, Emperor Wu "took as his weapons the two principles of clear distinction between gentry and commoners and bureaucratic recruitment based on ability and scholarship."[76] For instance, Yu Wuling 庾於陵, a northern immigrant and a member of the lower gentry, was appointed librarian of the crown prince (Taizi xima 太子洗馬).

All the posts in the Eastern Palace [the residence of the heir apparent] were "pure" posts; the librarian, who was in charge of secretarial duties, was considered particularly "pure." In recent history only a talented and reputable member of one of the top elite families would be granted such a post. Both Wuling and Zhou She had held this office. The Exalted Emperor [i.e., Emperor Wu] said: "An official post becomes 'pure' because of the person assigned to it. How could

74. *Nan shi* 75.1874–880.

75. Jansen (*Höfische Öffentlichkeit*, pp. 207–11) suggests that Emperor Wu's Tianjian reform was designed to strengthen the solidarity of the gentry against the commoners by making the hierarchy within the gentry class open to talent. It is a possible interpretation, but we know only the emperor's desire to make more efficient use of the gentry as a whole.

76. Yasuda Jirō, "The Changing Aristocratic," p. 52. Curiously, Ochi Shigeaki ("The Southern Dynasties," p. 58) states that Emperor Wu "reduced the class of 'lesser houses' (*hou-men* 後門), of commoner origin, to a class debarred from participation in government administration." But *houmen*, like *hanpin* 寒品 (humble rank), refers to the lesser gentry, not commoners; for another thing, Emperor Wu in a 509 edict explicitly encouraged employment of talented members of "lesser houses" in government administration (*Liang shu* 2.49). This edict is discussed below.

it be limited to the top elite clans." The comment was much admired in contemporary public opinion.[77]

東宮官屬通爲清選, 洗馬掌文翰, 尤其清者. 近世用人, 皆取甲族有才望, 時於陵與周捨並擢充職, 高祖曰: "官以人而清, 豈限以甲族." 時論以爲美.

"Pure" (*qing* 清) had been the term used since the second century to refer to a person's moral character as well as to the prestige of an official post (which was not necessarily proportional to the actual power of the post). Appointing someone from a "lesser family" to a "pure post" was an attempt to change the political culture as well as to improve the social image of the lower gentry.

Lodging the value of "purity" in the person instead of in the office was a smart move for the emperor, but sometimes he twisted the argument around. The southerner Zhang Shuai 張率 (475–527) was appointed vice director of the Palace Library (Bishucheng 秘書丞). Emperor Wu said to him: "Vice director of the Palace Library is a first-class pure position and has never been granted to the scions of southeastern families. Now I am appointing you to this position—to help establish your reputation."[78] When the prestigious office of the governor of Yangzhou 揚州 was left vacant by the death of Emperor Wu's younger brother in 526, "imperial relatives as well as princes and nobles all hoped to be promoted to the position." To everyone's surprise, Emperor Wu appointed Kong Xiuyuan 孔休源 (469–532), a native southerner.[79]

Emperor Wu also carried out various reforms regarding education and the recruitment system, closely related institutions with great cultural significance. The basic recruitment system used throughout the Southern Dynasties was the Nine Ranks System (*jiupin zhongzheng zhi* 九品中正制), first introduced in the Kingdom of Wei after 220. Under this system, each commandery had its own "arbiter" (Zhongzheng 中正), who ranked all candidates for office in his jurisdiction on a scale from one to nine: the first rank was the highest and reserved for "sages"; in reality the highest rank was the second. Candidates recommended for office were to be given an examination before they were appointed, although this was not consistently practiced during the course of the

77. *Liang shu* 49.689.
78. Ibid., 33.475.
79. Ibid., 36.521.

Southern Dynasties.[80] This recruitment system became increasingly closed to outsiders, as arbiters increasingly made "family background" the primary criterion.[81] This was what Emperor Wu was determined to change.

In 505 an imperial edict decreed that those who had not yet reached thirty or did not have a thorough understanding of at least one Confucian classic were not allowed to serve, unless the person had extraordinary talent.[82] At the same time Emperor Wu restored the National University, or the School for the Sons of the State (Guozi xue 國子學). The National University had experienced great vicissitudes in the Eastern Jin, Song, and Qi and had never acquired the same kind of prestige or influence that it would achieve in the Liang.[83] Erudites of the Five Classics (Wujing boshi 五經博士), a position established by Emperor Wu of the Han (r. 140–87 B.C.), were reinstated, with one person responsible for each classic and in charge of one academy. These academies together had had several hundred students, all of whom received a monthly stipend. The examination system was reinstated. "Those who answered the examination questions well and showed a good understanding of the Classics would be appointed to an official post. Within a dozen years, all those who carried the Classics and their book satchels gathered in the capital city."[84] The emperor also ordered that schools be set up in prefectures and commanderies. In 510 he decreed that all the sons of the crown prince, princes, and nobles should attend the National University for their education.[85]

---

80. See Tang Changru, "Nanbeichao houqi keju zhidu de mengya" 南北朝後期科舉制度的萌芽, in idem, *Wei Jin nanbeichao shi luncong*, pp. 578–86. See also Dien, "Civil Service Examination."

81. During the Qi, "the local selection did not check up on a candidate's talent or moral character. Marriage relations and lineage record became the crucial factors" (Du You, *Tong dian* 2.334–35). See also Xiong Deji, "Jiupin zhongzheng zhi kaoshi" 九品中正制考實, in idem, *Liuchao shi kaoshi*, pp. 201–21; and Tang Changru, "Jiupin zhongzheng zhidu shishi" 九品中正制度試釋, in idem, *Wei Jin nanbeichao shi luncong*, pp. 81–121.

82. *Liang shu* 2.41.

83. For the troubled history of the Guozi xue in the Eastern Jin and Song, see *Song shu* 14.357–67.

84. *Liang shu* 48.662.

85. Ibid., 2.49–59.

In 508, besides arbiters, the emperor established a "prefectural hope" (Zhouwang 州望) in each prefecture, a "commandery chief" (Junzong 郡宗) in each commandery, and a "district notable" (Xianghao 鄉豪) in each district; their job was to search for talented people and recommend them to the government. "There was no longer any distinction between the elite and the lesser families [i.e., the lower gentry]" 無復膏梁寒素之隔.[86] The same rule was applied to the National University. According to *The Sui History*, "In the past admission to the National University was limited to scions of the nobility. Emperor Wu desired to acquire young talents, and so all five academies let in gifted students of humble origin, and there was no enrollment limit."[87] An imperial edict of 509 stated:

> Anyone with a thorough understanding of one classic from beginning to end, after having answered the examination questions to our satisfaction, will be appointed according to his ability. Be he a cowherd or a sheep butcher, coming from a humble rank or from a lesser gentry family, he should be given a post befitting his talent. There shall be no omission.
>
> 其有能通一經、始末無倦者, 策實之後, 選可量加敘錄. 雖復牛監羊肆, 寒品後門, 並隨才試吏, 勿有遺隔.[88]

The official range of recruitment was much more open than in the past.

In the winter of 541, Emperor Wu, then in his seventies, completed a work in twenty scrolls entitled *The Corrective Word of Confucius* (*Kongzi zhengyan* 孔子正言) and wrote a poem to commemorate the occasion.[89] Dao Gai 到溉 (477–548), a renowned scholar and writer serving as the

86. Du You, *Tong dian* 2.335. See also *Liang shu* 2.47.

87. *Sui shu* 26.724. When the School for the Sons of the State (Guozi xue) was first established in 293, it was, according to Cao Sizong's 曹思宗 memorial in 498, an elite school intended to be different from the more inclusive National University (Taixue 太學). Only the sons of officials of the fifth rank and above were admitted into the Guozi xue. The Guozi xue of the Qi dynasty was established in 482, with an enrollment limit of 150 students; it was suspended at the emperor's death in the same year and restored in 485, with an enrollment of 200 students: the official ranks of the students' fathers were specified in both cases (*Nan Qi shu* 9.143–45).

88. *Liang shu* 2.49.

89. *Quan Liang shi* 1.1530. Jiang Zong 江總 (519–94), who was to become one of the last Chen emperor's favorite poets, wrote a poem in response and was much praised by Emperor Wu (*Chen shu* 27.343). Jiang's poem is no longer extant.

chancellor of the National University (Guozi jijiu 國子祭酒), asked permission to set up an erudite of the *Corrective Word* (*Zhengyan* boshi 正言博士), with two teaching assistants. The request was granted. Yuan Xian 袁憲 (529–98), a member of the Yuan clan of Chenjun 陳郡袁氏 (another one of the very top elite families), became a student specializing in the *Corrective Word*. His precocious intelligence impressed his supervisors. Zhou Hongzheng 周弘正 (496–574), erudite of the National University (Guozi boshi 國子博士), said to Yuan Xian's father, Yuan Junzheng 袁君正: "Would your son like to take the examination now?" Yuan Xian's father declined, saying that Xian was not yet well read enough. A few days later, Zhou was preparing to give a lecture. Many students were present. When Zhou saw Yuan Xian, he made Xian take the stand and invited two of his guests, Xie Qi 謝岐 (d. 561) and He Tuo 何妥 (d. 590s), to ask Xian "anything you want." The hall became packed with curious spectators, but Yuan Xian kept his cool and answered every question well. Finally Zhou Hongzheng himself joined the questioners, but nobody could best Yuan Xian. Later, Zhou told Yuan Xian's father: "This young man is already good enough to replace me and become an erudite of the National University!" Thereupon Yuan Xian's father decided to let Yuan Xian take the examination. "At the time, all students about to take the examination bribed the examiners, and Wenhao [Yuan Junzheng's retainer] asked Junzheng to prepare gifts for the teachers. Junzheng refused flatly, saying: 'How can I bear to acquire a passing grade for my son with money?' The teachers, much irritated, vied with one another to put difficult questions to Xian. Xian, however, answered each question clearly and fluently." He passed the examination with high honors and was married to then–Crown Prince Xiao Gang's daughter. Yuan Xian began his public career in 546 as an assistant in the Palace Library.[90] After the fall of the Liang, he served in the Chen dynasty and was portrayed as a capable and conscientious minister by the *Chen shu* and *Nan shi* historians.

The story about Yuan Xian gives us a glimpse of how the National University worked. Apparently students could take the examination

90. *Chen shu* 24.312. Also see *Nan shi* 26.718–19. Both histories mistook the era name of the year 546 as Datong 大同; it should have been Zhong datong 中大同. The first year of Datong was 535; Yuan Xian was only six then.

whenever they felt ready, and there was no age limit. Although Emperor Wu decreed that only those who had reached age thirty should be appointed (at the beginning of the Liang it was twenty-five), the rule did not apply to those with "extraordinary talent" or those who passed the examination on the Classics. As a result, many started off their official career at a much earlier age.

As Albert Dien points out, one sign of the cultural significance of examinations in this period was "the value that came to be placed on the literary quality of the questions posed to the candidates, as evidenced by the presence of the genre of examination questions (*cewen*) in the *Wen xuan*,"[91] the literary anthology compiled by Xiao Tong. But the fundamental aim of the educational project was to improve the existing recruitment system: cultural values and political values became closely intertwined. If, as Yan Zhitui said, scions of great houses, like sons of the "lesser families," had to take the exams, then even if they had to hire someone to write the answers or, as we have seen in Yuan Xian's story, to bribe the examiners, the message was nonetheless clear: lineage was no longer the only standard for judging a man.[92] In fact, during the Liang we begin to see a new criterion for evaluating people—the possession of *wen* 文: scholarly and literary accomplishments. This is an important point to bear in mind about the Liang.

Emperor Wu himself demonstrated a level of personal commitment to literary and scholarly pursuits rare for an emperor. He had been a competent poet since his youth, and he continued to compose poems after taking the throne. His collected literary works, now lost, included the large body of public documents he composed over nearly a half century of rule; even so, the size—120 scrolls—is remarkable. He was no less prolific as a commentator. Although we might expect the several hundred scrolls of commentary on Buddhist scripture from this Buddhist emperor, Emperor Wu also wrote a commentary on the Daoist classic *Laozi* and commentaries on a number of the Confucian classics, including *The Classic of Filial Piety*, *Annals of Springs and Autumns*, *The Classic*

91. Dien, "Civil Service Examination," p. 105; see pp. 105–6 for Dien's translation of "one of a set of three questions, dated to the early Liang (504) and written by Ren Fang (but in the voice of the emperor)" (ibid., pp. 105–6).

92. Yan Zhitui, *Yanshi jiaxun* 8.145.

of Poetry, *The Classic of Documents*, and *The Classic of Changes*. His exegesis of "The Doctrine of the Mean" ("Zhongyong" 中庸) was one of the few early independent commentaries on this text before it became part of the canonical Four Books in the twelfth century. He was, in addition, a great lover of music and invented new instruments for the performance of ritual music. To this, he added other gentlemanly skills of a southern aristocrat: chess, calligraphy, necromancy, riding, and archery. The extent of these accomplishments made Emperor Wu unique among Chinese emperors up to his day. Taken together, these accomplishments suggest a new view of the imperial role: the emperor rules by virtue of being an active representative of his culture.

Emperor Wu and his sons made a conscious effort to encourage culture, learning, and literature. At banquets and gatherings, the emperor invariably asked his ministers to compose poetry and would often join in himself. "On those whose writings stood out, [the emperor] would bestow gifts of gold and silk. To those who approached the court and presented a *fu* or an ode, he would often give audience."[93] In *The History of the Liang* and *The Southern History*, we find many anecdotes about the royal family's appreciation of ministers' literary talents. Emperor Wu frequently wrote poems to them, sometimes praising their writings, sometimes affectionately teasing their slowness in poetic composition. The circulation of these anecdotes lent an aura of cultural honor and privilege to literary ability, an aura unattainable through a noble lineage alone. As a result, when the renowned poet Wang Yun 王筠 (481–549) exhorted his sons to exert themselves in literature, even though he was a Langye Wang he chose to emphasize the family's literary rather than political achievements:

> The histories say that the Cui family of Anping and the Ying family of Ru'nan had literary talent for several generations . . . but they merely passed it on for two or three generations, quite unlike our family, which for seven generations has constantly renewed its reputation and virtue, with continuous officeholding and everyone producing his own collected literary works.[94]

> 史傳稱安平崔氏及汝南應氏並累世有文才. . . . 然不過父子兩三世耳; 非有七葉之中, 名德重光, 爵位相繼, 人人有集, 如吾門世者也.

---

93. *Liang shu* 49.685.
94. Ibid., 33.486–87.

It is particularly noteworthy that many of the writers and poets appreciated by the emperor were members of the lower gentry and native southerners who traditionally had been politically and culturally marginalized; now they seemed to make literature their "family business." The families of Dao Gai, Liu Xiaochuo 劉孝綽 (481–539), Zhang Shuai, Lu Chui (one of the Eight Companions of the Prince Jingling), Yu Wuling, Xu Chi, and Zhou She are all fine examples. By strategic intermarriage these families formed a new cultural elite, which is discussed in greater detail in Chapter 3.

Most of Emperor Wu's favorite ministers were, like the emperor himself, proficient in learning and literary writing. Zhou She left behind collected works in twenty scrolls, besides a *Commentary on Letter Writing* (*Shuyi shu* 書儀疏) in one scroll and a work on the rites in fifty-two scrolls. Xu Mian was prolific: the historian said that "even though he was trusted with state affairs, he never stopped writing."[95] His literary collection included a "Former Collection" of thirty-five scrolls and a "Latter Collection" of sixteen scrolls. Zhu Yi "studied the Five Classics and was particularly good at *The Record of Rites* and *The Classic of Changes*. He was not only widely read in literature and history but also skilled in miscellaneous arts: chess, writing, and arithmetic were all his specialties."[96] In 540 he lectured on Emperor Wu's *Commentary on Laozi* in front of an audience of over a thousand people; in 541 he lectured on Emperor Wu's *Exegesis of the "Doctrine of the Mean"* at the newly opened Elite Academy (Shilin guan 士林館); the crown prince also summoned him to the Mystery Garden (Xuanpu 玄圃) to lecture on *The Classic of Changes*.

Interestingly enough, the only one of the four powerful ministers of Emperor Wu's time who demonstrated no talent in literature (or, according to *The Southern History*, did not possess a high degree of learning) was He Jingrong, who was from one of the highest elite families. He Jingrong was a good minister, hard-working and responsible. Despite rumors about his greed and openness to bribery, when he was dismissed from his post and left the prime minister's residence, all he had were some everyday items and clothes: "the public admired him for it."[97] He

95. Ibid., 25.387.
96. Ibid., 38.537.
97. Ibid., 37.534. *Nan shi* 30.799.

was, however, also a target of savage satire. *The History of the Liang*, in its usual understated way, simply says: "Since the Jin and Song, all prime ministers found recreation in literature. Jingrong alone was diligent in official business and so was scorned by the world."[98] *The Southern History* was much more explicit: He Jingrong was "clumsy at calligraphy and shallow in learning." When signing his name, he wrote the characters in such a way that parts of them were disproportionately big or small.[99] It is clear that it was not just He Jingrong's "diligence in official business" that brought him so much ridicule—after all, Wang Dao 王導 (276–339) and Xie An 謝安 (320–85), the grand ancestors of the Wang and Xie clans, or even Wang Jian of the Qi, had been great ministers who took care of business, and yet they were much admired by the public; it was, rather, He Jingrong's lack of cultural refinement that damaged his reputation. This seems to have been particularly unforgivable in "a scion of an illustrious clan" like He Jingrong. From another perspective, however, we might say that precisely because He Jingrong was from a great family, he could afford not to possess the literary flair and learning of a Xu Mian or a Zhu Yi.

Cultural accomplishments, however, proved to be a much more important factor in the rise and fall of a clan than bloodline and pedigree. If the Xiao clan of Lanling 蘭陵蕭氏, of which Emperor Wu himself was a member, was considered on a par with such elite clans as the Wangs of Langye and the Xies and Yuans of Chenjun in the Tang dynasty,[100] it was primarily due to the fact that the Xiaos were able to maintain cultural eminence throughout political vicissitudes. After all, neither the Sima house of the Jin nor the Liu house of the Song acquired the same status. The Xiaos had been members of the lower gentry before they founded a dynasty,[101] but the Xiaos were a much more literary family. Long after the

98. *Liang shu* 37.532.

99. *Nan shi* 30.796–97.

100. See Liu Fang's "Xingxi lun" in *Xin Tang shu* 199.5677.

101. A remark by the founding emperor of the Qi portraying himself as *buyi suzu* 布衣素族 has often been misinterpreted as meaning "a man of a humble background." *Suzu*, "a pure clan," in fact refers to "a genteel lineage"; *buyi*, "plain clothes," is a term for being a civilian or a lowly official. *Buyi suzu* thus means a member of the gentry who does not hold a high office. In an attempt to clarify the misunderstanding accruing around the term *suzu*, Zhou Yiliang (*Lunji*, p. 82) listed

fall of the Liang, many of Emperor Wu's descendents continued to serve the state and were renowned cultural figures.[102]

Despite the emperor's support for the lower gentry and native southerners, there is no sign that he tried to suppress the northern immigrant elite by appointing them only to decorative but powerless posts. The case of He Jingrong testifies to his evenhanded approach to competing criteria for family status. The real problem seemed to be the frequent indifference of the members of the most elite families toward state service or their ineptitude in administrative matters. Wang Qian 王騫 (474–522), a member of the Langye Wang clan whose daughter was the crown princess, explicitly told his sons: "Ours is a so-called 'pure clan' [*suzu* 素族]. You should just follow the current and move upward step by step. There is no need to [actively] seek advancement."[103] Another member of the Wang clan, Wang Xi 王錫 (499–534), whose mother was Emperor Wu's sister, turned down the directorship of the Ministry of Personnel. Xie Ju 謝舉 (d. 548), a member of the Chenjun Xie clan, refused to deal with state affairs even though he was appointed a grand councilor. "He frequently requested to retire on the ground of illness, and the emperor would allow him sick leaves."[104] Some other members of the elite became resentful when appointed to minor posts and vented their resentment by neglecting their job. During his term as a county magistrate, the talented poet Wang Ji 王籍 (d. 547), one of the Langye Wangs, had everyone who filed a suit whipped.[105]

These great clans nevertheless continued to be privileged through the Liang. The imperial family chose marriage partners from these clans, and such alliances added to the glory of the imperial family as well as fortified the great clans' place at the top of the social strata. Therefore, when Hou Jing 侯景 (d. 552), a general who defected from the North, asked to

---

some examples of the usage of the term in the sense of "genteel lineage" in a footnote to his article. Another modern historian Tang Changru ("Du shi shi ci" 讀史釋辭, in *Wei Jin nanbeichao shilun shiyi*, pp. 249–53) agrees with Zhou Yiliang and supplements Zhou's explication by providing more examples.

102. This is discussed in greater detail in the Epilogue of this book.

103. *Liang shu* 7.159. Wang Qian was the eldest son of the powerful Qi minister Wang Jian.

104. Ibid., 37.530.

105. Ibid., 50.713.

marry a Langye Wang or a Chenjun Xie, Emperor Wu famously replied: "The Wang and Xie clans are too elevated to [supply your] spouse; you may seek [a spouse] from the Zhu and Zhang clans and below." Since both the Zhus and the Zhangs were southern elite clans, Emperor Wu's remark was a clear indication of the old hierarchy among the northern émigré and the native southerners. Hou Jing was understandably angered by the refusal and swore to "match the sons and daughters of the South with slaves."[106] Hou Jing did not exactly carry out his "matchmaking" promise, but the devastation he caused was much more effective in destroying the class system that had prevailed for over two hundred years in the South: a large number of gentry members either died during the ensuing wars or became captives and were taken north. Many great clans suffered multiple fatal blows. Wang Ke 王克, a descendent of Wang Dao and the vice director of the Imperial Secretariat, was "handsome in appearance and graceful in his manners," but he submitted to Hou Jing's authority when Hou Jing's army occupied the Palace City. Later, when General Wang Sengbian 王僧辯 recovered Jiankang, he mocked Wang Ke: "You must have had a hard time serving the barbarian lord!" Wang Ke could not answer a word. Then Wang Sengbian demanded to know where the imperial seal was; after a long silence, Wang Ke answered: "It was taken by Zhao, the magistrate of Pingyuan." Zhao was one of Hou Jing's most trusted confidants. Thereupon Wang Sengbian said: "The Wang family had been a noble clan for a hundred generations, but now it has fallen in one morning" 王氏百世卿族，便是一朝而墜![107] The image of the "fall" aptly describes the fate of the old elite clans in the South after the Hou Jing Rebellion.

THE EMPEROR BODHISATTVA

Any study of the Liang dynasty must include Buddhism. Emperor Wu's Buddhist faith was inseparable from his spiritual pursuits and his political aspirations. In many ways, his Buddhist enterprise should also be viewed as a competitive and imitative gesture, since the Northern Dynasty rulers were likewise passionately devoted to Buddhism and

106. *Nan shi* 80.1996.
107. Ibid., 23.637.

consistently advocated the notion that the "emperor *is* the Buddha."[108] But in his inventiveness as well as in his diligent observation of Buddhist precepts, Emperor Wu surpassed his northern counterparts. Institutionally, he exerted a vital influence on the subsequent development of Chinese Buddhism.[109]

It is necessary to begin a discussion of Emperor Wu's religious activities by clarifying one questionable event. An imperial edict recorded in *An Expansion of the Propagation of the Light* (*Guang hongming ji* 廣弘明集), a collection of Buddhist prose and poetry compiled by the Tang monk Daoxuan 道宣 (596–667), states that on the eighth day of the fourth month (Buddha's birthday) in the third year of the Tianjian era (May 7, 504), Emperor Wu not only formally converted to Buddhism and denounced Daoism but also demanded in a second edict that all members of the royal family as well as all courtiers convert as well. In no ambiguous terms, the emperor declared: "Although Laozi, the Duke of Zhou, and Confucius were disciples of the Buddha, they had deviated from the correct path. They represented the goodness of the mortal world but were unable to transcend the secular realm and attain sainthood."[110] The date of this event, however, has been proven unreliable by Japanese and Chinese scholars. This casts doubt on the veracity of the event itself. It is suggested that the whole document was fabricated by the editor of *Guang hongming ji* to exalt Buddhism.[111]

Although *Guang hongming ji* might not be the most reliable source, another modern scholar does not contest the authenticity of the imperial edict but believes that the date, the eighth day of the fourth month, should be moved to the eighteenth year of the Tianjian reign (519), a day when Emperor Wu did receive a set of Buddhist precepts and declared a general amnesty.[112] *Jie* 戒 (precept) is a broad term for rules of

108. See Yan Shangwen, "Liang Wudi huangdi."

109. There is much literature on Emperor Wu's religious endeavors. See, e.g., Yan Shangwen, *Liang Wudi*; and Janousch, "The Emperor as Bodhisattva."

110. Daoxuan, *Guang hongming ji*, *T* 52: 4.112.

111. Ōta Teizō, "Ryō Butei"; Xiong Qingyuan, "Liang Wudi Tianjian sannian."

112. See Zhao Yiwu, "Guanyu Liang Wudi." Interestingly, *Liang shu* did not record this event. It simply states that a general amnesty was declared on this day (*Liang shu* 2.59). It was *Nan shi* (6.197) that added the piece of information about receiving the Buddhist precepts.

conduct observed by Buddhist practitioners, be they monks, nuns, or lay believers. The process for a layman's reception of the precepts was quite elaborate, and there are many different sets of precepts, such as the Five Precepts, the Ten Precepts, and so forth. Many Mahāyāna Buddhist texts consider the observance of these precepts the first step toward enlightenment, after which comes *ding* 定 (Skt. *samādhi*, concentration) and *hui* 慧 (Skt. *prajñā*, wisdom). Before 519 Emperor Wu had spent about ten years compiling a treatise called *The Laws for Receiving Bodhisattva's Precepts for Monks, Nuns, and Lay People* (*Zaijia chujia shou pusa jie fa* 在家出家受菩薩戒法), of which a fragment is extant among the Dunhuang materials.[113] This treatise clearly served as a theoretical and ritual guide for his own reception of the Bodhisattva precepts in 519. In the treatise, the emperor made it clear that although a senior Buddhist monk was central to accomplishing the ceremony, the emperor received the precepts and the accompanying religious power *directly* from divine authority and not from a mortal priest. In other words, this treatise served as a theoretical basis for the emperor's later claim to be the highest authority in both the secular and the religious realms. He also had a round altar constructed for this special occasion.[114] As Yan Shangwen points out, the event that took place in 519 was not a casual gesture but had been carefully thought out and planned well in advance.[115] It was part of Emperor Wu's attempt to unify political and religious authorities into one supreme sovereignty, a decisive step in his construction of a new model for kingship. In the same year, the emperor changed the reign name from Tianjian to Putong 普通 (a Buddhist term, meaning "universal unimpediment")—an act of

113. Pelliot chinois 2196: *juan* 1 of *The Laws for Receiving Bodhisattva's Precepts for Monks, Nuns, and Lay People*. According to this fragment, the emperor compiled the treatise on the basis of his own synthesis of many different sūtras. See Yan Shangwen, "Liang Wudi shou pusa jie," pp. 48–49.

114. Dao Xuan, *Xu gaoseng zhuan*, *T* 50: 6.469. *Xu Gaoseng zhuan* placed the emperor's reception of the precepts in the Hall of Equal Enlightenment (Dengjue dian 等覺殿), which is referred to in *Nan shi* (6.197) as the Hall of No Obstruction (Wu'ai dian 無碍殿). "Wu'ai" is a Buddhist term referring to the absence of any obstruction of the highest Buddhist wisdom, which penetrates everything like rays of light.

115. Yan Shangwen, "Liang Wudi shou pusa jie," pp. 47–48.

commemoration and celebration, a mark of turning a new leaf in the imperial rule.[116]

According to "The Biography of Shi Huiyue" ("Shi Huiyue zhuan" 釋惠約傳) in *The Sequel to the Biographies of Eminent Monks* (*Xu Gaoseng zhuan* 續高僧傳), from the crown prince and members of the royal family and courtiers down to commoners, "48,000 people received precepts," following Emperor Wu's example.[117] The number may very well have been an exaggeration, but the emperor's decision to receive the Bodhisattva precepts clearly had a strong impact on Liang society. Crown Prince Xiao Tong constructed a Hall of Wisdom and Truth (Huiyi dian 慧義殿) in which he regularly discussed sūtras with eminent monks. In the fourth month of 520, "sweet dew descended in the Hall of Wisdom and Truth, and everyone thought it was heaven's response to the crown prince's supreme virtue."[118]

In such a context, the authenticity of the "conversion edict" recorded in *Guang hongming ji* is less important than what the edict reveals about the way in which the emperor's religious and political agenda was perceived by later generations. Even if the edict is a later fabrication, it indicates the extent to which the emperor was identified with his religious faith and how Buddhism was regarded *de facto* as the national religion of the Liang. Many elements of the edict can, in fact, be attested by other writings of Emperor Wu. Of these elements the most noteworthy is the implied trajectory of the evolution of the emperor's religious belief.[119]

By Emperor Wu's time the conversion model had already become a familiar one and was frequently associated with followers of Buddhism.

116. One may contrast it with Tianjian (heaven's inspection), a term found in Confucian classics such as the *Shijing*.

117. *T* 50: 6.469.

118. *Liang shu* 8.166.

119. The explicit rejection of Daoist practices, for example, stands out in the edict. It would be unwise to reject this claim as nothing more than Buddhist propaganda. In *Lidai sanbao ji* 歷代三寶記 (*T* 49: 3.38), a Buddhist work compiled in 597, Fei Changfang 費長房 recorded that Emperor Wu decreed a general abolition of Daoist establishments (*daoguan* 道館) in various prefectures in 517, the year before the emperor received the Buddhist precepts. Since the most famous Daoist practitioner of the day, Tao Hongjing 陶弘景 (456–536), received the Five Buddhist Precepts late in life, it seems only reasonable to conclude that the Buddhist influence was widespread in the Liang (*Liang shu* 51.743).

The famous Eastern Jin monk Huiyuan 慧遠 (334–416) began his career by studying the Confucian classics and was conversant with Lao-Zhuang philosophy. Circumstances made him a disciple of the monk Dao'an 道安 (312–85). His enlightenment upon listening to Dao'an's lectures was marked by these words: "[Compared to this,] Confucian and Daoist and all the other doctrines are mere husks [i.e., inessentials]."[120] Huiyuan once wrote in a letter to his friends:

> I often think back on the past when I immersed myself in the Classics of this mortal world. At that time, I thought it was the most glorious place to be. By the time I got to read *Laozi* and *Zhuangzi*, I realized that the Doctrine of Names (i.e., Confucianism) was no more than empty talk designed to respond to various changes. But nowadays, I have comprehended that in terms of the aura of the mysterious and metaphysical, how could one not take the Buddhist principles as the very foremost?[121]
>
> 每尋疇昔遊心世典，以爲當年之華苑也. 及見老莊，便悟名教是應變之虛談耳. 以今而觀，則知沈冥之趣，豈得不以佛理爲先?

It was also around the same time that the poet Tao Yuanming wrote about what I call "secular conversion" in his poetry: he declared that his public career had been a mistake and that he wanted to begin a new life of reclusion in "gardens and fields." Viewing one's life in such terms enables a person to make sense of sundry experiences and, more important, to construct a narrative of radical change. It is a mode of autobiography that would become quite influential in later writings.

Emperor Wu left the first poem in Chinese literary history on the experience of religious conversion. It may very well have been written around the time he received the Buddhist precepts:

會三教詩

A Poem Bringing Together the Three Doctrines[122]

少時學周孔	In my youth I emulated the Duke of Zhou and Confucius;
弱冠窮六經	at twenty I had exhausted the Six Classics.

120. See "The Biography of Huiyuan" in *Gaoseng zhuan* 高僧傳 (6.211) by the Liang monk Huijiao 慧皎 (497–554); also in *T* 50: 6.358.

121. *Quan Jin wen* 161.2390.

122. The text has many variants, which are not marked here; see *Quan Liang shi* 1.1531–32.

孝義連方册	Concepts of filial piety and righteousness fill the volumes,
仁恕滿丹青	acts of kindness and clemency pervade the histories.
踐言貴去伐	One carries out promise, values the elimination of pride;[123]
爲善在好生	doing good deeds means cherishing life.
中復觀道書	Then in mid-life I read Daoist tomes
有名與無名	on that which is named and that which is nameless.[124]
妙術鏤金版	Subtle methods are carved on golden tablets;
眞言隱上清	words of truth contained in the Exalted Clarity.[125]
密行貴陰德	Secret acts [of goodness] prize hidden virtues;
顯證表長齡	visible proof [of their effect] is manifested in longevity.
晚年開釋卷	In my old age I open the Buddhist scrolls:
猶月映群星	they are like the moon shining forth amidst stars.
苦集始覺知	I begin to understand suffering and its accumulation;[126]
因果方昭明	cause and effect are finally illuminated.
不毀惟平等	*Sāmānya* is the only thing that will not be destroyed,[127]
至理歸無生	the ultimate truth returns to Nirvana.

123. *The Record of Rites*: "Cultivating oneself and carrying out one's promises may be called good deeds" 脩身踐言謂之善行 (*Liji zhushu* 1.14). I take *fa* 伐 as "a sense of pride or self-complacency." The *Analects*: "I wish not to pride myself on being good or boast of my achievements" 願無伐善, 無施勞 (*Lunyu zhushu* 5.46).

124. A citation from *Laozi*: "The nameless was the beginning of heaven and earth; the named was the mother of the myriad things" 無名天地始, 有名萬物母 (*Laozi jiaoshi* 1.5).

125. "Exalted Clarity" is one of the three Daoist heavens. It is also the name of a Daoist sect founded in the third to fourth century and expanded by the Liang Daoist Tao Hongjing.

126. Suffering (*ku* 苦) and accumulation (*ji* 集) are two of the Four Noble Truths (*si sheng di* 四聖諦). "Suffering" is a necessary attribute of sentient existence; "accumulation" explains that accumulation of suffering is caused by passions.

127. *Sāmānya* is the realm of "equality" or "nondiscrimination" (i.e, considering everything as equal from the perspective of emptiness).

分别根難一	With discrimination, it is hard for *indriya* to remain intact;
執著性易驚	attachment to things easily causes surprises to one's nature.[128]
窮源無二聖	Going back to the origin, we do not find two sages,
測善非三英	when we measure the Good, the three doctrines do not differ.
大椿徑億尺	The big ailanthus tree grows to be a million feet straight up,
小草裁云萌	but the little grass has just sprouted.
大雲降大雨	From the great clouds comes a great shower,
隨分各受榮	all plants will receive their due, each according to its allotment.
心相起異解	From various minds arise diverse understandings;
報應有殊形	retribution also takes on varied forms.
差别豈作意	How could the differences be a result of deliberations?
深淺固物情	Profundity and shallowness are inherent in the nature of things.

The first part of the poem presents a linear course of spiritual growth; the second part makes it clear that although Buddhism is the moon outshining the stars that are Confucianism and Daoism, all three doctrines originate from the same source. The path to enlightenment is a process not of supplanting, but of integrating. In the final analysis, the three doctrines are no more than various manifestations of one great Truth, which is revealed differently according to the different capacity of each individual, just as each plant absorbs its own allotment of moisture in line with its receptivity. By positioning the study of Buddhism, the "greatest Rain of Dharma of all," in his old age, however, the poem seems to suggest that the individual intellectual capacity may expand with time, and that humans, unlike grass and ailanthus, may eventually transform themselves.

128. *Indriya* are the roots of plants, which enable them to grow; in this sense it means the capacity and abilities (classified into sharp, average, and dull) that enable a person to achieve a certain level of understanding. This couplet stresses the value of nondiscrimination and nonattachment, which open the way for the subsequent declaration that the three doctrines ultimately do not contradict one another.

Emperor Wu's reception of the Bodhisattva precepts in 519 constituted a watershed in his religious life. After 519 the emperor turned to more public, more spectacular forms of celebrating his Buddhist faith, which are discussed in greater detail later in this section. By contrast, the early years of his rule witnessed the most concentrated sponsorship of the composition, compilation, and cataloguing of various Buddhist works under imperial auspices. Of these works, two types deserve special attention: the so-called Buddhist encyclopedias and the biographies of eminent monks and nuns. Unlike the Buddhist scriptures and commentaries, which might prove too specialized for a layman, Buddhist encyclopedias and biographies were much more accessible to secular readers and, as a result, had a larger impact on the Liang cultural imagination. Both types are dealt with at greater length in the next chapter.

It was also in the early years of Emperor Wu's reign that he staged a large-scale ideological battle against anti-Buddhist sentiments, and nothing is more emblematic of Emperor Wu's integration of religious and political concerns than the case of Fan Zhen 范縝 (ca. 450–510), the person chosen by Emperor Wu as a target of attack in a sweeping Buddhist campaign. Fan Zhen was well known for his theatrical anti-Buddhist stance. During the Yongming era, he authored a treatise entitled "On the Mortality of the Soul" ("Shenmie lun" 神滅論), which had been the talk of the day and apparently incurred the great displeasure of the pious Prince of Jingling.[129] The Prince of Jingling summoned famous monks to debate with Fan Zhen and even enlisted a mutual friend to intervene, but Fan Zhen would not give up his views.[130] Some time between November 29, 507, and February 16, 508, Emperor Wu wrote a rebuttal to Fan Zhen's treatise known as "An Imperial Response to a Minister's Treatise on the Mortality of the Soul" ("Chi da chenxia Shenmie lun" 敕答臣下神滅論). This led to a flurry of rejoinders from sixty-two princes and ministers, all of which are preserved in *The Propagation of the Light* (*Hongming ji* 弘明集), a collection of writings on

129. *Liang shu* 48.665–70. For a discussion of the debate on the immortality of the soul, see Liebenthal, "The Immortality of the Soul" (Liebenthal erroneously dates Fan Zhen's treatise to 507); Lai, "Emperor Wu of Liang"; Jansen, *Höfische Öffentlichkeit*, pp. 215–18; and Zheng Jiliang, *Wei Jin nanbeichao*, pp. 367–455. For a translation into German of Fan Zhen's essay, see Balazs, "Der Philosoph."

130. *Liang shu* 48.670; *Zizhi tongjian* 136.4259–60.

Buddhism compiled by the monk Sengyou 僧祐 (445–518).[131] Emperor Wu's decision to single out Fan Zhen's treatise for criticism more than twenty years after it was first written and five years after he took the throne reveals much about the emperor's growing religious conviction and the maturity of his theory about the immortality of the soul, as well as about the intricacy of Liang court politics. We have to go back a few years and examine an incident that took place in 505.

That summer, at a court banquet, Fan Zhen offended the emperor deeply by speaking out for a minister in disfavor, Wang Liang 王亮 (d. 510), a prominent member of the Langye Wang clan. He had served the Qi as director of the Department of State Affairs. During Emperor Wu's conquest of the Qi capital, he was the only official who did not profess loyalty to the new emperor or welcome his army. In 503 Wang Liang did not attend the New Year's Day grand court banquet on the pretext of sickness, although it was later discovered that he had been in good health. He was censured for his "great disrespect" and deprived of all official titles. On the other hand, Emperor Wu accorded special favor and honor to Xie Fei 謝朏 (441–506), a descendent of the Chenjun Xie clan.[132] Fan Zhen, a close friend of Wang Liang's, criticized what he perceived to be the injustice of all this, much to the chagrin of the emperor. Thereupon Ren Fang, who was palace aide to the censor in chief at the time, filed a formal complaint against Fan Zhen, and the emperor himself not only endorsed Ren Fang's proposal to have Fan Zhen's case dealt with by the chamberlain for law enforcement, but took it upon himself to write a memo reprimanding Fan Zhen.[133] Soon afterward Fan Zhen was exiled to Guangzhou 廣州. In 507 he was summoned back to the capital to be a gentleman-attendant of the Secretariat (Zhongshulang 中書郎). Upon his return, however, Fan Zhen was greeted by a mass denunciation headed by the emperor and followed by

131. *T* 52: 10.60–68.

132. *Liang shu* 15.264. Cao Daoheng ("Lun dong Jin nanchao," p. 37) suggests that Emperor Wu respected Xie Fei because Xie Fei manifested loyalty to the Qi, but in fact Xie Fei had been a recluse since the last years of the Qi and refused several summons from the Qi court just as he refused Emperor Wu's. Cao also mistakes Wang Liang for a supporter of Emperor Wu's revolutionary army.

133. Both documents are preserved in "The Biography of Wang Liang" in *Liang shu* 16.268–70.

sixty-two courtiers, a "struggle session," so to speak, that confirmed the political and spiritual authority of the emperor.[134] Apart from their replies to the emperor's "Response," Xiao Chen, Cao Siwen 曹思文, and Shen Yue also wrote separate essays arguing against Fan Zhen.[135]

The much-revered monk Fayun 法雲 (467–529) played an important role in orchestrating the debate. Fayun apparently made the emperor's response to Fan Zhen's treatise available to the sixty-two courtiers, accompanied by a letter he had composed.[136] He probably did this with the emperor's tacit knowledge and approval, although Shen Yue's reply makes it clear that Fayun was not the only monk to receive a copy of the imperial response.[137] In any case, all the courtiers agreed with Emperor Wu's critique of Fan Zhen.[138] Many of them made specific references to Emperor Wu's "Response," and the emperor's two citations from a Confucian classic, *The Record of Rites*, were especially applauded: for the more Confucian-minded, it was seen as an affirmation of filial piety (the quotations involve making sacrifices to the spirits of ancestors) and the sacred nature of the Confucian classics; for the more Buddhist-minded, it was considered a good example of using expedient means to teach Buddhist truths. For both groups, it was an ingenious way of merging Buddhist and Confucian teachings and showing their "common origin."

134. Several replies by the courtiers referred to Fan Zhen as "Secretary Fan," which shows that the critique took place after Fan Zhen returned from the far South.

135. Xiao Chen's essay and Cao Siwen's two essays are included in Sengyou, *Hongming ji* (*T* 52: 9.54–60), along with Fan Zhen's rebuttal of Cao Siwen's first essay. Shen Yue's is included in the much later collection, Daoxuan, *Guang hongming ji* (*T* 52: 22.253–54). It is a mystery why Shen Yue's essay was excluded from *Hongming ji*. It might have been an accident, or it might have had something to do with Shen Yue's loss of the emperor's favor at the time of his death in 513.

136. *T* 52: 10.60.

137. Shen Yue said: "Recently Master Yue came from the court and he was also granted a copy of the imperial reply to the minister in question" 近約法師殿内出, 亦蒙敕答臣下一本 (*T* 52: 10.60). "Master Yue" refers to the monk Huiyue 慧約 (452–535), who was on close personal terms with Shen Yue.

138. Whalen Lai ("Emperor Wu of Liang," p. 167) remarks that "all except four of the respondents were on his [i.e. Emperor Wu's] side." Lai does not specify which four of the respondents expressed disapproval. My reading, however, shows that all courtiers supported the emperor's argument against Fan Zhen.

The carefully orchestrated debate marked the maturity of Emperor Wu's belief in the immortality of the soul, which he took to be the basis for obtaining Buddhahood. He expounded this belief in a treatise entitled "A Record of the Establishment of the Concept that 'The Luminous Spirit Is Able to Achieve Buddhahood'" ("Li shenming chengfo yi ji" 立神明成佛義記).[139] The vast scale of his pro-Buddhism campaign in the early years of his reign attests both to his efforts to build an ideological foundation for his unique vision of sovereignty and to the extent to which Buddhism was winning over the court.

Emperor Wu's public display of religious devotion had equally far-reaching consequences. Throughout the Liang, numerous Buddhist temples and monasteries had been constructed or converted from private residences. In the capital area alone, there were reportedly over five hundred of them.[140] The most famous was perhaps the Temple of Universal Peace (Tongtai si 同泰寺) built in 527, on the site now occupied by the Temple of the Cockcrow (Jiming si 雞鳴寺) in modern Nanjing. The temple boasted a nine-story pagoda, six large halls, and over ten smaller halls, all "in the shapes of the sun and moon."[141] As scholars point out, the temple was constructed in imitation of the structure of the Buddhist universe.[142] To have easy access to the temple, the emperor ordered a gate opened in the north wall of the Palace City (Taicheng 臺城); the gate was named the Great Pass (Datong men 大通門). In commemoration of the completion of the temple and the gate, the era name was changed to

139. For an English translation of this treatise, see Liebenthal, "The Immortality of the Soul," pp. 376–78; and Lai, "Emperor Wu of Liang," pp. 170–73. Lai, however, suggests that the sixty-two courtiers' replies were to this treatise, although in the replies there are many references to the emperor's "Response to a Minister's Treatise on the Mortality of the Soul," not to this treatise. See Lai, p. 167. In fact we do not know exactly in which year the emperor wrote the treatise, though it could have been written around the same time as the emperor wrote his "Response."

140. *Nan shi* 70.1721.

141. Xu Song, *Jiankang shilu* 17.478, citing *Yudi zhi* 輿地志 by Gu Yewang 顧野王 (518–81).

142. There was also a hemispherical dome (*gai tian yi* 蓋天儀) in the Tongtai Temple. The theory that the heavens were a hemisphere covering the earth had originated with *Zhou bi suan jing* 周髀算經, purportedly a Han work, but it corresponded to the cosmic vision expounded in Indian Buddhism; see Jiang Xiaoyuan and Niu Weixing, "Tianxueshi shang," pp. 134–35.

Datong in the spring of 527. In the Tongtai Temple, Emperor Wu gave public lectures on a variety of Buddhist scriptures; sometimes, a lecture series would continue for over a month. It was also in this temple that the emperor donned monk's robes and donated his body to the Buddha (*sheshen* 捨身) four times, in 527, 529, 546, and 547. Each time members of the royal family and courtiers "redeemed" him for huge sums of money.

The Tongtai Temple was also the site of a number of "unrestricted great assemblies" (*wuzhe dahui* 無遮大會) hosted by the emperor.[143] Monks and nuns, laymen and laywomen, were allowed to participate freely in these assemblies and hear the emperor preach, with food provided for all participants. Such assemblies, we are told, often attracted thousands of participants. *The History of the Liang* described one such assembly in some detail. In 537, arrangements were made to bring the Buddha's relics from the Temple of King Aśoka located south of the capital, into the imperial palace to be worshipped. On the fifth day of the ninth month (September 24), the emperor sent the heir apparent, princes, nobles, and courtiers to the temple to receive the relics. An unrestricted assembly was held at the temple. It was a beautiful late autumn day: "The weather was clear and mild, and the sun shone brightly. The capital was emptied of people, who all came out to witness the reception ceremony. There were hundreds of thousands of spectators."[144]

As Jinhua Chen points out, "The institution of the dharma-assembly was driven by the need for multidimensional and complex exchanges and interchanges between different classes in commodities that were both material and spiritual."[145] These theatrical performances united spiritual and secular leaders and diminished in some measure the distance between the monarch and his people, a distance difficult to bridge under Confucian rule: after all, the very concept of "no restriction" was in direct opposition to the Confucian emphasis on observing one's proper position in a strictly hierarchical society. But it is also true,

143. For a detailed account of Emperor Wu's Buddhist assemblies and a nice analysis of their religious, political, and economic significance, see Jinhua Chen, "*Pañcavārṣika* Assemblies." Emperor Wu was perhaps consciously emulating the Northern Wei rulers, who had also held "unrestricted assemblies," particularly during the rule of Empress Dowager Hu 胡太后 (d. 528) (*Wei shu* 19.480).

144. *Liang shu* 54.792.

145. Jinhua Chen, "*Pañcavārṣika* Assemblies," p. 101.

as Thomas Jansen suggests, that although the Buddhist ceremonies made Emperor Wu somewhat closer to the people, the emperor was arrogating to himself absolute spiritual power as well as secular power.[146] Yet, the effect of the ceremonies on the psychology of the people should not be underestimated.

According to the thirteenth-century monk Zhipan's 志磐 history of Buddhism, in 505 Emperor Wu inaugurated the Assembly of Water and Land (*shuilu dahui* 水陸大會 or *shuilu zhai* 水陸齋), a ritual that involves making food offerings to wandering water spirits and hungry ghosts on land. Inspired by a dream, the emperor reportedly spent three years studying various scriptures in order to create the proper ritual ceremony.[147] Zhipan's late date and the lack of corroborating evidence in dynastic histories compromise the veracity of his account; nevertheless, it is certain that Buddhist festivals flourished under Emperor Wu's rule.[148]

It is perhaps only fitting that the various religious festivities associated with Emperor Wu involved giving away food, since one of the most influential of Emperor Wu's religious policies had to do with food: he actively sought to impose a strict vegetarian diet on the Buddhist clergy. Before Emperor Wu's time, there had been no absolute prohibition against the eating of meat by Buddhist clergy, and "Three Purities Meat" (i.e., the eater had not seen the animal alive, had not heard its cries when it was slaughtered, and had no reason to suspect the animal was killed for his or her sake) had been deemed acceptable.[149] In 511 Emperor Wu began a campaign for vegetarianism. He wrote several long treatises addressed to all members of the Buddhist clergy prohibiting the eating of meat and fish as well as the consumption of alcohol and explaining in great detail why this was a desirable course.[150] Anyone caught violating these rules, he said, would be expelled from the

146. Jansen, *Höfische Öffentlichkeit*, pp. 211–15.

147. Zhipan, *Fozu tongji* 佛祖統記, *T* 49: 33.321.

148. The earliest mention of the celebration of the ghost festival or the Festival of All Souls (Yulanpen hui 盂蘭盆會) may be found in the Liang writer Zong Lin's 宗懍 (ca. 498–561) *Jingchu suishi ji* 荆楚歲時記; see Teiser, *The Ghost Festival in Medieval* China, pp. 56–58.

149. For a discussion of the Buddhists' eating of meat, see Kieschinick, *The Eminent Monk*, pp. 23–24. See also Mather, "The Bonze's Begging Bowl," p. 421.

150. "Duan jiu rou wen" 斷酒肉文, in *Quan Liang wen* 7.2988–91.

Buddhist clergy and punished by the secular authorities; elderly monks with the largest number of disciples would receive the most severe punishment. Two years later, perhaps under the emperor's influence, Shen Yue composed a treatise on the importance for the Buddhist clergy of having only one midday meal ("Shu seng zhongshi lun" 述僧中食論).[151] In 517 Emperor Wu issued an unprecedented edict ordering that the animal sacrifices made in ancestral temples be replaced with offerings of fruit and vegetables. The edict caused a great uproar and met with fierce resistance from alarmed courtiers, but the emperor was adamant.[152] This radical gesture represented the culmination of Emperor Wu's campaign for vegetarianism. Although it is difficult to ascertain the extent to which strict vegetarianism was practiced among the Buddhist clergy in the Liang, Emperor Wu's efforts no doubt contributed to making vegetarianism a much more conspicuous issue in Chinese Buddhist discourse and a permanent feature of Buddhist values.

The most remarkable aspect of the campaign was Emperor Wu's resolve to "teach by example." Calling all Buddhist deities and heavenly beings as witnesses in his treatises on giving up alcohol and meat, he swore to practice what he preached, and he abided by his vows. He adopted a strictly vegetarian diet and had only one meal a day; if he missed the midday meal, he did not eat for the rest of the day. He never drank wine. Except during state occasions and banquets, he did not listen to music. He also abstained from sexual intercourse after the age of fifty. He always dressed in plain cotton clothes and wore the same cap for three years before acquiring a new one. In contrast with his earlier years, the latter half of Emperor Wu's life was remarkably austere.[153] According to *The Record of the Three Treasures of All Ages* (*Lidai sanbao ji*), the Shu region (modern Sichuan) once presented the emperor with a tribute of taro roots, which the emperor found "as delicious as meat"; henceforth, he

---

151. *Quan Liang wen* 29.3122. Zhipan, *Fozu tongji* (*T* 49: 37.349), dates the treatise to 513. For a translation of the treatise into English, see Mather, *The Poet Shen Yüeh*, pp. 153–54.

152. *Liang shu* 2.57; *Nan shi* 6.196.

153. An incident recorded in *Liang shu* (7.230–31) shows that Emperor Wu was not naturally inclined toward an austere lifestyle. The emperor had become enamored of a palace lady from the last Qi emperor's harem; after Fan Yun remonstrated with him, he gave her away to a general.

ordered that no taro be sent as tribute—presumably to keep away from temptation. The compiler of *Lidai sanbao ji* said in amazement: "Being a monarch and yet achieving these deeds—he was indeed an incredible bodhisattva-emperor."[154]

Emperor Wu's religious faith was characterized by hybridity. On one hand, he accepted the Mahāyāna principle that all sentient beings could achieve Buddhahood; on the other hand, his belief in the immortality of the soul went against the grain of more "theoretical" Buddhism, which emphasized the absolute vacuity of all things. Some Buddhist scholars find Emperor Wu's understanding of Buddhism "rather superficial and obvious,"[155] but his religious undertakings nevertheless proved immensely popular among those seeking a more concrete, more "secular" way of embracing an esoteric religion. The various spectacular public assemblies and masses were an effective way of establishing a Buddhist kingdom in which every subject was saturated in Buddhist teachings and worshipped the Buddha, with the emperor himself as the *dharmarāja* (dharma king), who defended the Buddhist religion, protected his people, and was the ultimate source of both spiritual and secular authority in the mortal world.

In a great many ways, Emperor Wu deliberately acted as the highest Buddhist priest intervening on behalf of his people, both living and dead (it is not at all accidental that he was associated with masses dedicated to feeding hungry ghosts). This was, of course, also in perfect accord with the native Chinese view that the ruler was a mediator between heaven and men. In 521 Emperor Wu founded a home for poor, childless elderly people and the orphaned in the capital city, in the tradition of the Indian almsgiver Suddata.[156] In 529, when the capital city was afflicted with a plague, the emperor convened a deliverance assembly (*jiuku zhai* 救苦齋) in the Hall of Manifold Clouds (Chongyun dian 重雲殿) in the imperial park in which he prayed to the Buddha and asked to take all the sufferings of his people upon

154. *T* 49: 11.99.

155. Tang Yongtong, *Han Wei liang Jin*, p. 506. See also Fang Litian 方立天, "Liang Wudi Xiao Yan yu fojiao" 梁武帝蕭衍與佛教, in idem, *Wei Jin nanbeichao*, pp. 208–9.

156. *Liang shu* 3.64.

himself.[157] When Hou Jing's rebel army besieged the capital between 548 and 549, the emperor swore the same oath; at the time, even his six-year-old grandson, the Prince of Jianping, was moved to join him.[158]

Emperor Wu was perhaps the first Chinese emperor who consciously aspired to become a popular idol in the eyes of his people, not just a ruler presiding over them from a distance. To some degree he succeeded, and the establishment of religious regulations, rituals, and customs was a powerful way of institutionalizing Buddhism and making it accessible to all, be they members of the gentry or commoners.

Yet something more personally urgent than mere political aspiration seems to have motivated Emperor Wu to devote the late years of his life so passionately to Buddhism. The early Qing scholar Wang Fuzhi 王夫之 (1619–92) offered an interesting argument. Emperor Wu began his career studying the Confucian classics; the teachings of the Sage, though allowing one to correct past mistakes, show no mercy for rebellious subjects. Once Emperor Wu secured the throne through rebellion and usurpation, he could not but feel guilty and ashamed, knowing full well that "there would never be any place for him to feel at ease."[159] In contrast, Buddhism was a religion of compassion and emptiness: sins may either be explained away by reincarnation and karmic retribution or be expatiated by confession. In Wang Fuzhi's eyes, Emperor Wu, a complicated man burdened with his past, finally found his spiritual sanctuary—a resting place—in Buddhism.

THE LAST YEARS

Buddhist monks and nuns were a privileged and often wealthy class: like gentry families, monasteries owned large tracts of tax-exempt land and had laborers working the land for them. Monks and nuns were also exempt from corvée. In the early 520s, a man named Guo Zushen 郭祖深 wrote a memorial to the emperor concerning the management

157. *Nan shi* 7.206. See also Xu Song, *Jiankang shilu* 17.478. The first year of the Zhong datong 中大通 era was 529; Zhipan, *Fozu tongji*, *T* 49: 37.350, dates the event to 546, the first year of the Zhong datong 中大同 reign, which is presumably a mistake.

158. *Liang shu* 38.617–18.

159. Wang Fuzhi, *Du "Tongjian" lun*, pp. 567–68.

of the empire. Aware how outspoken his memorial was, he ordered a coffin to be carried after him when he presented the memorial, a conventional gesture implying that he was ready to be executed for his opinions. The gravamen of the memorial was a problem that plagued all the Southern Dynasties: how to increase the number of taxpaying households. Guo Zushen complained that "nearly half of the households of the empire" were lost to Buddhist monasteries. He asked for a national investigation, so that "monks and nuns who have no religious merit, if they are under forty, should be made to renounce their vows and become farmers." He also suggested ordering monks and nuns to adhere to vegetarianism, which in this case was clearly a request made out of economic, rather than ideological, concerns.[160] This shows that Emperor Wu's earlier imposition of vegetarianism on the Buddhist clergy had not taken full effect.

A much more pressing problem was, however, the issue of private armies (*buqu* 部曲, or more precisely, *jiabing* 家兵).[161] During the Southern Dynasties, local governors, magistrates, and powerful gentry families often had private armed forces. Just like the Buddhist clergy, these private soldiers constituted yet another part of the population that was exempt from taxes and corvée. The Qi and Liang dynastic histories make frequent references to private armies. The writer Zhang Shuai mentioned above was from a southern elite family; his father, Zhang Ying 張緱 (d. 505), had inherited several hundred soldiers from his own father, Zhang Yong 張永 (410–75), and always kept them on his estate.[162] One of the most famous generals of the Liang, Wei Rui 韋叡 (442–520), was a member of an illustrious northern immigrant family. When Emperor Wu rose against the Qi, Wei Rui came to his aid with a private army of some 2,000 soldiers and 200 horses. Xiahou Tan

160. *Nan shi* 70.1721–22.

161. For the issue of *buqu* or *jiabing*, see, e.g., Xiong Deji, "Liuchao de bingjia yu jiabing" 六朝的兵家與家兵, in idem, *Liuchao shi kaoshi*, particularly the section on "private soldiers," pp. 345–63. Here I am not concerned with "soldier households" (*bingjia* 兵家, *binghu* 兵户, or *shijia* 士家), that is, hereditary soldiers on "military registers" (*shiji* 士籍 or *bingji* 兵籍) and belonging, at least in name, to the state. These soldiers, though namely recruited by the state, often became loyal followers of their generals, who sometimes rebelled against the state.

162. *Nan Qi shu* 24.453.

夏侯亶 (483–538), the governor of Yuzhou, owned over 10,000 private soldiers and 2,000 horses. After he died, his son Xiahou Bo 夏侯譒 continued leading this large army and assisted in the prefecture's military defense. Later he attached himself to the rebel Hou Jing and followed Hou Jing in besieging the capital. He camped his army in the western branch of the Elite Academy and encouraged his soldiers to loot the residences of rich families. Yang Kan 羊侃 (496–549) was a northern general who defected to the Liang in 529. He stood out as the bravest and most resourceful leader defending the Palace City against Hou Jing's army. Emperor Wu presented him and his private army of more than a thousand soldiers with 5,000 taels of gold, 10,000 taels of silver, and 10,000 bolts of silk. Yang Kan refused the emperor's gift and used his own money to reward his troops. Zhang Xiaoxiu 張孝秀 (481–522), a reclusive gentry member living near the Dongling Temple (Donglin si 東林寺) at Mount Lu (Lushan 廬山), had several hundred private soldiers working his fields. The historian said that he used his surplus grain to provide for residents of the mountain area: "People near and far admired him; they became attached to him in great numbers."[163] Those people "attached to him" were, of course, dependent households who paid no taxes to the government. This is a classic example of how a local strongman gained wealth and power, all to the detriment of the state.

Private armies increasingly drew on voluntary recruits rather than "servile dependents whose status passed from father to son,"[164] although the hereditary retainer must still have existed. As the modern Six Dynasties historian Gao Min 高敏 says, soldiers recruited by generals and commanders to serve their own private purposes (*mubing* 募兵) gradually replaced part of the state army composed of members from the hereditary "soldier households."[165] The case of Lu Gao 陸杲 (459–532) is particularly telling: Lu Gao, an accomplished calligrapher and painter, was from a southern gentry family. In 521, he was appointed the administrator of Linchuan 臨川. According to *The Southern History*, upon taking leave of the emperor to take up his post, he requested the emperor's permission to recruit private soldiers. When the emperor asked him why

163. *Liang shu* 6.221, 22.422, 39.560, 45.752.
164. Graff, *Medieval Chinese Warfare*, p. 84.
165. Gao Min, *Wei Jin nanbeichao*, p. 295.

he had not presented his case through the proper channels, Lu Gao answered that they had not accepted his petition. "The emperor found this rather odd, but because Lu was leaving, he did not press the subject."[166] We do not know if Lu Gao got what he wanted, nor can we be certain what the emperor found odd—was it Lu Gao's request, or his claim that "those in charge of such matters" had refused him? But this incident does suggest two things: first, in order to recruit private soldiers, an official needed to present his case through "those in charge of such matters" and obtain the emperor's permission; second, even someone like Lu Gao, a devout Buddhist, described by the historian as "famous for his talent and learning," did not shy away from having private armed forces. At any rate, there is much evidence for the existence of private armies throughout the Southern Dynasties, contrary to the claim that "private militarization was largely an ephemeral response to temporary emergencies rather than a permanent and characteristic condition" of medieval China.[167]

Guo Zushen wrote in his memorial:

> The government appointed people with long-standing merit to posts in prefectures and commanderies on the three frontiers. They had no regard for the proper way of managing people but made greed and cruelty their priority. . . . When these people first began serving the state, they were entirely on their own, but as soon as they were appointed, they recruited private armed forces. The populace of Yangzhou and Xuzhou, faced with various corvée obligations, often responded to the recruitment and took advantage of the economic interest it brought them.[168]

> 朝廷擢用勳舊, 爲三陲州郡, 不顧御人之道, 唯以貪殘爲務. . . . 而此勳人投化之始, 但有一身, 及被任用, 皆募部曲. 而揚徐之人, 逼以眾役, 多投其募, 利其貨財.

He Zhiyuan 何之元 (500?–593), compiler of *Liang dian* 梁典, a history of the Liang, also noted the harm caused by the practice in his "General Commentary" ("Zonglun" 總論):

166. *Nan shi* 48.1204–5.
167. Holcombe, *In the Shadow*, p. 56.
168. *Nan shi* 70.1722.

The number of [taxpaying] households in the Liang was even smaller than that of a commandery of the Han: most of the population became private soldiers. They consumed food without plowing and wore clothes without tending to silkworms. Some of them served under princes and nobles, whereas others served under generals and commanders. They took their wives and children and followed their masters east and west.[169]

梁氏之有國, 少漢之一郡, 大半之人, 並爲部曲, 不耕而食, 不蠶而衣, 或事王侯, 或依將帥, 攜帶妻累, 隨逐東西.

Apart from voluntary recruitment, another source of private soldiers was the custom of "parting gifts" (*songgu* 送故), which had become firmly established by the Jin dynasty. Fan Ning's protest against the custom is often cited by historians:

Also, when prefectural governors leave their posts, all of them receive soldiers and weapons as parting gifts, not to mention an immeasurable quantity of rice and cloth. . . . The soldier households they receive may amount to over a thousand, and at the very least several dozens. These forces are controlled by private families, and yet they are subsidized by government salaries. . . . A meritorious minister is already rewarded with enfeoffment: why should he be granted soldiers in addition to being appointed to a local post? I suggest that the custom of "parting gifts" be brought under restraint, with three years [of serving in a post] as the basic minimum [for bestowing such gifts on a governor].[170]

又方鎮去官, 皆割精兵器仗以爲送故, 米布之屬不可稱計. . . . 送兵多者至有千餘家, 少者數十户. 既力入私門, 復資官廪布. . . . 若是功勳之臣, 則已享裂土之祚, 豈應封外復置吏兵乎? 謂送故之格宜爲節制, 以三年爲斷.

Although incensed by the custom, Fan Ning nevertheless did not ask the emperor to ban it outright, probably out of a pragmatic assessment of its deep-rooted and widespread influence.

At the very beginning of the Liang, Deng Yuanqi 鄧元起 (458–505), the governor of Yizhou 益州 (in modern Sichuan), asked to retire and return home to care for his aged mother. The request was granted, and Emperor Wu sent the young Xiao Yuanzao 蕭淵藻 (483–549), the

169. *Quan Chen wen* 5.3429.

170. *Jin shu* 75.1987. I differ from Gao Min (*Wei Jin nanbeichao*, pp. 290) in interpreting the last sentence, "with three years as minimum" 以三年爲斷. Gao seems to take it as referring to the number of years the soldiers were supposed to serve under the governor who received them as "parting gifts."

second son of his deceased brother Xiao Yi, to replace Deng Yuanqi.[171] "Yuanqi had worked assiduously on his 'return capital'—no grain or arms were left [in the storehouses]. When Yuanzao entered the city, he felt resentful at the state of affairs and threw Yuanqi into the prefectural prison."[172] *The History of the Liang* claims that Deng Yuanqi "hanged himself in prison," but *The Southern History* presents the incident in a different light:

> Xiao Yuanzao entered the city and asked Yuanqi for his good horses. Yuanqi said, "What does a youngster like you need horses for!" Yuanzao was infuriated; so he got Yuanqi drunk and had him killed. Yuanqi's soldiers surrounded the city, weeping for him and demanding to know why he had been killed. Yuanzao became afraid and said: "It is the will of the emperor." At this the soldiers disbanded.
>
> 蕭藻入城, 求其良馬, 元起曰: "年少郎子, 何用馬爲." 藻恚, 醉而殺之. 元起麾下圍城, 哭且問其故. 藻懼曰: "天子有詔." 乃散.

Later, when Emperor Wu learned the truth from Deng Yuanqi's former subordinate, he demoted his nephew and granted Yuanqi the posthumous title of "Loyal Marquis." The *Nan shi* historian seized the opportunity to deliver a moral lesson, criticizing Emperor Wu for his leniency to family members (demotion being too light a punishment in the historian's view); he considered such leniency a key factor in the fall of the Liang.[173] In fact, what we see here is a case of *songgu yingxin* 送故迎新 (seeing off the official leaving the post with gifts and welcoming the new one with supplies) gone bad. Deng Yuanqi was "known for his generous charitable deeds," and "many young men of his home region became attached to him." The facts that he was going to take all the provisions and weaponry with him and that his subordinates were capable of "surrounding the city" shows clearly that he had a private army of substantial size, which he intended to bring home on leaving (he had over 30,000 soldiers under his command when he first took Yizhou). Only with this in mind can we understand his earlier refusal to go to the rescue when Hanzhong 漢中 was besieged by the Northern Wei

171. Xiao Yuanzao's name was changed to Xiao Zao in *Nan shi* to avoid the taboo on the name of the founding emperor of the Tang, Li Yuan 李淵.

172. *Liang shu* 10.200.

173. *Nan shi* 55.1369, 1377.

army, even though his advisors urged him to do so: his refusal was presumably born of a desire to preserve his own armed forces.

The diffusion of military power had serious consequences for the Liang. When the Palace City was under siege between 548 and 549, the rescuing armies pouring in from all directions reportedly amounted to 300,000 men.[174] Even though this figure might be exaggerated, there is no question that the armies coming to the relief of the capital were more than Hou Jing's match in aggregate numbers. They were, however, under different leaders, and ultimately internal conflicts, poor organization, and low morale, as well as bad luck, led to the failure of the attempt to lift the siege.

Moreover, the fact that local governors, besides holding civil and administrative powers, were also in charge of the garrison troops (*fubing* 府兵) posed yet another potential problem for the central government. The "militarization of the local administrative powers," as a modern scholar points out, is a familiar topic in the historical studies of the Six Dynasties.[175] Emperor Wu followed the example of earlier dynasties in appointing his own family members to strategically important prefectures, but he would never have expected that during the Hou Jing Rebellion it would be his own sons—especially Xiao Yi, then governor of Jiangzhou, and Xiao Ji 蕭紀 (508–53), then governor of Yizhou, both controlling large armies—who were to disappoint him the most. Later, Xiao Yi's conflicts first with his nephew Xiao Yu 蕭譽 (d. 550, Xiao Tong's second son) and then with his brothers Xiao Lun 蕭綸 (507?–51) and Xiao Ji quickened the collapse of the empire.

Even without the Hou Jing Rebellion, the princes' military power would have posed a serious threat to the Liang court, perhaps not during Emperor Wu's lifetime, but certainly after his death. *The Southern History* states:

As the emperor was getting on in years, none of the princes submitted to one another. Even though Emperor Jianwen [Xiao Gang] at the time was the heir apparent, he did not feel at ease. He could not get along with the Prince of Shaoling 邵陵王 [i.e., Xiao Lun], the Minister of Works, in particular. Xiao Lun was the governor of Danyang, and his power kept the capital in dread.

174. Ibid., 7.222.
175. Tao Xinhua, *Wei Jin nanchao*, pp. 26–47.

Emperor Jianwen thereupon selected a troop of fine soldiers to defend the palace. The hostility between the brothers was known to all.[176]

時武帝年高, 諸王莫肯相服. 簡文雖居儲貳, 亦不自安, 而與司空邵陵王綸特相疑阻. 綸時爲丹陽尹, 威震都下. 簡文乃選精兵以衛宮内. 兄弟相貳, 聲聞四方.

But the Prince of Shaoling was certainly not the only one who thought himself superior to the other brothers or possessing a more valid claim to the throne.

At the time, many claimed to be soldiers and thus to be exempt from taxation and corvée, and yet never served in actuality. For fear of being discovered by the local authorities, they ran away from their hometowns. Thus we see the rise of a new kind of "immigrant household" (*qiaohu* 僑户), a term used by Guo Zushen to describe such vagrants. Emperor Wu issued a number of edicts encouraging vagrants to return to their home regions, first in 518 and then in 527, 541, 544, 546, and 547. The frequency of such edicts in the last years of his rule might be an indication of the increasing seriousness of the problem.

In the 540s, He Chen 賀琛 (ca. 482–550), a scholar well versed in the Confucian classics and particularly knowledgeable about ritual matters, wrote a memorial to the emperor in much the same vein as Guo Zushen had. The foremost item on his agenda was again the decrease in the number of taxpaying households. This time, however, Emperor Wu was infuriated by the critique and dictated a long response demanding He Chen to be precise in his accusations.[177] Emperor Wu's anger has often been interpreted as a sign of his love of obsequiousness in old age, but the emperor's response to He Chen's vague accusations and suggestions, which were based more on ideological concerns than on pragmatic calculations, was not entirely inappropriate. Unlike Guo Zushen, who was explicit and detailed in identifying the problems and how to deal with them, He Chen often became carried away by a self-righteous, pompous discourse about the vice of luxury, the callousness of local governors to people's sufferings, and the need to "save money" and cut down on unnecessary projects.

---

176. *Nan shi* 52.1296.

177. *Liang shu* 38.543–50.

If Emperor Wu did one thing amiss in his last years, it was the way in which he dealt with Hou Jing. In 534, the Northern Wei split into two kingdoms: the Western Wei, with its capital in Chang'an 長安 (modern Xi'an), and the Eastern Wei, with its capital in Ye 鄴 (in modern Hebei). Hou Jing first defected from the Eastern to the Western Wei; then he sent a memorial to Emperor Wu asking to surrender to the Liang. Emperor Wu accepted Hou Jing against the better judgment of some of his ministers. Later, after Emperor Wu negotiated a peace treaty with the Eastern Wei, Hou Jing feared that he would be sent back to the Eastern Wei and felt compelled to act. He rebelled in the autumn of 548 and soon advanced to the capital, Jiankang.

After a bloody siege lasting almost five months, the Palace City finally fell. On April 24, 549, Emperor Wu was resting when the Marquis of Yong'an, his grandson, came in and announced that the city had fallen. The emperor did not even stir, simply asking if there was a chance to fight one last battle. The answer was negative. At this he heaved a sigh, saying: "Founded by myself and lost by myself—what is there to regret?"[178]

The emperor gave an audience to Hou Jing, who arrived with 500 armed guards. The ceremonialist led him to the seat of the Three Dukes. With a calm demeanor, the emperor said to him: "You have been in the army for a long time. It must be quite exhausting for you." Hou Jing somehow could not manage to utter a word in reply. The emperor then asked him: "Where did you originally come from, that you had the nerve to do something like this? Are your wife and children still in the North?" Again Hou Jing could not bring himself to say anything, and an aide answered for him.[179] Later, Hou Jing went to see Crown Prince Xiao Gang, who treated him with the same composure and poise. Even Hu Sanxing, the usually stern Song historian, was moved to remark: "Xunzi once said, 'Those who are good at losing are not vanquished.' The emperor and the crown prince may have been vanquished, but they certainly did not lose their dignity. Alas, how sad!"[180]

178. Ibid., 29.437.
179. Ibid., 56.851.
180. *Zizhi tongjian* 162.5010.

Emperor Wu refused to submit to Hou Jing's will, and Hou Jing did not dare to force him. The end, however, was close for the eighty-five-year-old emperor. It is said that even his basic needs such as food and drink were often not satisfied, and that right before his death when he asked for some honey to alleviate the bitter taste in his mouth, it was not brought to him. A month after the fall of the Palace City, the emperor passed away in the Palace of Pure Abode (Jingju dian 淨居殿). Although the Liang survived for another forty years after him, the political power and cultural glory of the dynasty ended with Emperor Wu's death. Thousands of gentry members died or became slaves during the Hou Jing Rebellion or later in the conquest of Jiangling, the capital chosen by Xiao Yi, who ruled from 552 to 555. The social structure of the South, which had lasted for over two centuries, received a devastating blow from which it never recovered.

In retrospect, the Liang dynasty under the rule of Emperor Wu emerges as an age of vigor, aspiration, and achievement. Although the promotion of Buddhism was often cited as the emperor's "greatest failing," it was an ideologically ambitious undertaking, and it did not harm the state nearly as much as an entrenched political and social structure too deeply rooted to be removed without causing disturbances, insurgency, or even a civil war. Emperor Wu had done what he could to work effectively within the existing system, for he recognized, wisely, the limitations of imperial power that characterized all the Southern Dynasties.

"Pure Abode," the palace in which Emperor Wu breathed his last, is the name of the five heavens of purity where the saints who have transcended the cycle of reincarnation dwell. These saints are referred to as *anāgāmin*: those who have escaped the cycle of rebirth. Being an *anāgāmin* is only one step away from becoming an *arhat*, one who has achieved Nirvana. It was a fitting end for an emperor so devoted to Buddhism, whose life had turned out to be a grand Buddhist allegory. In Buddhist teachings, bitterness (*ku* 苦), the last taste in the emperor's mouth, constitutes the fundamental human condition, and the realm of appearances—including the imperial throne—is empty and unreal (*kong* 空). In both seventeenth-century fictional accounts of Emperor Wu's life, the emperor's death is portrayed not as a tragedy but as a release from the bounds of worldly attachments and suffering. To achieve such freedom, Emperor Wu had to pay the price, even if it was the loss of his empire.

CHAPTER TWO

Mapping the Cultural World (I)

Managing Texts

Around the middle of the sixth century, the northerner Yang Junzhi 陽俊之 wrote a set of poems in six-syllable lines. This set of poems, described by the compiler of *The Northern History* (*Bei shi* 北史) as "immoderate and clumsy," was dubbed "The Companion of Yang the Fifth" ("Yangwu banlü" 陽五伴侶). It became so popular in its day that not only was it often copied, but copies were sold in the market. One day, when Yang Junzhi was browsing through the book market, he discovered some errors in his poems. He told the bookseller and tried to make corrections. The bookseller refused him flatly: "Yang the Fifth, the author of these poems, was a worthy man from the past. What do *you* know, sir, that you dare to criticize them!" Yang Junzhi was immensely pleased with the bookseller's answer, although apparently he did not get to correct the errors in his own works.[1]

This was the age of manuscript culture. Texts were produced, circulated, and preserved by hand-copying. The anecdote about Yang Junzhi is important because it provides one of the earliest examples of textual fluidity in manuscript culture: what happened to a text during its transmission is a question that has profound implications for a better understanding of the early and medieval literary history. Liang scholars

1. *Bei shi* 47.1728–29.

were actively engaged in preserving and editing materials that, transmitted in manuscript form and surviving wars and natural disasters, were more often than not in textually problematic shape.

A poem written by Shen Yue during the Yongming era on the subject of the compilation of *An Epitome of Books of the Four Categories* allows us to catch a glimpse of the condition of some received texts:

披縢辨蠹冊	Untying the binding ropes, we decipher the worm-eaten scrolls;
酌醴訪深疑	over sips of sweet wine, we examine our deep doubts.[2]

In *The Master of the Golden Tower*, Xiao Yi described what faced the scholars of the Liang dynasty:

Philosophers emerged during the Warring States, and literary collections first flourished in the Han dynasty. Nowadays, each family produces writings, and every person has a collection. What is beautifully written may voice one's feelings and purify customs; what is badly written, on the other hand, proves no more than a waste of bamboo slips that will only tire the later-born. The texts of old pile up high, and more texts are being produced ceaselessly. One raises a foot and walks down the road of studying, and yet, even when one's hair is white, one has not exhausted everything. Sometimes what was valued in the past is looked down upon in the present, or what is prized today was scorned by the ancients. Alas, among the later-born gentlemen of broad knowledge, if there is one who can evaluate textual differences and similarities, edit and put in order what is chaotic and messy, so that each scroll of writings is free from blemishes, and there is no remaining task for the reader, then such a person may be well regarded as a scholar.[3]

諸子興於戰國, 文集盛於二漢, 至家家有製, 人人有集. 其美者足以敍情志, 敦風俗; 其弊者祇以煩簡牘, 疲後生. 往者既積, 來者未已. 翹足志學, 白首不遍. 或昔之所重, 今反輕; 今之所重, 古之所賤. 嗟我後生博達之士, 有能品藻異同, 删整蕪穢, 使卷無瑕玷, 覽無遺功, 可謂學矣.

This passage, typical of this period, shows an intense awareness of the changes taking place in literary history and the alterations in taste, as well as the unique standpoint of "modern" times; more important, it re-

2. *Quan Liang shi* 6.1642.
3. Xiao Yi, *Jinlouzi jiaozhu* 9.164.

veals that Liang scholars were consciously fixing things when dealing with texts. Many songs recorded in the "Treatise on Music" ("Yuezhi" 樂志) in Shen Yue's *Song shu* reappear in a much "neater" form in *The New Songs of the Jade Terrace*, compiled by Xu Ling toward the middle of the sixth century. As Stephen Owen says, "in these cases Xu Ling, the editor of *Yutai xinyong*, took texts from the 'Treatise on Music' and edited them for contemporary poetic taste."[4]

Liang literary writings were themselves transmitted in manuscript. Besides *Wen xuan* and *New Songs*, the two surviving literary anthologies from the Liang, the small fraction of the vast quantity of Liang literature that survives has been preserved primarily as excerpts in the Tang encyclopedias. These present standard problems of manuscript culture, such as dubious attributions and textual variants. The resolution of these issues in the printed editions of later times marked an attempt to write the cultural narrative of the Liang to conform to contemporary ideology.

This chapter and the next will draw a map of the cultural world of the Liang by examining textual production and circulation and book collecting and cataloguing and by delineating the literary and scholarly activities of the period and constructing a social context for prevailing literary tastes.

TEXTUAL PRODUCTION AND TRANSMISSION

In contrast to the age of print culture, the only medium for reproducing a text during this period was copying (*xie* 寫).[5] Many professional scribes made a living copying books for wealthy families. For men from poor gentry families, this not only was a way of supporting themselves but could also be a means of acquiring an education. In his youth, the scholar and poet Wang Sengru "copied books for others in order to

4. Owen, *The Making of Early Chinese Classical Poetry*, p. 6.

5. The phrase *xieshu* 寫書 has come to denote "writing a book" in later times, but in early medieval China it was strictly reserved for the meaning of "copying a book." It was also possible to reproduce a text through rubbings, but rubbing was limited to transmitting stone or metal inscriptions and not used as a primary means of textual circulation.

provide for his mother. After he finished copying a book, he was able to recite it."[6] Zhu Yi did the same.[7] Payment was made according to the number of scrolls (*juan* 卷) copied. Because of his excellent calligraphy, the northerner Liu Fang 劉芳 (b. 452) was paid one bolt of silk for each scroll of Buddhist scriptures and treatises, but this must have been an unusually high payment, not the average compensation for a common scribe. Liu Fang was able to procure over a hundred bolts of silk every year, and after several years, he became quite wealthy.[8] Even as a court gentleman for comprehensive duty (Tongzhilang 通直郎) serving in the Secretariat, the poet Yu Shiji 虞世基 (d. 618) copied books in his spare time to earn extra cash.[9]

Well-to-do families apparently kept scribes in their households. Zhao Yin 趙隱 (507–76) was a retainer of Sima Ziru 司馬子如 (d. 550s), the director of the Department of State Affairs of the Eastern Wei, and specialized in copying books. Zhao Yin was much appreciated by Sima Ziru because, unlike other scribes, he made few mistakes. The government also had its own scribes. During the Northern Wei, Jiang Shaoyou 蔣少游 (late 5th c.) was once summoned to be a Secretariat scribe (Zhongshu xieshusheng 中書寫書生). The northern minister Lang Ji 郎基 (6th c.) prided himself on being a conscientious official, whose only "abuse of power" involved having people copy books for him. In a well-known story of the period, a book trader offered to sell *The Comprehensive Epitome of the Park of Flowering Groves* (*Hualin bianlue* 華林遍略), a grand compendium commissioned by Emperor Wu of the Liang, to Gao Cheng 高澄 (521–49), the powerful Northern Wei minister and the elder brother of the founding emperor of the Northern Qi 北齊 (550–77). Gao Cheng asked the seller to leave the book with him for browsing. He then summoned several scribes and made a copy of the book within a single day and night. He returned the book to the seller the next day, saying: "I have no need for it."[10]

---

6. *Liang shu* 33.469.
7. Ibid., 62.1515.
8. *Bei shi* 42.1542.
9. Ibid., 83.2797.
10. Ibid., 55.2007, 90.2984, 55.2014, 47.1737.

Some copied books not for hire, but for pleasure. Xiao Jun 蕭鈞 (472–93), the eleventh son of the founding emperor of the Southern Qi, copied out the Five Classics in small script and put them in a "headband box" (*jinxiang* 巾箱), a box originally intended for containing headbands. When asked the reason, he answered: "This makes it easy to browse through the books and look things up. Besides, once one copies out something oneself, one will never forget it." All the other princes, upon hearing of this, imitated his practice. This was the origin of the term "Headband Box Five Classics" (*jinxiang wujing* 巾箱五經).[11]

Often the most economical way of acquiring a book was to borrow it from a friend and then make a copy of it. This was what Yuan Jun 袁峻 (fl. early 6th c.) did, imposing on himself the demand that he should fill fifty sheets of paper each day.[12] Zang Fengshi 臧逢世 borrowed *The History of the Han* (*Han shu* 漢書) from his brother-in-law Liu Huan 劉緩 (fl. 540) and made a copy of it using the blank margins of letters and calling cards.[13]

Tao Yuanming, the famous Eastern Jin poet, mentioned in the preface of a series of poems on drinking that he had asked his friend or friends to copy his poems "for amusement" (*yiwei huanxiao* 以爲歡笑).[14] However, in an age without printing, photocopying, and computers, hand-copying a text, regardless of the motive, was not "just for fun"—it was the only means of preservation and circulation. Usually the wider the circulation, the better the text's chance of being preserved. The dynastic histories record many examples of men whose literary collections did not survive simply because they did not keep a copy of a work after composing it.[15] The survival of texts from this period is not simply a matter of "natural selection," which implies that lost works must have been inferior in quality: it is instead a matter of deliberate care in preservation as well as sheer luck, a combination of human will *and* accident.[16]

11. *Nan shi* 41.1038.

12. *Liang shu* 49.688.

13. Yan Zhitui, *Yanshi jiaxun* 8.189.

14. *Quan Jin shi* 17.997.

15. For instance, Xiao Zike 蕭子恪 (478–529), in *Liang shu* 35.509; or Xiao Yuanzao, in ibid., 23.362.

16. In his illuminating lectures on lost books, Glen Dudbridge (*Lost Books*, p. 28) rightly points out that "books are transmitted only because someone wants to

A common practice in this period was not to copy out the entire work but parts of it—parts, no doubt, deemed important. This practice was known as "producing an epitome" (*chaoshu* 抄書), a phrase that simply means "copying a book" in modern Chinese but had a much narrower and more specific sense in the sixth century. The monk Sengyou gave a succinct definition of *chao* in the preface to a catalogue of "excerpted sūtras" (*chaojing lu* 抄經錄): "To *chao* a sūtra is to bring out the essence of its content" 抄經者, 蓋撮舉義要也.[17] There were two ways of "bringing out the essence" of a work: to summarize its content in one's own words and to copy out selected passages. Sengyou endorsed the first method, citing An Shigao's 安世高 (fl. 148–71) and Zhi Qian's 支謙 (fl. 222–54) translations of Buddhist scriptures; they "summarized the non-Chinese text in their translation, instead of cutting up the original scripture" 約寫胡本, 非割斷成經. Sengyou criticized the practice of his contemporaries, who would "sometimes break up various chapters [of a scripture] like scattered chess pieces, and sometimes cut up the text proper into bits and pieces like a melon."[18] And yet, copying out selected passages from a work seemed to be exactly what the Liang elite enjoyed doing. The famous court poet Wang Yun's account may serve as a general illustration of the custom of the time:

I have loved producing epitomes of books (*chaoshu*) since my youth. This love has only grown more intense as I get on in years. Even if it is a book I encounter by accident, I always make notes from it. When I read these notes later, my delight in them becomes deeper. This is a habit that has become second nature, and I do not feel tired of using my brush. From when I was thirteen or fourteen *sui*, which was in the *yihai* year of the Jianwu reign [495], till this year, which is the sixth year of the Datong reign of the Liang [540], forty-six years have been whiled away in this manner. When I read the Five Classics in my childhood, I went over each Classic seventy or eighty times. I am fond of *The Annals of Springs and Autumns*, a book I constantly recite and discuss. I read it over and over again and have copied out selected passages many times. From the other Classics, as well as from *The Offices of Zhou*, *Ritual Norms*, *The Discourses of the States*, *Erya*, *The Classic of Mountains and Seas*, *The Materia Medica*, I have twice

transmit them." The sheer contingency of the survival and extinction of certain books, however, should not be overlooked either.

17. Sengyou, *Chu sanzang ji ji* 5.217–18.

18. Ibid.

copied out selected passages. As for the works of the masters, histories, and various authors' literary collections, I copied out one set of selected passages from all. I have never asked others for help but have always done it myself. These epitomes, large or small, amount to over a hundred scrolls. Not good enough to pass on to fellow book-lovers, they just serve the purpose of refreshing my memory.[19]

余少好抄書, 老而彌篤, 雖偶見瞥觀, 皆即疏記. 後重省覽, 歡興彌深. 習與性成, 不覺筆倦. 自年十三四, 建武二年乙亥, 至梁大同六年, 四十六載矣. 幼年讀五經, 皆七八十遍. 愛左氏春秋, 吟諷常爲口實, 廣略去取, 凡三過五抄. 餘經及周官、儀禮、國語、爾雅、山海經、本草並再抄, 子史諸集皆一遍. 未嘗倩人假手, 並躬自抄錄, 大小百餘卷. 不足傳之好事, 蓋以備遺忘而已.

In the early years of his rule, Emperor Wu asked Dao Qia 到洽 (490–527) to produce an epitome of books in the "A" category (*jiabu shu* 甲部書, i.e., the Confucian Classics); Zhang Shuai was first put in charge of books in the "B" category (*yibu shu* 乙部書, the histories) and, then in 508, books in the "C" and "D" categories (*bing- dingbu shu* 丙丁部書, the works of the masters and literary writings, respectively).[20] Zhang Mian 張緬 (490–531) compiled excerpts from various prominent Eastern Han and Jin histories into *An Account of the Latter Han* (*Hou Han ji* 後漢紀) in forty scrolls and *An Epitome of the Jin Histories* (*Jin chao* 晉抄) in thirty scrolls. He was also engaged in making an epitome of the literary collections of writers of the Southern Dynasties, but he never finished the project.[21] Yu Zhongrong 庾仲容 (475–548) left behind *An Epitome of the Masters* (*Zi chao* 子抄) in thirty scrolls.[22]

No discussion of textual transmission would be complete without introducing the commerce in books during this period. We know regrettably little about it; yet there is enough to piece together a picture of a flourishing book trade both within the Liang empire and across the

19. *Liang shu* 33.486.

20. Ibid., 27.404, 33.475. The four categories of books were first devised by Xun Xu 荀勖 (d. 289), in the order of Classics, works of the masters, histories, and literary writings. The categories were modified by Li Chong 李充 (ca. 350s), and the new order was Classics (*jing* 經), histories (*shi* 史), works of the masters (*zi* 子), and literary collections (*ji* 集). Li Chong's categorization became the dominant mode of categorizing books, employed throughout imperial China.

21. Ibid., 34.492.

22. Ibid., 50.724.

North/South border. The monk Sengyou's *A Collection of the Records of Translated Tripitaka* (*Chu sanzang ji ji* 出三藏記集), an extraordinary work compiled during Emperor Wu's Tianjian era (502–19), was intended as a record of all Buddhist scriptures translated in the five hundred years since the introduction of Buddhism into China until the age of Sengyou, but quite inadvertently, it presents, as no secular source does, a treasure trove of data about textual transmission in early medieval China. It allows us to catch glimpses of a vast system of manuscripts being produced, reproduced, and circulated across Central Asia and China from the third to the sixth century, in short, of words in traffic.

Although Sengyou's work is concerned exclusively with Buddhist texts, we know from other sources that the traveling monks or merchants (*hushi ren* 互市人) mentioned by Sengyou also transported secular texts across extensive geographical regions. A northern monk came to Jiankang in 502 or 503, bringing with him an old copy of *The History of the Han*, which he claimed to be the "genuine version" (*zhenben* 眞本) of the author, Ban Gu 班固 (32–92). Xiao Chen, one of the Eight Companions of the Prince of Jingling, acquired it from the monk and gave it to Emperor Wu's nephew Xiao Fan 蕭範 in 510; Xiao Fan eventually presented it to the Crown Prince Xiao Tong.[23] The fact that someone tried to sell the Liang compendium *The Comprehensive Epitome of the Park of Flowering Groves* to the Northern Wei minister Gao Cheng also indicates a healthy book trade between the North and South. As we saw, Gao Cheng had scribes make a copy of the huge compendium within a day and night. Later, Zu Ting 祖珽 (d. 570s), a well-known northern writer, pawned several scrolls of that copy to get money for gambling. Zu Ting was given a good caning after Gao Cheng found out.[24]

Books were put up for sale in big cities from North to South. In *The Master of the Golden Tower*, Xiao Yi mentioned that he had sent someone to purchase books for him at Jiankang.[25] During the Yongming era of the Qi, the emperor's brothers were kept under tight control in terms of reading material. Beyond the Confucian Classics, they were allowed

23. *Liang shu* 26.397.
24. *Bei shi* 47.1737.
25. Xiao Yi, *Jinlouzi jiaozhu* 6.99.

only to look at portraits of filial sons. Xiao Feng 蕭鋒 (474–93), Prince of Jiangxia 江夏王, secretly instructed his subordinates to buy books for him in the marketplace. "Within a month he had procured almost everything."[26] We do not know what titles constituted "everything" in the late fifth century, but presumably it included the standard works of the masters, the histories, and the literary collections of famous writers. In the North, Cui Liang 崔亮 (b. 458) refused to become a retainer of the powerful minister Li Chong 李沖 simply for the sake of gaining access to Li's large book collection: "I can go and read books in the marketplace; so why should I subject myself to someone else?"[27]

Many writings apparently circulated as individual pieces, such as Wang Bin's 王斌 (fl. 490) "Treatise on the Four Tones" ("Sisheng lun" 四聲論) and Emperor Wu's second son Xiao Zong's 蕭綜 (502–30) "Treatise on the Money Fool" ("Qianyu lun" 錢愚論).[28] Some of them undoubtedly found their way into the book market and were put up for sale along with anthologies and collections. Yang Junzhi's set of songs in six-syllable lines, cited at the beginning of this chapter, was clearly one of the "best-sellers."

Some texts seemed to circulate very quickly. The famous court poet Liu Xiaochuo's compositions were so popular that every time he "finished [a piece] in the morning, it would become well known by evening."[29] Emperor Wu ordered that Xiao Zong's treatise "On the Money Fool," a satire aimed at his uncle Xiao Hong 蕭宏 (473–526), be "immediately destroyed," but "it had already spread far and wide."[30] In first-century B.C. Rome, an early version of Cicero's *On Moral Ends* was acquired by a friend, who subsequently copied the text. Cicero was worried that this draft, which he had not intended to reach the public, "might spread and displace his final 'edition.'"[31] Cicero's worry was typical of an age of active manuscript circulation and finds parallels in early medieval China.

26. *Nan shi* 43.1088.

27. *Bei shi* 44.1630.

28. *Nan shi* 48.1197, 51.1278.

29. *Liang shu* 33.483. This remark, though a cliché of popularity, does to a certain extent indicate the speed with which manuscripts circulated.

30. *Nan shi* 51.1278.

31. Fantham, *Roman Literary Culture*, p. 37.

COLLECTING AND CATALOGUING BOOKS

Book collections, private and public, reached a new height in the Liang. The imperial book collection of the Liang owed its start to a conflagration: at the end of the Qi dynasty, a fire broke out in the palace and destroyed many of the books in the imperial library. In 502, right after the Liang was founded, Wang Tai 王泰, who was then the director of the imperial library, obtained the emperor's permission to rebuild the collection. Scholars such as Liu Jun 劉峻 (462–521), He Zong 賀蹤, Ren Fang, and Yin Jun 殷鈞 (484–532) participated in the task. At the time, all Buddhist books were kept in the Park of Flowering Groves (Hualin yuan 華林園), and non-Buddhist books were kept in the Hall of Literary Virtue (Wende dian 文德殿) and the Quarters of the Imperial Secretariat (Shangshu ge 尚書閣). The non-Buddhist books, according to the "Bibliography" ("Jingji zhi" 經籍志) of *The History of the Sui* (*Sui shu* 隋書), occupied 23,106 scrolls. Compared to the 3,014 scrolls in the Eastern Jin imperial library in the fourth century (about one tenth the size of the Western Jin imperial collection), this was a great leap forward indeed. The number had also increased since the Yongming era, when the imperial book catalogue recorded no more than 18,010 scrolls.[32] As for the Buddhist works, a catalogue compiled by the monk Baochang 寶唱 in 518 recorded 54,000 scrolls.[33]

Although the Liang imperial library was no doubt impressive, many elite families had likewise built up sizable book collections during this period. Indeed, before the Qi and Liang there had never been so many private book collectors who gathered books on such a massive scale. As stated in *The History of the Sui*, "Emperor Wu of the Liang took great delight in poetry and the Classics, and the entire state was influenced by his predilections. Within the four borders, every household possessed literary writings and histories."[34] At the beginning of the Liang, Shen Yue's book collection boasted of 20,000 scrolls, which made him the

32. *Sui shu* 32.906–7.
33. Ibid., 35.1098.
34. Ibid., 32.907.

foremost private book collector in the capital area.[35] Next to him was Ren Fang, another of the Eight Companions of the Prince of Jingling, who had over 10,000 scrolls. Many of Ren Fang's books were "rare editions" (*yiben* 異本). Ren Fang also compiled a catalogue of his book collection, the earliest private book catalogue ever recorded in history. Upon Ren Fang's death in 508, Emperor Wu had Shen Yue and He Zong examine his catalogue and take whatever titles the imperial library did not have.[36] Both Zhang Mian and Wang Sengru, the two eminent Liang writers, had a library of over 10,000 scrolls. Wang Sengru's collection featured many "rare editions," which enabled him to frequently use "novel allusions" in his writings and surprise his readers.[37] Kong Xiuyuan had over 7,000 scrolls and was said to have collated them himself.[38]

In the royal family, both Crown Prince Xiao Tong and the Marquis of Wuping (Xiao Mai 蕭勱, Emperor Wu's cousin's son) had book collections totaling 30,000 scrolls.[39] But Xiao Yi was to outshine them both. In the chapter "Book Collecting" ("Jushu" 聚書) in *The Master of the Golden Tower*, he detailed his experience of amassing books over the years. His father, Emperor Wu, gave him his first books, the five Confucian Classics, at the age of six; thereafter he devoted considerable energy to book collecting. Some books were gifts from his relatives and friends; some were purchased from book markets; some had been copied from the book collections of various courtiers. By the time he wrote the chapter on book collecting in 553, one year before his death, he claimed to have a library of 80,000 scrolls.[40] In later times, particularly in Ming and Qing China, such stories of book collecting became common, but Xiao Yi's description remains the earliest account in Chinese history of how a collector assembled his collection.

35. *Liang shu* 13.242.
36. Ibid., 14.254.
37. Ibid., 34.492, 33.474.
38. Ibid., 36.522.
39. Ibid., 8.167; *Nan shi* 51.1263. Liu Zun 劉遵 (488–535) compiled a catalogue of Xiao Tong's books (*Liang donggong sibu mulu* 梁東宮四部目錄) in four scrolls (*Sui shu* 33.991).
40. Xiao Yi, *Jinlouzi jiaozhu* 6.98–102.

The Liang court poet Yu Jianwu's 庾肩吾 (487?–551) poem "A Companion Piece for His Honor Liu's Poem on 'Viewing the Book Collection of the Prince of Xiangdong'" ("He Liu mingfu guan Xiangdong wang shu" 和劉明府觀湘東王書) attests to the richness of Xiao Yi's library:[41]

陳王擅書府	The Prince of Chen excelled in book collection;
河間富典墳	the ruler of Hejian was rich in the classic canon.[42]
五車方累篋	Five carts of books fill one casket after another,[43]
七閣自連雲	and the seven storerooms reach the clouds.
松槧芳帙氣	Pine-ink adds a fragrance to the scrolls,
柏燻起廚文	the odor of cypress leaves protects the tomes in the cabinet from insects.
羽陵青簡出	From the Yu Mound azure bamboo slips have emerged;
嬀泉綠字分	green characters were recognized at the Gui River.[44]
方因接遊聖	Since you are in the company of a sage-prince,
暫得奉朝聞	for a short while you put the principle of "learning in the morning" in practice.[45]

41. *Quan Liang shi* 23.1991.

42. Prince of Chen was the poet Cao Zhi's 曹植 (192–232) title, and as such it is often used to refer to the younger brother of the crown prince. The Prince of Hejian (r. 155–130 B.C.) was Liu De 劉德, the son of Han Jingdi 景帝 (r. 156–141 B.C.). He loved learning and reportedly had a book collection as large as the imperial library (*Han shu* 53.2410).

43. Hui Shi 惠施, the Warring States sophist and a friend of Zhuangzi, owned five carts of books (*Zhuangzi jishi* 33.1102). "Five carts [of books]" became a habitual reference to describe a rich book collection or a broad learning.

44. Yuling, or the Yu Mound, was the place where the Zhou king sunned his insect-eaten books (*Mu tianzi zhuan* 5.45). The Gui River (in modern Shanxi 山西) is where the sage-emperor Shun took up residence. The green characters are apocryphal texts emerging from rivers as an auspicious sign. According to *Jin shu* 14.408, "In the past the grand sage-emperor Yu came to the Turbid River [i.e., the Yellow River] and received the green characters."

45. "Learning in the morning" is an abbreviation of the *Analects* quotation: "If I learn the Way in the morning, I would not mind dying at evening" (*Lunyu zhushu* 4.37).

櫶樓霞早發	At the Huan Tower morning clouds appear early,
林殿日先曛	the sun goes down first in the Forest Palace.
洛城復接眼	Your eyes are seeing the city of Luoyang again—
歸軒畏後群	but in the returning carriage, you are afraid you would fall behind the others.[46]

In his account of his collection, Xiao Yi did not mention the acquisition of a large hoard of books from Jiankang in 552. According to *The History of the Sui*, "After Emperor Yuan [i.e., Xiao Yi] defeated Hou Jing, he had the books of the Hall of Literary Virtue as well as other public and private book collections sent to Jiangling [Xiao Yi's headquarters]. There were more than 70,000 scrolls."[47] Niu Hong's 牛弘 (545–610) memorial to the founding emperor of the Sui made the same claim, though he mentioned that there were "duplicate copies" (*chongben* 重本) among these books.[48] If this number is accurate, and if the 80,000 scrolls in Xiao Yi's library included the books taken from Jiankang, then Xiao Yi's earlier collection would have come to no more than 10,000 scrolls. This is a much more realistic number, considering that even the imperial library had only 77,106 scrolls in the early years of Emperor Wu's rule, and that Crown Prince Xiao Tong's library had 30,000. On the other hand, even if the 80,000 scrolls did not include the 70,000 acquired from Jiankang, this extravagant number may still be explained by the inclusion of duplicate copies. But why did Xiao Yi not acknowledge the immense acquisition from Jiankang when he recorded every other instance of book acquisition in his life? The answer to this question may shed light on the nature of public and private book collecting in this period, and I will return to it after dealing with the issue of cataloguing—the natural step to take when facing a great store of books.

The compilation of a comprehensive bibliography of the imperial book collection had begun with the Western Han scholar Liu Xin's 劉歆

46. Luocheng, the city of Luo, is Luoyang, the old Eastern Han capital, here used to refer to the capital city, Jiankang. The last couplet seems to mean that they have to return to the capital now that they have browsed through the Prince of Xiangdong's book collection for the whole day, and yet the poet is lingering on, falling behind the others since he is unwilling to part from the books.

47. *Sui shu* 32.907.

48. Ibid., 49.1299.

(53 B.C.?–A.D. 23) *Seven Summaries* (*Qi lue* 七略). As Glen Dudbridge has pointed out, the influence of this project was far-reaching: "The managing and documenting of book collections were sponsored by the throne and made the responsibility of high-ranking officers of the state, and the state library became a symbol of national unity and culture, in the sense that it affirmed the ruling dynasty's legitimate inheritance and stewardship of written culture from the past."[49] Emperor Wu of the Liang was fully aware of the significance of the cultural power of the imperial library. When appointing the well-known court poet Liu Xiaochuo as director, the emperor reportedly said to the minister Zhou She: "The number-one office should be occupied by the number-one person" 第一官當用第一人.[50]

In 505, Liu Jun compiled *A Catalogue of Books of the Four Categories in the Hall of Literary Virtue of the Liang* (*Liang Wende dian sibu mulu* 梁文德殿四部目錄).[51] Books dealing with necromancy were considered as belonging to a separate category, whose catalogue was compiled by Zu Xuan 祖暅. In 507, Yin Jun compiled *A Catalogue of Books of the Four Categories* (*Liang Tianjian liunian sibu shu mulu* 梁天監六年四部書目錄), which, according to Ruan Xiaoxu 阮孝緒 (479–536), recorded fewer scrolls than Liu Jun's catalogue.[52] This was probably because Yin Jun eliminated duplicate titles. In 515, Emperor Wu commissioned the monk Sengshao 僧紹 to compile a catalogue of Buddhist scriptures in the imperial collection; the result was *A Catalogue of Buddhist Scriptures of the Park of Flowering Groves* (*Hualin fodian jingmu* 華林佛殿經目). Not completely satisfied, Emperor Wu asked the monk Baochang to put together a bibliography in four scrolls in 518. According to *The Sequel to the Biographies of Eminent Monks*, this bibliography was based on Sengshao's catalogue but added critical abstracts and "combined [same works under different titles] as well as separated [different works that had been mixed together]" 注述合離.[53]

---

49. Dudbridge, *Lost Books*, pp. 4–5.
50. *Liang shu* 33.480.
51. *Sui shu* 33.991. This catalogue was in four scrolls.
52. Ibid.; *Quan Liang wen* 66.3347.
53. *T* 50: 1.426.

Given the political and cultural importance of the imperial library, it is remarkable that the most impressive book catalogue of the Liang was compiled privately by an individual who had decided never to serve the state despite his illustrious family background. This man was Ruan Xiaoxu, who came from one of the highest elite families, the Ruan clan of Chenliu 陳留阮氏. He was related to the Langye Wangs, the Chenjun Xies, and the royal family of the Liang by marriage: his elder sister was married to Emperor Wu's brother, Xiao Hui 蕭恢 (476–526). Ruan Xiaoxu, however, chose to remain a recluse all his life. He avoided associating with his powerful relatives and devoted himself to scholarship and writing. His *Seven Records* (*Qi lu* 七錄) in twelve scrolls was an ambitious undertaking, in that it was intended to include all the books in the state of Liang. Although the catalogue itself has been lost, its preface, written in the spring of 524 at Jiankang, was preserved in the Tang Buddhist anthology *Guang hongming ji*. This preface is a fascinating document.

In the preface, Ruan Xiaoxu gave a brief history of book cataloguing from the Western Han; much of this information was later incorporated into the "Bibliography" of *The History of the Sui*. He then recounted how he had accomplished this grand task:

> I have a particular fondness for searching for forgotten writings and hidden records. If a household has had a book collection since the Song and Qi Dynasties, be it a princely residence or a gentleman's home, I always try to acquire its catalogue. Upon comparing the books I encountered—some being what I saw and some being what I heard of—with those recorded in the imperial catalogue, I have discovered many omissions in the latter. Therefore, I have gathered together various sources and compiled a new catalogue. . . . I hope that all the forgotten books and hidden records of this world have been included here.[54]

> 其遺文隱記，頗好搜集. 凡自宋齊已來，王公搢紳之館，苟能蓄聚墳籍，必思致其名簿. 凡在所遇，若見若聞，校之官目，多所遺漏. 遂總集眾家，更爲新錄. . . . 天下之遺書祕記庶幾窮于是矣.

Toward the end of the preface, Ruan mentioned that Liu Yao 劉杳 (487–536) had generously shown him his own, similar catalogue, which

54. *Quan Liang wen* 66.3346.

was subsequently incorporated into Ruan's *Seven Records*.[55] Ruan's catalogue recorded 44,526 scrolls, in 6,288 titles.[56] It is likely that it included the same works under different titles and various epitomes, books both extracted and expanded.

The division of Ruan's *Seven Records* was based on the subject classifications of Liu Xin's *Seven Summaries* as well as the Qi minister Wang Jian's *Seven Accounts* (*Qi zhi* 七志), with modifications. Books were divided into seven categories: the first five, classified as "Inner Chapters," were the Confucian classics, histories and biographies as well as genealogies, military works, literary anthologies and collections, and works on medical techniques and necromancy; the last two, the "Outer Chapters," were Buddhist and Daoist works. Ruan Xiaoxu explained in his preface that Wang Jian had not listed Buddhist works as a separate category; moreover, he had put Daoist works before Buddhist in his *Seven Accounts*, whereas Ruan Xiaoxu had reversed the order not only because "our beliefs differ" 所宗有不同 but also because "the teachings are poles apart in their depths" 其教有淺深也.[57] This suggests the proliferation of Buddhist scriptures and writings, as well as the high regard accorded to Buddhism in the Liang. Ruan would, of course, have never known that this remark earned his preface a place in a Buddhist anthology and ensured its survival.

From Ruan Xiaoxu's preface, we learn that many private book collections were large enough to warrant a private catalogue. This was the first time in Chinese history that private book catalogues were mentioned. Against such a larger background, Ruan Xiaoxu's private undertaking of compiling a catalogue of "all the books in the state" emerges as characteristic of his age: although the imperial catalogue was still used as a standard against which all private catalogues were measured, Ruan's project showed that the grand cultural task of comprehensively documenting book collections could be undertaken by a private

55. Liu Yao's book catalogue in five scrolls, *Gujin sibu shumu* 古今四部書目, circulated independently in the Liang (*Liang shu* 50.717). It seems to have been lost by the Sui, since it was not recorded in the *Sui shu* "Bibliography."

56. According to the Sui minister Niu Hong, Ruan Xiaoxu's catalogue recorded 30,000 scrolls rather than 40,000 (*Sui shu* 49.1299).

57. *Quan Liang wen* 66.2246.

individual, a lifelong recluse who was the antithesis of the public man of the state.

Nowhere did the conflict between private and public discourses find a more suggestive manifestation than in Xiao Yi's silence about his acquisition of the large imperial collection from Jiankang. By the time Xiao Yi wrote his chapter on book collecting, he had already ascended the throne in Jiangling; in fact, he would be better known to posterity not as Xiao Yi or the Prince of Xiangdong but as Emperor Yuan of the Liang 梁元帝, the title granted him after his death in 555. For a monarch, book collecting was part of the state-building project. As Dudbridge puts it, "The state library became a symbol of national unity and culture, in the sense that it affirmed the ruling dynasty's legitimate inheritance and stewardship of written culture from the past."[58] Attaining possession of the former imperial collection was therefore no light matter. When the remains of the state library were transported from Jiankang to the new Liang capital of Jiangling, it signified the rightful transference of power, and it would have been the proper job of a state historian to record such an event.

Herein, however, lies the problem. Xiao Yi's chapter on book collecting was part not of the dynastic history but of a work written in the tradition of the "masters." Xiao Yi was writing not as the emperor but as the Master of the Golden Tower, a private individual, an aficionado. This distinction seems to have been behind what he chose to include in this chapter and what he did not; in such a private context, the appropriation of the imperial collection would seem almost sacrilegious. Here we see a conflict of roles between his public role as a monarch and his private role as a great book collector. It is not that a monarch could not be a book lover; rather, the motivation and purpose implicit in the activity of book collecting for these two roles were different and could even be opposed: the monarch acted as the patron of arts and the legal guardian of culture; the private collector was someone who allowed an all-consuming passion to become the central expression of his individuality.

Xiao Yi intended *The Master of the Golden Tower* to be a highly individualized work. He took pains to explain to the reader why, unlike

58. Dudbridge, *Lost Books*, p. 5.

some ministers and princes of the past, he did not want to have his retainers write the work for him: "One cannot discuss the fineness of pure cotton with people who wear coarse cloth; those who eat boiled greens and wheat gruel do not know enough to talk about the taste of sacrificial offerings."[59] He did not even let his friends read his work while he was writing it and related a humorous story about people who, unaware what *Jinlouzi* was, kept asking to see "the tower made of gold."[60] Xiao Yi wanted the work to be his—not Emperor Yuan's. And if the author and book collector Xiao Yi did not want to say anything about the acquisition of the imperial library, it was because in the clash between the public and private values, the very nature of his work prevented him from speaking as an emperor. Indeed, one must not forget that Xiao Yi had begun to write *The Master of the Golden Tower* at the age of fourteen, long before he was burdened with the throne and certainly at a time when he had never expected to become emperor. *The Master of the Golden Tower* was the work of a private individual, meant eventually to be added to the imperial book collection; as such, there was no room in it for imperial discourse itself.[61]

Xiao Yi's father, Emperor Wu of the Liang, was one of the few Chinese emperors who managed to turn kingship into just one aspect of a complicated and larger-than-life personality. Most men, once they took on the role of sovereign, either lost their personality in it or encountered a disastrous end brought about by the collision of the two. Xiao Yi unfortunately belonged to the latter category. The irony of history made a great lover of books the great destroyer of books. On the eve of his

59. Xiao Yi, *Jinlouzi jiaozhu* 9.157.

60. Ibid., 9.157, 13.252.

61. After I wrote these passages, I came upon the first book-length study of *Jinlouzi* by contemporary scholar Zhong Shilun, *"Jinlouzi" yanjiu*. Zhong (p. 10) similarly observes that "it might not be appropriate to mention the public book collection [i.e., the imperial book collection] in a privately composed chapter on book collection." This point is made following Zhong's refutation (pp. 9–10) of another modern scholar Yu Jiaxi's 余嘉錫 questions about Xiao Yi's age at the time of writing this chapter. I discuss this point in greater detail in my paper, "The Twilight of Masters: Masters Literature (*zishu*) in Early Medieval China," presented at the Chinese Medieval Studies Workshop at Columbia University in December 2006 and forthcoming in the *Journal of the American Oriental Society*.

surrender to the Western Wei army, he set fire to his library; this act, probably the largest deliberate destruction of books in Chinese history, has more than anything else defined Xiao Yi's place in history.[62] The imperial book collection of the Liang, which began with a conflagration in the palace library in Jiankang, ended in flames in Jiangling.

The Summary Documents of the Three Kingdoms (*Sanguo dianlue* 三國典略) by a seventh-century historian named Qiu Yue 丘悅 gives a poignant account of the lowest moment in the history of the Liang—easily one of the lowest moments of Chinese civilization:

> The emperor [i.e., Emperor Yuan] entered the Bamboo Hall of the Eastern Palace and ordered his secretary Gao Shanbao to burn the 140,000 scrolls of books and charts, ancient and modern. He was going to throw himself into the flames as well but was stopped by the palace staff. He smashed his precious swords on the pillar, exclaiming with a sigh: "Civil and military culture has come to an end upon this night."[63]
>
> 帝入東閤竹殿，命舍人高善寶焚古今圖書十四萬卷，將自赴火，宮人左右共止之. 又以寶劍斫柱令折，歎曰："文武之道，今夜盡矣!"

The *Liang shu* authors, adhering to their usual reticence about the failings of the Liang royal family, were silent on Xiao Yi's burning of the books. It may very well have been that, as Dudbridge speculates, for "one of the historic disasters of Chinese civilization" to be inflicted "consciously and deliberately by an emperor, the trustee of that civilization in transmission and himself a writer of some importance—that is a disaster of another dimension."[64] For the historian Yao Cha 姚察 (533–606), who had served the Liang dynasty in his youth and expressed much sympathy for the ill-fated Liang emperors in his work, it may have also been easier to hide his sense of pain and horror in the historian's laconic, almost bare, formal prose.

---

62. The quantity of the books burned was certainly larger than the number burned by the First Emperor of the Qin.

63. *Taiping yulan* 619.2911; *Zizhi tongjian* 165.5121.

64. Dudbridge, *Lost Books*, p. 42.

LITERARY SCHOLARSHIP

The previous sections discuss textual production and transmission as well as book collecting and cataloguing. Cataloguing a book collection was only the first step in organizing and making sense of received knowledge. The compilation of anthologies (*zongji* 總集), literary collections of individual authors (*bieji* 別集), and books made up of quotations organized under a systematic set of headings (*leishu* 類書; commonly translated "encyclopedias") constitutes the subject of this section.[65] Through their intense literary and scholarly activities, Liang men of letters sought to find a place for every text. Texts that had been part of a scattered manuscript legacy were positioned in a lucidly constructed literary historical narrative and categorical structure of knowledge.

The birth of *leishu* was marked by the appearance of *The Imperial Overview* (*Huanglan* 皇覽), compiled between 220 and 222 by a group of renowned scholars under the auspices of Cao Pi 曹丕 (187–226), Emperor Wen of the Wei 魏文帝. According to the chronicles of the Wei in *The Records of the Three Kingdoms* (*Sanguo zhi* 三國志), "[The emperor] commissioned scholars to take excerpts from the Classics and transmitted records and then arrange them by categories, hence producing over a thousand sections."[66] After *The Imperial Overview*, it was not

65. It has been suggested that *leishu* bear a certain similarity to the European commonplace books. A commonplace book is essentially a scrapbook filled with miscellaneous items from poems and quotes to medical recipes, prayers, proverbs, and even tables of weights and measures. It served as an aid for remembering useful facts or concepts. Each commonplace book was made individually. Both commonplace books and *leishu* are a way of compiling knowledge, but their similarities end here. A *leishu* presents quotations from earlier writings in a series of carefully arranged categories; it is much more systematic than a typical commonplace book and often represents the collective efforts of many scholars rather than an individual compiler. Although "encyclopedia" is not a perfect rendition of *leishu*, a *leishu* is much more akin to an encyclopedia in terms of a comprehensive and systematic organization of knowledge than to a commonplace book.

66. *Sanguo zhi* 2.88. In the Liang, *The Imperial Overview* was still extant and spanned 680 scrolls. The Liu-Song scholar He Chengtian 何承天 (370–447) "compressed" (*he* 合) the original *Imperial Overview* into 123 scrolls, and Xu Yuan 徐爰 (394–475) further "compressed" it into 50 scrolls. Xiao Chen, one of the Eight Companions of the Prince of Jingling, made an epitome of 20 scrolls (*Huanglan chao* 皇覽抄), which was lost by the Sui. By the Sui only 120 scrolls of *The Imperial*

until the Liang that similar compilations begin to appear, this time not as an isolated case but in rapid succession.

One reason for the flourishing of encyclopedias was the increasingly heavy use of references and allusions in writing. The literary critic Liu Xie 劉勰 (ca. 465–522) devoted an entire chapter to the subject, "Categories of References" ("Shilei" 事類), in his *Literary Mind Carving the Dragon* (*Wenxin diaolong* 文心雕龍).[67] In the late fifth century, the minister Wang Jian as a pastime offered small prizes in the Imperial Secretariat for those who could come up with the largest number of citations concerning an object.[68] Once, Emperor Wu of the Liang, marveling at the size of a chestnut presented as a tributary gift from Yuzhou, reportedly asked his courtiers the following question at a banquet: "How many textual references to the chestnut are there?" Shen Yue came up with three fewer than the emperor. Afterward Shen Yue said to a friend: "That gentleman [i.e., the emperor] hates to be bested. If you don't let him come out on top, he would be embarrassed to death." When Emperor Wu heard of this comment, only Xu Mian's earnest intervention prevented the humiliated emperor from punishing his old friend for his insolence.[69] On another occasion, after other courtiers thought they had exhausted all the textual allusions to a "brocade coverlet," the scholar Liu Jun showed off his learning before Emperor Wu by listing more than ten further references.[70] As we will see in the next chapter, in the early years of the Liang it was fashionable to employ a large number of recondite allusions in one's poetry. The compilation of encyclopedias in this period was therefore very much a response to practical needs.

An encyclopedia is a special kind of anthology, representing the classification of knowledge and an understanding of the cosmos. We no longer have *The Imperial Overview* or any of the Liang encyclopedias,[71]

Overview were left from the original 680 scrolls (*Sui shu* 34.1009). Only He Chengtian and Xu Yuan's versions survived through the Tang in permuted forms, but they were subsequently lost during the Song.

67. *Wenxin diaolong yizheng* 38.1404–43.

68. *Nan shi* 48.1189.

69. *Liang shu* 13.243.

70. *Nan shi* 49.1219.

71. Some items from *The Imperial Overview* are preserved in various later compilations. In the early twentieth century, Luo Zhenyu 羅振玉 identified fragments of

but extant Tang dynasty encyclopedias such as *Classified Extracts from Literature* (*Yiwen leiju* 藝文類聚) exhibit a carefully organized system of things, a scheme of the universe as conceived in medieval China. As we shall see in Chapter 4, the categorical structure of an encyclopedia and the texts included under each subheading to be recycled by writers consulting the encyclopedia constitute a context within which any object or phenomenon was to be understood.

As the title *The Imperial Overview* indicates, an encyclopedia is also an affirmation of the emperor's power over knowledge and culture: like the extravagant Han *fu*, it promises to bring everything under the emperor's gaze, from the sun and moon down to the tiniest insect. If we bear this in mind, it may not be entirely unreasonable to speculate that the two most ambitious and best-known Liang encyclopedias might have been born from a rivalry, both between two brothers and between a prince and the emperor. Emperor Wu's younger brother Xiao Xiu 蕭秀 (475–518), the Prince of Ancheng 安成王, commissioned Liu Jun to compile an encyclopedia in 120 scrolls, *The Garden of Classified Extracts* (*Leiyuan* 類苑). Emperor Wu subsequently asked his minister Xu Mian to recommend scholars to compile an even grander encyclopedia. Xu Mian recommended five people, and the end result was *The Comprehensive Epitome of the Park of Flowering Groves* in 620 scrolls. The project took eight years to finish: it began in 516 and was not completed until 524.[72]

As one might expect, Buddhist encyclopedias also flourished in this period.[73] Not long after he took the throne, Emperor Wu had Zhou She, Yu Chan 虞闡, and Liu Gai 劉溉 (perhaps a typographic error for Dao Gai 到溉) assemble *The Record of the Buddha* (*Fo ji* 佛記) in thirty sections. Not satisfied with the preface they composed, however, Emperor

a pre-Tang encyclopedia discovered in Dunhuang as the Northern Qi encyclopedia *Xiuwendian yulan* 修文殿御覽, but William Hung (Hong Ye, "Suowei *Xiuwen dian yulan*") argued that the fragments are in fact from the Liang encyclopedia *Hualin bianlue*.

72. According to *Liang shu* and *Nan shi*, the five people recommended by Xu Mian were He Sicheng 何思澄 (ca. 479–532), Liu Yao, Gu Xie 顧協 (470–542), Zhong Yu 鍾嶼, and Wang Ziyun 王子雲 (*Liang shu* 50.716; *Nan shi* 72.1782–83). *Sui shu* 34.1009, however, gives another name, Xu Sengquan 徐僧權.

73. According to Chen Yuzhen ("Daoshi yu *Fayuan zhulin*," p. 249), *Fayuan jing* 法苑經 compiled in the Qi was the first Buddhist encyclopedia on record.

Wu asked Shen Yue to pen a new one.[74] Shen Yue duly complied, and the preface is preserved in its entirety in *Guang Hongming ji*. In the preface Shen Yue explained the nature of the compilation:

[The compilers] sought widely among the scriptures, searched and made selections from commentaries and treatises; then they distinguished the branches and divided the currents and attached them to different categories. Accomplishing much in a short period of time—this may describe [the reader's benefit from] such a project.

博尋經藏, 搜採注說, 條別流分, 各以類附, 日少功多, 可用譬此.

Shen Yue also clarified the editorial principles:

From similar incidents of stirring and response, only one example is chosen, and the rest have been left out. There are stories in which a person is resurrected from death and relates his or her after-death experiences; because these stories are, however, too far-fetched and fantastic and cannot be possibly verified, they are not included in the present volume and are considered as being open to doubt. Again there are stories in which a person is possessed and becomes a medium, or one's intense thoughts are materialized into dreams: such things are particularly difficult to believe or understand, and so none has been recorded.[75]

其有感應之流, 事類相似, 止取其一, 餘悉不書. 或後死而更生, 陳說經見, 事涉杳冥, 取驗無所, 亦皆靡載, 同之闕疑. 或憑人以言, 託想成夢, 尤難信曉, 一無所錄.

The absence of miracle tales distinguishes *The Record of the Buddha* from such later encyclopedic compilations as *A Forest of Pearls in the Garden of Dharma* (*Fayuan zhulin* 法苑珠林) from the seventh century.

In 516, Emperor Wu commissioned the monks Baochang, Senghao 僧豪, and Fasheng 法生 to compile another Buddhist encyclopedia in fifty scrolls, *Differentiated Manifestations of Sūtras and Laws* (*Jinglü yixiang* 經律異相), with a table of contents in five more scrolls. In the preface, the compilers stated that this epitome aimed to gather stories from various sūtras and classify them under different headings so that the reader might easily find things, and "students in the future age will be able to

74. For Emperor Wu's edict, see *Quan Liang wen* 5.2974.
75. Ibid., 30.3124–25.

become learned without much labor."[76] The promise of "quick profit," which likewise appears in Shen Yue's preface to *The Record of the Buddha*, seems to be a common feature of encyclopedic compilations. *Jinglü yixiang* is, however, the only extant Buddhist encyclopedia from this period. As such, it is invaluable for literary and religious scholars as well as for historians. Years later, another massive Buddhist encyclopedia in 300 scrolls, *Joined Jade-Disks from the Treasures of Dharma* (*Fabao lianbi* 法寶連璧), was commissioned by Xiao Gang and completed through the joint efforts of about forty courtiers. Only Xiao Yi's 534 preface survives.[77]

Apart from the compilation of encyclopedias, another important literary activity in the Liang was anthology making, which reached an unprecedented peak in Chinese literary history. The compilation of an individual author's collection of literary writings was either carried out by the author or by a friend after the author's death. As the editors of the eighteenth-century *Complete Books of the Four Categories* (*Siku quanshu* 四庫全書) observed, it was during the Qi and Liang dynasties that personal literary collections flourished and many forms and conventions (*tili* 體例) adopted by later editors of literary collections were established.[78] Zhang Rong 張融 (444–97) was the first Chinese writer we know of to give a title to his literary collection. When asked why he had named his collection *The Sea of Jade* (*Yuhai* 玉海), he replied: "Jade is a metaphor of virtue, and the sea expresses my admiration for the highest good."[79] *The History of the Sui* records two other collections by Zhang Rong, one of ten scrolls named *The Collection of the Great Marsh* (*Daze ji* 大澤集), and the other of sixty scrolls named *The Collection of the Golden Waves* (*Jinbo ji* 金波集).[80] Later, perhaps influenced by Zhang Rong, the imperial librarian Zhang Chi 張熾 named his collection *The River of Gold* (*Jinhe ji* 金河集).[81] Jiang Yan 江淹 (444–505) edited his writings into "The Former Collection" (*qianji* 前集) and "The

76. *T* 53: 1.1.

77. See *Quan Liang wen* 17.3051–53.

78. *Siku quanshu zongmu* 148.3101.

79. *Nan Qi shu* 41.730. Zhang Rong's reply contains an allusion to Laozi's remark: "The highest good is like water" (*Laozi jiaoshi* 8.31; *Sui shu* 35.1076).

80. *Sui shu* 35.1076.

81. Ibid., 35.1077.

Latter Collection" (*houji* 後集); Xu Mian and Liu Zhilin 劉之遴 (477–548) did the same.[82] The poet Wang Yun compiled a collection of his literary writings for each office he held, a practice that set an example for many later writers.[83] Emperor Wu had a separate collection of poetry and *fu* in twenty scrolls besides a regular collection of literary writings; he also had a collection of "miscellaneous prose" (*zawen* 雜文) in nine scrolls. This is one of the earliest cases in which an individual writer arranged his writings in different collections by genre.[84]

More significant than the appearance of individual literary collections were the many general collections in the Liang. By the sixth century, the compilation of literary anthologies had a long tradition. The earliest anthology is Zhi Yu's 摯虞 (d. 312?) *Collection of Literary Writings Divided by Genre* (*Wenzhang liubie ji* 文章流別集). Li Chong's *Forest of Writings* (*Han lin* 翰林), of which fifty-four scrolls were extant in the Liang and which was subsequently lost in the Sui, was probably also a collection of literary writings. During both the Song and the Qi dynasty, a large-scale general compilation was produced: Liu Yiqing's 劉義慶 (403–44) *Forest of Collections* (*Ji lin* 集林) in 200 scrolls and Kong Huan's 孔逭 (fl. 480s) *Garden of Literature* (*Wen yuan* 文苑) in 100 scrolls.[85] Their large size suggests that these were "collections" rather than "anthologies." Later, an epitome was produced for each collection. In the early fifth century, the poet Xie Lingyun compiled *A Collection of Fu* (*Fu ji* 賦集) in ninety-two scrolls as well as a *Collection of Poetry* (*Shi ji* 詩集) in fifty scrolls: both were apparently the first of their kind as single genre collections.[86]

In the Liang there was a proliferation of both general and single-genre anthologies. There were, among other works, *A Forest of Words* (*Ci lin* 詞林) in fifty-eight scrolls, *The Sea of Literature* (*Wen hai* 文海) in fifty scrolls, *A Collection of the Writings of Courtiers from the Wu*

82. *Liang shu* 14.251; *Sui shu* 35.1077, 35.1079.

83. *Liang shu* 33.487. For each of the seven successive offices he held, there were ten scrolls of poetry and prose; for his term of service in the Imperial Secretariat, there were thirty scrolls.

84. *Sui shu* 35.1076.

85. *Nan shi* 13.360; *Sui shu* 35.1082. Kong Huan was mentioned briefly in "The Biographies of Men of Letters" ("Wenxue zhuan" 文學傳) in *Nan shi* 72.1770.

86. *Sui shu* 35.1082.

Region (*Wu chaoshi wenji* 吳朝士文集) in ten scrolls, and *A Collection of Writings for the Headband Box* (*Jinxiang ji* 巾箱集) in seven scrolls. *Wu chaoshi wenji* is the earliest known regional anthology; its focus on authors who were native southerners betrays an intense awareness of a regional identity.[87]

The royal family was quite active in anthology making. Emperor Wu put together an anthology of *fu* entitled *Fu of Various Dynasties* (*Lidai fu* 歷代賦). Since it had only ten scrolls, it must have been a selection rather than a comprehensive collection like Xie Lingyun's anthology. Xiao Yi, Prince of Xiangdong, commanded Xiao Ben 蕭賁 to compile *A Collection of Stele Inscriptions* (*Bei ji* 碑集) in 100 scrolls.[88] Crown Prince Xiao Tong "compiled an anthology of past and present documents and writings in ten scrolls entitled *Correct Expressions* (*Zheng xu* 正序); an anthology of fine examples of poetry in the five-syllable line, *Prime Blossoms of Literary Writings* (*Wenzhang yinghua* 文章英華) in twenty scrolls; and *Wen xuan* in thirty scrolls."[89] Only the *Wen xuan* survives today. *Zheng xu* had already been lost by the Sui, since it is not recorded in the *Sui shu* "Bibliography."

We know little about *Prime Blossoms of Literary Writings*. It may have been the same work as another poetic anthology in twenty scrolls attributed to Xiao Tong, *Prime Blossoms of the Garden of Poetry from Past to Present* (*Gujin shiyuan yinghua* 古今詩苑英華), as recorded in the *Sui shu* "Bibliography" section.[90] Xiao Yi had asked for a copy of this work along with Xiao Tong's personal literary collection, and Xiao Tong readily agreed. Xiao Tong's letter to Xiao Yi is still extant; in it he expressed regret at the incompleteness of the anthology.[91]

87. *Sui shu* 35.1082.

88. Xiao Yi, *Jinlouzi jiaozhu* 10.200. The *Sui shu* "Bibliography" (35.1086) records a lost *Buddhist Stele Inscriptions* (*Shishi beiwen* 釋氏碑文) in thirty scrolls compiled by Xiao Yi. This may be the same as *A Collection of Stele Inscriptions from the Buddhist Canon* (*Neidian beiming jilin* 內典碑銘集林), whose preface by Xiao Yi is preserved in *Guang hongming ji*.

89. *Liang shu* 8.171.

90. *Sui shu* 35.1084; *Jiu Tang shu* 47.2080. The number of the scrolls recorded in the *Sui shu* "Bibliography" is nineteen, but one scroll may have been the table of contents, as is often the case.

91. *Quan Liang wen* 20.3064.

The History of the Sui records a lost *Wenzhang yinghua* by Xiao Tong, supposedly in thirty scrolls.[92] Nevertheless, the *Wenzhang yinghua* in twenty scrolls and the one in thirty scrolls might very well have been the same work: "two" (*er* 二) and "three" (*san* 三) are easily confused in copying; alternatively, the division into scrolls of the former anthology may have become changed during copying, a not uncommon phenomenon. Since the thirty-scroll work was already lost in the early seventh century, the *Sui shu* historian probably had never seen it and simply recorded the title from an earlier book catalogue; because of the different numbers of scrolls, the two versions of *Wenzhang yinghua* were recorded as two different works.

In the late sixth century, Yan Zhitui mentioned that Liu Xiaochuo had compiled an anthology entitled *The Garden of Poetry* (*Shiyuan* 詩苑). Since Liu Xiaochuo was an active participant in the compilation of *Wen xuan*, it would not be unreasonable to assume that *Gujin shiyuan yinghua* and *Shiyuan* might be the same work.[93] Yan Zhitui observed that Liu Xiaochuo selected only two poems by He Xun, whose fame at the time was equal to Liu Xiaochuo's own. "Contemporaries criticized [his anthology] for its narrow range."[94] This in fact recalls Xiao Tong's remark in his letter to Xiao Yi that he regretted the incompleteness of

92. *Sui shu* 35.1084. For a discussion of *Wenzhang yinghua* and *Gujin shiyuan yinghua*, see Cao Daoheng and Fu Gang, *Xiao Tong pingzhuan*, pp. 211–14. Cao Daoheng and Fu Gang believe that the *Sui shu* record of a *Wenzhang yinghua* in thirty scrolls came from Ruan Xiaoxu's *Seven Records* and claim that we must trust Ruan Xiaoxu's judgment (that *Wenzhang yinghua* and *Gujin shiyuan yinghua* were not the same). However, we cannot be certain about this. Ruan Xiaoxu may have simply recorded book titles without examining the content of the books, and if a book was recorded under different titles, a not uncommon phenomenon, then Ruan might have included both titles in his catalogue. Yu Shaochu 俞紹初 (in "*Wen xuan*" *xue xinlun*, p. 70) argues that, if the two books were indeed the same, the *Sui shu* compilers should have placed the title *Wenzhang yinghua* under the title *Gujin shiyuan yinghua*; but since the *Sui shu* compilers did not do so, the two books must have been different. This is a moot point, since the *Sui shu* compilers never saw the book called *Wenzhang yinghua*.

93. See "*Wen xuan*" *xue xinlun*, pp. 69–70; Cao Daoheng and Fu Gang, *Xiao Tong pingzhuan*, pp. 214–17.

94. Yan Zhitui, *Yanshi jiaxun* 9.276.

Gujin shiyuan yinghua, but before he could do anything about it, "the book had already gone into circulation."[95]

Poetry anthologies were very popular in the fifth and sixth centuries. Zhong Rong mentioned that Shen Yue had made an anthology of poetry, which is no longer extant.[96] In writing his critical work *Gradations of Poets* (alternatively known as *Shi ping* 詩評, *The Evaluation of Poetry*) Zhong Rong seemed to have been influenced by Shen Yue's selections. He claimed that in the past he had often ignored Fu Liang's 傅亮 (374–426) poetry, but after several poems by Fu Liang were included in Shen Yue's anthology, his attention was called to them.[97] He assigned Fu Liang to his lowest ranking, but it is clear that Fu Liang would not have made it even to the lowest rank if not for Shen Yue's anthology.

Among other poetry anthologies from the Liang are *A Collection of Poetry* (*Shi zuan* 詩纘) in thirteen scrolls, *Prime Blossoms of Various Poems* (*Zhongshi yinghua* 眾詩英華) in one scroll, *Poetry in Categories* (*Shi lei* 詩類) in six scrolls, and *New Songs of the Jade Terrace* (*Yutai xinyong*) in ten scrolls. Xiao Yi commanded Wang Xiaosi 王孝祀 to compile *Finest Blossoms of Poetry* (*Shiying* 詩英; ten scrolls); he also commanded Xiao Shu 蕭淑 to compile *New Writings from the Western Residence* (*Xifu xinwen* 西府新文; eleven scrolls) when the prince was the governor of Jingzhou (hence the "Western Residence" in the title, as Jingzhou was to the west of Jiankang). There were also poetry collections assembled by subject matter, such as a collection of Qi banquet poetry (*Qi yanhui shi* 齊讌會詩), or a collection of Qi libation banquet poetry (*Qi shidianhui shi* 齊釋奠會詩), both of which were presumably compiled during the Liang.[98]

95. *Quan Liang wen* 20.3064.

96. Zhong Rong, *Shi pin jizhu*, p. 397. Scholars assume that this anthology was either *An Epitome of Collections* (*Ji chao* 集鈔) in ten scrolls or *A Record of Song Literature* (*Song wenzhang zhi* 宋文章志) in thirty scrolls, both titles being recorded in the *Sui shu* "Bibliography" under Shen Yue's name. An alternative possibility is that the anthology had been lost by the Sui and so was not included in the *Sui shu* "Bibliography."

97. Zhong Rong (*Shi pin jizhu*, p. 397) described those poems as "average," but a textual variant, endorsed by several scholars as making the most sense in the context, has "level and graceful" 平美.

98. *Sui shu* 35.1084.

All the poetry anthologies cited above, except for *Yutai xinyong*, have been lost, and we know nothing about their compilers or their contents. Of *Xifu xinwen*, however, there is an interesting account preserved in Yan Zhitui's *Family Instructions of the Yan Clan* (*Yanshi jiaxun* 顏氏家訓). According to Yan Zhitui, his father Yan Xie 顏協 (498–539) was serving as secretary to Prince Xiao Yi when the anthology was being compiled:

> My late father's writings have always been decorous and appropriate instead of following the popular trend. When Emperor Yuan of the Liang [Xiao Yi] was a prince, he commissioned the compilation of *New Writings from the Western Residence*, which did not include a single piece by my father because his writings did not try to please the crowd and so lacked the echoes of Zheng and Wei [i.e., the "decadent" songs in *The Classic of Poetry*].[99]
>
> 吾家世文章，甚爲典正，不從流俗．梁孝元在蕃邸時，撰西府新文，訖無一篇見錄者，亦以不偶於世，無鄭衛之音故也．

Xifu xinwen therefore seems to have been an anthology of "popular" poetry. Since verse in the five-syllable line was the new vogue in the fifth and sixth centuries, we may assume that this anthology, with its claim to be "new," was composed primarily of such poems.

Only three Liang anthologies have survived: *Hongming ji*, *Wen xuan*, and *Yutai xinyong*. *Hongming ji*, compiled by the monk Sengyou, is a collection of Buddhist writings by both monks and laymen from the Eastern Han to the Liang. Most of the selected prose pieces are impassioned defenses of the religion against attacks by nonbelievers. Sengyou, however, also included writings by detractors, so that the reader has both sides of the argument. The anthology enables us to glimpse some of the most controversial issues in the early transmission of Buddhism in China, but its interest goes far beyond religious studies: it contains some of the best examples of analytical prose written in the Southern Dynasties. It also became the precedent for the seventh-century *Guang hongming ji*, which incorporated writings from more diverse genres, such as poems, inscriptions, and confessions, many of them written by Liang authors.

Wen xuan and *Yutai xinyong* are, on the other hand, both secular anthologies. *Wen xuan* is a general literary anthology arranged generically

99. Yan Zhitui, *Yanshi jiaxun* 9.251.

and, as such, is the oldest extant genre anthology.[100] It contains 761 pieces of prose and poetry by 130 authors, covering the period from the late Zhou to Xiao Tong's own time. In recent years, some scholars have argued that it was compiled on the basis of previous anthologies.[101] The major compilers of *Wen xuan* were Xiao Tong and his courtiers (most notably Liu Xiaochuo), although the extent to which the crown prince was involved in the editorial process is a point of fierce debate among modern scholars.[102] Although Xiao Tong did not specify the readership he had had in mind, the anthology was clearly intended for a general elite audience.

According to Dou Chang 竇常 (d. 825), *Wen xuan* made a point of excluding living authors.[103] This assertion, long accepted by *Wen xuan* scholars, has been challenged recently.[104] Indeed, unlike Zhong Rong, who spells out this editorial principle clearly in his preface to *Shi pin*,

100. There is a large body of literature about *Wen xuan*, which is the subject of modern scholarship dubbed *Xuan xue* 選學. For the compilation, content, selection standard, and other issues concerning *Wen xuan* editions and scholarship, see, e.g., *"Wen xuan" xue xinlun*; Fu Gang, *"Wen xuan" banben*; Wang Liqun, *"Wen xuan" chengshu*; Okamura Shigeru, *"Wen xuan" zhi yanjiu*; Shimizu Yoshio, *Shin "Monzen" gaku*; Knechtges, "Introduction" to his translation of *Wen xuan*; and idem, "Culling the Weeds."

101. Liu Liang 劉良, one of the "Five Ministers" who annotated *Wen xuan* in the early eighth century, first mentioned that *Wen xuan* followed "the editorial method of the previous worthies" in the case of Zhang Hua's poem "Da He Shao" 答何劭 (Xiao Tong, *Liuchen zhu*, p. 448). Okamura Shigeru (*"Wen xuan" zhi yanjiu*, pp. 59–95) speculated that *Wen xuan* was compiled on the basis of previous anthologies. This view is endorsed by a number of Chinese scholars, most notably Wang Liqun, who provided new supportive evidence in his *"Wen xuan" chengshu*, pp. 24–49, 266–77.

102. The Japanese monk Kūkai 空海 (774–835; *Wenjing mifu lun* [or *Bunkyō hifuron*], p. 354), citing Yuan Jing's 元兢 (fl. 675) preface to *Gujin shiren xiuju* 古今詩人秀句: "Xiao Tong, Crown Prince Zhaoming of the Liang, Liu Xiaochuo, and others compiled the *Wen xuan*." In the late twentieth century, the Japanese scholar Shimizu Yoshio (*Liuchao wenxue*, pp. 1–46) argued that Liu Xiaochuo was the actual editor of *Wen xuan*. Many Chinese scholars do not go quite this far, even though they acknowledge Liu's important role in the compilation of *Wen xuan*. For the argument against Shimizu's view, see *"Wen xuan" xue xinlun*, pp. 1–77.

103. Cited by Chao Gongwu 晁公武 (ca. 1105–80) in *Junzhai dushu zhi* 郡齋讀書志 20b.

104. See Wang Liqun, *"Wen xuan" chengshu*, pp. 140–53.

Xiao Tong never said anything about this in his preface to *Wen xuan*. Nevertheless, of the 130 *Wen xuan* authors, only ten lived into the sixth century, and the last to pass away was Lu Chui, who died in 526.[105] As such, *Wen xuan* illustrates the Liang consensus regarding the literary canon, but it reflects not so much the contemporary Liang literary scene as the Liang conception and evaluation of the literary past. Nor is there evidence that *Wen xuan* was particularly influential or more significant than other anthologies in the Liang dynasty,[106] although it became increasingly important in the late sixth century and exerted an immense influence in the Tang. *Wen xuan* was considered an important pre-Tang anthology throughout imperial China, even though it ceased being the predominant model for literary composition in the Northern Song.[107]

Yutai xinyong, on the other hand, is a single-genre anthology consisting of poems that are mainly in five-syllable lines and arranged more or less chronologically; moreover, the editor, Xu Ling, stated explicitly in the preface that the anthology was intended for a female readership, a unique perspective explored in greater detail later in this book. This anthology has long been associated with Prince Xiao Gang's literary salon and (mistakenly) with the rise of the poetic style that dominated the second half of the Liang, namely, the so-called Palace Style poetry.

---

105. *"Wen xuan" xue xinlun*, pp. 10–11. For this reason *Wen xuan* is surmised to have been completed between 526, the year of Lu Chui's death, and 531, the year of Xiao Tong's death. Wang Liqun (*"Wen xuan" chengshu*, pp. 140–53) suggests, on the other hand, that *Wen xuan* was compiled between 522 and 526.

106. There was no mention of *Wen xuan* in contemporary sources. Okamura Shigeru (*"Wen xuan" zhi yanjiu*, pp. 68–71, 88–91) notes that *Wen xuan* was received rather indifferently by its contemporaries and argues that *Wen xuan* had been hastily put together on the basis of earlier anthologies and was rather simple and short compared to earlier large anthologies.

107. The reception of *Wen xuan* was mixed in the Song. The literary master of the Northern Song, Su Shi 蘇軾 (1036–1101), criticized it rather severely, saying that it "had no proper editorial method and was inappropriate in its selections" (*Song shihua*, 1: 786). According to Lu You 陸游 (1122–1210; *Laoxue'an*, 8.100), *Wen xuan* was still highly esteemed at the beginning of the Northern Song, but its influence waned after the Qingli reign (1041–48), and Su Shi's influence dominated the Southern Song.

The history of *Yutai xinyong* editions is rather messy, but according to the 1633 reprint of a Song edition of *Yutai xinyong*, this anthology contains 654 poems by about 115 authors, 54 of whom were active in the sixth century, some of them remaining so through the end of the Liang and beyond.[108] In contrast with *Wen xuan*, many renowned contemporary poets, such as Liu Xiaochuo, Wang Yun, and the Xiao princes themselves, are amply represented in *Yutai xinyong*. In this sense, *Yutai xinyong* is more useful as an overview of the Liang literary landscape. For this reason, the focus in the current study is primarily on *Yutai xinyong* rather than on *Wen xuan*.

In *The Making of Early Classical Chinese Poetry*, Stephen Owen discusses how the men of letters in the fifth and sixth centuries "made" early classical poetry by editing received manuscripts, changing texts as they saw fit, assigning authorship, and writing a cultural narrative that defined their own place in literary history. Both anthologies from the Liang mediate our knowledge and perception of early Chinese classical literature. This is an important observation, but one already so well argued that I shall not spend time discussing it further in this book. Instead, I hope to call the reader's attention to another crucial point: both *Wen xuan* and *Yutai xinyong* were produced in a context of many other anthologies; moreover, they differ in a number of ways: the purpose of compilation, the range and standard of selection, and the intended readership. This context needs to be emphasized because many modern scholars draw general conclusions about the Liang literary scene based on a comparison of these two anthologies. Such a simplistic binary comparison without contextualization tells us more about the ideological presumptions underlying the writing of the cultural narrative by later generations than about the Liang. Although both *Wen xuan* and *Yutai xinyong* are immensely valuable in a variety of ways, their importance in the Liang dynasty itself should not be exaggerated. What we should bear in mind is that both anthologies are chance survivals from a sea of anthologies produced in the first half of the sixth century. In other words, the vast number of lost books from this period must remain

108. My calculation yields the number of 116 authors in the 1633 edition. The number of poems is based on the calculations in Liu Yuejin, "*Yutai xinyong*" *yanjiu*, pp. 43, 96. For a list of the 54 Liang authors in *Yutai xinyong*, see ibid., pp. 152–89.

the background against which we consider this period in Chinese literary history.

Yutai xinyong, however, did mark an interesting cultural moment: the emergence during the Liang of literary anthologies compiled explicitly for a female readership. This anthology, moreover, was put together for reading pleasure, not for a didactic purpose like *A Collection of Admonitions for Women* (*Furen xunjie ji* 婦人訓誡集) compiled by Xu Zhanzhi 徐湛之 (410–53). In addition to *Yutai xinyong*, there was also a collection simply entitled *Miscellaneous Prose* (*Zawen* 雜文) in sixteen scrolls; an appended note in the *Sui shu* "Bibliography" says that it was "composed for women" 爲婦人作.[109]

A number of upper-class women had their own literary collections.[110] Yin Chun 殷淳 (379–438) compiled *A Collection of Writings by Female Authors* (*Furen ji* 婦人集) in thirty scrolls; the Liang minister Xu Mian assembled a similar collection in ten scrolls.[111] The Liang in particular witnessed the appearance of many talented woman authors, beginning with the imperial court. In 503, Emperor Wu commissioned the writer Zhang Shuai to compile an encyclopedia of "textual references to women" (*furen shi* 婦人事) to "be distributed in the inner palace." This encyclopedia contained over 2,000 items and spanned a hundred scrolls; it was copied out by the finest calligraphers of the time.[112] As mentioned above, encyclopedias served the practical purpose of aiding a writer in composition, and so the compilation of an encyclopedia specifically for the "inner palace" indicated that many palace ladies tried their hand at writing. Among Emperor Wu's daughters, "the Princesses of Lin'an 臨安, Anji 安吉, and Changcheng 長城 all possessed literary talent; the Princess of Anji was the best known of them."[113] The

109. *Sui shu* 35.1082.

110. Ibid., 35.1070–71.

111. Ibid., 35.1082; *Liang shu* 25.387. The *Sui shu* "Bibliography" (35.1082) recorded *A Collection of Writings by Female Authors* (*Furen ji* 婦人集) in eleven scrolls and noted that it was no longer extant. It might have been the one compiled by Xu Mian, as the eleventh scroll would have been the table of contents.

112. *Liang shu* 33.475. The original text reads "over twenty items" (*ershi yu tiao* 二十餘條), which is clearly a textual error, since "ten" (*shi* 十) looks like "thousand" (*qian* 千), and "over twenty items" could not possibly have been divided into a hundred scrolls.

113. *Nan shi* 51.1278.

Princess of Lin'an's collection of literary writings in three scrolls was compiled posthumously by her brother Xiao Gang, who penned a preface for it. The preface is still extant.[114]

Literary composition was not, however, limited to members of the imperial family. In fact, the most famous woman writers of the Liang were from gentry families. Both Liu Lingxian 劉令嫻, sister of Liu Xiaochuo and wife of Xu Fei 徐悱 (495–524), and Shen Manyuan 沈滿願, Shen Yue's granddaughter, left collections of literary writings in three scrolls.[115] A handful of poems by them is still extant. Liu Lingxian's sacrificial essay for Xu Fei was so well written that her father-in-law, Xu Mian, gave up the notion of writing one himself.[116] In Chapter 4, we will return to the subject of elite Liang women's reading, writing, and anthology making.

114. *Quan Liang wen* 12.3017.

115. For an introduction and translation of Liu Lingxian's selected writings, see Idema and Grant, *The Red Brush*, pp. 146–53.

116. *Liang shu* 33.484; see also *Quan Liang wen* 68.3361.

CHAPTER THREE

Mapping the Cultural World (II)

Contextualizing Taste

This chapter turns from the material aspect of the Liang textual world investigated in Chapter 2 to its social context. Two central points emerge in this consideration of Liang society. The first half of the sixth century witnessed the rise of a cultural elite consisting of members of the lower gentry and native southerners. In the Liang, these politically and culturally marginalized social groups rose to prominent positions through their cultural accomplishments, in contrast with the old northern émigré aristocracy, which was defined primarily by pedigree. This shift coincided with what Yasuda Jirō has termed the "new aristocratic system" under Emperor Wu's rule. As Yasuda notes, through the Tianjian reform (see Chapter 1):

> Members of the lesser house (han-men) class, who even though they possessed ability had been constrained by their lesser background, were put on a par with the great bureaucratic houses and were transferred to the highest ranks of the executive class. From this new, expanded scholar-gentry class, officials were appointed with talent and scholarship as the selection criteria, in accordance with the new principle of state administration.[1]

Moreover, these members formed marriage alliances among themselves and over time became a considerable new social force distin-

1. Yasuda Jirō, "The Changing Aristocratic Society," p. 52.

guished by their cultural capital and by a network of affinal and agnatic relations.

Many scholars have discussed the literary groupings of the period.[2] What we see in the Liang, however, is something more than literary groups or even something else altogether, since many members of the Liang cultural elite were not confined to one literary group or another but moved freely across different "groups" and were widely admired by their contemporaries. This brings us to the second central point of this chapter: although the Liang literary scene has long been regarded as divided into several contending schools, a closer look reveals a set of shared beliefs concerning the nature of literature and the evaluation of the literary past. What have been construed as fundamental differences in theory and practice may be no more than changes in fashion and taste, diverse manifestations of individual penchants and talents, and the function of anthologies compiled for different purposes. The construction of a literary historical narrative about the rivalry among different camps serves an ideological purpose, which not only dictates the conclusion but, as we shall see, sometimes shapes the evidence as well.

THE RISE OF A CULTURAL ELITE

I begin by examining the backgrounds of two authors of works of literary criticism well known to any student of Chinese literature: Liu Xie, the author of *Literary Mind Carving the Dragon*, which was written at the turn of the sixth century; and Zhong Rong, the author of *Gradations of Poets*, which was completed between 513 and 518. *Literary Mind* is a fifty-chapter treatise discussing all aspects of literature, from genres to techniques; *Gradations of Poets* is divided into three sections, ranking 123 poets into three levels (top, middle, and lower) on the basis of their poetry in the five-syllable line.[3] Later in this chapter, I discuss the content of these two works; in this section, I focus on the social and political background of these two writers.

2. See, e.g., Morino Shigeo, *Rikuchō shi no kenkyū*, pp. 60–154; Cheng Zhangcan, *Shizu yu liuchao*, pp. 3–47; and Hu Dalei, *Zhonggu wenxue*.

3. The number of poets evaluated in *The Gradations of Poets* varies from edition to edition; see Zhong Rong, *Shi pin jizhu*, p. 10.

Liu Xie's grandfather, Liu Lingzhen 劉靈眞, was the brother of Liu Xiuzhi 劉秀之 (397–464), who had posthumously been granted the prestigious title of Minister of Works during the Song.[4] By Liu Xie's time, however, the Liu clan had suffered a series of mishaps and was long fallen from its former glory.[5] Liu Xie lost his father in childhood and never married because of strained financial circumstances. Instead, he went to live in a Buddhist temple, although at this early stage in his life he apparently did not take monastic vows. Liu Xie later embarked on an official career thanks to Shen Yue's recommendation, but he never reached a high position.[6] Zhong Rong, a descendent of Jin Palace Attendant Zhong Ya 鍾雅 (d. 329), presumably fared better materially, but the highest office he ever held was record keeper (Jishi 記室), a low-ranking secretary, under the Prince of Jin'an 晉安王 (Xiao Gang's title before he became the crown prince).[7] In an age characterized by a strict social hierarchy and an intense awareness of family status, it is a curious coincidence that Liu Xie and Zhong Rong, both minor figures in the sociopolitical world, wrote the two most ambitious works of literary criticism. And yet, as we move into the sixth century, we begin to see members of less prominent gentry families playing a much more visible role in shaping the culture of the age. Conscious of their less privileged social status, they strove for excellence in literature and learning and formed a close-knit literary community whose relations were frequently reinforced by intermarriage and blood ties. They made *wen* 文 not only a new criterion for evaluating people but also a "family business," and they often succeeded in translating their cultural capital into social and political prestige. The family politics of the great houses of previous eras was thus carried over into a new playing field.

4. *Song shu* 81.2075.

5. The posthumous ducal title granted to Liu Xiuzhi was passed to his son and then to his grandson, who was dispossessed of the title after the founding of the Qi in 479 (*Song shu* 81.2076). Liu Xiuzhi's uncle Liu Muzhi 劉穆之 (360–417) was one of the most trusted advisors of the founding emperor of the Song and was granted a posthumous ducal title, but his descendents were characterized by eccentricity and erratic behavior. By the late fifth century, several members of the Liu clan had been either demoted or sent into exile for misconduct (*Song shu* 42.1308–11; *Nan Qi shu* 36.639–43).

6. *Liang shu* 50.710–12.

7. Ibid., 49.694–97.

Shen Yue and Ren Fang, two members of the Eight Companions of the Prince of Jingling, were key figures in the formation of this cultural elite. Both were from lesser gentry families; Shen Yue was, moreover, a native southerner. Both men, however, achieved the status of grand masters at the turn of the century, and their eminence was confirmed, and indeed partially established, by their patronage of younger talents. A reading of *The History of the Liang* reveals that there was almost no contemporary writer who had not been generously praised by Shen Yue and/or Ren Fang. Indeed, a positive comment from either man was one of the *Liang shu* historian's rhetorical tactics for indicating the reputation of a man of letters.

The list of people Shen Yue recommended is quite long and includes most of the well-known writers from the late fifth to early sixth century.[8] Of Xie Tiao's poetry he said: "There has not been poetry like this in two hundred years."[9] He commented on Gu Xie's examination essay in similar terms: "Since [the Jin royal house] crossed the Yangzi River, there has not been anything like this."[10] He was particularly extravagant in praising Wang Yun, saying to Emperor Wu of the Liang: "Of famous personages lately, only Wang Yun is outstanding." He told Wang Yun, forty years his junior, that he would like to bequeath his large book collection to Wang, just as the famous late Eastern Han writer Cai Yong 蔡邕 (132–92) had given his books to the upcoming poet Wang Can 王粲 (177–217).[11] Shen Yue also liked to have accomplished calligraphers write his favorite poems on the walls of his suburban mansion; Wang Yun, Liu Xian, He Sicheng, and Liu Yao were the four authors whose writings enjoyed this honor.

8. Shen Yue spoke favorably of Yue Facai 樂法才 and his brother Yue Fazang 樂法藏, Zhang Shuai, Lu Chui, Liu Xiaochuo, Wang Yun, Xiao Zixian, Kong Xiuyuan, Jiang Ge 江革 (466?–535), Xie Ju, Zhu Yi, Liu Xian 劉顯 (481–543), Liu Zhilin, Liu Ru 劉孺 (483–541), Xiao Ji 蕭幾, He Xun, Wu Jun 吳均 (469–520), Liu Xie, Wang Ji, He Sicheng, and Liu Yao (*Liang shu* 19.303, 33.475, 33.479, 33.484–85, 35.511, 36.519, 36.523, 37.529, 38.537, 40.570, 40.572, 41.591, 41.596, 49.693, 49.698, 50.712, 50.714, 50.715).

9. *Nan Qi shu* 47.826.

10. *Liang shu* 30.445.

11. Ibid., 33.484–85.

As patrons of younger talents, Ren Fang and Shen Yue were often mentioned together. The *Liang shu* historian described Ren Fang as sociable and supportive of his friends: "Those he commended were often promoted, and thus members of gentry and nobility vied with one another to become acquainted with him. Dozens of guests were constantly in his house."[12] Ren Fang was particularly close to Yin Yun 殷芸 (471–529), Liu Bao 劉苞 (482–511), the brothers Dao Gai and Dao Qia, Liu Ru, Liu Xiaochuo, Liu Xian, Lu Chui, and Zhang Shuai. Their contemporaries referred to them as "those who have passed the Dragon Gate" (*Longmen zhi you* 龍門之游): Dragon Gate is the legendary gorge and falls on the Yellow River, and it was believed that carp who successfully swum through it would be transformed into dragons. We are told that, apart from the people mentioned above, "even scions of noble families could not become part of the group."[13] In 506 or earlier, Ren Fang's status as patron was further enhanced by his appointment as palace aide to the censor in chief, whose responsibility was to maintain disciplinary surveillance over court officials. Since the Censorate was called "the Orchid Terrace" (Lantai 蘭臺) in the Western Han, the group of young men of letters around Ren Fang was also known as "the assembly at the Orchid Terrace" (*Lantai ju* 蘭臺聚).[14] The exclusiveness of this group evoked an aura of cultural prestige that was expressly *not* contingent on family background. A new criterion of distinction was taking shape, a criterion that contested the conventional primacy of lineage.

Lu Chui presented a poem to Ren Fang, praising this select group:

和風雜美氣	A pleasant breeze is mixed with lovely vapors:
下有眞人遊	in the mortal world below roam immortal beings.
壯矣荀文若	How grand, a Xun Wenruo!
賢哉陳太丘	So admirable, a Chen Taiqiu.[15]
今則蘭臺聚	Today we gather at the Orchid Terrace,
方古信爲儔	which is surely a match for antiquity.

12. Ibid., 14.254.

13. *Nan shi* 48.1193, 25.678.

14. Ibid., 25.678.

15. Xun Wenruo is Xun Yu 荀彧 (163–212); Chen Taiqiu is Chen Shi 陳寔 (104–87). Both were renowned figures widely respected for their learning and their personal integrity.

任君本達識	Lord Ren is wise and knowledgeable;
張子復清修	Master Zhang again pure and refined.
既有絶塵到	There are the Dao brothers, transcending the dusty realm;
復見黄中劉	then again we see the Lius, the heart of the group.[16]

To describe their gathering as "a match for antiquity" was to affirm the values embodied by the group. Although nothing can redeem the poem from being a mediocre social piece, such self-representation was important in endowing their community with a cultural cachet, much like Shen Yue's implicit comparison of himself and Wang Yun to Cai Yong and Wang Can.

None of Ren Fang's select group came from the highest level of the social elite. Yin Yun was remotely related to Yin Jun, Emperor Wu's son-in-law, but none of Yin Yun's immediate family served in a prominent post. The Dao brothers were the great-grandsons of Dao Yanzhi 到彥之 (d. 433), a Song general of truly humble origin. He Jingrong, Emperor Wu's trusted minister, once said: "Dao Gai still emits a lingering stench, yet he thinks he can become a scion of a noble house by imitating one." He Jingrong's remark alluded to the fact that in his youth Dao Yanzhi had made a living by transporting human waste and selling it to farmers as fertilizer. The three cousins Liu Bao, Liu Ru, and Liu Xiaochuo were also from the nouveau riche: their ancestors were a minor gentry family from Pengcheng 彭城 (in modern Jiangsu); their grandfather, a general, had been granted the prestigious title of Minister of Works after his death during a prince's rebellion in 474. During the Qi, the Lius, mainly through maneuvers by Liu Ru's father, Liu Jun, became related to the royal family by marriage and gained higher social status. Both Lu Chui and Zhang Shuai, childhood friends related by marriage, were native southerners from Wu commandery, a fact that did not escape Shen Yue's notice. Shen Yue introduced them to Ren Fang with the remark: "These two talented young men [i.e., Lu and Zhang] are southern gold. You should befriend them."[17]

16. *Nan shi* 25.678.

17. *Liang shu* 33.475. The term "southern gold" comes from *The Classic of Poetry* and has much resonance (*Maoshi zhengyi* 21.770). It was used in a letter by the

Although no match for the Langye Wangs or Chenjun Xies in social and cultural prestige, the Daos, Lius, Lus, and Zhangs all played eminent roles in the sixth century after Ren Fang passed away in 508 and Shen Yue in 513. The following sketch of these four families illustrates the intricate world of Liang cultural politics.

LITERARY FAMILIES

The Dao brothers were successively appointed to the powerful post once occupied by Ren Fang: palace aide to the censor in chief. Dao Gai, an accomplished chess player, was particularly favored by Emperor Wu, himself a great chess aficionado. The two often spent the entire night playing chess. Once they made a bet, and the stakes were an unusual rock in Dao Gai's garden and a copy of *The Record of Rites*. Dao Gai lost, and the rock was transported into the palace and set up in front of the banquet hall in the Park of Flowering Groves. On the day the sixteen-foot-tall rock was transported from Dao Gai's residence to the palace, "people from all over the capital came to look. The rock was henceforth dubbed 'Lord Dao's Rock.'"[18] The passion for unusual rocks was later to become a popular obsession among Chinese literati, but this is the first account we have of a rock as an object of desire and, moreover, an object of public spectacle. The Liang was distinct from previous eras in its capacity to produce and display new forms of cultural value. There was no loser in the chess game.

Both Dao Gai's son Dao Jing 到鏡 and grandson Dao Jin 到藎 were skillful writers. Dao Jing died early; Dao Jin received the emperor's compliments for a poem he composed when following the emperor on a tour to the Tower of Looking North 北顧樓 in 544. He died during the conquest of Jiangling ten years later.

As a literary family, the Liu clan of Pengcheng was more influential. "There were about seventy clan members who were good at literary

---

prominent writer Zhang Hua in praise of gifted southerners such as the poet Lu Ji 陸機 (261–303). The phrase was again used by Lu Ji to refer to himself in a poem responding to the northern poet Pan Yue 潘岳 (247–300); see *Quan Jin shi*, 5.673–74. For a detailed discussion of Pan Yue and Lu Ji's poems and the issue of regional identity in the early medieval China, see Knechtges, "Sweet-peel Orange."

18. *Liang shu* 25.679.

writings, and this was quite exceptional in all of history."[19] Liu Xiaochuo was the most famous: indeed, Liu Xiaochuo and He Xun were considered the best poets of the times. He Xun's talent was widely acknowledged, and he was posthumously commended by Xiao Yi, but he was reportedly unpopular with Emperor Wu. Liu Xiaochuo, by contrast, was warmly received by both the emperor himself and the princes. "Every time Liu Xiaochuo composed a piece, if it was finished in the morning, it would become well known by evening. People recited or copied his poems, so that they were transmitted even to the far North and written everywhere on pillars or walls."[20] Xiaochuo's third brother, Liu Xiaoyi 劉孝儀 (484–550), excelled in prose, and his sixth brother, Liu Xiaowei 劉孝威 (496?–549), stood out in poetry: hence, Xiaochuo coined a phrase: "the [unrhymed] prose of the third and the poetry of the sixth" 三筆六詩.[21] Both brothers were members of Xiao Gang's literary entourage. Liu Zun, who compiled a catalogue of the crown prince's book collection, was a cousin of Liu Xiaochuo's and much admired by Xiao Gang. Liu Xiaochuo's sisters were likewise recognized for their literary talent. One of these sisters was Liu Lingxian. Two other sisters, one the wife of a Wang Shuying 王叔英 of Langye, the other the wife of Zhang Sheng 張嵊 (487–548), were also known for their talent and learning.[22]

Zhang Sheng was a member of the Zhang clan of Wu commandery 吳郡張氏, an illustrious southern family distinguished for both military and literary achievements. Zhang Sheng's grandfather was the versatile Zhang Yong, who was acclaimed for his skills in writing, calligraphy, music, riding, and architectural design. His monumental achievement in landscape architecture was the Xuanwu Lake (Xuanwu hu 玄武湖), still a popular attraction in modern Nanjing. Zhang Rong, the first writer who gave titles to his collections of literary writings, was a remote cousin of Zhang Sheng. He is remembered as the author of a large *fu* on the sea ("Hai fu" 海賦) and for his eccentric personality.

19. *Nan shi* 39.1012.
20. *Liang shu* 33.483.
21. Ibid., 41.594.
22. Ibid., 33.484; *Nan shi* 39.1012.

Another cousin was none other than Zhang Shuai, whom Shen Yue affectionately referred to as "southern gold." When still a child, Zhang Shuai made a rule of writing one poem each day; by the age of fifteen, he had reportedly composed over two thousand poems, odes, and prose pieces. According to one account, he showed his writings to a person named Yu Ne 虞訥, who criticized them harshly. Zhang Shuai thereupon burned them all and composed a new poem to show Yu Ne; this time, however, he claimed that the poem had been written by Shen Yue. Predictably, Yu Ne found every line and every single word simply wonderful.[23] In 505, Zhang Shuai was commanded by Emperor Wu to compose "*Fu* on the Dancing Horse" ("Wuma fu" 舞馬賦), which was much admired by the emperor. He was made vice director of the Palace Library, a "first-class pure position," to which, the emperor emphasized, no southerner had ever been appointed. Upon Zhang's death in 527, Xiao Tong wrote to Xiao Gang and praised him as "broad in talent and graceful in style."[24] Zhang Shuai was succeeded as palace librarian by his son Zhang Changgong 張長公. After Xiao Gang became the crown prince, he established a Department of Literary and Virtuous Expectant Officials (Wende daizhao sheng 文德待詔省), and Zhang Changgong was one of its members.

The Zhangs were connected by marriage to the Lu family of Wu commandery, another important southern clan. Lu Huixiao 陸慧曉 (440–501), a great-great-grandson of the Eastern Jin Defender in Chief Lu Wan 陸玩, had married the daughter of Zhang Dai 張岱 (412–84), Zhang Shuai's grand-uncle. When the Prince of Jingling gathered a group of scholars to compile the monumental bibliographical survey *Sibu yaolue*, Lu Huixiao was asked to participate in the project. Lu Chui, one of the prince's "Eight Companions," was Lu Huixiao's son. Lu Huixiao's nephew Lu Xian 陸閑 (d. 499) was a good friend of Zhang Dai's nephew Zhang Xu, who was widely recognized in the Qi for his exceptionally elegant manners and his discourse on *The Classic of Changes*. The eldest son of Lu Xian, Lu Jue 陸厥 (472–99), was the author of a famous letter to Shen Yue in 494, challenging Shen Yue on his claims about prosody. Lu Jue himself was an accomplished poet, and the

23. *Nan shi* 31.815.
24. *Liang shu* 33.479.

style of Lu Jue's poetry in the five-syllable line was considered "quite new and original."[25]

Lu Xian's grandson Lu Yungong 陸雲公 (511–47) was yet another well-known writer of the Liang. He had begun his official career by serving under the princes. In 536, the emperor's son-in-law Zhang Zuan, on his way back to the capital from Wuxing 吳興 (in modern Zhejiang), happened to read Lu Yungong's stele inscription for the temple of Taibo 太伯, the legendary founder of the kingdom of Wu and the uncle of the Confucian exemplar, King Wen of Zhou.[26] Taibo was more than just an ancestor for the people of Wu: he was their cultural hero, who had close blood ties with the rulers of the Central Domain (*zhongguo* 中國) but had broken away to establish a separate tradition in the South. He was the figure who legitimated Wu culture and made it unique. Writing a stele inscription for the temple of Taibo was therefore a gesture glorifying the author's Wu heritage. Zhang Zuan so much admired the piece that he recommended the young Lu Yungong to Emperor Wu, who then summoned Lu Yungong to the capital and made him a section director in the Bureau of Ministry Affairs. Like Dao Gai a good chess player, he soon became Emperor Wu's favorite and often played chess with the emperor till late at night.[27] Lu Yungong's son Lu Qiong 陸瓊 (537–86) and grandson Lu Congdian 陸從典, as well as his nephews Lu Yan 陸琰 (540–73), Lu Yu 陸瑜, and Lu Jie 陸玠 (540–76), were all celebrated literary figures.[28]

Another member of the Lu clan, Lu Rui 陸叡, was married to Zhang Rong's sister; his son Lu Gao's request for Emperor Wu's permission to recruit private soldiers was discussed in Chapter 1.[29] Lu Gao was an

25. *Nan Qi shu* 52.897. Only eleven poems by Lu Jue are still extant; some of them have lines of varying lengths, from three, four, five, to seven syllables.

26. Taibo, who was the legitimate heir to the throne of Zhou, ran away from the Chinese heartland along with his second younger brother, Zhongyong 仲雍, so that his father, King Tai 太王 (the Grand King), could pass the throne to their youngest brother. Taibo founded the state of Gouwu 句吳 in the South. Later the people of Gouwu moved to a city they called Wu (*Shi ji* 31.1445).

27. *Liang shu* 50.724.

28. *Nan shi* 48.1200–203.

29. Lu Gao's mannerisms allegedly resembled Zhang Rong's so much that there was a saying, "Under the sun there is no match for them—there are only the uncle and the nephew for each other" 無對日下，唯舅與甥 (ibid., 48.1204).

accomplished calligrapher and painter and the author of *The Biographies of Śramaṇa* (*Shamen zhuan* 沙門傳) in thirty scrolls. His only extant work is a collection of sixty-nine miracle tales, *More Records of Avalokiteśvara's Responsive Manifestations* (*Xi Guanshiyin yingyan ji* 繫觀世音應驗記). His preface, dated 499, relates the origin of the collection. The first person to collect stories of such a nature was Xie Fu 謝敷 (fl. late fourth century), an Eastern Jin recluse of Kuaiji 會稽, who sent them to Fu Yuan 傅瑗. The stories were subsequently lost during the Sun En Rebellion in 399. Fu Yuan's son Fu Liang later wrote down seven stories from memory. This was the original *Records of Avalokiteśvara's Responsive Manifestations*. Zhang Yan 張演, a cousin of Zhang Rong's father, subsequently wrote down another ten stories as a sequel, which was the *Continued Records of Avalokiteśvara's Responsive Manifestations* (*Xu Guanshiyin yingyan ji* 續觀世音應驗記).[30] In the preface, Zhang Yan claimed that belief in Buddhism was a family tradition. Indeed, according to *The Southern History*, Zhang Yan 張淹 (d. 466), Zhang Rong's brother and Lu Gao's maternal uncle, was such a fanatic believer that he once ordered all the clerks in his office to burn their arms "to illuminate the Buddha"; he also commanded that lawbreakers be required to make obeisances to the Buddha as punishment, sometimes several thousand times. He was eventually dismissed from office for such religious excesses.[31] During this period, religious belief seems to have been largely a family matter, and Lu Gao's collection of miracle tales should be regarded not only as a layman's efforts to accumulate merit but also as a continuation of the work of a kinsman.

Lu Gao's son Lu Zhao 陸罩 (487–after 541) served under Xiao Gang and was entrusted with the honor of writing a preface for Xiao Gang's literary collection. He was also one of the compilers of the Buddhist encyclopedia *Joined Jade-Disks from the Treasures of Dharma*. In the tradition of the many family histories composed in the Southern Dynasties, Lu Gao's brother Lu Xu 陸煦 compiled *A History of the Lu*

30. For a comprehensive modern edition, see Fu Liang et al., *Guanshiyin yingyan ji sanzhong yizhu*. See also Robert Campany's introduction and translation of a number of these stories in "The Earliest Tales."

31. *Nan shi* 32.833.

Clan (*Lu shi* 陸史) in fifteen scrolls.[32] Again, this was primarily a family undertaking.

This survey of the Daos, the Lius, the Zhangs, and the Lus shows literature not just as an individual means of attaining cultural and political prestige but as a "family business." Talent was presumed to be shared by the members of a literary family, and the literary prominence of individuals advanced the interests of the family as a whole. The first half of the sixth century witnessed the rise of another group of literary families: the Donghai Xus 東海徐氏, the Xinye Yus 新野庾氏 (an older but less powerful clan than the Yingchuan Yus 穎川庾氏),[33] and the Ru'nan Zhous 汝南周氏. All three clans, the Xus and Yus in particular, played prominent roles in the literary and political world of the Liang, and they, too, were related to one another through marriage.

The Xus were northern émigrés from Donghai (in modern Shandong). Xu Chi was a mentor of Xiao Gang. His mother was the sister of Zhou Yong, the author of *The Four Tones and the Rhymes* (*Sisheng qieyun* 四聲切韻). Zhou Yong worked closely with Shen Yue and Xie Tiao on matters of prosody during the Yongming era. His son, Zhou She, was one of Emperor Wu's most trusted advisors. It was Zhou She who recommended Xu Chi when Emperor Wu asked him to find a tutor for the young prince Xiao Gang.[34]

The Xus and Zhous were further related through intermarriage to another northern immigrant family, the Zangs of Dongwan (in modern Shandong) 東莞臧氏. Zhou Yong's mother was a granddaughter of Zang Tao 臧燾 (d. 423), the elder brother of Empress Zang of the Song founding emperor. Zang Tao's great-great-grandson Zang Dun 臧盾 (478–543) married his daughter to Xu Chi's son Xu Xiaoke 徐孝克 (527–99), whose lectures on the Buddhist scriptures and *The Record of Rites* reportedly attracted several hundred students. Among Zang Tao's descendents, his great-grandson Zang Yan 臧嚴 was well known in the Liang for his broad learning and especially for his familiarity with *The History of the Han*.[35]

32. *Nan shi* 48.1205.

33. See Tian Yuqing, *Dong Jin menfa*, p. 351; see also Lin Yi, *Yu Xin yanjiu*, pp. 4–5.

34. *Liang shu* 30.446–47.

35. Xiao Yi once tested Zang Yan's knowledge by asking him to identify a passage from each of the four categories of books (i.e., from the Confucian classics to

Zhou She's sons were mediocre, but three nephews, Zhou Hongzheng, Zhou Hongrang 周弘讓, and Zhou Hongzhi 周弘直, were renowned cultural figures. Zhou Hongzheng was a well-known writer and a great conversationalist, despite a stutter, on *Laozi*, *Zhuangzi*, and the Buddhist scriptures. Described by the *Nanshi* historian as "ugly but not unsightly," he also had sartorial panache. While still a youngster, he went to a large Buddhist lecture "wearing a pair of red pants, with his hair done in a 'brocade-twist' top-knot." When the scholar Liu Xian, a distant kinsman of the Zhous, was leaving the capital for a local post, he offered ten bolts of silk as a reward for the person who came to his farewell party dressed "in the most unusual clothes. All those who attended changed their attire in one way or another, most by simply modifying the length here and there. Liu Xian told them to wait and see. Finally Zhou Hongzheng showed up in a pair of green silk pants and wearing a dashing embroidered cape. He went directly to the prize and took it."[36] The historian Pei Ziye 裴子野 (469–530) admired the young man so much that he married his daughter to him. Zhou Hongzheng married his own daughter to Xu Jian 徐儉 (d. 588), the grandson of Xu Chi and the son of the influential court poet Xu Ling, the compiler of *New Songs of the Jade Terrace*. Xu Jian once composed a poem at a banquet at the command of Xiao Yi, who said admiringly: "The descendent of the Xu family continues to possess cultural accomplishments (*wen* 文)!"[37]

Along with Xu Chi and his son Xu Ling, Yu Jianwu and his son Yu Xin formed the core of Xiao Gang's literary salon. The Yus had immigrated from Xinye (in modern He'nan) to Jiangling at the beginning of the fourth century. Although a distinguished local clan, the Yus never held prominent offices before the Liang. Yu Jianwu's father, Yu Yi 庾易 (fl. 495), was a confirmed recluse, albeit a well-known

collections of literary writings); Zang Yan not only gave the source of each passage but also the author's name, without missing a single one (ibid., 50.719). As mentioned in Chapter 2, Zang Yan's son Zang Fengshi had once copied out the entire *Han shu* himself (Yan Zhitui, *Yanshi jiaxun* 8.189). Zang Fengshi's brother-in-law Liu Huan was the leading poet in the literary entourage of Xiao Yi. Liu Huan's father was Liu Zhao 劉昭, a cousin of the famous fifth-century poet Jiang Yan (*Liang shu* 49.692).

36. *Nan shi* 34.897–98.

37. Ibid., 62.1526.

one.[38] The family fortunes rose dramatically during the Liang. Yu Jianwu's brother Yu Qianlou 庾黔婁, known for his filial piety, was promoted to the powerful office of grand arbiter (Dazhongzheng 大中正) of Jingzhou, whose task was to recommend local talents for office;[39] another brother, Yu Wuling, was appointed librarian of the crown prince, a "pure" position usually occupied by members of the highest elite families. Emperor Wu remarked upon making this appointment: "An official post becomes 'pure' because of the person assigned to it. How could it be limited to the top elite clans?" (See Chapter 1.) This in itself is a good indication that the Yu clan belonged to the lesser gentry.[40] Both Yu Jianwu and Yu Xin were deeply appreciated by Xiao Gang for their literary accomplishments. As the *Zhou shu* historian said: "[The father and son] went in and out of the forbidden gates [of the crown prince's residence]; no one else enjoyed as much favor and respect as they did."[41]

These seven major literary families of the Liang illustrate the interconnections of the cultural world in this period. *Wen* 文, cultural accomplishments, provided a space in which earlier forms of family politics in the Southern Dynasties took an interesting turn; that is to say, through cultural capital, members of the lesser gentry and native southerners gained political power and social prestige, with intermarriage strengthening the connections among the powerful literary clans.

The first half of the sixth century witnessed the steady rise of a cultural elite. Families that had obtained recognition through military and political achievements in the fifth century now turned to literary and scholarly excellence. In many ways, Ren Fang's comment on the gifted Dao brothers, whose great-grandfather had been a transporter of human waste, was representative of the larger trend: "In my humble opinion, the Song dynasty benefited from the family's martial prowess, but the Liang gets to enjoy its literary attainments" 宋得其武, 梁得其文.[42] Even the

38. Yu Yi's short biography can be found in "The Biographies of Recluses" in *Nan Qi shu* 54.940.

39. *Liang shu* 47.651.

40. Ibid., 49.689.

41. *Zhou shu* 41.733.

42. *Liang shu* 27.404.

royal families of the Qi and Liang exemplify this process; coming from lesser gentry backgrounds, they not only obtained the highest political power but also became cultural trendsetters and the literary avant-garde.

AN IMAGINED RIVALRY

There has long been a conviction in scholarship on the Liang period that there were three rival literary "schools or camps."[43] One was the "archaic or traditionalist school," with Emperor Wu as its center (although Emperor Wu's "group identity" is sometimes disputed, as we shall see); another was the "compromise school," headed by Xiao Tong, Crown Prince Zhaoming; the third was the "avant-garde school" led by Xiao Gang and Xiao Yi. Despite disagreement on the membership of each group, certain writers and works have consistently been assigned to represent each of the "schools." A general consensus has Pei Ziye as the chief advocate of the "archaic school," primarily because of his treatise dubbed "On Carving Insects" ("Diaochong lun" 雕蟲論), but also because Xiao Gang once criticized his literary style as "too plain to be admired."[44] Xiao Tong's *Wen xuan* is considered the representative anthology of the "compromise school," and *Yutai xinyong* is regarded as the anthology par excellence of the "avant-garde" school, which is also known as the "Palace Style poetry group" (*gongti shi pai* 宮體詩派). Xiao Gang is believed to have been the inspiration behind the compilation of *Yutai xinyong*.[45] Sometimes the conflict perceived between the last two "schools" is tacitly understood as a sibling rivalry between Xiao Tong and Xiao Gang, a rivalry considered by some scholars as a literary

43. One of the earliest articles on the subject is Zhou Xunchu's "Liangdai wenlun sanpai shuyao" (A summary of the three schools in Liang literary theory). See also Wang Yunxi and Yang Ming, *Wei Jin nanbeichao*, pp. 182–88. This section, written by Wang Yunxi, is in fact frequently contradicted by later sections written by Yang Ming in the same volume when it comes to the analysis of individual writers in each "school." For a most recent reiteration of the view, see Fu Gang, "*Yutai xinyong* yu *Wen xuan*."

44. *Quan Liang wen* 53.3262, 11.3011.

45. The earliest mention of this relationship between Xiao Gang and *Yutai xinyong* was made by Liu Su 劉肅 (fl. early 9th century, in *Datang xinyu* 3.106). Liu Su's claims about *Yutai xinyong* will be discussed in greater detail in the next chapter.

disagreement, but occasionally the rivalry is even seen as going beyond the literary world.[46] As Okamura Shigeru states:

> Recently some scholars have made a new argument regarding the different political backgrounds of *Wen xuan* and *Yutai xinyong*. They presume an opposition between the old literary group of Xiao Tong and a new literary group of Xiao Gang and claim that *Yutai xinyong* was compiled by Xiao Gang's new literary group for the purpose of opposing the literary world centering around Emperor Wu and Crown Prince Zhaoming and advocating for the flourishing of the Palace Style.[47]

In this section, I argue that these three competing schools, which have been a commonplace of most literary scholarship since the 1960s, are largely imaginary.[48] Late imperial China witnessed many bitter feuds,

46. For instance, Shen Yucheng ("Gongti shi," p. 64) argues that Xiao Gang did a series of things, such as replacing Xiao Tong's staff members and asking Xu Ling to compile *Yutai xinyong*, after he became the crown prince in order to oppose consciously Xiao Tong's literary style, group, and anthologies. Fu Gang follows this argument in "*Yutai xinyong* yu *Wen xuan*," p. 18. However, it would not be up to Xiao Gang to change the staff members and reappoint them to various other posts, and it is doubtful that Xiao Gang was behind the compilation of *Yutai xinyong*. Cao Daoheng and Liu Yuejin (*Nanbeichao*, pp. 467–71) hint that several men of letters who were either close to Xiao Tong or counseled Xiao Gang to turn down the crown princedom were discriminated against after Xiao Tong died and Xiao Gang became the crown prince in 531. Wang Yun, Zhou Hongzheng, and Xiao Zifan 蕭子範 were singled out as examples. These claims do not bear close scrutiny. For Wang Yun's case, see the discussion below. Zhou Hongzheng "did not serve in any important post in Xiao Gang's Eastern Palace" not because he was ousted but because he became an active figure in the National University as well as the Elite Academy, nor did he "attach himself to Xiao Yi" until after the Hou Jing Rebellion. Xiao Zifan asked to compile a collection of Xiao Tong's works, and this, as Cao and Liu seem to intimate, prevented his poetry from being included in *Yutai xinyong*. The absence of Xiao Zifan's poetry shows that there was a division between the two ages: "the former was the age of *Wenxuan*, and the latter the age of *Yutai xinyong*." However, even Xu Chi, Xiao Gang's favorite poet, was not included in *Yutai xinyong*. In 549 Xiao Gang entrusted Xiao Zifan with the task of composing an elegy for his deceased wife, an elegy Xiao Gang admired so much that he said it was "the only thing" after the Hou Jing Rebellion that had preserved the aura of the formerly glorious Liang (*Liang shu* 35.510).

47. Okamura, "*Wen xuan*" *zhi yanjiu*, p. 98.

48. The only article I am aware of that explicitly points out that the "compromise and avant-garde schools" might have been more similar to each other than dif-

often with serious political consequences, among literary factions with opposing literary and political agendas, a phenomenon that continued into the modern period. This may be one reason why many modern Chinese scholars tend to project the notion of factional struggle onto earlier periods. An older and deeper motive for seeing the Liang literary world split among several "camps" is ideological, based on the conventional judgments of moral historiography. Xiao Tong's *Wen xuan* was seen as canonical and moral; Xiao Gang and his courtiers' Palace Style poetry as decadent and immoral.[49] In conjunction with this view, the salons of the two princes invited a dramatized but also much simplified literary historical account.

The evidence does not sustain the conventional agonistic account. Instead of a cultural landscape neatly divided into distinct "schools," the Liang literary world in fact shared a set of common expectations concerning what literature should be. Individual practice might vary with each writer's temperament and talent, as well as with changes in fashion and taste, but certain ideals continued to hold sway precisely because they were abstract principles.

A close look at the Liang literary world reveals that Emperor Wu, Xiao Tong, Xiao Gang, and Xiao Yi appreciated more or less the same group of contemporary men of letters. This point may be illustrated by the cases of two poets, Liu Xiaochuo and Wang Yun.

There is no doubt that Liu Xiaochuo was received with special favor by Xiao Tong. In 522 Liu Xiaochuo was singled out from all the men of letters serving in the Eastern Palace to compile Xiao Tong's literary collection and write a preface for it.[50] After Xiao Tong had the Hall of

ferent is an excellent article by the modern scholar Zhang Lei, "Bingfei ouran de qiaohe" (A not unaccidental coincidence). This article discusses the "overlapping selections" in *Wen xuan* and *Yutai xinyong* (i.e., sixty-four poems) and the significance of this phenomenon.

49. Zhou Xunchu, who had first advocated the "three Liang literary camps" theory in a 1964 article, "Liangdai wenlun sanpai shuyao," published an article in 1965 on Palace Style poetry, claiming that Xiao Gang's Palace Style poetry was not only sensuous but "pornographic" and that "the basic content of *Yutai xinyong* is filthy." He also explained in a footnote that he had been too positive in evaluating Palace Style poetry in the 1964 article ("Guanyu gongti shi," pp. 54–55).

50. The preface is extant; see *Quan Liang wen* 60.3312.

Enjoying the Worthies (Lexian tang 樂賢堂) constructed, Liu Xiaochuo was the first person whose portrait was painted and hung on the wall.[51] Xiao Gang had no less affection for Liu Xiaochuo. In a letter to Liu Xiaochuo written while Xiao Gang was serving as the governor of Yongzhou, Xiao Gang expressed how much he missed his old friend and desired to hear from him.[52] Emperor Wu also showed Liu Xiaochuo tremendous indulgence. When Dao Qia accused Liu Xiaochuo of committing incest with his younger sister, the emperor changed the accusation to something less offensive to spare Liu disgrace.[53] Although public opinion compelled the emperor to discharge Liu, he frequently sent Xu Mian to visit and console the mortified poet. Xiao Yi also wrote to Liu Xiaochuo upon the occasion and expressed his sympathy.[54] Shortly thereafter, Emperor Wu composed a poem entitled "Plowing the Field" ("Jitian" 籍田) and commanded dozens of courtiers to compose poems in response. Liu Xiaochuo's poem was considered the best, and he was immediately restored to office.[55]

More important than the personal favor showered upon Liu Xiaochuo by the royal family is the fact that Liu played an important role in the compilation of *Wen xuan*, and yet many of his poems found their way into *Yutai xinyong*, the "opposite anthology." Liu Xiaochuo's case is particularly interesting because of the confusion it has caused among modern scholars seeking a clear division of literary camps in the Liang. Some

51. *Liang shu* 33.480–81.

52. *Quan Liang wen* 11.3010.

53. According to the *Liang shu* historian, "At first, Xiaochuo was on good terms with Dao Qia, and both of them were guests at the Eastern Palace. Xiaochuo thought his writings superior to Dao Qia's and often expressed contempt for Dao's at banquets. Dao Qia became resentful. When Xiaochuo was appointed chamberlain of the court for the Palace Garrison, he took his concubine into the official residence while leaving his mother behind in his private residence. After Qia became palace aide to the censor in chief, he sent a clerk to investigate the matter, accusing Liu of 'taking his young sister to the magnificent residence, while abandoning his aged mother in the lesser abode.' In order to hide his blemish, Emperor Wu changed the character 'sister' (*mei* 妹) to 'beauty' (*shu* 姝)" (*Liang shu* 33.480–81). The *Nan shi* historian had stated clearly in his comment on Liu Xiaochuo: "Xiaochuo's incestuous affair was a stain on his character: he truly should be considered a man with no sense of decency" (*Nan shi* 39.1015).

54. *Liang shu* 33.481.

55. Ibid., 33.482.

scholars consider Liu's poems as possessing "a classic decorousness and appropriateness" (*dianzheng* 典正) and therefore consistent with the general inclination of Xiao Tong's "school";[56] others notice that Liu Xiaochuo left behind "sensuous Palace Style poems" (*gongti yanshi* 宮體豔詩).[57] In order to account for the perceived divergence in Liu Xiaochuo's oeuvre, some scholars have resorted to an ingenious solution by attributing the inconsistency to a change in style: the "sensuous Palace Style poems" are Liu Xiaochuo's "later works," written after the death of Xiao Tong.[58] There is, however, no evidence to support such a claim.

Wang Yun is another good example of the Liang royal family's shared assessment of contemporary writers. Along with Liu Xiaochuo, Wang Yun was a favorite of Xiao Tong. Once, at a party, Xiao Tong reportedly grabbed Wang Yun's sleeve with one hand and patted Liu Xiaochuo on the shoulder with another hand, citing a couplet from the Eastern Jin poet Guo Pu's 郭璞 (276–324) poem: "'On my left, I grasp Fuqiu's sleeve; / on my right, I pat Hongya on the shoulder." Both Fuqiu 浮丘 and Hongya 洪崖 are the names of immortals.[59] Shen Yue spoke highly of Wang Yun to Emperor Wu, who put Wang Yun's talent to good use.[60] In 514 Wang Yun was commissioned to write an epitaph for the eminent Buddhist monk Baozhi 寶誌 (d. 514); he was also ordered to compile a collection of memorials of the Secretariat in thirty scrolls. After Xiao Tong died in 531, Wang Yun composed an elegy, which was much admired by Emperor Wu. Shortly afterward, he was appointed the magistrate of Linhai. In 535, he was made an administrator to Xiao Huan 蕭歡 (d. 541), Xiao Tong's eldest son, and went on to become the director of the Palace Library, a prestigious position. From then on, he never left the capital. Cao Daoheng and Liu Yuejin, in their literary history of the Northern and Southern Dynasties, suggest that Wang Yun's political career floundered after the death of Xiao Tong; and yet,

---

56. Zhan Furui, "Liangdai gongti shiren," p. 131.

57. Qin Yueyu, "Liu Xiaochuo," p. 75.

58. Cao Daoheng and Shen Yucheng, *Nanbeichao wenxue shi*, p. 259. See also Qin Yueyu, "Liu Xiaochuo," p. 75; and Zhan Hong, "'Li er bu yin.'"

59. *Liang shu* 33.485. The couplet is from one of Guo Pu's poems on immortals, which is included in *Wen xuan*. See Xiao Tong, *Wen xuan* 21.1020; and *Quan Jin shi* 11.865.

60. *Liang shu* 33.485.

except for a lawsuit that temporarily prevented him from being promoted when he was magistrate of Linhai, there is no evidence that Wang Yun suffered any substantial political disadvantage.[61] More significant is a comment made by Xiao Gang on Wang Yun's poetry in 547. By that time Wang Yun had already come a long way from the young rising star praised by the venerable Shen Yue. Xie Gu 謝嘏 (d. 569), a Chenjun Xie serving as secretary to the crown prince, Xiao Gang, was appointed magistrate of Jian'an, and Xiao Gang held a farewell party for him, which Wang Yun attended. At the party Xiao Gang commanded everyone present to compose a poem to one of the fifteen difficult rhyme words being distributed. Later Xiao Gang wrote a note to his brother Xiao Yi, saying: "Wang Yun is certainly an old hand; among the up-and-comers, Xiao Kai is particularly admirable."[62] Xiao Kai 蕭愷 (506–49) was Xiao Zixian's son and the first to finish his assignment at the party. Xiao Gang's use of Wang Yun as the reference point for a rising star of the younger generation shows that Wang Yun, then in his sixties, was widely regarded as the grand old man of the literary world.

Zhou Xunchu, in his article on the "three camps" of the Liang, identifies Liu Xiaochuo and Wang Yun as major members of the "compromise" school, and yet he has to admit that both poets are represented in *Yutai xinyong*.[63] He also considers Liu Xie, Lu Chui, and Dao Qia as other major members of the "compromise school" and points out that their poems are not included in *Yutai xinyong*; this is a moot point because Liu Xie and Dao Qia are not included in *Wen xuan* either, and Lu Chui was commonly acknowledged as a master of prose, not of poetry. The two pieces by Lu Chui included in *Wen xuan* are stele inscriptions,

61. *Liang shu* 33.484–86. Cao Daoheng and Liu Yuejin, *Nanbeichao*, p. 467. Being appointed to a local post as magistrate was not necessarily an undesirable thing for an official. It depended on which commandery one was sent to. Appointment as the magistrate of a prosperous commandery could make one's fortune. The emperor knew this very well when he appointed Xiao Jie 蕭介 (ca. 477–549) to be the magistrate of Shixing in 536, saying: "Xiao Jie is very poor. He should be appointed to a commandery" (*Liang shu* 41.587). Wang Yun later declined appointment as the magistrate of Yongjia in 546 on the ground of illness, probably both because he was truly getting on in years and because he did not need the financial advantages brought by such a post.

62. *Liang shu* 35.513.

63. Zhou Xunchu, "Liangdai wenlun sanpai shuyao," pp. 240–42.

which, of course, would not have been included in *Yutai xinyong*, a poetic anthology.[64]

If the members of the Liang royal family largely agreed with one another in their evaluation of contemporary writers, there was also a general consensus concerning the literary past. In a well-known letter Xiao Gang wrote to his younger brother Xiao Yi, he listed the great literary names: Sima Xiangru 司馬相如 (179–117 B.C.), Yang Xiong 揚雄 (53 B.C.–A.D. 18), Cao Zhi, Wang Can, Pan Yue, Lu Ji, Yan Yanzhi 顏延之 (384–456), and Xie Lingyun.[65] These writers, whose value was clearly recognized by the cultural elite of the sixth century, are solidly represented in *Wen xuan* and would indeed have appeared in any general literary anthology put together by an average man of letters in the Liang. Among more recent authors, Xiao Gang cited the poetry of Xie Tiao and Shen Yue and the prose of Ren Fang and Lu Chui as the best exemplars of each genre. Again, each of these authors is not only well represented in *Wen xuan* but also anthologized more extensively in those genres perceived to be the specialty of each. The most telling case is Xiao Tong's and Xiao Gang's admiration of the Eastern Jin poet Tao Yuanming's works. Xiao Tong's appreciation of Tao Yuanming's writings on the reclusive life in a relatively unadorned style (compared with the intricate parallelism and rhetorical flourishes of the fifth and sixth centuries) has often been taken as evidence of his classic taste and puritanical impulse, but Xiao Gang, the allegedly "decadent" prince, was no less fond of Tao Yuanming, a fact often ignored by scholars who choose to see Xiao Gang as the polar opposite of Xiao Tong's elegant orthodoxy.[66]

---

64. Zhou Xunchu's claim ("Liangdai wenlun sanpai shuyao," pp. 241–42) that except for Liu Xiaochuo and Wang Yun, nobody from the "compromise school" is included in *Yutai xinyong* is also questionable, because he clearly counts Zhang Shuai, one of Xiao Tong's regular attendants in the Eastern Palace, as a member of Xiao Tong's "camp," and yet Zhang Shuai is well represented in *Yutai xinyong*.

65. *Liang shu* 49.690.

66. According to Yan Zhitui (*Yanshi jiaxun* 9.276): "Liu Xiaochuo, who was extremely famous at the time, did not care for any writer but Xie Tiao. He always kept Xie Tiao's poetry on the desk, reading and savoring them constantly. Emperor Jianwen [i.e., Xiao Gang] loved Tao Yuanming's writings in the same way." In order to explain Xiao Tong's love of Tao Yuanming, the modern scholar Li Jianfeng (*Yuanqian Tao Yuanming jieshou shi*, pp. 29, 84–97) portrays Xiao Tong as a suffering

This brings us to one of the major problems with the theory of the two princes' "rival camps," namely, the use of *Wen xuan* and *Yutai xinyong* as indicative of Xiao Tong and Xiao Gang's different literary views. First, although Xiao Tong certainly attached his name to *Wen xuan*, nothing in *Yutai xinyong* indicates Xiao Gang had anything to do with its compilation. Xiao Gang's alleged sponsorship of *Yutai xinyong* first surfaces in an unverifiable statement in an anecdotal account of four centuries later; moreover, other elements in the same account are clearly fanciful.[67] But even when we set aside Xiao Gang's role in the compilation of *Yutai xinyong*, the two anthologies are so utterly different in their natures, purposes, and editorial principles that they are not comparable. *Wen xuan* is a general genre anthology for a broad audience; *Yutai xinyong* is a single-genre collection of poetry for a specific readership. The disappearance of comparable anthologies should not prevent us from envisioning what we know was once there; different types of anthologies form the literary context from which the few preserved works emerged. It is easy to forget that *Wen xuan* and *Yutai xinyong* are chance survivals and draw absolute conclusions about "different moral and aesthetic values" represented by the two anthologies.[68] In fact, the proper question to ask is: What literary works would Xiao Gang have included if he had compiled a general anthology of literature like *Wen xuan*, an anthology intended to offer a balanced representation of the tradition? From what we know about Xiao Gang's predilection for past and present authors, it is quite unlikely that his selection would have differed radically from his brother's.

It is useful to examine the views on literature held by major members of the "compromise" and "avant-garde" schools, and see if they are indeed as far apart as commonly believed. The general statements about *wen*, for example, though formulaic, nevertheless tell us much about the common ground shared by the "different literary camps."

The opening of Xiao Tong's preface to the *Wen xuan* relates the genesis and significance of *wen*. Here *wen* is literature in the broadest sense—language and writing in general.

prince seeking peace in nature; but he says nothing of why Xiao Gang liked Tao Yuanming as well.

67. I discuss this account in greater detail in Chapter 4.

68. Zhou Jianjun, "Cong xuanshi."

Let us first examine the primordial origins of civilization,
And distantly observe the customs of the remote past—
Times when men dwelled in caves in winter, nests in summer,
It was a pristine age of simple people,
And writing had not yet been invented.
Then when Fu Xi ruled the empire,
He first
    Drew the Eight Trigrams,
    Created writing
To replace government by knotted ropes.
From this time written records came into existence.
The *Changes* says, "Observe the patterns (*wen*) of the sky
To ascertain the seasonal changes.
Observe the patterns (*wen*) of man
To transform the world."
The temporal significance of writing (*wen*) is far-reaching indeed![69]

A similar passage may be found in Xiao Gang's preface to *The Collection of Crown Prince Zhaoming* (*Zhaoming taizi ji* 昭明太子集), compiled after Xiao Tong's death and presented to the throne. The preface begins with a general statement about the importance of *wen*, which closely echoes Xiao Tong's preface: "In my humble opinion, the significance of *wen* is truly great and far-reaching." Xiao Gang then gave the same quotation from *The Classic of Changes* and set out to explain "the patterns of the sky" and "the patterns of man":

Written records were produced,
and writing created;
chanting and singing began,
descriptions and odes appeared.
They help people achieve filial piety
and change customs in the governing of the empire;
their ways extend into the eight directions,
and their principles touch the nine states,
assisting and moving gods above,
harmonizing bells and chimes—
these are the so-called patterns of man (*ren wen* 人文).

69. Translation from Knechtges, *Wen xuan*, 1: 17. *Quan Liang wen* 20.3067.

Like Xiao Tong, Xiao Gang emphasized the political and moral functions of *wen*. As Yang Ming has observed: "His [Xiao Gang's] argument [about "the patterns of the sky" and "the patterns of man"] is the same as [Xiao Tong's] in the *Wen xuan* preface."[70]

When it came to describing literature in the narrower sense, Xiao Tong wrote the following in a letter to Xiao Yi:

When literary writings possess a classic appropriateness, they might be burdened by being plain; when they are decorous and ornate, they could suffer from superficiality. If one's literary style may achieve ornamentation without being superficial and appropriateness without being plain, then content and form will be in a perfect balance, which is the very style of a gentleman. This is what I would like to accomplish in my own writings, but I regret to say that I am not quite there yet.[71]

夫文典則累野, 麗亦傷浮. 能麗而不浮, 典而不野, 文質彬彬, 有君子之致. 吾嘗欲爲之, 但恨未逮耳.

This passage, which is often cited to illustrate the literary ideal of the "compromise school," in fact represents values on which everyone in the Liang literary world agreed.[72] The "neither too X nor too Y" principle, couched in terms impossible to refute, appeared again and again in contemporary formulations of the ideal literary style. Xiao Yi, commonly recognized as a Palace Style poet, articulated his conception of literary style as follows:

As the generations pass, the principles of literary discussions do not remain the same; along with the changes in times and circumstances, the form of composing literary writings may also differ. However, if a piece is too verbose, then it may be hurt by being weak; if it is too concise, we may regret its crudity. Preserving the splendor, it may lose its normative form; emphasizing substance, it risks being flavorless. Some writings use allusions generously, which, however, all mean the same thing; some have original, extraordinary content but have no textual references on which to rely; some are orderly from beginning to end,

70. Wang Yunxi and Yang Ming, *Wei Jin nanbeichao*, p. 289.

71. *Quan Liang wen* 20.3064.

72. Zhou Xunchu ("Liangdai wenlun sanpai shuyao," p. 238) claims that Xiao Tong's "literary views are different from [the two core members of the "avant-garde" group] Emperor Jianwen's and the Prince of Xiangdong's" and cites this passage as evidence.

and yet their use of allusions is forced; some go back and forth and cover much ground, but their formal structure is not well crafted. Now suppose that a piece can be alluring without being garish, substantial without being plain, broad without being verbose, concise without being crude, patterned and yet possessing substance, succinct and yet smooth; that the trajectory of allusions follows one's intent, and the principles inherent in the words are profound—then this is what I would call the finest of all writings, and nothing could spoil it.[73]

夫世代亟改, 論文之理非一; 時事推移, 屬詞之體或異. 但繁則傷弱, 率則恨省; 存華則失體, 從實則無味. 或引事雖博, 其意猶同; 或新意雖奇, 無所倚約. 或首尾倫帖, 事似牽課; 或翻復博涉, 體製不工. 能使豔而不華, 質而不野, 博而不繁, 省而不率, 文而有質, 約而能潤, 事隨意轉, 理逐言深, 所謂菁華, 無以間也.

Yang Ming rightly observes that Xiao Yi's opinions were not only "consistent with Liu Xie and Xiao Tong's views" but also "shared by the Qi/Liang literati."[74]

The "neither/nor" prescription was reinforced in positive judgments passed on what were regarded as model writings at the time. In the late fifth century, Fan Yun commended He Xun's poetry because of its "just right" quality: "Observing literary men of late, I have noticed that if one's writings are substantial, they may become too scholarly; if they are alluring, they may be hurt by vulgarity. As for incorporating both clarity and substance, harmonizing modern and ancient styles, I have seen it in the young Master He" 頃觀文人, 質則過儒, 麗則傷俗, 其能含清濁, 中今古, 見之何生矣.[75] Indeed, despite Xiao Tong's modest claim that he had not quite achieved his literary ideal yet, his writings were being praised in exactly the same terms as those laid out in his letter to Xiao Yi. In the preface to Xiao Tong's collection compiled in 522, Liu Xiaochuo described Xiao Tong's writings as "possessing a classical appropriateness without being plain, unimpeded in their expression without lack of control, alluring and yet not excessive, succinct and yet not meager" 典而不埜, 遠而不放, 麗而不淫, 約而不儉.[76] Xiao Gang

73. From Xiao Yi's preface to *A Collection of Stele Inscriptions from the Buddhist Canon* (*Neidian beiming jilin* 內典碑銘集林), in *Quan Liang wen* 17.3053.

74. Wang Yunxi and Yang Ming, *Wei Jin nanbeichao*, p. 302.

75. *Liang shu* 43.693.

76. *Quan Liang wen* 60.3312.

likewise extolled Xiao Tong's writings for being "alluring and yet not excessive" 麗而不淫 in his preface to Xiao Tong's posthumous collection.[77] Rather than viewing these vaguely phrased qualities as reflecting the "true" characteristics of Xiao Tong's writings, we should regard them as expressions of values held in common by the Liang cultural elite.

Tracing the genesis of literature in the broad sense of the term to the rise of "the patterns of man," Liang writers were also interested in what prompted an individual to write. Here, too, there was a general consensus. Xiao Gang's take on the issue was eloquently expressed in a letter to his brother-in-law Zhang Zuan:

> As for times when the sun is setting in a spring courtyard and a swaying orchid welcomes the breeze; when the autumn rain is coming to an end and the sky is clearing up, and leaves from a *tong* tree have just begun to fall; when clouds arise from the horizons or bright moonlight enters the tower; when sometimes we gather together relatives and friends, setting out in carriages; when at parties we frequently sip from *chequ* goblets and empty the *yingwu* cups; or when I was at the frontier and surrounded with enemy troops on all sides, with the sky being covered with dust stirred up by the barbarian armies and military banners brushing the sun; when from time to time I heard the notes of a flute from the stronghold, and in the distance came the sound of a northern horn, which sometimes made me feel homesick, and yet at other times moved me to a heroic indignation at our foes: at times like these I would contemplate writing with my stunted quill and tried to compose some songs with mediocre tunes. As things meet my eyes, I jot down my feelings; I compose only upon being stimulated by some outer event.[78]
>
> 至如春庭落景, 轉蕙承風, 秋雨朝晴, 檐梧初下, 浮雲生野, 明月入樓; 時命親賓, 乍動嚴駕, 車渠屢酌, 鸚鵡驟傾. 伊昔三邊, 久留四戰. 胡霧連天, 征旗拂日. 時聞塢笛, 遙聽塞笳. 或鄉思悽然, 或雄心憤薄. 是以沈吟短翰, 補綴庸音, 寓目寫心, 因事而作.

In this passage, Xiao Gang listed the occasions that moved him to write. The implication is clear: literature, or more precisely poetry, was an expression of feelings stirred by changes in nature or by human affairs. Such a statement, derived from the canonical "Great Preface" to *The Classic of Poetry* and the "Record of Music" in *The Record of Rites*, was a

77. *Quan Liang wen* 12.3017.
78. Ibid., 11.3010.

familiar sentiment in the literary thought of the sixth century.[79] Zhong Rong uttered the following in the preface to *The Gradations of Poets*:

Spring breeze and birds, autumn moon and cicadas, summer clouds and showers, the bitter cold of the winter months: these are the stimuli for poetry in the four seasons. At happy meetings we express our affections with poems, or we voice our sadness when parting from friends. . . . All these occasions deeply touch our hearts. If not for poetry, how could we possibly describe them? If not for singing, how could we relieve our feelings?[80]

春風春鳥, 秋月秋蟬, 夏雲暑雨, 冬月祁寒, 斯四候之感諸詩者也. 嘉會寄詩以親, 離羣託詩以怨. . . . 凡斯種種, 感蕩心靈, 非陳詩何以展其義, 非長歌何以釋其情?

These claims again recall a passage from Xiao Tong's letter to Xiao Yi:

Sometimes, on a nice day, the natural world is bright and beautiful because of the spring sunshine. Trees bloom, and orioles sing in harmony; a warm breeze drifts, and brooks gush forth. Delighting in the pleasant month and going out on an outing, I would sit on the fragrant grass and gaze into the distance. Or as the vermilion heat of the summer is declining and the white depression of autumn marks the season, jade dew flows at night, and the metal wind starts blowing. Understanding the mood of the autumn hills, I climb high and lodge my feelings in the far distances. Or when the summer branches have grown so long that they become intertwined, I am tired of feeling melancholy and begin to write; when the winter clouds stretch a thousand miles, I compose songs on seeing the flustering snow. When close relatives depart, my hand is driven by my emotions; as brothers gather together, ink is spilled to express our intimacy.[81]

或日因春陽, 其物韶麗, 樹花發, 鶯鳴和, 春泉生, 暄風至. 陶嘉月而嬉遊, 藉芳草而眺矚. 或朱炎受謝, 白藏紀時, 玉露夕流, 金風多扇, 悟秋山之心,登高而遠託. 或夏條可結, 倦於邑而屬詞; 冬雲千里, 睹紛霏而興詠. 密親離則手爲心使, 昆弟晏則墨以親露.

---

79. "The affections are stirred within and take on form in words" 情動於中而形於言 (*Maoshi zhengyi* 1.13; translation from Owen, *Readings in Chinese Literary Thought*, p. 41). "All tones that arise are generated from the human mind. When the human mind is moved, some external thing has caused it. Stirred by external things into movement, it takes on form in sound" 凡音者, 生人心者也. 情動於中, 故形於聲 (*Liji zhushu* 37.663; translation from Owen, ibid., p. 51).

80. *Quan Liang wen* 55.3275–76.

81. Ibid., 20.3064.

In his "three camps" article, Zhou Xunchu claims that Xiao Gang advocates the expressive function of literature;[82] and yet, such a function seems to be something on which both Xiao Tong and Xiao Gang would readily agree.

The preceding discussions show that Liang writers classified into different "camps" in fact agreed on a variety of issues concerning literature, from the content of the canon to basic values. In studying Liang writers' articulation of their views of literature, however, one must avoid the pitfall of taking a text tied to particular circumstances as the authoritative statement of the author's general position; the same author might very well emphasize different aspects of an argument or even adopt different positions under different circumstances to suit the rhetorical purposes of the moment. A good example of this interpretive fallacy is to take Xiao Gang's letter to his cousin Xiao Ying 蕭暎, the Marquis of Xinyu 新渝侯, as "a summary of Xiao Gang's conception of Palace Style Poetry."[83] In this letter, Xiao Gang praised three poems by Xiao Ying, which had apparently been written in response to Xiao Gang's own compositions. Xiao Ying's poems are no longer extant, but their subjects, to judge from the context of the letter, were the loneliness of a palace lady and the mirror image of a beautiful woman.[84] Xiao Gang applauded the marquis's poems as displaying "extraordinary sentiments" (*xingqing zhuojue* 性情卓絶) and exemplifying "original, remarkable moods" (*xinzhi yingqi* 新致英奇). Yet it is clear that the letter was no more than a thank-you note offering polite compliments that may have been quite sincere in regard to these three *specific* poems. The letter was not, however, a declaration of what poetry, or even Palace Style poetry, should be.

In studying pre-Tang literature, it is important to bear in mind that we now have only a small fraction of the texts that once existed, and that this fraction has come to us primarily through encyclopedias, which often give excerpts rather than entire texts. In trying to reconstruct a comprehensive picture of the Liang from the fragmentary debris

82. Zhou Xunchu, "Liangdai wenlun sanpai shuyao," p. 250.
83. Wang Yunxi and Yang Ming, *Wei Jin nanbeichao*, p. 298.
84. *Quan Liang wen* 11.3011.

of a vastly larger textual world, we have to make use of all the bits and pieces at hand. There is, however, always a danger of overreading and overinterpreting precisely because the paucity of extant material invites us to vest every piece of information with more significance than it may have had in its original context. Texts are not self-enclosed constructs independent of context. Another example of this interpretive fallacy, which bears immediately on our discussion of Liang literary "schools," is Pei Ziye's treatise "On Carving Insects," which is usually considered a literary manifesto of the "archaic school."

"On Carving Insects" is preserved in two sources: the eighth-century historian Du You's 杜佑 (734–812) *A Comprehensive Canon of Administration* (*Tong dian* 通典), and the huge literary anthology *The Fine Blossoms of the Literary Garden* (*Wenyuan yinghua* 文苑英華), compiled between 982 and 987.[85] In *Tong dian*, Pei Ziye's treatise is included in "Miscellaneous Discussions" ("Zayilun" 雜議論) under the category of "Selection for Offices" ("Xuanju" 選舉), because Pei Ziye observed that during the Liu-Song period, "from the founding of the dynasty [420] till the Yuanjia era [424–53], people mostly devoted themselves to the Confucian classics and histories; by the Daming 大明 era [457–64], however, there rose a general penchant for literature."[86] The implication is that literary writings had replaced the study of the Confucian classics and dynastic histories as the standard for official appointment and promotion. Prior to citing Pei Ziye's "discussion" (*lun* 論), Du You had devoted a few lines to explaining Song Emperor Ming's (r. 465–72) excessive love of literature; this makes it quite clear that in the context of *Tong dian*, the quotation of Pei Ziye's criticism of the literary writings produced by the younger generation was aimed at the later years of the Liu-Song, not at the Liang. It is very likely that Pei Ziye's "discussion" was taken from his *Essential History of the Song* (*Song lue* 宋略); since this was completed in the late fifth century, he was not criticizing the Liang literary scene.[87] In the late 1970s, the Japanese scholar Hayashida

85. Du You, *Tong dian*, 16.389–90; *Wenyuan yinghua* 742.3873–74. See also *Quan Liang wen* 53.3262.

86. Du You, *Tong dian* 16.389.

87. Pei Ziye's *Song lue* was based on Shen Yue's *Song shu*, which was presented to the throne in 488 (*Liang shu* 30.442).

Shinnosuke did an excellent job of demonstrating that Pei Ziye's "treatise" was written in the late fifth century as part of *The Essential History of the Song*, and that the *Wenyuan yinghua* editors culled the text from Du You's *Tong dian* and gave it the title "On Carving Insects."[88] But more than two decades later, there are scholars who believe that Pei Ziye wrote his "treatise" in the 520s in order to criticize the poetic style of the contemporary "avant-garde" school.[89] In fact, the premise of Zhou Xunchu's "three camps" theory is the belief that Pei Ziye's "treatise" implicitly targets Xiao Gang.[90] What we see here is a historian's discussion of a specific period extracted from its context, made into a literary essay, and used anachronistically as a critique of a school whose "leader," Xiao Gang, was not even born yet.

In his day Pei Ziye was apparently admired for his learning and his public prose, not for his *fu* and poetry.[91] It seems rather arbitrary to refer to those who associated with him as a "literary group" (*wenxue jituan*) or a "faction" (*pai*), since Pei Ziye and his friends were engaged primarily in scholarly discussions of books (*taolun fenji* 討論坟籍), and it is clear from the dynastic histories that their interest was in scholarship and learning, not in literary composition. Of Pei Ziye's close associates, Liu Zhilin was the only one who "for the most part imitated the ancient style" in his writings, but again he struck up a friendship with Pei Ziye and Liu Xian because they "often discussed books together" (*gong taolun shuji* 共討論書籍), not because they composed *fu* and poetry together.[92] To portray

88. Hayashida Shinnosuke, *Chūgoku chūsei*, pp. 286–312. This section was translated into Chinese and published in *Gudai wenxue lilun yanjiu congkan* 古代文學理論研究叢刊 6 (1982): 231–50.

89. Yu Yuan and Zhang Minggao, *Wei Jin nanbeichao*, p. 327.

90. Zhou Xunchu, "Liangdai wenlun sanpai shuyao," p. 232.

91. Emperor Wu commissioned Pei Ziye to compose the proclamation against the Northern Wei on the eve of the northern campaign in 526; the proclamation was appreciated by the emperor, and Pei Ziye was subsequently entrusted with the task of drafting edicts and proclamations. This statement is immediately followed by the historian's discussion of Pei Ziye's composition style, which followed ancient models (*Liang shu* 30.443).

92. Ibid., 40.574. According to "The Biography of Pei Ziye," Liu Xian, Liu Zhilin, Yin Yun, Ruan Xiaoxu, Gu Xie, and Wei Leng 韋棱 were "all well read and had a deep admiration for Pei Ziye. Liu Xian was particularly respectful of Pei. At

Pei Ziye and Liu Zhilin as members of an "archaic school" evokes the Tang or Ming dynasty "archaic schools" (*fugu pai* 復古派), which consciously championed a "return to antiquity" in both literary theory and practice, and such an identification is anachronistic and lacks precision and does not reflect the literary scene of early medieval China. Indeed, if we must look to Pei Ziye's close friends to determine Pei's literary orientation, then we cannot ignore that Xiao Yi, the confirmed "Palace Style" practitioner, was just as fast a friend of Pei Ziye as was Liu Zhilin. Xiao Yi claimed that Pei Ziye was one of the four friends "who truly understood me," and his intimate association with Pei Ziye is well represented in *The Master of the Golden Tower*.[93] Xiao Yi's other three "bosom friends" were Liu Xian, Xiao Mai, and Zhang Zuan, all of whom would be classified as members of the "archaic school" in the "literary faction" theory. Yet another piece of evidence against Pei Ziye's place in the theory of factional struggle is the fact that one of Pei Ziye's poems appeared in the 1540 edition of *Yutai xinyong*—the very anthology thought to represent the rival school.[94]

Xiao Gang, in his letter to Xiao Yi written after he became crown prince in 531, criticized those who imitated Pei Ziye's "plain" literary style, and yet he acknowledged Pei Ziye as "a good historian."[95] Significantly, Xiao Gang attributed a particular strength or a talent in a specific genre to each writer mentioned in this letter. This was a familiar move, first seen in Cao Pi's "A Discourse on Literature" ("Lun wen" 論文),[96] but it also reflected the general tendency of an age that increasingly differentiated between belles lettres and public prose.[97] Xiao

---

the time, when Xiao Mai, the marquis of Wuping, and Zhang Zuan of Fanyang discussed books with Pei, both would look to Pei as judge" (ibid., 30.443).

93. *Quan Liang wen* 17.3051; Xiao Yi, *Jinlouzi jiaozhu* 9.155.

94. See Liu Yuejin, *"Yutai xinyong" yanjiu*, p. 53. More will be said about this edition later.

95. *Quan Liang wen* 11.3011.

96. *Quan Sanguo wen* 8.1097–98; Owen, *Readings in Chinese Literary Thought*, pp. 57–72.

97. Such a differentiation played into the distinction between *wen* 文 and *bi* 筆 in the Liang. In the late fifth century, *wen* was differentiated from *bi* on the basis of rhymes, as evidenced by Liu Xie's statement in *Wenxin diaolong* 44.1622: "In common parlance these days, a distinction is made between *wen* and *bi*, with *bi* as writing without rhyme and *wen* as writing with rhyme" (translation from Owen, *Read-*

Yi similarly agreed that those who were good at one were not necessarily skilled at the other.[98] To offer a critical assessment of one aspect of the oeuvre of an otherwise much admired older scholar, using a common form of judgment ("good at X but not at Y"), hardly constitutes factional polemics.

The inadequacy and anachronism of using "literary camps" to characterize the Liang literary scene can also be seen in scholars' disagreement on the "group identity" of Emperor Wu. Zhou Xunchu sees Emperor Wu as the central figure in the "archaist school."[99] Yan Caiping, in contrast, places Emperor Wu along with Xiao Tong in the "compromise school."[100] But because Emperor Wu composed some poems on the topic of palace ladies and romantic love, widely considered to be *the* characteristic subject matter of Palace Style poetry, Zhong Youmin identifies him as a Palace Style poet.[101] Cao Daoheng and Shen Yucheng group Emperor Wu with the other Palace Style poets such as Xiao Gang and Xiao Yi but admit that the emperor's "understanding of

---

ings in Chinese Literary Thought, p. 273). Later, Xiao Yi (*Jinlouzi jiaozhu* 9.190) further specified the definition of *wen*: he pointed out that writings serving pragmatic functions, such as memorials to the throne, were called *bi*, whereas *wen* must have "the exquisite beauty of fine silks, the alluring force of music, beautiful sound, and strong emotions" 惟須綺縠紛披，宮徵靡曼，唇吻遒會，情靈搖蕩. As Pauline Yu has observed, the *wen/bi* distinction indicates "the efforts of Six Dynasties literary critics to reduce the overly inclusive category of *wen* to an entity of somewhat more definite and manageable proportions" ("Formal Distinctions in Literary Theory," in Bush and Murck, eds., *Theories of the Arts in China*, p. 35).

98. Xiao Yi, *Jinlouzi jiaozhu* 9.189.

99. Zhou Xunchu, "Liangdai wenlun sanpai shuyao," pp. 235–36. Again, the examples cited by Zhou Xunchu are problematic. Emperor Wu's admiration of Pei Ziye was much emphasized, although the emperor showed appreciation only for Pei Ziye's public prose; there is no mention of his appreciation of Pei's *fu* and poetry. Xie Zheng's 謝徵 "friendliness" with Pei is taken to indicate his membership in the "archaic group," although there is no evidence that Xie Zheng's literary style was "archaic" (*Quan Liang wen* 50.718). Emperor Wu's favorable reception of Dao Gai and Liu Zhilin is regarded as proof of his "archaic" inclination, and yet Emperor Wu had shown similar favor to many other men of letters who might be properly considered members of the "compromise school" or "avant-garde school" (*Liang shu* 13.243).

100. Yan Caiping, *Qi Liang shige*, pp. 63–64.

101. Zhong Youmin, *Zhongguo shige shi*, pp. 343–44.

poetry tended to be conservative."[102] The disagreement not only demonstrates the contrived nature of the division of the Liang literary scene into schools but also accentuates the problems surrounding the definition of the term "Palace Style," which is the subject of the next chapter.

The ultimate weakness of Zhou Xunchu's "three camps" theory is the fact that it is predicated on the *contemporaneity* of the three "camps." Without the condition of simultaneity and a direct conflict of interests, there would be no "three camps." Rather, there would be only a change in tastes and fashions, which was in fact what happened in the Liang. Pei Ziye, who was born in 469 and died in 530, belonged to an older generation, as did Emperor Wu. Emperor Wu's lack of sympathy for the four tones advocated by Shen Yue is cited as a sign of his "archaic" tendency, but the immediate context of Emperor Wu's attitude was Shen Yue's loss of imperial favor in his last years.[103] Prosody, although important in its own right, was not all there was to the "Palace Style," as we shall see in Chapter 6. The emperor's lack of enthusiasm for the tonal theories of the Yongming poets and his ignoring of them in his own compositions do not mean that the emperor necessarily opposed poetry based on them. More important, Emperor Wu's dismissal of the four tones, like Zhong Rong's in the preface to *The Gradations of Poets*, occurred in the early years of the sixth century (Zhou She, with whom Emperor Wu had the conversation about the four tones, died in 524, but the conversation could have occurred much earlier). At this time, the Palace Style had not developed its mature form yet. Xiao Tong and particularly Xiao Gang and Xiao Yi, who lived into the 550s, represented a generation quite different from that of Emperor Wu or Pei Ziye. The changes in literary taste and fashions occurred over time, the subject of the last section of this chapter.

To recapitulate: despite differences in personal talents and interests and subtle variations in their evaluations of the literary past, there was a general consensus among Liang literati about the nature and function of literature as well as about the literary canon and values. The construction of the "three literary camps" of the Liang is anachronistic and does not bear close scrutiny, nor can it explain the theory and practice of the

102. Cao Daoheng and Shen Yucheng, *Nanbeichao wenxue shi*, p. 247.
103. See Emperor Wu's conversation with Zhou She in *Liang shu* 13.243.

Liang writers. And yet, the imagined differences among different group leaders have had some interesting consequences in terms of the treatment of the textual evidence.

XIAO TONG AND XIAO GANG: A CASE STUDY

Xiao Tong and Xiao Gang are generally considered polar opposites. This view did not begin with modern scholarship; it can be traced to the canonization of *Wen xuan* and the dismissal of Xiao Gang's Palace Style poetry in the official discourse of the early seventh century. This section takes a brief look at how the assumed "difference" between the brothers affected later editorial decisions concerning the authorship of a group of poems.

Neither Xiao Tong's nor Xiao Gang's collection has survived independently. *Yutai xinyong* is an important source for their poetry. Apart from a tiny fragment of a Tang manuscript copy of *Yutai xinyong* discovered in Dunhuang, the earliest extant versions of *Yutai xinyong* are from the Ming dynasty, that is to say, about a millennium after *Yutai xinyong* was compiled.[104] The 1540 edition is the earliest dated Ming edition.[105] This edition has largely been eclipsed by the 1633 edition printed by Zhao Jun 趙均 (courtesy name Lingjun 靈均, d. 1637). Zhao Jun claimed that his edition was a reprint of the Southern Song edition compiled by Chen Yufu 陳玉父. Yet Chen Yufu's edition itself was nothing but a patchwork. According to Chen Yufu's colophon, dated 1215, his edition was pieced together from three editions: two incomplete printed editions and one manuscript copy. Therefore, although the 1633 edition is now the most popular edition, it is far from reliable in its order of arrangement or contents. Interestingly, although the 1540 edition includes eight poems by Xiao Tong, the 1633 edition does not contain even one under Xiao Tong's name; and yet, of the eight poems attributed to Xiao Tong in the 1540 edition, seven appear in the 1633 edition under Xiao Gang's name.

104. For a detailed discussion of *Yutai xinyong* editions, see Liu Yuejin, *"Yutai xinyong" yanjiu*, pp. 3–64.

105. Ibid., p. 8.

Altogether, there are eleven poems assigned to both princes in various sources:

1. "Buying Lotus from a Passing Lotus Boat" ("Lianzhou maihe du" 蓮舟買荷度)
2. "Reflected in the Water, Looking at Her Fallen Hairpin" ("Zhaoliu kan luochai" 照流看落釵)
3. "On a Beauty Applying Her Morning Makeup" ("Meiren chenzhuang" 美人晨妝)
4. "On a Famed Gentleman Taking Delight in a Beautiful Woman" ("Mingshi yue qingcheng" 名士悦傾城)
5. "Singing Girls in the Grove" ("Linxia zuoji" 林下作伎)
6. "On a New Swallow" ("Yong xinyan" 詠新燕)

7–9. "Ditties of the Southland" ("Jiangnan nong" 江南弄), namely:
   A. "The Song of the Southland" ("Jiangnan qu" 江南曲)
   B. "The Song of the Dragon Flute" ("Longdi qu" 龍笛曲)
   C. "The Song of Picking Lotus" ("Cailian qu" 採蓮曲)

10. "In Imitation of Ancient Style" ("Nigu" 擬古)
11. "Late Spring" ("Wanchuan" 晚春)

Perhaps it is no surprise that the subjects of these poems are for the most part what an orthodox Confucian moralist would consider frivolous: palace ladies, singing girls, and romantic sentiment; in other words, a more "somber" poem would perhaps have had no trouble finding a place in Xiao Tong's collection. There is no definitive proof of the authorship of these eleven poems with dual attributions, although in some cases certain probabilities are larger than the others. What concern us here are the ideological implications of the editors' choices of authorship in the absence of an empirical basis for such choices. We shall examine the poems one by one.

Poems 1, 2, 3, and 4 appear in the fifth *juan* under Xiao Tong's name in the 1540 edition of *Yutai xinyong*, along with another poem, "Eternal Longing" ("Changxiangsi" 長相思, an undisputed Xiao Tong piece), although in the 1633 edition they become Xiao Gang's poems.[106] More compelling evidence for Xiao Tong's authorship is the fact that poems 2, 3, and 4 are attributed to Crown Prince Zhaoming (i.e., Xiao Tong) in

106. See ibid., p. 49.

Yiwen leiju, which was compiled in 624, a source, we suspect, less subject to manipulation than *Yutai xinyong*.[107]

In the 1633 edition of *Yutai xinyong*, the first two poems are entitled "Two of the Four Poems Written in Harmony with Yu Jianwu" ("Tong Yu Jianwu siyong ershou" 同庾肩吾四詠二首), and number 4 is entitled "Written in Harmony with the Prince of Xiangdong: On a Famed Gentleman Taking Delight in a Beautiful Woman" ("He Xiangdong wang 'Mingshi yue qingcheng'" 和湘東王名士悅傾城).[108] Feng Weine 馮惟訥 (1512–72), the compiler of the anthology *Record of Ancient Poetry* (*Gushi ji* 古詩紀), decreed that "since Jianwu was Xiao Gang's courtier, *Yutai* should be considered correct [as opposed to *Yiwen leiju*],"[109] although serving under one prince did not prevent an official from exchanging poetry with other princes.

For poems 3 and 4, Feng Weine did not even have evidence as flimsy as Yu Jianwu's being Xiao Gang's courtier, and yet he did not hesitate to declare in each case: "*Yiwen leiju* attributed it to [Crown Prince] Zhaoming—it is wrong."[110] Feng Weine cited no textual evidence to support his claims. The modern scholar Lu Qinli followed suit and assigned these poems to Xiao Gang in his monumental *The Poetry of Pre-Qin, Han, Wei, Jin, and the Southern and Northern Dynasties* (*Xian Qin Han Wei Jin nanbeichao shi* 先秦漢魏晉南北朝詩).[111] Indeed, these poems are now considered archetypal examples of Xiao Gang's "decadent" Palace Style poetry. Rather than the evidence leading to the conclusion, the desired conclusion can shape the evidence.

Poem 5, a poem about holding an evening banquet with singing girls performing in a grove, was attributed to Xiao Tong as early as in the Tang encyclopedia *A Primer for Beginners* (*Chuxue ji* 初學記).[112] It is preceded by Xiao Yi's poem "Written to the Command of the Crown Prince, in Harmony with His Poem on Singing Girls in the Grove" ("He linxia zuoji yingling" 和林下作妓應令). It is clear that Xiao Yi

107. *Yiwen leiju* 18.327–28, under the section "Beautiful Women."

108. Xiao Yi became the Prince of Xiangdong in 514. No poems under such titles are found in the extant collections of Yu Jianwu and Xiao Yi.

109. Feng Weine, *Gushi ji* 79.10a.

110. Ibid., 78.34.

111. *Quan Liang shi* 22.1953, 21.1938–39.

112. *Chuxue ji* 15.373

wrote the poem at the command of Xiao Tong in response to Xiao Tong's poem of the same title. That Xiao Tong's poem follows Xiao Yi's poem instead of the more logical temporal sequence is because Xiao Yi later became emperor and the writings of a crown prince always follow those of an emperor in premodern anthologies.[113]

The modern scholar Lu Qinli included the poem under both Xiao Tong and Xiao Gang, but he added a little note under the title of Xiao Yi's poem that it was "written to harmonize with a poem by Crown Prince Zhaoming,"[114] and the title of the poem under Xiao Gang is "Written at the Command of the Crown Prince, in Harmony with His Poem on Singing Girls in the Grove" ("He linxiaji yingling" 和林下妓應令). Even if we believe the poem was written by Xiao Gang, we have to assume that Xiao Tong first wrote a poem to the same title and then asked his two brothers to respond.

Poem 6 is a quatrain about a "new swallow" that flies into a tower, where it is startled by the sound of bracelets. *Yiwen leiju* attributed it to Xiao Gang, and *Wenyuan yinghua* to Xiao Tong.[115] Feng Weine stated that "*Yinghua* was wrong to identify it as Zhaoming's poem," but gave no reason for his opinion.[116] Lu Qinli followed Feng's judgment and placed the poem under Xiao Gang's name, without bothering to acknowledge the double attributions.[117]

Poems 7, 8, and 9 are three songs. The first is attributed to Xiao Gang in *Yiwen leiju* and *Wenyuan yinghua*.[118] The second appears under Xiao Gang's name in *Yiwen leiju*; a different, "fuller" version can be

113. In the tenth-century encyclopedia *Wenyuan yinghua* (213.1059), the title of Xiao Tong's poem is cited as "The Same as Before" ("Tongqian" 同前), and the poem preceding it is Xiao Yi's "Written at the Command of the Crown Prince, in Harmony with His Poem on Singing Girls in the Grove" ("He linxia yong ji yingling" 和林下詠妓應令). The modern scholar Yu Shaochu observes that if the poem was truly written "at the command of the Crown Prince," then it was not written by Xiao Tong (Xiao Tong, *Zhaoming taizi ji*, p. 224). But here it is obvious that the editors of *Wenyuan yinghua* replicated the order of the two poems in the earlier *Chuxue ji* and made a careless mistake.

114. *Quan Liang shi* 14.1800, 22.1954, 25.2051.

115. *Yiwen leiju* 92.1597; *Wenyuan yinghua* 329.1711–12.

116. Feng Weine, *Gushi ji* 79.17a.

117. *Quan Liang shi* 22.1974.

118. *Yiwen leiju* 42.765; *Wenyuan yinghua* 201.995.

found in the twelfth-century *Collection of Yuefu Poetry* (*Yuefu shiji* 樂府詩集).[119] The third song appears in *Wenyuan yinghua* under Xiao Gang, but a note acknowledges that it is attributed to Xiao Yi in *Yuefu shiji*.[120] In fact all three songs are attributed to Xiao Tong in a Song edition of *Yuefu shiji*, as they are in the 1540 edition of *Yutai xinyong*.[121] Feng Weine was aware of the Xiao Tong attribution in the various sources, but in this case he followed *Yiwen leiju*.[122] Feng apparently chose to follow a source not because of his faith in the source itself but because of a more subtle "standard" in his own mind. Since all three songs concern women, it may be that he decided Xiao Tong could not have written them. Lu Qinli also placed all three songs under Xiao Gang, explaining: "The old printed edition of *Yutai* listed [Emperor] Jianwen (i.e., Xiao Gang) as the crown prince, which is why later people mistakenly thought it referred to [Crown Prince] Zhaoming and the attributions were often confused."[123] This echoes the *Siku quanshu* editors' dismissal of the attribution of five poems (numbers 2, 3, 4, 5, and 10) to Xiao Tong in a Ming edition of *The Collection of Crown Prince Zhaoming* (*Zhaoming taizi ji* 昭明太子集) compiled by Ye Shaotai 葉紹泰 (fl. 1638),[124] but this does not adequately explain the early attributions of poems number 2, 3, 4, and 5 in *Yiwen leiju* and *Chuxue ji*, whose editors still had access to the collections of Xiao Tong, Xiao Gang, and Xiao Yi and did not have to cull poems from *Yutai xinyong*.

Poem 10, "In Imitation of Ancient Style," is a poem with irregular meters: 5 seven-syllable lines are followed by 2 five-syllable lines. The subject of the poem is a woman longing for her beloved. It is not found in sources other than *Yutai xinyong* (*juan* 9 of both the 1540 and the 1633 editions), which attributes it to Xiao Gang. Ye Shaotai's *Zhaoming taizi ji* nonetheless included it, presumably because Ye had access to sources unavailable to us. Ye did the same with poem 11, "Late Spring,"

119. *Yiwen leiju* 42.763; Guo Maoqian, *Yuefu shiji* 50.729.

120. *Wenyuan yinghua* 208.1032.

121. Guo Maoqian, *Yuefu shiji* 50.728–29; Liu Yuejin, *"Yutai xinyong" yanjiu*, p. 54. The *Wenyuan yinghua* editors must have seen the Xiao Yi attribution in some other source now lost to us.

122. Feng Weine, *Gushi ji* 77.20b.

123. *Quan Liang shi* 20.1924–25.

124. *Siku quanshu zongmu* 148.3109.

against the attribution of this poem to Xiao Gang in all earlier sources.[125] And yet, despite the relative lack of textual evidence, Lu Qinli placed poems 10 and 11 under both Xiao Tong and Xiao Gang, in glaring contrast with his attributions of poems 1–4 and 6–9: those poems have a better chance of being Xiao Tong's and yet appear under Xiao Gang only.[126] In the case of poem 10, Lu's decision might have been prompted by the title, "In Imitation of Ancient Style"; or it might be because this poem depicts a woman in sorrow and tears—in other words, it is an "expression of feelings," as opposed to the other poems, which described the physical beauty of women in detail. In the case of poem 11, we can only surmise that Lu's dual attribution arises because "Late Spring" is primarily a landscape poem that does not concern itself with women and romantic feelings, which are considered the usual topics of Xiao Gang's Palace Style poetry. Lu Qinli's influential editorial decisions derive from a belief in a certain kind of literary historical narrative and have in turn reinforced that narrative.

The multiple attributions of the eleven poems discussed in this section illustrate the problems particular to a manuscript culture: in the process of copying and transmitting, other poems easily became mixed with the original poems in an anthology or collection; authors sometimes were randomly assigned on the basis of impressions ("This looks like a Xiao Tong poem to me"); poems lost their authors, and authors lost their poems. The attribution of the poems to Xiao Tong or Xiao Gang in later anthologies was often determined not by textual evidence but by the qualities conventionally associated with the two brothers; such attributions in turn reinforced conventional judgments. In other words, the attribution of the poems is based on a set of values inscribed in the traditional account of literary history—Xiao Tong as moral and

125. "Late Spring" is attributed to Xiao Gang in *Yiwen leiju* (3.42), *Chuxue ji* (3.47), *Wenyuan yinghua* (157.738), and, according to Feng Weine (*Gushi ji* 76.9a), in *Yutai xinyong* as well. But the poem cannot be found in the 1540 and 1633 editions of *Yutai xinyong*; Lu Qinli did not give the bibliographical information about the *Yutai* inclusion (see *Quan Liang shi* 14.1799, 21.1946). Feng Weine either saw a different version of *Yutai* or made a mistake. On the attribution of this poem to Xiao Tong, Feng Weine commented: "Its style does not sound like [Xiao Tong's] at all" 語殊不類.

126. *Quan Liang shi* 14.1802, 22.1978.

orthodox, Xiao Gang as licentious and unrestrained; and these attributions, in turn, have become the evidence used to confirm the conventional narrative, still widely accepted as true.

LITERARY TASTES IN THE LIANG

Earlier in this chapter, I mentioned the two best-known works of literary criticism produced during this period: Liu Xie's *Literary Mind Carving the Dragon* and Zhong Rong's *Gradations of Poets*. Although Liu Xie's work remained relatively obscure for most of the imperial period, *Literary Mind Carving the Dragon* has attracted increasing attention since the late nineteenth century because its "grand critical system" has been perceived as closer to Western literary discourse than the unsystematic literary criticism scattered in "random notes" or individual essays.[127] It is, however, quite uncertain how much impact Liu Xie's work, or Zhong Rong's for that matter, had at the time it was written. Both Liu and Zhong were minor literary figures in their time. As a result of Liu Xie's immense fame in the twentieth century, however, scholars have tended to read his present reputation back into his own times and to suggest that his literary views shaped Xiao Tong's conception of literature in the compilation of *Wen xuan*. Such a claim is dubious at best, for, although Xiao Tong was said to have "received [Liu Xie] with deep admiration," Liu Xie was not a member of Xiao Tong's inner circle.[128] As David Knechtges has pointed out: "Although Liu Xie's views were undoubtedly known in his time, it is difficult to determine the extent of their influence on Xiao Tong."[129] Nor did Zhong Rong possess a grand stature in the Liang literary world. *The Southern History* asserts that Shen Yue's rejection of Zhong Rong's bid for patronage was the reason for Zhong's harsh evaluation of Shen Yue's poetry.[130] This anecdote might well be spurious, but it nevertheless reveals Zhong Rong's relative lack of literary status during his lifetime.

127. For a survey of the so-called Dragonology (*longxue* 龍學), see Cai Zong-qi's "Introduction" to *A Chinese Literary Mind*, pp. 2–5.

128. *Liang shu* 50.710.

129. Knechtges, *Wen xuan*, 1: 15.

130. *Nan shi* 72.1779.

Despite Liu Xie's theoretical endorsement of change, his impulse was to favor the conservative side when it came to judgments of recent literature. Liu Xie's vision of literary history was a continuous decline into increasing ornamentation and decadence. Literature began by being "plain and pure" (*chun er zhi* 淳而質) in distant antiquity and degenerated into being "deceptive and new" (*e er xin* 訛而新) in the Liu-Song period; indeed, "the nearer we are to our own times, the more insipid literature turns out to be."[131] In another chapter, he wrote:

> In recent times writers have generally showed a liking for the bizarre and artful. If we look to the origins of that form, it was in a mutation to a momentum inclined to the delusory. They grew sick of the old models and adopted whatever novelty they could get by any contrivance. If we examine their delusory concepts, what seems difficult is, in fact, nothing but an inversion of the proper.[132]
>
> 自近代辭人, 率好詭巧, 原其爲體, 訛勢所變, 厭黷舊式, 故穿鑿取新. 察其訛意, 似難而實無他術也, 反正而已.

Although Liu Xie admitted in principle that "transformation" was a positive value, in practice he seems not to have favored change, particularly that taking place in his own age.

Zhong Rong showed similar tendencies. His list of top-ranking poets ends with Xie Lingyun, who died in 433. He relegated all later poets, including Shen Yue and Xie Tiao, to the middle and lower ranks, in sharp contrast to Xiao Gang's assessment of Shen Yue's and Xie Tiao's poetry as "the crowning achievements of literature and models for later writings."[133] Xiao Yi likewise said that "the one who wrote poetry profusely and well was Shen Yue; those who wrote few poems but skillful ones were Xie Tiao and He Xun."[134]

Zhong Rong, however, was much more open-minded than Liu Xie in terms of generic preference. Whereas Liu Xie still insisted that "poetry in the four-syllable line is the normative form," Zhong Rong ranked all

---

131. Liu Xie, *Wenxin diaolong* 29.1089; translation from Owen, *Readings in Chinese Literary Thought*, p. 226. Owen translates the phrase *e er xin* 訛而新 as "things first became deceptive and a hunger for novelty appeared."

132. Liu Xie, *Wenxin diaolong* 30.1134; translation from Owen, *Readings in Chinese Literary Thought*, pp. 237–38.

133. *Quan Liang wen* 11.3011.

134. *Liang shu* 49.693.

poets on the merits of their five-syllable verse, saying that five-syllable verse "occupies the most important position in literature, being particularly flavorful among the various modes of literary expression."[135] Xiao Zixian also extolled poetry in the five-syllable line as "standing out alone among various genres."[136] During the Liang, literary criticism was applied most often to the sphere of poetry, particularly poetry in the five-syllable line.

Beginning in the second half of the fifth century, there was a keen awareness of the opposition between "old" (*gu* 古) and "modern" (*jin* 今).[137] Along with this awareness emerged a consciousness of the different values implicit in changing period tastes and individual styles, as well as a deliberate pursuit of novelty. Xiao Zixian's attitude is representative:

When it comes to literary writings, it is particularly undesirable that they should be ordinary and outdated. If a piece of writing does not manifest some new transformation, it cannot possibly replace the older writings to become the champion of its age. The poetry of the Jian'an period was of the same mode, and yet their advantages and disadvantages were brought forth by [Cao Pi's] *Discourse on Literature*; Pan [Yue] and Lu [Ji] were of equal fame, but [the styles of] their writings remain different. In the Eastern Jin dynasty Daoist discourse flourished: Guo Pu [in his poetry] specialized in its numinous transformations, and Xu Xun [fl. mid-fourth century] pushed its philosophical principles to the extreme. [Yin] Zhongwen's [d. 407] poetry did not entirely expel the metaphysical flavor; Xie Hun's [d. 412] sentiments were fresh, and he gained a moderate amount of fame. Yan [Yanzhi] and Xie [Lingyun] emerged at the same time, and each stood out as extraordinary poets. Tang [Hui]xiu [fl. early fifth

135. Liu Xie, *Wenxin diaolong* 6.210; Zhong Rong, *Shi pin jizhu*, p. 36. Poems in the seven-syllable line became increasingly popular in the sixth century, although the form did not reach its full splendor until the Tang.

136. *Nan Qi shu* 52.907.

137. Among the poetry anthologies recorded in the *Sui shu* "Bibliography" that can be roughly dated, works with titles like "ancient" and "modern" or "ancient and modern" first appear in the Qi and Liang. Moreover, we see a dramatic increase in the number of poems entitled *guyi* 古意 (an old motif or mood) in the Liang. If we discount the alternative title for Ji Kang's 嵇康 (223–62) poem presented to his brother (*Quan Wei shi* 9.485–86), *guyi* first appeared in the title of a poem by Yan Jun 顏竣 (d. 459) of the Liu Song, entitled "On Overwhelming Longing, with an Ancient Motif" ("Yinsi guyi" 淫思古意) (*Quan Song shi* 6.1242). Interestingly, *guyi* as a title is not found in extant Chen or Sui poetry.

century] and Bao [Zhao] appeared on the literary scene later, and both of them were remarkable. Vermilion and indigo are alike in their splendor, but they do not originate from each other.[138]

在乎文章, 彌患凡舊, 若無新變, 不能代雄. 建安一體, 典論短長互出; 潘、陸齊名, 機、岳之文永異. 江左風味, 盛道家之言, 郭璞舉其靈變, 許詢極其名理. 仲文玄氣, 猶不盡除; 謝混情新, 得名未盛. 顏、謝並起, 乃各擅奇; 休、鮑後出, 咸亦標世. 朱藍共妍, 不相祖述.

Xiao Zixian's positive emphasis on the value of originality and newness here forms a striking contrast with the views of Liu Xie, who, despite a theoretical approval of change, remained critical of recent writings.

In a postscript to "The Biography of Xie Lingyun" in *History of the Song*, Shen Yue described a similar trajectory in literary history. Tang Huixiu 湯惠休 and Bao Zhao, two popular early fifth-century poets, did not appear on Shen Yue's list of great names, probably because they were too close in time to the composition of the Song history.[139] But for Xiao Zixian, who compiled *The History of the Southern Qi* in the early sixth century, these two Liu-Song poets, with their large followings, had earned a legitimate place after Yan Yanzhi and Xie Lingyun, still considered the two greatest poets of the early fifth century. As the modern scholar Yang Ming has observed, both Xiao Zixian and Jiang Yan, who imitated Tang Huixiu and Bao Zhao in his group of poems entitled "Various Forms" ("Zati" 雜體), showed remarkable tolerance for different poetic styles.[140]

Xiao Zixian offered a general summary of poetic styles prevailing in the early sixth century by subsuming them under three broad types. For

138. Xiao Zixian's remarks constitute the historian's commentary on "The Biographies of Men of Letters" (*Nan Qi shu* 52.908).

139. *Song shu* 67.1778–79.

140. Wang Yunxi and Yang Ming, *Wei Jin nanbeichao*, p. 316. As Stephen Owen (*The Making of Early Chinese Classical Poetry*, p. 43) points out, Jiang Yan's "Various Forms," written in imitation of the styles of previous poets and arranged in chronological order, marked an important moment in literary history. "While Jiang Yan's series of imitations are not in themselves a history of poetry, they represent the condition within which a history of poetry is possible." Jiang Yan asked his readers to judge these different styles sympathetically, requesting "an understanding and appreciation of period differences that does not call for comparative judgment." For Jiang Yan's poems, see *Quan Liang shi* 4.1569–81; and Xiao Tong, *Wen xuan* 31.1452–86.

each type, he traced its "origin" to a poet of an earlier generation, just as Zhong Rong did in *The Gradations of Poets*. This gesture is very much part of the contemporary obsession with family trees and genealogies and reflects the political culture of the Six Dynasties.

In today's literary world there are many authors, but they can be roughly divided into three kinds. The first express their feelings leisurely and in flowery and detached language: although artful and decorative, in the end their works turn out to be lethargic and convoluted. [Such works] are suitable for public banquets but should not be upheld as a standard. Carelessness, sluggishness, and lack of energy and momentum constitute a fatal disease. Even though [this style's] classic correctness is admirable, it is dispassionate and does not move the reader. This style derives originally from Xie Lingyun.[141]

今之文章, 作者雖衆, 總而爲論, 略有三體. 一則啓心閑繹, 託辭華曠, 雖存巧綺, 終致迂回, 宜登公宴, 本非准的. 而疏慢闡緩, 膏肓之病. 典正可採, 酷不入情. 此體之源, 出靈運而成也.

Xie Lingyun exerted a strong influence on many poets from the late fifth to early sixth century. Xiao Ye, the fifth son of the founding emperor of the Qi and Xiao Zixian's uncle, once wrote a short poem in imitation of Xie Lingyun and presented it to the Qi emperor, who replied: "I have read your poem of twenty characters: it is the best among the poems by your brothers. However, Kangle [Xie Lingyun's ducal title] lacked restraint, and one cannot distinguish the beginning and end in his poetry. Anren [Pan Yue] and Shiheng [Lu Ji] are the ones you should really emulate; Yan Yanzhi might be considered next to them."[142] The Liang poets Fu Ting 伏挺 (484–548) and Wang Ji were known for imitating the "Xie Kangle style."[143] Wang Ji admired Xie Lingyun so much that "he felt no embarrassment when his lines overlapped [with Xie's]. His contemporaries all said that Kangle stood in the same relation to Wang Ji that Confucius had to [Zuo] Qiuming and Lao Dan had to Yan Zhou [Zhuangzi]."[144]

141. *Nan Qi shu* 52.908.

142. Ibid., 33.625. Xiao Ye was the Marquis of Wuling mentioned in Chapter 1.

143. For Fu Ting, see *Liang shu* 50.719. Wang Ji was one of the Langye Wangs mentioned in Chapter 1.

144. *Nan shi* 21.580–81. It was believed that Zhuangzi had expanded Laozi's teachings, and that Zuo Qiuming 左丘明 had elaborated *The Annals of Spring and Autumn* authored by Confucius into the *Zuo zhuan* 左傳.

The Qi emperor's comment on Xie Lingyun echoed a general sentiment about Xie Lingyun's poetry in the late fifth and early sixth centuries. Xie Lingyun's poetry was apparently regarded as occupying a distinguished place in literary history but not as being something that should be reproduced in modern times. Zhong Rong criticized Xie Lingyun for being "unrestrained" (*yidang* 逸蕩) as well as "lush and tangled" (*fanwu* 繁蕪), an image of plants growing wild. He added: "This man had broad learning and wide-ranging talent and would write down whatever met his eye; he neither ran out of inspiration nor left out anything in the natural world: it is only fitting that his poetry is diverse and opulent."[145] These views reappear in Xiao Gang's letter to Xiao Yi, in which Xiao Gang expressed disapproval of those who imitated Xie Lingyun's style:

Xie Ke [Xie Lingyun's baby name] wrote remarkable poetry with spontaneity; sometimes he became immoderate, wherein lies the weakness of his writings. . . . His followers fail to attain his strength but instead acquire only his longwindedness. . . . Xie's artfulness cannot be achieved [by imitation].[146]

謝客吐言天拔, 出於自然, 時有不拘, 是其糟粕. . . . 是爲學謝則不屆其精華, 但得其冗長. . . . 謝故巧不可階.

Xiao Gang praised Xie Lingyun for his "spontaneity," a corollary of his alleged "lack of restraint."[147] From Zhong Rong and Xiao Gang's

145. Zhong Rong, *Shi pin jizhu*, p. 160.

146. *Quan Liang wen* 11.3011. A couplet by Wang Ji, the avid student of the Xie Lingyun style, was nonetheless much admired by Xiao Gang, Xiao Yi, and others (*Nan shi* 21.581). The couplet is: "Cicadas sing—the groves become even quieter; / the hills grow more silent with birds' cry" 蟬噪林逾靜, 鳥鳴山更幽. Xiao Yi praised it as "never to be achieved again" (Yan Zhitui, *Yanshi jiaxun* 9.273). And yet, we can indeed detect the influence of earlier poetry in the very simplicity of its parallelism: that is, the two lines basically convey a single message—the sounds of nature only deepen the silence of the mountain and groves. Liang court poetry in the hands of Xiao Gang and his followers developed a much more elaborate parallel couplet.

147. Xie Lingyun's "spontaneity" was recognized in the famous comment by his contemporary poet Bao Zhao. Yan Yanzhi had reportedly asked Bao Zhao to compare Yan's poetry with Xie's; Bao Zhao answered that Xie's poetry in the five-syllable line was "like a newly blooming lotus, natural and lovely" 謝五言如初發芙蓉, 自然可愛, whereas Yan's was "like brocade and embroidery in display, with much ornate decoration" 若鋪錦列繡, 亦雕繢滿眼 (*Nan shi* 34.881). In *The*

comments, we can see that Xie Lingyun was revered for his achievements, but his style was considered out of date. By Xiao Gang's time, graceful restraint had become a dominant ideal in the Liang court poetry.[148] Yan Zhitui advised his children: "Composing a piece of writing is like riding a handsome steed: even if it has an untrammeled spirit, the rider should bring it under control with the reins, never allowing it to wander off aimlessly, to follow its whims and fall into a chasm."[149]

Xiao Zixian's second category of writings is much more bookish:

> Next we see a style that assembles allusions and brings together things of the same category for comparison. The author does not write anything without pairing up references. Although his broad knowledge is admirable, it eventually becomes a limitation. Sometimes one borrows the words of the ancients in their entirety to express the feelings of a modern person, which is like drawing a cart over a rugged road or a puppet talking. All the reader sees are allusions and references; clarity and embellishment are completely lost. This style originated from Fu Xian's [239–94] poems on the Five Classics and Ying Qu's [190–252] poems about contemporary affairs. Although they are not entirely the same, one can certainly make the association.[150]

> 次則緝事比類, 非對不發, 博物可嘉, 職成拘制. 或全借古語, 用申今情, 崎嶇牽引, 直爲偶說. 唯睹事例, 頓失清采. 此則傳咸五經, 應璩指事, 雖不全似, 可以類從.

Gradations of Poets, this comment is attributed to Tang Huixiu (Zhong Rong, *Shi pin jizhu* p. 270). Xu Song's *Jiankang shilu* (14.372) recorded a different version: Bao Zhao's comment was contextualized so that instead of being a general comment on Xie and Yan's poetry, it became a specific comment on the two poems composed by Yan Yanzhi and Xie Lingyun to the same topic.

148. Xiao Gang famously advised his son in a letter to be "unrestrained (*fangdang* 放蕩) in literary writings." This, however, cannot be understood as a request to relinquish artistic control; rather, it is, in the context of the letter, a call for unfettered imagination. See his "Letter to Daxin, the Duke of Dangyang" 誡當陽公大心書, in *Quan Liang wen* 11.3010. For more discussion of this letter, see Chapter 4.

149. Yan Zhitui, *Yanshi jiaxun* 9.248.

150. Fu Xian's extant poems on the Confucian classics are in the four-syllable line; see *Quan Jin shi* 3.603–4. By Ying Qu's poems, Xiao Zixian supposedly refers to his "Hundred and One Poems" (*Baiyi shi* 百一詩), which are in the five-syllable line; see *Quan Wei shi* 8.469–72. However, Ying Qu's extant poems, written in a straightforward and plain language, are not laden with allusions.

Xiao Zixian's description here suggests Ren Fang's poetic style. In his later years, Ren Fang was reportedly so irked by his contemporaries' praise of "Shen Yue's poetry and Ren Fang's prose" that he began to work on his versifying skills with the intention of outdoing Shen Yue. "He used too many allusions, and the phrasing of his poetry was not able to achieve fluency and smoothness. Since the younger generation of the capital area admired his style, he became even more contrived in his poetic compositions. Hence it was said that his talent had been used up."[151] Zhong Rong placed Ren Fang in the middle rank: "Since Fang had broad learning, he constantly used allusions and references in his poetry, which was why his poetry failed to be extraordinary. Those young people who imitate him are truly misled."[152] Zhong Rong's last remark confirms Xiao Zixian's statement that a reliance on allusions was prevalent in the early sixth century.

Zhong Rong attributed this kind of poetic practice to Yan Yanzhi and Xie Zhuang 謝莊 (421–66). He claimed that because of their influence "literary writings were almost like extracts from books" during the Daming and Taishi 泰始 (465–72) eras. He continued:

> In recent years Ren Fang and Wang Yuanchang [i.e., Wang Rong] did not value extraordinary expressions in their poetry but only pursued novel allusions. This has become customary among poets ever since. Hence not a single line lacks a phrase derived from some earlier source, and not a single phrase lacks a character derived from a source. The result is a patchwork, constrained and limited, which greatly damages literature. Rarely do we see a poet who deserves a name for spontaneous elegance.[153]

近任昉王元長等, 辭不貴奇, 競須新事. 爾來作者, 寖以成俗. 遂乃句無虛語, 語無虛字. 拘攣補衲, 蠹文已甚. 但自然英旨, 罕值其人.

Both Zhong Rong's and Xiao Zixian's objections to the extensive use of allusions in poetry suggest that "fluency and smoothness" (*liubian* 流便) had come to be regarded as an important value. In the late fifth century, Xie Tiao remarked that "a good poem should be as round and

151. *Nan shi* 59.1455.
152. Zhong Rong, *Shi pin jizhu*, p. 316.
153. Ibid., pp. 180–81.

smooth as a pellet."[154] Shen Yue was famous for advocating "easiness" (*yi* 易): "Writings should follow the rules of three kinds of easiness: an allusion should be easy to understand; words should be easy to recognize; the whole piece should be easy to read aloud."[155] Northern writers from the same period likewise prized the use of allusions without any overt trace (*yongshi bu shi ren jue* 用事不使人覺). Xing Shao 邢劭 (b. 496?) and Zu Ting both admired Shen Yue for such an ability.[156]

The third type of prevailing literary style, in Xiao Zixian's opinion, could be traced to Bao Zhao:

> Next there is the style that is startling in its phrasing, unconventional and sharp in its tone. Its artfully crafted language is immoderate and alluring, overwhelming one's mind and dazzling one's spirit. It is just like the five colors having pink and purple among them, and the eight tones including the sounds of Zheng and Wei. This is the legacy of Bao Zhao.
>
> 次則發唱驚挺，操調險急，雕藻淫豔，傾炫心魂．亦猶五色之有紅紫，八音之有鄭、衛，斯鮑照之遺烈也．

Pink and purple were not considered "correct colors" (*zhengse* 正色 or *zhengcai* 正采); likewise, the romantic songs of Zheng and Wei in *The Classic of Poetry* were regarded as "mutations," in contrast to the more decorous and proper odes. Bao Zhao, a Liu-Song poet who came from an obscure northern immigrant family, apparently enjoyed a large following in the late fifth century and early sixth century.[157] He died during a prince's rebellion in 466, and much of his writing was lost in the

154. *Nan shi* 22.609. This remark was cited by Shen Yue to praise Wang Yun's poetry.

155. Yan Zhitui, *Yanshi jiaxun* 9.253.

156. Ibid., 9.253.

157. Zhong Rong (*Shi pin jizhu* p. 58) wrote: "And then there are facetious people who laugh at Cao [Zhi] and Liu [Zhen] as ancient and clumsy; they consider Bao Zhao as a superior master from the golden age of the Fuxi emperor, and Xie Tiao as matchless from past to present. And yet when they emulate Bao Zhao, they never reach the level of 'At mid-day the market is crowded'; and when they imitate Xie Tiao, they only get such inferior lines as 'a yellow bird flies through the green boughs.'" Bao Zhao's line was taken from a *yuefu* poem "Jieke shaonian chang xing" 結客少年場行 (*Quan Song shi* 7.1267). It is also included in Xiao Tong, *Wen xuan* (28.1322). The "yellow bird" line was in fact written by Yu Yan, who edited Bao Zhao's posthumous collection; see *Quan Qi shi* 5.1459.

chaos. The Qi poet Yu Yan 虞炎 compiled Bao Zhao's collection, which, according to Yu Yan's preface, contained no more than half of his original oeuvre.

Although "extraordinary" (*qi* 奇) was a quality much admired in the Liang, its excessive form, *xian* 險 or *weize* 危仄 ("unconventional," or more precisely, "bizarre"), was open to criticism. This is also how Zhong Rong described Bao Zhao's poetry.[158] *Conversation's Underwood* (*Tan sou* 談藪), written by the northerner Yang Songjie 陽松玠 (late sixth century), recorded a story about an exchange between the poet Wu Jun and Shen Yue.

Wu Jun once wrote a couplet: "Autumn wind rushes the white water; / the feet of a wild goose printed on yellow sand." The Reticent Marquis [Shen Yue] said to him, "Printed on yellow sand—this phrase is too unconventional." Wu Jun said, "But I have read the following lines in your own poetry, 'Cherry blossoms in the mountains, newly blooming, are about to burst into flames.'" Yue said, "Mine are only *about* to burst into flames, but yours have *already* been printed."[159]

均又爲詩曰: "秋風瀧白水, 鴈足印黃沙." 沈隱侯約語之曰: "印黃沙語太險." 均曰: "亦見公詩云, '山櫻發欲然.'" 約曰: "我始欲然, 即已印訖."

Images like birds' imprints on the sand or burning flowers, which were to become commonplace in later poetry, were novel during this period and seemed a bit too peculiar. The Liang court poets sought a more balanced effect.

Xiao Zixian spelled out his paradigm for good poetry in clear terms:

Beyond the three styles described above, please allow me to lay out my own vision: a poetry that is born of natural instincts and yet consults the histories and biographies [for allusions and references]; a poetry that spontaneously responds to inspiration and is not premeditated; a poetry whose language is easy to understand and whose embellishment does not overwhelm its meaning; a poetry that disposes of the ore but keeps the gold; a poetry that is smooth, gentle, graceful, and passionate; a poetry that mixes in lines of ballads and is painless to read out aloud; a poetry that is neither too classic nor too popular, but suits the mind just right.

158. Zhong Rong, *Shi pin jizhu*, p. 290.
159. *Taiping guangji* 198.1483.

三體之外，請試妄談．若夫委自天機，參之史傳，應思悱來，勿先構聚．言尚易了，文憎過意，吐石含金，滋潤婉切．雜以風謠，輕脣利吻．不雅不俗，獨中胸懷．

Unlike Zhong Rong, who took a radical position against using allusions in poetry,[160] Xiao Zixian was more moderate, stressing inspiration and spontaneity but not downplaying the importance of "consulting the histories and biographies." Nevertheless, in this passage we see principles held in common: tonal harmony, resistance to obscure language and peculiar usages, the importance of feelings, and the exercise of restraint. These principles constitute a common poetic ideal characterized by grace.

Faced with a variety of styles and tastes, Xiao Gang, one of the most gifted and influential Liang poets, recommended wide reading and impartial absorption, a position evocative of Jiang Yan's sympathetic approach to different period and regional styles in his preface to "Various Forms."[161] In a treatise on practicing medicine, Xiao Gang made the following comment on his conception of literary writings:

It [practicing medicine] is like writing poetry: only by reading widely can one understand its principle. Whether ancient or modern, classic or popular, one must read them all without discrimination and learn their ways; then one can write beautiful poems on one's own and produce untrammeled tunes. How could one be good at poetry if one just holds the brush without being informed or be good at oratory if one shuts one's mouth and never speaks up? Yang Ziyun [Yang Xiong] once said: "Read a thousand *fu*, and then you will know how to write a *fu*."[162]

又若爲詩，則多須見意．或古或今，或雅或俗，皆須寓目，詳其去取，然後麗辭方吐，逸韻乃生．豈有秉筆不訊，而能善詩；塞兑不談，而能善義？楊子雲言：讀賦千首，則能爲賦．

Xiao Gang's observations reveal a consciousness of the literary past and various influences and are symptomatic of the passionate engagement of Liang writers, who faced a large repertoire of available texts.

---

160. Zhong Rong (*Shi pin jizhu*, p. 174) claimed that "great lines from past to present are mostly not patchworks of borrowed phrases but have come from directly writing down what one encounters."

161. *Quan Liang shi* 4.1569.

162. *Quan Liang wen* 11.3013.

CODA

In this chapter, I have sought to map out the rise of a cultural elite, whose members came from a previously marginalized background of lower gentry and native southerners. The literary landscape of the Liang, however, is much more difficult to define. The traditional practice of dividing it into antagonistic schools or camps and telling a simple literary historical story of the conflict between "classical orthodoxy" and "avant-garde decadence" turns out to be based more on prior assumptions than on actual facts and indeed has come to obscure or distort matters such as the attribution of authorship. Liang writers shared common values and terms regarding the genesis and function of literature, and the supposed leaders of the conflicting schools respected the same literary masters of the past. Even the different tastes and inclinations described in Xiao Zixian's essay reveal a deeper agreement among the Liang elite—an intense critical awareness of the continuity of a literary tradition as well as the diversity of styles available to be emulated.

Something new did, however, take place in the literature of what we may term the late Liang, namely, the innovations affected by Xiao Gang and his literary salon, which became the center of the Liang literary world after Xiao Gang returned to the capital from his provincial post at Xiangyang and was chosen as crown prince in 531. These innovations occurred in both poetry and prose (most notably *fu*), but, as noted in the Introduction, it was poetry that exerted the most far-reaching influence on later literature. Indeed, Xiao Gang's greatest contribution to the writing of *fu* was to take the formal poeticization of *fu* even further by mixing in five- and seven-syllable lines. The next two chapters examine Xiao Gang and his courtiers' Palace Style poetry closely in the hope of putting Palace Style poetry back into its cultural context and, in doing so, show it for what it once was: rather than the "flower of evil" fostered in a self-indulgent princely court, it developed out of an energetic cultural world open to "new transformation."

CHAPTER FOUR

The Pleasure of the Superfluous

Palace Style Poetry and Resistance to Canonization

This chapter explores the complicated history of how Palace Style poetry came to be understood as a poetry of decadence and how this interpretation was closely tied to a long-standing anxiety about the nature and function of literature in imperial China. To put it simply, classical Chinese literary theory, and to a large extent modern and contemporary Chinese literary theory as well, revolves around one central question: Is literature (*wen* 文) superfluous?

In reflecting on the place of *wen*, a word that refers to both cultural accomplishments in general and literature in particular, one may recall Confucius' remark in the first section of the *Analects*:

> A disciple should be filial at home and respectful of elders abroad. He should be prudent and keep his word. He should love people in general and cultivate the friendship of the benevolent. If he still has extra strength after having accomplished all these things, then he may use it to study *wen*.[1]
>
> 弟子入則孝, 出則悌, 謹而信, 汎愛眾而親仁. 行有餘力, 則以學文.

1. *Lunyu zhushu* 1.7.

Yu 餘, the word Confucius uses for "extra" here, is an interesting concept: it takes its origin from food, referring to food left over, because of an overabundance. In a poem from *The Classic of Poetry*, a guest laments that the host's hospitality has changed:

於我乎夏屋渠渠	Ah me, the plate was huge and deep,
今也每食無餘	nowadays no meal has leftovers.
于嗟乎不承權輿	Alas, what was begun is not continued!
於我乎每食四簋	Ah me, there were four dishes at every meal,
今也每食不飽	nowadays, at no meal do I get my fill,
于嗟乎不承權輿	Alas, what was begun is not continued![2]

The variation in the stanzas suggests a deterioration in the treatment of the guest. In the first stanza, the guest complains that there are no leftovers. In other words, "having no surplus" (*wuyu* 無餘) does not necessarily imply that one does not have enough: it simply means there is no extra. *Yu* therefore is something that is excessive, cannot be used up, and so is superfluous; yet it is also a necessity, something whose lack engenders feelings of anxiety and deprivation.

In the first poem of a pair entitled "Matching a Poem by Secretary Guo" ("He Guo zhubu" 和郭主簿), the Eastern Jin poet Tao Yuanming presented a picture of perfect contentment:

園蔬有餘滋	Of garden vegetables there is a surplus,
舊穀猶儲今	last year's grain is still in storage.
營己良有極	Providing for oneself does have a limit,
過足非所欽	more than enough is not my desire.
舂秫作美酒	Crushing rice to brew some wonderful ale,
酒熟吾自斟	I'll pour it myself when it is done.[3]

The surplus of garden produce and the overabundance of last year's grain form an ironic tension with the poet's declaration that "more than enough" is *not* what he wants at all. In fact, even ale itself is a luxury item, since it is made of grain. In the early third century, when the warlord Cao Cao banned spirits, Kong Rong 孔融 (153–208) saw through Cao's moralizing about the dangers of liquor and suggested the true reason for the ban: "I suspect that it is only because you begrudge the grain,

2. *Maoshi zhengyi* 614.246.
3. *Quan Jin shi* 16.978.

not because you take a lesson from those rulers who lost their states [through drinking]."[4]

The notion of "having just enough" (*zu* 足) recurs often in Tao Yuanming's poetry, but surplus (*yu*) seems to be a decisive element in constituting the sense of "having enough," as in the following dialogue from *Zhuangzi*:

Huizi said to Zhuangzi, "Your words are useless." Zhuangzi said, "Only when a person knows about uselessness can you talk to him about usefulness. It is not that heaven and earth are not vast and expansive, but what one can use of it is no more than the space to put one's feet on. And yet if you dig away the earth around the feet down to the Yellow Springs, is the ground under the feet still useful?" Huizi said, "It's useless." Zhuangzi said, "Then it is obvious how uselessness is useful."[5]

惠子謂莊子曰: "子言無用." 莊子曰: "知無用而始可與言用矣. 天地非不廣且大也, 人之所用容足耳. 然則廁足而墊之致黄泉, 人尚有用乎?" 惠子曰: "無用." 莊子曰: "然則無用之爲用也亦明矣."

As usual Huizi is trapped by Zhuangzi's sophistic argument. In a typical move, Zhuangzi contends that uselessness is in fact useful only by remaining useless. His example furnishes a good illustration of the function of "surplus" (*yu*). The "surplus ground" in his metaphor is literally *yudi* 餘地, still a resonant term today: it is the space one never occupies and yet must have in order to be able to enjoy what one does occupy.[6]

Pragmatists like Huizi always exist, and superfluity is always regarded with a sense of anxiety. It should be a good thing for a state to have extra grain in store, but even this can become a debatable point; superfluity, as opposed to mere sufficiency, may produce an excess of desire. Xunzi 荀子

4. *Quan hou Han wen* 83.923.

5. *Zhuangzi jishi* 26.936.

6. For the "surplus ground" metaphor, see also ibid., 24.871. Yan Zhitui (*Yanshi jiaxun* 10.280) took Zhuangzi's argument further: "A person's feet occupy no more than a few inches of ground, and yet if he walks on a path of a foot wide, he will certainly fall off the cliff; if he walks on a bridge made of a single narrow wood, he will certainly drown in the river. Why is this? Because there is no surplus ground around him. A gentleman, in establishing oneself, is the same: the most sincere words may not be necessarily trusted by people, and the most immaculate acts may sometimes arouse suspicion. This is all because one does not leave some extra room in one's words, actions, and reputation."

(ca. fourth–third century B.C.) advocated "overflowing surpluses" in material life (achieved through moderation), but he nevertheless warned, in the same chapter, that in matters other than material life, as in the case of music, "when they created bells, drums, flutes, chime stones, zithers, lutes, and reed pipes, they made them adequate to differentiate the auspicious from the inauspicious, to join together those who are merry and to establish harmony and nothing more, for they did not seek any surplus" (*buqiu qiyu* 不求其餘). Here the Tang commentator Yang Jing 楊倞 (ca. eighth–ninth century) annotated: "'Surplus' means 'excess' and indicates the sounds of Zheng and Wei."[7] "The sounds of Zheng and Wei" would come to be closely associated with Palace Style poetry of the Liang dynasty. Anxieties about surpluses extended to writing early on. Ban Gu, the Han historian, felt the need to defend his love of writing against an imagined interlocutor, who contemptuously referred to the activity of "composing and transmitting" as "a superfluous matter" (*yushi* 餘事).[8]

Within classical Chinese literary discourse itself, "surplus" became an important concept. The notion that poetry should not be mere surface but should have "a surplus/lingering taste" (*yuwei* 餘味) was a commonplace of later discourse on poetry. The concept of *yuwei* presents an interesting twist on the canonical statement in *The Classic of Changes* that "what is said cannot exhaust what is meant" (*yan bu jin yi* 言不盡意), a popular topic for discussion in the arcane discourse of the Eastern Jin period.[9] If "what is said cannot exhaust what is meant" conveys

7. *Xunzi jijie* 10.116.

8. *Quan hou Han wen* 25.609–10. The title of the essay is "Da bin xi" 答賓戲. The Eastern Jin writer Ge Hong 葛洪 (283–343; *Baopuzi waipian* 32.113) presented a similar hypothetical situation in which the Master had to defend literature. He argued: "Not all roots are necessarily precious, and not all branches are necessarily insignificant. It is like embroidery depending on plain silk, and pearls and jades being hidden within clams and rocks. Cloud and rain arise from one inch, and rivers begin with a foot-long stream. Although literature may be secondary to virtuous conduct, we nevertheless should not call it 'superfluous matter.'"

9. "What is written cannot exhaust what is said, and what is said cannot exhaust what is meant" (*Zhou yi* 7.157). Ouyang Jian 歐陽建 (270?–300) wrote a treatise entitled "What Is Said *Can* Exhaust What Is Meant" ("Yan jin yi lun" 言盡意論) to dispute the "common view held by the world" (*Quan Jin wen* 109.2084). "What is said can exhaust what is meant" was one of the three favorite subjects of discussion for the Eastern Jin minister Wang Dao; see Liu Yiqing, *Shishuo xinyu* 4.211.

the inadequacy of language to fully realize the intention of the speaker, then a "lingering taste" indicates the ability of language to carry more than its surface meaning, and the discrepancy between language and meaning becomes a positive value, rather than something to be deplored. This concept was first expounded by the literary critics Liu Xie and Zhong Rong.[10]

LIU XIE'S ANXIETY

Liu Xie's *Literary Mind Carving the Dragon* is an ambitious work, but perhaps because of its large scale and because of Liu Xie's use of parallel prose, it contains a number of internal inconsistencies and potential conflicts that modern scholars have tried to resolve by resorting to tortuous hypotheses and suggestions.[11] Liu Xie's plight sometimes arises from an unfortunate selection of words, words that have too much cultural and historical resonance to fit the context comfortably and so need to be fixed.

The opening chapter of this work, "Origin in the Way" ("Yuan dao" 原道), is meant to identify the source of literature and glorify its status in the cosmos. The grand argument of this chapter is that *wen* ("pattern" in general and literature in particular) is part of Nature and hence indispensable to human life:

> The human being is the flower of the elements: in fact, the mind of Heaven and Earth. When mind came into being, language was established; and with the establishment of language, pattern became manifest. This is the natural course of things, the Way. If we consider further the thousands of categories of things, each plant and animal has its own pattern. Dragon and phoenix display auspicious omens by their intricacy and bright colors; the visual appearance of a

10. See the "Encomium" to chapter 40 of *Wenxin diaolong*: "Deep writing has latent richness, / Lingering flavor folded minutely within" 深文隱蔚, 餘味曲包 (Liu Xie, *Wenxin diaolong* 40.1511; translation from Owen, *Readings in Chinese Literary Thought*, pp. 266–67). In the preface to *The Gradations of Poets*, Zhong Rong (*Shi pin jizhu*, p. 39) characterizes *xing* 興 ("affective image") as "what is said may be exhausted but what is meant lingers on" 文已盡而意有餘.

11. See Stephen Owen, "Liu Xie and the Discourse Machine" (in Cai Zong-qi, *A Chinese Literary Mind*, pp. 175–91), for a detailed discussion of the rhetorical mechanism of parallel exposition (the "discourse machine") and how it fights with the author for control over his work.

tiger is determined by its stripes, and that of a leopard, by its spots. The sculptured forms and colors of the clouds possess a subtlety that transcends the painter's craft; the intricate luxuriance of trees and plants does not depend upon the wondrous skill of an embroiderer. These are in no way external adornments: they are of Nature.[12]

[人]爲五行之秀, 實天地之心. 心生而言立, 言立而文明, 自然之道也. 傍及萬品, 動植皆文, 龍鳳以藻繪呈瑞, 虎豹以炳蔚凝姿; 雲霞雕色, 有踰畫工之妙; 草木賁華, 無待錦匠之奇. 夫豈外飾? 蓋自然耳.

Liu Xie was fond of using images taken from nature to describe literature, but when he tried to prove that everything in the universe, even inanimate things such as clouds and plants, possesses pattern (*wen*), he chose a rather troubling verb, *diao* 雕, "to sculpt," which indicates artifice and craft.

Even more troubling is the choice of the word *bi* (also pronounced *ben*) 賁, "to decorate," here translated as "intricate" in the phrase "the intricate luxuriance of trees and plants" (*caomu bihua* 草木賁華). *Bi* (or *ben*) is the name of a hexagram in *The Classic of Changes*, which the Confucian scholar Zheng Xuan 鄭玄 (127–200) glossed as "patterned ornamentation" (*wenshi* 文飾).[13] Liu Xie's awareness of the hexagram *bi* is clear from his direct reference to it in chapter 31 of his work, "The Affections and Coloration" ("Qingcai" 情采).[14] Liu Xie, an admirer of Confucius, would not have been ignorant of the story relating Confucius to this hexagram, which appears in several early works in slightly different versions:

Confucius divined and got the hexagram *bi*. He looked up and heaved a great sigh, feeling agitated. Zizhang came forward, raised his hand, and asked Confucius: "I have heard that *bi* is an auspicious hexagram. Why are you sighing?" Confucius said, "*Bi* is not the proper color. That is why I sighed. As I reflect on substance and plainness, white should be pure white and black should be pure black. So why did I get this *bi* hexagram? I have heard that red cinnabar and

12. Liu Xie, *Wenxin diaolong* 1.8; translation from Owen, *Readings in Chinese Literary Thought*, pp. 188–89.

13. *Zhou yi zhengyi* 3.62.

14. Liu Xie wrote in this chapter: "The Image of the hexagram *Bi* treats whiteness as the ultimate color: here a reversion to basics is valued" 賁象窮白, 貴乎反本 (*Wenxin diaolong* 31.1168; translation from Owen, *Readings in Chinese Literary Thought*, p. 244).

black lacquer are not patterned, white jade is not carved, and precious pearls are not decorated. This is because things that possess overabundant substance no longer receive ornamentation."[15]

孔子卦得賁，喟然仰而歎息，意不平．子張進，舉手而問曰："師聞賁者吉卦，而歎之乎?"孔子曰："賁非正色也，是以歎之．吾思夫質素，白當正白，黑當正黑，夫質[賁]又何也? 吾亦聞之，丹漆不文，白玉不彫，寶珠不飾，何也? 質有餘者，不受飾也."

Bi was generally understood as ornamentation, but it also functioned as a borrowed character for *ban* 斑, "variegated color."[16] This was why Confucius felt that *bi* violated the purity of colors and hence was not "proper." *Bi* is thus closely related to patterning, *wen* 文. Also of interest here is Confucius' comment on the relationship between substance and ornamentation: when something possesses "overabundant substance" (*zhi youyu* 質有餘), ornamentation is superfluous and unnecessary. Indeed, in a different context Confucius supposedly said: "The language is to be adequate to what is on the person's mind, and the patterning (*wen*) is to be adequate to the language. If a person does not use language, who will know what is on his mind? If the language lacks patterning, it will not go far."[17] Here patterning is understood as secondary to language, and language as secondary to "what is on the person's mind." Thrice removed from the center of concern, patterning, like a pretty piece of gift-wrapping paper, must prove adequate or sufficient to the language. Whenever the concept of "adequacy" surfaces, there is always the danger of overflowing and superfluity.

Confucius understood *bi* as precisely the outer ornamentation at risk of becoming superfluous. In the *Lüshi chunqiu* 呂氏春秋 version of the story, the disciple asking the question is Zigong, the most eloquent of Confucius' disciples. Zigong was the one who claimed that patterning was substance and substance was patterning; deprived of their patterned pelts, tigers and leopards would be no different from dogs and sheep.[18]

---

15. Liu Xiang, *Shuo yuan* 20.597. See also *Lüshi chunqiu* 22.1511; and *Kongzi jiayu* 2.61.

16. Knoblock and Riegel (*The Annals of Lü Buwei*, p. 577) translate *bi* as "variegated" in their translation of *Lüshi chunqiu*.

17. *Chunqiu Zuozhuan zhengyi* 36.623; translation from Owen, *Readings in Chinese Literary Thought*, p. 29.

18. *Lunyu zhushu* 12.107.

Zigong's comment is echoed in Liu Xie's praise for the stripes and spots of tigers and leopards.

Perhaps this explains Liu Xie's defensive conclusion: "These are in no way external adornments: they are of Nature." Both *bi* and *wen* have an unfortunate resonance. Always in danger of being considered "superfluous," they need constant justification.

PLAYING CHESS

Another problem in Liu Xie's model of "natural course of things" (*ziran zhi dao* 自然之道) is even more profound. Unlike tigers or leopards and trees or plants, a human being has neither a colorful pelt nor bright flowers. The "human pattern" (*ren wen* 人文) is manifested differently, not through the organic human body. Ideally it should "come forth from feeling" (*yuanqing* 緣情),[19] which ensures its "naturalness." As Liu Xie himself pointed out, however, there are always writers who "produce feeling for the sake of *wen*" (*wei wen er zao qing* 爲文而造情).[20] If *wen* can be produced out of feeling that is in turn produced for the sake of making *wen*, then *wen* risks being exterior to the writer: not just in the sense that, unlike the pattern and colors of tigers and clouds, it is on the outside of the human body rather than being an integral part of it, but also in the sense that *wen* is separated from the author and kept at a distance.

The mainstream of premodern Chinese literary theory held that poetry "sings forth one's feelings and innate nature" (*yinyong qingxing* 吟詠情性).[21] At the same time, however, there was an undercurrent of a different poetics, one in direct opposition to the established belief that writings should be a natural manifestation of the writer's feeling. This alternative poetics never became, or could become, canonical, but it derived its force exactly from its repression. Its marginalization created an eloquent tension in premodern Chinese literary discourse.

Zhong Rong's preface to *The Gradations of Poets* contains an unobtrusive passage:

19. Lu Ji, "*Fu* on Literature" ("Wen fu" 文賦), in *Quan Jin wen* 97.2013.
20. Liu Xie, *Wenxin diaolong* 31.1158.
21. See the "Great Preface" to *The Classic of Poetry* (*Maoshi zhengyi* 1.15).

In the past people were placed in nine categories, and gentlemen (*shi*) were divided into seven classes. But when we measure such evaluations by comparing reputation and reality, we discover that the two often do not match each other. Poetry, however, is a craft, and so can be clearly known. If we define poetry by categorical analogy, it is like the playing of chess.[22]

昔九品論人, 七略裁士, 校以賓實, 誠多未值. 至若詩之爲技, 較爾可知. 以類推之, 殆同博弈.

Chess playing is used in *Mencius* as an example of the importance of the ability to focus on studying: "Now chess playing is a minor skill, but if one does not focus one's mind on it, then one cannot acquire it."[23] Mencius tried to drive home the lesson that chess playing was a skill that could be mastered as long as one put one's heart into it. Clearly, characterizing the writing of poetry as akin to chess playing could be problematic. The writing of poetry would then be regarded as a skill (*ji* 技), or workmanship. Zhong Rong elsewhere voiced the conventional view that poetry sings forth one's feeling and one's nature, but here in the comparison to chess playing, poetry as a skill becomes separated from the poet. It is easier, Zhong Rong implies, to evaluate poetry than it is to evaluate people precisely because the performance of a skill, with its technical standards, is easier to judge than the behavior of a complex human being.

Contrary to the view of the modern scholar Cao Xu that "it was customary during the Six Dynasties to compare literature to chess playing,"[24] the only other example of this comparison in this period is found in the chapter of Liu Xie's *Literary Mind Carving the Dragon* entitled "The General Technique" ("Zong shu" 總術):

Thus to lay hold of these techniques and guide a piece is much like a chess master's full understanding of the methods of chess playing. To abandon the techniques and follow the dictates of the heart is like rolling the dice and hoping for good luck. Writing done by the roll of the dice may receive some fine points of art unexpectedly, but even though [such a writer] may achieve something in speeding ahead, he cannot continue it later on.[25]

---

22. Zhong Rong, *Shi pin jizhu*, p. 66.
23. *Mengzi zhushu* 11b.201.
24. Zhong Rong, *Shi pin jizhu*, p. 68.
25. Liu Xie, *Wenxin diaolong* 44.1642; translation (modified), from Owen, *Readings in Chinese Literary Thought*, p. 275.

是以執術馭篇，似善弈之窮數；棄術任心，如博塞之邀遇．故博塞之文，借巧儻來，雖前驅有功，而後援難繼．

Liu Xie's idea of "general technique" was vague enough to generate much discussion among later scholars, but one thing is clear: he did not endorse writing "at will" (*ren xin*, "following the dictates of the heart"). His ideal writer arranges things "by group and ranks, awaiting the proper conjunction of the affections" (*anbu zhengwu, yi dai qing hui* 按部整伍，以待情會).[26] Here Liu Xie employed a military metaphor as a continuation of the figure of chess playing, a competitive, militant game: a small army of words and stanzas, led by principles of organization, all at the writer-general's disposal, must wait quietly and patiently to merge forces with—or perhaps to ambush?—a lone sentiment innocently passing by. When "the timely moment" comes, these cunning soldiers should "seize the opportunity" and "never miss what is proper."[27] In these descriptions, like a general manipulating his army or a chess player moving his chess pieces, the writer bears a rather impersonal, tactical relationship to his writings.

Liu Xie insisted on the primacy of feeling in the production of *wen*, and he also apparently believed that for the reader this process also worked in the opposite direction in the sense that the reader could reach the feelings of the author through reading a literary work: "In the case of composing literary writings, the affections are stirred and words come forth; but in the case of reading a work of literature, one opens the text and enters the affections [of the writer], goes against the currents to find the source; and though it may [at first] be hidden, it will certainly become manifest."[28] Elsewhere Liu Xie confidently asserted that "a work may be clever, but one can recognize its falseness when examining its traces."[29] He even prescribed a six-step process that facilitated judgment of a piece of writing.[30] The six-step model is based

26. Liu Xie, *Wenxin diaolong* 44.1645; translation from Owen, *Readings in Chinese Literary Thought*, p. 276.

27. Liu Xie, *Wenxin diaolong* 44.1645; translation from Owen, *Readings in Chinese Literary Thought*, p. 276.

28. Liu Xie, *Wenxin diaolong* 48.1855; translation from Owen, *Readings in Chinese Literary Thought*, p. 290.

29. Liu Xie, *Wenxin diaolong* 18.699.

30. Ibid., 48.1853.

on the eight stages of knowing a person prescribed in Liu Shao's 劉邵 (ca. second–third century) *An Account of People* (*Renwu zhi* 人物志),[31] and Liu Xie's ultimate purpose indeed lies in "knowing the writer" through reading his works: "We shall never set eyes on their faces across the distance of many ages, but by looking at their writings, we may see their minds."[32] The question then becomes: what if the writer declares a total separation between his writing and himself?

Yan Zhitui, who started his official career in the South and later went North, observed in his *Family Instructions* a "cultural difference" between the two regions:

> In the South, when people write something, they want others to criticize it, so that they know what is wrong with it and can then correct it accordingly. This is what the Prince of Chen [Cao Zhi] once learned from Ding Yi.[33] In the North, people do not understand the point of offering criticism. When I first arrived at the City of Ye [the capital of the Northern Qi], I offended people because of my habit of criticizing people's writings, which I still regret even now.[34]
>
> 江南文制, 欲人彈射, 知有病累, 隨即改之, 陳王得之於丁廙也. 山東風俗, 不通擊難. 吾初入鄴, 遂嘗以此忤人, 至今爲悔.

In warning his children against the practice of criticism, Yan Zhitui recorded an interesting custom in the South: following others' suggestions in revising one's writings. If *wen* was the outer manifestation of a person's inner being, how could one allow others to participate in the process? A technical aspect to literary writings lurks uncomfortably

31. Liu Shao, *Renwu zhi*, pp. 154–96.

32. Ibid., 48.1855.

33. Ding Yi 丁廙 (d. 220) once asked Cao Zhi for help in revising his writings. Seeing Cao Zhi's hesitation, Ding Yi said, "Why should you hesitate? Whether my writings will turn out good or bad, it is my problem. Who in the later generations would know someone else had revised my writings?" Cao Zhi thought well of such open-mindedness (*Quan sanguo wen* 16.1140).

34. Yan Zhitui, *Yanshi jiaxun* 9.259. Interestingly, the modern scholar Wang Liqi (ibid., 9.260) tries to gloss the phrase *binglei* 病累 ("what is wrong with [a piece of writing]") as defects in metrics (*shengbing* 聲病), a minor aspect that would not influence the content of the writings. But such a reading is neither immediately clear from the context nor supported by Yan Zhitui's reference to Cao Zhi and Ding Yi, since a consciousness of "defects in metrics" was a late fifth-century phenomenon rather than a second- or third-century phenomenon.

beneath the canonical statements about what literature should be. It contravenes the claims that naturalness and authenticity are the most important values.

Literary writings can therefore open up a space in which a writer may assume a voice that is not his or her own. Yan Zhitui sensed danger in the practice of writing on behalf of someone else: "When you write on behalf of another person, you always assume that person's voice, which is only appropriate. But when it comes to words of sorrow upon encountering disasters and misfortunes, you should not utter them in another's place." He then listed a number of famous writers such as Cai Yong and Wang Can, who wrote prose and poetry commemorating another person's deceased parents or ancestors and then included these writings in their own collections. "Although the ancients carried out such a practice," Yan Zhitui continued, "nowadays it is forbidden."[35] The possibility of assuming another person's identity in a piece of writing was troubling—there is always anxiety about the simulation of a voice "not one's own."

Some time between 535 and 541, a father thus advised his teenage son in a letter:

> You are still very young, and what you lack is learning. The only thing that endures and glorifies the person is learning. That is why Confucius said, "I once did not eat all day and did not sleep all night, devoting myself to reflection; it had no benefit. It would have been better to study."[36] If one stands facing the wall and is like a monkey wearing a hat, this is what I would not approve. The way of establishing oneself is different from the way of writing. In establishing oneself, one should first of all be cautious and circumspect; in writing one needs to be free and uninhibited.[37]
>
> 汝年時尚幼, 所闕者學, 可久可大, 其唯學歟. 所以孔丘言: "吾嘗終日不食, 終夜不寢, 以思, 無益, 不如學也." 若使牆面而立, 沐猴而冠, 吾所不取. 立身之道, 與文章異: 立身先須謹重, 文章且須放蕩.

The father emphasized the importance of studying and used two allusions to enliven his sober counsels. In the first, he assumed the voice of another father—Confucius. Confucius had advised his own son to study the "Zhounan" and "Shaonan," the first two sections of *The Classic of*

---

35. Ibid., 9.260–61.
36. *Lunyu zhushu* 15.140.
37. *Quan Liang wen* 11.3010.

Poetry, saying that being unacquainted with the "Zhounan" and "Shaonan" was like standing with one's face to the wall.[38] The second allusion was to the warrior-general Xiang Yu 項羽 (232–202 BC). After Xiang Yu overthrew the Qin dynasty, he burned down its palaces, gathered up all his loot, and longed to go back to his home region in Chu, saying: "To become rich and powerful and yet not to go home is like putting on brocade clothes and walking in the dark night—who will know about it?" One of his advisors commented: "They say that the Chu people are like monkeys wearing hats; now I know what they mean."[39] A monkey would throw the hat away not long after putting it on, and so the saying seems to imply a lack of patience and persistence.

What has drawn attention throughout the ages is, however, not the father's exhortation to study, but the view expressed in the last sentences of the letter: "The way of establishing oneself is different from the way of writing. In establishing oneself, one should first of all be cautious and circumspect; in writing one needs to be free and uninhibited." The phrase "free and uninhibited" (*fangdang* 放蕩) has been interpreted variously, from licentious abandon to letting the literary imagination roam free.[40] More interesting is the opposition between the establishment of the self and literary writing. In this formula, *wen* is completely dissociated from the writer's self (*shen* 身).

APPRAISING THE BOIL: THE CASE OF XU CHI

The letter cited above was written by Xiao Gang to his second son, Xiao Daxin 蕭大心 (523–51), the Duke of Dangyang 當陽公.[41] In the eyes of the *Liang shu* historians, Yao Cha and Yao Silian 姚思廉 (557–637), Xiao Gang was nearly impeccable as a person: they portrayed him

38. *Lunyu zhushu* 17.156.

39. *Shi ji* 7.295–96, 7.315.

40. For the former viewpoint, see Gui Qing, "Wenzhang." For the latter viewpoint, see Xu Zhongyu, "Wenzhang"; and Zhao Changping, "Wenzhang."

41. Xiao Daxin was made the Duke of Dangyang in 532. He served as the governor of Yingzhou from 535 to 541 and then was called back to the capital until appointed governor of Jiangzhou in 547. Xiao Gang's letter was most likely written when Xiao Daxin was at Yingzhou.

as wise, learned, adept at managing civil and military affairs, filial, forgiving, articulate, and dignified; indeed, his only failing seems to have been his adoption of a "frivolous and alluring" poetic style.[42] Xiao Gang's letter is thus often taken to reflect both his own personality and his writing style: *fangdang*, translated above as "free and uninhibited," a term that came to be associated with sexual licentiousness only in later times, is regarded by many scholars as descriptive of the kind of poetry Xiao Gang was writing, the Palace Style.

What, after all, is the Palace Style (*gongti* 宮體)? The next chapter gives a much more detailed discussion of the nature of Palace Style poetry; here two essential facts about the Palace Style are pertinent. First, it is a historical term; to be precise, it is a name given to the poetry written by Xiao Gang and his courtiers in the last two decades of the Liang, with "palace" referring specifically to the Eastern Palace, the crown prince's residence. Second, the *ti* 體 in *gongti* indicates a style, a form, and does not necessarily have anything to do with the content or the subject matter of the poetry.[43]

The *Liang shu* historians attributed the origin of the term to Xu Chi, twenty-nine years Xiao Gang's senior and one of his most loyal courtiers:

> [Xu Chi] liked novel transformation in writing and was not constrained by the old styles. . . . Since Chi's style was so peculiar, everyone in the Spring Residence [the Crown Prince's residence] began to imitate it. The designation of "Palace Style" thus arose from this.[44]
>
> 屬文好爲新變,不拘舊體.... 摛文體既別,春坊盡學之,宮體之號,自斯而起.

All this is very vague: precisely what, for example, is meant by "novel transformation"? Yao Cha observed in the biography of another well-known Palace Style writer, Yu Jianwu: "During the Yongming era of the Qi, men of letters such as Wang Rong, Xie Tiao, and Shen Yue began using the four tones in their writing as a novel transformation. By this

42. *Liang shu* 4.109.

43. Shen Yucheng ("Gongti shi," p. 58) rightly points out that whereas Yao Cha considers Palace Style in formal terms, the Tang historians regard Palace Style as a poetry about women; he also admits that he sides with Yao Cha, although he still believes that "romantic love" is the most common topic in Palace Style poetry, a statement which I do not agree with. This is discussed below.

44. *Liang shu* 30.446–47.

time [531] they observed metrical rules even more strictly and admired ornate sumptuousness even more ardently than before."[45] This remark is often cited in defining the "Palace Style," but a stricter attention to metrical rules and greater rhetorical ornamentation developed over time in the course of the first half of the sixth century and have never been specified as the sort of "novel transformation" initiated by Xu Chi. In other words, the quantitative increase in attention to prosody and rhetorical ornamentation does not add up to an essentially qualitative innovation.

What, after all, set Xu Chi apart from his contemporaries or predecessors, many of whom had surely written about women and romantic love in a "frivolous and alluring" manner? What made Xu Chi's style so distinctive, so "peculiar," that it was imitated by everyone else? These questions lead us back to the frustratingly vague descriptions such as "more ornate and more sumptuous," which, as noted above, do not clarify the issue.

The almost complete loss of Xu Chi's literary corpus does not help either. There is, in fact, something rather strange about the silence surrounding Xu Chi's writings. *The History of the Liang* usually takes especial care to record the state of a person's literary writings at the end of his biography, but curiously not one word is recorded about Xu Chi's oeuvre.[46] Furthermore, the two leading Palace Style poets, Yu Jianwu and Xu Chi, receive different treatment in *The History of the Liang.* Unlike Yu Jianwu, Xu Chi's much more detailed biography was not included in the "Biographies of Men of Letters," an indication that he was regarded as more than a literary figure.

In 509 Xu Chi was assigned as tutor to the six-year-old Xiao Gang. From then on, Xu Chi almost never left the prince, apart from a few years while he was observing the mourning period for his parents or serving in a provincial post. He also won Emperor Wu over with his learning and eloquence. During the Hou Jing Rebellion, all the attendants fled as Hou Jing and his men marched into the imperial palace; Xu Chi was the only one who remained by Xiao Gang's side. He stood still and said to Hou Jing: "Mister Hou should seek audience [with the

45. *Liang shu* 49.690.
46. Ibid., 49.692.

crown prince] in an appropriate manner. How can you behave like this?" According to *The History of the Liang*, "Hou Jing's ferocity broke down, and he subsequently bowed to the crown prince. Henceforth he was always apprehensive of Xu Chi."[47] *The Southern History* says admiringly of Xu Chi: "Loyal and upright, this benevolent man indeed also possessed courage."[48] Later, Xu Chi fell ill after he was forbidden to see Xiao Gang and died at the age of seventy-six. We can be fairly certain that throughout his long career Xu Chi must have produced a fair amount of writing; yet not only do the dynastic biographies neglect to mention his literary collection, but even the comprehensive "Bibliography" in *The History of the Sui* compiled in the early seventh century fails to record a collection of Xu Chi's works. Perhaps the most striking fact is that despite his reputation as the initiator of the Palace Style, none of Xu Chi's poems was included in *Yutai xinyong*, which has always been considered *the* anthology of Palace Style poetry.

Why do we meet with this strange silence wherever we look for Xu Chi's works? Could they have been destroyed during the Hou Jing Rebellion? In 622, as a minister was transporting the Sui imperial book collection to the Tang capital of Chang'an, a boating accident caused the loss of 80–90 percent of the collection, and the catalogue of the collection was damaged as well. Could Xu Chi's collection have been among the lost books?[49]

The modern scholar Liu Yuejin speculates that one explanation for the omission of Xu Chi's poetry from *Yutai xinyong* might be that by the time Xu Ling compiled the anthology during the Chen dynasty all of Xu Chi's writings had been lost.[50] This is quite unlikely, because at least some of Xu Chi's works did survive the wars. A few extant pieces can be found in the two Tang encyclopedias: *Yiwen leiju* and *Chuxue ji*. *Yiwen leiju* contains one poem on curtain dust, one on a damaged bridge, and one on an orange, along with three couplets from a poem on a writing brush, and four lines from a "*Fu* on the Rolled Heart of a Winter

---

47. Ibid., 30.446–48.

48. *Nan shi*, 62.1531. This is an allusion to the *Analects*: "Confucius said, 'The benevolent man must also have courage, but the courageous one does not necessarily have benevolence'" (*Lunyu zhushu*, 14.123).

49. *Sui shu* 32.908.

50. Liu Yuejin, "*Yutai xinyong*" *yanjiu*, pp. 84–87.

Plantain" ("Dongjiao juanxin fu" 冬蕉卷心賦).[51] *Chuxue ji* contains what is apparently the entirety of the poem on a brush.[52] The Tang poet Bai Juyi 白居易 (772–846) was also acquainted with Xu Chi's poetry, although we do not know how much of Xu Chi's oeuvre Bai had seen. His *Baishi liutie shileiji* 白氏六帖事類集 includes one line from the poem on a brush,[53] but it is possible that Bai Juyi copied it from earlier encyclopedias rather than from a collection of Xu Chi's works.[54]

Since many early medieval literary works survive only because they were included in anthologies or encyclopedias, then one possible reason for the conspicuous absence of Xu Chi's writings might be that his subject matter did not fit the inclusion criteria of those sources. Like all anthologies, encyclopedias have an agenda. The first criterion for selecting a piece of writing is whether it can be accommodated under one of the categories in a topically arranged encyclopedia. Certain topics never qualified for inclusion. *Chuxue ji*, for instance, does not have a category on "illness." In *Yiwen leiju*, "illness" is a subdivision, along with medicine and divination, under the heading "Techniques" ("Fangshu" 方術), and not, as the *Siku quanshu* editors complained, under the more appropriate category of "Human Beings."[55] All the items under the subheading "Illness" deal with illness in general, rather than the particulars of specific diseases or concrete symptoms. Therefore, the fragment of a writing by Xu Chi, however highly regarded by contemporaries as a fine example of his "novel transformation," may well have never met the inclusion criteria of Tang encyclopedias.

The fragment in questions deals with the unseemly subject of a "boil" (*yong* 癰). Taken from a lost sixth-century work, *Conversation's Underwood* by Yang Songjie, it appears under the category of "Humor"

51. *Yiwen leiju* 6.110, 9.182, 86.1478, 58.1055, 87.1499.

52. *Chuxue ji* 1962; 21.516.

53. Bai Juyi, *Baishi liutie* 4.198.

54. The twelfth-century anthology *Yuefu shiji* has one *yuefu* poem by Xu Chi. Again, the compiler could have taken the poem from an earlier *yuefu* anthology rather than from Xu Chi's collection.

55. *Yiwen leiju*, p. 8. Instead of understanding categorization as a historical phenomenon reflecting the Tang people's view of the cosmos, the *Siku quanshu* editors raised a series of what they felt were "misjudgments" on the part of the *Yiwen leiju* editors in terms of categorization.

("Huixie" 詼諧) in the early Song compilation *Taiping guangji* (completed in 977) and is partially preserved in another Song encyclopedia, *Taiping yulan* (completed in 983) under the category of "Human Affairs: Liver" ("Renshi: gan" 人事: 肝).

The Palace Attendant of Liang Xu Chi of Donghai was the son of Xu Chao, the Senior Recorder. He was learned and talented. He favored novel transformation in his writings and was not constrained by old forms. He once described someone suffering from a boil: "The vermilion blood flows at night, and yellow pus pours out during the day. Looking from the side, one sees purple lungs; observing from the front, one catches sight of a red liver." And then, "A curtain hangs from the window—one clearly knows it is a bamboo screen; the swimming fish feels apprehensive about the net—obviously it has seen the fisherman's trap." And then, "His appearance is certainly not that of a fast horse, and yet his feet touch one another; his mat differs from that of a Confucian scholar, and yet he always reclines with the Classics."[56]

梁侍中東海徐摛, 散騎常侍超之子也. 博學多才, 好爲新變, 不拘舊體. 常體一人病癰曰: "朱血夜流, 黃膿晝瀉. 斜看紫肺, 正視紅肝." 又曰: "户上懸簾, 明知是箔; 魚游畏網, 判是見罾." 又曰: "狀非快馬, 蹋腳相連; 席異儒生, 帶經長臥."

Several things stand out in these lines: they strictly observe the metrical rules, they are marked by clever parallelism, and they contain ingenious puns. In the second passage cited by Yang Songjie, the bamboo screen, *bo* 箔, puns with 薄, "to despise," and so the couplet also means: "A curtain hangs from the window—[the condition of the boil] is clearly despised by others." However, *bo*, "to despise," also means "thin and light," which perfectly describes a bamboo screen. In the next couplet, the fisherman's trap, *zeng* 罾, puns with *zeng* 憎, "to be repulsed by," and so the couplet may also read: "A swimming fish is apprehensive of the net, which is clearly considered repulsive." What is considered "repulsive" here is the condition of the boil.

The third passage depicts the sufferer in a reclining position and curling up his legs, which makes him look like a galloping horse. According to the chapter on boils and sores in the medical work *The Inner Classic of the Yellow Emperor* (*Huangdi neijing* 黃帝內經), if a boil grows on the neck, it has to be treated immediately; if its "hot energy" goes

56. *Taiping guangji* 246.1909. See also *Taiping yulan* 376.1866.

into the liver and lungs, the person is beyond cure.[57] This is perhaps why the lungs and liver are mentioned in the passage cited above. Red and purple are, unlike vermilion and yellow, "improper colors."

The topic and the way in which the writer dealt with it are striking. An unpleasant and malodorous disease is portrayed in the most ornate parallel prose. The bursting of a boil, with the blood and pus pouring out, was often used as a metaphor for taking a painful but necessary step to end a thorny situation. Here its messiness is brought under tight linguistic control, producing a tension between the foulness of the disease and the "sumptuous" and "alluring" word play. This is the first time we see a writer applying the most decorous and mannered prose form to unseemly topics: blood, pus, slow suffering, and people's unsympathetic abhorrence of such a gruesome malady. This is also the first time a "boil" became an aesthetic topic, instead of a passing metaphor.

The literary discourse of disease is culturally and socially prescribed. An extensive account of a foul disease was never popular in classical Chinese literature, and the charm of later vernacular literature to a great extent lies in its breaking of the conventions of high literature, although even in this sphere disease and death are rarely treated in great detail. In early Chinese literature, illness is often described in vague, general terms; except in medical works, the depiction of diseases is highly conventionalized. Xu Chi's portrayal of a person suffering from a boil is therefore quite unprecedented. It is novel in its formal features as well as in its choice of subject matter. One possible reason for the paucity of extant works by Xu Chi might have been the peculiar quality of Xu Chi's choice of topics: there is no place, for instance, for the portrayal of a boil in either *Yiwen leiju* or *Chuxue ji*. Similarly, *Yutai xinyong* is an anthology whose selections were determined primarily by content, and the exclusion of the arch–Palace Style writer Xu Chi's poetry casts doubt on the assumption that *Yutai xinyong* was meant to be the representative anthology of Palace Style poetry.

Xu Chi's description of the boil is likewise missing in the monumental work *Complete Prose of Antiquity, the Three Dynasties, Qin, Han, the Three Kingdoms, and the Six Dynasties* (*Quan shanggu sandai Qin Han sanguo liuchao wen* 全上古三代秦漢三國六朝文) compiled by the Qing

57. *Huangdi neijing* 81.615.

scholar Yan Kejun 嚴可均 (1762–1843). Could Yan Kejun have overlooked it when he was combing through the Song encyclopedias? It is not impossible, but the more likely answer is that Yan Kejun saw the anecdote but did not consider Xu Chi's lines a piece of *wen*. He could have, for instance, regarded them as simply a "joke," the very category under which the anecdote was included in the *Taiping yulan*.

One of Xu Chi's two prose pieces that Yan Kejun did include is "A Disquisition on a Daughter-in-Law's Meeting with Her Parents-in-law" ("Fu jian jiugu yi" 婦見舅姑議), which he culled from Xu Chi's biography in *The History of the Liang*.[58] This piece is Xu Chi's discussion of a ritual topic on the occasion of the marriage of Xiao Gang's son Xiao Dalin 蕭大臨 (527–51). The question is whether the new daughter-in-law, three days after her wedding, should formally meet with her parents-in-law in the presence of wedding guests. "Disquisition" (*yi* 議) is listed as a genre in Cao Pi's "A Discourse on Literature," and an entire chapter of *Literary Mind Carving the Dragon* is devoted to the "disquisition and reply" ("Yidui" 議對).[59] In Xu Chi's biography, his "disquisition" on the ritual topic is presented as a direct answer to Xiao Gang's question in an apparently oral context; indeed, it is laid out in a straightforward, prosaic style. In every way Xu Chi's "disquisition" looks like an oral response, whereas his description of the boil, although presented in an anecdotal framework, can hardly be considered a verbal witticism because of its elaborate formal features, such as sophisticated parallelism. During the Liang, Xu Chi's portrayal of the boil would much more likely have been regarded as *wen* than would his discussion of the wedding rites. Yan Kejun's exclusion of the lines on the boil seems to reveal the ideological weight being carried into genre theory.

Xu Chi's portrayal of the boil, like a boil itself, becomes at last a superfluous thing, an excrescence. For later scholars, it floats outside the complex system of *wen*, unsure of its place between the liver—the source of that sanguine blood—and the darker humor arising therein. In a way, it is symbolic of the fate of Palace Style poetry: serving no practical function, it was caught up in a cultural system in which any surplus had to be appropriated and contained.

58. *Liang shu* 30.448.

59. *Quan sanguo wen* 8.1098; Liu Xie, *Wenxin diaolong* 18.669.

THE NORTHERNERS' VERDICT

As said above, the omission of any poem by Xu Chi, the originator of the Palace Style, from *Yutai xinyong* invites us to rethink the definition of Palace Style poetry as well as the claim that *Yutai xinyong* is its "representative" anthology.[60] The conventional definition of Palace Style poetry and the anthology reinforce each other and form a circle that is difficult to break. An examination of the history of this connection reveals some interesting junctures long obscured by a cultural tradition intensely opposed to the values represented by Palace Style poetry.

The Tang historian Wei Zheng 魏徵 (580–643) seems to have been the first person to associate Palace Style poetry explicitly with the boudoir:

When Emperor Jianwen of the Liang [Xiao Gang] was in the Eastern Palace, he also loved literary writings. The range of his lucid pieces and artful compositions was confined to pillows and mats; in his elaborate carvings and ornate words, his thoughts were limited to the boudoir. All the younger generation who loved such fuss and ado imitated his style, which was named the "Palace

60. In the twentieth century, Palace Style poetry is defined mainly by subject matter, since this seems to be the easiest way of discussing Palace Style poetry or poetry in general. Cao Daoheng and Shen Yucheng's (*Nanbeichao wenxue shi*, p. 241) definition probably best summarizes the mainstream conception of Palace Style poetry: (1) Palace Style poetry observes metrical rules more strictly; (2) its style progressed from "lightly decorated" to "heavily ornate"; (3) its subject matter is composed primarily of romantic feelings verging on eroticism (*yanqing* 艷情) and portrayal of (mostly boudoir) objects (*yongwu* 咏物). Ronald Miao ("Palace-Style Poetry," p. 1) has explicitly described Palace Style as "a thematic designation for Chinese verse centered on the life of the imperial residence." Anne Birrell (*Games Poets Play*, p. 5) also links Palace Style poetry with "a single, amatory theme." Depending on how Palace Style poetry is defined, some scholars believe that Palace Style had sprouted long before the Liang; see Liu Shipei, *Zhongguo zhonggu*, p. 97; Lin Wenyue, "Nanchao," pp. 406–58; and Shi Guanhai, *Gongti shipai*. Based on a thematic understanding of Palace Style poetry, Hu Dalei (*Gongti*) traces the "origin" back to *Shijing* and *Chuci*. For an overview of the study of Palace Style poetry in the twentieth century, see Xu Yuru, "Gongtishi"; Wang Shungui and Hu Jianci, "Ershi shiji"; and Wu Yun, *Wei Jin nanbeichao*, pp. 440–49. These overviews generally fail to take into consideration articles by Taiwan and overseas scholars.

Style" and known to courtiers and commoners. Its influence flowed on ceaselessly until the demise of the dynasty.[61]

梁簡文之在東宮, 亦好篇什, 清辭巧製, 止乎衽席之間; 彫琢蔓藻, 思極閨闈之內. 後生好事, 遞相仿習, 朝野紛紛, 號爲宮體, 流宕不已, 訖于喪亡.

As we can see, whereas the *Liang shu* historians considered the writing of Palace Style poetry as merely a regrettable blemish on the otherwise impeccable character of a fine prince, the Tang historian, operating from the moralistic standpoint of the conquest dynasty, interwove the description of the Palace Style into the narrative of dynastic fall.

About five centuries after the fall of the Liang, another historian, Sima Guang, again meted out a judgment against Xiao Gang; for Sima, he was the major culprit behind Palace Style poetry because Xiao Gang, unlike the other members of his coterie, would become an emperor. The judgment was, however, delivered in a strange fashion. It was couched in a letter addressed to Emperor Wu of the Liang by the rebel general Hou Jing, who had been besieging the Palace City for three months and, now reneging on his commitment to a truce, was preparing his final attack. The letter listed "ten mistakes" Hou Jing claimed Emperor Wu had made. *The History of the Liang* cites the letter in its entirety, but the eleventh-century historian Sima Guang included in the *Zizhi tongjian* only a passage he claimed that Hou Jing had added *after* listing the "ten mistakes," a passage found neither in *The History of the Liang* nor in *The Southern History*. Part of the passage directly concerns Xiao Gang:

The crown prince loves only pearls and jades and indulges in wine and women. When he speaks up, his speeches stop at being frivolous and shallow; when he writes, his compositions do not go beyond "In the Mulberries."[62]

皇太子珠玉是好, 酒色是耽. 吐言止于輕薄, 賦詠不出桑中.

According to Sima Guang, upon reading this letter, Emperor Wu was "both ashamed and angry." For fear that we might miss the subtle moral message, the commentator Hu Sanxing added a note here: "This

61. *Sui shu* 35.1090. Although the *Sui shu* was compiled by a number of historians, Wei Zheng was the supervisor of the project and authored all commentaries as well as the "Bibliography."

62. *Zizhi tongjian* 162.1278. "In the Mulberries" refers to Poem 48 in *The Classic of Poetry*, which deals with a romantic encounter.

means that all Hou Jing said was true, and so the emperor felt embarrassed and upset."

And yet, a comparison of Sima Guang's version of Hou Jing's letter with the letter preserved in *The History of the Liang* reveals some interesting discrepancies. At the beginning of the letter as recorded in *The History of the Liang*, Hou Jing wrote:

> Your Majesty is wise and talented in many things. In the past, when the world was in decline, you rose from the region of the Han and Mian rivers like a dragon and brought an end to disorder and chaos. . . . You took care of myriads of affairs and were diligent in pursuing the way of ruling in peace. You have collated the writings left behind by the Duke of Zhou and Confucius and expounded the mysteries of Buddhist truths. No monarch's arts and accomplishments could possibly compare with yours. That is why I leapt in joy in a distant corner of the world and sighed at the wind from the South. And yet, who would have expected that name did not accord with reality, and what one heard was different from what one sees.[63]
>
> 竊惟陛下睿智在躬, 多才多藝. 昔因世季, 龍翔漢、沔, 夷凶剪亂. . . . 躬覽萬機, 劬勞治道. 刊正周、孔之遺文, 訓釋眞如之祕奧. 享年長久, 本枝盤石. 人君藝業, 莫之與京. 臣所以踊躍一隅, 望南風而歎息也. 豈圖名與實爽, 聞見不同.

Hou Jing then engaged in a long tirade against Emperor Wu's "ten mistakes," all of which involved current events and issues directly touching on Hou Jing himself. The passage cited above is, however, completely missing from *Zizhi tongjian*. We know that Sima Guang used sources other than the standard dynastic histories, and it is quite possible that the part of Hou Jing's letter in *Zizhi tongjian* was taken from a now-lost source. And yet, in comparing the different parts of the letter, one cannot help noticing that Sima Guang's cutting and pasting produced dramatically different results. In *The History of the Liang* version, Hou Jing is saying that Emperor Wu, basically a good monarch, has done *him*, Hou Jing, wrong; in the *Zizhi tongjian* version, he is charging Emperor Wu with general misrule. Sima Guang, the stern Confucian moralist, seems to be using the opportunity to pass his own judgment on the Liang.

Written "history" is nothing more than a representation, shaped by vested interests and unstated motives. Lacking the source materials

63. *Liang shu* 56.846–47.

once accessible to Yao Cha or Sima Guang, we have no way of verifying the "truth" of Hou Jing's letter as realized so differently in their historical writings. What we do know, however, is that the selection of materials promoted different impressions that reflect the historians' different agendas. Furthermore, Sima Guang's phrasing of Hou Jing's criticism of Xiao Gang is remarkably similar to Wei Zheng's derogatory portrayal of Palace Style poetry. Both used words indicating spatial confinement such as "being limited to," "not going beyond," or "stopping at": a considerable failing for a future ruler whose concerns should extend to "all within the four seas." Both historians were northerners.

Wei Zheng's definition of Palace Style poetry, whose subject matter he claimed was confined to life in the boudoir, differs in a significant way from that of He Zhiyuan, expressed in the "General Commentary" of *Liang dian*:

> Taizong [Xiao Gang] was filial and benevolent. He was truly a monarch who could preserve [Emperor Wu of the Liang's] cultural achievements. It is regrettable that he was murdered by the rebels. As for his writings, they were alluring and ornate, responsible for the decline of established customs. They were recited by women but did not reach the ears of gentlemen. This is a profound failing in a man of letters, as well as a great blemish in the governing and moral cultivation of the people. The skill of carving insects has no relation to imperial rule. Even a stalwart man would not take up such a skill; what use should a monarch have for it?[64]
>
> 太宗孝慈仁愛, 實守文之君, 惜乎爲賊所殺. 至乎文章妖艷, 隳墜風典, 誦于婦人之口, 不及君子之聽. 斯乃文士之深病, 政教之厚疵. 然雕蟲之技, 非關治忽. 壯士不爲, 人君焉用?

Comparing this verdict with Wei Zheng's judgment, we see a subtle but important difference: for Wei Zheng, Xiao Gang's poetry was *about* women; but for He Zhiyuan, it was *read by* women. He Zhiyuan did not discuss the content of Xiao Gang's literary writings: his criticism was directed at their style and their audience.

What we see in all these accounts is that Palace Style poetry was defined by historians eager to justify the fall of the Liang and look for a scapegoat. At best this could be only a prejudicial endeavor.

64. *Quan Chen wen* 5.3430.

IDEOLOGICAL TRAPS: READING XU LING'S PREFACE

He Zhiyuan's comment on the audience for Xiao Gang's poetry would have reminded his contemporary readers of *Yutai xinyong*, whose preface, penned by Xu Ling, stated that the anthology was compiled for a female readership. In later times, however, many did not take Xu Ling's claim seriously.

An obscure Tang writer, Li Kangcheng 李康成 (fl. 778), compiled a *Latter Collection of the Jade Terrace* (*Yutai houji* 玉臺後集) in ten scrolls, which reportedly anthologized 670 poems by 209 writers from the Liang to Li Kangcheng's own age. Li Kangcheng claimed in the preface that he did not include any poet who had appeared in *Yutai xinyong* except for Xu Ling and Yu Xin.[65] Li Kangcheng said the following about Xu Ling in his preface:

During the Liang dynasty, Xu Ling and his father both served and were favored by the crown prince. The heir apparent loved literature, and particularly adored the Palace Style. Therefore, Xu Ling selected *yuefu* songs and sensuous poems written since the Western Han and compiled an anthology for [the crown prince] to read.[66]

昔陵在梁世，父子俱事東朝，特承優遇．時承平好文，雅尚宮體，故採西漢以來詞人所著樂府艷詩，以備諷覽．

Here we see a clear shift in the purported readership of *Yutai xinyong*: whereas Xu Ling had claimed the anthology was intended for palace ladies, Li Kangcheng believed that Xu had in fact compiled it for Xiao Gang himself.

The mid-eighth-century writer Liu Su offered another ingenious description of *Yutai xinyong*. The following passage is often cited by modern scholars, almost always in an excerpted form. Since it is an important early account of Xu Ling's anthology, it should be examined in its entirety:

65. The anthology is no longer extant; some ninety poems preserved in various sources have been collected in the modern scholar Fu Xuancong's *Tangren xuan*, pp. 315–60.

66. Ibid., p. 319.

Taizong [of the Tang, r. 627–49] told his courtiers: "I have composed a romantic song for fun." Yu Shinan remonstrated, saying: "Even though Your Majesty's piece is well crafted, the form of the poem is not of the orthodox sort. What the superior likes will invariably be imitated by his inferiors. Once this kind of writing enters circulation, I am afraid it will become very popular. From now on, please allow me not to obey Your Majesty's command to write poems like this." Taizong said: "I appreciate your sincerity and honesty. If every minister were like you, there would be no need to worry about misrule." He thereupon awarded fifty bolts of silk to Yu Shinan. Previously, when Emperor Jianwen of the Liang was still the crown prince, he loved to write sensuous poetry. People were influenced by him, and so the writing of sensuous poetry prevailed. It was dubbed the Palace Style. In his later years, Emperor Jianwen reformed his ways, but it was already too late; so he commissioned Xu Ling to compile *The Collection of the Jade Terrace* to glorify the style. Yongxing's [Yu Shinan] remonstrance with Taizong was largely caused by this past event.[67]

太宗謂侍臣曰: "朕戲作艷詩." 虞世南便諫曰: "聖作雖工, 體制非雅. 上之所好, 下必隨之. 此文一行, 恐致風靡. 而今而後, 請不奉詔." 太宗曰: "卿懇誠如此, 朕用嘉之. 羣臣皆若世南, 天下何憂不理?" 乃賜絹五十疋. 先是, 梁簡文帝爲太子, 好作艷詩, 境內化之, 浸以成俗, 謂之宮體. 晚年改作, 追之不及, 乃令徐陵撰玉臺集, 以大其體. 永興之諫, 頗因故事.

In this passage, Liu Su contrasted Tang Taizong's wise acceptance of his minister's criticism with Xiao Gang's ill-advised practice. For the first time in history, Xiao Gang was identified as the culprit behind the compilation of *Yutai xinyong*, a claim not found elsewhere in the earlier written record. Furthermore, completely ignoring Xu Ling's statement in the preface that this anthology had been compiled for the reading pleasure of palace ladies, Liu Su assigned a moral motivation for Xiao Gang's alleged command to Xu Ling to compile the anthology, a gesture of repentance for a youthful error. Again, we find no evidence in available historical sources for the assertion that Xiao Gang "regretted" his earlier writings. One question naturally arises: if Xiao Gang truly regretted the sensuous poems he had written earlier, why have them anthologized rather than destroyed? In a rather clumsy move, Liu Su would have us believe that the prince wanted to "glorify" or "aggrandize" his style, presumably by placing his poems side by side with classical

67. Liu Su (fl. 742–55), *Datang xinyu* 3.106.

precedents as well as the works of contemporary luminaries. In other words, Xiao Gang intended to cover up his error, because "it was too late" to correct it.

Zigong, Confucius' disciple, once said, "A gentleman's faults are like eclipses of the sun and moon: when he makes a mistake, everyone sees it; when he corrects it, everyone looks up to him." Earlier in the same section of the *Analects*, another disciple, Zixia, is quoted as saying, "When a small man makes a mistake, he is bent on embellishing it [i.e., covering it up with excuses]."[68] In Liu Su's narrative, Xiao Gang was literally trying to "embellish" (*wen* 文) his fault, and therefore he was at a moral disadvantage when compared with Tang Taizong, who corrected his mistake promptly and publicly by rewarding the remonstrator with fifty bolts of silk. The lesson of the story seems to be that any attempt to cover up one's faults is doomed to fail: both a sage-emperor's upright minister and the sagacious Liu Su himself saw through Xiao Gang's strategy. Note, however, that in his remonstration Yu Shinan did not mention Xiao Gang, Palace Style poetry, or *Yutai xinyong*. It was only through inference that Liu Su made the association, which helped drive home the moral message that *he*, Liu Su, wanted to convey through the story.

Many modern scholars also have trouble believing that a sixth-century courtier would have compiled an anthology "just for women," or that a female readership actually existed. In a strange act of misreading, Yang Ming claims that Xu Ling's preface "neither gives a truthful account of why the anthology was compiled nor articulates the compiler's literary views; instead, it employs the technique of fictionalization and asserts that *Yutai xinyong* was compiled by ladies in the harem whose 'matchless and peerless' beauty could 'overthrow a state and topple a city.'"[69] There is, however, no indication in Xu Ling's preface that the anthology was compiled *by* palace ladies. Yang Ming does grant that *Yutai xinyong* was compiled for reading pleasure, but, noticeably, he does not specify *whose* reading pleasure.

Other scholars similarly postulate that the female reader depicted in Xu Ling's preface is no more than a fabrication. For instance, Yu Yuan and Zhang Minggao state: "She not only was pretty but also possessed 'a

68. *Lunyu zhushu* 19.173, 19.171.
69. Wang Yunxi and Yang Ming, *Wei Jin nanbeichao*, p. 306.

wonderful understanding of literature' and excelled in 'writing poems and rhapsodies,' and was rich in 'talent and sensibility.' Peerless in good looks and literary skills: this was Xu Ling's ideal image of a beautiful woman."[70] Although they acknowledge the female authorship of some of the poems in *Yutai xinyong*, they regard the writing women portrayed in Xu Ling's preface as an "imaginary construct," effectively repudiating the very existence of a community of literary women during that period.

European and American scholars have added new twists to Xu Ling's much-discussed preface. Anne Birrell believes that Xu Ling uses palace ladies as a pretext to advocate a view that literature is entertainment and that "art is lightly to be pursued for art's sake." In order to oppose "dour academics who managed to find moral meaning everywhere," Xu Ling "mischievously pictures his readers as women indolently passing days and nights in luxurious harem boudoirs."[71] In her most recent book on Xu Ling's anthology, Birrell again proposes reading Xu Ling's preface as a subtle refutation of classical literary values, albeit granting more credit to the literary women celebrated in Xu Ling's preface.[72] Birrell has performed an important service to the field by rendering all of Xu Ling's anthology into English, but it is a risky business to read too much into Xu Ling's preface and to treat it as a covert literary manifesto with such anachronistic modern echoes as "art for art's sake." In the course of literary history, there certainly has been no lack of prefaces to poetry or prose anthologies that voice the writer's general views on literature, and yet we need to keep in mind the immediate context of the anthology at hand in order to avoid generalizing the authorial intent expressed in the preface.

Paul Rouzer argues that *Yutai xinyong*, ostensibly compiled for women, was intended to speak as much to men as to women and, in fact, provided a means for men to talk among themselves. In this literary community consisting largely of men, male poets not only bonded with one another but also tried to best one another in poetic craftsmanship; their desire to master the woman in the text became inseparably intertwined with their desire to master the text itself. Rouzer sees a close parallel between the palace lady in Xu Ling's preface and the male poet—both

70. Yu Yuan and Zhang Minggao, ed., *Wei Jin nanbeichao*, p. 386.
71. Birrell, trans., *New Songs from a Jade Terrace*, p. 6.
72. Birrell, *Games Poets Play*, pp. 279–303.

angling for the favor of her/his lord: if "a reading tradition already exists that suggests that 'cross-gendered' poetry is in fact the male speaking for 'himself,' then there is nothing that prevents us from seeing the preface otherwise: *Jade Terrace* tells of generations of male poets turning to lament and petition when they have been removed from office."[73] Rouzer also believes that "the readership would very obviously have been mostly male."[74]

And yet it is not at all "obvious" that the initial readership of *Yutai xinyong* would have been "mostly male." Many elite women in the Liang actively participated in contemporary literary life, and *Yutai xinyong* was not the first compilation to claim a female readership during this period. Upper-class women in early medieval China were generally very well educated.[75] Han Lanying 韓蘭英, a fifth-century woman writer listed in the lower rank by Zhong Rong in his *Gradations of Poets*, presented a "*Fu* on Restoration" ("Zhongxing fu" 中興賦) to Emperor Xiaowu of the Song and was thereupon admitted into the harem. She was appointed a teacher for palace ladies by Emperor Wu of the Qi and was respectfully addressed as "Master Han" (Han gong 韓公) because of her seniority and learning.[76] *The History of the Sui* records a literary collection by Han Lanying in four scrolls.[77] Liang Emperor Wu's commissioning of Zhang Shuai to compile an encyclopedia about women for his harem clearly indicates the general literacy of the palace ladies; it may also suggest that the compendium would be used for women's compositions. Chapter 2 mentions Emperor Wu's three literary daughters; his wife and concubines were equally accomplished. Empress Chi Hui was "a good calligrapher and well-read in histories and biographies."[78] Lady Ding Lingguang, Xiao Tong and Xiao Gang's mother, was well versed in

73. Rouzer, *Articulated Ladies*, p. 136.

74. Ibid., p. 132.

75. In a pioneering article, "The Education of Women in China During the Southern Dynasties," Beatrice Spade discusses Southern Dynasties women's educational opportunities as well as contributing social and cultural factors: for instance, instruction of their children; and religious environments such as Buddhist and Daoist establishments, where they could both study and teach.

76. *Nan Qi shu* 20.392.

77. *Sui shu* 35.1075.

78. *Liang shu* 7.157.

Buddhist scriptures, in particular the *Vimalakīrti Sūtra.*[79] Xiao Yi's mother, Lady Ruan Lingying 阮令嬴 (477–543), was able to recite Zuo Si's 左思 (ca. 250–305) "*Fu* on the Three Capitals" ("Sandu fu" 三都賦) as a child and was schooled in the Confucian classics. She authored an exegesis of *Saṁyuktābhidharma-hṛdaya-śāstra* (*Za apitan xin lun* 雜阿毗曇心論, a sūtra that was translated into Chinese in 435), and personally instructed Xiao Yi in *The Classic of Filial Piety*, *The Classic of Poetry*, and the *Analects*.[80]

Didactic works aimed at a female readership were available to gentry families during the Southern Dynasties. A cursory examination of the *Sui shu* "Bibliography" yields a number of titles, such as *A Mirror for Women* (*Nü jian* 女鑑), *Admonitions for Women* (*Nü xun* 女訓), *A Collection of Admonitions for Women* (*Furen xunjie ji* 婦人訓誡集), *Instructions for Sister-in-Laws* (*Disi xun* 娣姒訓), and *An Account of Chastity and Obedience* (*Zhenshun zhi* 貞順志).[81] Emperor Ming of the Song, repelled "by the extreme jealousy of the Song princesses," once commissioned Yu Tongzhi 虞通之 to compile *A Record of Jealous Women* (*Dufu ji* 妒婦記), which was intended to shame the princesses into "better behavior."[82]

As stated in Chapter 2, quite a few anthologies of women's writings circulated during the Liang. An epitome in two scrolls entitled *Furen ji chao* 婦人集鈔 was apparently produced from Yin Chun's *Collection of Writings by Female Authors*.[83] Xu Mian's *Collection of Women's Writings* (*Furen ji* 婦人集) in ten scrolls "was in wide circulation."[84] Indeed, when Xu Ling praised literary women in his *Yutai xinyong* preface, it was more a fact than an "imaginary construct." If the veracity of such titles as *Admonitions for Women* or *A Mirror for Women* goes unquestioned, why in regard to an anthology of poetry, would one refuse to believe the expressly stated editorial purpose and instead look for a hidden agenda,

79. Ibid., 7.161.

80. Xiao Yi, *Jinlouzi jiaozhu* 3.75.

81. *Sui shu* 34.999, 35.1086.

82. *Song shu* 41.1290.

83. *Sui shu* 35.1082.

84. *Liang shu* 25.387. Interestingly, in Xu Mian's biography in the *Nan shi* (60.1486), the historian did not mention this collection, but added to the list of Xu Mian's compilations a *Collection of Memorials to the Throne* (*Zhangbiao ji* 章表集) in ten scrolls instead.

even when there is overwhelming circumstantial evidence to the contrary? Is there a vested interest at play, and if so, what historical, cultural, and literary fallacies in *us*, not in Xu Ling's preface or anthology, does it betray?

Further questions arise. If, for instance, we believe that when a male courtier in premodern China wrote about a woman's longing for love he must have had the competition for imperial favor in mind, how do we account for the fact that many poems on such topics were authored by emperors and future emperors, as well as by women themselves? Such poems constitute a large portion of *Yutai xinyong*. The mode of allegorical reading assumes a parallel relationship between minister/ruler and wife/husband, but where exactly do we position such poems written by rulers themselves or by female poets?

There is, for instance, a poem by Xiao Gang praising a beautiful woman disappearing behind a screen after a musical performance. It was written to the *yuefu* title "On a Fair Lady" ("Meinü pian" 美女篇), whose most famous precedent would be the third-century poet Cao Zhi's poem of the same title. Cao Zhi's piece, which sings of a beautiful unmarried lady in her prime waiting for a proper suitor, has been customarily read as a "lament" about a virtuous, talented, but unrecognized man, and the woman in the poem is regarded as an allegorical figure standing for the poet himself. Such a reading may not be the only reading, but it is a possible reading. It is interesting therefore to observe how Xiao Gang's poem strenuously resists such an allegorical interpretation, nor does it work as a prince's admiration of a worthy courtier, if only for the simple reason that the depiction of the lady, unlike that in Cao Zhi's poem, is too detailed, sensuous, and circumstantial to qualify as an abstract allegorical figure.[85] Similarly, the "fair lady" in Xiao Zixian's poem of the same *yuefu* title is a tavern keeper who "sells Chengdu wine

85. The resistance to allegorical interpretation in Xiao Gang and other Liang court writers' poetry on the topic of "fair lady" is explored in greater detail in my dissertation, "Configuring the Feminine," pp. 169–84. Wu Fusheng makes a similar observation in *The Poetics of Decadence*, pp. 53–55. However, I disagree with Wu's conclusion that the woman in Xiao Gang's poem is as a result transformed "into an object." As a matter of fact, if the woman in Cao Zhi's poem cited above is usually read as a man in disguise (in fact the poet himself), then the woman in Xiao Gang's poem is portrayed as what she is: a real woman of flesh and blood.

during the day, / and counts Hejian coins at night"; this, too, can hardly be considered a courtier's self-portrait.[86]

This resistance to allegorical interpretation may partially explain why traditional readers were particularly averse to Xiao Gang: his poetry about women or written in a woman's voice would seem even more unpardonable than his courtiers' poems on the same topics precisely because his status as a future emperor ruined any possibility of salvaging such poetry by reading it as a courtier's lament and hence as "emotionally authentic." A number of poems in *Yutai xinyong* express male desire, but they are written in such a way that it is quite impossible to take them as political allegories. For instance, Liu Xiaowei wrote a long poem and sent it to his wife during a business trip. In this poem, entitled "Upon Seeing a Woman Weaving in the Ruo County, I Wrote This Poem Offhand to Send to My Wife" ("Ruoxian yujian ren zhi shuai'er ji fu" 鄀縣遇見人織率爾寄婦), the poet teased his wife with a lengthy description of a beautiful weaver he saw during his trip, but then he affirmed his love for her, telling her that he had wept so much thinking of her at night that his pillow was soaked. He assured her that he was not seeking a new lover and asked her to be faithful to him too, waiting for him to come back home and paint in her eyebrows for her.[87]

Yutai xinyong also includes a number of poems by women. Shen Manyuan, Shen Yue's granddaughter, sent a playful poem to a Lady Xiao, taunting her about her romantic relationship. Liu Lingxian addressed a poem to her friend Lady Tang, thanking her for a gift of an embroidery piece.[88] Poems such as these cannot be subsumed into the reading framework of a male homosocial community in which forms of symbolic bonding occurred. Nor should we essentialize *Yutai xinyong* by treating it as a collection of poems in which women are the passive objects of male desire and gaze.

The *Yutai xinyong* poems are in fact extremely diverse. A single-minded focus on the image of the languishing palace lady or a lonely woman pining for her absent beloved cannot do justice to the complex

86. *Quan Liang shi* 20.1908, 15.1816–17.
87. Ibid., 18.1877–78.
88. Ibid. 28.2134, 28.2131.

portrayal of women or gender relationships in this rich anthology of over 600 poems. Criticism of premodern Chinese society as patriarchal and male-centered, while correct in itself, often conditions us to see premodern women as nothing more than victims, and thus we often fail to take into account the complicated workings of power in social reality. When we believe a certain reading tradition to be exclusive, it is we, rather than the Liang poets, who are excluding other possible interpretations of a body of literature that is anything but conventional.

Once we accept Xu Ling's claim that *Yutai xinyong* was compiled for a female readership, more interesting problems surface. We may begin by asking, for instance, what it meant to include poems ostensibly about love affairs and trysts in an anthology intended for the reading pleasure of royal consorts, princesses, and other elite women. How would a female reader receive poems expressing male desire, anxiety, and pleading? How did the compiler of *Yutai xinyong* expect the female reader to react to a poem singing of the beauty of a catamite? What does it mean to have compiled an anthology of poetry to help palace ladies while away their surplus time? Toward the end of the preface, Xu Ling asked that his anthology be allowed to share the palace ladies' "cast-away days" (*qiri* 棄日), an elegant phrase that echoes the Han writer Sima Xiangru's "Zixu fu" 子虛賦: "And then, in the midst of drinking, during the rapture of music, the Son of Heaven becomes disconsolate, as if He had lost something. He says, 'Alas! This is too extravagant! During Our leisure moments from attending to state affairs, with nothing to do We cast away the days.'"[89] Interestingly, poetry was not only being granted a space separate from the male public sphere—namely the "inner palace"—but also being placed within a superfluous temporal frame; yet, among the poems were some authored by an emperor and a crown prince. In a tradition that had always foregrounded the political and moral functions of poetry and emphasized the weight of a ruler's words, this must be seen as a most subversive move on the *Yutai xinyong* editor's part.

In recent years, more and more Chinese scholars have come to accept that *Yutai xinyong* was indeed intended for a female readership.[90]

89. Translation from Knechtges, *Wen xuan*, 2: 109.

90. An article published in 1988 that accepts Xu Ling's professed compilation purpose is Shen Yucheng's "Gongti shi," p. 63. See also two articles reviewing the

One certainly should not exclude the probability that men read and enjoyed it too once it entered circulation, but the anthology was expressly compiled with a specific female audience in mind. To speculate on the deeper motives behind the compilation of such an anthology is not unlike always reading a poem about woman and desire as a mask for a male courtier's longing for imperial favor or lament over loss of that favor. The notion that such a lament is more serious, more emotionally authentic, and thus more admirable betrays a view of literature that is fundamentally based on the reading tenets of a patriarchal cultural tradition.

Yutai xinyong, a chance survival from numerous literary anthologies of the fifth and sixth centuries, was compiled for a female readership. It was not meant to be a "representative" anthology of Palace Style poetry, and this may in part explain why it contains no poem by Xu Chi, the reputed originator of the Palace Style. *Yutai xinyong* might well have been compiled with the tacit agreement of Xiao Gang, but since the preface mentions ladies in the harem, it might just as well have been sanctioned by Emperor Wu himself, who after all had commissioned an encyclopedia for his palace ladies. In fact, it could also have easily been demanded by one of the princesses, Xiao Gang's talented sisters. It should be emphasized, however, that agreement does not mean intervention. Sanctioning the compilation of an anthology for palace ladies is quite different from instilling a hidden agenda into it.

In any case, to describe Palace Style poetry, a poetry of "novel transformation," in more specific terms, we must look to the traces embedded in the poetic texts themselves as well as examine the larger cultural context of this period; this is the goal of the next chapter. For now, let us bear in mind that although the fundamental literary views of the Liang literati were not at odds with received values, it was nevertheless an age of brilliant innovations. A close examination of the contemporary scene shows more than a few points of departure from the literary past.

---

study of *Yutai xinyong* in premodern and modern China, Xu Yuru, "Jin ershinian," p. 226; and Zhang Lei, "*Yutai xinyong* yanjiu," p. 74.

WHEN DID THE SPRING FLOWERS FIRST FALL?

The falling of flowers is now such a commonplace in Chinese poetry that any Chinese reader immediately associates it with the end of spring, the passage of time, and the brevity of youth. From the Tang poet Du Fu's 杜甫 (712–70) famous line "One flower petal flies loose, and spring becomes less"[91] to the famous scene of the melancholy heroine of the eighteenth-century novel *The Dream of the Red Chamber* burying fallen flower petals and shedding tears, the image of fallen flowers has echoes in a long, rich tradition of texts and performances. The falling of flowers in spring is taken as a sign sent by nature to urge human beings to seize the day. But was it always so?

A cursory examination of early Chinese literature tells us otherwise. Flowers had certainly always withered but only in autumn, and, except for chrysanthemums, they usually did not fall. Indeed, flowers did not begin to fall in springtime until the Southern Dynasties.[92] Tao Yuanming mentioned falling peach blossoms in his "Account of the Peach Blossom Spring."[93] The description of the utopian community in this famous prose piece was written during an era when belief in the Pure Land (the Buddhist paradise) became prevalent among the Eastern Jin elite, especially in the Buddhist community in the Mount Lu area, where Tao Yuanming lived. In the lavish portrayal of the Pure Land in the Buddhist scriptures, fallen blossoms from the jeweled trees accumulate to a depth of four inches thick on the ground and are blown away by a heavenly wind every few hours. But the earliest datable "falling flowers" in the poetic tradition occurred as late as the fifth century. Xie Lingyun, Shen Yue, and Xie Tiao were among the first who wrote about the falling of spring flowers in poems; the best known example is

91. From No. 1 of "Qujiang ershou" 曲江二首, in *Quan Tang shi* 225.2409.

92. The poem "Dong Jiaorao" 董嬌嬈, attributed to Song Zihou 宋子侯 of the Eastern Han, mentions falling flowers in spring, but the flowers fall because the branches are broken off by a mulberry-picking girl, not because the season is coming to an end. Moreover, the earliest known source for this poem is *Yutai xinyong*.

93. *Quan Jin wen* 111.2098.

perhaps a couplet from Xie Tiao's "An Outing to the Eastern Fields" ("You Dongtian" 游東田):[94]

魚戲新荷動	Fish play, the new lotus leaves stir;
鳥散餘花落	Birds scatter—the remaining flowers fall.

The cyclic vitality of nature versus the implied unrepeatability of human experience, the harmonious relation between creatures of nature versus the lonely, intrusive human presence (indicated by the scattering birds), are embedded in an intricately structured parallel couplet.

The falling of spring flowers quietly marks an important moment in Chinese literary history. On the simplest level, it ends the conventional polarization of spring and autumn in an antithetical rhetorical structure (flourishing and decline) and adds new meaning to "spring" as a cultural sign. It serves as a dark token of death and decay in the most ebullient season and reminds people of nature's indifference to human feeling and desires. It also signifies, if not a new-born sensibility, then a new-born discourse on a sensibility. In Xiao Gang's writings, it coincides with the configuration of a feeling we refer to as "melancholy." The following is an excerpt from Xiao Gang's "*Fu* on Sorrow" ("Xuchou fu" 序愁賦):

情無所治	My feeling has nothing to attend to,
志無所求	nor is there anything I intend to seek.
不懷傷而忽恨	Not nursing a wound, I nevertheless suddenly feel resentful;
無驚猜而自愁	with no cause for alarm or suspicion, sorrow arises of its own accord.
玩飛花之入户	I amuse myself with the flying flower petals entering the window,
看斜暉之度寮	and watch the slanting rays cross over the lattice.
雖復玉觴浮椀	Despite jade goblets floating in the basin,
趙瑟含嬌	and the zither music of Zhao filled with charms,
未足以	they prove insufficient

94. *Quan Qi shi* 3.1425.

袪斯耿耿	to exorcise this disquietude in my mind,
息此長謠	or to put this long chanting to rest.[95]

Traditional Chinese poetics regards one's emotional response to the external world, be it political circumstance or changes in nature, as the origin of poetry. "The Record of Music" in *The Record of Rites* states: "All tones that arise are generated from the human mind. When the human mind is moved, some external thing has caused it." Then, after listing the six states of feeling—misery, happiness, delight, wrath, respectfulness, and fondness—it asserts: "These six conditions are not innate: they are stirred up and set in motion by external things."[96] Unlike previous writings about sorrow, in which we are almost always given some specific occasion or external reason for the depression,[97] the cause of sorrow in Xiao Gang's *fu* is not external. The author makes it clear from the outset that his feelings and intent remain self-contained, neither being set in motion by exterior things nor actively seeking them. Nothing is shown as lacking; sorrow arises suddenly, "of its own accord." The form of this sorrow is also intriguing: unlike the overwhelming sadness elaborately described in many literary precedents, there seems to be much "surplus ground" (*yudi* 餘地) for the speaker in his melancholy. *Wan* 玩, "to amuse oneself with," "to appreciate," or "to fondle," is an interesting verb: it has a temporal dimension; rather than

95. *Quan Liang wen* 8.2995.

96. *Liji zhushu* 37.663; translation from Owen, *Readings in Chinese Literary Thought*, p. 51.

97. For instance, Cao Zhi's "*Fu* on Sorrow" ("Xuchou fu" 敘愁賦) was written on behalf of his two sisters, whose sorrow was caused by being married away from their family. In his "Essay on Dispelling Sorrow" ("Shichou wen" 釋愁文), a Master Dark Void attributes the sorrow of the narrator to the chaos of the world and his pursuit of fame and benefit. The remedy suggested by the master is the herb of "nonaction" and the acupuncture needle of "dark void." The narrator follows the master's suggestion and is immediately cured. Cao Zhi also composed a "*Fu* on Nine Sorrows" ("Jiuchou fu" 九愁賦), in which sorrow is again shown as having a concrete cause (see *Quan sanguo wen* 13.1125, 19.1158). Jiang Yan's famous "*Fu* on Resentment" ("Hen fu" 恨賦) also lists specific events giving rise to the sentiment (*Quan Liang wen* 33.3142). Cao Pi once wrote in a *yuefu* poem "Ballad: Excellent!" ("Shanzai xing" 善哉行): "Worry comes from nowhere, / nobody knows its direction." The preceding stanzas, however, do hint at the reasons—hunger at dusk and a home far away (*Quan Wei shi* 4.390).

quick, instantaneous action, it implies duration. The speaker's encounter with the things of the world is thus characterized by a sense of leisure and contemplative idleness.[98]

玩飛花之入戶	I amuse myself with the flying flower petals entering the window,[99]
看斜暉之度寮	and watch the slanting rays cross over the lattice.

Flowers fall at an angle; the sun seems to do the same. The small, random fluttering of the flowers in the wind is contrasted with the sun's large, slow, and deliberate movement, and yet both are sinking into darkness and oblivion. They are saved, albeit temporarily, only by the quiet observer, held still in an exquisite balance of words bound together by the principle of parallelism. By directing his gaze toward the flower petals entering the room and the sunlight crossing the latticework, Xiao Gang turns the motion of the unfeeling things of nature into a lateral movement, imbued with a sense of direction and purpose, as if the flower petals and the sunlight were willfully entering this interior space to seek him out, the person whose feeling and intent are so perfectly self-contained that he needs nothing beyond himself. Everything is directed inward: just as nature crosses artificial barriers and moves in-

98. We may compare this line with a couplet in a Han rhymed prose piece in the *Chuci* meter, "Lamentation About the Times and My Fate" ("Ai shi ming" 哀時命): "Solitary and lonely, I have no friend, / who may share my delight in the sweetness remaining?" This in turn echoes the "Far Roaming" ("Yuanyou" 遠遊): "Who could share my delight in the sweetness remaining? / I faced the dawn winds and let feelings spread free" (*Chuci buzhu* 14.261, 5.165). The "sweetness remaining" refers to that of the fragrant plants withered by autumn frosts, not spring flowers, and the tone of both pieces is intensely desolate: the enjoyment of the lingering sweetness is phrased as a possibility in a rhetorical question, which points to impossibility.

99. The phrase "flying flower petals" (*feihua*), which in later poetry became a cliché, apparently first appeared in the Liang. Both Pei Ziye and Yu Jianwu used the image to describe snowflakes; see *Quan Liang shi* 14.1790, 23.1997. Xiao Gang seemed particularly fond of the image. In "*Fu* on the Zither" ("Zheng fu" 箏賦), he repeated the "flying flowers" line almost verbatim, but the context is the pleasure of a drinking banquet, which shows the neutrality of the appreciation (*wan*) of the falling flowers: "The white sun is slowly passing by: / time grows late but joy lasts long. / I appreciate the flying flowers crossing over the window, / and watch the spring wind enter the willow" 白日蹉跎, 時淹樂久. 翫飛花之度窗, 看春風之入柳 (*Quan Liang wen* 8.2996).

side to encounter his gaze, it is from the depths of the poet's being that a vague sense of restlessness and dissatisfaction arises. This is all the more disturbing because the sentiment originates from within, without having been motivated by any exterior lack.

雖復玉觴浮椀	Despite jade goblets floating in the basin,
趙瑟含嬌	and the zither music of Zhao filled with charms,
未足以	they prove insufficient
祛斯耿耿	to exorcize this disquietude in my mind,
息此長謠	or to put this long chanting to rest.

In these lines, Xiao Gang implies that his "long chanting" is a result of "this disquietude." This fits the canonical statement about poetry: "The poem articulates what is on the mind intently" (*shi yan zhi* 詩言志).[100] What is articulated here, however, is a troubling sort of "intent": without anything lacking or wanting to motivate it, it is an excessive, superfluous sentiment, a "luxury good." In later times, this sentiment would acquire an appropriate name: an idle melancholy (*xian chou* 閒愁). But Xiao Gang was the first writer to describe this strange kind of sorrow, which is left dangling in an uncomfortably superfluous space.

THE BROKEN BRIDGE AND SIX DUSTS

The image of "flying flowers" is a familiar one in Buddhist lore. When Buddha teaches, celestial flowers shower down from heaven in his honor. Some modern scholars have noticed a certain incongruity between the Buddhist faith prevailing in the Liang court and the writing of sensuous poetry and attributed this variously to the autonomous development of literature, the Chinese secularization of Buddhism, or the "flexibility" of Buddhism.[101] Such views fail to take into account the basic principle of Buddhist doctrine: that inherent in the sensory appearances of the physical world (*se* 色, Skt. *rūpa*) is emptiness (*kong* 空, Skt. *śūnyatā*). Buddhism is also known as the "Doctrine of Images" 像教,

100. *Shang shu* 3.46; translation from Owen, *Readings in Chinese Literary Thought*, p. 26.

101. See, e.g., Ma Jigao, "Lun gongti"; and Lu Yongfeng, "Fojiao."

and images are inevitably physical and sensuous, but the truth conveyed by them is one of emptiness and illusion.

When Xiao Gang was governor of Yongzhou, he ordered all statues in the Buddhist temples of Yongzhou to be displayed properly every day, not just on Buddhist festivals. His command stressed the importance of icons:[102]

The temples of this region exhibit the Buddha's statues only briefly, on the day of his nativity. Afterward the monks seal the statues in cases, even stripping them of the robes and taking off the pearls of flame from their coiffures. Sometimes the ten gods or five saints are put into one cabinet; sometimes, Mahāsattva and Śākyamuni stay in the same container.[103] This is indeed a case in which the heart and the act do not agree; it seems right on the surface, but the intention underneath is wrong. . . . Even painted portraits of magistrates and governors may enable clerks and commoners to learn reverence; melting bronze to cast the likeness of Fan Li kept him alive in the heart of the ruler of Yue.[104] If precious swords such as Longquan and Tai'e must leap from their scabbards, and if tigers and rhinoceros must break free from their cages, then how much more so should this be true of the Greatest and Most Perfectly Merciful, the Peerless Aggregation of Goodness? Upon hearing his Name, our cares are dispelled; when seeing the images, we enter the Way. How can we afford to neglect the fragrant carvings, conceal the sandalwood statues, cover the jade hair between Buddha's eyebrows, and obscure his Golden Palm?[105]

此土之寺, 止乎應生之日, 則蹔列形像. 自斯已後, 封以篋笥. 乃至棄服離身, 尋炎去頂. 或十尊五聖, 共處一廚; 或大士如來, 俱藏一櫃. 信可謂心與事背, 貌是情非. . . . 夫以畫像追陳, 尚使吏民識敬; 鎔金圖範, 終令越主懷思. 匹以龍阿, 尚能躍鞘; 方之虎兕, 猶稱出柙. 況復最大圓慈, 無上善聚, 聞名去煩, 見形入道, 而可慢此雕香, 蘊斯木櫁, 緘匿玉毫, 封印金掌?

102. *Quan Liang wen* 9.3001; translation (modified) from Marney, *Liang Chien-wen Ti*, pp. 132–33.

103. The ten gods may refer to the Buddha's ten chief disciples, each mastering one power or gift; the five saints may refer to the five bodhisattvas indicating five forms of wisdom and often displayed on the left side of the Buddha.

104. After the great minister Fan Li left the court to become a recluse, the King of Yue reportedly had his statue cast in the finest bronze and paid respects to it (*Guo yu* 21.659).

105. The Jade hair, or the white curl, grows between Śākyamuni's eyebrows, from which he sends out a ray of light to reveal all worlds.

The key statement in this passage is "when seeing the images, we enter the Way." Images serve a paradoxical function: they are an important vehicle for the Truth that signifies the emptiness of all images. This bears some similarity to Zhuangzi's argument that language, the means to obtain the meaning, is but a fish-trap; once the fish is caught, the fish-trap may be discarded.[106] But there is also a profound difference: in Buddhist doctrine images not only point to something beyond themselves, but this something signifies the very vanity of images. In this sense, images are the very means of their own annihilation. When we read the sensuous court poetry of the Liang, we must bear in mind the double-edged hermeneutic of an image in the context of Buddhism: at once significant and meaningless, both essential and superfluous.

Palace Style poetry is a poetry of images, and the images are often of an unusual kind. There are poems about ethereal, insubstantial, and elusive things such as shadows, dust, reflections in water, mist, coolness of air, or flickering candlelight. Along with poems about misperceptions and false impressions produced by the deluded senses, they speak to us about the immateriality of the world of the senses with its shifting shapes and dazzling colors, as in the following quatrain by Xiao Gang, "The Reflection of a Tower in Water" ("Shuizhong louying" 水中樓影):[107]

水底罘罳出	The watchtower comes out from the watery depths,
萍間反宇浮	the upturned eaves float among the duckweeds.
風生色不壞	Wind arises, but the colors are not destroyed;
浪去影恒留	the waves pass on, the reflection abides.

This quatrain is a perfect illustration of the Buddhist term "shadow matters" (*yingshi* 影事), which implies that all things are mere shadows. The reflection of a tower in water is the shadow of a shadow, emptiness within emptiness. It leaves the impression that the tower's colors (*se* 色), the very word for *rūpa*, do not perish despite the disrupting wind, and yet, such an impression itself is based on an illusive reflection, not on the real thing.

During the Southern Dynasties, the "Ten Mahāyāna Metaphors" became favorite motifs or images for poets. The ten metaphors compare

106. *Zhuangzi jishi* 9.944.
107. *Quan Liang shi* 22.1976.

the unreality of the phenomenal world to ten illusory objects: a magic show, flaming radiance, the moon reflected in water, void, echo, Gandharva city, dream, shadow, mirror image, and transformations. Poems on such topics must be viewed in the larger Buddhist context; Xiao Yi's poem "Gazing at the Reflection of the Moon in the River" ("Wang jiangzhong yueying" 望江中月影) is a fine example:[108]

澄江涵皓月	A limpid river harbors the bright moon:
水影若浮天	its reflection looks as if floating in the sky.
風來如可泛	As the wind blows, it seems to be drifting away;
流急不成圓	but currents are fast, and it fails to sustain roundness.
秦鏡斷復接	The Qin mirror is first shattered, then rejoined;[109]
和璧碎還聯	Bian He's jade disk is broken, but again restored.[110]
裂紈依岸草	A torn silk fan, right beside the grass on the bank,
斜桂逐行船	slanting cinnamon branch chases the sailing boat.
即此春江上	Right here, on this spring river,
無俟百枝然	there is no need for the lamp of hundred branches.[111]

A quick succession of metaphors compares the moon to the Qin mirror, the jade disk of Zhao, a broken round fan, and a slanting cinnamon branch. The changing reflection of the moon imitates the constant change of the moon itself. Indeed, for a while the eyes are almost deceived: "its reflection looks as if floating in the sky." The very speed with which the images dissolve into one another suggests the instability of the world of the senses and the erratic nature of human perception. Although the flowing river had been a symbol of the passage of time since the *Analects*, the fluttering of the waves causes the reflection of the moon to alter, and this reflects the larger movement of the heavenly body. All is in flux.

108. Ibid., 25.2045. The poem is attributed to Xiao Yi in *Yiwen leiju* (1.8) and *Chuxue ji* (1.10), but to Xiao Gang in the later *Wenyuan yinghua* (152.707).

109. Here I follow the *Chuxue ji* version and have "a Qin mirror" rather than "a Qin hook" 秦鉤, since the poem is about the full moon instead of a crescent moon. It is said that the first emperor of Qin possessed a magic mirror in which one could see through the person it was held up to; see *Xijing zaji*, p. 103.

110. Bian He's jade disk was a prized treasure in the Warring States period. The Zhao minister Lin Xiangru threatened to break it on a pillar when the King of Qin pressed him for it; see *Shi ji* 81.2440.

111. *Quan Liang shi* 25.2045.

Yu Jianwu's poem "A Companion Piece to 'Spring Night,' Respectfully Written at the Command of the Crown Prince" ("Fenghe chunye yingling" 奉和春夜應令) depicts a spring party lasting late into the night.[112] In this poem, knowledge dissolves and recedes from human grasp; the reader is left with a confusion of sensory responses and distorted perceptions:

春牖對芳洲	Spring window faces the fragrant isles,
珠簾新上鉤	the beaded curtain has just been rolled up.
燒香知夜漏	One burns incense to verify time told by the hourglass,
刻燭驗更籌	and marks a candle to confirm the night watches.[113]
天雞下北閣	The Celestial Rooster descends from the northern pavilion,
織女入西樓	while the Weaving Girl enters the western tower.[114]
月皎疑非夜	The moon is so bright, one suspects it is not really night;
林疏似更秋	the grove is sparse and seems like autumn again.
水光懸蕩壁	Watery light hangs from the wavering walls,
山翠下添流	mountain azure increases the currents.
詎假西園讌	Who would need the West Park banquet?
無勞飛蓋遊	Certainly we have no use for those flying canopies![115]

112. *Quan Liang shi* 23.1992.

113. One instrument used for measuring time was an incense stick. "Hourglass" here is actually a water clock (clepsydra). Marking a candle is also a device for telling the time. There were five watches during the night, but the length of the watch depended on the time of the year as well as on the place. A spring night is, of course, shorter than a winter night. From the image of the sparse grove, we know the poet is describing an early spring night, just as the night hours begin to become shorter. Each of the five watches is further divided into five smaller units called *dian* 點 or *chou* 籌. See the chapter "Telling the Time" in Wilkinson, *Chinese History*, pp. 199–223.

114. The Celestial Rooster, just like the Weaving Girl in the next line, is the name of a constellation, which was believed to be "in charge of waiting for the right time" (*zhu hou shi* 主候時; *Jin shu* 11.296, 300).

115. This is an allusion to the banquet poem written by Cao Zhi: "On a clear night we visit the West Park, / flying canopies follow one another" (*Quan Wei shi* 7.449).

The poem is remarkable for its obsession with time: in lines three to six, the poet lists at least five ways of measuring the passage of time. Yet time itself, from the small, local time that has to be verified and confirmed again and again to time in a larger sense, the shifting of the seasons, is very much distorted. The merrymakers want this spring night to last forever, even as it is slipping away, and in a moment of deluded perspective, the speaker suspects it is an autumn day rather than a spring night. Apart from the temporal distortion, there is also the mistake in spatial perception: the reflection in the water creates the illusion that the palace walls are faltering, with watery light emitting from them, and the volume of the water seems to have been increased by the greenery of the mountains reflected in the river below them.

Buddhist doctrine teaches that when a little child sees the moon in the water, he tries to grab it, and a wise adult laughs at him for doing so. The wise adult understands that the impulse to grab the moon in the water is a sign of one's deluded adherence to the sense of "I" and to consider "what I see" as reality, whereas in fact "I" is composed of the Five Skandhas, which are essentially illusive and transitory.[116] With this in mind, the following, apparently innocent quatrain by Xiao Gang, "On a Lone Duck" ("Yong dan fu" 詠單鳧), takes on a more complicated meaning, as the lonely duck, enamored of its own reflection, is sadly deluded in its attachment.

銜苔入淺水	It dives in shallows for beakfuls of moss,
刷羽向沙洲	heads to sandy isles to preen its feathers.
孤飛本欲去	It was ready to fly off all by itself,
得影更淹留	then found its reflection and lingered.[117]

The last line contains an unresolvable tension: the poet suggests that the discovery of its reflection prompts the duck to stay, and yet it is its staying that provides its reflection. The illusion of having a companion gives rise to fond attachment, and yet the attachment itself turns out to be the *raison d'être* for the creation and maintenance of that illusion. Cause (*yin* 因) and effect (*guo* 果) become hopelessly entangled.

116. The Five Skandhas, or the Five Aggregates, are form, feeling, perception, impulse, and consciousness. They are the components of a human being.

117. *Quan Liang shi* 22.1973; translation from Owen, ed. and trans., *An Anthology of Chinese Literature*, p. 327.

Shen Manyuan's "Song on Reflections in Water" ("Yingshui qu" 映水曲) portrays a woman's self-reflection in water:

輕鬢學浮雲	Light tresses mimic the drifting clouds,
雙蛾擬初月	her twin brows copy the crescent moon.
水澄正落釵	Where water clears, she straightens skewed hairpins;
萍開理垂髮	where duckweed opens, she smoothes tousled hair.[118]

The poem embodies a fleeting moment: both the drifting clouds and the crescent moon are transient, as are the lovely tresses and brows. It is not explained why her hairpins are skewed or her hair tousled, but we suspect that they may have to do with the aftermath of a languid nap on a summer afternoon, or the result of passion. The reflected image is a mere surface, but we have learned to infer what lies underneath.

The Liang court poet was fascinated by the appearances of things, especially fleeting, fragile, and superfluous things. Perhaps the best way to describe such a poet is to compare him to a collector, in the sense that the collector "'quotes' the object outside its context and in this way destroys the order inside which it finds its value and meaning" and "frees things from the 'slavery of usefulness' in the name of their authenticity, which alone legitimates their inclusion in the collection."[119] What other definition would befit the poet writing about a decrepit bridge—

虹飛亙林際	A rainbow soars at the edge of the forest;
星度斷山隅	the passageway of stars is broken by a hill.
斜梁懸水跡	Traces of water cling to the slanting plank;
畫柱脱輕朱	painted pillars have shed their pale vermilion.[120]

A bridge links what is separated by water. Even the celestial lovers—the Herd Boy and the Weaving Girl—need a bridge to cross the Heav-

118. *Quan Liang shi* 28.2133; translation from Owen, ed. and trans., *An Anthology of Chinese Literature*, p. 328.

119. Agamben, *The Man Without Content*, p. 105.

120. Xiao Gang, "Poem on a Damaged Bridge" ("Yong huaiqiao" 詠壞橋), in *Quan Liang shi* 22.1975. One of the few poems left by Xu Chi is also on a damaged bridge; see ibid., 19.1892.

enly River (the Milky Way) to meet each other. But this is a broken bridge: useless, deprived of its function, unable to join the worlds apart. Its body originally has been taken from the forest, and now it is being returned to its former state: a piece of slanting plank. The artificial traces of paint are now replaced by the natural traces of water. It is dangling in an intermediate state of being, a limbo.

Xu Chi wrote about curtain dust:[121]

朝逐珠胎卷	At dawn it rolls up with the pearl embryos;[122]
夜傍玉鉤垂	in the evening, it droops beside the jade clasp.
恆教羅袖拂	Always letting the gauze sleeves wipe it away,
不分秋風吹	it loathes to be blown off by the autumn wind.

Like the broken bridge, this is an unusual poetic topic, something that nobody had ever written about before, and in the context of this period it has a decidedly Buddhist flavor. Buddhists are ever vigilant against the Six Dusts, the six impurities of sight, sound, smell, taste, touch, and mind. But Xu Chi also made clever use of the literary tradition: Xie Tiao's poem "On the Mat" ("Yong xi" 詠席) ends with the lines "Always let the gauze dress brush it, / don't allow the pale dust to accumulate."[123] In Xu Chi's poem, however, it is the dust that yearns for the touch of the gauze sleeves.

Xiao Gang's "On Beam Dust" ("Liang chen" 梁塵) in a way answers the concern in Xu Chi's quatrain:[124]

依帷濛重翠	It clings to the curtain, dimming layers of kingfisher feathers;
帶日聚輕紅	catching the sunlight, clustering light red.
定爲歌聲起	It is surely stirred up by the singer's voice,
非關團扇風	not because of the breeze from the round fan.[125]

121. Xu Chi, "Composed to the Assigned Topic 'Dust on the Curtain'" ("Fude lian chen" 賦得簾塵), in ibid., 19.1892.

122. The curtain is made of stringed beads, which are being likened to pearls. A pearl is conceived inside the oyster, just as an embryo is in a woman's body, hence the term "pearl embryos."

123. *Quan Qi shi* 4.1454.

124. *Quan Liang shi* 22.1971.

125. A good singer's voice may agitate the dust on roof beams.

The last line alludes to a poem attributed to Lady Ban of the Western Han, in which the fan wishes the autumn wind would never arise, so that it would not be cast away.[126]

The motif of dust and singer is reminiscent of a poem by the venerable court poet Liu Xiaochuo entitled "A Companion Piece to 'On A Singer in a Spot of Sunlight'" ("Heyong geren piande rizhao" 和詠歌人偏得日照):[127]

獨明花裏翠	Singularly brightened, kingfisher feathers among flowers;
偏光粉上津	caught alone in the light, a glow on her powdered face.
屢將歌罷扇	Often she takes her fan, the singing done,
迴拂影中塵	and turns to brush away the dust motes in the beams.[128]

The fan, the singer's prop, is, in Stephen Owen's words, "an object left over from its primary purpose" after the singing is done.[129] But a fan's original function is to produce a breeze and cool off the summer heat; when it is being used as a singer's prop, it loses its pragmatic purpose and becomes an aesthetic fan.

Dust represents the impurity of the mortal world. It is a tacit reminder of the fragility of human order, a sign of the disharmony between man and nature. As such, it is an unwelcome nuisance. The broken bridge and the curtain dust provide two metaphors for Palace Style poetry: something freed from its practical function, something completely "use-less," superfluous, a cultural surplus. And yet, we, poetry-lovers, need a poetry that opens up a "superfluous" space in which literature is not sought out but simply rests in being found.

In the fourth year of the Kaihuang era (584), Yang Jian, the founding emperor of the Sui (r. 581–604), issued an edict ordering that all letters and documents, public or private, should be "plain factual records." In

126. *Quan Han shi* 2.117.
127. *Quan Liang shi* 16.1843.
128. Translation from Owen, "Dust Motes," pp. 66–70.
129. Ibid.

the ninth month of the same year, Sima Youzhi 司馬幼之, the governor of Sizhou 泗州, was imprisoned for writing a memorial that was "ornate and sumptuous."[130] This is the first case in Chinese history of punishing a person not because of what he wrote, but because of the way in which he wrote it. In other words, Sima Youzhi had committed a crime of style.

About eight centuries later, in the twenty-sixth year of the Zhizheng era (1366) of the last emperor of the Yuan, the Mongol dynasty, the scholar Tao Zongyi 陶宗儀 finished his *Notes Written During Breaks Between Plowing in the Southern Village* (*Nancun chuogeng lu* 南村輟耕錄). In this work he recorded the following anecdote:

One day the crown prince's tutor came to see the empress, saying, "The crown prince has been studying the Buddhist laws and feels enlightened. Now His Highness is going to be instructed in the way of Confucius. I am afraid that this would harm the true nature of the crown prince." The empress said, "Although I live secluded in the palace and do not know much about ethical codes, I have heard that from antiquity till today, the way of Confucius is essential in ruling the state. If one abandons it and seeks other doctrines, it would be heretical. Buddhism is certainly a good thing, but it is a superfluous matter and cannot be used to govern the world. How could you not let the crown prince read books?" Much embarrassed, the tutor submitted to the empress and withdrew.[131]

忽一日, 帝師來啓太子母后曰: "向者太子學佛法, 頓覺開悟. 今迺受孔子之教, 恐損太子眞性." 母后曰: "我雖居於深宮, 不知道德, 嘗聞自古及今, 治天下者須用孔子之道. 捨此它求, 即爲異端. 佛法雖好, 乃餘事耳, 不可以治天下. 安可使太子不讀書?" 帝師赧服而退.

The empress, "secluded in the palace" like the ladies praised in the *Yutai xinyong* preface, claimed that Confucianism was the only Way and relegated Buddhism to a "superfluous matter" (*yushi* 餘事). It is a "good" thing, but it is not useful in ruling the country, hence unimportant, inessential. She concluded with a rhetorical question: "How can you not let the crown prince read books?" Here "books" clearly refer to the Confucian canon, and it is interesting to notice that only the Confucian classics counted as "books." The crown prince in question, however, never got to rule the country. The year after Tao Zongyi finished his work, the dynasty collapsed.

130. *Sui shu* 66.1545.
131. Tao Zongyi, *Nancun* 2.21.

CODA

The Liang Palace Style poets heralded a new era in Chinese literary history. These poets took pleasure in words and invented a new way of making sense of the physical world, which the next chapter discusses in greater detail. Without these pioneering poets, we would never have had the great canon of classical Chinese poetry as it now exists. Yet these poets have long been excluded from the canon—with the exception perhaps of Yu Xin, a literary prodigal son who earned begrudging approval from scholars and critics. A perennial anxiety about the "use" of literature lies at the core of Chinese literary and cultural discourse from premodern to modern times. There is both an apprehension about superfluity and a mistrust of anything "left over," "alone," anything that does not "belong" or cannot be safely categorized, catalogued, and classified.

The perceived "superfluity" of the Liang Palace Style poetry is, however, created by the very function of the canon of classical Chinese poetry, for the existence of canon depends entirely on what is outside it, the "surplus ground" (*yudi*). By the same token, Liu Su, the Tang writer who first claimed that Xiao Gang had been behind the compilation of *Yutai xinyong*, needed Xiao Gang as a rhetorical prop for Emperor Taizong of the Tang in his neat little tale of perfect symmetry: the good ruler-minister team Taizong and Yu Shinan versus the bad ruler-minister Xiao Gang and Xu Ling. As a matter of fact, early Tang court poetry was nothing but a continuation of the Palace Style of the South, and the Tang encyclopedias are filled with quotations from southern literature and seldom cite northern writings. The northerners might pass judgment, but the southerners had their revenge.

Jiankang, the Liang capital, may have been trampled by Hou Jing's troops and later razed to the ground at the Sui emperor's edict, but Xiao Gang and his courtiers achieved what I would call a triumphant return of the words 文字的凱旋. In the long run, this, rather than the fall of an empire, is what matters.

CHAPTER FIVE

Illusion and Illumination

A New Poetics of Seeing

In the twentieth century, Palace Style poetry has largely been misunderstood as dealing primarily or even exclusively with the topics of women and romantic passions. However, as the modern scholar Hu Nianyi 胡念貽 has pointed out, Palace Style poetry covers all aspects of elite life, with poems on women and love accounting for only a small part of this genre.[1] As observed in the previous chapter, the *ti* 體 in the term *gongti* 宮體 indicates a style, a form, which does not necessarily stipulate the content. This chapter proposes that we think of Palace Style poetry not only in terms of subject matter but also in terms of its

1. Hu Nianyi, "Lun gongti," pp. 168–69. Hu shows that poems about romantic love occupy about one-third of Xiao Gang's extant poetic collection, one-fourth of Xiao Yi's, and one-tenth of Yu Jianwu's. Xiao Gang, Xiao Yi, and Yu Jianwu are all considered major Palace Style poets. Hu Nianyi's article on Palace Style poetry, published in 1964, advocates studying Palace Style poetry as a literary-historical phenomenon instead of simply dismissing it as "fundamentally reactionary." This article was severely criticized by Cao Daoheng ("'Pipan jicheng'"), Guo Yuheng ("Nenggou wu pipan"), and Zhou Xunchu ("Guanyu gongti shi") from a political (or "politically correct") point of view. Hu Nianyi's voice was completely overwhelmed. After the atmosphere of political pressure was over, Zhou Xunchu (*Wei Jin nanbeichao*, p. 303) subsequently expressed regret for having participated in the "joint attack."

formal aspects and that in considering its formal characteristics we ought to look at more than its exquisite parallelism or strict observation of tonal rules as then understood. At work in this poetry is something else, which goes beyond parallelism, prosodic ingenuities, and linguistic ornamentation. The Liang court poets were without question profoundly indebted to the poets of the late fifth century, who had developed a set of tonal regulations for writing poetry, but they were writing an altogether different kind of poetry in the 530s and 540s. One way to account for the distinctive features of Liang court poetry is to examine how the poets looked at things. Poetry in the Liang dynasty was more than an embodiment of a new prosody; at its foundation was an entirely new perception of the phenomenal world—and this was a change of major significance.

This chapter considers a group of Liang court poems on candlelight and candlelit scenes. I chose this group of texts because Palace Style poetry, which was profoundly influenced by Buddhist teachings about illusion, illumination, meditative concentration, and visualization, concerns highly particular moments; these moments are best illustrated by the fleeting images of light and shadow created by candles and observed by the poets with fascination and intensity.[2] These texts about candlelight and the mysterious shadows it produces capture the spirit of this unusually innovative poetry and illustrate most clearly the new poetics of seeing.[3]

---

2. In recent years, an increasing number of articles and book chapters have addressed the Buddhist influence on the Liang dynasty Palace Style poetry. See, e.g., Jiang Shuzhuo, "Qi Liang"; Wang Chunhong, "Lun fojiao"; Zhang Bowei, *Chan yu shixue*, pp. 268–76; Xu Yunhe, "Yuse," p. 153; and Pu Hui, *Nanchao fojiao*, p. 209. These works are, however, generally based on the problematic assumption that Palace Style poetry is about women and romantic passions, and they discuss the Buddhist influence in terms of Buddhist scriptures' lavish descriptions of women, from their psychological states (such as jealousy and desire) to their physical forms.

3. Another luminous image that repeatedly appears in the literature of the Six Dynasties period is the firefly, but this image functions differently from images of candles and lamps, even though fireflies were reportedly used as a reading lamp by Ju Yin 車胤 (d. ca. 401), who was too poor to buy lamp oil (*Jin shu* 83.2177). The firefly does not have the same religious significance as the lamp, which is an important Buddhist symbol; and the firefly's glow does not cast a shadow as candles and lamps do.

A BRIEF BIOGRAPHY OF THE CANDLE

The Liang court poets have long been accused of a sensuous love of artifacts, although our own world, in which artifacts are inseparable from their use-value and commodity value, may envy a time when people could relate to objects in a much more sensuous way. The understanding of the material culture of a historical period should enable us to better imagine a candlelit world radically different from our own, the world that forms the backdrop of the court literature of the Liang.

When we see the term "candle" (*zhu* 燭), we usually think of wax candles (*lazhu* 蠟燭), but in ancient China, a *zhu* was a torch made of animal fat and dried plants such as reeds or the stems of hemp.[4] Besides torches, lamps had also been in use since antiquity. Unlike early "torch" candles, lamps survive as artifacts. The earliest known lamps date to the Warring States period. They were made of pottery, bronze, or, more rarely, jade.[5] In fact, the first Chinese lamp might have been an instance of the "misuse" of a *dou* 豆, a shallow and tall stem dish used as a food container. Depending on the material of which it was made, such stem dishes had different names: a wooden one was called a *dou*, a pottery one was a *deng* 登, and the metal version of the *deng* was written *deng* 鐙, which is the character for "lamp," later commonly written with the fire radical 燈.

Lamps usually burned animal fat (*zhi* 脂 or *gao* 膏). Animal fat, however, had such a foul odor that people prepared it with oil extracted from fragrant plants to disguise its unpleasant smell. From the Eastern Han on, lamp oil was often extracted from various plants. Recent excavations of late Eastern Han tombs have unearthed a number of candlesticks obviously made for thin, long candles, and this has led some scholars to conclude that wax candles were already in use toward the end of the Eastern Han (second century A.D.).[6]

4. *Shanhai jing* 山海經 states: "Before the various plants are burnt into ashes, they are called 'candles' (*zhu*)" (*Shanhai jing* 2.32). A torch thus made is also called a *zheng* 蒸 or a *zheng zhu* 蒸燭. Kong Yingda's 孔穎達 (574–648) commentary on *The Record of Rites* says: "In the ancient times there were no wax candles; so people called the torch a candle (*zhu*)" (*Liji zhushu* 2.36).

5. Gao Feng and Sun Jianjun, *Zhongguo dengju*, pp. 10–15; Kong Chen and Li Yan, *Gu dengshi jianshang*, pp. 6–18.

6. Tang Xuanzhi and Liu Xinglin, "Zhongguo gudai," p. 61.

In the written record, wax candles are first mentioned in Six Dynasties sources. The "*Fu* on a Wax-Burning Lamp" ("Ladeng fu" 蠟燈賦) by Fan Jian 范堅 (fl. late third century) seems to describe some sort of a wax cake in a shallow dish rather than a thin, long, pillar-like wax candle. One of the earliest known mentions of the use of wax candles is found in the early fifth-century work *A New Account of the Tales of the World* (*Shishuo xinyu* 世說新語), which records Shi Chong's 石崇 (249–300) conspicuous consumption of wax candles as firewood.[7] Shi Chong's younger contemporary Zhou Song 周嵩 (d. 324) became upset with his brother Zhou Yi and hurled a burning "wax candle" at him.[8] That kind of temper tantrum was something only an aristocratic family could afford, since wax candles were expensive and unavailable to common people. Beginning in the Jin and throughout the Northern and Southern Dynasties, wax, along with other gifts such as money, cloth, and a court robe, was customarily granted by the emperor to the family of an important minister upon his death.[9]

PRE-LIANG WRITINGS ON LAMPS AND CANDLES

The oldest extant *fu* on the lamp, which is most likely a fragment of the original, is by Liu Xin. It describes a crane-shaped lamp:[10]

惟茲蒼鶴	Oh this dark crane
修麗以奇	is tall and beautiful, a true wonder.
身體剝削	Its body is cast into a slender shape,
頭頸委蛇	its head and neck extended and curved.
負斯明燭	Carrying this bright candle,

7. *Quan Jin wen* 124.2173; Liu Yiqing, *Shishuo xinyu* 30.878; *Jin shu* 33.1007.

8. *Jin shu* 69.1851. See also Liu Yiqing, *Shishuo xinyu* 6.363.

9. At the death of the grand statesman Xie An, his family was given "five hundred *jin* of wax" along with a court robe, a million cash, and other things (*Jin shu* 79.2076). The minister Liu Shilong's 柳世隆 (442–91) family, upon his death, was given "three hundred *jin* of wax" among other things (*Nan Qi shu* 23.430). The custom persisted throughout the Liang dynasty but seems to have disappeared in the late sixth century. No such imperial gift of wax is recorded in the histories of Sui and Tang dynasties.

10. Liu Xin, "Deng fu" 燈賦, in *Quan Han wen* 40.346.

躬含冰池	harboring inside an icy pool,
明無不見	it is dazzling and sheds light on all,
照察纖微	illuminating even the tiniest things.
以夜繼晝	As night succeeds day,
烈者所依	upon the lamp the brilliant one relies.

"Harboring inside an icy pool" refers to the body of the lamp, which is hollow and contains water. Liu Xin was apparently describing a particular kind of lamp called a *gang deng* 釭鐙. A *gang deng* usually has two parts: the lower part may be in the shape of a cauldron, and the upper part comprises a "plate" (for the lamp oil and the wick) and a shade, or an enclosed container with an opening. One or two pipes connect the two parts, channeling the rising smoke into the cauldron, where the soot would dissolve into the water. This arrangement keeps the air in the room clean from excess smoke and soot. The famous Changxin Palace Lamp, which was excavated in 1968 from the tomb of Dou Wan 竇綰, the wife of the Prince of Zhongshan 中山王 (r. 154–113 B.C.), and has subsequently appeared in many art books, is a *gang deng*, with the empty sleeve of the palace lady whose right hand is holding the lamp functioning as the pipe. In the lamp in Liu Xin's *fu*, the basin for the oil was probably located on the crane's back, and the crane's head and neck were turned backward and positioned over the basin to catch the smoke and direct it into the container of water in the crane's belly. The "bright candle" mentioned in the fifth line was most likely made of animal fat.

The point of this fragment of Liu Xin's *fu* is that nothing can hide from the lamp's illumination. The ability to illuminate everything is, of course, the attribute of a monarch or a sage, who presides over his people like the sun and moon, allowing nothing to escape his observation, while remaining impartial with his favors (as said in *The Record of Rites*, "The sun and moon illuminate [all] impartially"; *riyue wu sizhao* 日月無私照).[11] Only after seeing a bird-shaped *gang deng* from the Han, however, do we realize how precisely the author depicted this object.[12]

11. *Liji zhushu* 51.861.

12. The phoenix lamp excavated from a late Western Han tomb gives us a good idea of the crane lamp Liu Xin described in his *fu* (Kong Chen and Li Yan, *Gu dengshi jianshang*, pp. 27–28). Kang-i Sun Chang noticed the application of the same critical vocabulary, namely the "skill with words of verisimilitude in describing

An accurate description of this particular kind of lamp is also provided by the "*Fu* on the *gang* Lamp" ("Gang deng fu" 缸燈賦), composed by Xiahou Zhan 夏侯湛 (243–91):[13]

珠珍寶器	A bejeweled, precious vessel,
奇像妙工	an amazing image and wondrous craftsmanship,
取光藏煙	It gets light but hides the smoke,
致巧金銅	wrought skillfully with gilded bronze.
融冶甄流	Melted down and cast in a mold,
陶形定容	its shape is fashioned, its form set.
爾乃隱以金翳	And then it is hidden with gilded plates,
疏以華籠	and separated by a splendid shade.
融素膏于回槃	Pure white oil dissolves in the movable plate;
發朱耀于綺窗	crimson sparkle glistens on the window traceries.
宣耀蘭堂	It shines forth in the magnolia hall,
騰明廣宇	the brightness mounts up to the broad ceiling.
焰煜燴于茵筵	Its flames gleam on the banquet mats,
煥炤晰乎屏組	and radiate brilliance over the patterned screen.

The lamp plate on a bronze *gang* lamp excavated from the tomb of a Han princess has two small bronze plates that can be slid open or shut to control the amount of light;[14] the "gilded plates" mentioned in this *fu* likely refer to a similar device. The "splendid shade" is the cover over the lamp plate, which channels the rising smoke into the attached pipes. The lamp plate on both this lamp and the Changxin Palace Lamp can be rotated.

Also taking a lamp as its subject is an inscription by Li You 李尤 (first to second century A.D.). The piece is rather plain and straightfor-

things," to *fu* and poetry in the fifth and sixth centuries; see her "Description of Landscape in Early Six Dynasties Poetry," in Shuen-fu Lin and Stephen Owen, eds., *The Vitality of the Lyric Voice*, pp. 109–10.

13. *Quan Jin wen* 68.1851.

14. This lamp is now in the collection of the Department of History at Nanjing University (Kong Chen and Li Yan, *Gu dengshi jianshang*, pp. 20–24).

ward, with an emphasis on the moral function of the lamp—assisting "the worthy and wise" in their diligent labors:

金羊燈銘

Inscription on a Golden Ram Lamp[15]

賢哲勉務	The worthy and wise labor diligently,
惟日不足	for them daytime is not long enough.
金羊載耀	The golden ram carries flames on its back,
作明以續	producing light so that they may continue their work.

Fu Xuan 傅玄 (217–78) wrote inscriptions for both a lamp and a candle. "Inscription on a Candle" ("Zhu ming" 燭銘) is translated below:[16]

煌煌丹燭	Splendid is the vermilion candle,
焰焰飛光	set aflame it flashes light.
取則龍景	Taking its cue from the Dragon's glow,
擬象扶桑	it imitates the Fusang tree.[17]
照彼玄夜	Shining forth upon the dark night,
炳若朝陽	it is as bright as the morning sun.
焚刑監世	Burning its form, it watches over the world:
無隱不彰	there is nothing it does not illuminate.

Although called an "inscription," this composition might be seen as a miniature *fu* on an object (*yongwu fu* 詠物賦), since it describes the physical attributes of a candle, traces it to mythical, larger-than-life origins (as many *yongwu fu* are wont to do in order to exalt the object being praised), and recounts its function: to illuminate the night and "watch over the world."[18]

15. *Quan hou Han wen* 50.752.

16. *Quan Jin wen* 46.1725.

17. The Dragon refers to the mythical "Candle Dragon" in *Shanhai jing* (12.438, 4.260). It has a human face and a snake body. When it opens its eyes, it is day; when it closes its eyes, it is night. Some say it is a dragon holding a candle in its mouth. Fusang is a mythical tree in the east, from which ten suns rose and shone upon the world until the hero Yi 羿 shot nine suns down and ended the terrible drought.

18. Wan Guangzhi ("Handai song zan," p. 101) states that the Han inscriptions should also be regarded as "small *yongwu fu*" and argues that there was no strict boundary between *ming* and *fu* in the Han times. Indeed, despite its title, Liu Xin's "*Fu* on a Lamp" cited earlier reads more like an inscription (*ming*). Li Shibiao (*Wei Jin nanbeichao*, pp. 8–14) also points out how loosely and generally applied the

Fu Xuan's son Fu Xian also wrote a *fu* on the candle. What is left of this *fu* differs remarkably from the other pieces in that the author focuses on the circumstances of lighting the candle rather than on a detailed description of the object itself. If we had complete *fu* on candles, we might find that this was one of the usual phases of the exposition. The preface tells us about the occasion on which Fu Xian composed the *fu*:

I came to Chang'an to investigate a case. In this faraway place, I feel homesick and have night drinks with my fellow-travelers so as to forget sorrow. Seeing that candles within the enclosure burn themselves out in order to serve people, I feel this is just like sacrificing one's life for the sake of accomplishing good.[19]

余治獄至長安，在遠多懷，與同行夜飲以忘愁．顧帷燭之自焚以致用，亦猶殺身以成仁矣．

Fu Xian begins his *fu* with grand statements about the sources of light for day and night, moves on to the poet's sleeplessness and how he subsequently lights a candle. Finally, his sense of loneliness deepened by the shadows the candlelight has created, he summons his friends and starts a night banquet. That a candle burns itself out to fulfill its life's purpose echoes the more customary "*fu* on objects" in its emphasis on the practical functions (*yong* 用) of things. The parallel between the author (who undertook a trip on official business to distant Chang'an during the cold wintertime) and the candle devoting its life to serve the human need is unmistakable.

In the last decades of the late third century, Yin Ju 殷巨 wrote a *fu* on a whale-shaped lamp, an exotic item from the distant Roman empire (Daqin 大秦).[20] This piece praises the exquisite craftsmanship of the lamp only to emphasize toward the end that the real interest lies in the lamp's "function," rather than its decoration. And yet, the *fu* seems to belie the author's stated purport: preceding his claim of the primacy of the lamp's function are many elaborate lines describing the lamp's

generic term *fu* was in the Han times, in contrast with the much narrower meaning of the term in the Six Dynasties.

19. "Sacrificing one's life for the sake of accomplishing good" comes from the *Analects* (*Lunyu zhushu* 15.138).

20. Yin Ju left behind two *fu*: one on the whale-shaped lamp, and one on asbestos or fire-proof cloth ("Qibu fu" 奇布賦), which also came from Daqin and which he saw in the second year of the Taikang 太康 reign (281), according to his preface.

shape. Yin Ju is uncomfortably trapped between the utilitarian and the aesthetic values of the object:

鯨魚燈賦
Fu on a Whale Lamp[21]

橫海之魚	A fish spanning over the ocean
厥號爲鯨	is given the name "the whale."
普彼鱗族	Of all the scaled species
莫之與京	none may compete with it.
大秦美焉	The people of Daqin admired it so much
乃觀乃詳	that they observed it carefully.
寫載其形	They delineated its shape,
託于金燈	lodging it in a bronze lamp.
隆脊矜尾	Bulging is its spine and showy its tail,
鬐甲舒張	its whiskers and scales extend and open up.
垂首俛視	Lowering its head and looking down—
蟠于華房	how it coils in the splendid hall!
狀欣欣以竦峙	In high spirits it stands tall and upright,
若將飛而未翔	as if ready to fly away, and yet lingers on.
懷蘭膏于胸臆	Harboring orchid oil within its breasts,[22]
明制節之謹度	it illuminates the workers' careful measurements.
伊工巧之奇密	Ah, of all secret intricacies of craftsmanship,
莫尚美于斯器	nothing could be more beautiful than this vessel.
因綺麗以致用	With its ornamental beauty, it achieves its use,
設機變而罔匱	as it is designed with clever skill, it does not exhaust itself.
匪雕文之足瑋	It is not that we prize the elaborate decoration,
差利事之爲貴	but rather value the benefit of its function.
永作式于將來	Ever a model for the future generations,
跨千載而弗墜	spanning across a thousand years, it shall never fail.

No *fu* on lamps or candles are extant from the period between Fan Jian and Jiang Yan. Jiang Yan's *fu* on a lamp was deliberately modeled on "*Fu* on Wind" ("Feng fu" 風賦), which is attributed to Song Yu

21. *Quan Jin wen* 81.1928–29. Sun Hui 孫惠 (265–311) wrote a "Baizhi deng fu" 百枝燈賦, but only two sentences are extant (ibid., 115.2119).

22. What I translate "orchid" here is in fact thoroughwort (*Eupatorium japonicum*).

宋玉 (third century B.C.) but probably dates from the Western Han. Jiang Yan's *fu* differentiates "the prince's lamp" from "the commoner's lamp" and ends with the prince's appreciation of the minister composing the *fu*.[23] Also deserving mention is Xi Zuochi's 習鑿齒 (d. 382) fragmentary poem describing a lamp in the wind, which is included in the section on lamps in the early Tang encyclopedia *Yiwen leiju*. Xi Zuochi was a learned scholar who admired Buddhism and struck up a fast friendship with Dao'an, one of the most influential Chinese monks in the Eastern Jin. The lamp in the wind is a primarily Buddhist metaphor for the fragility and brevity of human life and the physical world.[24] In the fragment by Xi Zuochi, as the wind blows, making the flames flutter, the light gives shape to the invisible wind:

煌煌閒夜燈	Brilliant is the lamp during the quiet night;
脩脩樹間亮	how splendidly it glows among the trees.
燈隨風煒燁	The lamp flares up with the wind,
風與燈升降	the wind rises and falls with the lamplight.[25]

In the last decades of the fifth century, poetry on objects (*yongwu shi* 詠物詩) came into vogue. The first poems devoted exclusively to lamps or candles were written by Xie Tiao, who dominated the Yongming literary scene and, along with Shen Yue, exerted the strongest influence on the Liang court poets. As Kang-i Sun Chang has pointed out, Xie

23. *Quan Liang wen* 34.3148.

24. A candle or a lamp in the wind is a favorite Buddhist metaphor for the inconstant and illusive nature of physical reality. According to the *Mahāprājñāparamitā-śāstra* 大智度論, a commentary on the *Mahāprājñāparamitā-sūtra* 大品般若經 attributed to Nāgārjuna 龍樹 and translated by Kumārajīva 鳩摩羅什 (344–413) from 402 to 405: "The transformation and destruction of the world is like a lamp in the wind" (*T* 25: 23.229). But the Buddhist teachings were conveyed through oral preaching as often as through written texts, and so the metaphor of "lamp/candle in the wind" could have been familiar to Chinese audiences much earlier than the fourth century. The Wei poet Liu Zhen 劉楨 (d. 217) used this metaphor in an untitled fragmentary poem (*Quan Wei shi* 3.373). A *yuefu* poem entitled "Yuan shi xing" 怨詩行 (date unknown) compares human life to "a candle in the wind" 風吹燭 and encourages people to make the most of life. In this respect, it recalls the *yuefu* poem "Ximen xing" 西門行 as well as *Gushi shijiu shou* 古詩十九首 no. 15 (*Quan Han shi* 9.275, 9.269, 12.333).

25. The poem has been given no title; see *Yiwen leiju* 80.1368; and *Quan Jin shi* 14.922.

Tiao's poems on objects are social verse composed at banquets and parties in a salon setting.[26]

詠燈

On a Lamp[27]

發翠斜漢裏	Emitting blue iridescence from the Slanting River,[28]
蓄寶宕山峰	it harbors the treasure from the peak of Quarry Mountain.[29]
抽莖類仙掌	Its upright stalk resembles the stand of the bronze immortal,[30]
銜光似燭龍	and it holds light within like the Candle Dragon.
飛蛾再三繞	Fluttering moths circle it again and again,
輕花四五重	wispy blossoms four- or fivefold.
孤對相思夕	Alone, facing the lovesick evening,
空照舞衣縫	in vain it shines forth on the stitches of her dancing clothes.[31]

This standard *yongwu* poem resembles a miniature *fu* in that it lists the characteristics of the described object in what Cynthia Chennault has aptly called a "succession of images."[32] Like a mock epic, it creates a hyperbolic effect: it first shows the extraordinary origin of the lamp, not "in the wild," but in the celestial sphere or some transcendental realm,

26. Chang, *Six Dynasties Poetry*, p. 122.

27. *Quan Qi shi* 4.1452–53.

28. Slanting Stream (Xiexi) or Slanting River (Xiehan) is the Milky Way.

29. Quarry Mountain appears in *Liexian zhuan* 列仙傳, attributed to Liu Xiang 劉向 (79–8 B.C.). It was said to produce a great quantity of cinnabar, which was often used in making elixirs. When the local magistrate sealed off the mountain to prevent people from getting the cinnabar, it poured forth "flying like fire" (Liu Xiang, *Liexian zhuan*, p. 114).

30. Literally, "resembles the immortal's palm"; this refers to a bronze statue built by Emperor Wu of the Han standing on a tall column with outstretched palms to collect "sweet dew," which was thought to help obtain longevity.

31. A variant version reads: "In vain it shines forth—there are no clothes to stitch" 空照無衣縫 (*Chuxue ji* 25.616).

32. Chennault, "Odes on Objects," pp. 334. Kang-i Sun Chang (*Six Dynasties Poetry*, p. 93) has observed that "the concept of verisimilitude in *shih* is originally based upon the aesthetic principle of the descriptive *fu* in general." For the influence of *yongwu fu* on *yongwu shi*, see Liao Guodong, *Wei Jin yongwu*, pp. 544–48.

and then it likens the lamp to mythical Candle Dragon or the bronze immortal. The third couplet of the poem moves the rhetoric to a more mundane level, preparing the reader for the ending: a lonely evening of unsatisfied longing. With the ending, the poem returns to familiar *yongwu* territory: the human element sets in, and the depicted object is endowed with some sort of human emotion, be it loneliness, desire, or the feeling of insecurity that with the passing of a season, the lamp's utilitarian value will be exhausted and the owner will replace it with something else.

Xie Tiao's poem on a candle ("Yong zhu" 詠燭) is another typical *yongwu shi*:[33]

杏梁賓未散	Beneath the apricot beams, guests have not yet dispersed,[34]
桂宮明欲沈	the radiance of the Cinnamon Palace will sink into darkness soon.[35]
曖色輕幃裏	Its colors dimmed within the light curtain,
低光照寶琴	it lowers its light over an ornamented lute.
徘徊雲髻影	Back and forth, the silhouette of a cloud hairdo;
灼爍綺疏金	glimmering, gold on window tracery.
恨君秋月夜	I feel resentful that on a night of autumn moon,
遺我洞房陰	you should leave me behind in the dark shades of a secluded chamber.[36]

33. *Quan Qi shi* 4.1453.

34. "Apricot beams" echoes a line from the Han writer Sima Xiangru's "*Fu* on the Tall Gate Palace" ("Changmen fu" 長門賦): "Decorating the apricot wood for the beams" 飾文杏以爲梁 (*Quan Han wen* 22.245). By this period, "apricot beams" had become a common attribute of a luxurious building, as in Shen Yue's poem "Lamenting the Shedding Pawlonia Tree When Frost Descends" ("Shuang lai bei luo tong" 霜來悲落桐): "The apricot wood can be made into beams" 文杏堪作梁 (*Quan Liang shi* 7.1666).

35. Cinnamon Palace was the name of a Han palace, constructed in 101 B.C., to the north of the Weiyang Palace 未央宮 at Chang'an. Emperor Cheng of the Han (r. 33–7 B.C.) lived there when he was the crown prince; later it was the residence of several imperial consorts, including Emperor Ai's (r. 7–1 B.C.) empress (*Han shu*, 10.301, 12.347).

36. For annotated translations into English of both of Xie Tiao's poems, see Mather, trans., *The Age of Eternal Brilliance*, 2: 44–45.

The poem opens with a late night banquet scene: although the moon is about to set, the guests have not yet left. The time is perfect for lighting candles. The next couplet, however, moves away from the banquet to an intimate boudoir setting: here bright colors are toned down by faint candlelight, and the wavering shadow on the curtain exposes what is within, showing that the man is at the party while the woman is left alone. At first she plays the lute to amuse herself; then she gives up and begins pacing listlessly to and fro. The concluding couplet unifies the images of the candle and the woman.

The dark shades (*yin*) are a proper site for the candle: after all, it is a candle's function to illuminate a dark chamber. Here, however, it seems to cringe at such a prospect, as if it foresees that, with no one attending to it, it will flicker out. Without flame and light, it would be reduced to a mere candle, a dead thing.

The poems and poetic expositions on candles and lamps discussed so far share more or less the same basic structure: from the origins and characteristics of the object, they invariably come to its function of assisting the human world, its use-value. The following quatrain by Emperor Wu of the Liang is not very different. Emperor Wu was once, along with Xie Tiao and Shen Yue, one of the Eight Companions of the Prince of Jingling. Although he continued writing poetry till the 540s, his poetic style was more in line with that of the Yongming generation than of the literary community headed by his sons Xiao Gang and Xiao Yi.

詠燭

On a Candle[37]

堂中綺羅人	People wearing gauze and silk in the hall,
席上歌舞兒	dancers and singers on the mats:
待我光泛灩	wait till I send forth rippling rays,
爲君照參差	and illuminate the nooks and crannies for you.

This quatrain focuses on the candle's capacity to "illuminate" (*zhao* 照). The light of the candle turns the blur of a dim space into a complex space and brings out the irregular shapes of things. In an intensely Buddhist period, illumination could easily acquire a large significance both

37. *Quan Liang shi* 1.1536.

in an imperial and in a Buddhist context, for it is a manifestation of the particular attribute of a monarch and the wisdom achieved by a person in attaining Buddhist enlightenment.

SEEING THINGS AS THEY ARE: THE BUDDHIST CONCEPT OF ILLUMINATION

The way we see things is conditioned by our knowledge and beliefs. In "An Ode on a Lamp" ("Deng zan" 燈贊) by the Eastern Jin monk Zhi Tandi 支曇諦 (347–411), who originally came from Sogdiana, the lamp is, for the first time in Chinese literary history, explicitly represented as an aid to achieving Buddhist enlightenment:[38]

既明遠理	Shedding light upon distant principles,
亦弘近教	it also glorifies close teachings.
千燈同輝	A thousand lamps are a unified radiance;[39]
百枝並曜	a hundred branches equally glow.
飛煙清夜	Spreading smoke on a clear night,
流光洞照	it emanates light that illuminates all.
見形悦景	Seeing forms, delighting in its radiance,
悟旨測妙	one becomes enlightened and comprehends the subtle truth.

The lamp is one of the six offerings made to Buddha. According to Buddhist teachings, there are six means (that is, the Six Pāramitās 六波羅蜜) of crossing over (*du* 度) from this shore of birth and death to the other shore, which is Nirvana, and the sixth of these means is *prājña*, or wisdom.[40] Giving forth light and illuminating things, the lamp thus becomes the perfect symbol for *prājña*, the ability to understand the myr-

38. *Quan Jin wen* 165.2425.

39. "A thousand lamps" should have been a familiar image to Buddhists, because of the story about a king who decided to make an offering of a thousand lamps to Buddha by piercing a thousand holes in his own body. The story appears in *Da fangbian fo bao'en jing* 大方便佛報恩經, translated into Chinese in the second or third century, and later also in *Xianyu jing* 賢愚經, translated into Chinese in 445; see *T* 3: 2.133–35; 4:1.349–50. The stories are included in the Liang Buddhist encyclopedia *Jinglü yixiang* (*T* 53: 24.131–32, 25.136).

40. The first five are charity, receiving precepts, patience, devotion, and meditation.

iad phenomena of the universe exactly as they are. In praising the Buddha's image, Zhi Dun 支遁 (313?–66), the famous Eastern Jin monk poet, compared Buddha's wisdom to a brilliantly lit torch that illuminated his life's path in darkness.[41] Indeed, "the lamp of wisdom" (*hui ju* 慧炬 or *zhihui deng* 智慧燈) was a common phrase in the Southern Dynasties.[42] In the fifth century, the famous Daoist Lu Xiujing 陸修靜 (406–77) laid down a set of rules for what is known as "the lamp rite" 燈儀, a Daoist liturgy usually held after sunset and involving the use of lamps. His *Randeng lizhu weiyi* 燃燈禮祝威儀 is lost, but three "Odes to a Bright Lamp" ("Mingdeng zan" 明燈贊) from this liturgical text have been preserved in *Wushang huanglu dazhai lichengyi* 無上黃籙大齋立成儀, transmitted by the Southern Song Daoist Liu Yongguang 留用光 (d. 1225) and recorded by his disciple Jiang Shuyu 蔣叔輿 (1162–1223).[43] These odes in five-syllable lines liken "my body" to a burning lamp, which "forsakes [its] form and destroys the root of sufferings" (*shexing mie kugen* 舍形滅苦根).

The lamp, most importantly, emits light, enabling one to see in the dark. But sight can be deceiving. According to the Buddhist teachings, the "eye-consciousness" itself is unreal, and the physical things being seen are no more than illusory appearances. They belong to the realm of color and form 色, the object of eye-consciousness, which depends on causes and conditions to exist, and whose very existence is empty because it is impermanent. In a series of lectures on meditation, Zhiyi 智顗 (538–97), the founder of the Tiantai Sect (*Tiantai zong* 天臺宗), explicitly identified wisdom with *vipaśyanā* (*guan* 觀), the clear, penetrating, illuminating observation of the world as it is, that is, the world as transient, relative, constantly changing, and unreal. But how does

41. *Quan Jin wen* 157.2369.

42. For instance, Xiao Ziliang used the phrase *hui ju* in a letter (*Quan Qi wen* 7.2829). Huiju was the "dharma name" (*faming* 法名) of the prominent Liang court poet Wang Yun (*Quan Liang wen* 65.3337). Emperor Wu of the Liang used *zhihui deng* in his "Mohe banruo chanwen" 摩訶般若懺文 (*Quan Liang wen* 6.2987). Xi Zuochi, in a letter to the monk Dao'an dated 365, used the phrase "the lamp of bright wisdom" (*mingzhe zhi deng* 明哲之燈; *Quan Jin wen* 134.2230).

43. *Daozang* 9.584. Lu Xiujing's *Dongxuan lingbao zhai shuo guangzhu jiefa dengzhuyuanyi* 洞玄靈寶齋說光燭戒罰燈祝願儀 is still extant; in this work he introduced the term "Candle of the Law" (*fazhu* 法燭) and set up the office of lamp attendant (*shideng* 侍燈) in the ritual (*Daozang* 9.822, 9.825).

one achieve this illuminating observation? Using a remarkable metaphor, Zhiyi compared meditation (*dhyāna*) to a closed room and *vipaśyanā* to a bright lamp: "If one cultivates one's concentration (*ding* 定), then it is like a lamp in a closed room, which is capable of illumining great darkness."[44]

The word *ding* 定 is the same as *śamatha* (*zhi* 止), a state of deep concentration, which is also called *samādhi*, a Sanskrit word often transliterated *sanmei* 三昧. The cultivation of *samādhi* had a long history in China by the time of the Southern Dynasties. An Shigao, a Parthian monk and one of the earliest transmitters of Buddhism into China, translated the *Great Ānāpāna Sūtra* (*Da anban shouyi jing* 大安般守意經), which teaches breathing techniques to help one concentrate during meditation. In the Eastern Jin, *samādhi* acquired a new significance. In the fourth and the fifth centuries, the belief in the Pure Land (*jingtu* 淨土) of Amitābha Buddha 阿彌陀佛 was advocated by the famous monk Huiyuan and attracted many elite followers.[45] Amitābha Buddha is the Buddha of Infinite Life and Infinite Light; he resides in the Western Paradise, or the Pure Land (as opposed to the "impure land" of the mortal world), which is described in sumptuous terms in the "Three Sūtras of the Pure Land" (*jingtu sanbu jing* 淨土三部經): the *Sūtra of Infinite Life* (*Wuliangshou jing* 無量壽經), the *Sūtra of the Meditation on the Buddha* of *Immeasurable Life* (*Guan wuliangshou jing* 觀無量壽經), and the *Amitābha Sūtra* (*Amituo jing* 阿彌陀經). The first of these was translated in the third century, and the last two in the fifth century. According to these sūtras, meditating on Amitābha Buddha by calling out his name (*chengming nianfo* 稱名念佛) or visualizing his image (*guanxiang nianfo* 觀想念佛) enables a person to be reborn into a life of boundless joy in the Pure Land.[46]

---

44. *T* 46: 5.57.

45. Amitābha Buddha remains one of the most popular and best-known Buddhas in China. For the origin and propagation of the belief in the Pure Land of Amitābha during the Six Dynasties, see Wang Qing, *Wei Jin nanbeichao*, chap. 3.

46. There is also the third form of meditating: by contemplating the true, unchanging nature of Buddha (*shixiang nianfo* 實相念佛). This is the most abstract of the three forms of meditating, and also the least popular. Name-chanting was the most widespread form of practicing meditation, so much so that *nianfo* (meditating

On September 11, 402, Huiyuan assembled 123 monks and laymen in front of an image of Amitābha Buddha at Mount Lu to make a vow to be reborn in the Pure Land; he also composed a preface to a group of poems he and other fellow-believers had written on meditating on the Buddha and achieving *samādhi*.[47] The poems are no longer extant, save for four verses in four-syllable lines by a certain Wang Qizhi 王齊之, but the preface is preserved. There Huiyuan asserted that the writing of these poems was more than a literary exercise:

What is this concept called *samādhi*? It refers to the concentrating of the mind and the quieting of the thoughts. When the mind is concentrated, the will becomes one and undivided; when thoughts are quieted, energy becomes unoccupied and the spirit brightens. When the energy becomes unoccupied, wisdom quiets its glow; when the spirit brightens, no darkness is not illuminated. These two things [energy and the spirit] are the mysterious manifestations of nature: they come together and function.

夫稱三昧者何? 專思寂想之謂也. 思專則志一不分, 想寂則氣虛神朗. 氣虛則智恬其照, 神朗則無幽不徹. 斯二者, 自然之玄符, 會一而致用也.

The opening section explains the concept of *samādhi* and its significance. The phrase describing the state achieved by the spirit in concentration—"no darkness is not illuminated"—is reminiscent of Liu Xin's *fu* ("it is dazzling and sheds light on all, / illuminating even the tiniest things") and Fu Xuan's inscription ("there is nothing it does not illuminate").

Huiyuan went on to elucidate why, of different kinds of *samādhi*, meditation on the Buddha is the most commendable:

But then, there are many different kinds of *samādhi*, among which the most meritorious and yet the easiest to cultivate is to meditate on the Buddha. Why is this? He who exhausted the great mystery and reached Nirvana, is respectfully named Tathāgata;[48] his substance and spirit go along with transformations,

on the Buddha) had become synonymous with "chanting the name of the Buddha" and remains so in the modern Chinese vocabulary.

47. Huiyuan, "*Nianfo sanmei shiji* xu" 念佛三昧詩集序 (*Quan Jin wen* 162.2402). For Huiyuan's Amitābha belief and his method for achieving rebirth in the Pure Land, see also Zürcher, *The Buddhist Conquest*, pp. 219–23; and Fang Litian 方立天, *Huiyuan*, pp. 108–43.

48. Tathāgata, or "thus come" (如來), is the highest of a Buddha's titles. It is a special reference to Amitābha tathāgata 阿彌陀.

and his responses [to our call] do not come from one place. So he who enters this particular meditation will become oblivious [to the world around him] and forget knowledge. He will take the object of his meditation [*ālambana*] as a mirror; when the mirror is bright, his inner light shines forth, their rays joining, and myriad images are born, so that even without the help of ears and eyes, one can hear and see and act. Thereupon, he sees the true substance of the vacuous mirror in the profound absorption and becomes enlightened to the fact that the form of the luminary is lucid and whole, clear, radiant, and natural; he deeply observes the mysterious voice echoing in his mind, and thus concerns of this dusty world disappear, and blocked feelings become harmonious and open. If not for the method of the extreme subtlety, who could have been able to participate in this?

又諸三昧其名甚衆, 一功高易進, 念佛爲先. 何者? 窮元極寂, 尊號如來, 體神合變, 應不以方. 故令入斯定者, 昧然忘知. 即所緣以成鑒, 鑒明則内照交映, 而萬像生焉; 非耳目之所暨, 而聞見行焉. 於是睹夫淵凝虛鏡之體, 而悟靈相湛一, 清明自然; 察夫玄音之叩心聽, 則塵累每消, 滯情融朗. 非天下之至妙, 孰能與於此哉?

This passage offers a detailed description of the experience of meditation. The method of meditation adopted by Huiyuan is visualization, either of the Buddha himself or of the Pure Land. For the latter, the sūtra texts provide numerous striking images, such as "lotus flowers as large as a wheel" or "the four inches of fallen petals" that weave a soft, colorful, and fragrant carpet on the golden ground.[49] Huiyuan states that since the image of the Buddha is not fixed, each person should "take the object of meditation as a mirror"—which refers to an image being visualized in deep meditation. Because this object in itself has no material substance (it is just an image) and because it reflects everything clearly, it functions as an empty mirror: the reflection is not of the mere appearances of things, but of things as they really are, a clarification and an illumination. According to Huiyuan, the light of the mirror (that is, the shining image being contemplated) will commingle with the light emanating from the meditating subject, and then "myriad images will be born" in the mind; one will then realize the "true substance of the vacuous mirror," which is emptiness. In Huiyuan's description, the meditating subject and the object of his meditation seem eventually to

49. This is also evidenced by Wang Qizhi's poems (*Quan Jin shi* 14.939).

become one and the same in the image of the bright mirror. For Hui-yuan, this is the most effective way of achieving Nirvana.

In order for the object of meditation and eventually the meditative mind to become the all-illuminating mirror, one must cultivate concentration. The concept of *nian* 念 is of vital importance. The Chinese character *nian* means several things: chanting or vocalizing; concentrating the mind on one object (Skt. *smṛti*); an instant in time (Skt. *Kṣaṇa*; Ch. *cha'na* 剎那); and a thought. It is often understood as "a thought-instant," that is, a momentary thought *and* the fleeting moment such a thought takes.

The multiplicity of meanings of *nian* proves fruitful in an essay written by Shen Yue, one of the most revered predecessors of the literary circle surrounding the Liang princes. This essay, entitled "A Discourse on Body and Spirit" ("Xingshen lun" 形神論), has rightly been recognized by both Whalen Lai and Richard Mather as going beyond "the old body/spirit dichotomy."[50] Integrating Lao-Zhuang concepts and Buddhist discourse, the treatise is very much part of an extensive early medieval Chinese debate on the relationship between body and spirit and whether the spirit is immortal and separable from the body. In retrospect, it also sheds light on a new way of seeing in the Liang court literature.

Most relevant to the present discussion is the first part of this treatise:[51]

> During a single instant of concentrated thought, an ordinary person no longer feels the existence of his body. Although it is so for an ordinary person, the sage follows to the utmost every thought-instant. The sage has no self, and his body is as if empty in the first place. With a body that is as if empty, the sage encompasses myriad thought-instants that he would follow to the utmost.[52] This is how he differs from an ordinary person.

50. Mather, *The Poet Shen Yüeh*, p. 147; see also Lai, "Beyond the Debate."

51. The essay has been preserved in the Tang monk Daoxuan's *Guang hongming ji* (*T* 52: 22.253; *Quan Liang wen* 29.3120).

52. Unlike Whalen Lai ("Beyond the Debate," p. 152) and Richard Mather (*The Poet Shen Yüeh*, p. 148), I take *zong* here as the main verb (encompass), not *wu* (which Lai and Mather translated as "annihilate" or "terminate" respectively). The reason for this is that earlier in this passage we have *wu nian bu jin*: "[The sage has] no thought-instant [that he does] not exhaust or go to the end of."

凡人一念之時，七尺不復關所念之地．凡人一念，聖人則無念不盡．聖人無己，七尺本自若空．以若空之七尺，總無不盡之萬念，故能與凡夫異也．

For Shen Yue, the sage differs from an ordinary person not only in the ability to concentrate intensely and forget everything else (including the existence of his own body), but also in the ability to concentrate in a succession of thought-instants. In this way, the sage explores the limits of and exhausts the potentials offered by each and every thought-instant as well as by the myriad thought-instants. In other words, his consciousness is ever in an alert, focused state.

In Buddhism, it is not only "the sage" (i.e., the Buddha) who has no self, but also every human being. "Self" is an aggregate of the Four Great Elements—fire, water, earth, and wind—which are conditioned, impermanent, and so essentially empty. There is no such a thing as an inherent "self." Shen Yue's claim that the sage "has no self" (implying that an ordinary person does) shows clearly that he is using the term in Zhuangzi's sense rather than in the Buddhist sense. In "Free Wandering" ("Xiaoyao you" 逍遙遊) and other writings in *Zhuangzi*, that "the perfect man has no self" (*zhiren wu ji* 至人無己) is a recurring theme. In the Daoist context, it refers to transcending one's ego as well as the limitations imposed by the physical body and other material conditions, thus achieving the ultimate freedom in being one with the spirit of the universe.

In the next section Shen Yue explains that an ordinary person may have moments of "having no self," but whereas these moments are sporadic, the sage's "no-self" is a constant state:

> When an ordinary person during one thought-instant forgets his own body, then his eyes cease the function of seeing, and his feet cease the function of treading. When he thus forgets his eyes and his feet, what is the difference between this and having no eyes or feet? However, an ordinary person's temporary "not having" is actually grounded in "having," for hardly one moment of "not having" will have passed when "having" already succeeds it. When the thought-instant is disconnected from the body, one temporarily forgets [one's body/self]; when the thought-instant fades along with the mind, one again remembers it. When one concentrates one's thought on one part of the body, then all the other body parts are as if belonging to someone else, and this would be no different from the "non-self."

凡人一念，忘彼七尺之時，則目廢於視，足廢於踐．當其忘目忘足，與夫無目無足，亦何異哉？凡人之暫無，本實有，無未轉瞬，有已隨之．念與形乖則暫忘，念與心謝則復合．念在七尺之一處，則他處與異人同，則與非我不異．

Shen Yue considers the succession of thought-instants as the essential reason why the sage can maintain his state of "having no self." Ingeniously linking "non-self" (*fei wo* 非我), which is a Mahayāna Buddhist concept misused for the Lao-Zhuang term "having no self" (*wu ji* 無己), with "forgetting the self" (again a Zhuangzi term), Shen Yue postulates that "having no self" is the result of being able to *forget one's existence in a moment of intense concentration.*

But an ordinary person's nonbeing is only temporary, and the moment is fleeting; the sage's nonbeing lasts long and indeed reaches very far.[53] An ordinary person and a sage originally share one common path. Forgetting temporarily in one thought-instant marks the rank of the ordinary; forgetting everything in myriad thought-instants—that is a great sage.[54] If we consider [the dichotomy of form and spirit] in such terms, then it borders on causing confusion.[55]

但凡人之暫無，其無甚促；聖人長無，其無甚遠．凡之與聖，其路本同．一念而暫忘，則是凡品；萬念而都忘，則是大聖．以此爲言，則形神幾乎惑人．

In these lines, Shen Yue reiterates the difference between an ordinary person and a sage. He argues that the debate about body and spirit is

53. Here I follow the Taishō edition. *T* 52: 22.253. The *Sibu congkan* edition of *Guang hongming ji* (based on a Ming edition) has a different version: 但凡人之暫無<u>其無</u>，其無甚促；聖人長無<u>其無</u>，其無甚遠．

54. Whalen Lai ("Beyond the Debate," p. 152) renders the sentence as "When myriad *nien* are all forgotten, that is the way of the great sage." It is, however, *not* the myriad *nian* that the sage forgets; rather, he forgets everything continuously, in myriad thought-instants (in contrast with an ordinary person, who forgets everything in only one thought-instant).

55. Here I follow the *Sibu congkan* edition, which takes the penultimate character, *huo*, as "confusing" (*huo* 惑) instead of "some" (*huo* 或). If we follow the Taishō edition, then the punctuation would be different: 以此爲言，則形神幾乎．或人疑因果相主，毫分不爽．Whalen Lai's translation ("Beyond the Debate," p. 152) is based on the Taishō version: "If we follow this discourse, then the matter of spirit and form [soul and body] is well-nigh [understood]. Now there may be people who suspect that cause and effect." Richard Mather's (*The Poet Shen Yüeh*, pp. 148–49) translation also follows the Taishō version: "If we talk in this manner the problem of body and spirit will be near to solution. Some persons doubt the principle that the mutual interaction between cause and fruition never varies by the tiniest degree."

pointless because, in a constant state of intense concentration, the existence of body no longer matters and the sense of self is abolished.

In "A Discourse on the Spirit Being Immortal" ("Shen bu mie lun" 神不滅論), Shen Yue gives a detailed elucidation of the workings of concentration, which he believes is the only means of achieving the "correct enlightenment":

The sentient spirit is shallow and weak; worries and concerns confuse and distract [the mind]. If one thought can be all-encompassing, then worries and concerns have no way to reach the mind; but if it cannot be all-encompassing, then scattered thoughts will invade the mind. Before one thought is properly formed, many others will arise, and with the rising of a multitude of thoughts, it will be just like before. That a thought should fail to be all-encompassing is because of superficiality and confusion; shallowness and confusion are sicknesses caused by a delusional obsession with Being. To be neither superficial nor confused proceeds from total forgetting; only with this total forgetting will one gain a total illumination. Thus one may begin as an ordinary person but can end with correct enlightenment.[56]

情靈淺弱, 心慮雜擾, 一念而兼, 無由可至. 既不能兼, 紛糾遞襲. 一念未成, 他端互起. 互起眾端, 復同前矣. 不相兼之由, 由於淺惑. 惑淺爲病, 病於滯有. 不淺不惑, 出於兼忘. 以此兼忘, 得此兼照. 始自凡夫, 至於正覺.

This is Six Dynasties critical prose at its best: clear, precise, and incisive. Richard Mather is right in pointing out how "Zhuangzi-like" this passage is,[57] but the terseness and precision of its progressive argument are reminiscent more of a Buddhist exposition than of Zhuangzi's effusive discourse, in which the speaker often gets carried away by his own wit and passion for rhetoric.

Shen Yue shows us that it is easy to be beset with all kinds of thoughts and concerns and unable to focus on anything with profound concentration. This lack of focus is due to superficiality—an inability to penetrate deeply to the heart of an issue and pursue it to the point of completely exhausting its possibilities. Superficiality and confusion are signs of a more serious disease: obsession with Being—the antithesis of nothingness (*wu* 無) or emptiness (*kong* 空). The solution proposed by

56. *T* 52: 22.253; *Quan Liang wen* 29.3120.
57. Mather, *The Poet Shen Yüeh*, p. 151.

Shen Yue is a "total forgetting" of the self, which he believes will lead to a "total illumination."

Shen Yue's theory should be seen against the background of a widely held belief in the power of concentration during the Southern Dynasties. In the three collections of stories about the efficacy of Bodhisattva Avalokiteśvara, or Guanshiyin pusa 觀世音菩薩, written from the early fourth century to the year 501, the authors often emphasized an intense absorption in chanting the Bodhisattva's name, meditating on the Bodhisattva, or reciting the *Avalokiteśvara Sūtra* (*Guanshiyin jing* 觀世音經). A story from Lu Gao's collection, for instance, explicitly describes a devout layman's meditation on the Bodhisattva as "without break for even a single thought-instant" (*niannian xiangxu* 念念相續).[58] The intense concentration caused the man's shackles to fall off by themselves.

A POETRY OF ILLUMINATION

Shen Yue's understanding of Buddhism may be clouded by his use of such Lao-Zhuang concepts as "having no self" (*wu ji*) and "total forgetting" (*jian wang* 兼忘). Yet, it was characteristic of the elites of his age to mix the two doctrines freely into a hybrid theory, and his basic argument about concentration (*ding* 定) and illumination (*zhao* 照) harks back to Huiyuan. Both Huiyuan and Shen Yue believed that the power of concentration enables a person to achieve illumination. Shen Yue's unique contribution lies in his creative exploitation of the term *nian*, thought-instant. He broke the flow of time into myriad thought-instants (*wan nian* 萬念) and asked us to focus on each and every one of them. This idea is directly relevant to Liang Palace Style poetry: instead of being about women and romantic love, this poetry is about concentration, about a new, focused way of looking, and about the extraordinary, and yet often ignored, power of noticing.

58. Fu Liang et al., *Guanshiyin yingyan ji sanzhong yizhu*, p. 121. On the "presence" of Guanshiyin in early medieval China, see Campany, "The Real Presence." Particularly relevant to our discussion here is Campany's analysis of "the way in which devotion to Guanshiyin structured people's experience of time" (p. 245).

This poetry is intensely visual, not in the sense of presenting "pictorial images" but in the sense of seeing per se—what and how to see.[59] Wei-Jin poetry often describes things in generic and unspecific terms. Even the great poet Xie Lingyun sometimes lapsed into fragmentary descriptions of nature in his landscape poems, with a mountain scene in one line and a water scene in the next. The desire in these poems is to express the totality of the landscape. Such poems evoke another literary genre, the *fu*, a kind of "poetic exposition" designed to encompass all aspects of an object, a place, or an experience. In contrast, Liang court poetry in the tradition of Xie Tiao, Shen Yue, and He Xun works differently. This poetry puts the reader in a new relationship with things; it forces the reader to look at them on a temporally and spatially specific level. Instead of presenting a composite picture of disparate images, a Liang court poem has a center toward which everything in the poem gravitates. The poet's gaze is extremely focused, so much so that one feels the effect of illumination. The poem is an act of uncovering and unconcealing: the glowing contours of things begin to emerge against a dark background. The emergence betrays a keenly observant eye and often an unexpected perspective. The "dark background" is more than just a figure of speech. On one hand, it refers to the shadows in which things remain hidden until illuminated by the poet's intense gaze, which enables one to see the powder a butterfly's wings leave on flower petals or to notice the slower, heavier flight of birds in a fine drizzle. On the other hand, the dark background is the somber Buddhist mise-en-scène that constantly reminds both poet and reader that everything they see is impermanent and illusory and hence has no reality separate from the background against which it has emerged.

The things being seen in these Liang court poems exist on a temporally specific level. This view is opposed to the claim that the Liang

59. To emphasize the "visual" aspect of this poetry is not to downplay its auditory qualities, as one may clearly detect in this poetry the influence of the famous prosody theory, first explored by the poets of the Yongming generation, most notably Shen Yue and Wang Rong. Many scholars have argued that the attention to prosody in this period is related to the translating and chanting of Buddhist scriptures; see, e.g., Chen Yinke, "Sisheng san wen"; Rao Zongyi, "*Wenxin diaolong*"; and Sun Changwu, *Wen tan fo ying* 文壇佛影, pp. 155–77.

poems on objects are often "vapid still lifes."[60] This is a statement worth contesting, because by understanding that these poems are not "vapid still lifes," one may gain a clearer picture of what they actually are.

In the genre of still-life painting, things are often truly *still* in the sense that they are wrested out of the stream of life. A still-life painting of fruits and lobsters tells us nothing of time and place: there is nothing specific about the fruits and lobsters; they are "representative" of their species and are quasi platonic objects existing outside real lived time. In contrast, the Liang court poems are, to put it simply, "thought-instants." They attempt, often successfully, to present things as observed in living moments.[61] These moments are literally *arrested* in words, and words, much more so than pictures, have a temporal, dynamic quality. Words have more "movement" than pictures.

In the Liang court poems, there is often a fertile tension, which did not exist in earlier poetry, between the words of a line and between the lines of a couplet. It is difficult to explain this tension merely by attributing the effect to "a more exquisite parallelism," although parallelism does play an important role in creating this tension. By "tension," I mean an interaction between words and lines, a movement that cuts across time. This kind of interaction is what differentiates the parallelism of Liang court poetry from that of earlier poetry, which is usually more straightforward and simple.

60. Cynthia Chennault ("Odes on Objects," p. 392) borrows the term "still-life" and the word "vapid" from John Marney's characterization of the Liang "poetry on objects."

61. As scholars have pointed out, poetry in the fifth and sixth centuries had a tendency to become increasingly "compact." The reason why many surviving poems are "short" might simply be a function of the sources in which they are preserved—for example, Tang encyclopedias, which often included only excerpts of prose and poetry—and must be properly regarded as fragments. Still, shorter poems were undeniably becoming increasingly common in this period. Quatrains in particular enjoyed unprecedented popularity. Some scholars think this is due to the great influence of the Southern *yuefu* songs, which are usually five-syllable quatrains, and there is some truth to this claim. Nonetheless, I believe we should also consider the opposite possibility—that *yuefu* songs gained popularity at court because the elite loved the quatrain form.

Consider, for example, this fragment of a poem by the masterful poet Xiao Gang, entitled "Autumn Evening" 秋晚:[62]

浮雲出東嶺	Drifting clouds emerge from the eastern peaks,
落日下西江	in the west the sun descends to the river.
促陰橫隱壁	Hastening shadows stretch across and darken the walls;
長暉斜度窻	lengthened rays obliquely penetrate the window.
亂霞圓綠水	Tangled clouds, glowing red, are made circular by the clear water;
細葉影飛缸	tiny leaves outlined by a lamp in the air.

This is twilight, a time of division and ambiguity, when the day is ceasing to be day but the night is not yet quite begun. In the west the sun is setting; in the east we see no moon, only clouds pouring out from the mountains. Darkness is closing in all around. Shadows dominate. Xiao Gang was always fascinated with the play of shadow and light. Here shadows are darkening the walls, while the slanting rays of the setting sun penetrate the window: boundaries are being traversed.

The last two lines are hauntingly beautiful. Few poets before Xiao Gang had used the word "round" (*yuan* 圓) in the third position of a five-syllable line as a full verb, and in such a strange sense too. Because of the grammatical structure in the Chinese original, one might at first think the line means something like "tangled ruddy clouds make the clear water circular." One then realizes that the pool is circular, and so the clouds reflected in the pool, although tangled, are confined and given a shape—a roundness that indicates perfection. (In Buddhism *yuan* is used to describe perfect teachings or enlightenment.) Glowing red with the sunset, the clouds grant the pool a momentary splendor. This is the last light of nature. In the next line, the light in the water has already passed on and been transferred to something else. Lamps are being lit (reminding one of Xi Zuochi's poem about lanterns hanging from tree branches): a small, quiet indication of time's passage and the growing darkness. The poet notices the silhouettes of the tree leaves outlined by the lamplight. In a world gradually sinking into shadows, where boundaries begin to break down, the poet traces out

62. *Quan Liang shi* 21.1947.

luminous patterns and forms and affirms an order created by human efforts.

These lines by Xiao Gang are only a fragment of a poem. We do not know how the poem turned out, whether it fell flat or went into another direction. Yet, these lines suffice to intimate a peculiar vision of the world—and a peculiar way in which poetry is made to work. Compare Xiao Gang's lines to lines such as:

樹木發春華	Trees are blooming in spring splendor;
清池激長流	the clear pool stirs long currents.[63]

or

林壑斂暝色	Forests and ravines gather in the dusk colors,
雲霞收夕霏	clouds and vapors withdraw the sunset glow.[64]

These lines, representative to a certain degree of earlier poetic couplets, are taken from poems written by former masters. I am certainly not suggesting that they are inferior to Xiao Gang's lines, but they clearly belong to a different order. They are more straightforward and linear in their movement. In Xiao Gang's poem, even the first couplet, which is the simplest of the three, requires that one read back to grasp the picture. One understands the significance of the clouds in the eastern sky only after learning that the sun has sunk to the river's level in the west—only then does one realize that all around is darkness. The two lines are not merely parallel; rather, they interact with each other in a complex manner, creating a tension between the lines. The poem represents a moment when, at a time of decreasing visibility, vision is focused on even the smallest change in nature. As a result, nature becomes illuminated, just as the lamplight delineates the dark shapes of the tiny autumn leaves. The Liang court poems, in short, are made not from *sight* like a still-life painting, but from *experience*.

Fortuitously, Xiao Gang's poem ends abruptly with the image of a hanging lamp. Keeping in mind the Buddhist context, we begin to see why the topic of lamps and candles fascinated Liang writers. Lamps and

63. This couplet is taken from Cao Zhi's poem "Zeng Wang Can" 贈王粲 (*Quan Wei shi* 7.451).

64. This couplet is taken from Xie Lingyun's poem "Shibi jingshe huan huzhong zuo" 石壁精舍還湖中作 (*Quan Song shi* 2.1165).

candles are perfect symbols of light and vision; they exemplify the power of illumination achieved through an intensely concentrated and yet all-encompassing vision, and they demonstrate the play of light and shadows, which tricks human perception and creates mystery and illusion.

As noted in the previous chapter, later critics disliked Liang court poetry in part because it resists allegorization. If we temporarily set aside the serious/frivolous dichotomy (and consider what constitutes "seriousness" and why), we will find that one of the greatest virtues of Palace Style poetry is its resistance to allegorization. If allegory figures at all in this poetry, then it is a Buddhist one, concerning the essential unreality of all things, events, and human emotions. Buddhism also teaches that human perceptions are faulty and deluded, and that appearances and reality are not the same. In their prolonged, intense observation of the physical world, the Liang court poets offer a resigned, faintly sad illumination, which flickers like a candle in the wind.

FIRE, WIND, AND WATER: THE EXPERIENCE OF ILLUSION

The court poet Liu Xiaowei left two poems on candlelight. Here is the first one:

和簾裏燭詩
Companion Piece for
"On a Candle Behind the Curtains"[65]

開關簾影出	The door opens, curtain shadow comes out;
參差風焰斜	flickering back and forth, the flame in the wind is oblique.
浮光燭綺帶	Its drifting light shines on the brocade sash;
凝滴汙垂花	a congealed drop stains the hanging flowers.

The poem is not so much about an object as about a moment: when the door opens, a breeze slips in, the curtain is lifted up, and the candle flickers, casting wavering shadows, but also illuminating a presence. One may say many things about, if not the intended meaning, the

65. *Quan Liang shi* 18.1884.

significance of this little poem. One may, for instance, bring up the Buddhist metaphor of "a candle in the wind" or the Chinese *carpe diem* theme of lighting candles at night and seeking pleasure; or one might say, as a traditional Chinese critic would, that this is a mere poetic exercise, a frivolous social verse (as attested by its title), and therefore emotionless, meaningless, and, by implication, immoral. The truth is that this little poem represents no more than a moment of "enlightenment." First and foremost, however, it is about paying attention to the small details of life. It articulates a way of experiencing the physical world. What stands out in the poem is the texture of the textile: the embroidered sash, the flower patterns on the long trains of loose gowns or on the drapery (whose materiality is accentuated by the wax stain)—all unconcealed, as it were, by the incidentally revealed candlelight. This is how a Liang court poet typically looks at the world: things become illuminated in one precious, if brief, instant; and this instant is in motion, moving from a local scene to an even more minute detail, so minute in fact that one can hardly tell whether it is real or imaginary—although this imaginary is, like the powder left on petals by a butterfly's wings, grounded in the empirically true.

The revealing moment of a curtain being lifted up also figures in Xiao Yi's poem on the candle, which shares many of the elements of Liu Xiaowei's quatrain but turns out in a slightly different way:

古意詠燭詩

Candle: An Ancient Mood[66]

花中燭	Candle within a flower—
焰焰動簾風	bright and blazing, the wind blowing the curtain.
不見來人影	No silhouette of anyone coming,
迴光持向空	turning around its light, it faces the empty air.

Understanding the enigmatic first line, "Candle within a flower," requires some knowledge of the material culture of the period. During the Southern Dynasties, one popular decorative motif for porcelain vessels, including candlesticks, was the lotus.[67] The Chinese syntax of the second line (literally, "blazing flames move the curtain wind") creates the

66. Ibid., 25.2058.

67. See Lin Shimin, *Qingci yu Yue yao*, p. 39.

illusion that it is the flames of the candle that are making the wind in the curtain flicker. As in Xi Zuochi's poem, flames define and give shape to the wind, but Xiao Yi is much more sophisticated than Xi Zuochi in articulating this.

Xiao Yi's poem is about loneliness and the illusion produced by loneliness. Mistaking the movement of the curtain in the wind as a sign that someone is coming, the person holding the candle quickly turns around, but of course nobody is there. The candlelight illuminates an empty, unoccupied space—here *kong* 空 means sky or empty air, as well as nothingness, which is perhaps the most important Buddhist concept. "Silhouette" in Chinese is the same as "shadow" (*ying*): it is present in the poem only as an absence, that is, there is *no* silhouette of anyone coming. The loneliness thus described in Xiao Yi's poem evokes a *yuefu* song:

夜長不得眠	The night is long, I cannot sleep,
明月何灼灼	the bright moon, how brightly it shines!
想聞歡喚聲	I think I hear my sweetheart call out to me,
虛應空中諾	and I answer back—all for nothing—into the empty air.[68]

Commenting on these lines, Xiao Difei 蕭滌非, an eminent *yuefu* scholar, exclaims, "No one who had not experienced it in person could have uttered this."[69] However, anyone familiar with Buddhist texts would quickly associate this "realistic" song, as well as Xiao Yi's poem, with the famous Buddhist metaphor about a hallucination caused by an optical or aural disorder, which is likened to the unenlightened one's vain attachment to the illusory physical world.

Xiao Gang wrote a response to his brother Xiao Yi's poem:

和湘東王古意詠燭詩

A Companion Piece for the Prince of Xiangdong's "Candle: An Ancient Mood"[70]

花中燭	Candle within a flower—
似將人意同	as if it were sharing human feelings.

68. "Ziye ge" 子夜歌, no. 33, in *Quan Jin shi* 19.1042.

69. Xiao Difei, *Xiao Difei shuo yuefu*, p. 62.

70. *Quan Liang shi* 22.1977.

憶啼流膝上	Tears of longing flow onto the lap,
燭焰落花中	the candle's flares fall into the flower.

This poem explicitly displaces human feelings onto the candle: it is weeping wax tears, as though it were sharing human feelings and sympathizing with the person facing the candle (the third line deliberately plays with the double references of "tears"—both the wax tears of a candle and human tears).[71] The "sharing," however, grows ominous in the last line: the sparks falling into the flower-shaped candlestick are themselves referred to as "flowers," and their fall, as the candle is consuming itself, is illuminated by the burning flame and points to the approaching darkness.

It is difficult for us who live in an era of brilliant, glaring electric lighting to imagine an old world of shades, dim corners, and the large, distorted shadows cast on walls and rising up to the beams: the very kind of world that provided the material background for Liang Palace Style poetry. The paradox of a candle is that it creates shadow as well as light. Playing on this paradoxical nature, one of Shen Yue's quatrains on the old motif of longing for an absent lover achieves an unexpectedly novel effect:

夜夜曲
Song: Every Night[72]

北斗闌干去	The Dipper stretches across the sky,
夜夜心獨傷	every night the heart is suffering alone.
月輝橫射枕	Moonbeams obliquely strike the pillow,
燈光半隱牀	lamplight half hides the bed.

We assume that there is a woman because the image of the empty bed echoes the second of "Nineteen Old Poems,"[73] although we do not

71. This recalls the last couplet of a quatrain, "Zi jun zhi chu yi" 自君之出矣, by the last Chen emperor Chen Shubao 陳叔寶 (553–604): "My longing for you is like the night candle:/shedding tears till the rooster crows" (*Quan Chen shi* 4.2510). The image later returns in a famous quatrain, "Zeng bie" 贈別, by the Tang poet Du Mu 杜牧 (ca. 803–52). The last two lines of the quatrain read: "The wax candle has a heart and pities that we must part,/shedding tears on our behalf till the dawn breaks" (*Quan Tang shi* 523.5988). *Xin* 心 ("heart") puns on *xin* 芯 ("wick").

72. *Quan Liang shi* 6.1622.

73. *Quan Han shi* 12.329.

know on which side of the bed her body is. However, whether she is in the dark or in the light does not matter. What matters is the contrast between light and shadow, for it is this contrast that makes her feel more poignantly the emptiness of her bed.

For the Liang court poets, shadow was just as fascinating as illumination, for they knew that the latter depended on the former. Shadow is impermanent, conditional, and empty: contemplation on it leads to enlightenment. Shadow both is an illusion and produces illusions: we have all experienced how a familiar face or an ordinary object of daily life can be rendered mysterious, silent, and expressive to the point of being eloquent in semidarkness. In Chinese history, probably the best-known instance of creating illusions with the help of lamps and candles is the story in which a wizard claimed to be able to summon the soul of Lady Li, Han Emperor Wu's favorite consort, who had died young. The wizard set up a curtained enclosure, within which he hung up lamps and candles, and then he made the emperor sit in another curtained enclosure.

> Gazing from the distance, he [the emperor] saw a lovely woman, whose appearance was like that of Lady Li, walking around the place set for her within the curtains. But he could not go to take a closer look. The emperor then felt longing and sadness even more strongly, and wrote this poem: "Is it her / or is it not? / I stand and gaze at her, / yet she glides along, so slow in her coming."[74]
>
> 遙望好女如李夫人之貌，還幄坐而步. 又不得就視. 上愈益相思悲感，為作詩曰："是邪，非邪？立而望之，偏何姍姍其來遲！"

The historian Ban Gu was no Buddhist, but as a Confucian moralist, he nevertheless felt compelled to present the story of Lady Li as a tale of the illusory nature of romantic love: Emperor Wu's passion for Lady Li was exposed as a pursuit of shadows.[75] In many of the Liang court poems on candlelit scenes of passion, we hear echoes of the story of Lady Li. When unfulfilled, passion, itself illusory, creates illusions, as can be seen in Xiao Yi's quatrain on the candle, or in the last four lines of Wang

74. *Han shu* 97.3952; translation from Owen, ed. and trans., *An Anthology of Chinese Literature*, pp. 216–17.

75. See Owen, "One Sight."

Sengru's poem entitled "Night Sorrow: To Be Shown to My Guests" ("Yechou shi zhubin" 夜愁示諸賓):[76]

孤帳閉不開	The lonely curtains are all closed,
寒膏盡復續	cold oil burned out, more added.
誰知心眼亂	Who would understand that my heart and eyes are in such confusion—
看朱忽成碧	when I look at vermilion, it suddenly turns into emerald.

But more often than not the story of Lady Li is turned around, as the poet succeeds in taking a closer look. What fascinates the poet is the moment when the woman's face emerges from the dark and is completely illuminated by candlelight: the moment of unconcealment, when emotions can no longer be suppressed. Shen Yue describes such a moment in his "*Fu* on a Lovely Person" ("Liren fu" 麗人賦):[77]

響羅衣而不進	Her gauze clothes rustle, but she doesn't advance,
隱明燈而未前	hidden in the shadow of the bright lamp, not yet coming forward.
中步檐而一息	Midway upon the walkway she rests a while,
順長廊而迴歸	along the portico she turns around and goes back.
池翻荷而納影	Lotus leaves overturned in the pond, opening up a surface for her reflection;
風動竹而吹衣	a breeze stirs the bamboo grove, blowing on the clothes.
薄暮延佇	Since dusk I have been waiting,
宵分乃至	but she does not arrive until midnight.
出闇入光	Emerging from the darkness, stepping into light,
含羞隱媚	she bashfully conceals her charms.

The woman coming out of the shadows into the light also captures the poet's imagination in a quatrain by Liu Xiaowei's brother Liu Xiaochuo:

76. *Quan Liang shi* 12.1766. In *Yutai xinyong*, the title is simply "Night Sorrow," which would seem to create the impression that the speaker is a woman.

77. *Quan Liang wen* 25.3097.

詠姬人未肯出詩
On a Woman Unwilling to Come Forth[78]

帷開見釵影	Where the curtain opens, I see hairpin's shadow;
簾動聞釧聲	when the hangings stir, I hear bracelets' sound.
徘徊定不出	She hesitates and will not come forth,
常羞華燭明	always shy of the candle's light.

The woman's presence is conjured up like Lady Li's ghost. It is indicated by no more than a glimpse of shadows and some faint sounds. And yet, even as the poet is peeking, the woman behind the scene is also looking back at him. The poet is savoring the moment before revelation, and he knows it.

The following quatrain by Xiao Gang, focusing on the woman's face illuminated by the lamp, urges the eruption of passion—or does it?

烏棲曲
Song of the Roosting Crow[79]

織成屏風銀屈膝	The folding screen of brocade, with silver hinges—
朱唇玉面燈前出	her red lips and jade face emerge in lamplight.
相看氣息望君憐	They gaze at each other, breathing hard, expecting love—
誰能含羞不自前	who can be so shy, as not to come forward?

The woman in this poem has come forward from behind the screen and meets the man face to face. There is a pause, a mutual gaze (which is unusual in the Liang court poetry), and their breathing quickens as they stand so close to each other. But the anticipated advancing and embracing are displaced into the poet's rhetorical question put to her and to himself: at such a moment, who can still hold back? The displacement, the reader realizes, is only temporary in real time, but it becomes permanent in poetic time: the poem comes to an eternal standstill, like the love scene painted on Keats's Grecian urn, precariously positioned right on the verge of the headlong fall.

78. *Quan Liang shi* 16.1843.
79. Ibid., 20.1922.

Stephen Owen, in his reading of this poem, considers the woman a painted figure on the screen.[80] There is certainly an ambiguity in the poem that makes this reading possible. In this reading, the poem is suddenly tinged with a rich irony: the image in the second line becomes even more forceful, as the flooding lamplight brings forth the painted woman from the dark as if she were real; the closing question turns out to be self-mockery—the enlightened Buddhist layman looks at his secular self with a smile, as he comments on the foolishness of the viewer who, despite knowing better, still cannot help taking *śūnyatā* for *rūpa*, illusory appearances for reality.[81]

Apart from poems on lamps and candles, Xiao Gang composed a "*Fu* on Facing the Candle" ("Duizhu fu" 對燭賦),[82] which contains a few lines that are among the best in all Chinese writings on the candle. In the sensitive manner characteristic of Xiao Gang, they convey the trancelike state, the sensory illusions, induced by looking long and hard at dancing flames. The poet's attention is so intensely focused that any change in the phenomenal world—the passage of time, the passage of a breeze—is noticed only through the changes in the candle:

漸覺流珠走	After a while one feels the rush of flowing beads,
熟視絳花多	crimson flowers, stared at closely, multiply.
宵深色麗	Night grows deep—color is bright;
焰動風過	flame flickers—a breeze has just passed.

The "crimson flowers" are the sparks given off by the candle, but they could also be the spots of light in the eyes of the beholder gazing too intently at the flames. They remind one of the Buddhist phrase "sky flowers" (*kong hua* 空花), illusory flowers seen in the sky as the result of an optical disorder, which signify the empty nature of the physical world.

80. Owen, *Mi-Lou*, pp. 210–11.

81. In another poem, "Yong meiren kanhua" 詠美人看畫, Xiao Gang wrote about a palace lady looking at the portrait of a beautiful woman, suggesting that both were "painted" and thus unreal (*Quan Liang shi* 22.1953). This recalls a Buddhist story about how the recognition of the unreality of paintings and statues leads to enlightenment regarding the empty nature of the physical world. The story is included in the Liang Buddhist encyclopedia *Jinglü yixiang* (*T* 53: 44.229).

82. *Quan Liang wen* 8.2997.

The *fu* reads like a narrative poem, with alternating seven-, four-, six-, and five-syllable lines. The story is minimal and familiar: it is a chilly autumn night; a party that has gone on too long finally comes to an end; man and woman retire to the bedchamber, sharing an intimate moment alone:

雲母窗中合花毦	Behind mica windows is a space suitable for flowery rugs;
茱萸幔裏鋪錦筵	within ailanthus curtains, a sumptuous banquet is set up.[83]
照夜明珠且莫取	But let's not fetch those night-illuminating pearls,
金羊燈火不須然	and there is no need for lighting the golden ram lamp.
下弦三更未有月	At the third night watch, still no trace of the crescent moon;
中夜繁星徒依天	only a multitude of stars embracing the midnight sky.
於是	Thereupon
搖同心之明燭	swaying bright candles sharing the same heart-wick,
施雕金之麗盤	we put out dishes inlaid with gold.
眠龍傍繞	Slumbering dragons coil on the side,
倒鳳雙安	paired phoenixes, reversed, at peace.
轉辟邪而取正	Turning around the *bixie* candlestick, so it faces the right way;[84]
推櫺窗而畏寬	pushing open the window screen but worried the crack might be too wide.
綠炬懷翠	Emerald torches harboring kingfisher blue,
朱蠟含丹	vermilion wax contains scarlet;
豹脂宜火	Leopard lard is suitable for flames,
牛膝耐寒	and ox fat good for enduring the cold.
銅芝抱帶復纏柯	Bronze *zhi*-plants intertwine in a tight embrace and wrap around it,
金藕相縈共吐荷	golden lotus roots tangle, yielding lotus flowers.

83. Ailanthus curtains are curtains embroidered with ailanthus, a plant supposed to ward off evil. The sixth-century agricultural treatise *Qimin yaoshu* 齊民要術 by Jia Sixie 賈思勰 (fl. first half, 6th c.) claims that "if one hangs the seeds of ailanthus in one's house, then ghosts do not dare to enter" (Jia, *Qimin yaoshu*, p. 227).

84. *Bixie* is a mythical beast.

視橫芒之昭曜	Looking at the splendor of the oblique plumes of flame,
見蜜淚之躊跎	we see the hesitation of beeswax tears.
漸覺流珠走	After a while one feels the rush of flowing beads,
熟視絳花多	crimson flowers, stared at closely, multiply.
宵深色麗	Night grows deep—color is bright;
焰動風過	flame flickers—a breeze has just passed.
夜久惟煩鋏	Only as the night draws on does one need to bother with tongs;
天寒不畏蛾	weather being cold, have no fear of moths.
菖蒲傳酒座欲闌	When calamus wine is served, the banquet is coming to an end;[85]
碧玉舞罷羅衣單	after Green Jade finishes dancing, she feels the thinness of her gauze dress.[86]
影度臨長枕	A shadow crosses over, hovering over the long pillow;
煙生向果盤	wisps of smoke arise, drifting toward the fruit plate.
迴照金屏裏	Turning, it sheds light behind the golden screen:
脈脈兩相看	a mutual gaze, with unspoken feelings.

The *fu* once again abruptly stops at the point when the man and woman gaze at each other, and the built-up tension from holding back is deeply felt. What comes next will remain unspoken, which is only appropriate—it is irrelevant to the subject of the *fu*, for the candle is about to be extinguished.[87]

The French painter Georges La Tour (1593–1652) was famous for painting candlelit images. In one of his most famous paintings, *Magdalene with Two Flames*, the Magdalene sits at a table half turned away from the viewer, hands resting on a skull. On the table is a burning candle; in

85. Calamus was customarily immersed in wine and taken on the fifth day of the fifth month. See Zong Lin, *Jing Chu suishi ji*, p. 158.

86. "Green Jade" is supposed to have been the name of a singing girl in the Liu Song period. Her name became a *yuefu* song title.

87. Xiao Yi and Yu Xin both wrote a *fu* with the same title; see *Quan Liang wen* 15.3038 and *Quan hou Zhou wen* 9.3925–26. These pieces might have been composed on the same occasion. Due to space limitations, they are not discussed here.

front of the candle, a mirror. The flame is reflected in the mirror; hence the title of the painting.

The Magdalene, the reformed prostitute, is contemplating the vanity of the secular world and preparing herself for a religious life. The painter's choice of a mirrored candle corresponds curiously to the Liang court poets' fascination with candlelight reflected in water, perhaps because, as John Berger says, "When there is more than one figure, it is hard to be sure whether each is real or only the dream projection of the other. Every lit form proposes the possibility that it is no more than an apparition."[88] "Reflected image" is, in fact, one of the "Ten Mahāyāna Metaphors" for the essential emptiness of the phenomenal world: both Emperor Wu and Xiao Gang composed poems on these metaphors.[89]

Candlelight reflected in a mirror perfectly symbolizes the illusory nature of physical reality. Water, however, proves a much more unreliable mirror: it flows, undulates, quivers in the slightest wind, and causes distortions of reflected images. Candlelight shines on water but can never penetrate it. It remains a glittering surface, sparkling with burnished ripples.

The following example is a poem by Xiao Yi, "On the Reflection of Candlelight in the Pond" ("Yong chizhong zhuying" 詠池中燭影):[90]

魚燈且滅燼	Let the embers go out in the fish-form lamp,
鶴焰暫停輝	and the blaze of the crane lamp pause its radiance—
自有銜龍燭	there is, all by itself, the candle-holding dragon[91]
青火入朱扉	whose blue flame enters the vermilion gate.

88. Berger, *About Looking*, p. 116.

89. Of Xiao Yan's "Shiyu shi" 十喻詩, five are extant; see *Quan Liang shi* 1.1532–33. Six of Xiao Gang's "Shikong shi" 十空詩 are extant (ibid., 21.1937–38). Similar metaphors with some variations also appear in the *Vimalakīrti Sūtra*, which had been translated into Chinese at least six or seven times by the Liang dynasty. Xie Lingyun wrote a group of odes or encomiums (*zan* 讚) on these metaphors. Although treated as prose pieces by Yan Kejun, these odes are verses in rhymed five-syllable lines (*Quan Song wen* 33.2617).

90. *Quan Liang shi* 25.2047–48.

91. This line hints at the mythical "Candle Dragon," but dragon and phoenix also are the most common decorations for candlesticks.

映水疑三燭	Reflecting upon water, it seems like the Three Shinings,[92]
翻池類九微	churned in the waves, it resembles the Nine Branch Candelabra.
入林如燐影	Entering the grove like the shadowy will-o'-the-wisp;
度渚若螢飛	or crossing the islet, like fireflies.
河低扇月落	The Milky Way hangs low, fan-moon descends;
霧上珠星稀	fog rises, pearl stars scant.
章華終宴所	At the Zhanghua Terrace, when the banquet ends,[93]
飛蓋且相追	flying canopies pursue one another.

The poem begins with a rhetorical device not unlike a *priamel* (i.e., listing three nice things but then mentioning the fourth as the best). Then it offers a series of similes: the divine light on the Earth God altar, an object of artifice (the nine-branch candelabra), and things of nature (will-o'-the-wisp and fireflies). It also presents the movement of the party: entering the gate, lingering beside the pond, going into the grove, and then again crossing the islet. The couplet in lines 9 and 10 both marks the passage of time (the moon is descending, a late night or early morning fog is rising) and implies the increasing illusion of human perception (caused by the late hour and by the merrymaking and drinking). The reflections in the waters seem to have transformed the pond into the Milky Way—the speaker marvels at how low it is!—and so the human realm is turned into the heavenly sphere: as the singers and dancers grow tired, the round fan, resembling the moon, is laid down. The rising of the fog further confuses the senses: pearls worn by the palace ladies cannot be distinguished from the stars—both have become "scant." As the poet stops using such words as "seem," "resemble," or

92. It is said that Emperor Wu of the Han had seen a divine light ("shining three times during one night") appearing on the altar after he made sacrifice to the Earth God (*Han shu* 6.195).

93. Zhanghua Terrace was built by King Ling of Chu (r. 540–529 B.C.). In a *fu* on this terrace, Bian Rang 邊讓 (fl. late 2nd or early 3rd c.) described a great night banquet but ended with the king's "returning to his senses" in the morning and a praise of his sober rule of the country (*Quan hou Han wen* 84.929–30). In reality, King Ling of Chu met a tragic end.

"like," the rationality of the preceding four lines deteriorates, and the boundary between metaphor and reality becomes blurred.

Liu Xiaowei's quatrain in seven-syllable lines was written on the third day of the third month, a festival day celebrating the arrival of spring. The custom was to gather together by a winding stream (often man-made) and float wine cups on it; whenever a cup paused in front of someone, the person had to drink the wine, fill the cup with new wine, and let it drift on.

禊飲嘉樂殿詠曲水中燭影
On the Reflection of Candlelight in the
Winding Stream at the Jiale Palace at a Drinking Party on the
Third Day of the Third Month[94]

火浣花心猶未長	The fire-washed flower-heart has not yet grown very long,[95]
金枝密焰已流芳	fragrance already flows from the honeyed flames of golden branches.[96]
芙蓉池畔涵停影	The lotus pond saturates the abiding reflection,[97]
桃花水脈引行光	the peach-blossom waters lead the flowing light on and on.

The last couplet of the poem seems to balance the appearance of light in still water and in flowing water. In the tranquil "lotus pond," the reflection may be still, but the "peach blossom waters," a term referring to spring floods (which arrive when the peach trees are blossoming), are more appropriate for a winding stream. As the water flows on, the candlelight it reflects seems to be flowing too, and the crimson shimmering of the water inevitably reminds one of Tao Yuanming's "Peach Blossom

94. *Quan Liang shi* 18.1884.

95. "Fire-washed" alludes to asbestos, "cloth washable in fire" or "fire-proof cloth" 火浣布. There is a record of asbestos being used as lamp wicks in Wang Jia's 王嘉 (ca. fourth century) *Shiyi ji*, p. 225. The "flower-heart" refers to the candlewick. If it is made of asbestos, it does not burn away but seems to get longer as the candle burns.

96. Here *mi* 密 is a loan character for *mi* 蜜. The golden branches refer to a candelabra.

97. Both Cao Pi and Cao Zhi wrote poems with the title "Furong chi" 芙蓉池 (*Quan Wei shi* 4.400, 7.462).

Spring," a stream covered with peach blossoms that leads the inquisitive fisherman to a marvelous utopian realm.

Another poem on the same topic and also in seven-syllable lines was composed by Yu Jianwu. Whether the two poems were written on the same occasion is unknown, but both are concerned with illusion and inconstancy:

三日侍宴詠曲水中燭影

On the Reflection of Candlelight in the
Winding Stream at the Imperial Banquet on the
Third Day of the Third Month[98]

重燄垂花比芳樹	Manifold flames yield flowers like a fragrant tree,
風吹水動俱難住	wind blows, water stirs—both are hard to stay still.
春枝拂岸影上來	Spring boughs caress the riverbank, brushing over the reflections;
還杯繞客光中度	A returning wine cup flows around a guest, passing through light.

The burning candle is compared to a flowering tree in spring, its glory most fleeting. The candle is blown by the wind, and its reflection disrupted by the ripples. The "golden boughs" of the chandelier in Liu Xiaowei's poem are replaced by "spring boughs," perhaps those of willows brushing the water in the wind and disrupting the reflection, but the branches may also be a reference to the stems of the candelabra, in which case it would be their shadow on the ground that caresses the bank. The wine cup floating on the stream, itself a sparkling speck, is moving through currents of light. The poem itself is like a segment cut off from the stream of time: it does not stand still but is a fluid moment.

Xiao Gang's poem on sending a palace lady back to her boat at night adds a peculiar touch to the "candlelight in water" motif:

夜遣內人還後舟

Sending a Palace Lady Back by Night to the Rear Boat[99]

錦幔扶船列	Rows of brocade curtains shelter her barge,
蘭橈拂浪浮	magnolia oars float, brushing the waves.

98. *Quan Liang shi* 23.2004.

99. Ibid., 22.1969; translation from Owen, *An Anthology of Chinese Literature*, p. 327.

去燭猶文水	Her departing candle still patterns the waves;
餘香尚滿舟	her lingering scent still fills my boat.

The palace lady is departing in a barge and is well protected by the brocade curtains from prying eyes. Her absence is nonetheless very much present, filling up the entire space: her perfume permeates his boat, and her candle creates a shimmering pattern on the rippling water. Both effects—one of sight and the other of smell—are transitory (with the feeling of evanescence highlighted by the adverbs *you* and *shang*, "still"), but these fleeting signs of her absence insist on reminding us of her. The poem is an eloquent articulation of the unity of sensuous appearances (*se*) and emptiness (*kong*).

CODA: THE CHESSBOARD IN CANDLELIGHT

A poem on candlelight by the famous court poet Liu Xiaochuo, though hastily written to command on a social occasion, is nevertheless a good example of competent public performance, and in this sense it is representative of the average Southern Dynasties social verse. The poem, however, has a subject rich with associations and echoes, and it thus acquires a weight disproportionate to its origin when placed in its historical context. It is for this reason that I end the chapter with this poem:

賦得照棊燭詩刻五分成
A Poem Composed as Demanded on the
Candle Shining Forth on a Chessboard, Finished When
the Candle Burned Down by Half an Inch[100]

南皮弦吹罷	The string and woodwind instruments have stopped at Nanpi;[101]
終奕且留賓	the host urges the guests to stay and finish the chess game.

100. *Quan Liang shi* 16.1840.

101. Nanpi is the place where Cao Pi, when he was a young man, had parties with his literary friends. See his "Yu Wu Zhi shu" 與吳質書 (*Quan sanguo wen* 7.1089).

日下房櫳闇	As the sun goes down, the room darkens,
華燭命佳人	the beautiful lady is asked to bring in the sparkling candle.
側光全照局	Oblique light illuminates the entire chessboard;
回花半隱身	the flame twirls, her body half in shadow.
不辭纖手倦	She does not mind her slender hands growing tired—
羞令夜向晨	only regretting that night will be getting toward morning.

The fine moment of this poem comes in the third couplet: the chessboard, which is the center of attention, is illuminated—the only space of light in the surrounding dark. The woman holding the candle watches; since she is obviously standing, only parts of her body are illuminated by the candlelight, but her face remains in the shadow. The intensity of the game is thus brought forth in the play of shadow and light. The woman is so fascinated by the game that she worries that it will soon be dawn and, candle rendered unnecessary, she will be dismissed.

How would Liu Xiaochuo's immediate circle have reacted to this poem? We imagine that they would, first of all, applaud the speed with which the poem was composed. The recording of the exact composition time in the title indicates the pride the poet felt: the poem was, after all, an opportunity to show off his quick wit. It served the same purpose as swift, clever repartee, such as the examples admiringly recorded in the fifth-century compilation of anecdotes *Shishuo xinyu*.

The poet's contemporaries might also hear in Liu Xiaochuo's poem the echo of a popular *yuefu* song, and readers familiar with the literature of the period would likewise share such an association:

今日已歡別	Today I parted with my sweetheart;
合會在何時	when will we ever meet again?
明燈照空局	The bright lamp shines upon an empty chessboard—
悠然未有期	it shall be faraway, for there is no date yet![102]

102. "Ziye ge" 子夜歌, no. 9 (*Quan Jin shi* 19.1040). "Duqu ge" 讀曲歌, no. 62, is almost verbatim except for the first two characters of the opening line (*Quan Song shi* 11.1344).

Both the "bright lamp" and the "empty chessboard" are key images not only because they create a scene of loneliness and absence, but also because they are pivotal to the word play: *you ran* (faraway) puns on "oil burns" (*you ran* 油燃); *qi* 期 (tryst, appointment, date) on *qi* 棋 (chess pieces)—thus "no chess piece on the board" becomes "no date." When it is empty, the chessboard, originally a space of battle for domination, is inscribed with an erotic meaning.

The last line of Liu Xiaochuo's poem would likely have occasioned another recognition by educated readers both of his own time and of a later age: "night getting toward morning" 夜鄉晨 is a phrase appearing in a poem from *The Classic of Poetry*, "Torch in the Courtyard" ("Tingliao" 庭燎). As traditionally interpreted, this poem is supposed to be about a king who throughout the night constantly asked his attendant the time because he was anxious about being late for the morning court. Here is the last stanza of "Torch in the Courtyard":

夜如何其	How goes the night?
夜鄉晨	It is getting toward morning.
庭燎有煇	The torch is smoking in the courtyard.
君子至止	My princely men are arriving;—
言觀其旂	I see their banners.[103]

The political reading of this poem is evidenced by the surviving fragment of a verse of the same title by Fu Xuan of the Western Jin. Fu Xuan's poem describes a grand morning court scene on New Year's Day, with lamps and torches lit up and emissaries from various countries paying respects to the emperor.[104] It is certainly tempting to detect in Liu Xiaochuo's poem a "remonstrance" in the tradition of the *fu*, which was expected to counter the depiction of pleasure by concluding with a moral lesson. And yet one would be reading too much into this lighthearted social verse if one were to deduce that Liu Xiaochuo intended to warn the prince who had commanded the poem or his fellow officials against wasting time on trivial games. Besides, the phrase *ye xiang chen* might have been assimilated into contemporary literary vocabulary

103. *Maoshi zhengyi* 11.375; translation from Legge, *The Chinese Classics*, 4: 295.
104. *Quan Jin shi* 1.571.

without the author's or the reader's ever becoming conscious of its *locus classicus*.

In what light, then, may we now read Liu Xiaochuo's poem? In many ways, our reading is as much embedded in history as were the readings of Liu Xiaochuo's contemporaries. If hindsight offers us any advantage, then it has to be a retrospective viewpoint that Liu Xiaochuo's immediate audience would not possibly have possessed: in other words, we recognize this poem as a survivor. It survived historical events of a magnitude as yet unimaginable to its author: the destruction of the capital, Jiankang, during a siege, famine, plague, and slaughter; the Hou Jing Rebellion that split the country not into half but into many fragments and eventually led to the dynasty's downfall; the burning to ashes of tens of thousand books in the imperial library, twice, first in Jiankang and then in Jiangling. When, to the admiration of his imperial patrons, his brothers, and his friends, Liu Xiaochuo dashed off the poem on a candle lighting up the chessboard, he certainly did not anticipate how the match would end.

Of various forms of leisure activities, chess (sometimes translated "encirclement chess," or *go*) is perhaps most closely associated with martial accomplishments: moves in a chess game are paralleled with military maneuvers; defeat and victory seen as mirroring what happens on a real battlefield. As Zu-yan Chen says, chess is "intrinsically an antagonistic or warlike game, governed primarily by skills developed in handling strategic operations and tactical encounters."[105] Testimony to this is found in a number of *fu* on chess ("Weiqi fu" 圍棋賦)—by Liu Xiang, Ma Rong 馬融 (79–166), Cai Hong 蔡洪 (fl. third century), Cao Shu 曹攄 (d. 308), and Emperor Wu of the Liang himself, who was a great chess aficionado.[106] The political history of the Six Dynasties, apart from internal power struggles, had been a series of constant battles and diplomatic dealings with the northern military threat: the shadow of northern power, sometimes weakened, sometimes intensified, was nonetheless always present.

---

105. Zu-yan Chen, "The Art of Black and White."

106. *Quan Han wen* 35.321, 18.566; *Quan Jin wen* 81.1928, 107.2074–75; *Quan Liang wen* 1.2951. Emperor Wu reportedly obtained "the superior level" in chess skills (*Liang shu* 3.96).

For later generations, chess-playing was deeply embedded in the image of the Six Dynasties, partially because of the political instability and military strife that characterized much of the Six Dynasties, partially because of the defining role played by chess in a historical battle that decided the fate of the Southland. Xie An, the great minister of the Eastern Jin, was a chess lover. In the year 383, the northern ruler Fu Jian 符堅 stationed his army of reportedly a million soldiers on the Eastern Jin border, with the intent of destroying the Jin and unifying China. Against this background, Xie An played a game of chess with his nephew Xie Xuan 謝玄 (343–88), who was then in charge of the defending army of no more than 80,000 soldiers. They made a bet on Xie Xuan's villa. Xie Xuan had always been a much better chess player than his uncle, but on that day, nervous like everybody else in the capital city, he had difficulty concentrating and lost both the game and his villa to an unruffled Xie An. Turning to another nephew, Yang Tan 羊曇, Xie An said: "The villa now is all yours." He then went to the villa and held a big party. Only after midnight did he return home to deal with all the military matters awaiting his decisions. When the news of a grand victory later reached Xie An, he was again playing chess with a guest. He read the letter, indifferently put it aside, and resumed the game. Pressed by the anxious guest, he answered coolly: "Oh, the kids have smashed the intruders."[107]

Of all the stories about the panache (*fengliu* 風流) of the Six Dynasties, this probably represents the crowning moment. Xie An's cultivated coolness in the face of a powerful enemy is a favorite subject of later poetry. The best known is perhaps the late Tang poet Wen Tingyun's 溫庭筠 (ca. 812–70) "Song of Lord Xie's Villa" ("Xie gong shu ge" 謝公墅歌), which captures that famous moment in an elegantly drawn sketch of the chess-playing scene. The second part of the poem reads:

四座無喧梧竹靜	None of the guests made the least noise, beech and bamboo were hushed,
金蟬玉柄俱持頤	Lords of golden cicadas and scepters of jade, all rested their chins on hands.

107. Liu Yiqing, *Shishuo xinyu* 6.373; translation from Mather, trans., *A New Account*, p. 193. See also *Jin shu* 79.2075.

對局含嚬見千里	He faces the board, he knits his brows, he sees a thousand miles,
都城已得長蛇尾	and the capital has already seized the long serpent's tail.
江南王氣繫疎襟	The Southland's royal aura twines through his open lapels—
未許符堅過淮水	and he never let Fu Jian cross the river Huai.[108]

Two important things, immediately relevant to our view of Liu Xiaochuo's poem, stand out in the Xie An story. The first is the bet, which resulted in the changed ownership of the villa. Wen Tingyun grasped its significance, for it is cleverly reflected in the title of his poem—"*Lord* Xie's Villa"—and the second line of the poem, which states: "The *young Master* Xie's eastern villa" (Xie lang *dongshu* 謝郎東墅). The transition from one to the other is significant because, had Xie An not won the chess game, the panache with which he played would never have been recognized as such. Similarly, in the much larger "chess game," in which the bet was the fate of the Eastern Jin empire, it was again the final victory that served as the defining context for Xie An's flair. Without the victory, Xie An would have been seen as a fool.

How on earth did Xie An win? After all, he had far less skill in chess than his nephew, and the Eastern Jin army was not even one tenth of the size of the enemy forces. This leads us to the second important point of this story: Xie An won because he was able to concentrate, whereas his opponent could not.

Again, Wen Tingyun grasped this point. In his portrayal of Xie An, both the knitted eyebrows and the opened lapels indicate Xie An's deep absorption in the chessboard in front of him. Not even Fu Jian's powerful army could distract him.

The royal aura of the Southland, however, could not be sustained. For nearly half a century, the peaceful and prosperous reign of Emperor Wu of the Liang lulled the kingdom into a sense of security, but it all came to an end during the Hou Jing Rebellion. Looking back now, we see Liu Xiaochuo's poem on a chess game in a slightly different light

108. *Quan Tang shi* 5176.6702; translation from Owen, *An Anthology of Chinese Literature*, p. 332. For an excellent analysis of the poem, see Rouzer, *Writing Another's Dream*, pp. 130–31.

from his contemporaries. It, of course, can never compare with the chess game played with such aplomb by Xie An during the Battle of the Fei River: it was just an inconsequential chess game at one of those evening parties in a prince's salon or perhaps even in the imperial court. Whereas Xie An's chess-playing had a triumphant context, Liu Xiaochuo's poem has for its backdrop a dynasty's downfall. Therefore, it was doomed never to obtain the kind of panache characterizing Xie An and his version of the Six Dynasties; instead, it has acquired a lightness, a frivolity even, in the eyes of later generations.

To play a chess game and win requires concentration. For the Liang court poets, concentration on the myriad thought-instants had materialized into exquisitely crafted poems, each of which represented a moment of absorption in sensuous appearances and the ultimate emptiness of things. Is it really true then, as an austere Tang historian or a Northern Song neo-Confucian philosopher would have concluded, that the Liang fell because of a misdirection in attention? This, I think, is a myth, created by moralists looking for "a lesson" in every historical event, particularly the collapse of a state. Their goal is to teach their own dynasty how to avoid such pitfalls and thus to last forever. Without a doubt, one can always find what one is looking for, but the earnestness with which one searches may compromise the finding.

Xie An's lightness was made possible by the weight of a grand military victory;[109] in contrast, exactly because of the weight of history attached to it, Liu Xiaochuo's poem remains light—both in the sense of being weightless and inconsequential and in the sense of being luminous. Around its faint light, however, the room is darkened.

Literature, after all, represents a series of attempts on the part of humankind to resist what the modern writer Italo Calvino described as "the weight, the inertia, the opacity of the world."[110] The lightness of Liu Xiaochuo's poem, and all the little poems discussed in this chapter about lamps and candles written by the Liang court poets, to borrow a

---

109. The veracity of the accounts of the battle has, however, been questioned by some modern historians; see Rogers, "The Myth of the Battle." But Charles Holcombe (*In the Shadow*, p. 154) defends the view that an invasion took place. Perhaps the scale of the victory has been exaggerated.

110. Calvino, *Six Memos*, p. 4.

phrase from the thirteenth-century Italian poet Guido Cavalcanti, belongs to the lightness of "snow falling without wind."[111] It is not a scattered, chaotic, directionless kind of lightness but a focused lightness, which is achieved by way of a penetrating gaze and a belief in the emptiness of all things as taught by the Buddhists. Because of the court poets' intensely attentive way of seeing things, hitherto concealed patterns are unconcealed, and the world is illuminated.

111. Cited in ibid., p. 14.

CHAPTER SIX

"Suppression of the Light"

Xiao Gang, Prince and Poet

Since Xiao Gang has largely been regarded as a "Palace Style writer," with "Palace Style" conventionally misunderstood as concerned with boudoir life and romantic love, modern scholars' attention tends to be directed to poems with such subject matter when they discuss Xiao Gang's works. However, as the modern scholar Hu Nianyi has observed, about two-thirds of Xiao Gang's extant poems have nothing to do with such topics.[1] Indeed, even the fact that one-third of Xiao Gang's extant poems do treat boudoir themes is a function of the source that preserves them—*Yutai xinyong*, which was intended for a female readership. Such accidents of survival skew our perception of Xiao Gang and confirm the stereotyped image. Indeed, even in discussing the so-called decadent poems of Xiao Gang, scholars tend to cite the same small group of titillating poems as examples and ignore more intricate pieces that present a spirited portrait of female characters and a dramatic situation.[2]

1. Hu Nianyi, "Lun gongti," p. 168.

2. The poems cited most often to demonstrate the characteristic of Palace Style poetry are "On a Wife's Daytime Nap" ("Yong neiren zhoumian" 詠內人晝眠), or "On a Pretty Boy" ("Yong luantong" 詠孌童), or "On a Famed Gentleman Taking Delight in a Beautiful Woman" ("Mingshi yue qingcheng" 名士悅傾城) (which, for all we know, might have been written by Xiao Tong). More complex and subtle poems are pieces such as "A Companion Piece for 'Exchanging a Beloved Concubine for

Sometimes it seems that in order to make Palace Style poetry fit modern critical paradigms, critics look to poems that depict women "as objects" and deliberately neglect those with more psychological complexity and subtlety.

Xiao Gang, the most important figure in the sixth-century transformation of classical Chinese poetry, should be recognized as one of the greatest poets in classical Chinese literature: one whose life was cut short at the age of forty-eight and whose achievement was suppressed. Before he was murdered in the winter of 551, Xiao Gang wrote several hundred poems and prose pieces during the forty-five days of his imprisonment. Having no paper, he wrote on the walls and screens of his chamber. All these writings were effaced by Hou Jing's men; only a few have been transmitted to us. Xiao Gang's immense literary collection of 100 scrolls became dispersed and lost. His extant writings are largely preserved in encyclopedias; as a result, many of them are no more than excerpts.

Nevertheless, the total number of Xiao Gang's extant poems, over 250, still far exceeds any other poet's surviving oeuvre from the period. Only one copy of his collection reportedly survived the Hou Jing Rebellion; after the conquest of Jiangling, it was taken to the North and kept in the imperial library of the Western Wei.[3] The survival of a relatively large number of Xiao Gang's poems, compared with the fate of works by other Southern Dynasties writers, is more than a matter of luck or productivity; rather, it owes much to the abundant interest in his work among his contemporaries and subsequent generations. As Glen Dudbridge has said, "Transmission itself is not a wholly random process."[4]

---

a Horse'" ("He ren aiqie huan ma" 和人愛妾換馬), "Spring Boudoir Feelings" ("Chungui qing" 春閨情), "Looking for Plum Blossoms in the Snow" ("Xueli mi meihua" 雪里覓梅花), "Picking Mulberries" ("Caisang" 採桑), or "The Purple Steed" ("Zi liuma" 紫騮馬). Scholars also tend to avert their eyes from some genuinely wonderful love poems, such as "From the Camp Returning to the South of the City" ("Cong dun huan chengnan" 從頓還城南) or "Unclassified Song" ("Zayong" 雜詠).

3. *Zhou shu* 42.757. Xiao Dahuan 蕭大圜, Xiao Gang's youngest son, did not see his father's and grandfather's complete collections until he was appointed an academician by the Northern Zhou court in the early 560s; he then set out to copy the collections out by hand. It took him a year to finish.

4. Dudbridge, *Lost Books*, p. 27.

Xiao Gang was a poet's poet. A reader intent on finding a "message," moralistic or otherwise, or biographical revelations in Xiao Gang's poetry might be disappointed. Xiao Gang certainly composed many poems on social occasions such as court gatherings, farewell parties, or religious events, which have resulted in numerous trite and pedestrian works at the hands of lesser writers; yet Xiao Gang's poems on these and other subjects betray his most remarkable accomplishment—his attention to poetic language itself. Rarely before Xiao Gang had any poet been so sensitive to words and yet so bold and inventive with them.

The major concern of Xiao Gang's poetry is transience—in the sense not so much of taking mutability and mortality as his themes as of being intensely concerned with moments. His poetry catches fleeting moments in the flow of time and commits them to ink and paper. By portraying the world in terms of moments, Xiao Gang succeeded in making it both fragile and very much alive. This was perhaps why he was so fascinated with shadows: a shadow implies a specific time of the day, hence a specific moment.

Many have criticized Xiao Gang for being too delicate, a characteristic that suggests femininity in a patriarchal discourse and becomes a doubly suspicious trait in a ruler. Such a view often mistakes an extraordinary power of observation for delicacy. In the end, it is not Xiao Gang's poetry that is delicate, but the ephemeral, vibrant, and energetic world depicted in them.

THE EARLY YEARS

Like Xiao Tong, Xiao Gang was born of Lady Ding Lingguang. He was the third son of Emperor Wu.[5] He was born on December 2, 503, in the Xianyang Palace. On February 26, 506, he was enfeoffed as the Prince of Jin'an.

5. The second son, Xiao Zong, was born of Lady Wu Jinghui 吳景暉, who had been one of the favorites of the Marquis of Darkness in the East, the deposed Qi emperor. Xiao Zong was born in 502, seven months after Lady Wu was taken by Emperor Wu, and it was rumored that he had been sired by the late marquis. This rumor was never confirmed, but Xiao Zong, plagued by doubt, was alienated from Emperor Wu and defected to the Northern Wei in 525. He died of illness in the North in 529 or 530 (*Liang shu* 55.824; *Nan shi* 53.1318; *Wei shu* 59.1326).

As a boy Xiao Gang was precocious and reportedly began versification at the age of five (or six *sui* by Chinese reckoning). An incredulous Emperor Wu tested him in person, and Xiao Gang quickly composed a well-phrased piece. As the younger brother of the crown prince, he naturally received the appellation "the Prince of Dong'e,"[6] a title assumed by the prince and poet Cao Zhi, who was the younger brother of the heir apparent, Cao Pi.

In 509 Xiao Gang received his first administrative appointment: he was made General of the Cloud Banners and given command of the Stone Fort, a post held by his father from 495 to 497. At this point, he acquired his own staff. Xu Chi, the person who was to exert a large influence on Xiao Gang's development as a poet, was assigned as his tutor. Xu Chi and the young prince obviously formed a deep bond. It was perhaps not a coincidence that many years later Xiao Gang claimed that he had become obsessed with poetry at the age of six, the age at which Xu Chi became his mentor. Another well-known writer on Xiao Gang's staff was Zhang Shuai, who followed Xiao Gang to various posts for ten years and was a favorite of the young prince.[7]

About a year later, on January 27, 510, Xiao Gang was made the governor of South Yanzhou 南兗州. The district capital of South Yanzhou was Guangling 廣陵 (modern-day Yangzhou), just across the Yangzi River from the capital city, Jiankang. Nevertheless, this was the first time that Xiao Gang left the palace. He remained at Guangling for three years. In 512 he presumably came back to the capital for his marriage: his wife, Wang Lingbin 王靈賓 (505–49), was a member of the illustrious Langye Wang clan, descending from the Eastern Jin minister Wang Dao. Her grandfather was Wang Jian, the famous Qi statesman. Lady Wang bore Xiao Gang two sons and one daughter. She was to die in the siege of the Palace City in the spring of 549.

In 513 Xiao Gang was summoned back to the capital and appointed prefect of Danyang 丹陽, the larger metropolitan area of Jiankang. The ten-year-old Xiao Gang reportedly first tried his hand at administration around this time. A year later, he was made governor of Jingzhou

6. *Liang shu* 4.109; *Nan shi* 8.232.
7. *Liang shu* 33.478.

(whose capital lay in modern Hubei province). This office took him further away from home than did his previous appointments.

In the summer of 515, Xiao Gang was transferred to Jiangzhou (capital in Jiangxi province). Crown Prince Xiao Tong sent him a poem entitled "For [the General of the] Cloud Banners, My Younger Brother" 示雲麾弟, to which Xiao Gang responded in kind with a verse in the seven-syllable Chu song meter.[8] The meter might have been specially chosen to honor the occasion, since Jiangzhou was traditionally part of the Chu region. The opening of Xiao Tong's poem evokes "The Song of the Autumn Wind" ("Qiufeng ci" 秋風辭), attributed to Emperor Wu of the Han and now preserved through its appearance in none other than Xiao Tong's anthology *Wen xuan*.[9]

白雲飛兮江上阻	White clouds fly, blocking the view of the river;
北流分兮山風舉	the northern tributary branches off, the mountain wind arises.

This couplet echoes the first line of "The Song of the Autumn Wind": "The autumn wind arises, white clouds fly" 秋風起兮白雲飛. Xiao Gang's reply poem responds to the white cloud image and sends it in another direction:

蠡浦急兮川路長	The waves of the Pengli Lake are rapid, the river road is long,
白雲重兮出帝鄉	white clouds are many tiered, as I leave the land of the gods.

The second line alludes to *Zhuangzi*: "Riding the white clouds, he will arrive at the land of the gods."[10] But Xiao Gang gave a clever twist to the original: the white clouds transported him *out of* the land of the gods (here the imperial domain) and blocked his vision of the capital city. Xiao Gang's allusion to *Zhuangzi*, rather than to Emperor Wu of the Han's song, might not have been a purely literary choice; it could

8. From Xiao Tong's letter to Xiao Gang upon receiving the latter's poem, we know that Xiao Gang's poem, along with a letter no longer extant, had been sent to Xiao Tong on June 25, 515, twelve days after Xiao Gang's new assignment as the governor of Jiangzhou (Xiao Tong, *Zhaoming taizi ji*, p. 75).

9. Xiao Tong, *Wen xuan* 45.2025–26; *Quan Han shi* 1.94–95.

10. *Zhuangzi jishi* 12.421.

have been the consequence of his lack of access to the kind of textual sources available to Xiao Tong, who had one of the largest book collections at the time.[11]

Xiao Tong's poem may possibly suggest a wistful longing for all the "famous places" and "scenic spots" that his younger brother would be able to frequent. Whereas Xiao Tong used only vague terms such as "high peaks" and "Nine Tributaries" to describe the Chu landscape, Xiao Gang was much more specific with regard to geographical names in his reply poem, mentioning Pengli Lake, Mount Lu, Stone Mirror Hill, and Crane Ridge, all of which are in the region of Xunyang 尋陽, the district capital of Jiangzhou.[12] The younger brother may have lacked

11. The modern scholar Lu Qinli (*Quan Han shi* 1.95) has wondered why several sources, including the Song encyclopedia *Taiping yulan*, claim that "The Song of the Autumn Wind" is cited in *Han shu*, while it is nowhere to be found in the present version of *Han shu*. Interestingly, we may recall that in 510 Xiao Chen had acquired "a genuine version" of the *Han shu* from a Northern monk, which was later presented to Xiao Tong. Xiao Tong then asked several scholars, including Liu Zhilin and Dao Gai, to collate it with the current version of *Han shu*. Liu Zhilin reported "several dozens of differences" (*Nan shi* 18.506, 50.1251). *Liang shu* has "ten points of difference" (*Liang shu* 40.573). One of the *Han shu* versions seen by Xiao Tong might have contained this song. David Knechtges ("Han Wudi," pp. 10–11) speculates that *Wen xuan* may have culled the song from *Han Wu gushi* 漢武故事, a Han Wudi romance circulating in the Six Dynasties. This is very likely. If this song had been made up by the *Han Wu gushi* author, this would explain why it does not appear in *Han shu* and why it is about the wrong season: Emperor Wu of the Han supposedly composed the song while he was boating on the Fen River, and yet, according to *Han shu*, Emperor Wu never traveled on the Fen River during the autumn.

12. Xiao Tong addressed a poem to Xiao Gang in 521, in which he recounted their years together. It contains the following stanza about Xiao Gang's Jiangzhou post:

> A command came from heaven,
> and [you] again had to go to the Yunmeng Park [Jiangzhou].
> [We were once] overjoyed about sharing the same mat,
> so happy that we forgot to eat.
> Still you had to command the Nine Tributaries,
> and had not yet returned from the Three Rivers.
> For a long time you did not come back,
> how distant you were from me! (*Quan Liang shi* 14.1793)

The modern scholar Yu Shaochu (in Xiao Tong, *Zhaoming taizi ji*, p. 27) takes the subject of the second line as "I" (i.e., Xiao Tong himself) and hypothesizes that Xiao Tong might have taken a journey to Jiangzhou to visit Xiao Gang. This is highly unlikely. The activities of an heir apparent were highly regulated. There is

access to the sophisticated cultural atmosphere of the capital city, but he got to see the outside world. Indeed, the letter Xiao Tong wrote to Xiao Gang upon receiving Xiao Gang's reply poem contains the crown prince's apologia for his confinement to the capital area because of his status. After praising Xiao Gang's poem, Xiao Tong talked about his own leisure activities—mainly reading the Classics and histories, "fishing and hunting in the forest of phrases." He went on to argue for the advantages of mind travel:

> One does not have to step out of the courtyard, and yet hills and ravines are everywhere. Nothing can hide from a spiritual wanderer: mountains and forests all appear to his view. The cold spring and Stone Mirror [a place-name mentioned in Xiao Gang's poem]—seeing them is not necessarily better than hearing of them; pine forests and apricot groves—knowing about them might be superior to approaching them.[13]
>
> 不出户庭，觸地丘壑．天遊不能隱，山林在目中．冷泉石鏡，一見何必勝於傳聞；松塢杏林，知之恐有逾吾就．

Both Xiao Gang's innocent bragging about his travels and his elder brother's defensive reply were only natural: despite their precocity, the princes were, after all, two adolescent boys.

Xiao Gang was called back to the capital in 518 and was again given the command of the garrison at Stone Fort. The poetry critic Zhong Rong was assigned to serve as Xiao Gang's record keeper, and it is reasonable to assume that Xiao Gang read his *Gradations of Poets*, which had been completed recently or perhaps even under the aegis of Xiao Gang himself. Sima Jiong 司馬褧, an illustrious scholar on ritual matters, was appointed one of Xiao Gang's administrators. When Sima Jiong died not long afterward, Xiao Gang asked Yu Jianwu to compile a collection of his literary writings in ten scrolls. The young prince had already begun to show an active interest in literary activities.

Now that he was back to the capital area, Xiao Gang was able to participate fully in the literary and religious events at the crown prince's residence, which had become a major cultural center. It was presumably

no record in the histories of this period that a crown prince ever left the capital for a distant province, for business or pleasure.

13. *Quan Liang wen* 20.3064.

around this time that Xiao Tong compiled the poetry anthology *Prime Blossoms of the Garden of Poetry from Past to Present*. Xiao Tong must have exerted a strong influence on his younger brothers, particularly on Xiao Gang and Xiao Yi, who, besides Xiao Tong himself, were the most literary of Emperor Wu's sons. In the autumn of 518, Xiao Tong gave a lecture on the Two Satya (*erdi* 二諦; Two Truths) and the concept of Dharmakāya (*fashen* 法身; the Dharma Body) in the Mystery Garden: this must have been an exciting event, as attested by Xiao Tong's own poem about it, Xiao Gang's "Ode to the Lecture in the Mystery Garden" ("Xuanpu jiangsong" 玄圃講頌), and a *fu* by Xiao Ziyun 蕭子雲 (487–549).[14] The fifteen-year-old Xiao Gang presented his ode to his elder brother along with an admiring letter, and Xiao Tong responded kindly: "[The ode] is gracious in diction and sumptuous in phrasing; it is gentle and elegant. Finely decorated and substantial, it may be described as quite extraordinary!"[15]

The year 523 was an important one for the young prince. Already with a number of years as provincial governor behind him and with the birth of his first son, Xiao Daqi 蕭大器 (523–51), Xiao Gang was in every sense an adult, even though he had barely turned twenty. The emperor had made plans for him: he was appointed governor of Yongzhou (capital in modern Hubei province) and placed in command of the military forces of seven northern provinces. This was an important post. Situated on the frontier facing the Northern Wei, Yongzhou was the royal family's old power base: Emperor Wu had held the same post twenty-five years earlier and began his uprising from Yongzhou. Lady Ding, Xiao Gang's mother, was a native of Xiangyang, the provincial capital. Throughout Emperor Wu's rule, this governorship was held primarily by close relatives of the royal family, but Xiao Gang was the first person who remained in this post for as long as six years.

A poem written during this period, "Passing Through Pipa Gorge" ("Jing Pipa xia" 經琵琶峽), is worth citing in its entirety here.[16] Pipa Gorge is on the Yangzi River, between Jiangling and Xunyang. Xiao Gang would have had several opportunities to pass through Pipa Gorge,

14. Ibid., 10.3004, 12.3020–21, 23.3088.
15. Ibid., 19.3060.
16. *Quan Liang shi* 21.1934.

either on his way from Jiankang to Jiangling in 514, or from Jiangling to Xunyang in 515, or from Jiankang to Xiangyang in 523. Although not one of his best works, it demonstrates Xiao Gang's ability to learn from his literary predecessors and take fresh departures:

由來歷山川	In the past I have traveled through many mountains and rivers,
此地獨迴邅	but this place is particularly labyrinthine.
百嶺相紆蔽	A hundred ridges, winding, obscure one another;
千崖共隱天	the sky is concealed by a thousand precipices.
橫峯時礙水	Inclined peaks now and then impede the currents;
斜岸或通川	sometimes the slanting embankment leads the river through.
還瞻已迷向	Glancing back, I have already lost the direction;
直去復疑前	pressing ahead, I feel doubts about our progress.
夕波照孤月	The evening waves reflect a solitary moon,
山枝斂夜煙	mountain branches gather in nocturnal vapors.
此時愁緒密	At this moment sorrowful thoughts grow dense—
□□魂九遷	[. . .] the soul is transported nine times.

Liu Hui, father of the famous poet Liu Xiaochuo, addressed a poem to his friend Xie Tiao, entitled "Upon Entering Pipa Gorge and Gazing Toward the Jibu Mountain" ("Ru Pipa xia wang Jibu ji" 入琵琶峽望積布磯); Xie Tiao's reply poem is also extant.[17] The first couplet of Xiao Gang's poem clearly shows the influence of the opening lines of Liu Hui's poem: "Rivers and mountains indeed have much beauty,/but this place is the most wondrous of all" 江山信多美,/此地最爲神. But if Liu Hui and Xie Tiao stressed the hazards of the gorge, they also praised the attraction of the landscape. Liu Hui presented an alluring image of the gorge: "In dazzling brilliance, rainbow colors mingle,/interwoven like embroidered brocades on display" 照爛虹蜺雜,/交錯錦繡陳. In response, Xie Tiao wrote: "The reds and violets combine in mottled patterns;/Cloud-embroideries are mutually intertwined" 赬紫共彬駁,/雲錦相淩亂.[18] In contrast, Xiao Gang transformed the springtime loveliness of the landscape into a claustrophobic setting and a gothic night

17. *Quan Qi shi* 5.1468–69, 4.1443.
18. Translation from Mather, *The Age of Eternal Brilliance*, 2: 146.

scene, evoking the mystical atmosphere of the *Chuci*. The modern scholar Lin Dazhi 林大志 rightly detects in Xiao Gang's poem traces of "Crossing the River" ("Shejiang" 涉江) from the *Chuci*:[19]

入溆浦余儃佪兮	When I enter Xupu, I hesitate,
迷不知吾之所如	lost and not knowing where I am going.
深林杳以冥冥兮	In the deep woods it is dark and gloomy:
乃猨狖之所居	this is the monkeys' home.
山峻高以蔽日兮	The mountain is steep and high, and blocks the sun,
下幽晦以多雨	below it is dim, constantly raining.

Although Liu Hui had also described the steepness of the cliff ("Above us, the azure peaks obstruct the sun"), his use of bright colors produced a dramatically different effect from the melancholy picture presented by "Crossing the River." Xiao Gang's poem, on the other hand, intensifies the gloomy effect even further: "a hundred ridges" and "a thousand precipices" not only hinder the watercourse and thwart sunlight but also conceal the entire sky.

Even Xiao Gang's verbal echo of Liu Hui's poem has a new twist. Liu Hui had emphasized a sense of pleasant surprise: "Glancing back, it is not where we have come from;/looking ahead, the scenery is already fresh" 卻瞻了非向,/前觀復已新. Xiao Gang recycled this couplet but changed its phrasing ever so slightly; the new couplet was made to convey a sense of disorientation and loss: "Glancing back, I have already lost the direction;/pressing ahead, I feel doubts about our progress."

The next couplet shows a particular flair: "The evening waves reflect a solitary moon,/mountain branches gather in nocturnal vapors."[20] The image of light—a small luminous spot on the waters—forms a striking contrast with the ominous dark vapors "gathered" in the mountain trees.

19. Lin Dazhi, "Liang Jianwen di," p. 68; *Chuci buzhu* 4.130.

20. He Xun had written a famous couplet: "Light clouds emerge at the edge of the cliff;/a new moon ascends the sky in the waves" 薄雲巖際出,/初月波中上 (*Quan Liang shi* 8.1684). It has often been noted how this couplet must have influenced the Tang poet Du Fu's couplet: "Light clouds slumber at the edge of the cliff;/a solitary moon tossed over in the waves" 薄雲巖際宿,/孤月浪中翻 (from "Su jiangbian ge" 宿江邊閣; *Quan Tang shi* 229.2495). And yet, the image of a "solitary moon" tossed in the troubled waters also evokes Xiao Gang's line.

The fascination with the interplay of light and shadow, as well as with reflections and deluded senses, constitutes a hallmark of Xiao Gang's poetry.

THE YOUNG GOVERNOR OF YONGZHOU

A young man now, Xiao Gang must have played a more active role in administration than he had before; he also showed a young man's eagerness for military achievements. According to *The History of the Liang*,

> When he was governor at Xiangyang, [Xiao Gang] sent a memorial to the emperor asking permission to carry out a military campaign. He ordered Liu Jin, Dong Dangmen, Du Huaibao, Cao Yizong, and others to advance into the north, and they conquered Nanyang, Xinye, and other commandaries. Li Zhi, the Wei governor of South Jingzhou, eventually surrendered from Anchang. [Xiao Gang] enlarged the Liang territory by over a thousand square *li*.[21]
>
> 在襄陽拜表北伐，遣長史柳津、司馬董當門、壯武將軍杜懷寶、振遠將軍曹義宗等眾軍進討，剋平南陽、新野等郡. 魏南荊州刺史李志據安昌城降，拓地千餘里.

The military action took place in the spring of 525; Li Zhi surrendered in the summer of 528. Xiao Gang's letter to Li Zhi, persuading him to capitulate, is still extant.[22] In 529, in acknowledgment of Xiao Gang's accomplishments, Emperor Wu presented him with a military fife-and-drum band.

In a letter to his brother-in-law Zhang Zuan (cited in Chapter 3), Xiao Gang recounted how life in the army brought him poetic inspiration. He left behind a number of poems on frontier life and was one of the crucial figures in the establishment of what was to become an important poetic subgenre, "frontier poetry," which is discussed in greater

21. *Liang shu* 4.109.

22. *Quan Liang wen* 11.3010. A number of Xiao Gang's communiqués regarding his northern campaigns are preserved in the Tang anthology *Grove of Texts from the Literature Office* (*Wenguan cilin* 文館詞林). *Wenguan cilin* was compiled in 638 under Xu Jingzong 許敬宗 (592–672). Only 30 of the original 1,000 scrolls are extant in Japan. Most of Xiao Gang's communiqués do not appear in Yan Kejun's *Quan Liang wen*. See Luo Guowei, *Ricang*, p. 454–55, 474–75.

detail in the next chapter. Many of Xiao Gang's frontier poems describe the hardships of war and the soldier's valor and bravado, but occasionally he also gave voice to the psychology of a lover on being reunited with his beloved after a period of absence, as in the following quatrain entitled "From the Camp Returning to the South of the City" ("Cong dun huan chengnan" 從頓還城南):[23]

暫别雨成疑	A temporary parting—both become apprehensive;
開簾生舊憶	when the curtain opens, old memories return.
都如未有情	It is as if we were never in love before,
更似新相識	indeed more like having just met.

This little poem focuses on the moment when the curtain is drawn open and the lovers set their eyes on each other. Both have been tortured by an apprehension that the other might have a change of heart during their separation; now that they are together again, there is a moment of pause and hesitation, even a moment of shyness, before the old memories revive and their passion is wakened anew. Considerable skill is demonstrated in portraying the lovers' complex psychology in a mere twenty characters. Although the quatrain was written more than fifteen hundred years ago, the sentiments are as fresh and familiar as if the poem were composed only yesterday.

For all his engagement in military affairs, Xiao Gang did not neglect literary activities. He assembled ten scholars to compile epitomes from various books: Xu Chi, Yu Jianwu, Liu Xiaowei, Bao Zhi 鮑至, Jiang Boyao 江伯搖, Kong Jingtong 孔敬通, Shen Ziyue 申子悅, Xu Fang 徐防, Wang You 王囿, and Kong Shuo 孔鑠. "The prince provided them with sumptuous food and fruits, and they were known as the 'Scholars of the Lofty Studio'" (*gaozhai xueshi* 高齋學士).[24] In the Tang,

23. *Quan Liang shi* 22.1969. Xiao Gang had written another poem entitled "Returning Temporarily from the Camp to the City" ("Cong dun zan huan cheng" 從頓暫還城), which expressed a more conventional macho attitude of the soldier eagerly going off to war and leaving the woman behind ("Who cares about the one who keeps a lonely bed?"; *Quan Liang shi* 21.1940).

24. *Nan shi* 50.1246. According to a fragment preserved in *Taiping yulan* (185.1026b), it was Xu Chi's son Xu Ling, not Xu Chi himself, who was one of the "Scholars of the Lofty Studio," and they had "collated poetry collections" together. Jiang Boyao was also transcribed as Jiang Bocao 江伯操 and Shen Ziyue as Hui Ziyue 惠子悅.

however, Xiao Gang was already being confused with his more favorably received elder brother Xiao Tong: *Xiang Mian ji* 襄沔記, an early eighth-century account compiled by Wu Congzheng 吳從政 (fl. ca. 710), claimed that Crown Prince Zhaoming had compiled *Wen xuan* in the Lofty Studio.[25] This misinformation persisted in later times.[26]

A poem entitled "Making Offerings in the Temple of the Founding Emperor of Han" ("Han gao miao saishen" 漢高廟賽神), written during this period, testifies to Xiao Gang's maturing talent.[27] At least five courtiers wrote companion pieces for the poem,[28] but Xiao Gang's poem best captures the grandeur of the bygone dynasty and a strange sense of its presence:

玉軑朝行動	Jade wheel-locks are about to be released in the morning;
閶闔旦應開	the celestial gateway should be opening up as dawn breaks.
白雲蒼梧上	White clouds rise over the Cangwu plain,
丹霞咸陽來	cinnabar vapors pour out from Xianyang.[29]
日正山無影	Sun in mid-heaven, mountains deprived of their shadows;

25. Quoted in *Taiping yulan* 185.1026b.

26. Wang Xiangzhi's 王象之 (*jinshi* 1195) *Yudi jisheng* 輿地紀勝 (82.2664–65), for instance, regards the Scholars of the Lofty Studio as Xiao Tong's staff members who helped him in compiling the *Wen xuan*. The late Ming geographical treatise *Guang zhi yi* 廣志繹 (4.91) compiled by Wang Shixing 王士性 (*jinshi* 1577) repeats the mistake. For a discussion of this, see the introduction to Knechtges, *Wen xuan*, 1: 10. In 1990, the people of Xiangyang built a Zhaoming Terrace (Zhaoming tai 昭明臺) on the site of an old *Wen xuan* Tower (*Wen xuan* lou 文選樓), which was first constructed in the twelfth century and rebuilt many times over the centuries.

27. *Quan Liang shi* 21.1943. Xiangyang was part of the Hanzhong 漢中 area, which had been the Han emperor's fief before he ascended the throne.

28. The courtiers were Wang Taiqing 王臺卿, Liu Zun, Liu Xiaoyi, Yu Jianwu, and Xu Ling.

29. Cangwu is where the legendary sage-king Shun died and was buried (*Shi ji* 1.44). It is said that when Liu Bang, the founding emperor of the Han, was still a commoner, his wife could always find him no matter where he went into hiding. When he asked her how she did it, she said it was because there were always unusual clouds above where he was (ibid., 8.348). Xianyang was the Qin capital. Liu Bang's army, using red banners because Liu Bang was believed to be the son of the Red Emperor, was the first of all the rebel armies to enter Xianyang.

城斜漢屢廻	the city wall slanting, the Han River frequently twists and turns.
瞻流如地脈	When we look at the watercourse, it resembles earth's veins;
望嶺匹天台	we gaze toward the peaks—they match the Heavenly Terrace.[30]
欲祛九秋恨	To dispel this sorrow of late autumn,
聊舉十千杯	let us, for now, raise the cup filled with ten-thousand-cash wine.[31]

The first couplet effectively brings together the living and the dead: the jade wheel-locks belong to the carriage of the young prince, who has set out for the temple; he imagines that in response the soul of the departed emperor should be descending from heaven to accept the offerings made to him. The other poets writing to the same title referred to the soul of the Han emperor in explicit terms such as "immortal chariots" and "rainbow clothes." Such specific details, however, seem only to diminish the spiritual presence of the departed emperor. In contrast, with the word "should" in the second line, Xiao Gang appeals to the elusive nature of the spirit world. Yet his poem is pervaded by a haunting sense of mystic grandeur, all the more so because it always hovers over the boundary between the real and the imaginary, what is seen and what lies beyond the field of vision.

The defining line in this poem is in the middle couplet of the poem: "Sun in mid-heaven, mountains deprived of their shadows;/the city wall slanting, the Han River frequently twists and turns." The second line is merely clever—the Han River seems to be winding because of the city wall, rather than vice versa; the first line, however, is brilliant: time is passing, and the sun has risen to mid-heaven; the mountains are directly exposed to the white noon sun. It is a precise moment during the day, a fleeting moment, but also a moment of light, a moment that has no shadows. The season is deep autumn, and Yu Jianwu's companion piece talks about the trees shedding their leaves early; in Xiao

30. The Heavenly Terrace would be the Tiantai Mountain; see Sun Chuo's "*Fu* on Climbing the Tiantai Mountain" (*Quan Jin wen* 61.1806).

31. The wine-cup of ten thousand cash is an allusion to a line in Cao Zhi's *yuefu* "Song of the Renowned Capital" ("Mingdu pian" 名都篇): "Fine wine costs ten thousand cash for each *dou*" (*Quan Wei shi* 6.431).

Gang's poem, the mountains shed their shadows in the same way as the trees rid themselves of leaves and become naked. This moment of intense brightness is the last before the day slips toward dusk, the ritual ends, and the assembly disperses; it is also the last luminance before the impending winter, when everything, just like the soul of the departed Han emperor, will sink into darkness and oblivion. Yu Jianwu's poem describes the aftermath of the ritual: "Dust flies, the distant riders disappear; / the sun moves, half of the peak turning cold" 塵飛遠騎沒, / 日徙半峰寒. As the sun goes down behind the mountain, half of the peak is deprived of its light and warmth, growing cold and dark.

The ending of Xiao Gang's poem again forcefully brings together the worlds of the living and the dead: when the cup of "ten-thousand-cash wine" is being raised to the mouth, we do not know if it is the prince or the soul of the emperor who is moved to savor the offerings.

At Yongzhou, Xiao Gang suffered several family tragedies. In 525, his second elder brother Xiao Zong defected to the Northern Wei; then, on July 30, 529, the emperor's fourth son, Xiao Ji 蕭績 (505–29), died at the age of twenty-four. But what touched Xiao Gang most deeply was probably his mother's death in the winter of 525. Xiao Gang was consumed with grief. During the mourning period, "he became so emaciated that his bones stood out. Day and night he cried without cease. The mat on which he sat was soaked with tears and eventually became rotten."[32] He asked to resign his post on the occasion, but Emperor Wu rejected his request. He was to go back to Yongzhou and stay there for another three years.

Xiao Gang gradually grew restless. He seemed to be getting tired of life in the provinces and longing to return to the capital. A poem entitled "Thinking of the Shanglin Park on a Spring Day" ("Chunri xiang Shanglin" 春日想上林) reveals his homesickness quite clearly.[33] In a memorial to the emperor, he asked to be relieved of his duty on the ground of poor health (Xiao Gang seems to have suffered from rather serious illness more than once in his life). The memorial, though not dated, stated that he was about to turn thirty. We do not know if the

32. *Liang shu* 4.109.
33. *Quan Liang shi* 21.1944.

memorial had any effect, but in the early spring of 530, Xiao Gang was summoned back to the metropolitan area and appointed governor of Yangzhou, the region surrounding the Liang capital.

531: THE TURNING POINT

Xiao Gang finally returned to the capital in 531, after almost seven years of absence. He was a mature man by this point. According to his biography in *The Southern History*, the prince had a strong face, dark eyebrows, and a square chin; his glance was piercing, and his demeanor was "as dignified as a god."[34]

The Southern History records a dream Xiao Tong had before Xiao Gang was called back. In the dream, Xiao Tong is playing chess with Xiao Gang, and he gives his younger brother a patterned sword.[35] The patterned sword, made of wood since the Jin dynasty, was presented to high-ranking military officers with remarkable martial accomplishments as a mark of great honor. Shortly thereafter, Xiao Gang was granted the title of Cavalry General, but the dream seemed to bode more. In simple psychological terms, dreaming of playing chess with one's brother reveals a sense of competition; handing over the patterned sword is a symbolic transference of power. In his dream, the crown prince both usurped a power that did not belong to him (only the emperor could bestow such honors) and lost power at the same time.

There has been much speculation about the crown prince's untimely death. According to *The Southern History*, some time in April 531, Xiao Tong "went lotus picking in a boat with carved patterns" in the Rear Pond. A palace lady rocked the boat and capsized it. Xiao Tong fell into the water. Although promptly rescued, he had injured his leg. On May 7, 531, his condition suddenly worsened. The emperor, now finally learning of the seriousness of his son's illness, made ready to go and see him in person. But before he arrived, Xiao Tong had passed away.[36]

Palace gossip shrouds the death of the young prince. According to *The Southern History*, after Lady Ding, Xiao Tong and Xiao Gang's

34. *Liang shu* 4.109; *Nan shi* 8.232.
35. *Nan shi* 8.229.
36. Ibid., 53.1311.

mother, passed away in 525, her burial place was said to be inauspicious for the eldest son. Xiao Tong listened to the advice of a Daoist and buried "wax geese and other things" by the side of Lady Ding's tomb to counteract the bad *fengshui*. Bao Miaozhi 鮑邈之, a eunuch who was out of favor with Xiao Tong, reported this to Emperor Wu, hinting that the practice would harm the emperor himself. When the buried objects were unearthed, the emperor was shocked and intended to investigate the matter further, but desisted at Xu Mian's advice and had the Daoist executed.[37] This incident supposedly cast a shadow between father and son. To this day, scholars are still debating the veracity of the incident and whether Emperor Wu's subsequent choice of heir apparent had anything to do with the incident.[38] Xiao Tong's eldest son, Xiao Huan, would have been the legitimate heir to the throne. Xiao Huan was promptly summoned to the capital, but Emperor Wu procrastinated in proclaiming him the new crown prince. For nearly two months there was no announcement. On June 21, 531, the remains of Xiao Tong were interred. Only then did Emperor Wu finally come to a decision: instead of Xiao Huan, an imperial decree issued on June 27, 531, proclaimed Xiao Gang the new crown prince.

The Southern History speculates that it was partially due to the Wax Goose incident that Emperor Wu did not choose Xiao Tong's son as successor. And yet, the true reason for Emperor Wu's choice was probably that the aging emperor was worried about "having a juvenile ruler take over the empire."[39] Emperor Wu was already sixty-seven years old when Xiao Tong died. In an age when the average life expectancy was much lower, sixty-seven was very advanced in years, and, as the modern scholar Cao Daoheng has rightly pointed out in evaluating this matter, Emperor

37. *Nan shi* 53.1312–13. Later, after Xiao Gang became the crown prince, it happened that Bao Miaozhi, the eunuch who informed Emperor Wu of the wax geese, committed a misdemeanor. The misconduct was not serious enough in itself to warrant capital punishment, but, "moved by the wrongs his brother had suffered, [Xiao Gang] with tears in his eyes ordered Bao Miaozhi to be executed. The son of Miaozhi's elder brother, Senglong, had been a guard at the Eastern Palace; as soon as [Xiao Gang] learned that Senglong was Miaozhi's nephew, he immediately dismissed Senglong from duty."

38. See Mu Kehong, "Xiao Tong yanjiu," pp. 15–17; and Lin Dazhi and Lu Shengjiang, "'La'e shijian.'"

39. *Nan shi* 53.1313.

Wu certainly did not know that he was to sit on the throne for another two decades.[40] Emperor Wu had witnessed the disaster of an underage ruler: Crown Prince Wenhui of the Qi died before his father, and his teenage son, who succeeded to the throne, was overthrown within a year by a treacherous older cousin. The Marquis of Darkness in the East, the deposed emperor of the Qi, was another bad example. Having lived through those turbulent times and being surrounded by a number of ambitious nephews, Emperor Wu would not want to repeat that mistake.

Emperor Wu's unconventional decision took the court by surprise. One may well imagine that it must have been the hottest topic of the day. Xiao Gang's attitude was interesting. Earlier, when granted the martial band and named the governor of Yangzhou (a highly prestigious post), he had submitted a memorial declining the honor, a modest gesture demanded by etiquette. There is, however, no memorial turning down the crown princedom on record. Instead, we have a memorial from Xiao Gang expressing gratitude to the emperor for entrusting him with such a grave task; it also gave voice to his anxiety about being worthy of the charge.

It is, of course, always possible that a written request declining the position has been lost, but perhaps Xiao Gang accepted the appointment with no pretense of modesty because he understood the political situation. One may follow the conventions when being granted a martial band, but when the fate of the state is at stake, a false refusal would have been an insult to his father's decision, which had not been lightly made. Years later, Hou Jing's men forced Xiao Gang to copy out the edict of abdication they had prepared for him. When he came to the following sentences—"The departed emperor, bearing in mind the weightiness of the sacred vessels and wishing for the security of the altars of the state, promoted me out of turn, and thus I became the master of the Eastern Palace"—Xiao Gang could no longer control his emotions and burst into tears.[41]

On August 5, 531, Xiao Gang went through the ceremony of investiture. The Eastern Palace, where the crown prince resided, was currently undergoing repairs, and Xiao Gang temporarily moved into the Eastern

40. Cao Daoheng, "Zhaoming taizi," p. 53.

41. *Liang shu* 56.857; *Nan shi* 8.232.

Residence and lived there for a year. With the loss of a dear brother with whom he had shared so many interests, the radical change in the course of his life, and an awareness of many courtiers' dissatisfaction with the emperor's choice of heir, Xiao Gang seemed more burdened than elated by his new position. A long poem entitled "Receiving the Precepts in the Park of Flowering Groves" ("Meng Hualin yuan jie" 蒙華林園戒), written right after he became crown prince, enables us to catch a glimpse of Xiao Gang's feelings at this stage:[42]

庸夫耽世樂	An ordinary person indulges in worldly pleasures,
俗士重虛名	and a commonplace gentleman treasures empty fame.
三空既難了	The Three Emptinesses are difficult to comprehend,
八風恒易傾	while the Eight Winds always so easily move a person.[43]
伊余久齊物	I have long regarded all things as on the same level,
本自一枯榮	treating withering and flowering as equal.
弱齡愛箕潁	From a tender age I have loved the Ji and Ying,
由來重伯成	and always esteemed Bocheng.[44]
非爲樂肥遯	It is not that I take delight in being a recluse,
特是厭逢迎	but simply that I am weary of greetings and receptions.
執珪守藩國	Holding the jade plaque, I had been keeping guard of my fiefdom;
主器作元貞	now I am in charge of the sacrificial vessels as the crown prince.
昔日書銀字	In the past, when I was writing with silver ink,

42. *Quan Liang shi* 21.1936.

43. There are several different principles of Three Emptinesses. For instance, the emptiness of self, the emptiness of Dharma, and the emptiness of both; or the emptiness of giver, receiver, and that which is given. The sūtras teach that most people are usually moved by the winds of the eight directions: Praise, Ridicule, Suffering, Happiness, Benefit, Destruction, Gain, and Loss.

44. It is said that Xu You, the ancient recluse, lived at the foot of the Ji Mountain and to the south of the Ying River. Ji and Ying thereafter became a designation for reclusion. Bocheng was Bocheng Zigao 伯成子高, a lord in Yao and Shun's time who became a recluse under Shun's successor, Yu (*Zhuangzi* 5.423).

久自恧宗英	I had long felt ashamed in front of the flowers of the royal family;
斯焉佩金璽	now that I am bearing the golden seal,
何由廣德聲	by what means may I improve on my virtuous name?
居高常慮缺	In a high position I worry about imperfection;
持滿每憂盈	when holding a full vessel, I am anxious that it might spill over.
玆言信非矯	These words are indeed not false:
丹心良可明	this cinnabar heart can be read by all.
舟航奉睿訓	To board the boat of enlightenment, I receive the wise instruction,
接引降皇情	and am led onto the path of delivery by the imperial compassion.
心燈朗暗室	The heart lamp brightens in a dark chamber,
牢舟出愛瀛	a sturdy boat comes out from the River of Desires.
是節高秋晚	The season is the late autumn,
泬寥天氣清	the sky is expansive and empty, the air clear.
交門光景麗	The sun shines brightly over the Jiao Gate;
祈年雲霧生	at the Hall of Praying for Longevity, a mist rises.[45]
紅蕖間青瑣	Red lotus flowers joined with the azure traceries;
紫露濕丹楹	purple dews soak the cinnabar railings.
葉疏行逕出	Leaves turn sparse, a footpath is revealed;
泉溜遶山鳴	the spring flows, echoing around the hill.
綠衿依浦戍	Birds of emerald breasts rest by the riverbank,
絳顙拂林征	those with crimson heads flying past the groves.
庶蒙八解益	Hopefully, I will benefit from the Eight Liberations,[46]
方使六塵輕	and lighten up the load of the Six Dusts.
脫聞時可去	If one may be delivered upon hearing the Truth,
非吝舍重城	I don't begrudge giving cities away.

45. There was a Jiao Gate Palace in the Western Han, where Han Emperor Wu made sacrifices to gods and had a "Song of the Jiao Gate" 交門之歌 composed (*Han shu* 6.207). The Hall of Praying for Longevity was constructed by Liang Emperor Wu, presumably in 521 (*Sui shu* 7.144).

46. Eight kinds of liberation are based on meditation efforts.

In this poem, Xiao Gang expressed admiration for the quiet life not because, he emphasized, he wanted to be a recluse, but simply because he had always disliked social demands. Now put in charge of the "sacrificial vessels," he admitted he felt apprehensive and anxious. The reception of the Buddhist precepts in the late autumn of 531 was a welcome ritual, in which Xiao Gang found some measure of peace and solace.

A letter to Xiao Yi, then governor of Jingzhou, further reveals Xiao Gang's state of mind during this period: "Since I came to the capital, I have been agitated and distracted. I may open my mouth to laugh, but I do not feel genuine happiness."[47] He also complained about the loss of freedom and about the tiresome task of familiarizing himself with court etiquette while distancing himself from his former role as a military commander. He humorously confessed to Xiao Yi that as his head was being shaved during the reception of the Buddhist precepts, he felt an urge to have all of his hair cut off and become a real monk: "I would have had no doubt about Ma Yuan's remark about getting rid of lice, nor would I have cared about Mr. Ying's mockery of the 'polished pot.'"[48] Ma Yuan 馬援, an Eastern Han general, had once compared ridding a mountain of its trees to reveal bandits to shaving a baby's head to get at the lice;[49] Mr. Ying is the third-century Ying Qu, who compared the bald head of an old man to a "polished pot."[50]

Xiao Gang had always maintained an active correspondence with his younger brother Xiao Yi, a talented poet himself. After he became crown prince, Xiao Gang wrote Xiao Yi the famous letter in which he deplored the contemporary state of poetry in the capital area: "Nowadays, as I observe the literary styles at the capital, I cannot help noticing how utterly timid and uninspired they are, as writers compete in being superficial and careless and strive to be long-winded and lethargic."[51] He spoke out strongly against those who failed to recognize the independence of literary values and imitated the somber and archaic

47. *Quan Liang wen* 11.3012.

48. Ibid., 11.3012.

49. *Quan hou Han wen* 17.562.

50. *Quan Wei shi* 8.470.

51. *Quan Liang wen* 11.3011a–b. For a complete English translation, see Marney, *Liang Chien-wen ti*, pp. 80–83; or Siu-kit Wong, *Early Chinese Literary Criticism*, pp. 137–40.

styles of the Confucian classics. In order to fortify his argument, Xiao Gang listed the canonical writers—Yang Xiong, Sima Xiangru, Cao Zhi, Wang Can, Pan Yue, Lu Ji, Yan Yanzhi, and Xie Lingyun—as counter-examples: "In my view, the way in which they used words and employed their mind was totally different [from that of contemporary writers]." Such a stand, however, does not put Xiao Gang in the category of "traditionalist," as Siu-kit Wong has suggested,[52] for Xiao Gang was not advocating a return to the old styles; rather, he was using the former masters to illustrate how modern writers were misled in their idea of literature.

Xiao Gang soon turned his criticism to those who emulated the wrong models, one of which was the poetry of Xie Lingyun. As had Xiao Zixian, whom Xiao Gang held in high esteem, the crown prince charged Xie's imitators with writing that "though artful and decorative, in the end it is lethargic and convoluted. . . . Carelessness, sluggishness, and the lack of energy and momentum constitute a fatal disease. Even though its classic appropriateness is admirable, it is dispassionate and cannot move the reader."[53]

According to Xiao Gang, the other bad model was Pei Ziye. For Xiao Gang, Xie Lingyun was a gifted poet, but his epigones did not possess the same natural talent and ended up reproducing Xie Lingyun's shortcomings (i.e., long-windedness) without Xie Lingyun's sparkle. Pei Ziye, to the contrary, "had the ability of a good historian but did not achieve finesse in poetic compositions." Xiao Gang summarized his points succinctly: "Xie's artfulness cannot be achieved, and Pei's plainness should be no object of admiration."

Xiao Gang cited some positive models: Xie Tiao and Shen Yue were singled out for their poetry; Ren Fang and Lu Chui, for their prose. Zhang Shuai and Zhou She were praised for their rhapsodies (*fu*) and discursive treatises (*bian* 辯), respectively.[54] Xiao Gang not only accorded poetry a separate realm but also implied that a writer often

52. Siu-kit Wong, *Early Chinese Literary Criticism*, p. 144.

53. See Chapter 3 for a discussion of Xiao Zixian's commentary.

54. Zhang Shuai's "*Fu* on the Dancing Horse," which received the emperor's approval, is recorded in his biography in the *Liang shu* 33.475–78. Zhou She was said to be "particularly good at exegesis and analysis" (ibid., 25.375).

excelled in one particular genre. Noticeably, all the positive models given by Xiao Gang were contemporaries. In this, Xiao Gang differed sharply from the other two well-known critics of the Liang, Liu Xie and Zhong Rong.

Toward the end of the letter, Xiao Gang exhorted Xiao Yi to lead the fight against what he saw correctly as the abuse of literature. But being the crown prince put Xiao Gang in a much better position to be a leader than his younger brother, who was posted in one of the provinces. The name "Palace Style" refers to the Eastern Palace, the official residence of the heir apparent. Gradually, it was to become the "new transformative style" that every fashionable young nobleman wanted to emulate. Thanks to his privileged position and his immense talent, Xiao Gang was able to begin changing the direction of literature. Although he did not leave behind much theoretical writing on poetry, Xiao Gang was fully conscious that he and his brother were writing a different sort of poetry.

THE YEARS AT THE SPRING RESIDENCE

Xiao Gang's official biographies jump from 532, the year when he formally moved into the Eastern Palace, to 549, when he ascended the throne. The seventeen years in between are largely left blank except for the following remarks:

> When he was put in the position of guarding the state [i.e., when he became the crown prince], he pardoned many offenders; and yet, in dealing with administrative affairs, he could not be deceived in the smallest detail. He never tired of receiving men of letters and discussing literature with them. Once, in the Mystery Garden, he lectured on Emperor Wu's exegesis on the Five Classics, and the whole court was emptied [to listen to him].[55]
>
> 及居監撫, 多所弘宥, 文案簿領, 纖豪必察. 弘納文學之士, 賞接無倦. 嘗於玄圃述武帝所製五經講疏, 聽者傾朝野.

Since Emperor Wu was getting on in years, Xiao Gang no doubt took over more and more administrative duties, but his power was limited,

55. *Nan shi* 8.232–33.

and Emperor Wu remained the one who made final decisions on important affairs of the state. The first few years in the capital were hard for Xiao Gang. Although he had yearned to return to the capital before, now that he was crown prince, he seemed to miss his days as a provincial governor. Xiao Gang's rejoinder to Xu Chi, presumably written when Xu Chi was away from the capital between late 531 and 534, reveals a profound sense of dissatisfaction with his situation:

> Shan Tao once said: "The crown prince should focus only on cultivating his virtue." But the present times are different from the old days. I have been entrusted with the responsibility for guarding the state, and yet I cannot oust the wicked and support the good or assist in some small way in state legislation; nor can I promote what is right and replace what is wrong and contribute to sagely government. Because of this, I feel guilty and ashamed and cannot forget my worries even at night.[56]
>
> 山濤有言, 東宮養德而已. 但今與古殊. 時有監撫之務, 竟不能黜邪進善, 少助國章, 獻可替不, 仰禆聖政, 以此慚惶, 無忘夕惕.

With fresh memories of life in the provinces, in the same letter Xiao Gang also expressed his indignation at some of the "complacent and smug" court officials who lacked field experience and did little in their comfortable positions:

> [In the past] I traveled in the Five Ridges and was in the military for ten years. I have experienced all sorts of perils and hardships. When I look at ministers who know only to protect their own lives and occupy positions for nothing and those petty clerks with their brushes, I see that they have never known the topography of mountains and rivers, the pains of soldiers in armor, the sufferings of the common people, or the like of local customs. And yet they frequent the lofty palaces, prizing themselves highly between the tall gates, with jade cookware set in front of them and yellow gold in their hands. Complacent and smug, they feel that since the times of the Yellow Emperor and Emperor Fuxi, there has been only one person worth noting [i.e., themselves]. This cannot but draw long sighs from me.
>
> 驅馳五嶺, 在戎十年, 險阻艱難, 備更之矣. 觀夫全軀具臣, 刀筆小吏, 未嘗識山川之形勢, 介冑之勤勞, 細民之疾苦, 風俗之嗜好. 高閣之間可來, 高門之地徒重. 玉饌羅前, 黃金在握, 浞訾栗斯, 容與自喜, 亦復言軒羲以來, 一人而已. 使人見此, 良足長歎.

---

56. *Quan Liang wen* 11.3010a.

Xiao Gang's sense of impotence as crown prince is supported by a letter of condolence he wrote to Liu Xiaoyi in 535, upon the death of the latter's cousin Liu Zun, who had been one of Xiao Gang's staff members at Yongzhou:

After I moved into the Spring Residence, we were able to see each other again. The Bowang Palace has no obligation to receive guests;[57] the cultivation of virtue [on the part of the crown prince] must follow much etiquette. I can only rely on my old friends to associate with me from time to time [to bring me pleasure]. Yet this man passed away, which is truly saddening. . . . Yesterday I was going to write a tomb inscription for him, as well as compile his literary writings into a collection. Inferior and mediocre as I am, I could not honor and elevate him while he was alive so that he might have made use of his talent; now, although I may write his tomb inscription and compile his writings, what good does this do for the deceased? It is for this reason that my sorrow and regret have no end.[58]

比在春坊, 載獲申晤, 博望無通賓之務, 司成多節文之科. 所賴故人, 時相媲偶. 而此子溘然. 實可嗟痛. . . . 吾昨欲爲誌銘, 並爲撰集. 吾之劣薄, 其生也不能揄揚吹獻, 使得騁其才用, 今者爲銘爲集, 何益既往? 故爲痛惜之情, 不能已已耳.

Xiao Gang did not, however, idle away the years in the Eastern Palace. He was actively engaged in literary and scholarly undertakings. As noted in Chapter 3, he established a Department of Literary and Virtuous Expectant Officials, whose members included many of the younger generation, such as Xu Chi's son Xu Ling, Yu Jianwu's son Yu Xin, and Zhang Shuai's son Zhang Changgong. In 531, shortly after becoming crown prince, Xiao Gang assembled a group of scholars, old and young, to begin compiling *The Record of the Discourse at the Hall of Eternal Spring* (*Changchun dian yiji* 長春殿義記), for which Xu Ling wrote a preface. Spanning 100 scrolls, this record may have been an account of astronomical discussions held at the Hall of Eternal Spring led by Emperor Wu, along with other esoteric subjects.[59] Another large compilation project, begun in Yongzhou, the *Joined Jade-Disks from the Treasures*

57. Bowang Palace was constructed by Emperor Wu of the Han for the crown prince.

58. *Liang shu* 41.593–94.

59. Ibid., 40.579; *Chen shu* 26.326.

of Dharma, was finally completed in 534. During this period, Xiao Gang also authored or compiled a prolific body of works, among which were commentaries on Confucian and Daoist classics, a selection of Xie Lingyun's writings (possibly annotated), a manual on jousting, treatises on topics ranging from vinegar and bathing to chess and pellet chess, and a volume of medical prescriptions. Most impressive of all was a collection of his own literary writings in 100 scrolls.[60]

Some of Xiao Gang's poems may safely be dated to this period. "Enjoying the Cool in the Mystery Garden" ("Xuanpu naliang" 玄圃納涼), a fragment, is one of them.[61] The Mystery Garden, located to the northeast of the Palace City, was part of the Eastern Palace compound. In the late fifth century, Crown Prince Wenhui of the Qi had expanded it, with new towers and terraces surrounded by strange-looking rocks and streams.

登山想劍閣	I think of Jian'ge when ascending a hill;
逗浦憶辰陽	lingering by the ford, I recall Chenyang.
飛流如湅雨	Waterfalls are like pouring rain;
夜月似秋霜	moonlight resembles autumn frost.
螢翻競晚熱	Fireflies flit, chasing evening heat;
蟲思引秋涼	insects chirp with longing, bringing in the cool of the fall.
鳴波如礙石	Waves splash, as if impeded by rocks;
闇草別蘭香	amid plants in the dark, one distinguishes the orchid fragrance.

In this poem Xiao Gang evokes an imaginary space beyond the immediate purview of the senses. Jian'ge, a mountain in modern Sichuan, was famous for its steepness; Chenyang, a place in modern Hunan, alludes to a line from the *Chuci* poem "Crossing the River" ("Shejiang" 涉江): "In the morning I left Wangzhu, / in the evening I stay over at Chenyang."[62] Chenyang is frequently cited in later poetry to express the

60. *Nan shi* 8.233. All these works have been lost; only the prefaces to *The Manual of Jousting* and to *The Manual of Pellet Chess* are extant.

61. *Quan Liang shi* 22.1957.

62. *Chuci buzhu* 4.130.

homesickness of a traveler.[63] Here, however, Xiao Gang subverts the order of the allusion: whereas in other poems Chenyang is the present point from which the poet longs for home, in Xiao Gang's poem it is relocated, displaced, receding to memory and imagination. Xiao Tong once stressed to Xiao Gang that mind travel was superior to physical travel; now that Xiao Gang was likewise confined to the Eastern Palace, might he have recalled what his elder brother, who had lived in the Eastern Palace for twenty-five years, said to him? And yet, if Xiao Tong's argument for mind travel affirms the value of staying put, Xiao Gang's couplet conveys a vague sense of listlessness.

The next couplet, touching on the title "Enjoying the Cool," continues the imaginary scene. "Pouring rain" (*dongyu* 凍雨) once again has a *Chuci* echo, but in the southern dialect it also referred to a summer thunderstorm.[64] The novel simile—moonlight resembling autumn frost—was later transformed by the Tang poet Li Bai 李白 (701–62) into one of the best-known couplets in Chinese literary history: "In front of my bed, the bright moonlight: / I suspect it is frost on the floor" 床前明月光, / 疑是地上霜.[65]

What is remarkable about Xiao Gang's poem is the interplay between the reality of a hot, sultry summer night and the frequent figurative evocation of autumn chill. As the glowworms flicker in the darkness, even such tiny dots of fire seem to intensify the heat. Only by being perfectly still is the poet able to feel cool. In the meantime, his senses of hearing and smell are sharpened because of his stillness and the growing dark. What he hears and smells begin to reveal things he cannot see: the rocks in the stream and the orchid among the plants. The last line pays homage to Tao Yuanming, one of Xiao Gang's favorite poets:

幽蘭生前庭	A hidden orchid grows in the front yard,
含薰待清風	holding back its fragrance, awaiting a fresh breeze.

63. Jiang Yan's poem "On Returning to My Home Garden" ("Huan guyuan" 還故園) begins with the couplet: "The minister of Han wept at Changsha, / and the traveler of Chu felt sad at Chenyang" (*Quan Liang shi* 3.1560). During a period of exile from the capital, Liu Xiaochuo wrote a poem entitled "Staying over at the Fanchang Ford at Evening" 夕逗繁昌浦, which contains the lines: "I feel like staying over at Chenyang, / at this place the lonely boat lingers" (ibid., 16.1832).

64. *Erya zhushu* 6.97.

65. *Quan Tang shi* 165.1709.

清風脫然至	Once the fresh breeze comes,
見別蕭艾中	the orchid will be distinguished from the weeds.[66]

What Tao Yuanming states explicitly in his poem is only implied in Xiao Gang's couplet, that a breeze enables the poet to distinguish the scent of the orchid in the dark. This breeze must be more than welcome on such a hot summer night, and yet, it is so faint that the poet notices it only by way of a wafting aroma. It is a special kind of synaesthesia.

Enjoying the cool on a hot summer day seems to have been a popular topic with Xiao Gang. In many ways, this is a topic that involves being still: one cannot cool down on a hot day if one is in motion, and physical stillness enables the poet to better observe the world around him. Here is the beginning of another poem entitled "Enjoying the Cool" ("Naliang" 納涼), also written during this period:[67]

斜日晚駸駸	The slanting sun is racing toward evening,
池塘生半陰	partial shades growing by the pool.
避暑高梧側	Escaping the summer heat beneath a tall wutong tree,
輕風時入襟	a light breeze from time to time enters my robe.
落花還就影	A falling petal still drawing near its shadow;
驚蟬乍失林	a cicada, startled, suddenly loses the grove.

Startled perhaps by the approach of the poet, the cicada suddenly stops singing, or perhaps it has lost its hold and fallen from the tree. A stillness sets in, and the summer heat subsides with the disappearance of the noise. In the silence of the cicada's choked cry, the loss of the grove is intensely felt.

The remarkably beautiful fifth line follows the delicate trajectory of a falling petal. As the poet seeks to avoid the summer heat in the shade of a tall *wutong* tree, it seems to him, in a moment of sympathy with nature, that even the flower petal is trying to take refuge in the shadow it casts. It does not know, however, that it is chasing an illusion: the shadow will disappear the moment it is captured, as it becomes one with the flower petal.

66. From no. 17 of Tao Yuanming's "Yinjiu" 飲酒 series (*Quan Jin shi* 17.1000).
67. *Quan Liang shi* 21.1946.

"Suffering from Heat" ("Kure" 苦熱) had become an established poetic topic in the Six Dynasties, but the Liang first saw a large number of poems about enjoying the cool on a hot summer day. Among Xiao Gang's extant poems is another entitled "Enjoying the Evening Cool" ("Wanjing naliang" 晚景納涼).[68] The poem begins unassumingly enough:

日移涼氣散	The sun moves away, cool air spreads,
懷抱信悠哉	a peaceful mood truly descends on me.
珠簾影空捲	Pearl curtains rolled up, shadowing the sky,
桂户向池開	cinnamon windows opening toward the pond.

Unlike other poems on the same topic, this one touches on the theme only in the first line; the rest of the poem portrays a night scene, and coolness is once again implied in stillness and quiet.

烏棲星欲見	Crows are roosting, stars about to appear,
河淨月應來	the river clear, the moon should come forth.
横階入細笋	The stairs are penetrated by fine bamboo shoots;
蔽地濕輕苔	covering up the ground, light moss becomes wet.

This is a dark moment: the sun has set, but the moon has not come out yet, and the stars are only "about to appear." As the night deepens, measured by the nesting of the crows and the dew on the moss, it grows increasingly quiet, and the poet's senses become increasingly acute, leading to distorted perceptions and almost surreal delusions:

草化飛爲火	Plants transform into flying balls of fire;
蚊聲合似雷	the humming of mosquitoes gathers like thunderclaps.

Glowworms were believed to metamorphose from rotten plants. In the sight and hearing of the poet immersed in the silence of the dark night, the tiny flickering lights are exaggerated into flames, and the sound of mosquitoes, thunderclaps. The tranquil summer night is suddenly filled with sound and fury—but the poet just as abruptly brings them to an end:

68. *Quan Liang shi* 21.1947.

於茲靜聞見	Right at this spot, I calm my listening and watching,
自此歇氛埃	dust and noise are settled from now on.

Xiao Gang's couplet on the glowworms and mosquitoes recalls a *Liezi* passage, which describes insects so tiny that they may live "on the eyelashes of a mosquito" and yet the mosquito is unaware of them. But the Yellow Emperor and his friend Rongchengzi are able to detect them. The two sages, after three months of fasting, "extinguished their minds and relinquished their bodies; gradually they began to look with their spirits [instead of with their eyes], and they saw the insects being as lofty as the peak of Mount Song; they listened with their *qi* [instead of with their ears], and they heard the insects being as loud as the sound of thunderclaps."[69] In other words, only by quieting one's physical senses can one achieve true knowledge and understanding of the physical world and a spiritual peace, as hinted in the concluding lines of Xiao Gang's poem.

By exaggerating the humming of mosquitoes, Xiao Gang's couplet reduces the size of the listener, who feels small as he is wrapped up in the dark summer night, with bamboo shoots growing around him and fireflies flickering with their specks of light. The quietness is accentuated by the thundering of the mosquitoes. We must not forget one of Xiao Gang's favorite couplets by his contemporary poet Wang Ji:

蟬噪林逾靜	Cicadas sing—the grove becomes even quieter;
鳥鳴山更幽	the hills grow more silent with birds' cry.[70]

69. *Liezi* 5.418. The couplet on the glowworms and mosquitoes is also reminiscent of a poetic game called "Big Words" (*dayan* 大言) and "Small Words" (*xiaoyan* 小言), which uses hyperbolic language to talk about largeness and smallness. Xiao Tong, when still a boy, had asked his courtiers to compose to these topics. Since Shen Yue was one of the courtiers who wrote at the crown prince's command, this incident must have occurred before his death in 513. Other courtiers writing on the same topics included Wang Xi, Wang Gui 王規 (492–536), Zhang Zuan, and Yin Jun. Wang Xi was appointed to Xiao Tong's staff in 512 at the age of thirteen. So this group of poems might have been composed around this time. See *Quan Liang shi* 7.1656, 14.1802, 15.1805, 15.1808, 18.1861–62.

70. *Quan Liang shi* 17.1854.

According to Yan Zhitui, Xiao Gang recited the couplet constantly, unable to get it out of his mind.[71]

PERCEPTIONS AND REPRESENTATIONS

A great many poems by Xiao Gang, most of them undatable, deal with the perception of objects and their representation in poetry. "Ascending the City Wall" ("Dengcheng" 登城) is an interesting piece, because it is a poem about writing poetry, or, more precisely, about the inability to write poetry.[72] Depending on our reading of the last line, it also touches on poetry's inability to capture the complexity of human emotions. The poem is, in some ways, an ingenious rewriting of the Western Jin writer Lu Ji's famous "*Fu* on Literature," with a particular Xiao Gang twist.

日影半東簷	As the sunlight is divided by the eastern eaves,
靖念空杼柚	I calm my thoughts, the loom of composition, bare.
小堂倦縹書	I tire of the volumes bound in green silk in the little studio,
華池厭修竹	and grow weary of the tall bamboos by the lovely pond.
寂寞既寡悰	Quiet and desolate as it is, joys are few,
登城望原陸	I ascend the city wall, gazing at the plain.
遙山半吐雲	Distant mountains are half disgorging clouds,
嚴飈時響谷	a gusty wind at times echoes in the valley.
靡靡見虛煙	I see the empty vapors, widespread,
森森視寒木	dense and tall are the cold trees.
落霞乍續斷	Sunset clouds, now continuous, now broken;
晚浪時迴復	evening waves at times flow and ebb.
遠矚既濡翰	After gazing afar, I moisten the brush,
徒自勞心目	but have labored my heart and eyes to no avail:
短歌雖可裁	although a short song may be cut to order,
緣情非霧縠	the piece "following from the affections" is no misty crepe.

71. Yan Zhitui, *Yanshi jiaxun* 9.273.
72. *Quan Liang shi* 21.1932.

The poem begins with shadows cast by the sun, which indicate a specific time in a day, in this case mid-morning. The bare loom of composition (literally, "weaving in vain") in the second line uses weaving as a metaphor for writing, and a clever pun is intended: threads or silk, *si* 絲, the raw material for weaving, puns with "thought" (*si* 思), here given as its synonym, *nian* 念.[73] "Calming one's thoughts" refers to the act of concentrating on the task at hand and forgetting the outside world, and calming one's thoughts in order to write recalls the opening passage of Lu Ji's "*Fu* on Literature":

其始也，皆收視反聽	Thus it begins: retraction of vision, reversion of listening,
耽思傍訊	Absorbed in thought, seeking all around,
精騖八極	My essence galloping to the world's eight bounds,
心遊萬仞	My mind roaming ten thousand yards, up and down.

What Lu Ji describes here is, as Stephen Owen explains, the "process of meditation or speculation that precedes an individual act of composition."[74] But before this process happens, a writer must first go through the stages of "nourishing feeling and intent in the ancient canons" and "roaming in the groves and treasure houses of literary works," as well as the stage of observing and experiencing the empirical world: "He moves along with the four seasons and sighs at their passing on, / Peers on all the things of the world, broods on their profusions" 遵四時以嘆逝，/瞻萬物而思紛.[75] These very activities, intended to prepare the poet for the act of composition are, however, rejected by Xiao Gang:

小堂倦縹書	I tire of the volumes bound in green silk in the little studio,
華池厭修竹	and grow weary of the tall bamboos by the lovely pond.

73. Lu Ji also uses "shuttle and loom" to refer to literary composition: "Even if the shuttle and loom were in my own feelings, / I must dread lest others have preceded me" 雖杼軸於予懷，/怵他人之我先 (*Quan Jin wen* 97.2013; translation from Owen, *Readings in Chinese Literary Thought*, p. 150).

74. Owen, *Readings in Chinese Literary Thought*, p. 96.

75. Ibid., pp. 87–90.

The poet then ascends the city wall in the hope of finding poetic inspiration. Time passes; the day is coming to an end, indicated by the sunset clouds and the "evening waves." His solution has failed.

遠矚既濡翰	After gazing afar, I moisten the brush,
徒自勞心目	but have labored my heart and eyes to no avail:

"Moistening the brush" again echoes, but also subverts, a couplet by Lu Ji: "At first it [i.e., literary composition] hesitates on his dry lips, / But finally flows freely through the moist brush" 始躑躅於燥吻, / 終流離於濡翰.[76] The free flow of creativity after the initial dry barrenness is the ideal outcome after the writer's strenuous efforts, but Xiao Gang indicates that he is not so lucky, because

短歌雖可裁	although a short song may be cut to order,
緣情非霧縠	the piece "following from the affections" is no misty crepe.

To understand the last line, we again have to resort to Lu Ji's "*Fu* on Literature," which was certainly familiar to Xiao Gang's contemporaries. Lu Ji describes the generic characteristic of poetry thus: "The poem follows from the affections and is sensuously intricate" ("shi yuanqing er qimi" 詩緣情而綺靡).[77] *Qi* 綺, here rendered "intricate," refers to patterned silk. "Misty crepe" evokes Yang Xiong's comparison of *fu* to "misty crepe" (*wuhu* 霧縠) in *Fayan* 法言.[78] In the *Fayan* passage, Yang Xiong famously repents his youthful passion for *fu*, mistrusting its seductive power. When an imaginary interlocutor suggests that *fu* is as beautiful as misty crepe, Yang Xiong disparages it as a "borer worm for women's needlework" (*nügong zhi du* 女工之蠹).[79] The topic of Xiao Gang's poem, "ascending the city wall," strengthens the association of "misty crepe" with *fu*, since it

76. Owen, *Readings in Chinese Literary Thought*, p. 110. I changed Owen's translation of *han* 翰 as "pen" to "brush" to reflect the verbal echo; the original Chinese texts for "moisten the brush / the moist pen" are identical in Xiao Gang's poem and Lu Ji's *fu*.

77. Ibid., p. 130.

78. I am grateful to David Knechtges for pointing out this reference.

79. This phrase echoes a remark from Liu An's 劉安 (179–122 B.C.) *Huainanzi*: "Brocade and exquisite embroidery are what bring harm to women's needlework" 錦繡纂組, 害女工者也 (*Huainanzi* 11.376). The remark also appears verbatim in an edict issued by Emperor Jing of the Han in 142 B.C. (*Zizhi tongjian* 16.544).

serves as a reminder of the ancient saying: "He who can climb to a high place and recite *fu* can become a grand master" 登高能賦可以爲大夫.[80] The last line thus presents a contrast between poetry and *fu*. What Xiao Gang seems to be saying here is that his feelings may be expressed in poetry, especially a short song, which "follows from the affections," but not in the more extravagant rhetorical beauty of *fu*. The fabric metaphor is nicely sustained throughout the poem.

Whereas Lu Ji admits at the end of "*Fu* on Literature" that he does not always know how to overcome writer's block, Xiao Gang's poem is interesting in being an eloquent discourse on the inability to write and the special function of poetry, perhaps short lyric poetry in particular. The landscape description embedded in the poem serves an interesting purpose: unlike most poetic landscapes, it does not "stir" the poet's feelings and provoke him to "respond" in writing. In the end, he does write, but he writes about the futility of looking for poetic inspiration in the standard sources of books or nature. Poetry is, as traditional poetics insists, still occasioned by empirical experience, but the experience turns out to be the poet's self-reflexive frustration about not being able to write.

Another poem, entitled "Evening Sun in the Rear Hall" ("Wanri houtang" 晚日後堂), also touches on the issue of poetic composition, but here the process of composition is displaced in the progress of the poem itself.[81]

幔陰通碧砌	As awning shades pass over the emerald stairs,
日影度城隅	the sunlight is crossing the corner of the city wall.
岸柳垂長葉	Willows on the bank droop long leaves;
窗桃落細跗	peach blossoms by the window shed delicate calyxes.
花留蛺蝶粉	A flower retains the butterfly's powder;
竹翳蜻蜓珠	the bamboo conceals the dragonfly pearl.
賞心無與共	There is no understanding friend to share with—
染翰獨踟躕	moistening the brush, I linger alone.

Once again, the poem opens with the movement of shadows, which connects two far-apart spaces: the emerald stairs seen by the poet, and

80. *Han shu* 30.1755.
81. *Quan Liang shi* 22.1955.

the corner of the city wall, which seems to be an imagined scene, inferred from the shadows cast and the position of the sun. From this point on, boundaries become blurred. As the poet's eyes linger over the tiniest detail in the world of nature, it becomes difficult to distinguish what he actually sees from what he imagines. Willows on the bank, a distant scene, are juxtaposed with an adjacent one: the peach blossoms by the window. The poet is so close to the peach blossoms that he claims that he can even see their shedding of the delicate calyxes. This couplet reminds the reader: just as the sun is sinking, springtime is also coming to an end.

The next couplet is characterized by Xiao Gang's masterful command of parallelism. According to Zhang Hua's *Bowu zhi* 博物志, a work recording strange phenomena, "On the fifth day of the fifth month, if one buries the head of a dragonfly under a west-facing window, after three days of not eating anything, it will turn into a green pearl."[82] Now, a butterfly does have powder on its wings, but the "dragonfly pearl" is certainly a fiction. And the poet ingeniously claims that it is "concealed" by the growing bamboo—even as the image is being evoked, it is negated. A figment of the poet's imagination deriving from a textual image is bound with an object that empirically exists by the formal requirements of parallelism ("butterfly's powder" being counterbalanced by "dragonfly pearl") and so takes on an appearance of physical reality.

And yet, is the stain on a flower left by the powder on a butterfly's wings visible to even the most perceptive human eyes? The scene depicted in this couplet seems more a consequence of the poetic imagination than a result of even the most careful observation. It is in this sense that the process of poetic composition is being embedded in the progress of the poem itself: the act of looking and seeing turns out to be one and the same as the act of fantasizing and creating, and it is impossible to separate perception and representation. Precisely for this reason the poet has trouble finding an "appreciative friend" to share his vision, since he is seeing things that cannot be perceived with the physical eyes. Xie Lingyun once famously said that a fine hour, beautiful scenery, an appreciative friend, and enjoyable activities were four things hard to

82. Zhang Hua, *Bowu zhi* 4.50.

come by together.[83] Sitting alone in the late afternoon, with the sun going down and springtime ending, Xiao Gang realizes that the only enjoyable matter is to moisten the brush and write.

The world perceived and represented by Xiao Gang consists of fleeting moments, and this is especially true with his "poetry on objects." As Cynthia Chennault notes, "Instead of things that stand free in nature, the new trend of Southern Qi odes was to depict small decorative items which had incidental uses, such as musical instruments, utensils for a banquet, a lady's toiletry articles, and so on."[84] But of the more than forty poems on objects by Xiao Gang, only one-fifth are about inanimate objects. Xiao Gang was far more interested in portraying natural phenomena or living things, such as horses, birds, flowers, and insects. And they are depicted not as static, inanimate, and generic objects but as specific, particular, and vulnerable to the flow of time, as, for instance, in this short poem, "On a Climbing Vine" ("Yong teng" 詠藤):[85]

纖條寄喬木	Slender vine lodging on a lofty tree,
弱影掣風斜	its pliant shadow pulling the wind aslant.
標春抽曉翠	Marking spring, sprouting morning green;
出霧掛懸花	emerging from mist, suspended flowers hanging from it.

The poet chooses to write about the climbing vine as of an early spring morning, when the fog has not yet entirely cleared up. But the wind is blowing, and the sun shines through, casting shadows on the ground. Although in reality it is the wind that pulls at the vine, the second line creates the illusion that it is the vine pulling the wind and drawing the wind "aslant." By representing the thing of nature as being in constant motion, the poet emphasizes the fragility of the vine as well as its suppleness.

Xiao Gang's fascination with the specifics of the physical world instead of generalities is demonstrated by his obsession with the play of light and shadow, which reappears in "On the Rose" ("Yong qiangwei" 詠薔薇):[86]

83. *Quan Song shi* 3.1181.
84. Chennault, "Odes on Objects," p. 332.
85. *Quan Liang shi* 22.1973.
86. Ibid., 22.1972–73.

燕來枝益軟	Swallows come, the branches even softer;
風飄花轉光	wind blows, the flowers more radiant.
氤氳不肯去	Aroma lingers, refusing to leave,
還來階上香	it comes back, drifting upstairs.

Again, the poet portrays the rose at a specific moment and in a specific situation: the rose in the wind. Wind turns the flowers around so they are fully exposed to the sun and become even more resplendent. It is also the wind that carries the sweet scent of the flowers up the stairs, although the fragrance is being personified as lingering around and even ascending the stairs.

"On Gardenia" ("Yong zhizihua" 詠梔子花), likely a fragment, is as much about the flowers as about the shadows of the flowers:[87]

素華偏可憙	White blossoms are most lovely,
的的半臨池	bright and luminous, it half faces the pond.
疑爲霜裏葉	One suspects the leaves are wrapped in frost,
復類雪封枝	or snow is encasing the branches.
日斜光隱見	Sun slanting, light hidden and then visible;
風還影合離	as wind returns, shadows meet and part.

In a famous metaphor comparing snowflakes to willow catkins, the Eastern Jin woman poet Xie Daoyun 謝道蘊 (ca. late fourth century) turned a winter scene into a spring one. Xiao Gang did the opposite in this poem: the white flowers of gardenia are likened to snow and frost, both of which easily melt under the sun. Only the leaves and branches are of any substance in this poem: the white flowers seem transformed into a radiant white light, which is intensified by the presence of shadow.

Many poems on objects could have been written without the poet ever setting eyes on the objects at all, since the poems usually serve to demonstrate the poet's erudition by piling up allusions to previous literary writings. The more successful of Xiao Gang's *yongwu* poems, however, do not accumulate allusions or mechanically enumerate the characteristics of the object being portrayed. Instead, they exemplify the poet's keenness in observing the world around him. The following couplet sensitively depicts a fine drizzle:

87. *Quan Liang shi* 22.1965–66.

漬花枝覺重	Moistening flowers—the branches feel heavy;
濕鳥羽飛遲	damping the plumage of birds, slowing down their flight.

The couplet is echoed in the great Tang poet Du Fu's well-known poem, "Delighted in the Rain on a Spring Night" ("Chunye xiyu" 春夜喜雨): "In the morning one looks at where the red becomes wet: / flowers growing heavy in the Brocade City" 曉看紅濕處，/ 花重錦官城.[88]

"On Clouds" ("Yong yun" 詠雲), a poem about the mortality and fragility of the physical world, is an example of Xiao Gang's best *yongwu* poetry:

浮雲舒五色	Floating clouds unfold in five colors—
瑪瑙映霜天	agate shining against the frosty sky.
玉葉散秋影	Leaves of jade scattering autumn shadows;
金風飄紫煙	a metal wind sending purple mist adrift.

This poem demonstrates Xiao Gang's familiarity with the literary tradition and his ability to make it new. In his "*Fu* on the Floating Clouds" ("Fuyun fu" 浮雲賦), Lu Ji compared the clouds of "five colors" to lotus flower, rose-of-sharon, agate, and carnelian. He also described the clouds as "leaves of jade" being blown off "golden boughs."[89] It is interesting to observe what Xiao Gang takes from Lu Ji: instead of organic plants such as lotus and rose-of-sharon, he chooses jade and carnelian, raw materials of nature whose hard texture is effectively contrasted with the shifting forms of clouds in Xiao Gang's poem. On one hand, the poet uses words of insubstantiality such as "floating," "shadow," "mist," and "adrift"; on the other hand, he stresses the solidity of minerals. That the sky is "frosty" intensifies the sense of coldness and hardness.

The clouds depicted in this poem are season-specific: they are autumn clouds. Real leaves decay and rot in autumn, but not "leaves of jade." And yet, with the blowing of the "metal wind" (autumn being

88. *Quan Tang shi* 226.2439.

89. *Quan Jin wen* 96.2008. Lu Ji's description was in turn inspired by a passage in the late second-century scholar Ying Shao's 應劭 *Fengsu tongyi* 風俗通義: "As the Yellow Emperor fought Chiyou at Zhuolu, there was always a five-colored cloud resembling golden boughs and leaves of jade that hovered above the Yellow Emperor" (Ying, *Fengsu tongyi*, p. 407).

the season of metal according to the Chinese cosmology of five elements), even leaves of jade are scattered and eventually turned into what they really are: insubstantial, ethereal mist.

The Buddhist paradise known as the Pure Land is described as a diamond realm and decorated lavishly with the Seven Jewels, which include agate, carnelian, jade, and gold (also *jin* in Chinese). In this land, even the trees are made of precious gems, such as beryl, crystal, and pearl. For some lay readers, this might seem unnatural or artificial, and yet, what are beryl, crystal, and pearl if not things of nature as well? Their only difference from trees of the mortal world is that they do not decay: hence, they are beyond life and death. Xiao Gang was obviously fascinated by the land of bliss sumptuously portrayed in the sūtra texts. In his poem "Riding in the Western Residence" ("Xizhai xingma" 西齋行馬), we see another couplet that evokes such a beautiful, eternal world: "Clouds open up like agate leaves;/clear are the waters of glass" 雲開瑪瑙葉,/水淨琉璃波.[90] Viewed in a Buddhist context, Xiao Gang's poem on clouds becomes poignant. As the "leaves of jade" turn into a mist dispelled by the autumn wind, we see the contrast between the solidity of the diamond land inhabited by Heavenly Beings and the insubstantiality and vulnerability of the human world.

Many of Xiao Gang's poems are informed by his intimate knowledge of Buddhism. "On a Fair Lady Looking at a Painting" ("Yong meiren kanhua" 詠美人看畫) illustrates the illusory nature of the physical world:[91]

殿上圖神女	In the hall a portrait of a divine woman;
宮裏出佳人	From the palace emerges a fair lady.
可憐俱是畫	So lovely, both are painted;
誰能辨僞眞	who could distinguish real from unreal?
分明淨眉眼	Both have bright eyes and neat brows;
一種細腰身	Their slender waists are one and the same.
所可持爲異	How do we separate the two?
長有好精神	One is always in good spirits.

Rather humorously, Xiao Gang points out that both women, inside and outside the painting, are "painted," alluding to the court lady's heavy

90. *Quan Liang shi* 21.1950.
91. Ibid., 22.1953.

makeup. The last couplet, as Kang-i Sun Chang has said, underlines the "permanent value of art": only one of the two women, the painted one, is "always" in good spirits.[92] One may object that Xiao Gang is treating the real woman like an object of art by comparing her to a painting, and yet, nowhere else can we see more clearly the immense energy and fragility of the human condition: unlike the painted beauty, the real woman can fall sick, grow old, become angry or sad, and easily lose her "good spirits," which only a painted image is privileged to possess forever. Indeed, for readers like members of the Liang nobility saturated in Buddhist teachings and frequently in attendance at Buddhist lectures, the very statement that "one is always in good spirits" is tongue-in-cheek: painting is one of the best-known metaphors in Buddhist scriptures for the illusory nature of the physical world. Thus, the permanence of a painting is itself an illusion, conditioned by the brevity of human life. The poem in fact recalls a Buddhist story about the mutual deception of a carpenter and a painter. In the story, the carpenter made a wooden statue of a pretty girl. It was so life-like that the painter took it to be a real girl and fell in love with her. After learning of his error, the embarrassed painter decided to get back at his friend. He drew a life-size painting of hanging himself, which led the carpenter to think that the painter had committed suicide. Terrified, the carpenter tried to cut the rope, only to discover it was a painting. Because of the incident, both friends were enlightened about the unreal nature of the physical world, and they became monks.[93]

"Reflected in the Water, Looking at Her Fallen Hairpin" ("Zhaoliu kan luochai" 照流看落釵) explores a favorite poetic subject in the Liang, a reflection in water:[94]

92. Chang, *Six Dynasties Poetry*, p. 156.

93. The story is from *Za piyu jing* 雜譬喻經 and included in *Jinglü yixiang* (*T* 53: 44.229).

94. *Quan Liang shi* 22.1964. An otherwise unknown Liang poet Tang Sengji 湯僧濟 wrote a poem, "On Discovering a Gold Hairpin When Cleaning a Well" ("Yong xiejing de jinchai" 詠渫井得金釵; *Quan Liang shi* 28.2119). Xiao Gang's and Tang Sengji's poems are antecedents of Du Fu's poem "Bronze Jar" ("Tongping" 銅瓶), which is about a bronze jar found in a well in the imperial palace after the An Lushan Rebellion (*Quan Tang shi* 225.2425).

相隨照綠水	They follow one another to look into the clear water,
意欲重涼風	for they all value the cool breeze.
流搖粧影壞	The currents waver, the makeup is ruined;
釵落鬢華空	hairpin falls, her tresses become empty.
佳期在何許	When is that lovely time going to be?
徒傷心不同	In vain she laments that his heart is not the same.

Both *huai* 壞, "to ruin or destroy," and *kong* 空, "empty," are technical terms in Buddhist scriptures. *Huai* refers to the ruination of destructible things, such as the human body, the things of nature, and the universe. According to the sūtras, there are three kinds of sufferings, the third of which is *huaiku* 壞苦, suffering experienced due to the annihilation of things one is attached to.

Chapter 4 discusses Xiao Gang's poem on a lone duck seduced by its reflection in water. Several other poems feature a lonely bird: a crane in "Upon Hearing a Solitary Crane on the River Isle" ("Yong zhou wen duhe" 詠洲聞獨鶴), and a wild goose in "Gazing at a Wild Goose Flying Alone at Night" ("Ye wang dan fei yan" 夜望單飛雁).[95] The latter is a quatrain in seven-character lines, still a novel poetic form in the Liang:

天霜河白夜星稀	The sky is frosty, the Milky Way pale, the evening stars few,
一雁聲嘶何處歸	a wild goose cries a mournful note: where can he go?
早知半路應相失	If he had known he would lose his companions halfway,
不如從來本獨飛	it would have been better for him to have always flown by himself.

The power of this poem lies in the directness of the last two lines, which present an effective emotional response to the situation. We cannot help wondering what keeps the speaker up as late as the lonely wild goose, even as the Milky Way grows pale in the dawn light.

95. *Quan Liang shi* 22.1960, 22.1978. For the former I follow the title given in *Yiwen leiju* 90.1566.

547–52: THE FINAL YEARS

Seventeen years as a crown prince in the shadow of a vigorous father is not the most desirable situation for a grown man, but Xiao Gang made the best of it. He not only assisted Emperor Wu in administration but also devoted much time to literary and scholarly activities. In the early summer of 547, "a marvelous stallion appeared [i.e., a good omen], and the crown prince presented 'An Ode to the Treasured Steed' ('Baoma song' 寶馬頌) to the throne."[96] The ode praised the peace and prosperity of the state as well as the sagely rule of the emperor in extravagant terms. And yet, earlier that year, driven by his ambition to conquer the North and inspired by a dream of unifying China, Emperor Wu had made the fatal mistake of accepting Hou Jing's capitulation, against the better judgment of several courtiers: it was the beginning of the collapse of the Liang.

That same year, Xiao Gang gave many lectures on the *Laozi* and *Zhuangzi* in the Eastern Palace. The former prime minister He Jingrong expressed a worry to a friend: if absorption in Lao-Zhuang discourse had led to the fall of the Western Jin to the northern barbarians, it might cause the same thing to happen again.[97] In peaceful times, such a remark would have gone unremembered, but with hindsight, historians recorded it as an insightful prediction.

Blaming the collapse of a state on Lao-Zhuang discourse or Buddhism was no more than a cultural myth. Hou Jing's rebellion was the direct consequence of his own ambitious, his fickle nature, and some bad political decisions made by the Liang court. In September 548, Hou Jing declared war under the pretext of ridding the court of evildoers. Having secured Xiao Zhengde 蕭正德, Emperor Wu's nephew, as an ally, Hou Jing and his advisor Wang Wei 王偉 devised a daring plan to head directly for the capital city. The rebel army met with surprisingly little resistance. In a matter of two months, Hou Jing and his 8,000 men stood outside Jiankang. On the evening of December 7, 548, the court declared martial law. The people of Jiankang panicked, and riots broke out in streets. The imperial boulevard was blocked.

---

96. *Nan shi* 7.219. The ode is preserved in *Wenyuan yinghua* under the title of "Mabao song" 馬寶頌; see *Quan Liang wen* 12.3020.

97. *Quan Liang wen* 37.533.

Seeing how urgent the situation was, Xiao Gang went to see the emperor and asked to be given total command. The emperor replied, "This is naturally your responsibility. There is no need to ask." At that time, still oblivious to the treachery of Xiao Zhengde, Xiao Gang ordered him to guard the Red Sparrow Gate to the south of Jiankang. Xiao Gang's eldest son, Xiao Daqi, was put in charge of the military defense of the capital, aided by the loyal and resourceful general Yang Kan, who was to distinguish himself as a true hero in the siege of the Palace City. Xiao Tui 蕭推 (d. 548), one of Xiao Gang's favorite cousins, was commissioned to guard the Eastern Residence City, the small satellite city to the southeast of the Palace City.

On December 9, Hou Jing's army reached the Red Sparrow Pontoon Bridge. Yu Xin, charged with severing the bridge, withdrew at the sight of Hou Jing's warriors. Xiao Zhengde's men reopened the bridge and brought Hou Jing across. To the west, Xiao Dachun 蕭大春 (530–51), Xiao Gang's sixth son, fled from the Stone Fort; to the north, Xie Xi 謝禧 (b. 509) and Yuan Zhen 元貞 abandoned Baixia, the other fortress defending Jiankang. Jiankang was exposed to the enemy on three sides now. Within Jiankang itself, Xiao Gang had commissioned Wang Zhi 王質 (511–70) to aid Yu Xin, but Wang Zhi fell back upon encountering the enemy. By this point, no one had put up a real fight against Hou Jing.

John Marney sees this as a consequence of Xiao Gang's poor deployment of personnel,[98] but the fact is that the Liang court was completely unprepared for such a crisis. As Zhuang Tie 莊鐵 (d. 550), the Liyang magistrate who was among the first to surrender to Hou Jing, put it, "The country has lived in peace for many years, and people are not used to warfare. When they hear Your Highness has raised an army, they are shaken with amazement and terror." The daring gamble devised by a desperate and determined Hou Jing and his advisors—to cut straight to the heart of the Liang empire with no more than 8,000 soldiers and several hundred horses—worked to their advantage.

Everyone retreated into the Palace City. A bloody siege ensued, during which many acts of heroism and betrayal occurred. At one point, Song Yi 宋嶷, the supervisor of construction, deserted and advised Hou Jing to flood the Palace City with the waters of Xuanwu Lake, and all

98. Marney, *Liang Chien-wen Ti*, p. 142.

the avenues leading to the imperial palace were turned into rivers.[99] Many people in the Palace City, aristocrat and commoner alike, died of hunger or disease, including Xiao Gang's wife, Lady Wang, who passed away in the spring of 549. In the meantime, rescue armies poured into the capital area, only to be rendered powerless by internal factions, defeats, and much bad luck. On April 24, 549, after a drawn-out resistance of nearly five months, the Palace City fell.

The saving grace for the emperor and the crown prince was their utter composure in the face of disaster. Both received Hou Jing with dignity, and it was Hou Jing who found himself nervous and speechless. The absence of fear in the royal persons deeply impressed Yuan Xian, a smart young man who had entered the civil service at the age of seventeen and married Xiao Gang's daughter, the Princess of Nansha. Forty years later, in 589, when the Sui army marched into the Chen imperial palace, he tried to persuade the last Chen emperor to emulate Emperor Wu of the Liang in his reception of Hou Jing. Instead, the Chen emperor hid himself, along with two of his favorite palace ladies, in a dried-up well, from which he was pulled by the Sui soldiers.[100] His lack of dignity has become notorious ever since.

On June 12, Emperor Wu passed away. On July 7, Hou Jing disclosed the news of the emperor's death, and Xiao Gang was proclaimed emperor. Thus began Xiao Gang's two and a half years of nominal rule under the domination of Hou Jing. The story about Xiao Gang's choice of reign title may best reflect his state of mind. At first, he was going to use Wenming 文明 (Luminous Cultivation), a phrase taken from the hexagram Mingyi 明夷 (Suppression of the Light) in *The Classic of Changes*,[101] which is about remaining constant in the face of adversity: "When the light goes into the earth, there is suppression of the light. Inside it is all luminous cultivation; outside, yielding and obeisance: in this way one endures great adversity. King Wen [of Zhou] was like this."[102] But Xiao Gang abandoned this choice because he was afraid

99. *Liang shu* 56.844.
100. *Chen shu* 24.314.
101. *Nan shi* 8.233.
102. *Zhou yi zhengyi* 4.88. King Wen of Zhou suffered years of imprisonment under the tyrannical rule of the last Shang king. He was the father of King Wu, who eventually overthrew the Shang dynasty.

that Hou Jing, or more precisely his well-educated advisor Wang Wei, would detect the hidden message. Instead he chose Dabao 大寶 (Great Treasure). This phrase comes from the "Commentary on Appended Phrases" in *The Classic of Changes*: "The great treasure of the sage is called [his] position."[103]

Appearances were initially more or less maintained, although not without a sense that things had gone terribly awry. On April 6, 550, Hou Jing invited Xiao Gang to hold the traditional banquet in celebration of the Lustration Festival in Leyou Park 樂遊苑. By that time Hou Jing had taken Xiao Gang's daughter, the beautiful Princess of Liyang, as his favorite concubine. Xiao Gang returned to the palace toward dawn; afterward, Hou Jing and the princess sat side by side on the imperial couch facing south, with all the civil and military officials present.[104] On May 28, Hou Jing invited Xiao Gang and Lady Fan, the Princess of Liyang's mother, to a party at Western Isle. Xiao Gang, still in mourning dress, showed up in a plain coach with about 400 attendants, whereas Hou Jing and his officers were followed by several thousand warriors in shiny iron armor. When the musicians played the traditional Liang state banquet music, Xiao Gang shed tears.[105]

An inscription on Xiulin Hill 秀林山, attributed to Xiao Gang, testifies to an imperial outing on April 16, 550.[106] Gracefully phrased, it reveals nothing about the author's terrible situation. Literary conventions effectively helped maintain the refined, glossy surface of the sophisticated Liang court.[107] This seems to illustrate Xiao Gang's original choice of reign title: "Inside it is all luminous cultivation; outside, yielding and obeisance."

In late 550, Xiao Huili 蕭會理 (519–50), Xiao Gang's nephew, initiated a failed coup against Hou Jing. Hou Jing henceforth grew

103. *Zhou yi zhengyi* 8.166.

104. *Nan shi* 80.2008.

105. Ibid., 80.2009; *Sui shu* 13.304.

106. *Quan Liang wen* 13.3025.

107. John Marney (*Liang Jian-wen Ti*, p. 165) was led to believe that Xiao Gang had enjoyed a certain degree of freedom because of the following remark: "Taking advantage of leisure time after taking care of state affairs, I summon my carriage for an outing." But this is in fact a conventional way to begin an outing narrative and has nothing to do with reality.

apprehensive of Xiao Gang. Previously Wang Ke, Yin Buhai 殷不害 (505–89), and Xiao Zi 蕭諮 had been the only courtiers permitted to see Xiao Gang alone.[108] After the coup, Wang Ke and Yin Buhai kept their distance out of fear, but Xiao Zi still came to the palace every day. Hou Jing finally had Xiao Zi assassinated. Upon learning of Xiao Zi's death, Xiao Gang knew that his own end was drawing near. Pointing to the hall in which he lived, he told Yin Buhai: "'Pang Juan shall die right here.'"[109]

In the spring of 551, Hou Jing went to the rescue of his general Ren Yue 任約, who was fighting against Xiao Yi's army, and did not return to Jiankang till late summer, having been defeated in the campaign. Since Hou Jing had always held immense contempt for the southerners, believing they were easy to vanquish, he intended to postpone his enthronement until conquering the entire South. Now that he had lost many of his capable officers in battle, he advanced his schedule. On October 2, 551, Xiao Gang was deposed and put under house arrest. Xiao Dong 蕭棟 (d. 552), a grandson of Xiao Tong, was proclaimed emperor. Many princes were murdered at this juncture, including Xiao Daqi, Xiao Gang's eldest son, who had given up an opportunity to escape in order to be with his father and had kept his dignity throughout imprisonment.[110]

Having no paper, Xiao Gang reportedly wrote several hundred poems and prose pieces on the walls and wooden screens between the

108. *Nan shi* 52.1298.

109. *Liang shu* 56.858; *Nan shi* 8.233. Pang Juan was a general in the Warring States period. His adversary carved the words on a tree: "Pang Juan shall die underneath this tree." Pang Juan ordered his soldier to light up a torch and read the words. The torchlight at night became a signal to the enemy to begin the ambush, which resulted in Pang Juan's death (*Shi ji* 65.2164).

110. *Liang shu* 8.172. Someone asked the prince why he was not afraid. He replied, "I reckon I will die before the rebels do. If my uncles can destroy them, they will kill me first; if not, they will also kill me to clear the way. Why should I indulge in needless sorrow over a doomed life?" On the day of his death, he was lecturing on the *Laozi*. When the executioner arrived, he said, "I have anticipated this day for a long time; I am surprised how slow it comes." The executioners were going to strangle the prince with his own belt. Ever poised and calm, he told them that the sash was too fragile and would not work and asked to have curtain cords brought forth instead.

pillars during the days of confinement. On the evening of November 15, Wang Wei and two of his men, Peng Juan 彭雋 and Wang Xiuzuan 王脩纂, brought some wine to Xiao Gang, claiming Hou Jing had sent them to wish His Majesty a long life. Xiao Gang said with a smile: "I have already been dethroned, so why do you still address me as 'Your Majesty'? Won't life end with this 'wine for long life'?" He nevertheless drank merrily, even quoting the *Analects* and commenting ironically on Peng Juan's playing a crooked-necked lute: "I didn't know that music could attain such a level."[111] After he retired, Wang Xiuzuan suffocated Xiao Gang with a bag filled with dirt. His body was left in a wine-cellar to the north of the city. Later, Wang Wei came in and examined Xiao Gang's writings on the walls and screens. "Disturbed by their extreme sentiments," Wang Wei had them scraped off immediately. One of his people "memorized three linked-pearl pieces, four poems, and five quatrains, all of which were very sad."[112]

A fragment is preserved in Xiao Gang's *Liang shu* biography:

> I, Xiao Shizan of Lanling, am an honorable man of the Liang. From beginning to end, I have remained constant in establishing myself and practicing the Way. 'In the wind and rain it is all dark, and the cock crows without ceasing.' I do not attempt to deceive even in a darkened room, let alone under the Three Lights [of sun, moon, and stars]. And yet I am destined to come to such an end: such is the working of Fate—what is to be done!
>
> 有梁正士蘭陵蕭世讚, 立身行道, 終始如一, 風雨如晦, 雞鳴不已. 弗欺暗室, 豈況三光. 數至於此, 命也如何!

"In the wind and rain it is all dark, and the cock crows without ceasing" are lines from the poem "Wind and Rain" ("Fengyu" 風雨) in *The Classic of Poetry*. According to the traditional interpretation, this poem "reflects on how a gentleman remains steadfast in chaotic times."[113]

One poem survives, preserved in the Buddhist anthology *Guang Hongming ji*:

恍忽煙霞散	Dimly, the mists and rosy clouds have dispersed,
颸颼松柏陰	wind rustling in the shades of pines and cypresses.

111. *Lunyu zhushu* 7.13.
112. *Liang shu* 4.108; *Nan shi* 8.233–34.
113. *Maoshi zhengyi* 4.179.

幽山白楊古	In desolate hills, poplars grow old;
野路黃塵深	yellow dust lying deep on deserted road.
終無千月命	Never destined for a thousand-month life,
安用九丹金	what need for the Nine Elixirs' gold?
闕里長蕪沒	Queli has long been overgrown with weeds,
蒼天空照心	the gray heavens show forth this heart to no purpose.[114]

Queli was Confucius' native place. Pines and cypresses, like poplars, were trees planted by tombs. The fifth line recalls a couplet by the Eastern Jin poet Guo Pu: "One lives in the world for no more than a thousand months: / human life is like the stalk of an autumn leaf" 在世無千月,/命如秋葉蒂.[115] Any of the Nine Elixirs, according to the Daoist Ge Hong, enables one to become an immortal. After taking the elixir, one may either ascend to heaven or remain in the human world, impervious to harm. These elixirs can also be transformed into gold.[116]

In a commentary on this poem, the early Qing critic Wang Fuzhi said with admiration: "Even though he faced such great sorrows, its tone and rhythm are not disordered. Brooding, calm, and yet full of feelings, it can still move us even after a thousand years. 'In the wind and rain it is all dark, and the cock crows without ceasing.' What he said of himself is no lie. Possessing such a quality, if not for his unlucky fate, might not he be considered as having had the capacity to rule an empire?"[117] Indeed, in this poem one may see most clearly Xiao Gang's remarkable self-possession, his artistic control, and his strength of character, which had been cultivated since early childhood. The first line of the poem summarizes the life of the unfortunate prince-poet: it had been a life of "mists and rosy clouds," resplendent, but unreal, finally sent adrift by the metal wind. The gray heavens were revealed, but with the shades of pines and cypresses spreading, it would soon be dark.

Finally, on April 30, 552, Xiao Yi's general Wang Sengbian, whose army recovered Jiankang, escorted Xiao Gang's casket back to the court and led civil and military officials in weeping and obeisance according

114. *Quan Liang shi* 22.1979.
115. *Quan Jin shi* 11.867.
116. See Ge Hong, *Baopuzi neipian* 4.65.
117. Wang Fuzhi, *Gushi pingxuan*, p. 303.

to ritual etiquette. According to the modern calendar, this day marked the fiftieth anniversary of the founding of the Liang. On May 26, Hou Jing was killed attempting to escape to the North. His body was displayed on the streets of Jiankang and soon thereafter torn to shreds and "eaten up" by the people of Jiankang.[118]

On June 5, 552, Xiao Gang's sarcophagus was interred in Zhuangling 莊陵 next to that of his wife. Xiao Yi changed the posthumous title conferred by Hou Jing, Mingdi 明帝 (the Bright Emperor), to Jianwendi 簡文帝. The bleak picture envisioned by Xiao Gang—the desolate hills, the rustling of the poplars, the deep accumulation of dust on the deserted road—is not far from reality. Today, in the suburbs of Nanjing, we can still see the last trace of the ruins of Xiao Gang's mausoleum: a large stone unicorn standing tall in the fields, but broken and fragmented.

CODA

Xiao Gang once gave a definition of poetry in a comment on the poem "Tomb Gate" ("Mumen" 墓門) in *The Classic of Poetry*.[119] The following passage is an elucidation of the line: "I sing [this song] to inform him" ("Ge yi xun zhi" 歌以訊之).[120]

> The poem is thought (*si*); it is also words (*ci*). Concerns come forth in one's mind and are called thought; articulation reveals one's bosom. Expressed in words, it is a poem; expressed in music, it is a song: their origin is the same. Therefore it says: make a good song to inform him.
>
> 詩者, 思也, 辭也. 發慮在心謂之思; 言, 見其懷抱者也. 在辭爲詩, 在樂爲歌, 其本一也. 故云: 作好歌以訊之.

This passage both echoes traditional poetics and goes beyond it. *Si*, unlike feeling (*qing* 情) or aims (*zhi* 志), stresses the rational operation of the mind. Xiao Gang's equivalence of the poem with "words" in the

118. *Liang shu* 56.862.

119. This comment is from Xiao Gang's exegesis on *The Classic of Poetry*, *Maoshi shiwu guofeng yi* 毛詩十五國風義. The fragment is preserved in *Maoshi zhishuo* 毛詩指說 by the Tang scholar Cheng Boyu 成伯璵, and collected in the Qing scholar Ma Guohan's 馬國翰 (1794–1857) *Yuhan shanfang ji yishu* 16.48a.

120. *Maoshi zhengyi* 711.254.

second part of the definition is equally worthy of note, since it emphasizes the importance of language. In the traditional conceptualization of poetry, a poem is what is intently on the mind; in Xiao Gang's definition, a poem is also just words. This points to a poetics of treating poetry as a reflective craft, not as a transparent, immediate expression of experience. Such a poetics was to become a formidable alternative voice in the literary tradition in the ninth century,[121] but Xiao Gang's concept of poetry as "thought and words" was too advanced for his own age. He did well in the protected world of the free-spirited Liang court, but once removed from that context, his poetry became an easy target for later critics, who had little sympathy or tolerance for, not just any prince, but a crown prince harboring unconventional ideas about writing.

Wang Fuzhi was one of the few Chinese critics to praise Southern Dynasties poetry highly. In evaluating a couplet by Xiao Gang, he said:

> Only Du Zimei [Du Fu] in his early years could have constructed such lines. Taibai [Li Bai] and Mojie [Wang Wei 王維 (701–61)] sometimes come close. As for the rest, they have long been bending over under his wind.[122]
>
> 唯杜子美早年足構此句，太白、摩詰時差參近之，餘子望風而靡久矣.

Xiao Gang's brilliance has long been suppressed by misunderstanding and misrepresentation. Only when we look closely at his poetry do we see a world intensely luminous in its delicacy and vulnerability. We have observed his fascination with the representation of shadow; and yet, what is shadow but the obstruction, hence confirmation, of light?

121. See Owen, *The End of the Chinese "Middle Ages,"* pp. 107–29.
122. Wang Fuzhi, *Gushi pingxuan*, p. 301.

CHAPTER SEVEN

The Cultural Construction of the North and South

In 1998, *Yellow River Literature*, a provincial magazine founded by the Shanxi Writers' Association, published a novella entitled "The Water Town of My Dreams" ("Mengzhong shuixiang" 夢中水鄉). In this *bildungsroman*, the protagonist narrates what prompted him to apply for Nanjing University during his high school years.

> When I was reading literary and historical works, what took the strongest hold of me was the Southland. The beautiful scenery such as described in "River blossoms at dawn-break are more fiery than flames; / the spring river is of an emerald green," the Yue girl of tender sensibilities singing "Trees grow on the hill, branches grow on the tree; / my heart delights in my lord, but my lord does not know," and the sweet lotus-picking songs as soft as moonlight drifting in the waves—all of these enraptured me, intoxicated me. Yes, I thought to myself, I will go to college in the Southland![1]

This rather effusive passage presents a common fantasy about the highly romanticized Southland (Jiangnan), an image conjured up here by a medley of literary and historical texts. Particularly noteworthy is the close association between the Southland and feminine beauty.

The images of the North and the South in the Chinese cultural imagination have become standardized by now: the North is tough,

1. *Huanghe wenxue* 黃河文學 1998, no. 2 (1998): 153.

harsh, austere; the South, warm, soft, sensuous. It is not difficult to identify these two sets of attributes with conventional gender characteristics and to conceive the North as masculine, the South as feminine. This chapter argues that these images, instead of "reflecting reality," are no more than cultural constructs first formed during the Northern and Southern Dynasties. The process culminated in the sixth century and was firmly established in the Sui and Tang, the two conquest dynasties that unified China and brought the North and South together.

The South (*nanfang* 南方), sometimes referred to as Jiangnan 江南 (literally, "the [area] south of the Yangzi River"), was traditionally designated *Jiangdong* 江東, "the [area] east of the Yangzi River," because between the two cities of Wuhu 蕪湖 (in modern Anhui province) and Nanjing, the Yangzi River flows south–north. It was alternatively known as Jiangzuo 江左, the "left side of the Yangzi River," a term that began to appear more frequently in written records after the Eastern Jin. Since the emperor always "faced south" on his throne, the area east of the Yangzi (Jiangdong) would be "the left side of the river." But whereas "Jiangzuo" was commonly used in prose pieces and dynastic histories from the fourth to the sixth century to refer to the territory under the control of the Southern court, the term used in poetry to designate the South was "Jiangnan." Indeed, Jiangnan appears most often in the poetry of the Liang dynasty, when the romanticized image of the South was being established.

Several things, however, must be clarified from the outset. First, "North" (*beifang* 北方) and "South" (*nanfang*) in the Chinese cultural imagination do not have a fixed, clear-cut geographical border. They correspond only roughly to geographical locations, and even this correspondence has changed from one historical period to another. These are vague cultural terms that evoke generalized associations, and as such, they are both difficult and fascinating to analyze. The Yangzi River might be taken as a sort of boundary between "South" and "North," but the area to the south of the Yangzi River is vast, and the Far South, such as the modern Guangdong province, or the Southwest, such as Sichuan (then known as Shu), do not figure prominently in the cultural imagination about the "South," or Jiangnan. The Yangzi Delta is the locus of this cultural fantasy about Jiangnan, although, as mentioned above, the geographical range of the terms "North" and "South" changed with the real boundaries of the Chinese empire. For instance, for a modern Chinese, the three Northeastern provinces, Heilongjiang, Jilin, and Liaoning, certainly would be included in a general reference to the "North," but in the fifth century the "North" was identified primarily with whatever territory was then controlled by the Northern Wei state.

This leads to the second point of clarification, which is the use of these two terms in the Northern and Southern Dynasties. The actual geographical boundary between North and South China was fluid throughout the fourth, fifth, and sixth centuries, as territorial wars were constantly being fought and land frequently changed hands. Nevertheless, because of the political situation, a strong consciousness of the "North" and "South," regardless of the exact physical boundary, was being formed and developed in this period. One thing worth noting is that the terms "northerners" (*beiren* 北人 or *beishi* 北士) and "southerners" (*nanren* 南人 or *nanshi* 南士) were employed with more regularity than ever before. Granted, as we saw in Chapter 1, when people in the South used the terms "southerner" and "northerner," they sometimes referred to the native southerners as opposed to northern émigrés. Or when the writer Jiang Yan wrote his "*Fu* on Awaiting Chastisement in the South and Longing to Return North" ("Daizui jiangnan si beigui fu" 待罪江南思北歸賦) in the late fifth century, by "south" he meant modern Fujian province, where he was in exile, and by "north" he meant the capital city of Jiankang, which was north of where he was.[2] It is therefore important to contextualize the terms "North" and "South," and yet, it is undeniable that during this period there was a larger conception of "South vs. North" in the sense of a political North dominated by non-Han Chinese and a political South dominated by what was perceived as orthodox Han Chinese culture. People in the fifth and sixth centuries often consciously compared the North and South; this phenomenon culminated in Yan Zhitui's *Family Instructions*, in which Yan Zhitui, a southerner (in fact the descendent of a very early northern immigrant) going North, contrasted "northern" and "southern" customs in many places. In this specific context, as in many others from the period, the terms "North" and "South" were used to refer not to exact geographical

2. *Quan Liang wen* 33.3142.

locations with fixed geographical boundaries but to political and cultural loci—the North and the South, which had been divided since the beginning of the fourth century. The central point is that the two terms are relational, not only to each other but also intrinsically by their very nature. In this chapter, when I speak of the "North" and the "South," I use the terms not only in the contemporary sense of the larger South/North division in the fifth and sixth centuries but also with the understanding that both terms are cultural constructions dependent on political boundaries rather than on precise geographical boundaries. One of the central arguments of this chapter is that the North (*beifang*) and South (*nanfang*, or more specifically Jiangnan), which still figure prominently in the Chinese cultural imagination today, as we see in the passage cited at the beginning of this chapter, were first shaped during the Northern and Southern Dynasties.

The last point to be clarified is a historical one. As early as the *Shijing* and *Chuci*, there was already a discourse on the South. There is, however, a significant point of difference between the South in the earlier cultural discourse and that in later times: namely, in the earlier period, the relational term to the South was not the "North" but the Central States of the Chinese heartland. In other words, the South did not become a political and cultural center for the Han Chinese until the Six Dynasties period. This is why I posit that the construction of the North and South as two large cultural terms fundamentally began in the Northern and Southern Dynasties, when North and South China, despite their mutual contempt and despite the claims of each that it represented orthodoxy, were on a par in their political and cultural status, especially from the fifth century on.

The chapter begins by giving a brief account of the long-term conflict between the North and South and then describes the conquest dynasties' mediation in the transmission and evaluation of the literary output of the North and South. The rest of the chapter is divided into four sections, each devoted to a group of texts that played a key role in shaping the images of the North and the South. The first section traces the origin and development of "frontier poetry." In this poetry, "frontier" is identified with a specific locale: the far north or the northwest. Neither the real geographical division line between the North and South during this period nor the southern or the southwestern borderlands ever constituted part of this poetic tradition. The early frontier poetry, written by southerners who had never been to the far north, was both a result of the development of its internal generic history and an attempt of Southern Dynasties literati to construct a space "out there"—distant, inaccessible, and exotic. The "frontier" in the frontier poetry represents a North perceived and constructed as a cultural other.

The next section takes up a group of "northern" *yuefu* songs from this period. These songs are prized for representing the rigorous and hardy northern style; yet they were for the most part performed and preserved by Liang court musicians. To what extent, then, may we consider them as representing the North, and to what extent should we think of them as presenting a North as perceived and constructed by the southerners?

The third section deals with a group of poems on lotus flowers and lotus picking. In the native Chinese literary tradition, lotus had long been associated with the South. The plant acquired a particular religious significance in this period because of its rich Buddhist connotations. Sensuous and yet spiritual, lotus caught the imagination of the southern poets, who made the lotus flower the embodiment of the Southland or Jiangnan.

The last section of this chapter treats the southern *yuefu* quatrains. Although Lu Qinli lumped most of the southern *yuefu* songs under the Jin dynasty in his monumental work *Xian Qin Han Wei Jin nanbeichao shi*, there is often no way of telling in which dynasty these songs were produced. Even if a tune title might have first been created in the Jin dynasty, the lyrics to the same title could have been composed in a much later era. For the most part passionate love songs in five-character lines, they are usually regarded as embodying the voice of a lower-class female. A close examination, however, shows that the songs might not have been so much the creation of the common folk as that of the aristocratic imagination; moreover, the gender identity of the speaker in these songs is often ambiguous. The question is what motivates modern scholars to read these songs not only as gender specific but also as female, and what purposes such a reading serves.

A BRIEF ACCOUNT OF THE NORTH/SOUTH CONFLICT

Although in a general sense "South" (Jiangnan) refers to the entire area lying to the south of the Yangzi River, in a narrower sense or as a cultural term, "Jiangnan" indicates the regions of Wu and Yue (modern Jiangsu and Zhejiang provinces). Wu and Yue were two pre-Qin domains regarded as "southern barbarians" by the Central States of the Chinese heartland. Nevertheless, Wu claimed descent from Taibo 太伯 and Zhongyong 仲雍, sons of the Zhou ancestor Gugong Danfu 古公亶父, and the Yue princes considered themselves the offspring of an even more ancient and venerable personage, King Yu, the legendary founder of the Xia dynasty.[3] During the Six Dynasties, many elite families of the South continued to assert a distinguished northern lineage, thus maintaining a double claim to the orthodox Han Chinese cultural heritage and to a southern identity.[4]

The South developed economically throughout the Han dynasty, but it was not until the Kingdom of Wu established its capital at Jianye 建業 (Jiangkang) in the third century that the South could boast an imperial court and a cultural center apart from those in the Chinese heartland. After the Western Jin conquered Wu in 280, many members of the southern elite went to the capital of Luoyang and served in the Jin court, and clashes ensued from their encounter with the northern gentry.[5] This tendency became even more pronounced after the Jin royal house fled to the South during the invasion of the northern "barbarian" tribes in the early fourth century. Although the Prince of Langye, later Emperor Yuan of the Jin (r. 317–23), secured the support of the southern elite with the help of the minister Wang Dao, he was intensely aware that he was "lodging in other people's land."[6]

During the period of division, the North-South rivalry was twofold: in the South, the northern émigré families and the native southern

3. *Shi ji* 31.1445, 41.1739.

4. For the proclaimed ancestral roots of the Southern elite families, see Fang Beichen, *Wei Jin nanchao*, pp. 7–15.

5. See Satō Toshiyuki, *Sei Shin bungaku*; and Knechtges, "Sweet-peel Orange."

6. Liu Yiqing, *Shishuo xinyu* 2.91.

gentry competed for political privileges;[7] at the same time, the South and North, divided by the Yangzi River, contended for military dominance and, as the Northern Wei underwent sinicization during the reign of Emperor Xiaowen (r. 471–99), cultural authority. From the fifth century on, diplomatic missions, among other forms of communication across the border, became increasingly frequent.[8] Both emissaries and "receptionists" (*zhuke* 主客) were chosen for their learning, literary talent, and eloquence.[9] The ability to offer a witty repartee or compose an elegant occasional poem was considered quite important in diplomatic situations. In 549, for example, when Xu Ling was visiting the Eastern Wei as an envoy, Wei Shou 魏收 (506–72) teased him, saying that he had brought the southern heat to the North. Xu Ling replied, "When Wang Su came to this land, he taught the Wei people about rites and righteousness; today, my presence makes you realize the existence of four seasons."[10] Wei Shou, unable to think of a retort, was greatly embarrassed. Later, he was thrown into jail by the then-minister Gao Cheng as a punishment for his verbal ineptitude.[11]

The representation of North and South in a given anecdote by and large depends on who recorded the anecdote and why: whether to honor or insult one or the other region, or to applaud or disparage an individual. In *A Record of Buddhist Monasteries in Luoyang* (*Luoyang qielan ji* 洛陽伽藍記; preface dated 547) the northerner Yang Xuanzhi 楊衒之 gives a full account of a long speech by the Northern Wei minister Yang Yuanshen 楊元慎 about the moral decline and cultural inferiority of the South, delivered to the southerner Chen Qingzhi. After

7. See Tang Changru, "Du *Baopuzi* tuilun nanbei xuefeng de yitong" 讀抱朴子推論南北學風的異同, in idem, *Wei Jin nanbeichao shi luncong*, pp. 337–67; and Zhou Yiliang, "*Nan Qi shu* Qiu Lingju zhuan," in idem, *Lunji*, pp. 102–26.

8. For a detailed account of north–south communications, see Xu Baoyu, *Yu Xin*, pp. 1–49.

9. The poet Xie Tiao once sought to turn down the task of receiving the Northern Wei emissaries on the ground of "lack of eloquence," although his request was denied (*Nan Qi shu* 47.826).

10. Wang Su 王肅 (464–501), a Southern Qi nobleman, defected to the Northern Wei in 493 and was instrumental in assisting Emperor Xiaowen to carry out the sinicization reforms.

11. *Nan shi* 62.1523.

relating another incident to the discredit of the South, Yang Xuanzhi concluded that "the Wu chaps no longer dared to say anything [against the North] after that."[12]

Chen Qingzhi was a famous Liang general who conquered Luoyang in 529 in one of the Liang's most successful campaigns. He was reportedly impressed by the northerners during his stay in the North. After returning to the South, he treated northerners with great respect, and even adopted northern attire. When the minister Zhu Yi asked Chen Qingzhi why he admired northerners so much, he replied that he had learned to appreciate the cultural superiority of the Central States. However, the southerners' general perception of the North was unwittingly demonstrated by Chen Qingzhi's remark: "Since the [Eastern] Jin and Song dynasties, Luoyang has been called a wasteland, and all those living to the north of the Yangzi River have been regarded as barbarians" 自晉宋以来, 號洛陽為荒土, 此中謂長江以北, 盡是夷狄.[13]

As stated above, it was during the Southern Dynasties that the South ceased being peripheral to the Chinese heartland. The southern emperors saw themselves as the upholders of the Chinese cultural tradition during an era when the Chinese heartland had fallen into the hands of "barbarians." During the first half of the sixth century, the cultural program of Emperor Wu of the Liang was so successful that even many northerners tended to agree. As the Eastern Wei minister Gao Huan 高歡 (495–547) said, "To the east of the River, there is Xiao Yan, that old man of Wu, who is bent on cultivating rituals and music. Gentlemen of the Central States look up to him as the orthodox lineage. If I tighten up the control of law, then I am afraid that all my generals would defect to Heita 黑獺 [Yuwen Tai 宇文泰, 507–56, the powerful minister of the Western Wei] and all my civil officials to Xiao Yan."[14]

12. Yang Xuanzhi, *Luoyang qielan*, pp. 117–19.

13. Ibid., p. 119. Chen Qingzhi's son Chen Xuan 陳暄 also liked to dress in northern clothes (i.e., knee-high boots and ankle-length robes). In a letter to a friend, Xu Ling had described Chen Xuan as wearing "nomad boots" (*huxue* 胡靴) and "barbarian robes" (*lupao* 虜袍; *Quan Chen wen* 9.3451). The *Nan shi* (61.1503) historian, writing in the early Tang, used the same phrases to describe Chen Xuan's attire but dropped the pejoratives "nomad" and "barbarian."

14. *Bei Qi shu* 24.347–48.

But cultural splendor did not necessarily ensure imperial legitimacy. The conquest dynasties, Sui and Tang, regarded the Southern Dynasties as illegitimate kingdoms, with the Mandate of Heaven passing from the Eastern Jin to the Northern Wei, then to the Western Wei and the Northern Zhou, and finally to themselves. This view did not change until the Northern Song, when the Han Chinese realms were privileged over the non-Han powers.[15]

To a certain degree it was in the Sui and Tang, the two dynasties that unified China, that a comparison between the North and the South as two cultural alternatives—not, or not just as, "us" and "them"—became fully possible. The comparison had begun after the fall of the Liang. As more and more southerners migrated to the North, the mixing of the southern and northern populations led to a deeper mutual understanding and a stronger awareness of their different cultural identities.

Commenting on the different customs in the North and South in the *Yanshi jiaxun*, Yan Zhitui noted that, among other things, northerners and southerners seemed to have different literary tastes. He cited a couplet by Xiao Que 蕭慤, which he claimed was not received sympathetically by northern writers but was much admired by southerners like himself.[16] In the preface to Xiao Que's collection, the northern poet Xing Shao explicitly stated the point: "From the Han dynasty to the Jin dynasty, feeling and appreciation could not be brought into harmony; in the North and in the South, intention and design should naturally differ" 自漢逮晉，情賞猶自不諧；江北江南，意製本應相詭.[17] And yet, Xing Shao's insistence, a judgment expressed in an individual case, should best be regarded as a gesture to reinforce the cultural identity of the North. As we shall see, the southern court style exerted a powerful influence in the North.

15. In discussing *The Summary Documents of the Three Kingdoms*, Glen Dudbridge (*Lost Books*, p. 35) points out that Qiu Yue, a Han Chinese himself, considered the Western Wei and the Northern Zhou as rightful and the Liang and the Chen as secondary kingdoms, "for reasons to do with the succession of power."

16. Xiao Que's father was a nephew of Emperor Wu of the Liang (Yan Zhitui, *Yanshi jiaxun* 9.275).

17. *Quan bei Qi wen* 3.3842.

THE CONQUEST DYNASTIES' IMPRINT ON LITERATURE

The fact that both the Sui and the Tang were northern dynasties has a significant bearing on our understanding of early medieval Chinese literature. Official Sui/Tang discourse severely criticized the court poetry of the late Southern Dynasties, particularly Liang Palace Style poetry, and such criticism was to become mainstream opinion for over a millennium. Before we take northern contempt for southern court literature for granted, we should, however, consider some interesting statistics.

The historian's preface to "The Biographies of Men of Letters" in *The Southern History* is a mere tenth of the length of the same historian's preface to "The Biographies of Men of Letters" in *The Northern History*. The disparity forcefully demonstrates that more significance was assigned to the northern than to the southern literati. In terms of the surviving literary works, however, the situation is completely reversed: northern poetry survives only in extremely meager quantities, and the same may be said of northern prose.[18] Xing Shao, Wei Shou, and Wen Zisheng 溫子昇 (495–547), the "Three Talents of the North," were all active during the sixth century and all fell under the influence of Liang court style.[19] Wen Zisheng's extant poems (including fragments) number eleven; Xing Shao's, nine; Wei Shou's, sixteen. These meager survivals contrast with the large quantities of literary writings each man produced. Wen Zisheng left a collection in thirty-nine scrolls; Xing Shao, in thirty-one scrolls; Wei Shou, in sixty-eight scrolls.[20]

Since many of their poems are preserved in encyclopedia sources, we cannot help noticing the gap between the official discourse in the

18. That is, barring several book-length works such as *The Commentary on the Classic of Waters* (*Shuijing zhu* 水經注), *A Record of Buddhist Monasteries in Luoyang* (*Luoyang qielan ji*), *The History of the Wei* (*Wei shu* 魏書), as well as the agricultural treatise *Essential Techniques for the Peasantry* (*Qimin yaoshu*). If not for the oeuvres of Yu Xin, Wang Bao 王褒 (513?–76), and a few other southerners who went to the North, the extant northern literary output would have been even smaller.

19. *Wei shu* 104.2325; *Bei Qi shu* 37.484; *Bei shi* 56.2027. Xing Shao was an admirer and avid emulator of Shen Yue; Wei Shou, of Ren Fang (Yan Zhitui, *Yanshi jiaxun* 9.254).

20. These figures are according to the "Bibliography" of the *Sui shu* 35.1079.

dynastic histories and the practice of Tang encyclopedias such as *Yiwen leiju* and *Chuxue ji*, two of the most important sources of pre-Tang poetry and prose. Whereas the historians passed negative judgments on southern literature, the compilers of the two encyclopedias elected to include far more writings by southerners than by northerners. The case of Xiao Gang is especially instructive: although the dynastic histories censure Xiao Gang for his writings, a large number of his poems and prose pieces found their way into the *Yiwen leiju*, and over 250 of his poems are extant, an impressive number for an early medieval writer. In contrast, although the North produced a large output of literary work, only a small amount has been preserved; and even this owes much to *The History of the Wei* compiled by Wei Shou, himself a writer.[21] In other words, the Tang encyclopedias show a strong bias against northern literature.

Liu Su's 劉餗 (ca. 742–55) anecdotal collection *Sui Tang jiahua* 隋唐嘉話 records a story about the Liang poet Xu Ling's treatment of Wei Shou's writings. When Xu Ling had accomplished his diplomatic mission and was getting ready to go home, Wei Shou reportedly asked Xu Ling to transmit his literary collection to the South. Xu Ling agreed, but on the way back to Jiangkang dumped Wei Shou's collection into the Yangzi River. His attendant, horrified, asked Xu Ling what he was doing, to which Xu Ling replied, "I was getting rid of an embarrassment for Mr. Wei, that's all."[22] We cannot verify the historical accuracy of

21. The prose pieces included in the *Wei shu* are more often than not memorials to the throne and other kinds of political documents. This may have contributed to the false impression that the northern literary writings stressed pragmatic functions over aesthetic values (see Wu Xianning, *Beichao*, p. 116). Moreover, the standard dynastic histories tend to include *fu* and prose pieces such as letters but rarely quote poetry. Such a practice is also largely responsible for creating another false impression, namely, that *fu* and prose flourished in the North, but not poetry.

22. Liu Su (ca. 742–55), *Sui Tang* 3.55. The southerners' alleged contempt for northern literary achievements is further reflected in a story recorded in Zhang Zhuo's 張鷟 (658–730) *Chaoye qianzai* 朝野僉載 (6.140): "When Yu Xin of the Liang first came to the North from the South, he was not respected by the literary men. So Yu Xin showed them his '*Fu* on the Barren Tree'; from that point on, nobody dared to say anything anymore. At the time Wen Zisheng composed an inscription for the Temple of the Hanling Mountain. Yu Xin read it and copied it out. The southerners asked Yu Xin: 'How are the Northern writers?' Xin answered:

this story, but the incident is in a way symbolic of what happened to the northern literature: it was suppressed even before being given a chance. Zhang Yi 張彝 (461–519), for instance, presented the Northern Wei emperor with seven scrolls of poems he claimed to have collected in the provinces. This poetry collection would have been of great interest to literary scholars, but unfortunately, except for Zhang Yi's memorial to the throne accompanying the collection, it has vanished without a trace.[23] In writing literary history, it is important to take into account lost books.

Although the head compiler of *Yiwen leiju* was the southerner Ouyang Xun 歐陽詢 (557–641), the editorial team included several northerners.[24] The general exclusion of northern literary writings, therefore, is a case not of a southerner conspiracy but of literary taste overwhelming political judgment. The fall of the Liang brought many a southerner to the North, and the Liang court style was avidly emulated by the Northern Zhou princes and nobles. As *The History of the Sui* noted: "Ever since the Zhou swallowed the old territories of the Liang and the Jing [the Later Liang], that style became prevalent in the Northwest."[25] Indeed, the early Tang court style was very much a continuation of that of the Liang and the Chen.

Literary practice apart, the opinion of the early Tang historians was nevertheless crucial in the construction of the images of the North and South. The judgment passed in the preface to "The Biographies of Men of Letters" in *The History of the Sui*, repeated in *The Northern History*, set the tone for the later perception of the northern and southern literatures:

'There is only one piece of stone from the Hanling Mountain that is worth speaking of. Xue Daoheng 薛道衡 [540–609] and Lu Sidao 盧思道 [535–86] barely know how to hold their brushes. As for the rest, they are like donkeys braying and dogs barking—merely making noises.'"

23. Zhang Yi's memorial is preserved in his biography in *The History of the Wei* (*Wei shu* 64.1430–31).

24. In addition to Ouyang Xun, of the dozen people who participated in the compilation project, we know the names of five: Pei Ju 裴矩 (d. 627), Zhao Hongzhi 趙弘智 (572–653), and Linghu Defen 令狐德棻 (563–666) were northerners; Chen Shuda 陳叔達 (d. 635) and Yuan Lang 袁朗 were from the South.

25. *Sui shu* 76.1730.

To the left side of the Yangzi River [i.e., the South], the tunes of *gong* and *shang* are set forth, and pure sumptuousness is valued; to the north of the Yellow River, the intent of writings is virtuous and hardy, and people prize vital force and substance. When vital force and substance are prized, principle may overwhelm the phrasing; if pure sumptuousness is valued, then ornament may exceed meaning. Those writings with profound principles are suitable for being put to contemporary use; those with sumptuous ornamentation are appropriate for chanting and singing. This is a general comparison between the advantages and disadvantages of the northern and southern writers.[26]

江左宮商發越，貴於清綺；河朔詞義貞剛，重乎氣質．氣質則理勝其詞，清綺則文過其意，理深者便於時用，文華者宜於詠歌，此其南北詞人得失之大較也．

The attributes "sumptuousness" (*qi* 綺) and "hardiness" (*gang* 剛) could easily slip into gender categories, with the conquered South seen as sensuous and effeminate, and the conquering North as tough and masculine. The writings of Liang writers such as Xiao Gang, Xiao Yi, Yu Xin, and Xu Ling were singled out for condemnation and described as "the sound of a fallen state" (*wangguo zhi yin* 亡國之音). This view still holds sway over Chinese literary scholars even today.

The historian then envisioned a poetry that joined the South and North:

If one could take the pure sound from that side and cut down long-winded sentences on this side, so that each discards its failing and the strengths are combined, then patterning and substance will be balanced, and perfection reached.

若能掇彼清音，簡茲累句，各去所短，合其兩長，則文質斌斌，盡善盡美矣．

Joining patterning (*wen*) with substance (*zhi*) was not exactly a novel idea, but viewed in the historical context of the early Tang, the fusion represented the poetics of a unified empire: to identify the South with *wen* and the North with *zhi* was a particular move, an interesting and important assertion when the long period of division came to an end. The picture of the North and South presented in the histories is, however, much complicated when checked against a series of texts.

26. *Sui shu* 76.1730; *Bei shi* 83.2781–82.

IMAGINING THE NORTH: THE BIRTH OF FRONTIER POETRY

Representation of empirical experience has always been valued positively in Chinese literary theory, and yet, the birth of the poetic subgenre later dubbed "frontier poetry" had little to do with experiential genuineness. As Stephen Owen has pointed out, "The Central Asia of poetry was primarily a literary topic: the styles associated with it, the elements that constituted a frontier scene, and the appropriate responses have developed out of a long tradition of poems by men who had never been anywhere near the frontiers."[27]

It should be stressed that in frontier poetry proper the "frontier" (*biansai* 邊塞) is identified with a specific locale: the far north or the northwest of China.[28] In this sense, the Southern Dynasties poets who engaged in writing "frontier poetry" had no real-life experiences of what they depicted in great detail in their poems. The southern borderlands never constituted part of the frontier poetry tradition, even though territorial wars had been fought in the deep south or the southwest since the Han as often as in the North. Frontier poetry became a notable phenomenon in the Liang, but as the modern scholar Liu Hanchu has rightly observed, Bao Zhao, the poet of the early fifth century, was the first who "made it big."[29] Before Bao Zhao, there were a small number of poems about military campaigns, but the conventions of frontier poetry

27. Owen, *The Great Age*, p. 174. Yan Caiping ("Liang Chen," p. 45) and Liu Hanchu 劉漢初 ("Liang Chen biansai shi xiaolun" 梁陳邊塞詩小論, in *Wei Jin nanbeichao wenxue lunji*, pp. 77–79) have also observed the lack of "realistic" basis for Liang and Chen "frontier poetry."

28. The "frontier" in "frontier poetry" has been defined by a modern scholar as "the borderland along the Great Wall and in the Hexi and Longyou regions [in modern Gansu]" (Tan Youxue 譚優學, "Biansai shi fanlun" 邊塞詩泛論, in *Tangdai biansai shi*, p. 2). But certainly Liaoxi (in modern Liaoning) and the old state of Yan (in modern Hebei) also feature prominently in frontier poetry.

29. Liu Hanchu, "Liang Chen," pp. 72–73 (see note 27 to this chapter). Bao Zhao's innovation was already noticed by his contemporaries. When Jiang Yan did his famous series "Various Forms," he chose one topic for each poet he imitated, and the topic for Bao Zhao was "Military Campaign" ("Ronghang" 戎行) (*Quan Liang shi* 4.1580).

had not been fully established, and the "frontier" was by no means pinned down to a particular region. In contrast, Bao Zhao was largely preoccupied with the far north. "To 'Going Out from the Northern Ji Gate'" ("Dai chuzi Jibeimen xing" 代出自薊北門行) is a typical example, with its stylized description of the austerity of army life and the harsh weather of the North.[30] The poem ends with a vow to repay the grace of one's ruler and sacrifice one's life for the state. In "To Prince Si of Chen's 'Ballad on the White Horse'" ("Dai Chen Siwang baima pian" 代陳思王白馬篇), the speaker assumes the voice of a chivalrous hero pursuing military glory on the frontier.[31] In both ballads, Bao Zhao's imagination is engaged primarily with the North, and temporally the poems are set in the distant Han dynasty. For Bao Zhao, "the frontier" evokes another time, another place.

In a study on Southern Dynasties frontier poetry, the modern scholar Wang Wenjin comments that it conjures up "a world far away from the South itself in both spatial and temporal terms,"[32] which Wang attributes to the southern poets' attachment to the heartland and their desire to recover the lost North.[33] More important, however, frontier poetry is about the construction of a space "out there," a space that is distant and exotic. For the southern poets, alluding to contemporary frontier warfare in terms of the Han army fighting against the Xiongnu undoubtedly

30. *Quan Song shi* 7.1262. The place-names mentioned in the poem are all northern: Xianyang (in modern Shaanxi), Guangwu (in modern Shanxi), and Shuofang (in modern Inner Mongolia). The Ji in the title refers the capital of the ancient state of Yan, whose site is in modern Beijing.

31. *Quan Song shi* 7.1264.

32. Wang Wenjin, *Nanchao*, p. 84.

33. Ibid., pp. 78–82. Yan Caiping ("Liang Chen," pp. 47–51) and Liu Hanchu ("Liang Chen," p. 81; see note 27 to this chapter) also speculate on the reason for the flourishing of the frontier *yuefu* in the South in the sixth century. Liu makes much of Liang poets' penchant for group compositions and "treating literature as play." Yan, on the other hand, argues for the influence of northern *yuefu* songs coming to the South. For this, however, we do not have sufficient textual evidence. For one thing, the Liang and Chen frontier poems are nothing like the extant *yuefu* songs that supposedly came from the North; for another thing, many of the *yuefu* titles adopted by the Liang and Chen poets are from the Han and Wei music repertoire preserved as much in the South as in the North. Yan cites the use of northern place-names (especially from the northwest frontier) in the southern frontier poetry, but these names are common allusions to dynastic histories and earlier literature.

carried the implication that the southern empire possessed the imperial legitimacy that the northern "barbarians" did not. The pleasure of writing, however, lies in the detailed depiction of the bitter cold of the North and the enumeration of foreign place-names: this is the fashioning of a cultural other at work, which in turn reinforces one's own cultural and regional identity. The same role-playing impulse and the desire for identity building, as we shall see in the last section of this chapter, also figure in their writing, performance, and appreciation of southern *yuefu* songs.

A good case in point is the transformation of a *yuefu* title, "Ballad of Joining the Army" ("Congjun xing" 從軍行), in the hands of Southern Dynasties poets. One of the earliest examples is a fragment attributed to a Wei musician, Zuo Yannian 左延年 (fl. 220s), which begins by lamenting the sufferings of soldiers: "How sad—those serving on the frontier" 苦哉邊地人.[34] The opening line was subsequently adopted by the southern poet Lu Ji in his "Ballad of Joining the Army" with a slight variation:[35]

苦哉遠征人	How sad—those on a far-flung campaign!
飄飄窮西河	Swept along all the way to Xihe.
南陟五嶺巔	To the south they ascend the Five Peaks;
北戍長城阿	to the north they defend the Great Wall.
深谷邈無底	Valleys are deep, bottomless pits;
崇山鬱嵯峨	lofty mountains are towering and grand.
奮臂攀喬木	When climbing, they strive to hold on to the tall trees;
振跡涉流沙	leaving behind foot tracks as they cross flowing sand.
隆暑固已慘	The heat of summer is miserable enough;
涼風嚴且苛	chilly wind, stern and cruel.
夏條焦鮮藻	Fresh blooms are scorched on summer branches;
寒冰結衝波	cold ice freezes rushing currents.

34. *Quan Wei shi* 5.411. The poet Wang Can wrote several poems to the title "Joining the Army" during Cao Cao's campaigns to the Southwest and Southeast. Although appearing in *Yuefu shiji* under the title "Ballad of Joining the Army," they differ from the *yuefu* ballads in that the speaker in Wang Can's poems is no imaginary persona (*Quan Wei shi* 2.361–63; Guo Maoqian, *Yuefu shiji* 32.475–77).

35. *Quan Jin shi* 5.656–57.

胡馬如雲屯	Barbarian horses gather like clouds;
越旗亦星羅	Yue banners everywhere, like profuse stars.
飛鋒無絕影	Flying blades cast no shadows;
鳴鏑自相和	sounding arrowheads sing in harmony.
朝食不免冑	Even at breakfast they don't take off their armor;
夕息常負戈	when resting at evening, they still carry the halberds.
苦哉遠征人	How sad—those on a far-flung campaign,
撫心悲如何	striking their chests, they grieve with no end.

Lu Ji's description of the military life alternates between south and north, summer and winter, land and river, making it clear that the poem aims for the totality of the soldier's experience.

In the fifth century, Yan Yanzhi and Shen Yue wrote to the same title in close imitation of Lu Ji's poem,[36] depicting the soldier's experience in broad strokes and encompassing both northern and southern campaigns. Wu Jun's poem to the same title shows interesting deviations:[37]

男兒亦可憐	A man is truly a sorry creature—
立功在北邊	seeking glory on the northern frontier.
陣頭橫卻月	The army formation is shaped like a crescent moon;
馬腹帶連錢	his horse belly patterned like strings of cash.
懷戈發隴坻	Holding a halberd, he sets out from Longdi;
乘凍至遼川	in the freezing cold he arrives at Liaochuan.
微誠君不愛	Even if his lord does not appreciate his loyalty,
終自直如弦	he shall be ever "as straight as the bow string."

All the essential elements of the earlier poems are here: horse, halberd, cold, and exotic place names such as Longdi and Liaochuan. Even the opening lamentation over the soldier's fate echoes the "original" *yuefu* poem. But Wu Jun's is a much shorter poem, less elevated in diction, and much more self-conscious in adopting the plain-spoken style generally associated with old ballads, a trait that had won his poetry a

36. *Quan Song shi* 5.1228; *Quan Liang shi* 6.1615.
37. *Quan Liang shi* 10.1721.

reputation for possessing an "ancient aura."[38] More important, the locus for military action is identified with the North and the North only.[39]

Liang frontier poetry emphasizes the elements of heroism and stoicism, although the hardship of military life is ever present. The imagined frontier scene, firmly established in the far north by now, is couched in well-crafted couplets, such as He Xun's:

陣雲橫塞起	Cloud formation rises, stretching across the frontier,
赤日下城圓	the crimson sun, round, sets on the city wall.[40]

The horizontality of the clouds, so massive that they resemble an army formation, is countered by the downward movement of the sun. The juxtaposition of *yuan* (round) with *qi* (rise) is striking, for the principle of parallelism demands that "round" be read as a verb rather than an adjective, thus anticipating Xiao Gang's use of *yuan* as a full verb discussed in an earlier chapter. He Xun's couplet clearly inspired the great Tang poet Wang Wei, who wrote in "The Envoy Arrives at the Frontier" ("Shi zhi saishang" 使至塞上): "In the great desert, a single column of smoke rises straight; / the sun setting on the long river, round" 大漠孤煙直, / 長河落日圓.[41] The late Tang poet Li He 李賀 (791–817) transformed the images of the sun and dark clouds into a striking couplet in one of his well-known *yuefu* poems, "The Ballad of the Yanmen Magistrate" ("Yanmen taishou xing" 雁門太守行), a title that first become associated with the frontier theme in the Liang: "Black clouds press on the city wall, the city wall about to crumble; / the light of armor

38. *Liang shu* 49.698. Several poems at the turn of the sixth century claiming to be imitations of the "ancient style" depict the northern frontier life, such as Fan Yun's "Xiao gu" 傚古 or He Xun's "Xue gu" 學古 (*Quan Liang shi* 2.1547, 8.1693–94).

39. The first line of the poem evokes a ballad from the "Liang Songs for Fife and Drum," which begins with the statement: "A man is a sorry creature" 男兒可憐蟲 (*Quan Liang shi*, 29.2152). The last line is an allusion to an Eastern Han "children's song": "Straight as the bow string, / and die by the roadside. / Crooked as a hook, / and you'll become a lord" (*Hou Han shu* 13.3281).

40. From He Xun's "Xue gu," no. 1 (*Quan Liang shi* 8.1693).

41. *Quan Tang shi* 126.1279.

catches the sun, golden scales open up" 黑雲壓城城欲摧,/甲光向日金鱗開.[42]

Xiao Gang, in the generation after He Xun, used the image of the "cloud formation" in his "Ballad of Joining the Army," but the oppressive quality of the dark clouds is much lessened in Xiao Gang's flamboyant treatment of the military campaign:[43]

雲中亭障羽檄驚	Feathered dispatches startle the fortresses of Yunzhong,[44]
甘泉烽火通夜明	the beacon fires of Sweet Springs blazing bright all night.
貳師將軍新築營	The Ershi General has just built a new camp,
嫖姚校尉初出征	the Commandant of Piaoyao is on his first campaign.[45]
復有山西將	There again are the officers from the northwest,
絶世愛雄名	who love the name of "hero" all their lives.[46]
三門應遁甲	The Three Gates correspond to Evading the Cyclical Signs;
五壘學神兵	one learns the divine military strategies from Five Fortresses.[47]
白雲隨陣色	White clouds imitate the color of the formation;
蒼山答鼓聲	blue mountains respond to the sound of drums.
邐迤觀鵝翼	One witnesses the "Goose Wing" stretching long;

42. *Quan Tang shi* 390.4395.

43. *Quan Liang shi* 20.1904.

44. Yunzhong, literally "Amid the Clouds," was the name of a northern commandery in the Han dynasty, often invaded by the Xiongnu.

45. The Ershi General was Li Guangli 李廣利; the Commandant of Piaoyao was Huo Qubing 霍去病. Both were renowned generals from the time of Emperor Wu of the Han.

46. According to *Han shu* (69.2998): "Since the Qin and Han dynasties, the northeast produced prime ministers, and the northwest produced generals" 秦漢已來, 山東出相, 山西出將.

47. The Three Gates are the Gate of Life 生門, the Gate of Rest 休門, and the Gate of Opening 開門, which are the three auspicious "gates" in such military strategies as "Marvelous Gates and Evading the Cyclical Signs" 奇門遁甲. "Evading the Cyclical Signs" refers to a type of divination used to determine military strategy. The *Sui shu* "Bibliography" (*Sui shu* 34.1013) records a military strategy manual called "The Chart of Five Fortresses of the Old Man of Yellow Stone" ("Huangshigong wuleitu" 黃石公五壘圖) in one scroll.

參差睹雁行	or lined up unevenly, like a row of wild geese.
先平小月陣	First we shall destroy the army of Xiao Yue;
卻滅大宛城	then we shall conquer the city of Dawan.[48]
善馬還長樂	Fine stallions are brought back to the Palace of Eternal Joy;
黄金付水衡	yellow gold, entrusted to the Director of Imperial Parks.[49]
小婦趙人能鼓瑟	The young wife, a native of Zhao, skilled at the harp;
侍婢初笄解鄭聲	the maid with newly bound hair knows the music of Zheng.
庭前柳絮飛欲合	Catkins in the front yard, blown around, about to commingle;
必應紅妝起見迎	certainly she will dress up and meet her beloved.

In contrast with the ballads of his literary predecessors, Xiao Gang's poem to the traditional *yuefu* title has a new, contemporary tone, with its mixture of seven- and five-syllable lines, its feisty, upbeat rhythm, and its clear story line. The free juxtaposition of places far apart in reality might have incurred the disapproval of a critic like Yan Zhitui, who insisted on referential accuracy, but it reveals the exotic place-names as no more than names and signs.[50] Taken from dynastic histories or geographical records, they constitute a literary landscape.

Xiao Gang's ballad noticeably ends with a description of the general's wife. In the last four lines, the poet imagines that as the man comes home from the frontier, his wife, attended by her maid, would apply her makeup for the occasion and greet him. The mingling of the

48. Xiao Yue was Xiao Yuezhi 小月氏 or Gandhāra, the name of a kingdom to the east of present-day Afghanistan. Dawan was Ferghana in Central Asia.

49. The Palace of Eternal Joy was constructed by the first Han emperor.

50. Yan Zhitui (*Yanshi jiaxun* 9.271) states that "the geographical descriptions in one's literary writings must be correct and appropriate" and singles out two couplets from Xiao Gang's "Ballad of the Yanmen Magistrate" for criticism. The two couplets are attributed to a poem of the same title by Chu Xiang 褚翔 (505–48) in Guo Maoqian, *Yuefu shiji* 39.575. However, since an excerpt from the poem that does not include the two couplets is attributed to Xiao Gang in *Yiwen leiju* 42.758, the poem seems to be by Xiao Gang after all.

catkins has a sexual undertone. And yet, the integration of the "boudoir lament" into an ostensibly "frontier poem" is not just a rhetorical device.[51] The delineation of home and hearth or the woman's space is in fact almost an essential part of frontier poetry, for it serves to accentuate a distant, exotic space "out there" that belongs exclusively to men. This male space is characterized by an escape from family obligations and monotonous everyday routine; a man could, if fortunate enough, always come back to his wife, and the freedom of his movement is contrasted with the woman's confinement to home and indeed exists only in relation to it. By depicting a man's moving back and forth between these two spaces, the southern male poet manages to inhabit both worlds, but also, perhaps inadvertently, creates a gender split between the harsh, cold North of military might and a warm, sensuous South of home and hearth.

Xiao Gang's "Ballad of Joining the Army" left an indelible mark on the poem to the same title by his younger contemporary Lu Sidao, a famous northern poet. A pastiche of various recurring elements of frontier poetry, including place-names, images, and allusions, Lu Sidao's poem is informed not so much by his empirical knowledge of the North as by his familiarity with literary conventions. As Xiaorong Zheng observes, "Images and geographical terms in this poem appear to be all associated with the Han dynasty, which suggests that the poem was not used to portray a real experience or event that occurred at the time."[52]

51. Wang Wenjin (*Nanchao*, pp. 98–121) has a nice discussion of the prominence of the "boudoir lament" motif in Southern Dynasties frontier poetry. He argues that the integration of the two motifs manifests the aesthetic style of "hardness and softness complementing each other."

52. Xiaorong Zheng, "A History," p. 367. Zheng also provides a partial translation of the poem and gives a nice analysis. However, I disagree with Zheng's statement that what distinguishes Lu Sidao's poem from its southern counterparts is the fact that "there is neither a female lover nor feminine tone" in Lu's poem, which is "in masculine tone." This statement is contradicted by lines 13–14 and 17–18 of Lu Sidao's poem, which make reference to the "marvelous tree" in the courtyard and facing the moon "among sweet-smelling flowers." Both of these images imply a female presence (see note 56 below). Lines 17–18 are omitted from Zheng's translation.

朔方烽火照甘泉	Beacon fires of Shuofang shine at the Sweet Springs,
長安飛將出祁連	the winged general of Chang'an emerges from Mount Qilian.[53]
犀渠玉劍良家子	Rhinoceros-hide shields, jade-encrusted swords, sons of good families;
白馬金羈俠少年	white horses, gilded reins, chivalrous lads.[54]
平明偃月屯右地	At early dawn, the encampment of Crescent Moon guards the western territory;
薄暮魚麗逐左賢	the formation of fish scales pursues the Xiongnu prince at dusk.
谷中石虎經銜箭	The stone tiger in the valley has taken an arrow;
山上金人曾祭天	the bronze statue on the mountain was used in making sacrifices.[55]
天涯一去無窮已	Once they depart to the end of the world, there's no end to it;
薊門迢遞三千里	Jimen is distant, three thousand miles away.
朝見馬嶺黃沙合	In the morning they see the yellow sand gathering at the Horse Ridge;
夕望龍城陣雲起	at evening, gaze toward the cloud formation at the Dragon City.
庭中奇樹已堪攀	The branches of the marvelous tree in the courtyard have grown long;[56]
塞外征人殊未還	the man going on a campaign past the frontier has not returned.
白雪初下天山外	White snow has first fallen beyond the Tianshan Mountain,

53. The "winged general" was the nickname given to the famous Han general Li Guang 李廣 by the Xiongnu people (*Shi ji* 109.2871).

54. This is an allusion to Cao Zhi's "Baima pian" 白馬篇: "White horse decorated with gilded reins" (*Quan Wei shi* 6.432).

55. The first line in this couplet refers to the famous story about Li Guang, who shot an arrow into what he thought was a tiger at night; in the morning it turned out to be a tiger-like rock, the arrow deeply buried in it (*Shi ji* 109.2871). The second line refers to the bronze statue the Xiongnu set up on the mountain in their sacrificial ritual. It was obtained by the Han general Huo Qubing (*Shi ji* 110.2908).

56. Number 9 of the "Nineteen Old Poems" begins with the line, "There is a marvelous tree in the courtyard." The poem goes on to say that the speaker wants to snap a bough and send it to the absent beloved (*Quan Han shi* 12.331).

浮雲直上五原間	floating clouds rising straight up toward the Five Plains.[57]
關山萬里不可越	The mountains and passes, stretching ten thousand miles, cannot be crossed over;
誰能坐對芳菲月	and yet who can sit and face the moon among the sweet-smelling flowers?
流水本自斷人腸	The flowing water naturally breaks one's heart;
堅冰舊來傷馬骨	hard ice has been known to wound the horse's bones.[58]
邊庭節物與華異	Seasons and sceneries on the frontier all differ from the Chinese land;
冬霰秋霜春不歇	winter sleet and autumn frost do not cease even in spring months.
長風蕭蕭渡水來	A steady wind crosses the river with a rustling sound;
歸鴈連連映天沒	wild geese returning to the South, one after another, disappear into the distant sky.
從軍行	Join the army, march on—
軍行萬里出龍庭	the army marches ten thousand miles, repairing to Dragon Court.[59]
單于渭橋今已拜	Now that the khan has bowed to the emperor at the Wei Bridge,[60]
將軍何處覓功名	where will the general go and look for accomplishments and fame?[61]

57. The Five Plains, Wuyuan, was a frontier fortress in the Han (*Shi ji* 110.2918). It is in modern Inner Mongolia.

58. The "flowing water" refers to the soldier's song about the "flowing water of Longtou" (*Longtou liushui* 隴頭流水; *Quan Jin shi* 18.1020). That the ice wounds the bones of the horse drinking from the currents alludes to the ballad attributed to the Wei poet Chen Lin 陳琳 (d. 217), "Yinma Changcheng ku" 飲馬長城窟 (*Quan Wei shi* 3.367).

59. The Dragon Court was where the Xiongnu people gathered and made sacrifices every year. Ban Gu in the inscription of the Yanran Mountain commemorating the Han general Dou Xian's 竇憲 great victory over the Xiongnu wrote that "the Dragon Court of Laoshang [the title of the Xiongnu khan] has been burned down" (*Hou Han shu* 23.815).

60. *Han shu* 8.271.

61. *Quan Sui shi* 1.2631.

Among other things, one cannot help noticing the similarity between the opening of Lu Sidao's poem and that of Xiao Gang's.[62] Both poets opt for a dramatized beginning, focusing on the blazing beacon fires. Lu Sidao's "Ballad of Joining the Army" is distinguished by the poet's demonstration of considerable skill in weaving received images and motifs into a smooth, eloquent flow.

The conventions of frontier poetry had been so well established by the Liang that very few poems portrayed southern campaigns. In the one poem entitled "Southern Campaign" ("Nanzheng" 南征) by a certain Su Ziqing 蘇子卿 (fl. sixth century), the southern frontier is described only in negative terms, such as the absence of cold.

一朝遊桂水	One morning one travels to the Cassia River;
萬里別長安	taking leave of Chang'an, going ten thousand miles away.
故鄉夢中近	Homeland is close in dreams;
邊愁酒上寬	sorrows on the frontier are lessened by wine.
劍鋒但須利	All one ever wants is for the sword blade to be sharp—
戎衣不畏單	no need to fear the thinness of army clothes:
南中地氣暖	earth vapors being warm in the South,
少婦莫愁寒	the young wife doesn't have to worry about cold.[63]

The Sui poet Xue Daoheng's *yuefu* poem, "The Ballad of Yuzhang" ("Yuzhang xing" 豫章行), juxtaposes the theme of the military campaign against the backdrop of the South. And yet, except for the first three couplets, this poem of twenty-eight lines is devoted to the description of the soldier's wife left at home. It is, on the whole, more of a "boudoir lament" poem than a frontier poem, and one looks in it for images of the "southern frontier" in vain.[64]

62. A fragment from "The Ballad of Joining the Army" by Yuwen Zhao 宇文招 (d. 580), a Northern Zhou prince, is extant, and its opening is almost a verbatim repetition of the first line of Lu Sidao's piece: "The beacon fires of Liaodong shine upon the Sweet Springs" 遼東烽火照甘泉 (*Bei Zhou shi* 1.2344–45).

63. *Quan Chen shi* 9.2601–2.

64. An interesting piece on the "military" experience at the southern frontier was written by the Sui poet Sun Wanshou 孫萬壽 (fl. early seventh century), who was sent into exile in the South for violating the dress code when he served under

In the second half of the sixth century, the northern army made repeated attempts on the South. "The Ballad of Joining the Army" by Ming Yuqing 明餘慶 (d. 618?), a southerner who went North, offers a unique perspective on southern campaigns.[65]

三邊烽亂驚	On the three frontiers disquieting beacon fires blaze in chaos;
十萬且橫行	an army of ten thousand soldiers begins a fearless march.
風卷常山陣	A blast furls the Formation of Changshan;[66]
笳喧細柳營	reed pipes sound off at the Camp at Slender Willows.[67]
劍花寒不落	Sword sparkles blossoming, though cold, do not wither;
弓月曉逾明	the bow moon becomes ever brighter at dawn.
會取淮南地	We will certainly conquer the land to the south of the Huai River,
持作朔方城	and make it into our Shuofang fortress.[68]

The poet cannot help alluding to "cold," and yet the only thing cold in this poem is the "blossom" of the sword, a metaphor for the sparkling of the blade. Shuofang was the name of a northern frontier commandery in the Han. From a northerner's point of view, the South was naturally the ultimate frontier; and yet, the poet had to deploy a northern place-name to convey the sense of distance and foreignness he felt about the South.

The Southern Dynasties poets were, as scholars have pointed out, true pioneers in their invention and exploration of the literary northern

the Prince of Teng. It is a long poem, of some eighty lines, but the major portion is devoted to the expression of the poet's homesickness (*Quan Sui shi* 1.2638).

65. Ibid., 2.2646.

66. The Formation of Changshan is named after a legendary Chang Snake, whose head and tail can come to each other's rescue if attacked; see Sun Wu, *Sunzi* 11.197.

67. "Slender Willows" was the place where the Han general Zhou Yafu 周亞夫 camped his army (*Shi ji* 57.2074).

68. Huainan, "to the south of the Huai River," has a textual variant, Hexi 河西, in the late Ming anthology *Gushi ji* compiled by Feng Weine (136.15b). However, both earlier sources, *Wenyuan yinghua* (199.983), and Guo Maoqian, *Yuefu shiji* (32.483), have Huainan. Indeed, the last couplet of the poem would have made little sense with Hexi, a region in the northwest.

frontier. Frontier poetry was an attempt of the Southern Dynasties literati to construct a space "out there"—distant, inaccessible, exotic. The southern poets' obsession with the far north in their frontier poetry represents a desire to fashion a cultural other, which is part of a larger attempt to construct their own cultural identity. In the end, even the northern poets adopted the vocabulary of poetic images of the northern frontier by the southern poets, and empirical experiences fell short of powerful literary models. The image of the North as constructed by the southerners in early medieval China has had a lasting impact on the Chinese cultural imagination. The northerners conquered the South, but it was the South that articulated the North.

When Xiao Yi was in Jiangling, his courtier Wang Bao composed a poem to the *yuefu* title "Yan'ge xing" 燕歌行 and "depicted the cold and miseries of the frontier." Emperor Yuan and many of his courtiers wrote poems to the same title in response. Later, when Jiangling fell to the Western Wei, Wang Bao was captured and taken to the North. The historian commented that Wang Bao's poem turned out to be a poetic prophecy that "became fulfilled only now."[69] In more than one sense, life had imitated art.

MANNERED MACHISMO: SONGS OF THE "NORTH"

The image of a macho North was reinforced in a group of *yuefu* poems generally known as "the folk songs of the North" (*beichao min'ge* 北朝民歌). All these songs, however, have their textual source in the "Liang Songs for Fife and Drum" ("Liang gujiao hengchui qu" 梁鼓角横吹曲), recorded in *A Record of Music Past and Present* (*Gujin yuelu* 古今樂錄) compiled by the southern monk Zhijiang 智匠 (fl. ca. 568) and preserved in *Yuefu shiji*.[70] Songs for fife and drum were "military music," performed by musicians on horseback in court rituals or as part of an imperial procession. These were sometimes granted as a high honor to princes and ministers.

69. *Zhou shu* 41.731.
70. Guo Maoqian, *Yuefu shiji* 25.362–72.

Current scholarship, in the tradition of premodern Chinese commentators, tends to overemphasize the northern aspect of these songs and sees them as reflecting the "essence" of the North and the "spirit" of non-Han ethnic peoples, both fundamentally different from the "soft" nature of the South.[71] One major flaw of this binary approach is its failure to take into account the musical categories into which the northern and southern songs fall. In other words, the northern songs included in the "Liang Songs for Fife and Drum" should not be regarded as representative of the "typical northern music" (if there was indeed such a thing). Since "songs for fife and drum" were military music, it is no wonder that the songs selected for this purpose sing of battles, manly courage, and a love of weaponry.

Two points need to be stressed before we delve into a more detailed analysis of the songs. First, we do not know for certain the origin of many of these songs (indeed, some of them might well have migrated from the North), and it is not the purpose of this section to argue that these songs were "actually" produced by southerners. The focus of this section is, rather, the role of southerners in choosing, performing, preserving, and transmitting these songs. In other words, the mediation of southerners, which is often ignored or glossed over in standard accounts of these songs, must be taken seriously, and its significance carefully considered. The proper question to ask is therefore not whether these songs were originally northern or southern, but why they were chosen by southerners for performance in the southern court. Second, we should separate the issues of music and lyrics in dealing with these songs. That is, the *music* of these songs might well have integrated non-Han music motifs from the North, but the adaptation of the lyrics is a different matter.[72] In most cases, we do not have definitive evidence for the northern origin of the lyrics.

71. Just to cite a few examples, see Li Kaiyuan and Guan Furong, *Bei Wei*, pp. 78–80, 101–3; Wang Yunxi, *Yuefu shi*, pp. 472–73; Zhou Jianjiang, *Bei Wei*, p. 217; and Cao Daoheng, *Nanchao wenxue*, p. 267. For a concentrated discussion of the differences between northern and southern songs, see Tan Runsheng, *Beichao*, pp. 316–34.

72. For the performance of the non-Han music from the North, see *Nan Qi shu* 1.10, 7.103, 24.449. The southern music also penetrated into the North. According to *Wei shu*, the northern court acquired the southern music, including "The Sound of Wu" and "The Western Tunes," during the military campaigns carried out under

Because these Liang songs for fife and drum are filled with northern place-names such as Chang'an, the Wei River, Guangping, Julu, Longtou, and Dongping, some scholars take this as indisputable evidence that the songs originated in the North.[73] However, as the preceding discussion of frontier poetry shows, a generous use of northern place-names does not rule out the possibility that the songs were composed by southerners who had never been to the North. In fact, the very couplet "I am a lad of barbarian origin,/I do not understand the songs of the Han lads" 我是虜家兒,/不解漢兒歌, which is often taken as proof that this was a northern song, poses many questions.[74] No northerner from this period would have referred to himself or herself as *lu* 虜, a pejorative term used to designate the non-Han people of the North and loosely translated as "barbarian." It is argued that this song might have been translated into Chinese from the Xianbei 鮮卑 language and that the translator used the word *lu* to translate the ethnic term (whatever it was) the Xianbei singer employed to designate himself. This proposition is not entirely implausible, but it only leads to further questions. Why would a Xianbei singer compose a song about not being able to comprehend Han Chinese songs? Is the mood of this song one of pride and contempt, as some scholars have suggested, or one of humility and anxiety, even of nostalgia, as the "barbarian" lad looks at the lush growth of willows near Luoyang, which presents a sharp contrast with the treeless, barren expanse of his steppe homeland?[75] These are open-ended questions; we could certainly construct many hypothetical contexts for the composition of the song, but the point is that there are no definitive answers. More important, we should be asking why, of all "northern songs," this particular one was selected by the southern court musicians? Why were southerners interested in hearing such

Emperor Xiaowen and Emperor Xuanwu (r. 500–515) of the Northern Wei (*Wei shu* 109.2843).

73. For instance, see Xiao Difei, *Han Wei liuchao*, p. 272.

74. *Quan Liang shi* 29.2158.

75. Xiao Difei (*Han Wei liuchao*, p. 280) argues that the term "Han'er" (Han lad) was a derogatory term used by the Xianbei people in the North and gives several examples from the dynastic histories to prove his case. However, the meaning of a term such as "Han lad," unlike *lu*, is context bound, and at least in one case it was used in an apparently neutral sense (*Beishi* 30.1108).

declarations? One thing is certain: while the northern "barbarian" proclaims his inability to understand the Han Chinese songs, the Han Chinese audience of this song understands *him* perfectly and hence enjoys a cultural superiority over the "barbarian" lad. In the end, it is less important to know whether these songs are from the North than to recognize that they are *about* the North: they represent the Liang imagination of the North, and of what a "typical northerner" was like.

The compilation of *Gujin yuelu* in 568 is a terminus ad quem; we do not know how long before that the songs were composed. The only songs whose date is reasonably certain are "The Gaoyang Musicians' Songs" ("Gaoyang yueren ge" 高陽樂人歌), and then only if we can trust Zhijiang's identification of "Gaoyang" as the Prince of Gaoyang of the Northern Wei, who was most likely Yuan Yong 元雍 (d. 528).[76]

In the Western Han, the musician Li Yannian 李延年 reportedly composed twenty-eight tunes for the martial band based on "barbarian music" (*Huqu* 胡曲) brought back from the Western Region. In the Wei and Jin dynasties, ten out of the tunes were still being performed.[77] Of these ten, both "Breaking the Willow Branches" ("Zhe yangliu" 折楊柳) and "Longtou" 隴頭 feature in the extant "Liang Songs for Fife and Drum." As we read these songs now, we should bear in mind that the lyrics, even those to the same tune title, were not necessarily from the same period or composed by the same person.

The first tune title in the "Liang Songs" is "Qiyu" 企喻, under which four songs are listed. The title "Qiyu," commonly assumed to be a transliteration of a Xianbei word, also appears in the "Perfected Being's Songs of Dai" ("Zhenren Dai ge" 眞人代歌), a set of 150 songs singing of the history of the Wei royal house and performed in the Wei palace

76. Yuan Yong was said to be an extravagant prince whose household boasted "five hundred female performers." After he died, all the female performers were forced to become Buddhist nuns. Some of them later married officials (Yang Xuanzhi, *Luoyang qielan*, p. 177).

77. The ten tunes are "Yellow Swan" ("Huanghu" 黃鵠), "Longtou," "Going Out of the Pass" ("Chu guan" 出關), "Entering the Pass" ("Ru guan" 入關), "Going Out of the Frontier" ("Chu sai" 出塞), "Entering the Frontier" ("Ru sai" 入塞), "Breaking the Willow Branches," "Huangtanzi" 黃覃子, "Chi zhi yang" 赤之揚, and "Expecting the Traveler" ("Wang xingren" 望行人); see *Jin shu* 23.715–16.

and on state occasions.[78] However, we do not know if the lyrics under this tune title in the "Liang Songs for Fife and Drum" constitute part of the original "Songs of Dai," of which, according to *The Old Tang History* (*Jiu Tang shu* 舊唐書), fifty-three survived into the Tang. Only six of the fifty-three had comprehensible titles, including "Qiyu."[79] In fact, the modern Six Dynasties historian Tian Yuqing strongly argues that the "Qiyu" songs in the "Liang Songs" have nothing to do with the "Songs of Dai."[80] Depending on how one punctuates the text, the passage in "The Monograph on Music" in *The Old Tang History* may be understood as saying that the tune of Qiyu in the "Liang Songs" was "quite different" from that of the northern songs.[81]

The next tune title is "Langye W/wang" 琅琊王, under which we find eight songs. The eighth song contains the following lines: "Who can ride such a horse?/There is only the Duke of Guangping" 誰能騎此馬? 唯有廣平公.[82] *Yuefu shiji* identifies the Duke of Guangping as Yao Bi 姚弼 (d. 416), a northern general.[83] There were, however, a number of dukes of Guangping from the fourth to the sixth century,[84] and it remains uncertain to which duke this song was referring.

The first song in the set expresses a man's fondness for his weapon:

新買五尺刀	I have just purchased a blade of five feet,
懸著中梁柱	and I hang it on the central pillar.

78. *Wei shu* 109.2828. For an account of the "Songs of Dai," see Tian Xuqing, *Tuoba*, pp. 217–25.

79. *Jiu Tang shu* 29.1072. The other five titles are: "Murong Khan" ("Murong kehan" 慕容可汗), "Tuyuhun" 吐谷渾, "Buluoji" 部落稽, "The Princess of Julu" ("Julu gongzhu" 鉅鹿公主), and "King Suddhodhana's Heir Apparent" ("Baijingwang taizi" 白淨王太子). King Suddhodhana's heir apparent was the Śākyamuni Buddha.

80. Tian Yuqing, *Tuoba*, p. 219.

81. "The Liang *yuefu* songs for fife and drum also had songs of 'Major Song of King Suddhodhana's Heir Apparent,' 'Minor Song of King Suddhodhana's Heir Apparent,' 'Qiyu,' and others. The Sui songs for fife and drum included the song of 'King Suddhodhana's Heir Apparent.' Compared with northern songs, their tunes were all different" 梁樂府鼓吹又有大白淨皇太子、小白淨皇太子、企喻等曲. 隋鼓吹有白淨皇太子曲. 與北歌校之, 其音皆異 (*Jiu Tang shu* 29.1072).

82. *Quan Liang shi* 29.2153.

83. Guo Maoqian, *Yuefu shiji* 25.364.

84. They included Shi Le 石勒 (274–333), Fu Xi 符熙 (fl. 4th c.), Zhang Li 張黎 (ca. 5th c.), You Minggen 游明根 (419–99), and even a member of the Northern Qi royal family, Gao Sheng 高盛 (d. 536).

一日三摩娑	I stroke it three times a day,
劇於十五女	more often than I would a maiden of fifteen.

Such an exaggerated image of masculinity is built on the subversion of the "effeminate" man indulging in women and wine and can easily be cited as an example of the "typical northerner"—or, more precisely, of what might fit the southern imagination of the "typical northerner." Indeed, a southern poet like Wu Jun, who loved extravagant gestures of bravado himself, could have easily composed such a poem.

Most of the "Langye W/wang" songs cannot, however, be readily identified as "northern," such as the second one:

琅琊復琅琊	Langye, oh Langye,
琅琊大道王	a prince on the great road of Langye,
陽春二三月	in the second and third months of the sunny spring,
單衫繡裲襠	wearing a light shirt, with embroidered vest.

The third line often appears verbatim in southern *yuefu* songs; in fact, it recalls the opening line of a song whose title is "Song of the Great Road" ("Dadao qu" 大道曲), attributed to the Eastern Jin nobleman Xie Shang 謝尚 (308–57).[85] This poem highlights the ambiguity of the title of the song set. During the Southern Dynasties, the most immediate association with the title would have been the famous Wang clan from Langye 琅琊王氏. The title can, of course, also mean "the Prince of Langye." Again, however, the Prince of Langye would have been associated primarily with the South, even though "Langye" as a physical place was in the North. Six Eastern Jin emperors, including the dynastic founder, had been Princes of Langye before ascending the throne, and being named the Prince of Langye was politically significant in this period.[86] One does not have to look to the North for a Prince of Langye, however, and in any case there were fewer Princes of Langye in the North than in the South.[87]

---

85. *Quan Jin shi* 12.878.

86. They were Yuandi 元帝 (r. 317–22), Kangdi 康帝 (r. 343–45), Aidi 哀帝 (r. 362–66), the Abdicating Emperor 廢帝 (r. 366–71), Jianwen 簡文帝 (r. 371–73), and Gongdi 恭帝 (r. 419–20).

87. There was Sima Chuzhi 司馬楚之 (d. 464), who was made the Prince of Langye primarily because of his southern origin: he was a member of the Jin royal

The next tune title is "Song Lyrics of the Princess of Julu" ("Julu gongzhu geci" 鉅鹿公主歌辭).[88] Each of the three songs under this title consists of two seven-syllable lines, and together they read more like three stanzas of one song than like three separate songs. The *Jiu Tang shu* historian did not explain his reasons for saying that this song set "seemed" to be from the time of Yao Chang 姚萇 (330–94); the rest of his statement is likewise ambiguous: "The lyrics are in Chinese, differing from the northern songs."[89]

Both of the next two tune titles are called "The Purple Steed" ("Zi liuma" 紫騮馬). Zhijiang appended a note to the second one, marking it as "different from the previous tune."[90] The lyrics of the two sets contain no obvious differences; perhaps Zhijiang was referring to the music, which is now lost. Of the six songs in the first set, the last four read like a continuous sixteen-line poem with a clear narrative line: a man leaves home at fifteen to join the army and returns at eighty only to find his house ruined and his family no more.[91] In contrast, the song to the next tune title is a simple love song; again, it is remarkably similar to numerous southern *yuefu* quatrains. Another striking thing about "The Purple Steed" is that this *yuefu* title began to appear in court poetry only in the Liang. Both Xiao Gang and Xiao Yi composed to the title, and Xiao Gang's "Purple Steed" poem was in fact one of the "Three Companion Pieces for the Prince of Xiangdong's 'Songs for the Fife'" ("He Xiang-

family who escaped to the North after the Jin was replaced by the Song in 420; there was Yuan Chuo 元綽, who was made the Prince of Langye in 535; in the Northern Qi, there was Gao Yan 高儼 (557–71), whose enfeoffment nevertheless came much too late (in 569) for the "Liang Songs for Fife and Drum."

88. *Quan Liang shi* 29.2153–54.

89. *Jiu Tang shu* 29.1072.

90. Guo Maoqian, *Yuefu shiji* 25.365; *Quan Liang shi* 29.2154.

91. Zhijiang's note says: "From the line 'Joining the army at fifteen' down is an old poem" 十五從軍征以下是古詩 (*Quan Liang shi* 29.2154). The lines from "Joining the army at fifteen" down have been duly printed as a complete poem in Feng Weine's *Gushi ji* and Zhang Zhixiang's 張之象 (1507–87) *Gushi leiyuan* 古詩類苑 (printed in 1602) and classified as a "Han poem" by Lu Qinli (*Quan Han shi* 12.335–36). It is certainly interesting to observe that any poem called an "old poem" is automatically treated as a Han poem, even though "old poem" was nothing but a vague reference to a poem that had lost its place in time and so could be from anywhere from the third to the fifth century.

dong wang 'Hengchui qu' sanshou" 和湘東王橫吹曲三首).[92] It is hard to ascertain whether the prince's poems were inspired by the *yuefu* songs, or vice versa.

The next tune title, "Song Lyrics of Huangdansi" ("Huangdansi ge" 黃淡思歌), does not make much sense.[93] Zhijiang suspected that Huangdansi derived from "Huangtanzi" 黄覃子, a tune created by the Han musician Li Yannian.[94] In any case, all the songs under this title are love songs, and the third song sings of a fancy boat made in Guangzhou: "Its sail post is made of ivory, / with ropes made of green silk" 象牙作帆檣, / 綠絲作幃繂.[95]

"The Song of Master Liu of Dongping" has only three lines: "Master Liu of Dongping, the son of Andong. / Trees are sparse. / Nobody in the house—whom to look at?" 東平劉生安東子, / 樹木稀, / 屋里無人看阿誰? According to *Yuefu shiji*:

> *Yuefu jieti* 樂府解題 says that no one knows when Master Liu lived. Those who composed to the title "Master Liu" 劉生 since Qi and Liang all portray Master Liu as a chivalrous, bold, and uninhibited man traveling in the region of the Five Mounds and Three Qins [i.e., the Chang'an area]. Some say that he held a sword and went on military campaigns as an officer in charge of tallies. The details, however, remain unclear. The editor [of *Yuefu shiji*] notes: There is a "Song of Master Liu of Dongping" in the "Liang Songs for Fife and Drum," which I suspect is the same as "Master Liu."[96]
>
> 樂府解題曰: "劉生不知何代人, 齊梁已來爲'劉生'辭者, 皆稱其任俠豪放, 周遊五陵三秦之地. 或云抱劍專征, 爲符節官, 所未詳也." 按古今樂錄曰: 梁鼓角橫吹曲有"東平劉生歌", 疑即此"劉生"也.

Almost all the extant songs to the title "Master Liu" are authored by sixth-century southern poets, beginning with Xiao Yi. In addition, there is a song entitled "An Dongping" 安東平 in "The Western Tunes"

92. *Quan Liang shi* 20.1911.

93. Ibid., 29.2155.

94. *Jin shu* 28.847 records a Jingzhou ballad in the fourth century called "Huangtanzi" 黄曇子.

95. Longzhou 龍洲 in the text is emended to the "dragon boat" 龍舟 (*Quan Liang shi* 29.2155). Both Wang Yunxi (*Yuefu shi*, p. 474) and Tan Runsheng (*Beichao*, pp. 58–59) have cited this song in their brief discussions of the southern elements or what they see as a "southern influence" in the "Liang Songs."

96. *Yuefu shiji* 24.359.

of the South, which contains the following lines: "Master Liu of Dongping/again moves one's heart" 東平劉生,/復感人情.[97] This is clearly associated with "The Song of Master Liu of Dongping." All evidence thus seems to point to the southern origin of the song about Master Liu or at the very least a strong southern interest in the figure of Master Liu as a traditional *yuefu* role type: the chivalrous, swashbuckling knight roaming the region around Chang'an.

"Breaking the Willow Branches" had a long history before this song became part of the "Liang Songs for Fife and Drum."[98] "The Ballad of Breaking the Willow Branches" ("Zhe yangliu xing" 折楊柳行) is an old *yuefu* title going back at least to the third century. *The History of the Jin* (*Jin shu* 晉書) mentions a "Song of Breaking the Willow Branches" in the capital area from the Taikang era (280–90) of the Western Jin, which "began with words of the misery of warfare and ended with matters such as capturing and slaughtering."[99] For the first song of the set, the "Treatise on Music" in *Jiu Tang shu* records a slightly different version, claiming that the lyrics "originally came from the North."[100] The song cited above, "I am a lad of barbarian origin," is also from this song set.

Interestingly, two songs under this tune title appear in transformed form in the presumably much later ballad "Mulan" 木蘭. One suspects that the *yuefu* quatrains function as building blocks: they can be sung separately and independently, but, when necessary, they become stanzas stitched together to contribute to a longer narrative.

"The Ballads of the Horse-Riding Retainer of Youzhou" ("Youzhou make yin" 幽州馬客吟) could have been another old tune title.[101] A fragment from "The Unofficial Biography of Chen Wu" ("Chen Wu biezhuan" 陳武別傳) preserved in *Yiwen leiju* states that Chen Wu, a "barbarian" from Xiutu 休屠 who lived in the fourth century, learned many songs from his fellow shepherds, such as "The Ballad of Liangfu of

97. *Quan Jin shi* 19.1063.

98. *Quan Liang shi* 29.2158.

99. *Jin shu* 18.844. In the "Yuejie zhe yangliu ge shisanqu" 月節折楊柳歌十三曲 of "The Western Tunes," the refrain, "Break the willow branches," occurs in each of the thirteen songs; see *Quan Jin shi* 19.1066–69. The same refrain also appears in another southern song set, "Solo Songs" 讀曲歌 (*Quan Song shi* 11.1341).

100. *Jiu Tang shu* 29.1075.

101. *Quan Liang shi* 29.2159.

Taishan" ("Taishan Liangfu yin" 太山梁父吟), "The Ballad of the Horse-Riding Retainer of Youzhou," and "Hard Traveling" ("Xinglu nan" 行路難).[102] "The Ballad of Liangfu" was a favorite song of Zhuge Liang 諸葛亮 (181–234), and "Hard Traveling" was an "old song" refined by the Eastern Jin minister Yuan Shansong 袁山松 (d. 401).[103]

Five songs are included in "The Ballads of the Horse-Riding Retainer of Youzhou" song set; the third, fourth, and fifth are love songs. Although Tan Runsheng judges these songs to be primarily "northern songs," he believes that they manifest a "southern influence" because of lines such as "The lad wears a purple vest, / the girl puts on a colored skirt" 郎著紫袴褶, / 女著彩裌裙, or "The yellow flowers shine with a golden color, / a green snake holds in its mouth a crimson pearl" 黃花鬱金色, / 綠蛇銜珠丹. The argument is that such "artful and flashy words" signify a loss of "innocent feelings."[104] The North/South and nature/culture binarism has such a strong hold on our cultural imagination that the North, construed as cold, barren, a sort of a desolate "wild west," is not even allowed any colors (figurative and literal) in its image.

The preceding analysis of some of the songs labeled "northern" draws a picture of songs of mixed, ambiguous origins. And yet, the most powerful myth shrouding these songs is summarized in the famous scholar Liu Dajie's 劉大杰 (1904–77) bald statement: "Northerners' feelings are often expressed directly, like a linear line; [for the northerners,] there is no such roundabout, metaphoric way [of expression] as adopted in the South. It is not that the northerners could not fall in love; it is simply that their way of demonstrating love was different from that of the southerners."[105] This essentializing view has been widely shared among scholars.[106] Sometimes the "difference" between northern and southern *yuefu* songs is also understood as an ethnic difference: the simplicity, innocence, and lack of cultivation of the Xianbei people on one side; the veiled, tortuously expressed Han Chinese sensibility on the other.[107] These theories of environmental and ethnic determinism would have

102. *Yiwen leiju* 19.352.
103. *Sanguo zhi* 35.911; *Jin shu* 83.2169.
104. *Beichao*, pp. 66–67.
105. Liu Dajie, *Zhongguo wenxue fazhanshi*, p. 343.
106. See, e.g., Cao Daoheng, *Nanchao wenxue*, p. 267.
107. See, e.g., Li Kaiyuan and Guan Furong, *Bei Wei*, p. 101.

been more convincing with solid evidence, of which, regrettably, there is little, if any.

The third song from "The Horse-Riding Retainer of Youzhou" set reads as follows:

南山自言高	The south mountain says of itself that it is tall,
只與北山齊	but it is only as tall as the north mountain.[108]
女兒自言好	A girl says of herself that she is pretty,
故入郎君懷	so she casts herself in her lover's arms.

Compare this with the "Song of Green Jade" ("Biyu ge" 碧玉歌) attributed to the Eastern Jin elite poet Sun Chuo 孫綽 (314–71):[109]

碧玉破瓜時	Green Jade is sixteen,
相爲情顛倒	she and her lover are infatuated with each other.
感郎不羞難	Moved by her lover, she does not feel shy—
回身就郎抱	turning around, she throws herself in his arms.

Or "The Song of Meng Zhu" ("Mengzhu" 孟珠):[110]

望歡四五年	I have waiting for my sweetie for four or five years;
實情將懊惱	this love of ours has been truly frustrated.
願得無人處	How I wish that we were alone,
回身與郎抱	I'd turn around and take him in my arms!

Or one of the "Songs of Front Stream" ("Qianxi ge" 前溪歌), which seems to sing of an illicit affair:[111]

黄葛生爛熳	The yellow kudzu grow lushly—
誰能斷葛根	who can cut off their roots?
寧斷嬌兒乳	I would rather cut off my baby's milk,
不斷郎殷勤	but will not cut off my lover's devotion.

The expression of fiery sentiments in these southern songs is by no means "roundabout."

Indeed, a song attributed to the Empress Dowager Hu of the Northern Wei, reportedly composed in fond memory of her lover Yang Hua

108. Tan Runsheng (*Beichao*, p. 66) judges this song to be from the North on the basis of this couplet. His reasoning escapes me.

109. *Quan Jin shi* 13.902.

110. Ibid., 19.1065.

111. Ibid., 19.1051.

楊華, who defected to the South, is filled with sentimentality and tenderness.[112] Baffled by how ill it befits the stereotypical image of the tough northern woman, scholars could only resort to the explanation that the song had been influenced by the southern style.[113] Opening with a line commonly seen in the *yuefu* songs of this period, the song is built around a pun on the lover's name, Yang Hua, which also means "willow catkins."

陽春二三月	In the second and third months of sunny spring,
楊柳齊作花	willow trees all turn out catkins.
春風一夜入閨闥	Spring breeze enters the boudoir overnight;
楊花飄蕩落南家	the catkins flutter and float, falling into the southern household.
含情出户腳無力	Filled with longing, I go out the door, my feet having no strength to support me;
拾得楊花淚沾臆	I pick up the catkins from the ground, tears drenching my breast.
秋去春還雙燕子	The swallow couple, you who leave in autumn but return in spring—
願銜楊花入窠裏	I wish you would carry the catkins back to the nest!

LOTUS PICKING: CONFIGURING THE SOUTH

Ming Yuqing, the author of "Ballad of Joining the Army," was the grandson of the famous Liang scholar Ming Shanbin 明山賓 (443–527). His father, Ming Kerang 明克讓 (525–94), was taken to the North after the Liang fell and served first the Zhou and then the Sui before his death. Ming Yuqing might easily have felt a strong identification with the North despite his Southern connections. After all, the Ming family had come to the South only after the prefectures to the north of the Huai River were lost to the Northern Wei in 466. Their experience mirrored many northern immigrant families since the Eastern Jin: a large part of the southern elite was not native to the South but were

112. The song is entitled "Yang baihua ge" 楊白華歌 (*Quan bei Wei shi* 3.2246).
113. See Zhou Jianjiang, *Bei Wei*, p. 217.

settlers in a land that had long been considered peripheral to the Central States, "a land of pestilential vapors" (*zhangli di* 瘴癘地). Transforming it into a meaningful cultural space, a center of the Han civilization of which they saw themselves as the rightful owners and upholders, was a weighty task faced by the northern immigrants who came to inhabit the South. They found a way in the glorification of one central poetic image: the lotus.

In the southern *yuefu* songs, the lotus provides a rich range of possibilities for double entendres about romantic entanglements: "lotus," *lian* 蓮, puns with "love" (*lian* 憐), "lotus seed," *lianzi* 蓮子, with "love or cherish you" (*lian zi* 憐子), "lotus root," *ou* 藕, with "lover/spouse/couple" (*ou* 偶), and the filaments in the lotus root (*si* 絲), whose suppleness enables them to stretch without breaking, with "love-longing" (*si* 思).

The lotus is also rich in religious connotations. In the Buddhist context, the lotus symbolizes purity and enlightenment, since the lotus grows out of the mud but remains uncontaminated by it. In the Pure Land of Amitābha Buddha, men and women are born from lotus flowers without going through childbirth.[114] One of the most influential Buddhist texts in the Southern Dynasties was *The Lotus Sūtra*. The fourth-century monk Sengrui 僧叡 wrote in a colophon to *The Lotus Sūtra*:

> Among all flowers, the lotus is the most sumptuous. When it first opens and is not yet in full bloom, it is called Mukula; when it is already open and about to wither, it is called Kāmalā; when it is in full bloom, it is called Puṇḍarīka. The stage of first opening is a metaphor for the Two Ways; the stage of its being about to wither, for Nirvana; and the stage of being in full bloom, for this scripture itself.[115]
>
> 諸華之中, 蓮華最勝. 華而未敷, 名屈摩羅; 敷而將落, 名迦摩羅; 處中盛時, 名分陀利. 未敷喻二道, 將落譬泥洹. 榮曜獨足, 以喻斯典.

114. Zhi Dun mentioned this in the preface to his "Amituofo xiangzan" 阿彌陀佛像讚 (*Quan Jin wen* 157.2369).

115. Ibid., 160.2386. "Two Ways" could mean many things, such as "the Difficult Way" (*nanxing dao* 難行道) versus "the Easy Way" (*yixing dao* 易行道). The former requires one to accumulate merit in this world and obtain enlightenment; the latter asks one to contemplate the Buddha and be reborn in the Pure Land.

Naming the scripture *Lotus Sūtra* both indicated the special place it held in the Buddhist canon and granted the lotus a privileged position in the world of flora and fauna.

The lotus was frequently mentioned in sūtras, painted in temple murals, and carved out of wood or stone to accompany Buddhist statues. When the Marquis of Darkness in the East made his beloved consort, Pan Yu'er 潘玉兒, walk on lotuses made of gold and referred to this as "producing a lotus blossom at every step," he was sacrilegiously inspired by Buddhist scriptures—lotuses had sprouted wherever the Śākyamuni Buddha's feet touched the ground when he was first born.[116] "Lotus" is also a common female name in sūtras. Several stories relate how a woman called Lotus became enlightened to the vanities of the mortal world and decided to give up secular life for Buddhism.[117] In these cases, the name is evidently symbolic.

For people in the Liang, the lotus with its sumptuous beauty and religious significance must have evoked the essential teaching of the Buddha, that sensuous forms and emptiness are one and the same. The image of the lotus represents both sensual desires and the transcendence of such desires. A *yuefu* song attributed to Emperor Wu of the Liang illustrates the double facets of the lotus.[118]

豔豔金樓女	Splendid is the lady of the golden tower.
心如玉池蓮	Her heart is like a lotus in the jade pond.
持底報郎恩	How do I ever repay my love's grace?
俱期遊梵天	We make a date for roaming in the Brahma Heaven together.[119]

116. *Nan shi* 5.154. The name of the most notorious female character in Chinese literary history, Pan Jinlian 潘金蓮 (Pan the Golden Lotus), from the Ming novels *Shuihu zhuan* 水滸傳 and *Jin ping mei* 金瓶梅, was clearly a composite name inspired by the *Nan shi* anecdote, although the historical Pan Yu'er defended her chastity by committing suicide after the Qi fell and Emperor Wu of the Liang decided to give her away to one of his generals (*Nan shi* 55.1352).

117. The stories are included in the *Jinglü yixiang* (*T* 53: 23.123).

118. *Quan Liang shi* 1.1518.

119. A similar motif can be found in the "Yuejie zhe yangliu ge shisanqu": "The lotus begins to blossom. / Where do we pledge our love? / We expect to be reborn in front of the World Honored One. / Break the willow branches! / Holding the incense and scattering famed flowers, / we want to belong to each other for ever" 芙蓉

Brahma Heaven is in the Realm of Form. It is quiet, pure, far away from the Kāmadhātu, the Realm of Desires (*yujie* 欲界).

In the native Chinese tradition, the lotus had a particular affinity with the Southland. In the *Chuci*, the "songs of the South," the lotus symbolizes moral purity. But it was a song entitled "The Southland" ("Jiangnan" 江南) that proved most compelling for the southern literati's imagination. The song was first recorded in the "Treatise on Music" in Shen Yue's *History of the Song*.[120]

江南可採蓮	In the Southland one can pick lotus,
蓮葉何田田	how spreading the lotus leaves are!
魚戲蓮葉間	Fish play among the lotus leaves.
魚戲蓮葉東	Fish play east of the lotus leaves,
魚戲蓮葉西	fish play west of the lotus leaves.
魚戲蓮葉南	Fish play south of the lotus leaves,
魚戲蓮葉北	fish play north of the lotus leaves.

Tiantian 田田 in the second line of the poem is a highly unusual compound.[121] What is noteworthy is that the compound was first used for describing lotus leaves only in the late fifth century, at about the same time when Shen Yue was compiling *The History of the Song*;[122] and again exclusively by poets from Shen Yue's social circle, such as Xie Tiao, Lu Jue, and Wang Yun.[123]

始懷蓮,/何處結同心?/俱生世尊前./折楊柳./捻香散名花,/志得長相取 (*Quan Jin shi* 19.1067). The World Honored One is one of the titles of Śākyamuni Buddha.

120. *Song shu* 21.605; *Quan Han shi* 9.256.

121. *Tian tian* rarely appears in earlier literature. It is used once in the *Record of Rites* as onomatopoeia (*Liji zhushu* 56.948). One meaning of *tian* is "many in number," and so *tian tian* could refer to the density of the lotus leaves.

122. *Song shu* was commissioned by the Qi emperor in 487 and presented to the throne in 488, but the treatises or monographs were completed later. Based on the avoidance of certain taboo characters in the monographs, it is assumed that the compilation of the monographs, barring the two on "Celestial Configurations" and "Musical Pitches and the Calendar" produced earlier by He Chengtian, had continued throughout the Qi and was not finished until after the founding of the Liang in 502.

123. Xie Tiao used *tian tian* to depict lotus leaves in a *yuefu* poem, "Song of the River" ("Jiangshang qu" 江上曲), and then in "*Fu* on Longing to Return" ("Sigui fu" 思歸賦) and "*Fu* on Roaming in the Rear Garden" ("You houyuan fu" 遊後園賦) (*Quan Qi shi* 3.1417; *Quan Qi wen* 23.2919, 23.2920). Lu Jue, who once wrote to Shen Yue contesting his theory of tonal rules, used *tian tian* to describe

Shen Yue's sources for the "Treatise on Music" are unclear. He could have acquired the text of "The Southland" from court musicians, or some old manuscript in the imperial library, or anywhere else. He listed the song as an "old lyric" (*guci* 古詞) and claimed, rather vaguely, that it was a "Han street ballad."[124] The Northern Song compilation *Yuefu shiji* appended a note to the song, saying that it was "performed by Wei and Jin musicians."[125] We do not know how trustworthy this statement is, but one thing is quite clear: this song was seldom performed, if at all, in the fifth century.[126] That poets in Shen Yue's social circle began to allude to the old "Han song" in the late fifth century, but not before, seems to suggest that they had gained access to the song only through Shen Yue. If this inference is true, it may help explain why poetry on lotus picking, not just poetry on the lotus, suddenly became so popular in the same period: the latter is a "poetry on objects" type, whereas the former shifts the focus to action and human interaction with the lotus plant. That an "old" song, believed to be from the Han dynasty, delineated a special relationship between the lotus and the Southland, fascinated the southern poets.

Picking lotus to send to one's beloved is the topic of one of the "Nineteen Old Poems,"[127] and yet, perhaps only a Liang poet could give an ingenious twist to the theme by linking lotus picking with the frontier narrative. In Wu Jun's "Song of Picking Lotus" ("Cailian qu" 採蓮

lotus leaves in a poem presented to his brother-in-law, 奉答內兄希叔 (*Quan Qi shi* 5.1467). Lu Jue was also the author of a *yuefu* song entitled "Song of South Commandery" ("Nanjun ge" 南郡歌), which begins with the line "In the Southland one can pick lotus" 江南可採蓮 (*Quan Qi shi* 5.1464). Wang Yun also used *tian tian* to describe lotus leaves (*Quan Liang shi* 24.2013).

124. *Song shu* 19.549.

125. Ibid., 26.384.

126. A fragmentary poem by the Western Jin poet Fu Xuan begins with: "We cross to the south of the river, and pick lotus" 渡江南, 採蓮花 (*Quan Jin shi* 1.568). The phrasing is similar to the first line of "The Southland": 江南可採蓮. But it is difficult to talk about "echoes" or "influence" when the date of "The Southland" is in doubt. As a matter of fact, Fu Xuan's opening lines evoke the fifth of the "Nineteen Old Poems," known to Fu Xuan's contemporary Lu Ji (see the following footnote).

127. This poem is No. 5 of the "Nineteen Old Poems." It was chosen to be imitated by Lu Ji (*Quan Han shi* 12.330; *Quan Jin shi* 5.687). Both the original and Lu Ji's imitation were included in the *Wen xuan*.

曲), the lotus is identified as that of the Southland, and the beloved, a soldier going on a campaign to the northeast.[128]

錦帶雜花鈿	Brocade sash mixed with flowered hairpins,
羅衣垂綠川	gauze robe hanging in the green river.
問子今何去	I ask you where are you going now?
出采江南蓮	I'm going out to pick the lotus of the Southland.
遼西三千里	Liaoxi is three thousand miles away,
欲寄無因緣	I want to send the lotus to him but have no means.
願君早旋反	I wish that you would come back soon
及此荷花鮮	in time to see the fresh lotus flowers.

Wu Jun, whose poetry was known for its "ancient aura," was nevertheless the only Liang poet to incorporate the motif of an "old poem" in his "Song of Picking Lotus." The Liang texts on lotus picking, unlike Wu Jun's relatively unadorned poem, share a much more intricate and sensuous vocabulary.

The earliest datable "Song of Picking Lotus" was written by Emperor Wu of the Liang in the winter of 512 or early 513, as one of a set of seven songs entitled "Ditties of the Southland" ("Jiangnan nong" 江南弄).[129]

游戲五湖采蓮歸	Sporting on the Five Lakes, I return from lotus picking:
發花田葉芳襲衣	blooming flowers and spreading leaves, their aroma pervades my clothes.
爲君儂歌世所希	For you, my lord, I'll sing a song that everyone cherishes.
世所希	Everyone cherishes it
有如玉	as they cherish jade:
江南弄	the "Ditties of the Southland,"
采蓮曲	the "Song of Picking Lotus."

In the second line, the word for "spreading," *tian*, echoes "The Southland," but the sporting fish darting in five directions are displaced by the lotus-picking girls "sporting on the Five Lakes." In the third line,

128. *Quan Liang shi* 10.1724.
129. Ibid., 1.1522.

the use of the southern dialectal *nong* 儂 (I) reinforces the local flavor. It is a song about the Southland as much as about a song about the Southland. Such self-reflexivity points to a conscious fashioning of the image of the Southland.

"One Can Pick Lotus in the Southland" ("Jiangnan ke cailian" 江南可採蓮), a poem written by Liu Huan, a member of Xiao Yi's salon, offers a romanticized celebration of the Southland as the land of romance:

春初北岸涸	In early springtime, the northern shore is dry,
夏月南湖通	but in summer months one can pass through South Lake.
卷荷舒欲倚	Folded lotus leaves now open up, about to become slanting;
芙蓉生即紅	lotus blossoms are already red as soon as they bloom.
楫小宜迴逕	Oars are small, proper for a winding stream;
船輕好入叢	boat is light, easily entering the clumps.
釵光逐影亂	The luster of the hairpins chases the confused reflections in water;
衣香隨逆風	the scent of the dresses following the opposing wind.
江南少許地	The Southland is a little region:[130]
年年情不窮	but year after year, love never comes to an end.[131]

In the background of the last couplet is a remark by Wang Xun 王珣 (350–401), the grandson of the Eastern Jin minister Wang Dao: "The land to the south of the Yangzi River is small and cannot be compared to the Central Domain" 江左地促, 不如中國.[132] But Wang Xun went on to praise his grandfather's urban design for the capital of Jiankang: by making the streets winding and twisting, Wang Dao had, so Wang

130. This alludes to a story in the commentary to the *Shi ji* (59.2100). Emperor Jing of the Han once asked all his sons to sing and dance at a party. The Prince of Changsha (in present Hu'nan, the old Chu region) only raised his hands slightly. Everyone laughed at his clumsiness, and the emperor was moved to ask him why. The prince answered: "The kingdom of your subject is small and the land is narrow, insufficient for turning and whirling around." The emperor henceforth granted him three more commanderies.

131. *Quan Liang shi* 1848.

132. Liu Yiqing, *Shishuo xinyu* 2.156.

Xun argued, succeeded in making the capital impenetrable and unfathomable, instead of a city that could be comprehended in one glance. In the same way, Liu Huan maintained that even though the Southland was a "little region," it was a land of intricacies, niceties, and endless romantic sentiments.

Xiao Gang's "*Fu* on Picking Lotus" ("Cailian fu" 採蓮賦) best illustrates the emblematic power of the lotus.[133] The opening lines present a sweeping view of the Southland, only to be counterbalanced by the immediate and close-at-hand:

望江南兮清且空	I gaze at the Southland, pure and empty;
對荷華兮丹復紅	I face the lotus blossoms, vermilion and red.

Wang, "to gaze," suggests looking out at a wide expanse of landscape, and *dui*, "to face," a much closer view. The poet moves from the panorama of the Southland to a close-up of the lotus blossoms, and yet, the vast background is always there: the poet's choice of words, "pure and empty," recalls both aristocratic and Buddhist values. Then, a scene of lush vegetative entanglements, with its erotic overtones, replaces the clarity of the boundless landscape.

臥蓮葉而覆水	Lotus leaves recline and cover the waters,
亂高房而出叢	high pods tangled up, rise above the clumps.
楚王暇日之歡	The delight of Chu kings in their leisure days;
麗人妖艷之質	the beguiling substance of beautiful women.
且棄垂釣之魚	Let us discard the fish caught by the dangling hook,[134]
未論芳萍之實	not to mention the fruit of the fragrant duckweed,[135]

133. *Quan Liang wen* 8.2998.

134. "The fish caught by the dangling hook" alludes to the story of Lord Longyang 龍陽君, the lover of the King of Wei. He wept during fishing; when asked the reason by the king, he answered that it was because he feared he might be discarded by the king just as "a former fish" is tossed back when new fishes are caught (*Zhanguo ce* 25.917).

135. "The fruit of the fragrant duckweed" refers to a story recorded in *Kongzi jiayu* (2.18). The Chu king found a strange-looking melon in the river, but no one could identify it except Confucius, who recognized it as the fruit of the duckweed, a rare fruit and a good omen for the country.

唯欲回渡輕船	desiring only to turn our light boat across the water
共采新蓮	and pick the fresh lotus together.
傍斜山而屢轉	We turn often as we follow along meandering hills;
乘橫流而不前	then, riding the contrary currents, we stop advancing.
於是素腕舉	Thereupon pale wrists are lifted,
紅袖長	red sleeves hang long,
回巧笑	coy smiles are flashed,
墮明璫	bright earrings drop.
荷稠刺密	The lotuses are thick, the thorns dense,
亟牽衣而綰裳	urgently pulling on dresses and tugging at skirts;
....	[one missing line]
惜虧朱而壞妝	what a pity—the rouge is spoiled, and makeup ruined.

All embark on a boat trip on a winding stream, ending in a spellbound world. The red sleeves echo the vermilion blossoms; the lifted wrists recall the rising stalks. The stillness of the boat is balanced by an array of actions. As the world of vegetation fights back, appearances can no longer be maintained, and chaos erupts. The erotic implication of ruined makeup and exposed flesh is overwhelmed by the Buddhist connotation of the word *huai* 壞, which points to the destruction of the ephemeral physical world of Form and Color (*wuse* 物色). The poet tarries, until he, too, surrenders to the forces of nature.

物色雖晚	Though too late to observe the forms and colors of things,
徘徊未反	we linger on, not yet turning back.
畏風多而榜危	We dread lest winds be strong and the oars unsteady;
驚舟移而花遠	then taken by surprise when the boat, jolted, moves on, and the flowers grow distant.

The act of zooming in on the lotus blossoms in the opening couplet is now being reversed: the flowers become distant and hazy, disappearing into the night.

At this moment, a voice is heard singing in the dark:

歌曰	The song goes:
常聞蕖可愛	I have always heard that lotuses are lovely,
采擷欲爲裙	so I picked and gathered them to make a skirt.
葉滑不留綖	The leaves were slippery, the thread wouldn't stay,
心忙無假薰	the stalks/hearts were flustered, having no need for incense.
千春誰與樂	For a thousand springs who will join you in pleasure?
唯有妾隨君	There is only I, my lord, who will go along with you.

To make a skirt out of lotuses reminds one of the high-minded gentleman in the *Chuci*; in Six Dynasties lore, however, wearing clothes made of lotus leaves is the customary way in which an animal spirit, usually an otter, transforms itself into an alluring woman who seduces hapless mortal males.[136] The concluding song of Xiao Gang's *fu* is, then, a siren's call to the world of sensuous forms, colors, and illusions. The promise to follow her lord "for a thousand springs" is a hollow one, however reassuring at the end of the day.

Xiao Gang's *fu* presents a powerful vision of the Southland, with the lotus as the central image. The key to this *fu* is the synchronicity of the "forms and colors of things" and the larger background that is "pure and empty" (*qingkong* 清空). Each defines and is defined by the other; neither can exist alone. Always a land of sensuous pleasures, the Southland also awakens one to the vanity of such pleasures. For the later-born, however, there is an added historical dimension to the Southland, and the "emptiness" of its pleasures is rendered literal by our knowledge of the conquest of the Southern Dynasties and the devastation of the South. If for Xiao Gang and his contemporaries the Southland represented a world of immediacy, the image of the Southland they fabricated came to be tinted with an elegiac tone in the later ages.

In the sixth century, lotus picking was the main constituent in the northerners' image of the South. It was perhaps no coincidence that the tunes composed by Yang Kan, the northern general who defected to

136. See Gan Bao (fl. fourth c.), *Soushen ji*, p. 228; and Liu Yiqing's *Youming lu*, p. 73.

the Liang in 529, were none other than "Picking Lotus" ("Cailian" 採蓮) and "Song of Oars" ("Zhaoge" 棹歌).[137] As the images of lotus picking emigrated to the North, it would also have been impossible to distinguish Lu Sidao's "Song of Picking Lotus" from a southern court poet's writings. It, in many ways, resembles a poetic rewriting of Xiao Gang's *fu* on picking lotus.

曲浦戲妖姬	By the winding river a beautiful girl playfully roams,
輕盈不自持	so light and delicate, she can hardly support herself.
擎荷愛圓水	Holding up the lotus, she is in love with the round dews;
折藕弄長絲	breaking a lotus root, playing with the long filaments.
珮動裙風入	Pendants stir, as a breeze enters her skirt;
妝銷粉汗滋	as perspiration glows, makeup is melting away.
菱歌惜不唱	She begrudges singing the "Song of Water Chestnuts,"
須待暝歸時	for she must wait till it is dark, when she returns.[138]

For southerners detained in the North, the "Song of Picking Lotus" evoked a lost land, a lost era. After the fall of the South, Jiang Zong, who had successively served Liang and Chen, was taken to Chang'an. Some time between 589 and 593, he joined two northern poets, Yuan Xinggong and Xue Daoheng, in writing on the sights of Chang'an.[139]

137. *Liang shu* 39.561. Yang Kan was known for his love of luxury and extravagant display of wealth. His river outings, with bejeweled boats, brocade screens, and an orchestra of female musicians, were grand spectacles that attracted thousands of spectators. His personal ensemble included the famous dancer Zhang Jingwan 張靜婉, who inspired the Tang poet Wen Tingyun to write "Zhang Jingwan: Song of Picking Lotus" 張靜婉採蓮曲.

138. *Quan Sui shi* 1.2631.

139. Yuan Xinggong was a Northern Qi minister well known for his literary talent. He and Xue Daogeng had been taken to Chang'an after Emperor Wu of Zhou (r. 561–79) conquered the Northern Qi in 577. For their poems, see *Quan Sui shi* 2.2654, 4.2683.

秋日昆明池詩
The Kunming Pool on an Autumn Day[140]

玄沼蕭條望	Bleakly looking over the dark pool,[141]
遊人意緒多	the sightseer has much on his mind.
終南雲影落	Cloud shadows fall on the Zhongnan Mountain;
渭北雨聲過	the sound of rain passes by the north shore of the Wei River.
蟬噪金堤柳	Cicadas make noises on the willows by the metal dike;[142]
鷺飲石鯨波	egrets drink from the waves by the stone whale.[143]
珠來照似月	The pearls are shining like the moon;
織處寫成河	where the Weaving Girl weaves, a river flows.[144]
此時臨水歎	Upon this day, I sigh by the water—
非復採蓮歌	there is no longer a "Song of Picking Lotus."

The dewdrops or raindrops on the lotus leaves are mentioned explicitly in the two northern poets' poems, but only indirectly in the image of the pearl moon in Jiang Zong's. Furthermore, the lotus is referred to not as a real presence but as part of a song title, framed in terms of loss. Interestingly, it was not the lotus itself that was found missing at the Kunming Pool, but the *song* about picking lotus. The lotus, though physically present, became no more than an index of absence. What mattered was never the flower itself, no matter how splendidly it

140. *Quan Chen shi* 8.2579.

141. "Dark pool" has a textual variant: "divine pool" (*lingzhao* 靈沼). A line in Zhang Heng's 張衡 (78–139) "*Fu* on the Western Metropolis" ("Xijing fu" 西京賦) reads: "Then, there was / The divine pool of Kunming, / With its Black Water and Dark Foot Shrine" 迺有昆明靈沼，/黑水玄阯 (*Quan hou Han wen* 52.763; translation from Knechtges, *Wen xuan*, 1: 209). The Black Water comes out of the Kunlun Mountain (*Shanhai jing* 2.48).

142. The "metal dike" indicates the sturdiness of the embankment. See Zhang Heng's "*Fu* on the Western Metropolis": "It was surrounded by a 'metal' dike, / Planted with weeping willow and purple osier" 周以金堤，/樹以柳杞 (*Quan hou Han wen*, 52.763; translation from Knechtges, *Wen xuan*, 1: 211).

143. It is said that Emperor Wu of the Han had a whale carved out of jadeite at the Kunming Pool, whose scales moved during thunderstorms.

144. On the eastern and western shores of the Kunming Pool were erected stone statues of the mythical lovers Weaving Girl and the Cowherd; the river in the eighth line refers to the Heavenly River (the Milky Way), which separates the lovers.

bloomed, but a tune, a mood, an aura of a place that had invented itself successfully in the image of the lotus blossom.

In later times, poets continued to write about lotus, lotus picking, and the Southland, Jiangnan.[145] However, after the Southern Dynasties, no one could ever inhabit the Southland again, for it had become a land of the past. Xiao Gang and his contemporaries were celebrating, creating, and experiencing the South all at once, but the later-born could never look at a lotus-picking girl again without thinking of *the* lotus-picking girl who embodied the sensuous, alluring, lost Southland.

Precisely because she is not an individual person, the lotus-picking girl lives on. Even in the twentieth century, we can still recognize her despite her transformation into a member of a people's commune in the poetry of a socialist poet.[146] She lingers on into the new millennium, in the postmodern world with its tacky plastic lotuses, reportedly planted at an unspecified tourist site in the Southland.

PERFORMING WOMEN: SONGS OF THE SOUTH

This discussion of the cultural construction of the Chinese South would not be complete without a consideration of a group of southern *yuefu* songs, not only because these songs played a crucial role in the southern court's imaginary construction of a local South of commoners, but also because the interpretive tradition formed around these songs in the twentieth century constitutes part of an ongoing cultural construction of the North and South.

145. For songs of lotus picking from the Tang, see Guo Maoqian, *Yuefu shiji* 50.733–37; and Owen, ed. and trans., *An Anthology of Chinese Literature*, pp. 381–83.

146. A collection of poetry by the modern poet Yan Zhen 嚴陣 (1931–) is entitled *Jiangnan qu* 江南曲, which includes a "Song of Picking Lotus" and a "Song of Gathering Water Chestnuts," written in the modern vernacular Chinese and free verse form. The ending of the "Song of Picking Lotus" gives a new twist to the traditional theme: "Never fear that the lotus leaves may block the way home: / the red flag of the commune is waving and beckoning" 別擔心荷葉遮住了歸路, / 公社的紅旗正在飄動 (Yan Zhen, *Jiangnan*, p. 80).

There are two major groups of southern *yuefu* songs: "The Sound of Wu" ("Wu sheng" 吳聲), and "The Western Tunes" ("Xi qu" 西曲). The "Wu sheng" songs, of which there are about 330, are believed to represent the Wu region of the lower Yangzi River, particularly the Jiankang area; the "Xi qu" songs, originating from the central Yangzi region, particularly the Jiangling and Xiangyang areas, number about 140. Both groups are mostly quatrains in the five-syllable line; they have a penchant for using puns and typically sing of romantic love.

Modern scholars generally regard these songs as representing the spontaneous, innocent voice of a lower-class woman, unsullied by the refined but decadent male aristocrats who treated women as playthings and love as a game. In early twentieth-century China, when folk literature was prized over elite literature, this conviction prompted scholars to hail these southern *yuefu* songs as among the most splendid achievements of Six Dynasties literature.[147] This conviction has grown into a minor interpretive tradition that itself requires attention and reevaluation. But first we must ask: What is at stake if it turns out that the claim about the female voice is based on shaky ground?

The most frequently cited internal evidence for the claim is that the first-person pronoun *nong* in these songs is used by a woman and the term *huan* 歡 (sweetie) refers to her male lover.[148] But the argument does not stand close scrutiny.[149] In fact, Wu Zeng 吳曾 (fl. ca. 1157) even maintained that in the "Wu sheng" songs *huan* refers to a woman and *nong* a man.[150] He then gave a series of examples to illustrate his point. Wu Zeng's statement is eloquent testimony that the southern songs present an inherent gender ambiguity and that they have not always been read as female songs.

147. See Zheng Zhenduo, *Chatuben*, p. 196.

148. Ge Xiaoyin, *Badai*, p. 164.

149. Examples abound in writings from this period. Sima Daozi 司馬道子, the Eastern Jin prince, had used *nong* to refer to himself when he said in the Wu dialect, "I know, I know" 儂知儂知 (*Jin shu* 64.1733). Sometimes the prefix *a* 阿 is added to *nong*. In the Tang dynasty compilation, Du You, *Tong dian* (145.3705), the definition of *huan* is simply given as "a form of address for one's beloved in the South," with no indication of the gender of the beloved.

150. Wu Zeng, *Nenggaizhai manlu*, 3: 2997.

Many of the southern songs were composed in an interesting form, "paired" or "matching songs" (*duige* 對歌).[151] In this form, the voices of a man and a woman usually engage in a dialogue. One well-known example is the first two songs in the "Ziye ge" 子夜歌 set.[152]

落日出前門	At sunset I come out the front door,
瞻矚見子度	looking around, I see you pass by.
冶容多姿鬢	Pretty looks, charming hairdo—
芳香已盈路	your sweet scent fills the road.

芳是香所為	Sweet scent comes from perfume;
冶容不敢當	pretty looks—I dare not claim.
天不奪人願	Heaven does not oppose one's wish,
故使儂見郎	and makes me run into you.

Sometimes it would be impossible to understand the meaning of one song without its matching song, as in the following pair.[153]

寡婦哭城頹	A widow weeps till the city wall crumbles—
此情非虛假	such a love is not false.
相樂不相得	If we delight in each other, but cannot be together;
抱恨黃泉下	I'd feel regret even in the Yellow Springs.

內心百際起	A hundred sorrows rise in the heart;
外形空殷勤	on the outside, assiduous in vain.
既就頹城感	Since you swear by the crumbling city wall,
敢言浮花言	how dare I use superficial words?

Here the lovers are apparently trapped in a hopeless situation. In the first song, the woman affirms her love by alluding to Qiliang Zhi's 杞梁殖 widow, who, upon receiving the news of her husband's death, wept so bitterly that the city wall was literally moved by her tears and collapsed. She eventually committed suicide.[154] In the second song, the man replies that he will repay her love with the same passion. "Superficial words" in the last line are literally "flowery words."

151. For a perceptive article on *duige* in the "Wu sheng" songs, see Yu Guanying, "Wusheng gequ li de nannü zengda" 吳聲歌曲裡的男女贈答, in idem, *Han Wei liuchao*, pp. 60–69.

152. *Quan Jin shi* 19.1040.

153. Ibid., 19.1057.

154. Liu Xiang, *Lienü zhuan* 4.81–82.

Another pair of songs portrays two lovers suffering from a misunderstanding, and one is explaining himself or herself to the other.[155]

儂心常慊慊	My heart is always affectionate,
歡行由豫情	while your feelings, my love, are hesitant.
霧露隱芙蓉	Mist and dews conceal the lotus—
見蓮詎分明	how can one see the blossoms clearly?
非歡獨慊慊	You, my love, are not affectionate alone:
儂意亦驅驅	my feelings are likewise earnest.
雙燈俱時盡	The twin lamps burn themselves out together—
奈許兩無由	what can be done when both run out of lamp-oil?

The first song makes use of the commonplace pun, *lian*, lotus/ love, and the last line also means: "Your love is not clearly demonstrated." In the second song, "oil" (*you* 油) puns with "reason or means" (*you* 由); the beloved defends him- or herself by saying that circumstances prevent him/her from showing his/her love.

These examples show us that the male voice is just as prominent in the southern songs as the female voice. Further illustrating this point is a couplet from "Ziye ge" no. 31: "You sing songs of a subtle sense, / and I, too, give forth sweet lyrics" 郎歌妙意曲,/儂亦吐芳詞.[156] "You" as *lang* 郎 is marked as male here, explicitly represented as a singer. The male voice does not have to occur only in matching songs, as in the following:[157]

蹔請半日給	I asked for a half-day leave,
徙倚娘店前	lingering in front of my girl's shop.
目作宴瑱飽	My eyes feast on her beauty;
腹作宛惱饑	my stomach suffers from starvation.

This song is reminiscent of a well-known story from the period about a pretty girl selling "barbarian powder."[158] A young man secretly falls in love with her; he goes to her shop and buys a packet of powder from her

155. *Quan Song shi* 11.1343.
156. *Quan Jin shi* 19.1042.
157. To the tune title "Xi wu ye fei" 西烏夜飛 (*Quan Song shi* 11.1349).
158. *You ming lu*, p. 3. For a full English translation of the story, see Kao, *Classical Chinese Tales*, pp. 143–44.

every day. The *yuefu* song cited above would be the perfect illustration of the young man's situation.

In the story, the girl finally becomes suspicious and questions the young man, who then tells her the truth. The girl is so touched that she makes a tryst with him. She then goes to his house at dusk. It is worth noting that the girl goes to the young man's house, not vice versa. Many southern songs are about keeping and breaking trysts, waiting for one's beloved, and feeling sorrow upon separating at dawn. The question is: If these songs often do not have a clear gender marker, why, then, are they so commonly regarded by modern scholars as embodying a female voice?

It seems that a particular range of feelings is considered, either explicitly or implicitly, as an internal gender marker of the *yuefu* songs. That is, the expression of pain, longing, anger, and fear of betrayal is usually attributed to a woman. The social, economic, and political inequality of men and women is interiorized as an essential difference between the two sexes, and emotional unfaithfulness is construed as one form of gender oppression. Scholars subjecting the interpretation of the southern songs to the political and social interests of the modern world are somehow trapped in a circular logic. The speaker in most of the songs is considered to be female because the songs manifest a set of culturally, socially, and historically constructed "feminine traits" such as weeping and complaining. Then, these "female songs" are taken as incontestable proof of female subjugation, and as such, they reinforce the view that women were not only politically and economically oppressed but also emotional exploited. Such an essentializing feminism runs the risk of becoming an inverted form of sexism. As Judith Butler aptly put it, "The insistence upon the coherence and unity of the category of women has effectively refused the multiplicity of cultural, social, and political intersections in which the concrete array of 'women' are [*sic*] constructed."[159] Since powdering one's face was not a practice confined to women in early medieval China and weeping at parting was part of the required social decorum for men in the South, many kinds of behavior and feelings labeled as "feminine" or "female" need to be placed in their sociohistorical context for us to understand their true meanings.

---

159. Butler, *Gender Trouble*, p. 14.

The issue is further complicated by the fact that even as the songs were being performed in a contemporary context, there was much at stake in determining who was speaking to whom in the songs. The circumstantial text for a pair of songs from the late fifth century best illustrates the sort of "gender trouble" involved. As the story goes, Zhu Shuoxian 朱碩仙 was a famous singer of "Wu sheng" songs in the Southern Qi court. Once, Emperor Wu of the Qi went to the Zhongshan Mountain and paid a visit to the tomb of Lady He, one of his favorite consorts. The emperor commanded Zhu Shuoxian to improvise a song on the occasion, and Zhu offered the following:

一憶所歡時	Whenever I miss my sweetie,
緣山破芿荏	I climb the mountain, breaking through the wild thickets.
山神感儂意	The mountain god is so moved by my love—
盤石銳鋒動	even the craggy rocks are shaken up.

The emperor was visibly vexed. "What impudence!" he reportedly said, "This lowborn person is mocking me!" Seeing the emperor's displeasure, another singer, Zhu Zishang 朱子尚, sang a different song:

暧暧日欲冥	Darkly, oh darkly, the sun is about to set;
歡騎立踟躅	my sweetie's steed is lingering on.
太陽猶尚可	The sun is still quite bright—
且願停須臾	I wish you will stay for a while.

The emperor was greatly pleased, and both singers were handsomely rewarded.[160]

An emperor has a right to be capricious. Nevertheless, one is tempted to ask what in the two songs could have triggered such drastically different responses. The answer is to be found in the identity of the speaker. In the first song, the singer is evidently speaking in the voice of the emperor, portrayed in this case as an infatuated lover. The second song, however, is from Lady He's point of view, as her spirit

160. Guo Maoqian, *Yuefu shiji* 46.671; *Quan Qi shi* 6.1475. Xiao Yi (*Jinlouzi* 2.66) recorded a different version of this story. He gave the name of the singer as Chen Shang 陳尚 with no mention of Zhu Shuoxian. The gifts presented to the singer were 30,000 cash and twenty bolts of silk. Xiao Yi also referred to Chen Shang's song as "a vulgar 'Wu sheng' tune" ("Wu sheng" *biqu* 吳聲鄙曲).

expresses a desire for the emperor to stay. Therefore, whereas in the first song the man is seen as chasing after the phantom of his beloved, the second song reverses the situation by rendering the woman a suppliant figure. The emperor is no longer at the mercy of either the mountain god or, for that matter, death, but can freely choose whether to gratify the woman's wish or not. Paradoxically, being the object of desire puts the man in the position of power.

To Emperor Wu of the Qi, the court singer was "a lowborn person" (*xiaoren* 小人), a resonant term in the hierarchical Southern Dynasties society. For a lowborn person to assume the voice of the emperor was at best impudent and at worst subversive. In this case, the authorial voice is closely associated with authority, and the issue of class, not that of gender, emerges in the foreground. To repair this disruption of social order, the second singer, Zhu Zishang, must speak to the emperor from a suppliant female position. In doing so, Zhu creates a pair of matching songs running parallel to each other, and restores the imperial dignity.

Just as it is misguided to take the pleading female voice in the second song as representative of the entire corpus of southern songs, it is likewise unfeasible to regard the southern songs as originating from common folk. Many tune titles and song lyrics in the "Wu sheng" and "Xi qu" sets were composed by nobles, princes, or even emperors; if some of these works were indeed folk songs, it must be remembered that they were performed for the pleasure of the Southern Dynasties elite as well as preserved by them.[161] It would be much more productive, therefore, to explore the symbolic significance of these songs as "feminine," since they occupied the peripheral position of "popular/vulgar" music (*suyue* 俗樂) as opposed to the normative, elegant music (*yayue* 雅樂), and because they were, and still are, taken to represent southern culture. If the feminine may be predicated as a marginal position in a cultural and social structure, then the songs certainly constitute a distinct feminine space deployed for various purposes.[162] As Stephen Owen has said, "The

161. The set of songs under "Ziye sishi ge" 子夜四時歌, for instance, is characterized by highly elegant diction and allusions to the classical literary tradition. For a discussion of this phenomenon, see Cao Daoheng, "Tan nanchao yuefu min'ge" 談南朝樂府民歌 in idem, *Zhonggu wenxue*, pp. 298–99.

162. There was, for example, Xie Shang's "class cross-dressing" when he sat on a folding chair, playing the *pipa* and singing "The Song of the Great Road" on the

émigré elite needed the imagined cultural world of the southern commoner as much as they depended on them socially. This was a fantasy necessary to the constitution of their own cultural whole." The songs became what he described as "a theatre of plebeian culture," in which the culture of the local commoners was imagined to be more primitive, more "natural," more passionate and spontaneous.[163]

Indeed, the writing, performing, and enjoying of such songs were compelled by the same desire that prompted the southern aristocrats to write frontier poetry and play the role of macho military men. When some of the southern emperors and nobles set up marketplaces and shops in their parks,[164] it was not because the Southern Dynasties court was going through "vulgarization" or even "commercialization," but because imagining and playing out the social and cultural other was a way of constructing and confirming their own cultural identity.

CODA

The binary structure North/South was first formed in the Period of Disunion and still dominates Chinese cultural discourse, both on this period and on later periods. As we have seen, the binary opposition of North and South began as a political and geographical partition that was quickly transformed into a cultural division. Both southern and northern regimes consciously and actively engaged in the construction of their cultural images in opposition to their political rival and imagined cultural other. On one hand, the southern court, particularly during the long reign of Emperor Wu of the Liang, was dedicated to the

gate tower of a Buddhist monastery in the marketplace; no one in the marketplace recognized him as a high-ranking statesman. And ironically, Xie Shang's song is about the pleasures of going incognito; see Pei Qi, *Pei Qi yu lin*, p. 91. There was Wang Zhongxiong 王仲雄, Xie Tiao's brother-in-law, who sang the song, "Woe Is Me!" ("Ao'nong qu" 懊儂曲), in the presence of Emperor Ming of the Qi. The song embedded or was believed to embed the ruler-minister relation in the lover's discourse, putting Wang Zhongxiong the singer in the position of a woman speaking to her fickle lover; see *Nan Qi shu* 26.485; and *Nan shi* 45.1131.

163. Owen, "Gone South: Fantasies of the Eastern Jin Plebeian," unpublished paper, delivered at the Workshop on the Eastern Jin held at Harvard University on May 6, 2005.

164. See *Jin shu* 64.1734; *Song shu* 4.66; *Nan shi* 5.155.

establishment of cultural achievements (*wen* 文) as a strategy to set itself above its northern rival, often referred to as "barbarian" (*lu* 虜); on the other hand, the North argued its own position as the legitimate inheritor of Han Chinese civilization by cultivating learning in the Confucian classics and likewise regarded its southern opponents as "barbarians" (*yi* 夷).[165] After the unification of China under the Sui and Tang dynasties, the paradigm of southern culturalism/northern martialism (*wen* 文 vs. *wu* 武) promoted by the southern court was displaced into another pair of binary terms, pattern/substance (*wen* 文 vs. *zhi* 質). This pair of loaded concepts already had a long history. Whereas "substance" (*zhi*) was considered the fundamental term and the privileged basis for "pattern" (*wen*), the importance of *wen* nevertheless remained in the foreground, and it was fully recognized that "substance" without "pattern" ran the risk of being uncouth or, even worse, losing one's distinct identity.[166] The adoption of this particular binary framework placed Early Tang historians in a bind, resulting in an ambivalent attitude toward southern culture ("refined" or "decadent"), even as they identified the North with "substance."

In later times, the cultural images constructed and promoted during the Period of Disunion not only constituted part and parcel of the common perception of the North and South but contributed to the shaping of social reality. Images generated in writings became criteria for judgment and expectations in social life, which in turn determined behavior. Contrary to the claim that culture comes from nature and literary output reflects social reality, we should consider how, in more than one sense, nature is produced by culture. We need to think outside of the binary frameworks of North/South and nature/culture and examine how such pairs of terms came into being.

---

165. For northern studies of the Confucian classics, see Wu Xianning, *Beichao*, pp. 32–37. For a detailed discussion of the system of the National University of the Northern Wei, see Zhang Jinlong, "Bei Wei Taixue yu zhengzhi, wenhua" 北魏太學與政治、文化, in idem, *Bei Wei*, pp. 221–43.

166. The famous passage from the *Analects* 13.8 fully testifies to the ambivalence inherent in the attitude toward pattern and substance. Ji Zicheng once blurted, "All a gentleman needs is substance—what use does he have for pattern?" Zigong retorted, "Substance is as pattern, and pattern is as substance. [Without pattern,] the hide of a tiger or a leopard would be no different from that of a dog or a sheep."

CHAPTER EIGHT
Parting Ways

December 9, 548, was a day that Yu Xin would remember for the rest of his life. Hou Jing's rebel army had penetrated to the capital city Jiankang. Xiao Gang put Yu Xin, then thirty-five years old and the mayor of Jiankang, in charge of a thousand soldiers defending the Red Sparrow Pontoon Bridge to the south of the Palace City. Xiao Gang had ordered Yu Xin to sever the great pontoon, but Xiao Zhengde, Emperor Wu's nephew who was conspiring with Hou Jing, opposed the decision on the grounds that it would send the people of Jiankang into a panic. Unaware of Xiao Zhengde's collusion with the enemy, Xiao Gang took his advice, and Yu Xin just waited by the Qinhuai River with his soldiers.

As the Qinhuai River glistened in the cold December sun, Yu Xin was chewing on a stick of sugarcane, which, like the betel nut, was a favorite Southern snack, believed to "dispel irritability and alleviate hangovers."[1] A big fellow with a stout build, Yu Xin was no stereotypical "effeminate southerner" or man of letters.[2] Nor was he a stranger to warfare: in 542, when a rebellion broke out in Jiangzhou, he had discussed "river battles" with Xiao Yi, then the governor of Jiangzhou.[3] That rebellion was suppressed within two months, and Emperor Wu

1. *Zizhi tongjian* 161.4986.

2. Yu Xin's dynastic biography describes him as being "of a height of over six feet and having a waist of ten armfuls" (*Zhou shu* 41.733).

3. Yuwen You 宇文逌, "Preface to Yu Xin's Collection," *Quan hou Zhou wen* 4.3902.

reportedly praised Yu Xin for his military astuteness. Xiao Gang no doubt had faith in Yu Xin's ability to prevent Hou Jing from crossing the Qinhuai River; Yu Xin perhaps trusted himself no less.

As soon as Hou Jing's army appeared on the south shore, Yu Xin ordered his soldiers to sever the pontoon. They had scarcely cut away one of the floats when Hou Jing's men, wearing armor under their dark green robes, loomed into full view. At the sight of their iron masks, Yu Xin and his soldiers fell back to the Red Sparrow Gate. An arrow struck the gate pillar, and the sugarcane in Yu Xin's hand fell to the ground at the twang of bowstrings. At that point, he turned and fled, followed by his troops, and the defense collapsed.

The rest was history. With no defenders left on the north shore, a member of Xiao Zhengde's faction had the pontoon bridge reconnected; Hou Jing's army crossed the Qinhuai River effortlessly and joined forces with Xiao Zhengde. Xiao Zhengde's men had been clothed in crimson robes with green linings; they reversed their robes so that the lining faced out and completely merged with Hou Jing's warriors. They advanced to the Xuanyang Gate of the Palace City, meeting little resistance on the way. A five-month siege began, which was to end with the disintegration of the Liang empire and the ruin of the South.

After Jiankang fell, Yu Xin escaped to Jiangling and joined the entourage of Xiao Yi, who was crowned emperor in 553. In the early summer of 554, Yu Xin was sent to Chang'an, the capital of the Western Wei, as an envoy. Five months later, when Yu Xin was still in Chang'an, the Western Wei launched a massive attack on Jiangling. In early January 555, Xiao Yi was captured and killed. Yu Xin was detained in Chang'an and never again returned to the South.

Yu Xin and his father, Yu Jianwu, along with Xu Ling and his father, Xu Chi, were the most prominent members of Xiao Gang's literary salon, so much so that the Palace Style was also known as the "Xu-Yu Style" (*Xu Yu ti* 徐庾體). Both Xu Chi and Yu Jianwu passed away not long after the Hou Jing Rebellion, but the fates of Xu Ling and Yu Xin mirrored each other like a finely wrought parallel couplet. Xu Ling had been sent on a diplomatic mission to the Eastern Wei in the summer of 548 shortly before the Hou Jing Rebellion broke out. Xu Ling was trapped in the North, unable to go back. In 550, the Eastern Wei emperor abdicated in favor of the powerful minister Gao Yang 高洋 (529–

59), who founded the Northern Qi. Xu Ling was detained, and his repeated pleas to be allowed to return to the South fell on deaf ears. In a letter he wrote to Yang Yin 楊愔, vice director of the Imperial Secretariat, Xu Ling described his state of mind as being so beset with sorrows that "I no longer know whether I am still alive or dead."[4] Yang Yin, however, never responded. It was not until 555 that Xu Ling was finally sent back to the South. He would serve the Chen for sixteen years before he passed away in 581.

Thus Xu Ling and Yu Xin, scions of the two grand literary families of the Liang, went separate ways: one managed to go home to the war-torn and devastated South; the other remained in the North. Back in the southern court, Xu Ling was revered as the grand literary master, but it was Yu Xin, in the North, who made the most of his life situation. A complicated man, Yu Xin seemed constantly tortured by guilt, shame, regret, and homesickness. These sentiments are reflected not only in his monumental *fu* "The Lament for the South" ("Ai Jiangnan fu" 哀江南賦)[5] but also in his shorter prose pieces and poetry as well. Perhaps because he spent the rest of his life in the North, Yu Xin had the time and distance to reflect on the fall of the Liang, and he saw the impending doom of the South more clearly than did Xu Ling. Dying within two years of each other, neither lived to see the unification of China under Emperor Wen of the Sui, but if Xu Ling might still have entertained the illusion of a lasting southern court, Yu Xin finally brought himself face to face with the northerners—this time without the iron masks or a river between them. He came to recognize their ruthlessness, their determination, their untiring persistence. The last datable poem in his corpus, written in the last months of his life, envisioned the end of the South in no sentimental terms. It may be fashionable to state that how one tells one's life matters more than how one lives it, but the statement is not true, because how one lives one's life ultimately informs the way in which one tells it.

4. *Quan Chen wen* 7.3440.

5. Since this *fu* has been amply analyzed by scholars, I do not discuss it in this chapter. The *fu* has been translated in its entirety and analyzed in detail by William Graham in *The Lament for the South*. See also Xu Donghai, *Yu Xin shengping*, pp. 209–37.

Yu Xin was not alone in giving account of his age. The Chen dynasty, an afterglow of the refined southern court, which had reached the zenith of its glory in the Liang, barely lasted thirty years. After its fall in 589, the emperor, members of the royal family, and all court officials were taken to the North in a procession reportedly extending five hundred miles.[6] Many of the Chen courtiers had begun their careers in the Liang; although they had managed to escape dislocation following the Hou Jing Rebellion, in the end they, too, fell prey to the northern conquerors. This chapter is devoted to the aftermath of the Hou Jing Rebellion, and examines a number of mid- to late sixth-century poems and prose pieces by southern writers responding to the devastation of the South. Driven by a need to make sense of what had happened to the state, the family, and the self, these texts articulate a framework for the destruction of the old social and cultural order. Viewed against this background, Yu Xin's poetry stands out, not just because its emotional force is intensified by a remarkable formal control, but also because its poignancy is deepened by the author's reflective distance across time and space.

SURVIVORS' ACCOUNTS I: YAN ZHITUI

After the fall of Jiangling in January 555, Yin Buhai, one of the few courtiers allowed to see Xiao Gang during his last days, lost his mother in the chaos. It was bitterly cold at the time, raining snow and sleet, and the streets were filled with frozen corpses. Yin Buhai searched for his mother throughout the city, turning over every corpse in the ditches. He found her body after seven days.[7]

At Jiangling, many people died at the swords of the Western Wei soldiers. Three brothers who begged to die in place of one another ended up being killed together.[8] A large number of survivors, about a hundred thousand in all, were taken to the North as captives. Because of the inclement weather and the harsh treatment, two or three out of every ten died on the way; the rest, except for top-level officials and

6. *Nan shi* 10.309.
7. *Chen shu* 32.424–25.
8. Yan Zhitui, *Yanshi jiaxun* 1.44–45.

their families, became slaves. Only a few were eventually released and made their way back to the South.[9] Among the captives, there was a gentry member surnamed Liu who had lost his family during the Hou Jing Rebellion and only had his youngest son with him. He carried the child in his arms and was unable to advance quickly because of the muddy road. Liang Yuanhui 梁元暉, a northern general, forced him to abandon the child. Liu begged to no avail: the soldiers snatched the boy from Liu's arms and tossed him in the snow. As he was being beaten and dragged away, Liu looked back at every step, crying his son's name and weeping. Because of the physical abuse, fatigue, and sorrow, he died in a few days.

This anecdote was recorded by a fellow captive, Yan Zhitui, a well-known writer and scholar, in a work entitled *The Record of the Wronged Souls* (*Yuanhun zhi* 冤魂志).[10] A devout Buddhist who believed in divine justice, Yan Zhitui added that Liu's ghost appeared to Liang Yuanhui every night and asked for his son's life. Liang fell ill and died a year later.

Yan Zhitui's account, intended to illustrate the principle of retribution, inadvertently preserves a local detail—the tragedy of one man and his little boy—from a vast canvas of brutality and devastation. Yan Zhitui himself and his family were among the captives traveling the hard winter road north. But he was one of the lucky ones: his literary talent was appreciated by the Western Wei general Li Mu 李穆 (510–86), who dispatched him to Hongnong 弘農 (in He'nan province) to be a secretary to his brother Li Yuan 李遠 (d. 557), the Duke of Yangping.

In 555, the Northern Qi sent Xiao Yuanming 蕭淵明, a nephew of Emperor Wu of the Liang, to the South to be the new emperor of the Liang, along with many detained Liang courtiers, including Xu Ling. Yan Zhitui heard the news and thought that he might have a better chance to return to the South if he were in the Northern Qi. Taking advantage of the rise of the Yellow River, he gathered his family onto a

9. Yuwen Tai, the Western Wei minister, freed several thousand gentry members from slavery in response to a remonstrance from the Liang official Yu Jicai 庾季才 (d. 603) (*Bei shi* 89.2948).

10. Also known as *The Record of Retribution for Grievances* (*Huanyuan zhi* 還冤志 or *Huanyuan ji* 還冤記); see Yan Zhitui, *Yuanhun zhi*, pp. 88–89; and Wang Guoliang, *Yan Zhitui*, p. 115.

boat and escaped to the Qi capital, an act of courage much admired by his contemporaries.[11]

Unfortunately, not long after Yan Zhitui arrived at the Qi court, the political situation in the South underwent a radical change: Chen Baxian 陳霸先 (503–59) killed Wang Sengbian, the general who supported Xiao Yuanming, deposed Xiao, and established Xiao Yi's teenage son as the new emperor. Liang and Qi were soon at war. In the winter of 557, Chen Baxian dethroned the Liang emperor and founded the Chen dynasty. The stateless Yan Zhitui stayed on at the Northern Qi. Twenty years later, on the eve of the fall of the Northern Qi, Yan Zhitui advised the Qi emperor Gao Wei 高緯 (r. 565–76) to flee to the South. His advice, although favored by the emperor, was opposed by the ministers, all of whom were Northerners. Yan Zhitui missed his last chance to return to the South. After the Qi fell, he was taken as a prisoner of war to Chang'an and given a minor post several years later.

A middle-aged man now, Yan Zhitui composed a *fu* entitled "Contemplating My Life" ("Guan wo sheng fu" 觀我生賦), giving a detailed biographical account of his life during this chaotic age.[12] To highlight the autobiographical aspect, Yan Zhitui annotated the *fu* with comments in unrhymed prose, explaining references and furnishing details. These annotations recount the author's personal circumstances and explain larger historical events. Yan Zhitui was clearly writing with an audience in mind—people who he feared might not be acquainted with what had transpired in the South: northerners perhaps, but also future generations.

11. A poem entitled "Passing Dizhu at Night on My Way from Zhou to Qi" ("Cong Zhou ru Qi ye du Dizhu" 從周入齊夜度砥柱) and attributed to Yan Zhitui in *Wenyuan yinghua* supposedly relates the poet's night-time escape. However, this poem appears as an anonymous piece in the Tang work *Wenjing mifu lun* 文鏡秘府論, and, under a different title, is attributed to the monk Huimu 惠慕 in the Ming anthology *Gushi ji*. See *Quan bei Qi shi* 2.2283.

12. Toward the end of this *fu*, Yan Zhitui lamented that "I have one life, but went through three transformations," referring to Hou Jing's assassination of Emperor Jianwen, the death of Emperor Yuan, and the fall of the Northern Qi. We thus know that the *fu* must have been written before the new dynasty he was serving, Zhou, was overthrown in 581. For the text of the *fu*, see *Bei Qi shu* 45.618–26; and *Quan Sui wen* 13.4088–90. For an English translation of this *fu*, see Dien, *Pei ch'i shu*.

Like Yu Xin in "The Lament for the South," Yan Zhitui tried to rationalize the fall of the Liang by enumerating what Emperor Wu had done wrong. This was done in the spirit not of angry finger-pointing but of regret and disappointment. Beneath the polished surface of the courtier's stylized prose, one hears the painful question: "How could all this have happened?" In the following translation, Yan Zhitui's annotations are enclosed in parentheses.

養傅翼之飛虎	Nurturing a flying tiger endowed with wings,

(梁武帝納亡人侯景, 授其命, 遂爲反叛之基. Emperor Wu of the Liang accepted the refugee Hou Jing and gave him command, which became the foundation of Hou's later rebellion.)

子貪心之野狼	the emperor adopted a greedy wild wolf as his son.

(武帝初養臨川王子正德爲嗣, 生昭明後, 正德還本, 特封臨賀王. 猶懷怨恨. 徑叛入北而還, 積財養士, 每有異志也. At first, Emperor Wu adopted Zhengde, the son of the Prince of Linchuan, as his heir; after Crown Prince Zhaoming was born, Zhengde was returned to his natal family and received the special title of the Prince of Linhe. Feeling resentful, Zhengde once defected to the North. After he came back to the South, he accumulated wealth and gathered soldiers, always harboring evil intentions.)

初召禍於絶域	He first courted disaster from a faraway region,
重發釁於蕭牆	then again brewed trouble within palace walls.

(正德求征侯景, 至新林, 叛投景, 景立爲主, 以攻臺城. Zhengde asked the emperor's permission to fight against Hou Jing. When he arrived at Xinlin with his forces, he defected to Hou Jing, who then set up Zhengde as his master and attacked the Palace City.)

雖萬里而作限	Although separated by the river of ten thousand miles,
聊一葦而可航	one reed leaf helped them cross over.
指金闕以長鎩	Aiming at the golden tower with their long spears,
向王路而蹶張	the rebels opened their strong bows on the imperial boulevard.
勤王踰於十萬	Over a hundred thousand troops came to the rescue,
曾不解其搤吭	but none of them could relieve the strangled throat.

嗟將相之骨鯁	How sad that those upright generals and ministers
皆屈體於犬羊	should all bend their knees to some dog and sheep.

(臺城陷, 援軍並問訊二宮, 致敬於侯景也. After the Palace City fell, the rescue armies all sent greetings to the emperor and the crown prince and paid their respects to Hou Jing.)

武皇忽以厭世	The Martial Emperor suddenly grew weary of the world,
白日黯而無光	the white sun was eclipsed and lost its brilliance.[13]
既饗國而五十	He had enjoyed the throne for fifty years—
何克終之弗康	how could the end have not come off well?
嗣君聽於巨猾	His successor submitted to the great evildoer,
每凜然而負芒	ever anxious and uneasy, as if with thorns on his back.
自東晉之違難	The Eastern Jin had sought a shelter from the catastrophe,
寓禮樂於江湘	and lodged the rites and music at the Yangzi and Xiang rivers.
迄此幾於三百	Since then, it had been almost three hundred years,
左衽浹於四方	while those wearing lapels on the left spread to all sides.[14]
詠苦胡而永歎	I chant the poem about suffering from the barbarian invasion, and heave long sighs;
吟微管而增傷	I recite Confucius' remark about Guan Zhong, which only increases my grievances.[15]

Yan Zhitui went on to describe the fall of Jiangling:

13. "Growing weary of the world" is a euphemism for death.

14. "Wearing lapels on the left" was a way of "barbarian" dress.

15. The poems about suffering from the "barbarians" refer to the two poems attributed to the Eastern Han woman writer Cai Yan 蔡琰 (*Hou Han shu* 84.2801). Confucius said of Guan Zhong, the prime minister of the state of Qi: "If not for Guan Zhong, all of us would have spread our hair and bared our left shoulders by now" (*Lunyu zhushu* 14.127). To spread one's hair and bare one's left shoulder was a non-Han custom; Confucius implied that the Chinese heartland would have fallen under "barbarian" rule if not for Guan Zhong.

民百萬而囚虜	A hundred thousand people became captives;
書千兩而煙煬	a thousand carts of books turned into ashes.
溥天之下	Under the vast sky,
斯文盡喪	this culture of ours had come to total ruin.

(北於墳籍少於江東三分之一，梁氏剝亂，散逸湮亡，唯孝元鳩合，通重十餘萬，史籍以來，未之有也．兵敗悉焚之，海內無復書府. The North has less than one-third the number of books that once existed in the South. During the fall of the Liang, the southern book collection became scattered and lost. Emperor Yuan gathered the remaining books, which amounted to over a hundred thousand scrolls: an unprecedented number in history. He had all of them burned after his defeat; so there is no more library within the four seas now.)

憐嬰孺之何辜	I pitied the innocent young children,
矜老疾之無狀	and was moved by the cruelties shown to the elderly and sick:
奪諸懷而棄草	babies were snatched from parents' arms and abandoned in grass;
踣於塗而受掠	the elderly and sick fell on the road, their possessions robbed.

Yan Zhitui's narration of the fall of the Northern Qi in the second half of his *fu* does not come close to this passionate lament over the destruction of "this culture of ours." To him, the fall of the Liang seemed to equal the devastation of civilization itself, and he felt its impact in a much more cosmic way than he did the collapse of one dynasty:

若乃五牛之旌	As for the banners carried by the five oxen,
九龍之路	the imperial carriage drawn by the nine dragons,[16]
土圭測影	the gnomon template used for measuring the sun's shadow,
璿璣審度	the astrolabe for calculating the stars—
或先聖之規模	they were either fashioned and designed by the former sages,
乍前王之典故	or created as canons and precedents by the previous kings,

16. The five oxen drawing the imperial carriage carried banners on their backs (*Jin shu* 25.754). The nine dragons refer to the legendary steeds acquired by Emperor Wen of the Han (*Xijing zaji*, p. 52). Wang Liqi believed that the nine dragons were patterns decorating the imperial carriage (Yan Zhitui, *Yanshi jiaxun*, p. 610).

與神鼎而偕沒	but now have all but vanished with the divine cauldrons,
切仙弓之永慕	evoking our eternal longing for the immortal bow.[17]

Yan Zhitui also related how he had felt upon first setting foot on northern soil. What he had read about only in history books suddenly became real in front of his eyes, and yet, only the geography remained the same as before, not the "customs and teachings" of the ancient times. We see in this a gap opening between book knowledge and empirical experience. Although the author "knew better," he was unable to reconcile the North he saw with the source of orthodox Chinese civilization he had read about.

爾其十六國之風教	The customs and teachings of the sixteen states,
七十代之州壤	the land passed down by the seventy generations,[18]
接耳目而不通	though separated from the ear and eye in the past,
詠圖書而可想	were well imagined in the course of my readings.
何黎氓之匪昔	Yet how different are their people today—
徒山川之猶曩	only mountains and rivers still retain their former looks.

Yan Zhitui claimed that he had contemplated becoming a recluse but was afraid that it might get him in trouble; yet, even as he served the Wei, he yearned for his homeland.

每結思於江湖	I often thought of withdrawing to the rivers and lakes,
將取弊於羅網	but I feared ending up in traps and nets.

17. The "divine cauldrons," the symbol of imperial power, disappeared in chaotic times and reappeared in an age of peace and prosperity. The "immortal bow" belonged to the Yellow Emperor; it dropped to the ground when he ascended to Heaven, and those of his courtiers who were unable to follow him clasped the bow and wept over his departure (*Shi ji* 12.465, 28.1394).

18. "The sixteen states" were enfeoffed to the sons of King Wen of Zhou (*Chunqiu Zuozhuan zhengyi* 15.255). The phrase "seventy generations" alludes to the descendents of the legendary Shennong emperor (*Taiping yulan* 78.494). The Qing commentator Lu Wenchao 盧文弨 (1717–96) believed that it refers to seventy-two ancient lords who held the *fengshan* ritual at Mount Tai (Yan Zhitui, *Yanshi jiaxun*, p. 611). Both the sixteen states and seventy generations indicate the ancient Han civilization of the Chinese heartland.

聆代竹之哀怨	I listened to the sad music of the Dai,
聽出塞之嘹朗	or the clear, sharp sound of "Going Out of the Frontier."
對皓月以增愁	Facing the bright moon added to my sorrow;
臨芳樽而無賞	even sweet wine failed to bring relief.

In *Family Instructions of the Yan Clan*, Yan Zhitui explained in greater detail why he and his brothers decided to serve in the North:

My brothers and I would not have entered public service except for the decline of the fortunes of our clan. We have few powerful clansmen and few close relatives. Wandering off to a foreign land, we were no longer protected by our family heritage. I feared that you might be degraded to becoming servants and grooms and bring shame to our ancestors. For this reason, we risked the shame of advancing in the society and did not dare to let our family status fall. Besides, the political culture in the North is so stern and harsh that no one there goes into reclusion.[19]

計吾兄弟不當仕進, 但以門衰, 骨肉單弱, 五服之內傍無一人, 播越他鄉, 無復資廕, 使汝等沈淪廝役, 以為先世之恥, 故靦冒人間, 不敢墜失. 兼以北方政教嚴切, 全無隱退者故也.

What this passage reveals is that one's responsibility to family and clan transcend that to the state. Although this would be frowned upon by austere Confucian moralists in later times, it reflected the social reality of the Six Dynasties.

Toward the end of the *fu*, Yan Zhitui reflected somberly on his experiences. Instead of complaining about cosmic or divine injustice, he was full of self-reproach—a final attempt to make sense of what had happened. In a way, it would have been much more comforting for Yan Zhitui and many other survivors of the Hou Jing Rebellion to believe that human error, rather than the will of Heaven, had caused all the misfortunes.

予一生而三化	This one life of mine has undergone three transformations,
備荼苦而蓼辛	filled with bitterness, sufferings, and hardships.

19. Yan Zhitui, *Yanshi jiaxun* 20.534. Yan Zhitui had two elder brothers: Yan Zhiyi 顏之儀 (523–91) and Yan Zhishan 顏之善.

(在揚都值侯景殺簡文而篡位，於江陵逢孝元覆滅，至此而三爲亡國之人. When I was in Jiankang, Hou Jing assassinated Emperor Jianwen and usurped the throne; then, at Jiangling, Emperor Yuan was defeated and killed; by now [i.e., the fall of the Northern Qi] I have been a man of the fallen state thrice.)

鳥焚林而鎩翮	A bird of the burned forest has its wings clipped,
魚奪水而暴鱗	a fish taken out of water exposes its scales in the sun.
嗟宇宙之遼曠	I lament and feel ashamed that in such a vast universe,
愧無所而容身	there should be no place to lodge this body of mine.
. . . .	
向使潛於草茅之下	Suppose that I had hidden myself under a thatched hut,
甘爲畎畝之人	content to be a man plowing the fields,
無讀書而學劍	having never had studied books or practiced swordsmanship,
莫抵掌以膏身	nor clasped my hands and pursued self-interest,
委明珠而樂賤	but rather let this bright pearl be abandoned and take pleasure in debasement,
辭白璧以安貧	turning down the offer of the white jade and remaining complacent in poverty,
堯舜不能榮其素樸	then even [sage emperors like] Yao and Shun could not have brought glory to my simplicity,
桀紂無以汙其清塵	nor could [tyrants like] Jie and Zhou stain my purity;
此窮何由而至	and where would this adversity have come from,
茲辱安所自臻	and how could I have suffered from humiliation?
而今而後	Thus, from now on,
不敢怨天而泣麟也	I shall not complain of heaven or weep for the captured unicorn.[20]

Despite his claim that he would have been better off had he been an ignorant man, Yan Zhitui exhorted his sons to study. The author was compelled by the need to give an explanation for his sufferings in an autobiographical account contemplating his life, but in giving

20. Confucius had wept at the capture of a unicorn, an auspicious beast appearing only in times of peace and prosperity (*Chunqiu Gongyang* 28.356).

instructions to his sons, he had to fulfill the role of a responsible father, who wants the best for his children.

The Family Instructions of the Yan Clan may have been written over a long period of time, from the 570s when Yan Zhitui was serving the Northern Qi till after the Sui unified China in 589.[21] In this work, Yan Zhitui laid out a series of rules of conduct for his descendents. The man emerging from these lucid, well-written essays provides a fascinating character study. In many ways, Yan Zhitui represented the "average" Southern Dynasties courtier: he was a learned scholar and a talented writer, and yet he lacked the flair of a Yu Xin or a Xu Ling; admitting that he had no interest in the abstract discourse of *Laozi* and *Zhuangzi*, he manifested a down-to-earth, pragmatic bent in his philosophy of life.[22] The topics discussed in this work range from children's education to household management, remarriage, scholarship, literary writing, maintenance of good health, mastery of miscellaneous arts such as calligraphy and painting, and various ethical codes. The work demonstrates a sixth-century Chinese man's vision of the world and shows a displaced southerner's self-conscious comparison of the South and the North. More important, Yan Zhitui's *Family Instructions* is characterized by his quest for an honorable *and* safe way of life in a dangerous age and by his painful attempt to establish an enduring value system when everything familiar had crumbled and things were in constant flux.

Going from the South to the North, Yan Zhitui witnessed the degradation of many members of the southern elite and the rise of those who had been commoners: a change in social order that would have been unimaginable for a southerner if not for the devastation of the South. "In these chaotic times," he said, "I have seen many captives. Those who could read the *Analects* and *The Classic of Filial Piety*, despite being [descended from] low-born men for a hundred generations, became instructors; those who knew nothing about reading or writing, even though descended from a noble lineage of a thousand years, had no

21. Yan Zhitui said, "I was recently appointed a gentleman of the palace gate [i.e., one of the imperial secretaries]"; this occurred in 572. In the last chapter, he mentioned the unification of China, which took place in 589 (*Yanshi jiaxun* 13.319, 20.534).

22. Ibid., 1.179.

choice but to plow the fields or herd horses." This led him to counsel his sons to acquire useful skills, and "of valuable skills easy to acquire, nothing compares to reading books."[23]

Yan Zhitui's grandfather had starved himself to death to protest Emperor Wu of the Liang's deposing of the last Qi emperor,[24] but Yan Zhitui expressed a rather different attitude toward the issue of loyalty to the state:

> Not surrendering to monarchs with different surnames—this is the integrity of a Boyi and a Shuqi; whoever one serves is one's ruler—this demonstrates the righteousness of a Yi Yin and a Jizi. Ever since the Spring and Autumn period, there have been many [cases of] families becoming split and going into exile, and of states being conquered and destroyed: there is no constant relationship between a prince and his subject.
>
> 不屈二姓, 夷、齊之節也; 何事非君, 伊、箕之義也. 自春秋已來, 家有奔亡, 國有吞滅, 君臣固無常分矣.

Such a statement might be offensive to a neo-Confucian philosopher and even sound jarring to an orthodox-minded modern scholar; it nevertheless reveals the state of mind of many a Six Dynasties courtier. Yan Zhitui went on to advise his sons to avoid denouncing one's former ruler if they ever found themselves in such a situation: "However, when a gentleman breaks off friendship with a person, he does not speak ill of the latter. If one has to bend one's knees and serve another, he should not change his thoughts [about his former ruler] even if [his former state] no longer exists."[25] This, Yan Zhitui decided, was the best one could do. Again, this might fall short of neo-Confucian moral standards, but Yan Zhitui was setting rules for his children on pragmatic grounds. There is nothing pretentious and high-sounding here, for the twelve-chapter work is more than a patriarch's "family instructions"—it is a survival guide.

Yet, when he was penning this guide, Yan Zhitui could not have foreseen the fate of his second son Minchu 愍楚.[26] Minchu was a well-

23. *Yanshi jiaxun* 8.153.

24. *Liang shu* 44.727.

25. Yan Zhitui, *Yanshi jiaxun* 9.240.

26. Minchu's name literally means "feeling sad for the Chu," Chu being a reference to Jiangling, a city in the ancient Chu region.

known scholar at the Sui court and authored a work on pronunciation.[27] In the chaos ensuing from the collapse of the Sui in 617, he was captured by a ruthless rebel general, Zhu Can 朱粲 (d. 621). At first, Zhu Can treated Minchu with respect, but as his army ran out of food, Zhu Can ordered his troops to make food of people. Minchu and his family were eaten by Zhu Can's soldiers.[28]

SURVIVORS' ACCOUNTS II: SHEN JIONG

Yan Minchu's sad end was a painful irony. Had Yan Zhitui known what would befall Minchu, he might have regretted asking his sons to pursue studies instead of plowing in the fields. A decision by one of Yan Zhitui's fellow captives to conceal his literary talents reportedly helped his speedy return to the South. This lucky captive was Shen Jiong, a well-known Liang writer.

After the fall of Jiankang, one of Hou Jing's generals, Song Zixian 宋子仙, tried to make Shen Jiong his secretary; Shen Jiong refused and was preparing to die, but Song Zixian pardoned him at the last minute. Later, Wang Sengbian defeated Song Zixian and awarded 100,000 cash to the soldier who found Shen Jiong. Thereafter Shen Jiong drafted all Wang Sengbian's correspondence, proclamations, and documents. After Xiao Gang's death, Wang Sengbian urged Xiao Yi to take the throne, and Shen Jiong composed all of Wang's memorials. *The History of the Chen* praised Shen Jiong's writings as "unmatched at the time."[29]

Shen Jiong's wife and son had been killed by Hou Jing, and his younger brother had escaped with their mother. Xiao Yi felt sorry for Shen Jiong's family tragedy and made him the County Marquis of Yuanxiang. An admirer of Shen Jiong's writings, Xiao Yi asked Wang Sengbian to send Shen Jiong and another minister, Kong Huan 孔奐 (514–83), to his court at Jiangling. A reluctant Wang Sengbian wrote to the emperor several times trying to retain the pair, but a handwritten

27. *Jiu Tang shu* 46.1985.
28. Ibid., 56.2275.
29. *Chen shu* 19.253.

note from the emperor saying, "I'd like to borrow the two gentlemen, Shen and Kong, from you," finally persuaded him.[30]

Shen Jiong was among the captives taken to the North after Jiangling fell. While there, "he was afraid that the Wei court might detain him because of his literary talents; so he kept his door closed and swept the courtyard, making no social calls and receiving no visitors. If he ever wrote anything, he would destroy the draft afterward instead of allowing it to spread."[31] However, a sacrificial essay addressing the spirit of Emperor Wu of the Han, composed by Shen Jiong at the site of the Tongtian Terrace (two hundred miles from Chang'an), is included in Shen Jiong's biography in *The History of the Chen*. In this essay, Shen Jiong expressed his desire to return to his homeland. That same night, the story goes, Shen Jiong dreamed of arriving at a heavily guarded imperial palace. He made his plea again and heard a voice telling him, "We have no regret letting you go; you will be back in no time." Indeed, in a matter of days, he was released, along with some other Liang courtiers. Shen Jiong arrived at Jiankang in 556 and served the Chen for four years before he passed away at the age of fifty-eight.

On the way back to Jiankang, Shen Jiong passed through Yingzhou (in modern Hubei), and wrote a poem entitled "Gazing at the City of Yingzhou" ("Wang Yingzhou cheng" 望郢州城).[32]

魂兮何處返	Where did my soul just come back from?
非死復非仙	Neither from death nor the immortal land.
坐柯如昨日	Sitting with the ax seems like yesterday,
合石未淹年	and the rocks were closed off hardly a year ago;[33]

30. *Chen shu* 21.284.

31. Ibid., 19.254.

32. *Quan Chen shi* 1.2445.

33. According to *Dongyang ji* 東陽記 by Zheng Jizhi 鄭緝之 (fl. late fourth c.), a Jin woodcutter named Wang Zhi encountered four lads playing zithers and singing in the mountain. Wang Zhi leaned on his ax and listened to them. After a while, he got up to leave, only to discover the wooden handle of his ax had rotten away. He went home and found that dozens of years had elapsed while he was in the mountain, and all his relatives and friends had died (*Taiping yulan* 762.3517). I was unable to locate the allusion to the closing of the rocks, but the Song scholar Wu Zeng (*Nenggaizhai manlu*, 3: 3057–58) recorded a local legend about Yingzhou, which tells how an old soldier followed three Daoists into a cave and was given a

歷陽頓成浦	and yet Liyang has suddenly become a lake,[34]
東海果爲田	and the Eastern Sea has truly turned into land.
空憶扶風詠	In vain I think of the ballad of Fufeng;
誰見峴山傳	who has seen the steles of the Mount Xian?[35]
世變才良改	The world is altered, so are talented, good men;
時移民物遷	as time goes on, people and things change.
悲哉孫驃騎	How sad was Cavalry General Sun—
悠悠哭彼天	shedding tears over that distant Heaven.

Cavalry General Sun is Sun Xiu 孫秀 (d. 302), the grandson of a brother of the Wu emperor Sun Quan 孫權 (r. 222–52). Suspected of conspiracy by the last Wu emperor, Sun Hao 孫皓 (r. 264–80), Sun Xiu defected to the Western Jin in 270 and was made a general of the cavalry. When the Wu was conquered by the Western Jin ten years later, Sun Xiu claimed illness, refusing to go to court and offer the Jin emperor his congratulations. He said in tears, "In the past, the General of Suppressing the Rebels [i.e., Sun Ce 孫策] founded the dynasty in his twenties, when he was a mere commandant. The last emperor owned the entire South, and yet he abandoned it. Our ancestral temples and tombs will lie in ruins. 'Thou distant azure Heaven, / what sort of man is he?' "[36] The citation is from the poem "Shuli" 黍離, in *The Classic of Poetry*, which was interpreted by traditional commentators as a lament for the devastation of the old Zhou capital.[37]

The first couplet of Shen Jiong's poem echoes the *Chuci* song "Summoning the Soul" ("Zhaohun" 招魂), which ends with the line: "Come back, O soul! I grieve over the Southland" 魂兮歸來哀江南.

stone that turned to gold. After the old soldier left the cave, the rocks behind him closed off, and there was no way to go back in.

34. This is an allusion to *Huainanzi* 2.76: "The city of Liyang turned into a lake overnight."

35. The "Song of Fufeng" ("Fufeng ge" 扶風歌), written by Liu Kun 劉琨 (271–318), sings of the sorrows of being away from home (*Quan Jin shi* 11.849–50). The Jin general Du Yu 杜預 (222–84), when stationed at Xiangyang, had two steles made on which he carved a record of his accomplishments. He sank one into the river beneath Mount Wan and set the other up on the top of Mount Xian, saying: "How do we know that in the future the river will not turn into a hill and the hill into a valley?" (*Jin shu* 34.1031).

36. *Wu shu* 51.1213.

37. *Maoshi zhengyi* 4.147.

The second and third couplets highlight the poet's sense of disorientation, caused by the quick succession of earth-shattering changes. At a time like this, the past is best preserved in individual memory, not by stele inscriptions. The poem ends with the citation of a citation, which not only describes the ruined state of Yingzhou but also foreshadows the fall of the South.

Shen Jiong wrote another poem as he was approaching Jiankang. Square Hill is an extinct volcano a few miles away from the capital; the Qinhuai River winds around it.

長安還至方山愴然自傷

Feeling Sad upon Arriving at Square Hill on
My Way Back from Chang'an[38]

秦軍坑趙卒	The army of Qin buried the Zhao soldiers alive:
遂有一人生	there was one person who survived.[39]
雖還舊鄉里	Though I have returned to my homeland,
危心曾未平	this fearful heart is not yet at peace.
淮源比桐柏	The source of the Huai River is comparable with Mount Tongbo;
方山似削成	Square Hill seems to have been chiseled.[40]
猶疑屯虜騎	Still apprehensive about the barbarian cavalry,
尚畏値胡兵	I am ever wary of encountering nomad troops.
空村餘拱木	Only large trees remain in the empty village;
廢邑有頹城	deserted towns are left with crumpling city walls.
舊識莫不盡	None of my old friends can be found;
新知皆異名	all my new acquaintances have different names.
百年三萬日	A hundred years, thirty thousand days in all,
處處此傷情	this heart-wrenching sorrow in each and every one of them.

This poem presents a complex psychological portrait of a survivor, who feels a range of emotions upon returning alive to his homeland. The Huai River in the third couplet is another name for the Qinhuai River: both are familiar landmarks in the environs of Jiankang. This Huai

38. *Quan Chen shi* 1.2445.

39. The Qin general Bai Qi 白起 reportedly buried 400,000 Zhao soldiers alive at Changping (*Shi ji* 43.1826).

40. "The Mount Taihua is [as if] chiseled: square on all four sides" (*Shanhai jing* 2.22).

River evokes the other, much larger Huai River, whose source is Mount Tongbo on the border between modern He'nan and Hubei. Shen Jiong might also be thinking of the Mount Tongbo in his home area—like Shen Yue, Shen Jiong was from Wukang county in the Wuxing commandery (in modern Zhejiang), where Mount Tongbo was a famous Daoist site celebrated for its beautiful, numinous scenery; in fact, it was considered nothing short of a Daoist paradise.[41] Square Hill, on the other hand, reminds the poet of Mount Taihua, better known as Mount Hua, another famous mountain with a spiritual, mystical aura and

41. This was the site of a famous Daoist temple known as the Golden Court Temple (Jinting guan 金庭館). Shen Yue wrote a stele inscription for it ("Tongbo shan Jinting guan bei" 桐柏山金庭館碑) in 501 (*Quan Liang wen* 31.3130). The composition date is usually given as 498; here I follow Zhao Mingcheng's 趙明誠 (1081–1129) *Jin shi lu* 金石錄 2.9a, and Chen Si's 陳思 (fl. 1259) *Baoke congbian* 寶刻叢編 13.4a–b. Some scholars are skeptical about the authenticity of the attribution, since the prose account preceding the tetrasyllabic inscription is a first-person narrative of the head Daoist priest at the Golden Court Temple, which contradicts Shen Yue's biography; some scholars also identify (mistakenly) Mount Tongbo as the one in He'nan. For a discussion of this point, see Lin Jiali, *Shen Yue yanjiu*, pp. 52–54. I believe that Shen Yue wrote the prose account on behalf of the head Daoist priest (i.e., in the priest's voice). The line "I, with my lack of talent, am the first to undertake this task" 越以不才，首膺斯任, remains the same in several Northern and Southern Song sources, but becomes "I, Yue, with my lack of talent" (約以不才) in Ming sources, which may have emended the earlier *yue* 越 to Yue 約 to fit Shen Yue's name; see Kong Yanzhi, *Kuaiji duoyong zongji* 16.12a; Shi Su et al., *Jiatai Kuaiji zhi* 20.7077; and Gao Sisun, *Shan lu* 5.7228. *Yue* 越 could be the Daoist priest's first name; it could also function as a particle with no real meaning. The Golden Court Temple also features in Shen Yue's poem entitled "Enjoying the Temple of the Daoist Priest Shen" 遊沈道士館 (*Quan Liang shi* 6.1637). The title of this poem is alternatively given as "Enjoying the Daoist Priest Shen's Golden Court Temple" 遊沈道士金庭館 in Kong Yanzhi, *Kuaiji* 9.16a–b; Shi Su et al., *Jiatai* 20.7090; and Gao Sisun, *Shan lu* 6A.7232. One of the Tang *Wen xuan* commentators identifies the Daoist priest in this poem as a certain Shen Gong 沈恭 (Xiao Tong, *Liuchen zhu* 22.30a). Mather (*The Age of Eternal Brilliance*, 1: 266) identifies Shen Gong as a recluse recorded in *Nan Qi shu* 54.944, but the recluse in *Nan Qi shu* was named Shen Yanzhi 沈儼之, with a courtesy name Shigong 士恭. In any case, given the Wuxing Shen clan's strong Daoist connections and the proximity of Mount Tongbo to Wuxing, it would be reasonable to speculate that the Daoist priest or priests residing at the Golden Court Temple at Mount Tongbo were distantly related to the Shen clan of Wuxing, to which both Shen Yue and Shen Jiong belonged.

regarded as the haunt of immortals. But once again the poet seems to be intending a double entendre: east of Jiankang there is a mountain of the same name, Mount Hua; the Qinhuai River flows from it, and it was the site of a Daoist temple in the fifth and sixth centuries.[42] A descendent of the Shen clan of Wuxing traditionally known for their Daoist beliefs, Shen Jiong might well be making use of the Daoist associations of Mount Tongbo and Mount Hua to express his ecstatic feelings upon coming home: the very landscape of the Jiankang area looks like a paradise to him. In fact, he articulated this sentiment quite explicitly in his "*Fu* on the Returned Soul" ("Guihun fu" 歸魂賦), saying that upon entering the Liang court, he felts as if he had obtained paradise: "How could immortality be worth pursuing?/*This* feels like wearing a robe of cloud and a gown of rainbows" 何神僊之足學,/此即雲衣而虹裳也.[43]

But in the poem on Square Hill, Shen Jiong's ecstasy upon homecoming is mixed with lingering fear, as the southern landscape still seems full of perils in the eyes of the former captive:

猶疑屯虜騎	Still apprehensive about the barbarian cavalry,
尚畏値胡兵	I am ever wary of encountering nomad troops.

The feeling of entering an immortal paradise also gives way to a sense of horror as the poet opens his eyes to the reality of a land devastated by war and famine:

空村餘拱木	Only large trees remain in the empty village;
廢邑有頹城	deserted towns are left with crumpling city walls.

Even sadder is the change that had occurred in his social circle:

舊識莫不盡	None of my old friends can be found;
新知皆異名	all my new acquaintances have different names.

By this point, the poet's initial happiness has all but turned into a profound sense of melancholy and loss:

42. Again Shen Yue has left a poem about the Daoist temple at Mount Hua: "In a Temple on Mount Hua, Working for Merit on Behalf of the State and [Royal] Family" ("Huashan guan wei guojia ying gongde" 華山館爲國家營功德) (*Quan Liang shi* 7.1660; for a translation, see Mather, *The Age of Eternal Brilliance*, 1: 268).

43. *Quan Chen wen* 14.3478.

百年三萬日	A hundred years, thirty thousand days in all,
處處此傷情	this heart-wrenching sorrow in each and every one of them.

Shen Jiong's "*Fu* on the Returned Soul," of which only parts have survived, portrays in greater detail his experiences during and after the Hou Jing Rebellion.[44] Particularly remarkable is his description of the landscape on his forced march to the North after the fall of Jiangling. Of all the places he passed through, Yongzhou, the old power base of the Liang, touched the author most deeply. This was where Emperor Wu of the Liang had begun his "imperial enterprise," and where Xiao Gang, here referred to as Taizong, won several military victories over the Northern Wei while he served as governor.

余既長于克民	I grew up during Emperor Wu's reign;
覺何從而掩泗	wiping away tears, where could I follow him?
淯水兮深且清	The Wei River is deep and clear,
宛水兮澄復明	the Wan River, limpid and sparkling.
昔南陽之穰縣	In the past, this was the Rang county of Nanyang,
今百雉之都城	today it is a city with walls of a hundred feet.
我太宗之威武	Oh, the martial prowess of our Emperor Taizong!
遏宛淯而陳兵	He deployed his troops and stopped the rivers from flowing.
百萬之虜	A hundred thousand barbarian soldiers
俄成魚鱉	were reduced to fish and turtles in an instant;
千仞之阜	The peaks of a thousand meters
倏似滄瀛	suddenly turned into the great seas.
雖德刑成于赦服	Though his virtuous castigation was accomplished by forgiving his conquered foes,
故蠻狄震乎雄名	the barbarian people were nevertheless awestruck by his heroic name.

As his journey went on, Shen Jiong was impressed by the northern landscape, previously known only through books. It is interesting to observe that he noticed and recorded only those places whose names already existed in earlier texts. In many ways, this was a travel back in time, as the author kept discovering the landmarks of Qin and Han

44. Ibid., 14.3477–78.

dynasties, and his book knowledge was being checked against, and verified by, empirical experience.

訪軹道之長組	I looked for the long rope of Zhidao,
拾藍田之璵璠	and picked up jade from Lantian.[45]
無故老之可訊	I found no elderly people to ask about the sites,
並膴膴之空原	just empty plains, overgrown with vegetation.
登未央之北闕	Climbing onto the northern watchtower of the Weiyang Palace,
望長樂之基趾	I looked toward the foundation of Changle.[46]
伊太后之所居	At the place where the Empress Dowager used to live,
築旗亭而成市	now a banner-pavilion was built, a marketplace formed.[47]
槐路鬱以三條	The three lanes were still lined up with locust trees;[48]
方塗坦而九軌	large, flat roads nine carriage-gauge wide.[49]
覿阡陌之遺蹤	I observed the remaining traces of the former streets—
實不乖乎前史	indeed they fit the descriptions of the histories.

Sometimes, past and present became intertwined:

傍直城而北轉	One followed the Zhicheng Gate and turned to the north,
臨橫門而左趨	or bearing left after emerging from Hengmen;[50]

45. Zhidao was the place where the last Qin emperor tied a rope around his neck (as a sign of surrender and captivity) and presented the imperial seal to Liu Bang, who was to found the Han dynasty (*Shi ji* 6.275). Lantian, in the vicinity of Chang'an, was famous for producing fine jade.

46. Weiyang and Changle were names of Han palaces. The Changle Palace was where Liu Bang's principal wife, Empress Lü, once lived.

47. A "banner-pavilion" was a construction built in the marketplace, with a banner or banners set up on it.

48. Each of the avenues running from Chang'an's gates had three lanes. The middle lane was used by the emperor only; the left for traffic entering the city and the right for traffic leaving the city. This is mentioned in Ban Gu's "*Fu* on the Western Capital" ("Xidu fu" 西都賦) (*Quan hou Han wen* 24.602; see Knechtges, trans., *Wen xuan*, 1: 105).

49. According to *The Rites of Zhou*, the streets of the capital city were supposed to be able to accommodate nine carriages traveling abreast (*Zhouli zhushu* 41.642).

50. Both Zhicheng and Hengmen were names of city gates in Chang'an.

南則董卓之塢	to the south was the citadel of Dong Zhuo;
北則符堅所居	in the north, where Fu Jian had lived.
即二賊之墟壘	The castles of these two thieves
爲彼主之庭除	became the very courtyard of that ruler of theirs.

Dong Zhuo was the general who seized the last Han emperor, sacked Luoyang, and re-established Chang'an as the capital in 189; Fu Jian, the northern emperor who lost the battle of the Fei River to the Eastern Jin army. Shen Jiong's patent distaste for the Western Wei in his reference to "that ruler of theirs" contrasts sharply with the way in which he alluded to the Liang emperors. With an ingenious twist, he managed to separate Chang'an the capital of the Han dynasty from the Chang'an of such illegitimate insurgents as Dong Zhuo and Fu Jian and identified contemporary Chang'an, the capital of the Western Wei, with the latter.

The last part of Shen Jiong's *fu* describes his homesickness and his trip home. The detailed and sometimes painfully labored portrayal of the landscape on his way to Chang'an is now replaced with a rapid succession of the names of places he passes through, suggesting lightheartedness as well as eagerness.

Shen Jiong's *fu* does not deal with human encounters during the author's captivity. Chang'an is a city of sites and ruins. As the author moved about, he attempted to assuage his own sense of displacement by displacing Chang'an into the past, because that was the only Chang'an he knew—a city that for most southerners had existed only in texts.

SURVIVORS' ACCOUNTS III: YU XIN

Not many classical Chinese poets have stirred such opposite reactions as Yu Xin did. Du Fu, arguably the greatest Chinese poet, deeply admired Yu Xin, but the Qing historian Quan Zuwang 全祖望 (1705–55) claimed that Yu Xin was simply a shameless man, and Lu Tongqun, a modern scholar who wrote a critical biography of Yu Xin, tried hard to see the worst motives behind many of Yu Xin's poems and prose pieces, even interpreting "The Lament for the South" as a veiled request for office in the northern court.[51] What has troubled people about Yu Xin is perhaps not the fact that he served the enemy of his state, but that he kept vocalizing his feelings of guilt and shame in a body of extraordinary writings—extraordinary in no small measure due to the pain and regret expressed in them. Sometimes one cannot help wondering if Yu Xin preferred to stay in the north just so that he could write about it.

According to *The History of the Zhou* (*Zhou shu* 周書) and *The Northern History*, after Chen and Zhou renewed diplomatic relations, the Chen court asked for the release of Wang Bao, Yu Xin, and a dozen others, but Emperor Wu of the Zhou "begrudged [Wang and Yu] and did not send them back, only releasing people such as Wang Ke and Yin Buhai."[52] Wang Ke had, in fact, been released in 555, before Emperor Wu of the Zhou was enthroned, and Yin Buhai returned to the South as late as 575. Emperor Xuan of the Chen (r. 569–82) did make an attempt to get Wang Bao and Yu Xin back in the early 570s; his request was immediately blocked by the Zhou emissary.[53]

There is, of course, no reason to doubt that Yu Xin was forcibly detained by the northerners, especially when he first arrived in the Western Wei court as the Liang envoy, but it would also be perfectly understandable if Yu Xin did not want to return to the South after a number of years, for he had nothing to go back to. Whereas Xu Ling's family remained in the South for the entire time of his detainment, Yu Xin's family was brought to Chang'an after the fall of Jiangling; soon after that, the Liang collapsed—which had not yet happened when Xu Ling and Shen Jiong returned to the South. Moreover, Yu Xin was no common Liang courtier: he had been close to the top members of the Liang royal house. Without Xiao Gang and Xiao Yi, the South would never have been the same for Yu Xin, not to mention the fact that the Liang had been overthrown by the Chen. With no family and state to beckon Yu Xin, it was as he said in the twentieth poem of the "In Imitation of Linked Pearls" ("Ni lianzhu" 擬連珠) series:[54]

51. Lu Tongqun, *Yu Xin*, pp. 160–61, 356.

52. *Zhou shu* 41.734; *Bei shi* 83.2794.

53. *Zhou shu* 39.703.

54. *Quan hou Zhou wen* 11.3938–39. "Linked Pearls" is a genre. For a discussion of Yu Xin's "Ni lianzhu," see Wang Cicheng 王次澄, "Yu Xin 'Ni lianzhu' xilun" 庾信擬連珠析論, in *Disanjie*, pp. 127–64.

楚塹既塡	When the moats of Chu are flattened out,
遊魚無託	the roaming fish has no place to lodge itself;
吳宮已火	the palace of Wu has been burned down,
歸燕何巢	so where should the returning swallow nest?

And again in the last piece of the same series:

烏江艤檝	As the boat moored on the Wu River,
知無路可歸	one already knew that there was no way to return;
白雁抱書	the white wild goose clutched a letter,
定無家可寄	and yet, there was no family to carry it to.

Xiang Yu was defeated by the founding emperor of the Han and chased to the shores of the Wu River. Turning down the village head's invitation to cross the river in the only boat available, Xiang Yu said:

It is heaven's will to destroy me; what good would it do to cross the river? Besides, in the old days I have crossed the river and marched west with eight thousand sons from the land east of the river; now if I return alone, even if their fathers and elder brothers take pity on me and make me their king, how could I bear to face them? Even if they don't say a word, wouldn't I feel ashamed?[55]

天之亡我，我何渡爲？且籍與江東子弟八千人渡江而西，今無一人還，縱江東父兄憐而王我，我何面目見之？縱彼不言，籍獨不愧於心乎？

Xiang Yu committed suicide by the Wu River. The wild goose alludes to Su Wu 蘇武 (ca. 143–60 B.C.), the loyal Han envoy detained by the Xiongnu. When a Han emissary demanded Su Wu's return, the Xiongnu court claimed that Su Wu had died. The Han emissary countered the lie by making up a story about the Han emperor shooting down a wild goose with a letter attached to its feet—a letter written by none other than Su Wu. The Xiongnu court gasped, and Su Wu was henceforth released.[56]

Yu Xin was neither Xiang Yu nor Su Wu, although he shared Xiang Yu's shame and Su Wu's homesickness. *The History of the Zhou* makes a famous comment on Yu Xin: despite the prominent status he achieved

55. *Shi ji* 7.336.
56. *Han shu* 54.2466.

in the North, "he always harbored thoughts of homeland."[57] And yet, Yu Xin's homesickness was of a rather different quality than Su Wu's: to Yu Xin, the South was not merely a physical space, it was also a land of the past. What Yu Xin had lost and lamented was more than his state, even more than his prince; it was an entire era, a way of life. Such a sense of loss is more profound than that brought about by separation from one's native land.

Yu Xin's twenty-seven poems in the series "In Imitation of 'Singing of My Feelings'" have often been cited as best illustrating his "hopeless regret for what has happened, hopeless frustration with the present,"[58] and yet, despite their fame, these poems are not Yu Xin at his finest or his most characteristic. They are passionate outbursts uttered with too much agitation and disquietude to translate into successful poetry. The reader may be touched by the poet's anguish, but it is hard to suppress the feeling that the poetry suffers somewhat from absence of restraint.[59] Indeed, Yu Xin was at his best only when he maintained his cultivated grace, framing the intensity of his emotions with that elegant discretion characteristic of a Liang court poet.

The following poem is entitled "Encountering Snow When I Was in the Suburbs" ("Jiaoxing zhixue" 郊行值雪).[60]

風雲俱慘慘	Wind and clouds—both harsh and bleak;
原野共茫茫	the plain, a blurred expanse.
雪花開六出	The snow flowers blossom in six petals;
冰珠映九光	pearls of ice shining like the lamp of nine lights.
還如驅玉馬	It is like driving a horse of jade,
暫似獵銀獐	and, for a while, hunting silver roebucks.
陣雲全不動	Formation of clouds remain entirely still;
寒山無物香	nothing in the cold mountain is fragrant.

57. *Zhou shu* 41.734.

58. See Graham and Hightower, "Yu Hsin's 'Songs of Sorrow,'" p. 6. The entire set has been translated into English by Graham and Hightower.

59. The early Qing critic Wang Fuzhi (*Gushi pingxuan*, p. 290) offered an interesting analysis of this poem series. He singled out No. 21 for praise. "As for the rest, it is not that they do not have coherence of thought, but on the whole they are too scattered and cannot be discussed as poetry."

60. *Quan bei Zhou shi* 3.2381.

薛君一狐白	The one white fox fur coat of the Lord of Xue;
唐侯兩驌驦	a pair of frosty chargers of the Marquis of Tang.
寒關日欲暮	At the cold pass, it is about to turn dark;
披雪上河梁	braving the snow, I walk onto the river bridge.

The poem opens with a desolate scene only to subvert it in the next couplet: suddenly, snow flakes become spring flowers, and ice glistens like pearls in the lamplight. The "harsh and bleak" wintry landscape is transformed into an enchanted world of light and delight, and the magic continues as the poet feels, with almost a childlike joy, that he is riding on a horse of jade, chasing after a silver roebuck.

The phrase "for a while" (*zan* 暫) in the sixth line is crucial, since it reveals the temporary nature of the magical ambiance. As the roebuck runs away, it shakes off whatever snow had clung to its back. The spell is broken. Clouds, like formations of soldiers, remain ominous still and bode more snow, but the snowflakes no longer seem like flowers, for, after all, they are cold and give off no sweet scent. The poet pauses on the snowy plain: both sky and mountain are cold, immense, and immobile, pressing down on him with a primitive, threatening force. It is at this moment that he thinks of something warm—

薛君一狐白	The one white fox fur coat of the Lord of Xue;

The Lord of Xue, better known as the Lord of Mengchang 孟嘗君, was a prince of Qi who lived in the third century B.C. and was detained in the state of Qin. The Qin king imprisoned the Lord of Mengchang and planned to have him killed. The Lord of Mengchang sent one of his retainers to the king's favorite palace lady and asked for her help; the lady requested the Lord of Mengchang's white fox fur coat in return. Unfortunately since the fur coat had been presented to the king as a gift, another retainer had to steal the coat from the palace storage and give it to the lady. The lady, as promised, put in a good word for the Lord of Mengchang, who was released and went back to his home state.[61]

The snow, the cold, and perhaps the silver roebuck being hunted make the poet yearn for the white fox fur coat, but he is no Lord of Mengchang. After all, that legendary white fox fur coat was one of a kind: "It was worth a thousand in gold," the historian said, "and was

61. *Shi ji* 75.2354.

absolutely peerless in the whole world. After presenting it to King Zhao of Qin, [the Lord of Mengchang] had not another fur coat left." The poet longs for the fur coat in vain—after all, the Lord of Mengchang had used it up—there is no going home.

But the poet's imagination has been stimulated, and he keeps on dreaming in the snow:

唐侯兩驌驦	a pair of frosty chargers of the Marquis of Tang.

In a *Zuozhuan* story, the Marquis of Tang had a pair of frost-colored horses. Zichang 子常, the powerful minister of Chu, coveted them, but the marquis refused to give them to him. Thereupon Zichang had the marquis detained in Chu for three years. Finally, the people of Tang stole the horses and presented them to Zichang, who then let the marquis go.[62] Again, the poet is not as fortunate as the marquis.

The horse of jade and roebuck of silver in the real world are bound up with legendary animals in the poet's imagination. These beautiful white animals, as soon as they are conjured up by the poet's word magic, are negated by a reminder of their uniqueness, which makes them unobtainable. They disappear into the snow-covered plains.

The last couplet echoes the opening lines of a poem attributed to Li Ling 李陵 (d. 74 B.C.), the Han general who was captured by the Xiongnu army, surrendered, and remained in the Xiongnu court for the rest of his life: "Hand in hand, we walk onto the river bridge: / it is dusk now—where is the wanderer going?" 攜手上河梁,/遊子暮何之? The poem was supposedly addressed to Su Wu right before his return home.[63] Yu Xin's couplet changes these lines slightly, but significantly:

寒關日欲暮	At the cold pass, it is about to turn dark;
披雪上河梁	braving the snow, I walk onto the river bridge.

In a world that is growing dark, the poet steps onto the river bridge, alone. The question put forth in the original poem, "Where is the

62. *Chunqiu Zuozhuan zhengyi* 54.944.

63. The attribution is almost certainly spurious, but what mattered was that people believed in it. Xiao Tong's *Wen xuan* (29.1353) contains a series of poems by Li Ling and Su Wu, including the one to which Yu Xin alludes. See also *Quan Han shi* 12.337.

wanderer going?" is merely implied here, but becomes more poignant in its repression.

Yu Xin's forlornness is expressed just as effectively in a lavishly depicted spring scene, as in the following poem, "Seeing People Going on a Spring Outing" ("Jian youchun ren" 見遊春人).[64]

長安有狹斜	Chang'an has narrow lanes,
金穴盛豪華	the Golden Grotto abounds in luxuries.[65]
連盃勸上馬	Before mounting the steed, one is urged to drink many a cup;
亂果擲行車	fruits are tossed at random toward the moving carriages.[66]
深紅蓮子豔	Dark red: the allure of the lotus seed;
細錦鳳凰花	fine brocade with the pattern of phoenix.
那能學噀酒	How could I learn spewing the wine?
無處似欒巴	There is no way to imitate Luan Ba.

The poet appears in this poem as an observer: he looks on at the flirtatious drinking and fruit tossing, neither joining in the jovial crowd nor sharing their lightheartedness. The second couplet uses several verbs to describe a series of actions; in contrast, the third couplet is striking in its sudden stillness, since it is composed of only nouns and adjectives. A sensuous, yet enigmatic detail: lotus seeds are, so far as we know, never "dark red," and we can only assume that the color reminds the poet of something as "alluring" (*yan* 艷) as lotus seeds, *lianzi*, which puns with "loving you." The next line confirms the impression that the poet is talking about fabric—a fine brocade imprinted with a phoenix pattern. Perhaps the clothing worn by one of the people on the spring outing has caught the poet's eye. The abrupt transfer from the hustle and bustle of the merrymaking crowd to a still close-up of a textile creates an

64. *Quan bei Zhou shi* 4.2386–87.

65. "Chang'an has narrow lanes" is a line from a *yuefu* poem (*Quan Han shi* 9.266). "Golden Grotto" was used to refer to the house of Guo Kuang 郭況, the brother of Empress Guo in the Eastern Han (*Han shu* 10.403).

66. This alludes to the Pan Yue story. Pan Yue, the Western Jin poet, was a good-looking man. When he went out, women always tossed fruit into his carriage to show their admiration of him, and he would come home with a carriage full of fruit (*Jin shu* 55.1507).

unexpected effect; in this moment of focused vision, the poet's mood seemingly also experiences a shift.

As in most of Yu Xin's poems, the reader's familiarity with the allusions ultimately provides the key to understanding the message of the poem. The last couplet refers to the story of the Eastern Han official Luan Ba 欒巴. At the grand court gathering on New Year's Day, Luan Ba, a Daoist adept, was the last to arrive. At the banquet, instead of drinking the liquor, he spewed it out toward the southwest. He was subsequently charged with showing disrespect. Luan Ba defended himself by saying that his hometown, Chengdu, was having a fire, and so he spat out the liquor in order to make it rain and put out the fire. The emperor sent an emissary to Chengdu, and it turned out that on New Year's Day a fire had indeed broken out in the Chengdu marketplace, but at dinnertime a rain came from the northeast and extinguished the fire. Moreover, the rain smelled like liquor. Luan Ba was exonerated. Later, during a great thunderstorm, Luan Ba disappeared into the fog. Not long after, it turned out that he had returned to Chengdu on that day and taken leave of his relatives and friends, saying that he would not come back again. The historical Luan Ba committed suicide while imprisoned for a memorial he wrote to Emperor Ling of the Han (r. A.D. 168–89), but according to Daoist legend Luan Ba ascended to heaven as an immortal.[67]

In the last couplet of his poem, Yu Xin claimed that he could not imitate Luan Ba: there was a lot of drinking going on around him, and he was probably drinking too, but he had no magic power to make rain with his liquor and assuage the sufferings of his homeland, nor could he disappear, return to his hometown, and bid farewell to his relatives and friends. The emotional force of the ending couplet very much depends, however, on the build-up in the preceding lines. The cheerful, flirtatious crowd enjoying a spring outing reminds the poet of something unseasonal and out-of-reach: lotus seeds, which with all their amorous implications evoke the sensuous allure of the South. The third couplet is the pivotal point: the poem would be dominated by the giddiness of the crowd without these lines, which exemplify the focused attention on a

67. *Hou Han shu* 57.1842; Ge Hong, *Shenxian zhuan*, p. 285. For an English translation of Luan Ba's hagiography, see Campany, trans., *To Live*, pp. 252–54.

detail characteristic of Liang court poetry. The textile provides a still center for the poet's longing as well as a figure for his pain, whose intensity is woven into beautiful patterns, controlled and balanced.

Yu Xin's two sons and one of his daughters died during the Hou Jing Rebellion. After he went to the North, a grown-up daughter and a grandson also passed away. He wrote "*Fu* on a Grief-stricken Heart" ("Shangxin fu" 傷心賦) to mourn their untimely deaths. But even in the most melancholy life, there can be some small measure of joy. When a son was born to him in his middle age, he wrote an unusually jubilant poem, "Getting Drunk upon a Happy Occasion" ("Youxi zhizui" 有喜致醉), in celebration. Fortunately for Yu Xin, he never lived to see what was to happen to his son.

Sometimes pleasure had a bittersweet flavor to it, as he caught sight of a popular southern fruit in the North.

忽見檳榔
Upon Suddenly Seeing the Betel Nut[68]

綠房千子熟	Green pod with a thousand ripe nuts;
紫穗百花開	on a purple stalk, a hundred flowers blossoming.
莫言行萬里	Don't tell me that you have traveled ten thousand miles—
曾經相識來	once upon a time, we were acquaintances.

The use of a numeral in each line, except for the last, creates an unexpected twist and effectively builds up the momentum of the ending.

Sometimes the poet imagined that he was still in the South, as in "Gazing at the Wei River" ("Wang Wei shui" 望渭水).[69]

樹似新亭岸	Trees are like those on the shore of Xinting;
沙如龍尾灣	sand seems to be of the Dragon Tail Harbor.
猶言今暝浦	One still thinks that at today's darkening ford,
應有落帆還	there should be a returning boat with dropped sails.

Both Xinting and Dragon Tail Harbor were southern place-names. Xinting, a suburb of Jiankang, had a special association. A *Shishuo xinyu* story relates that in the early fourth century northern refugees would

68. *Quan bei Zhou shi* 4.2408.
69. Ibid., 4.2406.

often gather on the grass at Xinting, drinking and feasting. On one occasion, Zhou Yi remarked with a sigh: "The scenery is not dissimilar [from that of the old capital], and yet the mountains and rivers are different!"[70] Everyone present was moved to tears, except for Wang Dao, who changed his countenance and said: "We should strive together to work for the royal house and recover the sacred prefectures; what is the point of sitting here and facing one another like the captives of Chu?"[71] Yu Xin's quatrain is an ironic reversal of the *Shishuo xinyu* story: the poet is in the North now, and the scenery took on a likeness of the southern landscape in his eyes.

The last two lines of the quatrain allude to a poem by the Liang poet He Xun, "Sleeping Over at the Southern Isle Ford" ("Su Nanzhou pu" 宿南洲浦).[72] This poem describes the traveler's hardship and homesickness, ending with the statement: "I sit up at night, with tears flowing;/on this evening, I have a particular longing for my hometown." The second couplet of He Xun's poem inspired Yu Xin's lines:

解纜及朝風	We untied the boat in time for the morning breeze,
落帆依瞑浦	and dropped sails at the darkening ford.

Imagining that he will see a returning boat with dropped sails "at today's darkening ford," Yu Xin not only fuses North and South but also past and present.[73]

From time to time, southern envoys visited Chang'an; among them were Yu Xin's old friends Zhou Hongzheng and Xu Bao 徐報.[74] Yu Xin must have asked one of them to take this poem to Xu Ling:

70. The Western Jin capital of Luoyang resembled Jiankang geographically in that it was surrounded by mountains with rivers running through it; hence Zhou Yi's remark about the scenery being similar. But the names of the mountains and rivers were different.

71. Liu Yiqing, *Shishuo xinyu* 2.92.

72. *Quan Liang shi* 8.1691–92.

73. The third line of Yu Xin's quatrain has a textual variant: "One still thinks of chanting poetry at the darkening ford" 猶言吟瞑浦. This would evoke the earlier poet's presence in a more explicit manner.

74. According to Yan Zhitui's annotation to "*Fu* on Contemplating My Life," Xu Bao had participated in book collation along with Yu Xin when what was left of the Jiankang imperial library was transported to Jiangling. Since Xu Ling's eldest

故人倘思我	If my old friend ever misses me,
及此平生時	please do so while I am alive.
莫待山陽路	Don't wait till you are on the Shanyang road,
空聞吹笛悲	grieving to no avail over the flute melody.[75]

Xiang Xiu 向秀 (ca. 221–300), Ji Kang, and Lü An 呂安 (d. 262) were good friends when they lived in reclusion at Shanyang. Later, both Ji Kang and Lü An were executed by the powerful Sima clan, and Xiang Xiu was forced to enter public service. When passing through Shanyang on a business trip, he heard someone playing a flute and composed the famous "*Fu* on Remembering Old Friends" ("Sijiu fu" 思舊賦).[76]

It was hard for Yu Xin not to think of death. He was getting on in years, and, acknowledged as one of the best writers of his time, he was often asked to write tomb inscriptions or grave memoirs (*muzhiming* 墓誌銘) for high-status northern princes, generals, ministers, and their wives. These inscriptions are usually composed of two parts. The first part, in unrhymed prose, is the *zhi* and gives details on the identity, family background, and accomplishments of the deceased. The second part, in rhymed four-syllable lines, is the *ming*, and it praises the life of the deceased and expresses the grief of the living. Unlike epitaphs (*beiming* 碑銘), which were inscribed on a stone stele placed outside the grave, tomb inscriptions were buried with the dead.[77] In literary historical terms, the most significant thing about the tomb inscription is that only in the late fifth century did it begin to be treated as a literary genre and enter personal literary collections.[78] The tomb inscriptions composed by Yu Xin are well crafted, enriched with remarkable imagery.[79]

son, Xu Jian, like Xu Bao, also served as the director of the Treasury Bureau under Xiao Yi, Xu Bao and Xu Jian might very well be the same person (*Chen shu* 26.335). In fact, *Nan shi* 62.1525 gives another version of Xu Jian's name as Xu Bao.

75. *Quan bei Zhou shi* 4.2400.

76. *Quan Jin wen* 72.1876.

77. See Li Shibiao, *Wei Jin nanbeichao*, pp. 96–98.

78. According to the Qi minister Wang Jian, Yan Yanzhi composed a stele inscription for Wang Qiu 王球 (393–441) (*Nan Qi shu* 10.158). It is no longer extant. Emperor Xiaowu of the Song composed a tomb inscription for his favorite half-brother, the Prince of Jianping (*Song shu* 72.1680). This inscription is preserved (perhaps only partially) in *Yiwen leiju* 48.866. For the origin of the tomb inscription, see Cheng Zhangcan, "Muzhi qiyuan kao" 墓誌起源考, in idem, *Shixue*, pp. 1–12. Cheng believes the term *muzhi* was first used as a title in Yan Yanzhi's stele

Some of the tomb inscriptions were composed for southern detainees like himself, such as Xiao Tai 蕭太 (520–70, a nephew of Emperor Wu of the Liang), Liu Xia 柳遐 (501–72), and Wu Mingche 吳明徹 (513–80). The tomb inscription for Wu Mingche is worth particular mention. Wu Mingche was a famous Chen general who won many battles against the northerners but was finally defeated and sent to Chang'an as a captive in 578; he was also the general who had captured and executed Wang Lin 王琳, a Liang loyalist, in 573. Wang Lin was Yu Xin's friend, a gracious, fair-minded general beloved by civilians and soldiers alike.[80] Yu Xin's feelings toward Wu Mingche were understandably complicated. On one hand, Yu Xin related in blunt terms Wu Mingche's defeat by the Zhou army, not resorting to euphemism, apology, or excuse—"Conceited about his talent, showing off his aptitude, he took risks and overestimated his power";[81] on the other hand, he also empathized with the general's fall. Toward the end, the poet gave way to a moving lament, which goes beyond his usually more formal style in this genre and rings painfully personal.

壯志沈淪	His stalwart aspirations were shattered,
雄圖埋沒	his heroic plans, buried and gone.
西隴足抵	He stretched his feet in the western fields,
黄塵碎骨	his bones were crushed by yellow earth.
何處池臺	Where are those ponds and terraces he once roamed?
誰家風月	Which household now gets to enjoy the wind and moon?

inscription for Wang Qiu. This is very doubtful, for the earliest sources, in citing Wang Jian's remark, only refer to Yan's inscription as "stele inscription" (*shi zhi* 石誌), not *muzhi*. Moreover, quotations in premodern Chinese sources are not necessarily verbatim, indeed often are not.

79. The well-known modern Chinese writer Feiming 廢名 (1901–67; *Feiming wenji*, p. 191) once even said that no Chinese writer but Yu Xin could have produced the following lines: "The frost, imitating the willows, turns pale; / the moon follows the grave mound in becoming round" 霜隨柳白, / 月逐墳圓. The couplet is from "Zhou Piaoji da jiangjun kaifu Houmochen Daosheng muzhiming" 周驃騎大將軍開府侯莫陳道生墓誌銘 (*Quan hou Zhou wen* 9.3961).

80. A poem in Yu Xin's collection was addressed to Wang Lin (*Quan bei Zhou shi* 4.2401).

81. *Quan hou Zhou wen* 16.3962–63.

墳隧羈遠	The underground vault detains the one from afar;
營魂流寓	his innermost soul is lodged in a foreign land.
霸岸無封	No grave mound was built on the bank of Ba;
平陵不樹	nor were trees planted in the Pingling.
壯士之隴	The mausoleum of a stouthearted man,
將軍之墓	the resting place of a general—
何代何年	in what generation, during what year,
還成武庫	would it be ever turned into an armory again?[82]

Although Yu Xin did not live to see the conquest of the South, he most likely saw it coming. In 577 the Northern Qi capital fell to the Zhou; a grand victory over the Chen army and the capture of Wu Mingche took place in the following spring. The unification of China seemed imminent.[83]

The end was not to come quite so soon. In the summer of 578, Emperor Wu of the Zhou died; his son, Emperor Xuan 宣帝 (559–80), was a ruthless and senseless young man. He had always been apprehensive of his uncle, the astute and capable Prince of Qi, and the first thing he did after being enthroned was to have the prince strangled. He delegated more and more power to his father-in-law, Yang Jian, and commanded his surviving uncles, including the Prince of Teng and the Prince of Zhao, both generous patrons of Yu Xin, to leave the capital for their fiefdoms on June 30, 579. The Prince of Teng edited Yu Xin's literary writings into a collection in twenty scrolls and sent it to Yu Xin from his fiefdom. In a letter expressing his gratitude, Yu Xin revealed that he had not been in good health.[84]

82. Shulizi 樗里子 (d. 300 B.C.) was the younger brother of King Hui of Qin. Before he died, he predicted that in a hundred years imperial palaces would be erected on both sides of his tomb. During the Han dynasty, the Weiyang Palace was built to the west of his tomb, and the Changle Palace, to the east; the imperial armory was directly facing his tomb (*Shi ji* 71.2310).

83. The historian thus described Emperor Wu of the Zhou: "After the conquest of the Northern Qi, he planned to exploit the full potential of his army to overpower the Turks as well as subdue the South, so as to unify the entire world within a couple of years—such were his aspirations" (*Zhou shu* 6.107).

84. *Quan hou Zhou wen* 10.3933.

Some time that year or the next, Yu Xin decided to retire. Old age and deteriorating health were, however, not the only factors in his decision. A more important concern was probably with the state of the court. Emperor Xuan was a tyrant, and his mind was focused on trivial matters such as devising various titles for himself and his four empresses or building extravagant palaces and inventing elaborate dress codes. On April 1, 579, he ceded the throne to his young son and proclaimed himself "Emperor of Heavenly Beginning" (*Tianyuan huangdi* 天元皇帝).[85] As was customary, Yu Xin wrote a memorial congratulating the emperor on what he referred to as an "extraordinary affair."[86]

Yu Xin had lived through enough political coups by now to recognize that the Zhou ruling house was having serious problems. In September 579, he composed "Returning from Tongzhou" ("Tongzhou huan" 同州還).[87] This poem gives an account of one of Emperor Xuan's many trips to Tongzhou and conveys a strong sense of anxiety about the trouble brewing just underneath the flashy surface of the imperial outing:

赤岸繞新村	The Crimson Embankment winds around a new village,
青城臨綺門	the emerald city wall rises with its splendid gate.[88]

85. *Zhou shu* 7.119.

86. *Quan hou Zhou wen* 9.3928.

87. Tongzhou was the former place of residence of the Zhou royal family and the birthplace of Emperor Xuan. The Zhou emperors made frequent trips to Tongzhou. This poem has been dated to the year 580, because in the *Zhou shu* biography of Emperor Xuan, a passage about an outing to Tongzhou in 580 mentions "the Marsh of Crimson Embankment" (Chi'an ze 赤岸澤); see Lin Yi, *Yu Xin yanjiu*, p. 163. This trip lasted from April 5 till April 14 (*Zhou shu* 7.123). But Emperor Xuan would have passed by the Marsh of Crimson Embankment on every Tongzhou trip. He visited Tongzhou twice in 570: once from September 7 till September 19; once from December 14 till December 18. The phrasing in Yu Xin's poem corroborates the dating of this poem to September 579, both because of the reference to contemporary affairs and because autumn is the traditional hunting season.

88. The Emerald City Gate (Qingcheng men 青城門) was one of the city gates of Chang'an, also known as the Splendid Emerald Gate (Qingqi men 青綺門); see Li Daoyuan, *Shuijing zhushu* 19.1585. The gate's spontaneous collapse in 577 was considered a bad omen (*Bei shi* 10.369). *Sui shu* 22.632 claimed that it did not bode well for the crown prince (later Emperor Xuan), for emerald was the color of spring, and the crown prince's palace was usually referred to as the Spring Residence.

范雎新入相	Fan Ju was recently appointed the prime minister,
穰侯始出蕃	while the Marquis of Rang has just left for his fiefdom.
上林催獵響	In the Shanglin Park, the clamor of hunting;
河橋爭渡喧	people competing for crossing, noise on the river bridge.
竄雉飛橫澗	Fleeing pheasants fly across the stretching ravine;
藏狐入斷原	a fox in hiding enters the broken plain.
將軍高宴晚	The general's lofty banquet lasts late into the night,
來過青竹園	and he pays a visit to the park of emerald bamboos.

The Marquis of Rang was the maternal uncle of King Zhao of Qin. Fan Ju, newly appointed the prime minister, persuaded the king to reduce the power of the marquis, and in 271 B.C., the Marquis of Rang was sent away from the capital to his fiefdom. This couplet is generally understood as an allusion to Emperor Xuan's appointment of Yang Jian as one of the four prime ministers on February 12, 579, and his rustication of the princes to their fiefdoms a few months later. What deserves note is the subtext of this allusion. At the end of "The Biography of the Marquis of Rang" in *Shi ji*, the historian makes the following comments about the marquis: "He was the very reason why the state of Qin could expand its eastern territory and weaken the other states, so that the whole world bowed to Qin. When his status and wealth reached their zenith, one man gave the king some advice, and then the marquis was deprived of his power and eventually died of distress. [If this was what happened to someone as close to the king as the marquis,] how much more so for a minister serving in a foreign state?"[89] "A minister serving in a foreign state" was exactly how Yu Xin always regarded himself. The hunt, an intimate part of the elite life in the North, seems ominous against such a political background. As pheasants and foxes sought shelter, the poet was probably thinking of withdrawing from public life as well.

89. *Shi ji* 72.2329–30.

The last couplet of Yu Xin's poem refers to the Qi Park: the Qi Park in the old Shang capital of Zhaoge was famous for its bamboo groves. The Eastern Han general Kou Xun 寇恂 (d. 36) ordered his soldiers to cut down the bamboos in the park and had a million arrows made out of them for the purpose of defending the prefecture of He'nei against rebel troops.[90] With this hint at preparations for war, Yu Xin's poem ends on a menacing note. Indeed, despite all the palace intrigues, the Zhou never slowed its pace in attempting to unify the realm. In December 579, Zhou generals captured three Chen cities, including Guangling, which was right across the Yangzi River from Jiankang.[91] With the capture of these cities, all the land to the north of the Yangzi River was in northern hands.

It was perhaps in the early summer of 580 that Yu Xin wrote a poem in response to Yan Zhitui's brother Yan Zhiyi, "A Companion Piece for Grand Master Yan's 'Newly Cleared Skies'" ("Tong Yan dafu chuqing" 同顏大夫初晴).[92]

夕陽含水氣	Vapors over water consume evening's light,
反景照河隄	rays thrown back shine on the river's high banks.
濕花飛未遠	Sopping petals blow away, but not far,
陰雲斂尚低	shadowy clouds draw in, though still hanging low.
燕燥還爲石	Swallows dry up and again turn to stone,
龍殘更是泥	the dragon falls apart and once more is mud.[93]

90. *Hou Han shu* 16.621.

91. *Zhou shu* 7.121. Guangling was the capitol of South Yanzhou in the Liang, where Xiao Gang had served as governor from 510 to 513 (see Chapter 6).

92. *Quan bei Zhou shi* 3.2380; translation (modified) from Owen, ed. and trans., *An Anthology of Chinese Literature*, p. 330. Yan Zhiyi, who had been tutor to the crown prince, was made Grand Master after Emperor Xuan took the throne in 578. The season of the poem is clearly early summer. The poem hints at a drought before the rain and the ritual of praying for rain, which might refer to the drought that had led Emperor Xuan to issue an amnesty edict on May 23, 580, and to pray for rain three days later. It rained on that day (*Zhou shu* 7.123–24).

93. According to a legend, the stone swallows of Lingling turned into real swallows when it rained and then became stone again after the rain stopped. Dragons made of clay were used in sacrifices for rain.

香泉酌冷澗	A sweet-smelling spring pours a chilly torrent,
小艇釣蓮溪	a small skiff fishes in a brook of lotuses.
但使心齊物	If only the mind could take all things as equal—
何愁物不齊	why feel distress that things are not equal at all?

There might be a touch of irony directed at the ritual of praying for rain in the sixth line: if the poem was indeed written in the summer of 580, Yu Xin is discreetly mocking the young emperor's supplications for rain on behalf of the people he hardly cared about. The metamorphoses of swallow into rock and dragon into clay are nevertheless wonderful illustrations of the last couplet, which echoes Zhuangzi's argument that all things, good or bad, beautiful or ugly, are on the same level. The poet seems to be suggesting to Yan Zhiyi to go with the flow; and yet, the advice about tolerance and acceptance is shadowed by the question: "Why feel distress that things are not equal at all?" In reality, things are "not equal," and this cannot but affect a person's equanimity.

On June 22, 580, the young Emperor Xuan died. Power fell completely into the hands of Yang Jian. The Prince of Zhao and the Prince of Teng were killed on charges of conspiring against Yang Jian. In the following spring, Yang Jian forced the abdication of the child emperor. He assumed the throne himself and founded the Sui dynasty.

A few months later, the Sui emperor launched a massive military campaign against the Chen, appointing Gao Jiong 高熲 as the commander in chief. Yu Xin's friend Liu Zhen 劉臻 (d. 598) was made Gao Jiong's secretary.[94] Liu Zhen, like Yu Xin, had served under Xiao Yi, and was taken to the North after the fall of Jiangling. Before embarking on the journey, he exchanged poetry with Yu Xin, who composed a quatrain, "In Reply to Director Liu Zhen" ("He Liu Yitong Zhen" 和劉儀同臻). This was the last known poem written by Yu Xin.

94. Liu Zhen's father, Liu Xian, was among the group of literary men known as "those who passed the Dragon Gate" in the early sixth century (see Chapter 3). Liu Zhen himself was an expert in the studies of the *Han shu* and *Hou Han shu* (*Bei shi* 83.2809).

南登廣陵岸	To the south I climbed the banks of Guangling,
回首落星城	and turned my head to gaze on the Shooting Star Fortress:
不言臨舊浦	who would have thought of facing the former shore again
烽火照江明	only to see beacon fires illuminating the river?[95]

In this quatrain of twenty characters are two place-names: Guangling and the Shooting Star Fortress. The Shooting Star Fortress was to the west of Jiankang; Guangling was north of the Yangzi River and had been taken over by the Zhou army in 579. Yu Xin had never participated in any of the campaigns; his description of Guangling and the Shooting Star Fortress was imagined from his friend's perspective.

The first two lines are directly taken from Wang Can's well-known poem "Seven Sorrows" ("Qi ai shi" 七哀詩). In 192, during the chaos of a civil war, Wang Can was forced to flee Chang'an and went to the South. On his way, he turned back and looked at the once-prosperous metropolis for the last time:

南登霸陵岸	To the south I climbed the slope of Ba Mound
回首望長安	and turned my head to gaze on Chang'an.
悟彼下泉人	And I understood why someone wrote "Falling Stream"—
喟然傷心肝	I gasped and felt that pain within.[96]

The Ba Mound, or Baling, was the tomb of Emperor Wen of the Han (r. 179–157 B.C.), whose peaceful reign formed a poignant contrast with the present war-torn Chang'an. The "Falling Stream" ("Xia quan" 下泉) is the title of a poem in *The Classic of Poetry*, which, according to traditional commentators, expresses longing for a wise king:

洌彼下泉	Biting chill, that falling stream
浸彼苞蕭	that soaks the clumps of asphodel.
愾我寤嘆	O how I lie awake and sigh,
念彼京周	thinking of Zhou's capital.[97]

95. *Quan bei Zhou shi* 4.2401.

96. Translation from Owen, ed. and trans., *An Anthology of Chinese Literature*, p. 252.

Yu Xin's quatrain is thus like a "Chinese box," with one layer containing another containing another. And yet, these literary echoes would have been so obvious to Yu Xin's contemporaries or any educated premodern Chinese reader that the quatrain, rich with associations, remained transparent. Just as Wang Can looked back at the old capital at Chang'an before going to the barbarian South, Yu Xin imagined his friend ascending the riverbank at Guangling to gaze on the Shooting Star Fortress, the very place where the Liang troops had eventually overpowered Hou Jing's rebel army. As a matter of fact, the general who set up a camp at the Hill of the Shooting Star was none other than Chen Baxian, who later founded the Chen. Of all the place-names in the vicinity of Jiankang, Yu Xin chose the Shooting Star Fortress: Was this an acknowledgment of the supreme irony of history—that the Chen was facing its own nemesis now? Perhaps. Yu Xin could also have selected this place-name simply to avoid a direct reference to Jiankang, or because the image of the shooting star matches so beautifully with that of the beacon fires raging along the Yangzi River.

In many ways, Jiankang itself was a shooting star of a city, whose brilliance was transient. Capital of the Six Dynasties for four hundred years, it was once the "jewel in the crown of south China's commercial empire," and its population "topped one million individuals, including Han Chinese, aboriginal peoples, and foreigners."[98] During the reign of Emperor Wu of the Liang, Jiankang reached a dazzling height of cultural glory. But in the late sixth century, Jiankang had already fallen from its former splendor: devastated by the Hou Jing Rebellion, its light had long dimmed. Eight years after Yu Xin's death, following the conquest of the Chen, Yang Jian, now Emperor Wen of the Sui, ordered the destruction of the entire city: its walls, palaces, and houses were all to be demolished and the land returned to agriculture.[99] Yu Xin's quatrain turned out to be a "poetic prophecy" (*shichen* 詩讖) in a way he would never have intended: the star had fallen from the sky; once the raging beacon fires died out, it would be dark.

97. Ibid., p. 253.
98. Shufen Liu, "Jiankang and the Commercial Empire," pp. 35–36.
99. *Zizhi tongjian* 177.5516.

From the time when he left Jiangling in 554 until his death in 581, Yu Xin not only never returned to the South but never even got close to Jiankang or Guangling. His last datable poem envisioned his old capital engulfed in a night illuminated by a blazing light. The pathos was born not just of witnessing the destruction of one's birthplace but also of the fall of an empire, the end of an era. The Chinese like to situate a poem in the context of a poet's life and age: indeed, without the background story, we would never know how much emotional power, intensified by restraint, is packed into a quatrain of twenty words.

CODA I: THE WILLOW SONG

Cui Tu 崔塗 was a southerner living in the late ninth century and took first place in the civil service examination in 888. To him was attributed the following poem, "Upon Reading Yu Xin's Collection" ("Du Yu Xin ji" 讀庾信集).[100]

四朝十帝盡風流	Four dynasties, ten emperors— you lived through all of them with panache;
建業長安兩醉遊	wandering, inebriated, in both Jianye and Chang'an.
唯有一篇楊柳曲	There is, however, just this one "Willow Song"
江南江北爲君愁	that makes one sad for you, from South to North.

One detects a hint of irony in describing Yu Xin's life in Jiankang and Chang'an as inebriated wandering,[101] but the Tang poet's attitude toward Yu Xin is more complicated than simple disapproval, since he singles out the "Willow Song" ("Yangliu ge" 楊柳歌) in Yu Xin's collection and expresses sympathy for its author. Yu Xin was famous for using tree imagery—barren, half-dead trees—to convey his sense of failure, loss of vitality, and lack of joy. His "*Fu* on the Barren Tree" ("Kushu fu"

100. *Quan Tang shi* 679.7785. Also attributed to an anonymous author (ibid., 785.8863).

101. Yu Xin made frequent references to drinking in his poems written in the North. In his "Willow Song," cited below, he explicitly states that one had better drown one's sorrows in drinking.

枯樹賦) is perhaps the best-known example,[102] and the "Willow Song" may well be considered its poetic counterpart.

The "Willow Song" opens with the figure of a willow tree growing by the river, threatened by wind and waves. Such an allegorical treatment of a plant lodging its roots in the wrong place already had a long tradition,[103] but Yu Xin's poem soon departs from the willow and goes into a labyrinth of fragmentary, metaphorical images of memory and pain. In the dazzling display of textual allusions, wit, and linguistic ingenuity, we can nevertheless discern a narrative thread: the poet is reminiscing about his youthful years, the Liang court, and the Liang princes, perhaps especially Xiao Gang, Yu Xin's "understanding friend,"[104] whose tragic fate is epitomized in a powerful poetic image of a white jade tablet falling into the gaping mouth of a bronze beast.

河邊楊柳百丈枝	The willow tree by the river had boughs of a hundred feet,
別有長條踠地垂	its long branches hanging curling to the ground.
河水衝激根株危	The currents rushing and dashing, the roots of the willow in danger,
倏忽河中風浪吹	suddenly it was blown by wind and waves into the river.
可憐巢裏鳳凰兒	How pitiful—the young phoenix in the nest on the willow tree!
無故當年生別離	Somehow, back then, it was severed from its home.
流槎一去上天池	Once the drifting log went off, it rose to the Pool of Stars,
織女支機當見隨	and should be taking away the loom-stone of the Weaver.[105]

102. For a full English translation of this *fu*, see Owen, "Deadwood."

103. See Po Qin's 繁欽 (d. 218) poem "On Sweet Basil" ("Yong hui" 詠蕙; *Quan Wei shi* 3.385). Also see Tao Yuanming's no. 9 of "Imitations of Old Poems" ("Ni gu" 擬古; *Quan Jin shi* 17.1005).

104. No. 6 of Yu Xin's "In Imitation of 'Singing of My Feelings'" begins with these lines: "In the past I was treated as a gentleman of the state; / all my life I am grateful to a lord who understood me" (*Quan bei Zhou shi* 3.2368).

105. Legend has it that as the Han envoy Zhang Qian was looking for the source of the Yellow River, his raft arrived at the Heavenly River, and he obtained the

誰信從來蔭數國	Who would believe that all it needed to shelter several states
直用東南一小枝	was only one little southeastern branch?[106]
昔日公子出南皮	The young lord who in the old days made outings at Nanpi,
何處相尋玄武陂	where can one find him now on the banks of Xuanwu Pond?
駿馬翩翩西北馳	A handsome charger galloping toward the northwest,
左右彎弧仰月支	to left and right the rider arched his bow, shooting at Yuezhi.[107]
連錢障泥渡水騎	The mudguard patterned with stringed coins got soiled in crossing the brook,
白玉手板落盤螭	and the white jade tablet fell into the mouth of the coiled dragon.[108]
鳳凰新管簫史吹	New pipes of the phoenix, Xiao Shi had played them;
朱鳥春窓玉女窺	through the spring window of vermilion bird, the Jade Maiden was peeping.[109]

stone used by the Weaving Girl to support her loom (*Taiping yulan* 51.379, citing Zong Lin's *Jing Chu suishi ji*).

106. In a fragment from Sun Chuo's *Sunzi*, a man of the mountain tells a man of the sea that a huge tree of the Deng Grove may shelter several states (*Quan Jin wen* 62.1815). This couplet refers to the former might of the willow tree and suggests the past power and glory of the Liang.

107. In these lines Yu Xin alludes to a number of writings by the Cao princes: in one of his letters, Cao Pi recalled their outings at Nanpi in the old days; Cao Pi's poem "Written at the Xuanwu Pond" ("Yu Xuanwu pi zuo" 於玄武陂作) begins with the line: "Brothers go on an outing together." Cao Zhi's "Ballad on the White Horse" describes the military accomplishments of a chivalrous knight-errant; see *Quan sanguo wen* 7.1089; and *Quan Wei shi* 4.400, 6.432–33.

108. It was said that the minister Wang Ji's horse refused to cross a stream for fear of staining the precious mudguard it was wearing (*Jin shu* 42.1206). Emperor Ming of the Jin (r. 322–24), while still a little boy and the crown prince, put his white jade tablet in the open mouth of a bronze coiled dragon; the jade tablet slipped in and could not be recovered (*Taiping yulan* 692.3222).

109. Xiao Shi was the son-in-law of Duke Mu of Qin. Playing on his panpipes, he summoned a phoenix and rode away with his wife (*Taiping guangji* 4.25). In *Han Wu gushi*, Dongfang Shuo 東方朔 was said to have peeped at the Queen Mother of the West through the vermilion bird window (Lu Xun, *Gu xiaoshuo*, p. 346). The peeping Jade Maiden is an allusion to a line from the Eastern Han writer Wang

銜雲酒盃赤瑪瑙	The wine goblet containing clouds was made of red agate;
照日食螺紫琉璃	the food vessel of purple glass reflected the sun.
君言丈夫無意氣	If you think that a man has no ambition,
試問燕山那得碑	let me ask you—how did Mount Yan acquire its stone stele?[110]
百年霜露奄離披	And yet, what has lasted a hundred years of frost and dews all at once withers,
一旦功名不可爲	suddenly on one morning, accomplishments and fame are out of reach.
定是懷王作計誤	It must be that King Huai had erred in his plan,
無事翻覆用張儀	recanting for no reason and trusting Zhang Yi.[111]
不如飲酒高陽池	Ah, one had better get drunk at the Gaoyang Pond,
日暮歸時倒接離	coming back at day's end, wearing one's cap upside down.[112]
武昌城下誰見移	Who had transplanted the willow from the Wuchang city gate?
官渡營前那可知	How could one still recognize it in front of the Guandu encampment?[113]

Yanshou's 王延壽 (fl. 163) "Rhapsody on the Hall of Numinous Brilliance in Lu" ("Lu Lingguang dian fu" 魯靈光殿賦): "The Jade Girl, peeping from a window, looks below" (*Quan hou Han wen* 58.790; translation from Knechtges, trans., *Wen xuan*, 2: 263).

110. The Eastern Han general Dou Xian inscribed his grand victory over the Xiongnu army on a stone stele on Mount Yanran 燕然 (*Hou Han shu* 23.814).

111. King Huai of Chu was duped by the Qin minister Zhang Yi and severed relations with the state of Qi. King Huai later died in Qin (*Shi ji* 40.1724).

112. Toward the end of the Western Jin, the state was beset with troubles, but Shan Jian 山簡, the governor of Xiangyang, cared only about drinking. He often drank by a scenic local pond, which he referred to as his "Gaoyang Pond," Gaoyang being a reference to the Western Han figure Li Yiji 酈食其, the self-styled "Drunkard of Gaoyang." A song was made about Shan Jian coming home drunk and wearing his cap upside down (*Jin shu* 43.1229–30).

113. The Eastern Jin general Tao Kan once recognized a willow transplanted from the west city gate of Wuchang. See *Jin yangqiu* 晉陽秋, cited in Liu Jun's annotation in Liu Yiqing, *Shishuo xinyu* 3.179. Cao Pi, in the preface to his "*Fu* on the Willow" ("Liu fu" 柳賦), relates that he had planted a willow at Guandu in 200; now, fifteen years later, the tree had grown a great deal, and "many of my followers had died" (*Quan Wei wen* 4.1075).

獨憶飛絮鵝毛下	I alone still remember the days when its catkins were blown around like goose feathers;
非復青絲馬尾垂	today, there are no more silk threads hanging like the green horse-binders.
欲與梅花留一曲	I would like to leave a song about the willow, a companion piece for "Plum Blossoms,"
共將長笛管中吹	so as to play the tunes together on a long flute.[114]

The figure of the willow tree returns toward the end of the poem, in allusions of uprooting, transplantation, and metamorphosis. The willow is now barren: its green leaves all gone, the catkins dispersed by a gusty wind. The only consolation is to write a song about it—*this* song—a self-referential gesture typical of the Liang *yuefu* poetry.

CODA II: HOW IT REALLY ENDED

The Old Tang History contains the biography of a northern rebel general Xue Ju 薛舉, who started an uprising in 617, one year before the Sui fell. Xue Ju's son, Xue Ren'gao 薛仁杲, was described as a greedy and ruthless man who enjoyed killing. In an offhand note, the historian stated that Xue Ren'gao captured Yu Xin's son, Yu Li 庾立. Enraged by Yu Li's refusal to surrender, Xue Ren'gao had Yu Li spitted over an open fire, sliced, and fed to his soldiers.[115]

There seems to be a dark humor in the turn of events, as the offspring of southern writers such as Yan Zhitui and Yu Xin were literally ingested and consumed by the northerners—a peculiar gastronomic unification of China. Hu Sanxing, the *Zizhi tongjian* commentator who was ever keen to uncover moral lessons in history, added this note to the narrative of the Yu Li incident: "The historian shows us that Xue Ren'gao could not gather upright men of letters around him and honor them. This was why he came to a bad end."[116] Such a reading was no doubt intended to bring out the cosmic justice inherent in the workings

114. Both "Breaking the Willow Branches" and "Plum Blossoms Fall" ("Meihua luo" 梅花落) were popular *yuefu* titles in the Southern Dynasties.

115. *Jiu Tang shu* 55.2247.

116. *Zizhi tongjian* 184.5746.

of human history, but it in fact exposes the commentator's deep-seated anxiety about the essential irrationality and senselessness of the grand scheme of things. Just as Yu Xin had said in a poem presented to the Marquis of Yongfeng, a member of the Liang royal family who eventually surrendered to the Western Wei, "Benevolence and righteousness, to one's surprise, destroyed the state of Xu" 仁義反亡徐.[117] In the end, Yu Li's fate only serves to illustrate the violence of the age and the triumph, however temporary, of sheer brutal force.

Yu Xin might have been ashamed of his flight from Hou Jing's warriors on that fatal day in the winter of 548, and yet, we should be grateful that he did not hold out like his son, for he would almost certainly have been killed. And if Yu Xin had died that day, we would have been deprived of one of the best chroniclers of the conquest of the South and of the life of an individual at a time of profound historical changes. In the final analysis, that moment when the Liang court poet laid eyes on the iron masks of Hou Jing's troops summed up the encounter between the North and South. Yu Xin was to win the ultimate victory, but his conquest was of a different kind: much less tangible, much slower, and bringing almost no joy to the victor.

117. *Quan bei Zhou shi* 4.2390. When the state of Xu was being invaded, King Yan, who "practiced benevolence and righteousness," did not want to involve his people in battle and was subsequently conquered (*Hou Han shu* 85.2808).

EPILOGUE

The Aftermath and the Romanticization of the Liang

With the Hou Jing Rebellion and the fall of the Liang, the cultural world of the Southern Dynasties came to an end—the Chen was but a fading echo of the Liang. But if the Liang officially ended in 557, its life continued long afterward, both politically and culturally. After the sacking of Jiangling in 555, the Western Wei set up Xiao Cha 蕭詧, Xiao Tong's third son, as the new ruler of Liang; his territory was limited to Jingzhou and sandwiched between the Western Wei, the Eastern Wei, and the Chen. Although subordinated to the Western Wei, Xiao Cha nevertheless ruled over the small portion of land as emperor, and his dynasty is known as the Latter Liang 後梁. It lasted thirty-three years, almost as long as the Liang itself. Xiao Cha died at the age of forty-three in 562 and received the posthumous title, Emperor Xuan 宣帝.

The throne passed to his third son, Xiao Kui 蕭巋, Emperor Ming 明帝. In 582 Xiao Kui's daughter was chosen to be the consort of the Sui prince Yang Guang 楊廣, better known as Emperor Yang of the Sui or Sui Yangdi 隋煬帝 (r. 605–17). Emperor Wen of the Sui treated Xiao Kui with exceptional generosity; at the suggestion of his wife, Empress Yang, he even dismissed the Sui army stationed in the Western City of Jiangling. He also told Xiao Kui that he would conquer the Chen and escort Xiao Kui back to Jiankang. But Xiao Kui did not live to see that day. Like his father, he died at forty-three. The year was 585, three years before Emperor Wen unified China. Xiao Kui's son Xiao Cong 蕭琮 succeeded him.

Any illusion that the Sui would grant autonomous power to the Liang ruler soon vanished. In 587 Xiao Cong was summoned to the Sui capital, Chang'an. The people of Jiangling, sensing the end was drawing near, wept at his departure, saying, "Our prince is not coming back!" After Xiao Cong set out, the Sui emperor sent an army to take over the Liang defenses; Xiao Cong's uncle Xiao Yan 蕭巖 and his son Xiao Huan 蕭瓛 rebelled and in the end escaped to the Chen. The state of the Latter Liang was thereupon abolished.

Long after the splendid reign of Emperor Wu of the Liang was over, the people of the South retained their affection for the Liang. When Xiao Huan was appointed governor of Wuzhou by the Chen emperor, the elders of the three Wu regions fondly referred to him as "the son of our sovereign." A superstitious belief contributed to Xiao Huan's popularity in the South: just like Emperor Wu, Xiao Gang, Xiao Cha, and Xiao Kui, Xiao Huan was the third son in his family. After the Sui conquest of the Chen in 589, the Wu people made Xiao Huan their leader and opposed the Sui rule. After a brief period of resistance, Xiao Huan's army was crushed, and he was executed in Chang'an at the age of twenty.

Xiao Huan was not the last hope for a Liang renaissance. In 617, as the Sui was being torn apart by insurgencies, a group of military officers at Yuezhou 岳州 (in modern Hu'nan) plotted a rebellion. When they tried to put one Dong Jingzhen 董景珍 in charge, Dong Jingzhen declined, saying that his family origins were too humble for him to be a commanding presence. He suggested instead a descendent of the Liang royal family, Xiao Xian 蕭銑 (584–621), the then-magistrate of Luochuan 羅川 (in modern Hu'nan), arguing that Xiao Xian was "tolerant, kind, and gracious, very much resembling Emperor Wu."[1] Xiao Xian was a great-grandson of Xiao Cha; his grandfather Xiao Yan had been executed by the Sui army in 587. Xiao Xian grew up in straitened circumstances and made a living as a scribe. It was only because a cousin of his father was the empress of Sui Yangdi that he had been granted a low office. Accepting the request to be the rebel leader, Xiao Xian showed remarkable diplomatic talent at the beginning of his career. In

1. *Jiu Tang shu* 56.2263.

618 he ascended the throne as the new ruler of the Liang. He soon conquered a large part of the South and set up his court at Jiangling. Xiao Xian held out for five years until Jiangling was besieged by the Tang army in 621. Losing hope for rescue, he decided to surrender in order to protect the city from slaughter. He was brought to Chang'an and executed there. True to family tradition, Xiao Xian retained his grace and poise to the very end.[2]

If the Liang royal house did not do well in safeguarding the throne, they more than adequately compensated in other arenas. The Xiao clan flourished throughout the Sui and Tang. Empress Xiao, the wife of Sui Yangdi, was a refined and talented woman; her "*Fu* on Expressing My Intent" ("Shuzhi fu" 述志賦) is preserved in *The History of the Sui*.[3] It was both because of her and because of Yangdi's fascination with the southern culture that many members of the Xiao clan held offices in the Sui court. The Xiao continued to be prominent in the Tang and married into the Tang royal family. Among the descendents of Xiao Tong, there were nine prime ministers from the seventh to the tenth centuries. Xiao Yingshi 蕭穎士 (708–59), a ninth-generation descendent of Emperor Wu's brother Xiao Hui, was a well-known writer.

Meanwhile, the Liang dynasty was becoming romanticized in the popular imagination. A number of extant Tang stories give fantastic accounts of Emperor Wu or of his ministers, or use the Liang as the narrative backdrop. "Supplementing Jiang Zong's 'Story of the White Gibbon'" ("Bu Jiang Zong baiyuan zhuan" 補江總白猿傳) by an anonymous author is set anachronistically in the last years of the Datong era (535–546) of Emperor Wu. It relates that while General Ouyang He 歐陽紇 (548–70) was away on a military campaign, his wife was abducted by a gibbon and gave birth to a son, Ouyang Xun, who later compiled *Yiwen leiju*.[4] A more complicated and intriguing Liang

2. For Xiao Xian's biography, see ibid., 56.2263–66.

3. *Sui shu* 36.1111–12.

4. *Quan Tang wudai xiaoshuo*, 1: 23–26. As a matter of fact, Ouyang Xun was born in 557, long after the Datong reign. Ouyang He's expedition against the Southern minorities occurred in 556, the last year of the Liang dynasty, under the leadership of his father, Ouyang Wei 歐陽頠 (498–563). (*Chen shu* 9.157). For a study of the various anachronisms in this story, see Jue Chen, "Calculated Anachronisms."

romance is "An Account of the Four Gentlemen of Liang" ("Liang sigong ji" 梁四公記), variously attributed to Zhang Yue 張說 (667–730), Liang Zaiyan 梁載言 (*jinshi* 675), or Lu Shen 盧詵.[5] This story is preserved as fragments in various Song encyclopedias and anecdotal collections.[6] In it, four elderly gentlemen appear at Emperor Wu's court during the Tianjian era; they awe and embarrass the emperor and his courtiers, as well as foreign emissaries, with their superior knowledge on all subjects, from the mundane to the esoteric. The only figure in the Liang court who is portrayed positively is Xiao Tong. He alone recognizes the four gentlemen and treats them with great respect; he deciphers the unusual characters constituting the names of the four gentlemen and identifies their sources in classical and literary texts. As a result, "the four men were delighted and bowed to the crown prince as if he were an old friend. They were regarded as the Four Noble Scions." Although the term "Four Noble Scions" (*si gongzi* 四公子) is, as Dudbridge rightly points out, reminiscent of the Four Noble Scions of the Warring States, their association with Crown Prince Zhaoming harks back to the famous Four White Heads of Shang Mountain (*Shangshan sihao* 商山四皓) from the Western Han, whose friendship with Crown Prince Liu Ying 劉盈 (later Emperor Xiaohui, r. 194–188 B.C.) saved him from being deposed by the emperor in favor of his younger brother. We can only wonder whether the missing potions of the narrative mentioned the four gentlemen's role in Xiao Tong's untimely death and Emperor Wu's subsequent choice of Xiao Gang as heir. If the story was indeed authored in the late seventh or early eighth century, it should come as no surprise that a story about the Liang would cast Crown Prince Zhaoming in a positive light since a number of Xiao Tong's descendents occupied prominent positions in the Tang court.

Despite the narrator's ironic attitude toward Emperor Wu and his courtiers, one nevertheless notices an obsessive fascination with the Liang. The four extraordinary men choose to come to Emperor Wu in response to his "deferential treatment of gentlemen"; this decision

5. *Quan Tang wudai xiaoshuo*, 1: 160–71.

6. For an excellent study of this story, see Dudbridge, "Classification: The Case of 'The Four Gentlemen of Liang,'" in idem, *Lost Books*, pp. 53–71.

makes the Liang court the center of everything that happens. It does not matter that the four gentlemen best the emperor and his courtiers with their knowledge: their very presence attests that the Liang is superior to all its neighboring states. In the larger scheme of things, these men serve the needs of the emperor. The Liang comes across as a sophisticated, dynamic empire attracting exotic and extraordinary people and things from afar. The only other pre-Tang era that became the object of a vivid historical imagination was the reign of Emperor Wu of the Han, who was known for his long, colorful, and prosperous rule, just like Emperor Wu of the Liang.

Whereas Emperor Wu of the Han is always associated with the pursuit of immortality, it is impossible to separate Emperor Wu of the Liang from his Buddhist faith. He is the protagonist in several stories of reincarnation and retribution. In one story, the emperor promises an old acquaintance appointment as a county magistrate, but for one reason or another the promise is never realized. The eminent monk Baozhi explains the reason to the person: in his previous life he had promised to donate 500 cash to the emperor, who was hosting a vegetarian feast for the Buddhist clergy, but he never carried out his promise.[7] In another story, the emperor is playing chess when a monk named Kowtow Master comes to see him. The emperor, absorbed in the chessboard, says, "Kill this one off," referring to the "killing off" of a pawn. The attendants, however, misunderstand and subsequently have Kowtow Master executed. Before he dies, Kowtow Master tells the executioner that in a previous life he had accidentally killed an earthworm that was the emperor's former self. An apparently random act of killing is thus rationalized into an act of karmic retribution.[8] In the Tang, there already existed an inherent conflict in Emperor Wu's image: on one hand, he was regarded as a saintly patron of Buddhism; on the other hand, he was a convenient bad example whenever a Confucian statesman needed to

7. *Quan Tang wudai xiaoshuo*, 1: 31. The story was recorded in Tang Lin's 唐臨 (600–659) story collection, *Mingbao ji* 冥報記.

8. This story is from Zhang Zhuo's *Chaoye qianzai* (*Quan Tang wudai xiaoshuo*, 5: 2906). It is incorporated into the Ming writer Feng Menglong's vernacular story, "Emperor Wu of the Liang Returns to the Land of Extreme Bliss Through Ceaseless Cultivation."

make a point about the shortcomings of Buddhism.[9] This conflict is most obvious in the seventeenth-century novel *The Romance of Emperor Wu of the Liang Coming from the West*, in which the narrator struggles to make sense of the character of Emperor Wu in terms of the various conflicting stereotypes of dynastic founder, failed last ruler, and devout Buddhist disciple.

After the An Lushan Rebellion in 755, which dealt a severe blow to the Tang empire, stories about the Liang lost their earlier exuberance and dynamism. An elegiac tone set in. The Southern Dynasties, especially the Qi, Liang, and Chen, were portrayed as decadent, dissolute, and doomed. In both prose accounts and poetic representations of the Liang from the mid-eighth century on, one detects a sense of melancholy, which reflects the cultural ambiance of the late Tang rather than that of the Liang. A story by Dai Fu 戴孚 (*jinshi* 757) tells how a native of Jiankang named Chang Yi 常夷, who lived near the Blue Stream, became a fast friend of the ghost of the Liang minister Zhu Yi's nephew, Zhu Xiu 朱秀, a fictional character (unless Dai Fu had access to historical records lost to us). The ghost often reminisces about the Liang and Chen and relates a number of anecdotes that "were left out in the histories." These anecdotes, although apparently ordered randomly, are in fact organized according to a more or less chronological scheme, ranging from the opulence of the Liang court to the devastation caused by the Hou Jing Rebellion. The decline of the Liang from its former splendor caught the imagination of Tang writers, who experienced a similar cycle after the An Lushan Rebellion.[10]

Sometimes the cultural imagination focused on an actual historical person. A story by Zhang Du 張讀 (834–86) tells of the protagonist Lu Qiao's 陸喬 encounter with the ghosts of Shen Yue and Fan Yun.[11] Shen Yue presents his son, Qingxiang 青箱, who died young. Qingxiang recites a poem he composed upon visiting the ruins of the Palace City. Lu Qiao praises the poem but cannot help noticing that it is metrically a regulated poem (*lüshi*), something that he considers an

9. Han Yu's famous memorial on the Buddha's bones is one of the many examples (*Quan Tang wen* 548.5552).

10. *Quan Tang wudai xiaoshuo*, 1: 406–8.

11. Ibid., 3: 1641–43.

anachronism in the context of Qi-Liang poetry. Shen Yue explains that Qingxiang is merely following contemporary (i.e., Tang) customs. Shen Yue and Fan Yun then recall the "good old days" when both were guests at the residence of the Prince of Jingling. Shen Yue says: "From the Liang till today, it has been more than four hundred years. The rivers, the mountains, the wind, and the moon are no different from those of the old times, and yet, people have changed. How can one not feel sad about this!" The story ends with a revelation by Shen Yue: within two years a war will break out in Lu Qiao's home region of Danyang. A year later, the governor, Li Qi 李錡, rebels (an event that happened in 807); in another year, Lu Qiao himself passes on.

But even in the midst of sentimental nostalgia there was space for macabre humor. Xue Yongruo's 薛用弱 (fl. 817–31) account of an event in the life of the writer Xiao Yingshi, the descendent of Emperor Wu's brother Xiao Hui, adds a delicious twist to an otherwise commonplace story. During his travels, Xiao Yingshi meets two young men in the boat, who stare at him and say to each other: "This person very much resembles Prince Zhonglie of Boyang." Xiao Yingshi, a descendent of the prince, immediately introduces himself to the young men, who say: "We have known your ancestor for a long time." Xiao Yingshi does not want to make further inquiries in the presence of the other people in the boat, but as soon as they arrive at the riverbank, the two young men leave in a hurry. Convinced that they are immortals or gods, Xiao Yingshi is filled with regret that he could not talk with them further. A year later, he returns from the South. As he is visiting a local magistrate, the clerk reports that five or six grave-robbers have just been caught, and behold—two of them are none other than the young men from the boat. Just as Xiao Yingshi is trying to explain to the magistrate that there must have been a mix-up, the grave-robbers confess that they had opened up the tomb of the Prince of Boyang, and that in the tomb they saw the corpse of a nobleman lying on a stone couch. His visage was as if alive and bore a remarkable resemblance to Xiao Yingshi. This, they said, was how they had "recognized" Xiao Yingshi in the boat.[12]

12. Ibid., 2: 786–87.

In general, the most powerful and evocative images of the Liang and of the Southern Dynasties come from poetry. As the Tang empire was gradually disintegrating, the Southern Dynasties constituted a favorite object of somber reflection for the late Tang poet. Li Shangyin 李商隱 (813–58), well known for his "poetry on history" (*yongshi shi* 詠史詩), left a sarcastic sketch of the Southland in a quatrain entitled "The Southern Dynasties" ("Nanchao" 南朝).[13]

地險悠悠天險長	The Earthly Barrier is extended, the Heavenly Barrier stretches long;[14]
金陵王氣應瑤光	the imperial aura of Jinling corresponds to the Star of Yaoguang.[15]
休誇此地分天下	Do not boast that this land had taken up half of the empire—
只得徐妃半面妝	it only got to be the makeup applied on Lady Xu's one cheek.

Lady Xu Zhaopei 徐昭佩, Xiao Yi's wife, was not loved by the prince, who visited her quarters only once every two or three years. Whenever she heard he was coming, she would put makeup on half of her face—a defiant mockery of the prince, who was blind in one eye.[16] In Li Shangyin's quatrain, the Southland is introduced in virile military and political terms only to be turned into a lurid, effeminate image: the partial makeup on a woman's face. Yaoguang was also the name of a Buddhist temple in Jingzhou, and Lady Xu was said to have had an affair with a monk of this temple.[17] It seems that the poet might be intending a clever double entendre, and indeed, as the Liang ended with Xiao Yi's short reign, so did the "imperial aura" of the Southland.

Nevertheless, irony and moral didacticism frequently give way to an elegiac mood in poems dealing with the Liang. Li He had composed many sensuous poems inspired by the Southern Dynasties. One of them,

---

13. *Quan Tang shi* 540.6183.

14. The Heavenly Barrier is another name for the Yangzi River.

15. Jinling is an old name for Jiankang. The Yaoguang Star is the seventh star of the Big Dipper.

16. *Nan shi* 12.341. In 549, after Lady Xu's only son (Xiao Yi's eldest son) died in battle against Hou Jing, Xiao Yi forced her to commit suicide.

17. Ibid., 12.342.

"Song on Returning from Kuaiji" ("Huanzi Kuaiji ge" 還自會稽歌), was written "on behalf of" the court poet Yu Jianwu.[18] In the preface, the poet explained the purpose behind his composition.

During the Liang dynasty, Yu Jianwu used to compose poems in the Palace Style as companion pieces written at the command of the crown prince. When the dynasty fell, Yu Jianwu took refuge at Kuaiji and only later returned home. It has been my opinion that he must have written something from that time; only now it cannot be found. Therefore I composed "Song on Returning from Kuaiji" to supplement what is missing regarding his sorrow.

庾肩吾於梁時, 嘗作宮體謠引以應和皇子. 及國勢淪敗, 肩吾先潛難會稽, 後始還家.僕意其必有遺文, 今無得焉, 故作"還自會稽歌"以補其悲.

The poem itself presents a mournful picture of decrepitude, ruins, and aging.

野粉椒壁黃	The peppered walls, brown with moldy spots;[19]
濕螢滿梁殿	wet fireflies fill the Liang palace.
臺城應教人	He who composed to command in the Palace City
秋衾夢銅輦	under autumn blankets dreams of the bronze palanquin.[20]
吳霜點歸鬢	The frost of Wu speckles the tresses of the returning man,
身與塘蒲晚	his body growing old together with the reeds in the pool.
脈脈辭金魚	With yearning he takes leave of the golden fish,[21]
羈臣守迍賤	wandering courtier, holding to his helplessness and humble station.

The Liang palace is overgrown with weeds and becomes the breeding ground for fireflies. The court poet is overtaken by the season of autumn, wasting away like a reed suffering from the frost—an allusion to his white hair.

18. *Quan Tang shi* 390.4392–93. The translation is Stephen Owen's.

19. "Peppered walls" refers to the imperial harem: pepper was mixed into the plaster to make the rooms aromatic (*Jin shu* 49.1374).

20. The bronze palanquin is the carriage of the crown prince.

21. The "golden fish" was a badge worn by high officials in the Tang.

Li He's poem was probably inspired by a quatrain attributed to Yu Jianwu. According to Qiu Yue's *Summary Documents of the Three Kingdoms*, Yu Jianwu was captured by Hou Jing's general Song Zixian at Kuaiji. Song Zixian ordered Yu Jianwu to write a poem on the spot; otherwise he would execute him. Yu Jianwu composed the following quatrain and was subsequently released.

髮與年俱暮	My hair and age both tend toward dusk;
愁將罪共深	sorrow and guilt grow deep together.
聊持轉風燭	I will just hold a candle flickering in the wind
暫映廣陵琴	to illuminate, for a little while, the zither of Guangling.[22]

Although the story is most likely apocryphal, it must have been well known to a Tang reader interested in Liang lore. A poem saving a person's life seems to be a favorite trope, although the Buddhist metaphor for human life—a flickering candle in the wind—does recall the many Palace Style poems composed at the Liang court on candles and candlelight; what distinguishes this quatrain is that it is less about illuminating the zither than about the imminent darkness.

Jiankang was destined to become a capital city again, first of the Southern Tang in the tenth century, then briefly of the Ming in the fourteenth century, and finally of the Southern Ming in the seventeenth century when the Manchu army occupied the North. Even in modern times, it was once the chosen capital of the Republic of China under the name Nanjing, the Southern Capital. The "imperial aura" of Jinling outlived the Southern Dynasties, and yet, on each occasion history repeated itself, people saw in the fate of the Southern Dynasties the reflection of their own situation.

The Liang, however, was anything but decadent. Decadence signifies a process of decay, a fading away, "the end of something"; decadence in literature is characterized by an ennui born from powerlessness and helplessness and from the wearisome feeling of having experienced it all before and the best part being over. Nothing can be further from the truth for the Liang. That melancholy sense of loss, of vanished

22. The zither of Guangling refers to the "Tune of Guangling," played by the poet Ji Kang right before his execution.

splendors, remained alien to the Liang itself. Despite what everyone said *after* the Hou Jing Rebellion, no one had ever seen it coming; indeed, for Liang writers, their age was marked by beginnings, innovations, "new transformation," and energetic undertakings. They lived in intensely experienced moments, in the here and now, and were sophisticated innocents. The cultural spirit of the Liang can therefore be best summed up as robust.

The Hou Jing Rebellion struck the fatal blow that destroyed the entrenched social structure; it also destroyed the panache of the Southern Dynasties. The fact that the last Chen emperor hid in a well in an attempt to escape the Sui army epitomizes the essential difference between the Liang and the Chen, for at the very moment he lowered himself into the well, the dashing world of the Southern Dynasties was forever lost.

Scattered in the suburbs of modern Nanjing are colossal stone chimeras guarding the mausoleums of Liang royalty; these mythical beasts form a glaring contrast with the surrounding crops and the farmland on which they stand. Majestic and impenetrable even in their ruin, they are indices of absence and loss, silently but eloquently testifying to the cultural vigor and self-assurance of a glorious age.

Reference Matter

Works Cited

Agamben, Giorgio. *The Man Without Content*. Trans. Georgia Albert. Stanford: Stanford University Press, 1999.

Bai Juyi 白居易, comp. *Baishi liutie shilei ji* 白氏六帖事類集. Taibei: Xinxing shuju, 1975.

Balázs, Stefan. "Der Philosoph Fan Tschen und sein Traktat gegen den Buddhismus." *Sinica* 7 (1932): 220–34.

Bei Qi shu 北齊書. Beijing: Zhonghua shuju, 1972.

Bei shi 北史. Comp. Li Yanshou 李延壽. Beijing: Zhonghua shuju, 1974.

Berger, John. *About Looking*. New York: Vintage, 1980.

Birrell, Anne. *Games Poets Play: Readings in Medieval Chinese Poetry*. Cambridge, Eng.: McGuinness China Monographs, 2004.

Birrell, Anne, trans. *New Songs from a Jade Terrace: An Anthology of Early Chinese Love Poetry*. Harmondsworth, Eng.: Penguin Books, 1986.

Bush, Susan, and Christian Murck, eds. *Theories of the Arts in China*. Princeton: Princeton University Press, 1983.

Butler, Judith. *Gender Trouble: Feminism and the Subversion of Identity*. New York: Routledge, 1990.

Cai Zong-qi, ed. *A Chinese Literary Mind: Culture, Creativity, and Rhetoric in "Wenxin Diaolong."* Stanford: Stanford University Press, 2001.

Calvino, Italo. *Six Memos for the Next Millennium*. New York: Vintage, 1988.

Campany, Robert Ford. "The Earliest Tales of the Bodhisattva Guanshiyin." In *Religions of China in Practice*, ed. Donald S. Lopez. Princeton University Press: 1996, pp. 82–96.

———. "The Real Presence." *History of Religions* 32, no. 3 (1993): 233–72.

Campany, Robert Ford. trans., *To Live as Long as Heaven and Earth: A Translation and Study of Ge Hong's "Traditions of Divine Transcendents."* Berkeley: University of California Press, 2002.

Cao Daoheng 曹道衡. *Lanling Xiao shi yu nanchao wenxue* 蘭陵蕭氏與南朝文學. Beijing: Zhonghua shuju, 2004.

———. "Liang Wudi yu Jingling bayou" 梁武帝與竟陵八友. *Qilu xuekan* 齊魯學刊 1995, no. 5: 46–53.

———. "Lun Dong Jin nanchao zhengquan yu shizu de guanxi jiqi dui wenxue de yingxiang" 論東晉南朝政權與士族的關係及其對文學的影響. *Wenxue yichan* 文學遺產 2003, no. 5 (2003): 29–38.

———. *Nanchao wenxue yu beichao wenxue yanjiu* 南朝文學與北朝文學研究. Nanjing: Jiangsu guji chubanshe, 1998.

———. "'Pipan jicheng' haishi 'jianrong bingxu?'" 批判繼承還是兼容並蓄? *Xin jianshe* 新建設 1964, nos. 10–11: 96–104.

———. "Zhaoming taizi he Liang Wudi de jianchu wenti" 昭明太子和梁武帝的建儲問題. *Zhengzhou daxue xuebao* 鄭州大學學報 1994, no. 1: 47–53.

———. *Zhonggu wenxue shi lunwen ji xubian* 中古文學史論文集續編. Taibei: Wenjin chubanshe, 1994.

Cao Daoheng 曹道衡 and Fu Gang 傅剛. *Xiao Tong pingzhuan* 蕭統評傳. Nanjing: Nanjing daxue chubanshe, 2001.

Cao Daoheng 曹道衡 and Liu Yuejin 劉躍進. *Nanbeichao wenxue biannian shi* 南北朝文學編年史. Beijing: Renmin wenxue chubanshe, 2000.

Cao Daoheng 曹道衡 and Shen Yucheng 沈玉成. *Nanbeichao wenxue shi* 南北朝文學史. Beijing: Renmin wenxue chubanshe, 1991.

Chang, Kang-i Sun. *Six Dynasties Poetry*. Princeton: Princeton University Press, 1986.

Chao Gongwu 晁公武. *Junzhai dushu zhi* 郡齋讀書志. Taibei: Guangwen shuju, 1966.

Chen, Jinhua. "*Pañcavārṣika* Assemblies in Liang Wudi's Buddhist Palace Chapel." *Harvard Journal of Asiatic Studies* 66, no. 1 (June 2006): 43–103.

Chen, Jue. "Calculated Anachronisms and Intertextual Echoes in 'Bu Jiang Zong baiyuan zhuan.'" *T'ang Studies* 14 (1996): 67–97.

Chen shu 陳書. Comp. Yao Silian 姚思廉. Beijing: Zhonghua shuju, 1972.

Chen Si 陳思. *Baoke congbian* 寶刻叢編. *Siku quanshu* ed.

Chen Yinke 陳寅恪. "Sisheng san wen" 四聲三問. In *Chen Yinke xiansheng wen shi lunji* 陳寅恪先生文史論集. Hong Kong: Wen Wen Publications, 1973, pp. 205–18.

Chen Yuzhen 陳昱珍. "Daoshi yu *Fayuan zhulin*" 道世與法苑珠林. *Zhonghua foxue xuebao* 中華佛學學報 1992, no. 5: 233–62.

Chen, Zu-yan. "The Art of Black and White: *Wei-ch'i* in Chinese Poetry." *Journal of the American Oriental Society* 117, no. 4 (1997): 643–53.

Cheng Zhangcan 程章燦. *Shixue luncong* 石學論叢. Taibei: Da'an chubanshe, 1999.

———. *Shizu yu liuchao wenxue* 世族與六朝文學. Ha'erbin: Heilongjiang jiaoyu chubanshe, 1998.

Chennault, Cynthia. "Odes on Objects and Patronage During the Southern Qi." In *Studies in Early Medieval Chinese Literature and Cultural History: In Honor of Richard B. Mather and Donald Holzman*, ed. Paul W. Kroll and David R. Knechtges. Provo, UT: T'ang Studies Society, 2003, pp. 331–98.

Chuci buzhu 楚辭補注. Annot. Hong Xingzu 洪興祖. Taibei: Tiangong shuju, 1989.

Chūgoku chūseishi kenkyū: Rikuchō Zui Tō no shakai to bunka 中國中世史研究: 六朝隋唐の社会と文化. Tokyo: Tōkai daigaku shuppankai, 1970.

Chunqiu Gongyang zhuan zhushu 春秋公羊傳注疏. See *Shisanjing zhushu*.

Chunqiu Zuozhuan zhengyi 春秋左傳正義. See *Shisanjing zhushu*.

Chuxue ji 初學記. Comp. Xu Jian 徐堅 et al. Beijing: Zhonghua shuju, 1962.

Crowell, William. "Northern Émigrés and the Problems of Census Registration." In *State and Society in Early Medieval China*, ed. Albert Dien. Stanford: Stanford Univesity Press, 1990, pp. 171–209.

Daoxuan 道宣, comp. *Guang Hongming ji* 廣弘明集. In *Taishō shinshū Daizōkyō* 52.

———. *Xu Gaoseng zhuan* 續高僧傳. In *Taishō shinshū Daizōkyō* 50.

Daozang 道藏. Beijing: Wenwu chubanshe; Shanghai: Shanghai shudian; Tianjin: Tianjin guji chubanshe, 1987.

Dien, Albert E. "Civil Service Examination: Evidence from the Northwest." In *Culture and Power in the Reconstitution of the Chinese Realm, 200–600*, ed. Scott Pearce, Audrey Shapiro, and Patricia Ebrey. Cambridge: Harvard University Asia Center, 2001, pp. 99–121.

———. *Pei Ch'i shu 45: Biography of Yen Chih-t'ui*. Bern: Herbert Lang, 1976.

Ding Fulin 丁福林. *Dong Jin nanchao de Xieshi wenxue jituan* 東晉南朝的謝氏文學集團. Ha'erbin: Heilongjiang jiaoyu chubanshe, 1998.

Disanjie Wei Jin nanbeichao wenxue guoji xueshu yantaohui lunwenji 第三屆魏晉南北朝文學國際學術研討會論文集. Taibei: Wenshizhe chubanshe, 1998.

Du You 杜佑. *Tong dian* 通典. Beijing: Zhonghua shuju, 1988.

Dudbridge, Glen. *Lost Books of Medieval China*. London: British Library, 2000.

Erya zhushu 爾雅注疏. See *Shisanjing zhushu*.

Fang Beichen 方北辰. *Wei Jin nanchao jiangdong shijia dazu shulun* 魏晉南朝江東世家大族述論. Taibei: Wenjin chubanshe, 1991.

Fang Litian 方立天. *Huiyuan jiqi foxue* 慧遠及其佛學. Beijing: Zhongguo renmin daxue chubanshe, 1984.

———. *Wei Jin nanbeichao fojiao luncong* 魏晉南北朝佛教論叢. Beijing: Zhonghua shuju, 2002.

Fantham, Elaine. *Roman Literary Culture: From Cicero to Apuleius*. Baltimore: John Hopkins University Press, 1996.

Fei Changfang 費長房, comp. *Lidai sanbao ji* 歷代三寶記. In *Taishō shinshū Daizōkyō* 49.

Feiming 廢名. *Feiming wenji* 廢名文集. Beijing: Dongfang chubanshe, 2000.

Feng Menglong 馮夢龍. *Stories Old and New: A Ming Dynasty Collection*. Trans. Shuhui Yang and Yunqin Yang. Seattle: University of Washington Press, 2000.

Feng Weine 馮惟訥, comp. *Gushi ji* 古詩紀. *Siku quanshu* ed.

Fu Gang 傅剛. *"Wen xuan" banben yanjiu* 文選版本研究. Beijing: Beijing daxue chubanshe, 2000.

———. "*Yutai xinyong* yu *Wen xuan*" 玉臺新詠與文選. *Zhongguo dianji yu wenhua* 中國典籍與文化 2003, no. 1: 15–20. The same article was published under the title "*Wen xuan* yu *Yutai xinyong*" 文選與玉台新詠 in *Zhenjiang gaozhuan xuebao* 鎮江高專學報 16, no. 4 (Oct. 2003): 18–22.

Fu Liang 傅亮, Zhang Yan 張演, and Lu Gao 陸杲. *Guanshiyin yingyan ji sanzhong yizhu* 觀世音應驗記三種譯注. Annot. Dong Zhiqiao 董志翹. Nanjing: Jiangsu guji chubanshe, 2002.

Gan Bao 干寶. *Soushen ji* 搜神記. Ed. Wang Shaoying 汪紹楹. Beijing: Zhonghua shuju, 1979.

Gao Feng 高豐 and Sun Jianjun 孫建君. *Zhongguo dengju jianshi* 中國燈具簡史. Beijing: Beijing gongyi meishu chubanshe, 1992.

Gao Min 高敏. *Wei Jin nanbeichao bingzhi yanjiu* 魏晉南北朝兵制研究. He'nan: Daxiang chubanshe, 2000.

Gao Sisun 高似孫. *Shan lu* 剡錄. Beijing: Zhonghua shuju, 1990.

Ge Hong 葛洪. *Baopuzi neipian jiaoshi* 抱朴子内篇校釋. Annot. Wang Ming 王明. Beijing: Zhonghua shuju, 1985.

———. *Baopuzi waipian jiaojian* 抱朴子外篇校箋. Annot. Yang Mingzhao 楊明照. 2 vols. Beijing: Zhonghua shuju, 1991.

———. *Shenxian zhuan* 神仙傳. In *Liexian zhuan jinyi / Shenxian zhuan jinyi* 列仙傳今譯神仙傳今譯, annot. Qiu Heting 邱鶴亭. Beijing: Zhongguo shehui kexue chubanshe, 1996.

Ge Xiaoyin 葛曉音. *Badai shishi* 八代詩史. Xi'an: Shaanxi renmin chubanshe, 1986.

Graff, David A. *Medieval Chinese Warfare, 300–900*. New York: Routledge, 2002.

Graham, William T., Jr., trans. and annot. *The Lament for the South: Yü Hsin's "Ai Chiang-nan fu."* Cambridge: Cambridge University Press, 1980.

Graham, William T., Jr., and James Hightower. "Yü Hsin's 'Songs of Sorrow.'" *Harvard Journal of Asiatic Studies* 43, no. 1 (June 1983): 5–55.

Gui Qing 歸青. "Wenzhang qie xu fangdang bian" 文章且須放蕩辨. *Shanghai daxue xuebao* 上海大學學報 1994, no. 6: 41–47.

Guo Maoqian 郭茂倩, comp. *Yuefu shiji* 樂府詩集. Beijing: Zhonghua shuju, 1979.

Guo yu 國語. Shanghai: Shanghai guji chubanshe, 1978.

Guo Yuheng 郭預衡. "Nenggou wu pipan di 'jianrong bingxu' ma?" 能夠無批判地"兼容並蓄"嗎? *Xin jianshe* 新建設 1965, no. 1: 33–42.

Han shu 漢書. Comp. Ban Gu 班固. Beijing: Zhonghua shuju, 1962.

Hayashida Shinnosuke 林田愼之助. *Chūgoku chūsei bungaku hyōronshi* 中國中世文學評論史. Tokyo: Sōbunsha, 1979.

———. "Pei Ziye 'Diaochong lun' kaozheng: Guanyu 'Diaochong lun' de xiezuo niandai jiqi fugu wenxue lun" 裴子野雕蟲論考證: 關於雕蟲論的寫作年代及其復古文學論. Trans. Chen Xizhong 陳曦鐘. *Gudai wenxue lilun yanjiu congkan* 古代文學理論研究叢刊 6 (1982): 231–50.

He Wenhuan 何文煥, comp. *Lidai shihua kaosuo* 歷代詩話考索. Beijing: Zhonghua shuju, 1981.

Holcombe, Charles. *In the Shadow of the Han: Literati Thought and Society at the Beginning of the Southern Dynasties*. Honolulu: University of Hawai'i Press, 1994.

Hong Ye 洪業 (William Hung). "Suowei *Xiuwen dian yulan*" 所謂修文殿御覽. *Yanjing xuebao* 燕京學報 12 (1932): 2499–558. Reprinted in *Yiwen leiju fu suoyin leishu shizhong* 藝文類聚坿索引類書十種. 5 vols. Taibei: Wenguang chubanshe, 1977, 4: 2343–402.

Hou Han shu 後漢書. Comp. Fan Ye 范曄. Beijing: Zhonghua shuju, 1965.

Hu Dalei 胡大雷. *Gongti shi yanjiu* 宮體詩研究. Beijing: Shangwu yinshuguan, 2004.

———. *Zhonggu wenxue jituan* 中古文學集團. Guilin: Guangxi shifan daxue chubanshe, 1996.

Hu Nianyi 胡念貽. "Lun gongti shi de wenti" 論宮體詩的問題. *Xin jianshe* 新建設 1964, nos. 5–6: 167–73.

Huangdi neijing 黃帝內經. Annot. Yang Weijie 楊維傑. Taibei: Tailian guofeng chubanshe, 1984.

Huijiao 慧皎. *Gaoseng zhuan* 高僧傳. Beijing: Zhonghua shuju, 1992. Also in *Taishō shinshū Daizōkyō* 50.

Idema, Wilt, and Beata Grant, trans. and eds. *The Red Brush: Writing Women of Imperial China*. Cambridge: Harvard University Asia Center, 2004.

Janousch, Andreas. "The Emperor as Bodhisattva: The Bodhisattva Ordination and Ritual Assemblies of Emperor Wu of the Liang Dynasty." In *State and Court Ritual in China*, ed. Joseph P. McDermott. Cambridge: Cambridge University Press, 1999, pp. 112–49.

Jansen, Thomas. *Höfische Öffentlichkeit im frühmittelalterlichen China: Debatten im Salon des Prinzen Xiao Ziliang*. Freiburg: Rombach, 2000.

Jia Sixie 賈思勰. *Qimin yaoshu jiaoshi* 齊民要術校釋. Annot. Miao Qiyu 繆啓愉. Beijing: Nongye chubanshe, 1982.

Jiang Lansheng 江藍生. *Wei Jin nanbeichao xiaoshuo ciyu huishi* 魏晉南北朝小說詞語匯釋. Beijing: Yuwen chubanshe, 1988.

Jiang Shuzhuo 蔣述卓. "Qi Liang fuyan wenfeng yu fojiao" 齊梁浮艷文風與佛教. *Huadong shifan daxue xuebao* 華東師範大學學報 1988, no. 1: 29–36.

Jiang Xiaoyuan 江曉原 and Niu Weixing 鈕衛星. "Tianxueshi shang de Liang Wudi" 天學史上的梁武帝. *Zhongguo wenhua* 中國文化 1997, nos. 15–16: 8–40.

Jin shu 晉書. Comp. Fang Xuanling 房玄齡 et al. Beijing: Zhonghua shuju, 1974.

Jinglü yixiang 經律異相. Comp. Baochang 寶唱 et al. Taibei: Fotuo jiaoyu jijinhui, Chubanbu, 1988.

Jiu Tang shu 舊唐書. Comp. Liu Xu 劉昫 et al. Beijing: Zhonghua shuju, 1975.

Johnson, David. *The Medieval Chinese Oligarchy*. Boulder, CO: Westview Press, 1977.

Kao, Karl S. Y., ed. and trans. *Classical Chinese Tales of the Supernatural and the Fantastic: Selections from the Third to the Tenth Century*. Bloomington: Indiana University Press, 1985.

Kieschinick, John. *The Eminent Monk: Buddhist Ideals in Medieval Chinese Hagiography*. Honululu: University of Hawai'i Press, 1997.

Knechtges, David R. *Court Culture and Literature in Early China*. Variorum Collected Studies Series. Aldershot, Eng.: Ashgate Publishing, 2002.

———. "Culling the Weeds and Selecting Prime Blossoms: The Anthology in Early Medieval China." In *Culture and Power in the Reconstitution of the Chinese Realm, 200–600*, ed. Scott Pearce, Audrey Shapiro, and Patricia Ebrey. Cambridge: Harvard University Asia Center, 2001, pp. 240–41.

———. "Han Wudi de fu" 漢武帝的賦. In *Disanjie guoji cifu xue xueshu yantaohui lunwenji* 第三屆國際辭賦學學術研討會論文集. Taiwan: Guoli zhengzhi daxue, Wenxueyuan, 1996, pp. 1–14.

———. "Sweet-peel Orange or Southern Gold? Regional Identity in Western Jin literature." In *Studies in Early Medieval Chinese Literature and Cultural History: In Honor of Richard B. Mather and Donald Holzman*, ed. Paul W. Kroll and David R. Knechtges. Provo, UT: T'ang Studies Society, 2003, pp. 27–79.

Knechtges, David, trans. *Wen xuan or Selections of Refined Literature*. Vols. 1–2. Princeton: Princeton University Press, 1982, 1987.

Knoblock, John, and Jeffrey Riegel, trans. *The Annals of Lü Buwei: A Complete Translation and Study*. Stanford: Stanford University Press, 2000.

Kong Chen 孔晨 and Li Yan 李燕. *Gu dengshi jianshang yu shoucang* 古燈飾鑑賞與收藏. Changchun: Jilin kexue jishu chubanshe, 1996.

Kong Yanzhi 孔延之. *Kuaiji duoying zongji* 會稽掇英總集. *Siku quanshu* ed.

Kongzi jiayu shuzheng 孔子家語疏證. Annot. Chen Shike 陳士珂. Shanghai shudian, 1987.

Kūkai 空海. *Wenjing mifu lun (Bunkyō hifuron) jiaozhu* 文鏡祕府論校注. Annot. Wang Liqi 王利器. Beijing: Zhongguo shehui kexue chubanshe, 1983.

Lai, Whalen. "Beyond the Debate on 'The Immortality of the Soul': Recovering an Essay by Shen Yüeh." *Journal of Oriental Studies* (Hong Kong) 19, no. 2 (1981): 138–57.

———. "Emperor Wu of Liang on the Immortal Soul, *Shen Pu Mieh*." *Journal of the American Oriental Society* 101, no. 2 (Apr.–June 1981): 167–75.

Laozi jiaoshi 老子校釋. Annot. Zhu Qianzhi 朱謙之. Beijing: Zhonghua shuju, 1984.

Legge, James, trans. *The Chinese Classics*, vol. 4, *Shijing* 詩經. Taibei: Jinxue shuju, 1969.

Li Chuanyin 李傳印. "Nanchao puxue yu zhengzhi" 南朝譜學與政治. *Shixue lilun yanjiu* 史學理論研究 2003, no. 2: 75–85.

Li Daoyuan 酈道元. *Shuijing zhushu* 水經注疏. Nanjing: Jiangsu guji chubanshe, 1989.

Li Jianfeng 李劍峰. *Yuanqian Tao Yuanming jieshou shi* 元前陶淵明接受史. Jinan: Qilu shushe, 2002.

Li Kaiyuan 李開元 and Guan Furong 管芙蓉. *Bei Wei wenxue jianshi* 北魏文學簡史. Taiyuan: Shanxi renmin chubanshe, 1993.

Li Ruiliang 李瑞良. *Zhongguo gudai tushu liutong shi* 中國古代圖書流通史. Shanghai: Shanghai renmin chubanshe, 2000.

Li Shibiao 李士彪. *Wei Jin nanbeichao wenti xue* 魏晉南北朝文體學. Shanghai: Shanghai guji chubanshe, 2004.

Liang shu 梁書. Comp. Yao Cha 姚察 and Yao Silian 姚思廉. Beijing: Zhonghua shuju, 1973.

Liao Guodong 廖國棟. *Wei Jin yongwu fu yanjiu* 魏晉詠物賦研究. Taibei: Wenshizhe chubanshe, 1990.

Liebenthal, Walter. "The Immortality of the Soul in Chinese Thought." *Monumenta Nipponica* 8, no. 1/2 (1952): 327–97.

Liezi guzhu jinyi 列子古注今譯. Annot. and trans. Xiao Dengfu 蕭登福. Taibei: Wenjin chubanshe, 1990.

Liji zhushu 禮記注疏. See *Shisanjing zhushu*.

Lin Dazhi 林大志. "Liang Jianwen di 'Jing Pipa xia shi' fawei" 梁簡文帝經琵琶峽詩發微. *Chenzhou shifan gaodeng zhuanke xuexiao xuebao* 郴州師范高等專科學校學報 24, no. 4 (Aug. 2003): 67–68.

Lin Dazhi 林大志 and Lu Shengjiang 盧盛江. "La'e shijian zhenwei yu Zhaoming taizi houqi chujing" 蠟鵝事件眞僞與昭明太子後期處境. *Wenxuan yichan* 文學遺產 2004, no. 6: 117–19.

Lin Jiali 林家驪. *Shen Yue yanjiu* 沈約研究. Hangzhou: Hangzhou daxue chubanshe, 1999.

Lin Shimin 林士民. *Qingci yu Yue yao* 青瓷與越窰. Shanghai: Shanghai guji chubanshe, 1999.

Lin, Shuen-fu, and Stephen Owen, eds. *The Vitality of the Lyric Voice: Shih Poetry from the Late Han to the T'ang*. Princeton: Princeton University Press, 1986.

Lin Wenyue 林文月. "Nanchao gongti shi yanjiu" 南朝宮體詩研究. *Wen shi zhe xuebao* 文史哲學報 1966, no. 15: 406–58.

Lin Yi 林怡. *Yu Xin yanjiu* 庾信研究. Beijing: Renmin wenxue chubanshe, 2000.

Liu An 劉安. *Huainanzi* 淮南子. Taibei: Zhonghua shuju, 1981.

Liu Dajie 劉大杰. *Zhongguo wenxue fazhanshi* 中國文學發展史. Taibei: Zhonghua shuju, 1995.

Liu Shao 劉卲. *Renwu zhi jiaojian* 人物志校箋. Annot. Li Chongzhi 李崇智. Chengdu: Bashu shushe, 2001.

Liu Shipei 劉師培. *Zhongguo zhonggu wenxue shi jiangyi* 中國中古文學史講義. Shanghai: Shanghai guji, 2000.

Liu, Shufen. "Jiankang and the Commercial Empire of the Southern Dynasties: Change and Continuity in Medieval Chinese Economic History." In *Culture and Power in the Reconstitution of the Chinese Realm: 200–600*, ed. Scott Pearce, Audrey Shapiro, and Patricia Ebrey. Cambridge: Harvard University Asia Center, 2000, pp. 35–52.

Liu Su 劉餗 (fl. 742–55). *Sui Tang jiahua* 隋唐嘉話. Beijing: Zhonghua shuju, 1979.

Liu Su 劉肅 (fl. 806–20). *Datang xinyu* 大唐新語. Guilin: Guangxi shifan daxue chubanshe, 1998.

Liu Xiang 劉向. *Lienü zhuan* 列女傳. Taibei: Zhonghua shuju, 1981.

———. *Liexian zhuan jiaojian* 列仙傳校箋. Annot. Wang Shumin 王叔岷. Taibei: Zhongyang yanjiuyuan, 1995.

———. *Shuo yuan shuzheng* 說苑疏證. Annot. Zhao Shanyi 趙善詒. Shanghai: Huadong shifan daxue chubanshe, 1985.

Liu Xie 劉勰. *Wenxin diaolong yizheng* 文心雕龍義證. Annot. Zhan Ying 詹鍈. Shanghai: Shanghai guji chubanshe, 1989.

Liu Yiqing 劉義慶. *Shishuo xinyu jianshu* 世說新語箋疏. Annot. Yu Jiaxi 余嘉錫. Shanghai: Shanghai guji, 1993.

———. *You ming lu* 幽明錄. Beijing: Wenhua yishu chubanshe, 1988.

Liu Yuejin 劉躍進. *Menfashizu yu Yongming wenxue* 門閥士族與永明文學. Beijing: Sanlian, 1996.

———. *"Yutai xinyong" yanjiu* 玉臺新詠研究. Beijing: Zhonghua shuju, 2000.

Lu Qinli 逯欽立, ed. *Xian Qin Han Wei Jin nanbeichao shi* 先秦漢魏晉南北朝詩. Beijing: Zhonghua shuju, 1995.

Lu Tongqun 魯同群. *Yu Xin zhuan lun* 庾信傳論. Tianjin: Tianjin renmin chubanshe, 1997.

Lu Xun 魯迅, ed. *Gu xiaoshuo gouchen* 古小說鉤沉. Taibei: Pangeng chubanshe, 1978.

Lu Yongfeng 陸永峰. "Fojiao yu yanshi" 佛教與豔詩. *Zhonghua foxue yanjiu* 中華佛學研究 2002, no. 6: 419–43.

Lu You 陸游. *Laoxue'an biji* 老學庵筆記. Beijing: Zhonghua shuju, 1979.

Lü Buwei 呂不韋. *Lüshi chunqiu jiaoshi* 呂氏春秋校釋. Annot. Chen Qiyou 陳奇猷. Shanghai: Xuelin chubanshe, 1984.

Luo Guowei 羅國威. *Ricang Hongren ben Wenguan cilin jiaozheng* 日藏弘仁本文館詞林校證. Beijing: Zhonghua shuju, 2001.

Lunyu zhushu 論語注疏. See *Shisanjing zhushu*.

Ma Duanlin 馬端臨. *Wenxian tongkao* 文獻通考. Taiwan: Shangwu yinshuguan, 1987.

Ma Guohan 馬國翰. *Yuhan shanfang ji yishu* 玉函山房輯佚書. Changsha: Langhuan guan, 1883.

Ma Jigao 馬積高. *Lidai cifu yanjiu shiliao gaishu* 歷代辭賦研究史料概述. Beijing: Zhonghua shuju, 2001.

———. "Lun gongti yu fojiao" 論宮體與佛教. *Qiusuo* 求索 1990, no. 6: 86–92.

Maoshi zhengyi 毛詩正義. See *Shisanjing zhushu*.

Marney, John. *Liang Chien-wen Ti*. Boston: Twayne Publishers, 1976.

Marney, John, trans. *Beyond the Mulberries: An Anthology of Palace Style Poetry*. San Francisco: China Materials Center, 1982.

Mather, Richard B. "The Bonze's Begging Bowl: Eating Practices in the Buddhist Monasteries of Medieval China." *Journal of the American Oriental Society* 101, no. 4 (1981): 417–23.

———. "Intermarriage as a Gauge of Family Status in the Southern Dynasties." In *State and Society in Early Medieval China*, ed. Albert Dien. Stanford: Stanford Univesity Press, 1990, pp. 211–28.

———. *The Poet Shen Yüeh (441–513): The Reticent Marquis*. Princeton: Princeton University Press, 1988.

Mather, Richard B., trans. *The Age of Eternal Brilliance: Three Lyric Poets of the Yung-ming Era (483–493)*. 2 vols. Leiden: Brill, 2003.

———. *A New Account of Tales of the World*. Minneapolis: University of Minnesota Press, 1976.

Mengzi zhushu 孟子注疏. See *Shisanjing zhushu*.

Miao, Ronald. "Palace-Style Poetry: The Courtly Treatment of Glamour and Love." In *Studies in Chinese Poetry and Poetics*. San Francisco: China Materials Center, 1978, pp. 1–42.

Morino Shigeo 森野繁夫. *Rikuchō shi no kenkyū: "shūdan no bungaku" to "kojin no bungaku"* 六朝詩の研究: "集団の文学"と "個人の文学." Tokyo: Daiichi gakushūsha, 1976.

Mu Kehong 穆克宏. "Xiao Tong yanjiu santi" 蕭統研究三題. *Wenxue yichan* 文學遺產 2002, no. 3: 12–22.

Mu tianzi zhuan 穆天子傳. *Sibu beiyao* ed. Shanghai: Shanghai shudian, 1989 reprint.

Nan Qi shu 南齊書. Comp. Xiao Zixian 蕭子顯. Beijing: Zhonghua shuju, 1972.

Nan shi 南史. Comp. Li Yanshou 李延壽. Beijing: Zhonghua shuju, 1975.

Ochi Shigeaki 越智重明. "The Southern Dynasties Aristocratic System and Dynastic Change." *Acta Asiatica* 60 (1991): 54–77.

Okamura Shigeru 岡村繁. *"Wen xuan" zhi yanjiu* 文選之研究. Trans. Lu Xiaoguang 陸曉光. Shanghai: Shanghai guji chubanshe, 2002.

Ōta Teizō 太田悌藏. "Ryō Butei no shadō hōbutsu ni tsuite utagau" 梁武帝の捨道奉仏について疑う. In *Yūki kyōju shōju kinen: bukkyō shisōshi ronshū* 結城教授頌壽記念仏教思想史論集. Tokyo: Daizōshuppan, 1964; pp. 417–32.

Owen, Stephen. "Deadwood: The Barren Tree from Yü Hsin to Han Yü." *CLEAR* 1, no. 2 (1979): 157–79.

———. "Dust Motes." In *Institutions and Originality: Occasional Papers*. Seattle: Walter Chapin Simpson Center for the Humanities, 1998; pp. 65–77.

———. *The End of the Chinese "Middle Ages": Essays in Mid-Tang Literary Culture*. Stanford: Stanford University Press, 1996.

———. *The Great Age of Chinese Poetry: The High T'ang*. New Haven: Yale University, 1981.

———. *The Making of Early Chinese Classical Poetry*. Cambridge: Harvard University Asia Center, 2006.

———. *Mi-Lou: Poetry and the Labyrinth of Desire*. Cambridge: Harvard University Press, 1989.

———. "One Sight: The *Han shu* Biography of Lady Li." In *Rhetoric and Discourses of Power in Court Culture*, ed. David Knechtges and Eugene Vance. Seattle: University of Washington Press, 2005, pp. 239–59.

———. *Readings in Chinese Literary Thought*. Cambridge: Harvard University, Council on East Asian Studies, 1992.

Owen, Stephen, ed. and trans. *An Anthology of Chinese Literature: Beginnings to 1911*. New York: W. W. Norton, 1996.

Pei Qi 裴啓. *Pei Qi yu lin* 裴啓語林. Beijing: Wenhua yishu chubanshe, 1988.

Pu Hui 普慧. *Nanchao fojiao yu wenxue* 南朝佛教與文學. Beijing: Zhonghua shuju, 2002.

Qin Yueyu 秦躍宇. "Liu Xiaochuo yu Liangdai zhongqi wenxue" 劉孝綽與梁代中期文學. *Sichuan shifan xueyuan xuebao* 四川師範學院學報 4, no. 4 (2002): 72–76.

Quan Tang shi 全唐詩. Beijing: Zhonghua shuju, 1960.

Quan Tang wen 全唐文. Beijing: Zhonghua shuju, 1983.

Quan Tang wudai xiaoshuo 全唐五代小說. Ed. Li Shiren 李時人. 5 vols. Xi'an: Shaanxi renmin chubanshe, 1998.

Rao Zongyi 饒宗頤. "*Wenxin diaolong* 'Shenglü pian' yu Jiumoluoshi *Tongyun*—lun sisheng shuo yu Xitan zhi guanxi jian tan Wang Bin, Liu Shanjing, Shen Yue youguan wenti" 文心雕龍聲律篇與鳩摩羅什通韻—論四聲說與悉曇之關係兼談王斌劉善經沈約有關問題. *Zhonghua wenshi luncong* 中華文史論叢 1985, no. 3: 215–36.

Rogers, Michael. "The Myth of the Battle of the Fei River [A.D. 383]." *T'oung pao* 54, no. 1/3 (1968): 50–72.

Rouzer, Paul. *Articulated Ladies: Gender and the Male Community in Early Chinese Texts*. Cambridge: Harvard University Asia Center, 2001.

———. *Writing Another's Dream: The Poetry of Wen Tingyun*. Stanford: Stanford University Press, 1993.

Sanguo zhi 三國志. Comp. Chen Shou 陳壽. Beijing: Zhonghua shuju, 1959.

Satō Toshiyuki 佐藤利行. *Sei Shin bungaku kenkyū: Riku Ki o chūshin to shite* 西晉文學研究: 陸機を中心として. Tokyo: Hakuteisha, 1995.

Sengyou 僧祐, comp. *Chu sanzang ji ji* 出三藏記集. Annot. Su Jinren 蘇晉仁 and Xiao Lianzi 蕭錬子. Beijing: Zhonghua shuju, 1995.

———, comp. *Hongming ji* 弘明集. In *Taishō shinshū Daizōkyō* 52.

Shang shu 尚書. See *Shisanjing zhushu*.

Shanhai jing jiaozhu 山海經校註. Annot. Yuan Ke 袁珂. Shanghai: Shanghai guji chubanshe, 1980.

Shen Yucheng 沈玉成. "Gongti shi yu *Yutai xinyong*" 宮體詩與玉台新詠. *Wenxue yichan* 文學遺產 1988, no. 6: 55–65.

Shi Guanhai 石觀海. *Gongti shipai yanjiu* 宮體詩派研究. Wuhan: Wuhan daxue chubanshe, 2003.

Shi ji 史記. Comp. Sima Qian 司馬遷. Beijing: Zhonghua shuju, 1959.

Shi Su 施宿 et al. *Jiatai Kuaiji zhi* 嘉泰會稽志. Beijing: Zhonghua shuju, 1990.

Shimizu Yoshio 清水凱夫. *Liuchao wenxue lunwenji* 六朝文學論文集. Trans. Han Jiguo 韓基國. Sichuan: Chongqing chubanshe, 1989.

———. *Shin "Monzen" gaku: "Monzen" no shinkenkyū* 新文選學: 文選の新研究. Tokyo: Kenbun Shuppan, 1999.

Shisanjing zhushu 十三經注疏. Comp. Ruan Yuan 阮元. Taibei: Yiwen yinshuguan, 1955.

Siku quanshu zongmu tiyao 四庫全書總目提要. Shanghai: Shangwu yinshuguan, 1933.

Song shihua quanbian 宋詩話全編. Ed. Wu Wenzhi 吳文治. 10 vols. Nanjing: Jiangsu guji chubanshe, 1998.

Song shu 宋書. Comp. Shen Yue 沈約. Beijing: Zhonghua shuju, 1974.

Spade, Beatrice. "The Education of Women in China During the Southern Dynasties." *Journal of Asian History* 13, no. 1 (1979): 15–41.

Sui shu 隋書. Comp. Wei Zheng 魏徵 et al. Beijing: Zhonghua shuju, 1973.

Sun Changwu 孫昌武. *Wen tan fo ying* 文壇佛影. Beijing: Zhonghua shuju, 2001.

Sun Wu 孫武. *Sunzi* 孫子. Taibei: Shangwu yinshuguan, 1991.

Taiping guangji 太平廣記. Comp. Li Fang 李昉 et al. Beijing: Zhonghua shuju, 1981.

Taiping yulan 太平御覽. Taibei: Shangwu yinshuguan, 1974 reprint.

Taishō shinshū Daizōkyō 大正新修大藏經. Taibei: Shihua yinshua qiye, 1990.

Tan Runsheng 譚潤生. *Beichao min'ge* 北朝民歌. Taibei: Dongda tushu, 1997.

Tang Changru 唐長孺. "Clients and Bound Retainers in the Six Dynasties Period." In *State and Society in Early Medieval China*, ed. Albert Dien. Stanford: Stanford University Press, 1990, pp. 111–38.

———. *Wei Jin nanbeichao shi luncong* 魏晉南北朝史論叢. Shijiazhuang: Hebei jiaoyu chubanshe, 2000.

———. *Wei Jin nanbeichao shilun shiyi* 魏晉南北朝史論拾遺. Beijing: Zhonghua shuju, 1983.

Tang Xuanzhi 唐玄之 and Liu Xinglin 劉興林. "Zhongguo gudai deng zhu yuanshi" 中國古代燈燭原始. *Zhongguo keji shiliao* 中國科技史料 19, no. 12 (1998): 57–67.

Tang Yongtong 湯用彤. *Han Wei liang Jin nanbeichao fojiao shi* 漢魏兩晉南北朝佛教史. Beijing: Beijing daxue chubanshe, 1997.

Tangdai biansai shi yanjiu lunwen xuancui 唐代邊塞詩研究論文選粹. Lanzhou: Gansu jiaoyu chubanshe, 1988.

Tangren xuan Tangshi xinbian 唐人選唐詩新編. Ed. Fu Xuancong 傅璇琮. Xi'an: Shaanxi renmin jiaoyu chubanshe, 1996.

Tao Xinhua 陶新華. *Wei Jin nanchao zhongyang dui difang junzhengguan de guanli zhidu yanjiu* 魏晉南朝中央對地方軍政官的管理制度研究. Chengdu: Bashu shushe, 2003.

Tao Zongyi 陶宗儀. *Nancun chuogeng lu* 南村輟耕錄. Beijing: Zhonghua shuju, 1997.

Teiser, Stephen F. *The Ghost Festival in Medieval China*. Princeton: Princeton University Press, 1988.

Tian Xiaofei. "Configuring the Feminine: Gender and Literary Transvestitism in the Southern Dynasties Poetry." Ph.D. diss., Harvard University, 1998.

Tian Yuqing 田餘慶. *Dong Jin menfa zhengzhi* 東晉門閥政治. Beijing: Beijing daxue chubanshe, 1996.

———. *Tuoba shi tan* 拓跋史探. Beijing: Sanlian shudian, 2003.

Tianhuazang zhuren 天花藏主人. *Liang Wudi xilai yanyi* 梁武帝西來演義. *Guben xiaoshuo jicheng* 古今小說集成 12–13. Shanghai: Shanghai guji, 1992.

Wan Guangzhi 萬光治. "Handai song zan ming zhen yu tongti yiyong" 漢代頌贊銘箴與同體異用. *Shehui kexue yanjiu* 社會科學研究 45, no. 4 (1986): 87–102.

Wang Chunhong 汪春泓. "Lun fojiao yu Liangdai gongti shi de chansheng" 論佛教與梁代宮體詩的產生. *Wenxue pinglun* 文學評論 1991, no 5: 40–56.

Wang Fuzhi 王夫之. *Du "Tongjian" lun* 讀通鑒論. Taibei: Liren shuju, 1985.

———. *Gushi pingxuan* 古詩評選. Ed. Zhang Guoxing 張國星. Beijing: Wenhua yishu chubanshe, 1997.

Wang Guoliang 王國良. *Yan Zhitui "Huanyuan zhi" yanjiu* 顏之推還冤志研究. Taibei: Wenshizhe chubanshe, 1995.

Wang Jia 王嘉. *Shiyi ji* 拾遺記. Beijing: Zhonghua shuju, 1981.

Wang Lin 王琳. *Liuchao cifu shi* 六朝辭賦史. Ha'erbin: Heilongjiang jiaoyu chubanshe, 1998.

Wang Liqun 王立群. *"Wen xuan" chengshu yanjiu* 文選成書研究. Beijing: Shangwu yinshuguan, 2005.

Wang Qing 王青. *Wei Jin nanbeichao shiqi de fojiao xinyang yu shenhua* 魏晉南北朝時期的佛教信仰與神話. Beijing: Zhongguo shehui kexue chubanshe, 2001.

Wang Shixing 王士性, comp. *Guang zhi yi* 廣志繹. Beijing: Zhonghua shuju, 1997.

Wang Shungui 王順貴 and Hu Jianci 胡建次. "Ershi shiji gongti shi yanjiu" 二十世紀宮體詩研究. *Ningxia daxue xuebao* 寧夏大學學報 25, no. 4 (2003): 71–76.

Wang Wenjin 王文進. *Nanchao biansai shi xinlun* 南朝邊塞詩新論. Taibei: Liren shuju, 2000.

Wang Xiangzhi 王象之. *Yudi jisheng* 輿地紀勝. Beijing: Zhonghua shuju, 1992.

Wang Yunxi 王運熙. *Yuefu shi shulun* 樂府詩述論. Shanghai: Shanghai guji chubanshe, 1996.

Wang Yunxi 王運熙 and Yang Ming 楊明. *Wei Jin nanbeichao wenxue piping shi* 魏晉南北朝文學批評史. Shanghai: Shanghai guji chubanshe, 1989.

Wang Zhongluo 王仲荦. *Wei Jin nanbeichao shi* 魏晉南北朝史. Shanghai: Shanghai renmin chubanshe, 2004.

Wei Jin nanbeichao wenxue lunji 魏晉南北朝文學論集. Taibei: Wenshizhe chubanshe, 1994.

Wei shu 魏書. Comp. Wei Shou 魏收. Beijing: Zhonghua shuju, 1974.

"Wen xuan" xue xinlun 文選學新論. Zhengzhou: Zhongzhou guji chubanshe, 1997.

Wenyuan yinghua 文苑英華. Ed. Li Fang 李昉 et al. Taibei: Xinwenfeng chuban, 1979.

Wilkinson, Endymion. *Chinese History: A Manual.* Cambridge: Harvard University Asia Center, 1998.

Wong, Siu-kit, trans. *Early Chinese Literary Criticism*. Hong Kong: Joint Publishing, 1983.

Wu Fusheng. *The Poetics of Decadence: Chinese Poetry of the Southern Dynasties and Late Tang Poetics*. Albany: SUNY Press, 1998.

Wu Jianhui 吳建輝. "Lun Shen Yue de mendi guan, zhengzhi diwei, wenxue diwei jiqi guanxi" 論沈約的門第觀、政治地位、文學地位及其關係. *Xiangtan daxue shehui kexue xuebao* 湘潭大學社會科學學報 24, no. 2 (Apr. 2000): 30–33.

Wu Xianning 吳先寧. *Beichao wenxue yanjiu* 北朝文學研究. Taibei: Wenjin chubanshe, 1993.

Wu Yun 吳雲. *Wei Jin nanbeichao wenxue yanjiu* 魏晉南北朝文學研究. Beijing: Beijing chubanshe, 2001.

Wu Zeng 吳曾. *Nenggaizhai manlu* 能改齋漫錄. In *Song shihua quanbian* 宋詩話全編, vol. 3. Ed. Wu Wenzhi 吳文治. Nanjing: Jiangsu guji chubanshe, 1998.

Xiao Difei 蕭滌非. *Han Wei liuchao yuefu wenxue shi* 漢魏六朝樂府文學史. Beijing: Renmin wenxue chubanshe, 1984.

———. *Xiao Difei shuo yuefu* 蕭滌非說樂府. Shanghai: Shanghai guji chubanshe, 2002.

Xiao Tong 蕭統. *Zhaoming taizi ji jiaozhu* 昭明太子集校注. Annot. Yu Shaochu 俞紹初. Zhengzhou: Zhongzhou guji, 2001.

Xiao Tong 蕭統, ed. *Liuchen zhu Wen xuan* 六臣注文選. Beijing: Zhonghua shuju, 1987.

———. *Wen xuan* 文選. Shanghai: Shanghai guji chubanshe, 1994.

Xiao Yi 蕭繹. *Jinlouzi jiaozhu* 金樓子校注. Annot. Xu Deping 許德平. Taibei: Jiaxin shuini gongsi wenhua jijinhui, 1969.

Xijing zaji quanyi 西京雜記全譯. Annot. and trans. Cheng Lin 成林 and Cheng Zhangcan 程章燦. Guiyang: Guizhou renmin chubanshe, 1993.

Xin Tang shu 新唐書. Comp. Ouyang Xiu 歐陽修 et al. Beijing: Zhonghua shuju, 1975.

Xiong Deji 熊德基. *Liuchao shi kaoshi* 六朝史考實. Beijing: Zhonghua shuju, 2000.

Xiong Qingyuan 熊清元. "Liang Wudi Tianjian sannian 'sheshi Lilao daofa' shi zhengwei" 梁武帝天監三年"捨事李老道法"事證僞. *Huanggang shizhuan xuebao* 黄岡師專學報 18, no. 2 (1998): 67–70.

Xu Baoyu 徐寶余. *Yu Xin yanjiu* 庾信研究. Beijing: Xuelin chubanshe, 2003.

Xu Donghai 許東海. *Yu Xin shengping jiqi fu zhi yanjiu* 庾信生平及其賦之研究. Taibei: Wenshizhe chubanshe, 1984.

Xu Ling 徐陵, ed. *Yutai xinyong jianzhu* 玉臺新詠箋注. Annot. Wu Zhaoyi 吳兆宜 and Cheng Yan 程琰. Beijing: Zhonghua shuju, 1985.

Xu Liqiang 徐立強. "*Liang huang chan* chutan" 梁皇懺初探. *Zhonghua foxue yanjiu* 中華佛學研究 1998, no. 2: 177–206.

Xu Song 許嵩. *Jiankang shilu* 建康實錄. Shanghai: Shanghai guji chubanshe, 1987.

Xu Yuru 徐玉如. "Gongti shi yanjiu de xianzhuang yu fansi" 宮體詩研究的現狀與反思. *Jianghai xuekan* 江海學刊 2001, no. 4: 162–66.

———. "Jin ershinian *Yutai xinyong* yanjiu" 近二十年玉臺新詠研究. *Huaiyin shifan xueyuan xuebao* 淮陰師范學院學報 2001, no. 2: 225–29.

Xu Yunhe 許雲和. "Yuse yixiang yu Liangdai gongti shi" 欲色異相與梁代宮體詩. *Wenxue pinglun* 文學評論 1996, no. 5: 145–53.

Xu Zhongyu 徐中玉. "Wenzhang qie xu fangdang" 文章且須放蕩. In *Gudai wenxue chuangzuo lunji* 古代文學創作論集. Beijing: Zhongguo shehui kexue chubanshe, 1985, pp. 19–39.

Xunzi jijie 荀子集解. Comp. Wang Xianqian 王先謙. Taibei: Shijie shuju, 1969.

Yan Caiping 閻采平. "Liang Chen biansai yuefu lun" 梁陳邊塞樂府論. *Wenxue yichan* 文學遺產 1988, no. 6: 45–54.

———. *Qi Liang shige yanjiu* 齊梁詩歌研究. Beijing: Beijing daxue chubanshe, 1994.

Yan Kejun 嚴可均, comp. *Quan shanggu sandai Qin Han sanguo liuchao wen* 全上古三代秦漢三國六朝文. Beijing: Zhonghua shuju, 1987.

Yan Shangwen 顏尚文. *Liang Wudi* 梁武帝. Taibei: Dongda tushu, 1999.

———. "Liang Wudi huangdi pusa linian xingcheng de shidai beijing" 梁武帝皇帝菩薩理念形成的時代背景. In *Fojiao de sixiang yu wenhua: Yinshun daoshi bazhi jin liu shouqing lunwenji* 佛教的思想與文化: 印順導師八秩晉六壽慶論文集. Taibei: Faguang wenhua chubanshe, 1991, pp. 123–64.

———. "Liang Wudi shou pusa jie ji sheshen Tongtai si yu 'huangdi pusa' diwen de jianli" 梁武帝受菩薩戒及捨身同泰寺與"皇帝菩薩"地位的建立. *Dongfang zongjiao yanjiu* 東方宗教研究 1990, no. 10: 43–89.

———. "Liang Wudi zhujie *Dapin banruo jing* yu fojiao guojia de jianli" 梁武帝註解大品般若經與佛教國家的建立. *Foxue yanjiu zhongxin xuebao* 佛學研究中心學報 1998, no. 3: 99–128.

Yan Zhen 嚴陣. *Jiangnan qu* 江南曲. Shanghai: Zuojia chubanshe, 1964.

Yan Zhitui 顏之推. *Yanshi jiaxun jijie* 顏氏家訓集解. Annot. Wang Liqi 王利器. Shanghai: Shanghai guji chubanshe, 1980.

———. *Yuanhun zhi jiaozhu* 冤魂志校注. Annot. Luo Guowei 羅國威. Chengdu: Bashu shushe, 2001.

Yang Xiong 揚雄. *Fayan yishu* 法言義疏. Annot. Wang Rongbao 汪榮寶. Beijing: Zhonghua shuju, 1987.

Yang Xuanzhi 楊衒之. *Luoyang qielan ji jiaozhu* 洛陽伽藍記校注. Annot. Fan Xiangyong 范祥雍. Shanghai: Shanghai guji chubanshe, 1999.

Yasuda Jirō. "The Changing Aristocratic Society of the Southern Dynasties and Regional Society: Particularly in the Hsiang-yang Region." *Acta Asiatica* 60 (1991): 25–53.

Ying Shao 應劭. *Fengsu tongyi jiaoshi* 風俗通義校釋. Annot. Wu Shuping 吳樹平. Tianjin: Tianjin guji chubanshe, 1988.

Yiwen leiju 藝文類聚. Comp. Ouyang Xun 歐陽詢 et al. Taibei: Wenguang chubanshe, 1974.

Yu Guanying 余冠英. *Han Wei liuchao shi luncong* 漢魏六朝詩論叢. Hong Kong: Nandao chubanshe, 1971.

Yu Xin 庾信. *Yu Zishan jizhu* 庾子山集注. Annot. Ni Fan 倪璠. Beijing: Zhonghua shuju, 1980.

Yu Yuan 郁沅 and Zhang Minggao 張明高, eds. *Wei Jin nanbeichao wenlun xuan* 魏晉南北朝文論選. Beijing: Renmin wenxue chubanshe, 1996.

Zhan Furui 詹福瑞. "Liangdai gongti shiren luekao" 梁代宮體詩人略考. *Hebei daxue xuebao* 河北大學學報 1996, no. 2: 3–6.

Zhan Hong 詹鴻. "'Li er bu yin, yue er bu jian': lun zhanzhuan yu Xiao shi menxia de Liu Xiaochuo jiqi shige zhuangzuo" 麗而不淫, 約而不儉: 論輾轉於蕭氏門下的劉孝綽及其詩歌創作. *Longyan shifan xuebao* 龍岩師範學報 16, no. 4 (1998): 43–45.

Zhang Bowei 張伯偉. *Chan yu shixue* 禪與詩學. Taibei: Yangzhi wenhua, 1995.

Zhang Hua 張華. *Bowu zhi jiaozheng* 博物志校證. Annot. Fan Ning 范寧. Beijing: Zhonghua shuju, 1980.

Zhang Jinlong 張金龍. *Bei Wei zhengzhi yu zhidu lungao* 北魏政治與制度論稿. Lanzhou: Gansu jiaoyu chubanshe, 2003.

Zhang Lei 張蕾. "Bingfei ouran de qiaohe: *Yutai xinyong* yu *Wen xuan* xuanshi xiangchong xianxiang xi" 並非偶然的巧合：玉台新咏與文選選詩相重現象析. *Zhengzhou daxue xuebao* 鄭州大學學報 36, no. 6 (Nov. 2003): 16–19.

———. "*Yutai xinyong* yanjiu shuyao" 玉台新咏研究述要. *Hebei shifan daxue xuebao* 河北師範大學學報 27, no. 2 (2004): 72–76.

Zhang Yihe 章義和. *Diyu jituan yu nanchao zhengzhi* 地域集團與南朝政治. Shanghai: Huadong shifan daxue chubanshe, 2002.

Zhang Zhuo 張鷟. *Chaoye qianzai* 朝野僉載. Beijing: Zhonghua shuju, 1979.

Zhanguo ce 戰國策. Shanghai: Shanghai guji chubanshe, 1978.

Zhao Changping 趙昌平. "'Wenzhang qiexu fangdang' bian" 文章且須放蕩辨. In *Gudai wenxue lilun yanjiu* 古代文學理論研究 1984, no. 9: 92–98.

Zhao Mingcheng 趙明誠. *Jin shi lu* 金石錄. *Siku quanshu* ed.

Zhao Yiwu 趙以武. "Guanyu Liang Wudi 'she dao shi fo' de shijian jiqi yuanyin" 關於梁武帝"捨道事佛"的時間及其原因. *Jiaying daxue xuebao* 17, no. 5 (1999): 1–5.

Zheng Jiliang 鄭基良. *Wei Jin nanbeichao xingjin shenmie huo xingjin shenbumie de sixiang lunzheng* 魏晉南北朝形盡神滅或形盡神不滅的思想論證. Taibei: Wenshizhe chubanshe, 2002.

Zheng, Xiaorong. "A History of Northern Dynasties Literature." Ph.D. diss., University of Washington, 2002.

Zheng Xin 鄭欣. *Wei Jin nanbeichao shi tansuo* 魏晉南北朝史探索. Shandong: Shandong daxue chubanshe, 2004.

Zheng Zhenduo 鄭振鐸. *Chatuben Zhongguo wenxue shi* 插圖本中國文學史. Beijing: Wenxue guji kanxingshe, 1959.

Zhipan 志磐. *Fozu tongji* 佛祖統記. In *Taishō shinshū Daizōkyō*.

Zhong Rong 鍾嶸. *Shi pin jizhu* 詩品集注. Annot. Cao Xu 曹旭. Shanghai: Shanghai guji chubanshe, 1994.

Zhong Shilun 鍾仕倫. *"Jinlouzi" yanjiu* 金樓子研究. Beijing: Zhonghua shuju, 2004.

Zhong Youmin 鍾優民. *Zhongguo shige shi (Wei Jin nanbeichao)* 中國詩歌史(魏晉南北朝). Changchun: Jilin daxue chubanshe, 1989.

Zhou Jianjiang 周建江. *Bei Wei wenxue shi* 北魏文學史. Beijing: Zhongguo shehui kexue chubanshe, 1997.

Zhou Jianjun 周建軍. "Cong xuanshi zhi chayi kan *Wen xuan*, *Yutai xinyong* de wenxue piping yiyi" 從選詩之差異看文選、玉台新詠的文學批評意義. *Qiusuo* 求索 4 (2002): 140–42.

Zhou li zhushu 周禮注疏. See *Shisanjing zhushu*.

Zhou shu 周書. Beijing: Zhonghua shuju, 1971.

Zhou Xunchu 周勛初. "Guanyu gongti shi de ruogan wenti" 關於宮體詩的若干問題. *Xin jian she* 新建設 1965, no. 3: 54–61.

———. "Liangdai wenlun sanpai shuyao" 梁代文論三派述要. *Zhonghua wenshi luncong* 中華文史論叢 1964, no. 5: 195–221. Reprinted in Zhou Xunchu, *Wei Jin nanbeichao wenxue luncong* 魏晉南北朝文學論叢. Nanjing: Jiangsu guji chubanshe, 1999, pp. 230–53.

Zhou yi zhengyi 周易正義. See *Shisanjing zhushu*.

Zhou Yiliang 周一良. *Wei Jin nanbeichao shi lunji* 魏晉南北朝史論集. Beijing: Beijing daxue chubanshe, 1997.

———. *Wei Jin nanbeichao shi zhaji* 魏晉南北朝史札記. Beijing: Zhonghua shuju, 1985.

Zhu Dawei 朱大渭. *Liuchao shilun* 六朝史論. Beijing: Zhonghua shuju, 1998.

Zhuangzi jishi 莊子集釋. Comp. Guo Qingfan 郭慶藩. Beijing: Zhonghua shuju, 1961.

Zizhi tongjian 資治通鑑. Comp. Sima Guang 司馬光. Beijing: Guji chubanshe, 1956.

Zong Lin 宗懍. *Jing Chu suishi ji jiaozhu* 荊楚歲時記校注. Annot. Wang Yurong 王毓榮. Taibei: Wenjin chubanshe, 1988.

Zürcher, Erik. *The Buddhist Conquest of China: The Spread and Adaptation of Buddhism in Early Medieval China*. Leiden: Brill, 1972.

Index

Harvard-Yenching Institute Monographs Series

(Titles now in print)

11. *Han Shi Wai Chuan: Han Ying's Illustrations of the Didactic Application of the Classic of Songs*, translated and annotated by James Robert Hightower
21. *The Chinese Short Story: Studies in Dating, Authorship, and Composition*, by Patrick Hanan
22. *Songs of Flying Dragons: A Critical Reading*, by Peter H. Lee
24. *Population, Disease, and Land in Early Japan, 645–900*, by William Wayne Farris
25. *Shikitei Sanba and the Comic Tradition in Edo Fiction*, by Robert W. Leutner
26. *Washing Silk: The Life and Selected Poetry of Wei Chuang (834?–910)*, by Robin D. S. Yates
27. *National Polity and Local Power: The Transformation of Late Imperial China*, by Min Tu-ki
28. *Tang Transformation Texts: A Study of the Buddhist Contribution to the Rise of Vernacular Fiction and Drama in China*, by Victor H. Mair
29. *Mongolian Rule in China: Local Administration in the Yuan Dynasty*, by Elizabeth Endicott-West
30. *Readings in Chinese Literary Thought*, by Stephen Owen
31. *Remembering Paradise: Nativism and Nostalgia in Eighteenth-Century Japan*, by Peter Nosco
32. *Taxing Heaven's Storehouse: Horses, Bureaucrats, and the Destruction of the Sichuan Tea Industry, 1074–1224*, by Paul J. Smith
33. *Escape from the Wasteland: Romanticism and Realism in the Fiction of Mishima Yukio and Oe Kenzaburo*, by Susan Jolliffe Napier

34. *Inside a Service Trade: Studies in Contemporary Chinese Prose*, by Rudolf G. Wagner
35. *The Willow in Autumn: Ryutei Tanehiko, 1783–1842*, by Andrew Lawrence Markus
36. *The Confucian Transformation of Korea: A Study of Society and Ideology*, by Martina Deuchler
37. *The Korean Singer of Tales*, by Marshall R. Pihl
38. *Praying for Power: Buddhism and the Formation of Gentry Society in Late-Ming China*, by Timothy Brook
39. *Word, Image, and Deed in the Life of Su Shi*, by Ronald C. Egan
40. *The Chinese Virago: A Literary Theme*, by Yenna Wu
41. *Studies in the Comic Spirit in Modern Japanese Fiction*, by Joel R. Cohn
42. *Wind Against the Mountain: The Crisis of Politics and Culture in Thirteenth-Century China*, by Richard L. Davis
43. *Powerful Relations: Kinship, Status, and the State in Sung China (960–1279)*, by Beverly Bossler
44. *Limited Views: Essays on Ideas and Letters*, by Qian Zhongshu; selected and translated by Ronald Egan
45. *Sugar and Society in China: Peasants, Technology, and the World Market*, by Sucheta Mazumdar
46. *Chinese History: A Manual*, by Endymion Wilkinson
47. *Studies in Chinese Poetry*, by James R. Hightower and Florence Chia-Ying Yeh
48. *Crazy Ji: Chinese Religion and Popular Literature*, by Meir Shahar
49. *Precious Volumes: An Introduction to Chinese Sectarian Scriptures from the Sixteenth and Seventeenth Centuries*, by Daniel L. Overmyer
50. *Poetry and Painting in Song China: The Subtle Art of Dissent*, by Alfreda Murck
51. *Evil and/or/as the Good: Omnicentrism, Intersubjectivity, and Value Paradox in Tiantai Buddhist Thought*, by Brook Ziporyn
52. *Chinese History: A Manual, Revised and Enlarged Edition*, by Endymion Wilkinson
53. *Articulated Ladies: Gender and the Male Community in Early Chinese Texts*, by Paul Rouzer
54. *Politics and Prayer: Shrines to Local Former Worthies in Sung China*, by Ellen Neskar
55. *Allegories of Desire: Esoteric Literary Commentaries of Medieval Japan*, by Susan Blakeley Klein
56. *Printing for Profit: The Commercial Publishers of Jianyang, Fujian (11th–17th Centuries)*, by Lucille Chia
57. *To Become a God: Cosmology, Sacrifice, and Self-Divinization in Early China*, by Michael J. Puett

58. *Writing and Materiality in China: Essays in Honor of Patrick Hanan*, edited by Judith T. Zeitlin and Lydia H. Liu
59. *Rulin waishi and Cultural Transformation in Late Imperial China*, by Shang Wei
60. *Words Well Put: Visions of Poetic Competence in the Chinese Tradition*, by Graham Sanders
61. *Householders: The Reizei Family in Japanese History*, by Steven D. Carter
62. *The Divine Nature of Power: Chinese Ritual Architecture at the Sacred Site of Jinci*, by Tracy Miller
63. *Beacon Fire and Shooting Star: The Literary Culture of the Liang (502–557)*, by Xiaofei Tian